MARRIAGE STABILITY, DIVORCE, AND THE LAW

Max Rheinstein

MARRIAGE STABILITY, DIVORCE, AND THE LAW

The University of Chicago Press
Chicago and London

THE UNIVERSITY OF CHICAGO PRESS, CHICAGO 60637
THE UNIVERSITY OF CHICAGO PRESS, LTD., LONDON

© *1972 by The University of Chicago*
All rights reserved. Published 1972
Printed in the United States of America

International Standard Book Number: 0-226-71773-9
Library of Congress Catalog Card Number: 79-169582

Contents

PREFACE   vii

I THE AMERICAN SCENE
  1. What This Book Is About   3
  2. From Free to Indissoluble to Terminable Marriage   7
  3. Divorce in the United States: Liberal Attack and Conservative Defense   28
  4. Our Dual Law of Divorce: The Law of the Books and the Law in Action   51

II DIVORCE IN THE CULTURAL CONTEXT
  5. A Non-Christian Country: Japan   109
  6. Liberalism Dominant: Sweden   126
  7. Marriage Breakdown in a Divorceless Country: Italy   158
  8. Divorce in a Split Society: Les Deux Frances   194
  9. Land of Socialist Experimentation: The Soviet Union   222

III THE PROBLEM RESTATED
  10. The Democratic Compromise   247
  11. What Is the Evil: Divorce or Marriage Breakdown?   261
  12. Does Divorce Breed Breakdown?   277

IV THE CULTURAL BREAKTHROUGH
  13. A Change of Climate   311
  14. The Liberal Breakthrough, I: England and New York   317
  15. The Liberal Breakthrough, II: California, the Commissioners on Uniform State Laws, and the Federal Republic of Germany   367
  16. What to Do about Marriage Breakdown   406

Appendix A. Marriage Disruption and Divorce Laws in
   the United States   444

Appendix B. The English Divorce Reform Act of 1969   470

Index   473

Table of Cases   479

Preface

"Revolution in Divorce" was the title under which the American Academy of Matrimonial Lawyers announced, in October 1970, its Seventh Annual Institute in Chicago. Perhaps the word "revolution" is bandied around a bit too easily these days. But the changes that the law of divorce is undergoing are indeed sensational. The idea that, if allowed at all, divorce shall be granted solely upon the ground of one spouse's serious misconduct is being jettisoned.

Judicial search for guilt has long been reduced in the Scandinavian countries, in Switzerland, Germany, Austria, and in all the socialist countries. Now England, Australia, and Canada have followed suit. In the United States divorce after a certain period of separation has become possible in thirty jurisdictions without investigation of fault. Under the California Family Law Act of 1970, the Iowa Dissolution of Marriage Act of 1970, and the Texas Family Code of 1969, allegation and investigation of guilt is eliminated radically. The same aim is pursued in the draft law produced in 1970 by the National Conference of Commissioners on Uniform State Laws, the draft that was published in the same year by the minister of justice of the Federal Republic of Germany, and in discussions that are under way in the Netherlands and in Sweden. In New York, where since 1787 divorce had been limited to the single ground of adultery, new grounds were added in 1966, among them that of three years' separation without investigation of guilt.[1] Even in Italy, where divorce has not been admitted on any ground, the dam broke when, again in 1970, both houses of Parliament passed a law admitting divorce not only in certain cases of grave misconduct but also without investigation of guilt, after a separation of the spouses that has lasted several years. How has all this change come about? What does it signify? How will it affect the stability of mar-

---

1. Four years later the period was shortened to one year.

riage, the family, and the home? These are the problems which are treated in this book.

My interest in the relationship between marriage stability and the law of divorce grew out of my membership in the Interprofessional Commission on Marriage and Divorce. That body was established under the sponsorship of the American Bar Association shortly after the divorce rate in the United States had, in 1946, reached its all-time high of 4.4 per 1,000 population, when statistics seemed to indicate that one divorce occurred for every three marriages newly concluded, and when public sentiment demanded that something be done "to stem the rising tide of divorce." It was taken for granted that the end could be achieved through a properly drafted law on marriage and divorce, and the Interprofessional Commission was expected to draft the model law that would protect the American family from threatened ruin. The commission was in existence for more than ten years, but no model law emerged from it. At an early time the members reached the conclusion that no sensible law could be drafted without knowledge of the social facts more extensive and more accurate than that existing at the time. It was, in fact, felt that misconceptions had to be dispelled before meaningful data could be gathered. Extensive research thus appeared necessary to provide the basis for a proposed solution. Efforts of the commission to obtain funds for research failed. From the numerous foundations that were approached funds were obtained for just one item, a field study of metropolitan diverce courts.[2] So I decided to have some of the work carried on at the University of Chicago Comparative Law Research Center. Material was assembled with the assistance of Mr. Nils Beckman, Mr. Friedrich E. v. Fischer, Dr. Samuel Stoljar, and Dr. Alexander Broel-Plateris, and several seminars were conducted, one of them jointly with my faculty colleague Karl N. Llewellyn. Participants in another were Professor Thorkild Jacobsen, expert on ancient Mesopotamia, Professor Ross Snyder of Chicago Theological Seminary, Professor Ernst Wolf of the University of Frankfurt am Main, Germany, his then assistants, Dr. Gerhard Lüke (lawyer) and Herbert Hax (statistician) and, as sociologist, Dr. Gerhard Baumert, also of Frankfurt am Main. In 1953, a seminar at the Johann Wolfgang Goethe University in Frankfurt was conducted jointly with Professor Max Horkheimer, philosopher-sociologist, Professor Ernst Wolf of the Faculty of Law, and Professor Everett C. Hughes of the Department of Sociology of the University of Chicago. The Chicagoans were in Frankfurt under the auspices of the Chicago-Frankfurt Aca-

2. M. B. VIRTUE, FAMILY CASES IN COURT (1956).

demic Exchange Scheme, together with Dr. Samuel Stoljar, Mr. Eugene Litwak, and Mr. Gerhard O. W. Mueller as assistants. When under the auspices of the John Simon Guggenheim Memorial Foundation I spent the autumn of 1955 as a visiting professor at the University of Cambridge, England, and, under the Fulbright program the spring of 1961 in Japan, I was able to observe family law and practice in these countries.

The following publications grew out of the work of the University of Chicago Comparative Law Research Center:

1. M. Rheinstein. *Trends in Marriage and Divorce Laws in Western Countries*, 18 LAW & CONTEMP. PROB. 3–19 (1953).
2. M. Rheinstein. *The Law of Divorce and the Problem of Marriage Stability*, 9 VAND. L. REV. 633–64 (1956).
3. M. Rheinstein. *The Code and the Family*, in: NEW YORK UNIVERSITY INSTITUTE OF COMPARATIVE LAW, THE CODE NAPOLEON AND THE COMMON LAW WORLD 139–61 (1956).
4. G. O. W. Mueller. *Inquiry into the State of a Divorceless Society: Domestic Relations Law and Morals in England from 1660–1857*, 18 U. PITT. L. REV. 545–78 (1957).
5. E. Wolf, G. Lüke & H. Hax. SCHEIDUNG UND SCHEIDUNGSRECHT. 485 pp. TUBINGEN, 1959.
6. M. Rheinstein. *Divorce and the Law in Germany*, 65 AM. J. OF SOCIOLOGY 489–98 (review of the book just listed) (1960).
7. M. RHEINSTEIN. LECTURES ON MARRIAGE AND DIVORCE (in Japanese, with English summary). Tokyo, 1963.
8. Y. WATANABE & M. RHEINSTEIN. *The Family and the Law: The Individualistic Premise and Modern Japanese Family Law*, in A. Von Mehren, ed., LAW IN JAPAN: THE LEGAL ORDER IN A CHANGING SOCIETY 364–98 (1963).
9. M. Rheinstein. *Modern Civil Law — Family Law and Succession*, in YIANNOPOULOS, ed., CIVIL LAW IN THE MODERN WORLD 27–57 (1965).
10. M. Rheinstein. *An Inquiry into the State of Marriage Stability in the Swiss and the Italian parts of the Italian-Swiss Border Region*, in: FESTSCHRIFT FÜR HANS G. FICKER 385–409 (1967).

Two international *colloques* of experts were organized by the International Association of Legal Science, a branch of UNESCO. The first of these convened, on 5, 6, and 7 September 1956, in Santiago de Compostela, Spain; the second, from 9 to 16 September 1957, in Chicago, Illinois. The papers presented to the first *colloque* are published in *Revista del Instituto de derecho comparado* (Barcelona), no. 8–9, pp. 467–726 (1957):

W. Czachorski, *Les moyens juridiques, directs et indirects, d'assurer la stabilité de la famille en Pologne*;
J. L. Aguilar Gorrondona, *Contribución venezolana al estudio comparativo de los medios juridicos, directos o indirectos, para lograr la establilidad de la familia*;

B. Tabbah, *La stabilité de la famille — Réponses au questionnaire*;
L. de Luca, *Mezzi giuridici diretti o indiretti per assicurare la stabilità della famiglia nell' ordinamento italiano*;
P. G. Vallindas, B. Lambadarios, P. Dagtoglou, N. Deloukas, E. Krispi-Nicole-Topoulou, D. Tsiropinas, A. Tsoutsos, P. Yotis, D. Zervos, *La stabilité de la famille*;
J. Limpens, *Moyens juridiques susceptibles de promouvoir la stabilité du mariage. Rapport belge*;
R. H. Graveson, *Answers to Questionnaire concerning Legal Devices to Promote Marriage Stability. England*;
G. Marty, *Les moyens juridiques pour favoriser la stabilité de l'union conjugale*;
Z. Nakagawa, *On Japanese Marriage and Divorce Law*;
C. J. Arnholm, *Answers to Questionnaire concerning Legal Devices to Promote Marriage Stability. Norway*;
F. Schmidt, *Legal Devices to Promote Marriage Stability. Sweden*;
K. Redden, T. Esener, N. Seymen, *Legal Devices to Promote Marriage Stability in Turkey*;
B. T. Blagojevic, *La stabilité de la famille et le droit de divorce*;
G. M. Swerdlow, *Moyens juridiques, directs, et indirects, contribuant à la stabilisation de la famille en U.R.S.S.*;
M. Rheinstein, *Comparative Study of the Legal Means, Direct or Indirect, to Promote the Stability of the Family*.

The papers of the Chicago *colloque* are published in volume 9 of the *Annales de la Faculté de droit d'Istanbul* (8ᵉ année, no. 13), pp. 1–381 (1960):

M. Rheinstein, *The Stability of the Family*;
M. Rheinstein, *Marriage Stability and Law on Divorce*;
W. E. McCurdy, *Divorce: A Suggested Approach with Particular Reference to Dissolution for Living Separate and Apart*;
D. Johnston, *Marriage Counseling and Family Life Education in the United States*;
H. Ficker, *A Survey of Marriage and Educational Counseling in the Federal Republic of Germany*;
H. Hinderling & L. Duc, *Marriage Counseling in Switzerland*;
J. M. Mogey, *The State of Marriage Counseling and Family Life Education in England in 1957*;
T. Sameshima, *The Japanese Family Court*;
P. V. Alexander, *The Family Court — an Obstacle Race?*;
O. Johnstone, *The Family Court*;
G. Marty, *Le conseil au mariage en France*;
G. Marty, *La politique juridique française en faveur de la famille*;
I. Melander, *Marriage Counseling and Conciliation Proceedings in Finland*;
G. Karlsson, *Social Policies and Marriage Stability in Sweden*;
B. T. Blagojevic, *Données statistiques*;
A. Plateris, *Statistical Data on Marriage Stability*;
W. Czachorski, *Données statistiques sur le divorce en Pologne*;

E. W. Burgess, *Personality Goals and Roles of Family Members*;
J. P. Spiegel, *The Psychiatric Aspects of Marital Stability: Introductory Formulation to the Problem*;
J. P. Spiegel, *The Resolution of Role Conflict within the Family*;
W. Bonac, *Die Ehetrennungen in der Föderativen Volksrepublik Jugoslavien.*

On 29 February 1952, a Conference on Divorce was held at the Law School of the University of Chicago. The presentations made at this conference are published in the Law School of the University of Chicago Conference Series No. 9 (1952):

Karl N. Llewellyn, *Introductory Remarks*;
E. A. Robson, *The Law and Practice of Divorce*;
W. C. Boyden, *The Property Aspects of Divorce*;
H. J. Rudick, *The Tax Aspects of Divorce*;
M. Rheinstein, *Our Dual Law of Divorce: The Law in Action versus the Law of the Books*;
P. W. Alexander, *A Therapeutic Approach*;
M. F. Nimkoff, *Contributions to a Therapeutic Solution to the Divorce Problem: Sociology*;
T. M. French, M.D., *Contributions to a Therapeutic Solution to the Divorce Problem: Psychiatry*;
E. H. Mudd, *Contributions to a Therapeutic Solution to the Divorce Problem: Social Work and Marriage Counseling*;
F. J. Nosek & S. Schaar, *Discussion*;
A. M. Kross, *Therapeutic Solution of Family Conflicts*;
H. F. Goodrich, *Migratory Divorce*;
K. N. Llewellyn, *Summary.*

The extensive research has, I hope, helped to clarify the problems. To me it has been a stimulus to formulate the propositions stated in this book. They are tentative. Our factual knowledge is still incomplete.

If we were to fill all the gaps or even fully to bring up to date the material collected, the book would never be completed. Since its inception, the methods of social science research have been refined and elaborated. As one whose training has been in the law, I recognize the insufficiency of my familiarity with these methods. I am neither a statistician nor a sociologist. I have tried to make use of the comparative method of legal research. I hope to demonstrate that, through it, insights can be obtained that may be of use to social scientists, to lawyers, to lawmakers, and generally to people interested in the topic.

Heartfelt thanks are expressed to all who gave assistance or information, to the John Simon Guggenheim Memorial Foundation, which made possible a three months' stay in England, and to the Center for Advanced Study in the Behavioral Sciences, at Stanford, California, for an academic year's stay during which the accumulated material could be sifted.

I

THE AMERICAN SCENE

1
What This Book Is About

Marriages, at least most of them, are still intended to be for life. "We take each other to love and to cherish, in sickness and health, for better, for worse, until death do us part." Even where this time-honored formula of the Christian marriage ritual is not used, the parties expect, or hope, that their marriage will last. But not all marriages do last. Some marriages collapse; in fact, a great many do. And when a marriage collapses, problems arise, for the spouses, their children, and the community. Hopes are dashed, a home is destroyed, and with it the economic basis of a family. Readjustments must be made, children have to be taken care of, wounds should be prevented from festering.

How do we deal with these problems? Not very intelligently. In fact, the traditional approach is perhaps the least effective that one can imagine for the industrialized society of the twentieth century. For ages Western society adhered to the idea that the best way to deal with marriage breakdown was to prevent it; and the method of prevention was deterrence. He who is at fault in bringing about the collapse of a marriage is a wrongdoer who is to be punished. A third party who interferes with a marriage relation by alienating the affections of one spouse from the other, or by committing adultery with the wife, or, in later times, with either spouse, is to pay damages, not only compensatory but also punitive. A spouse who has so misbehaved himself as to render intolerable to the other the continuance of the marital community may be driven out into the cold.

Repression through deterrence worked fairly well, although never completely, in the comparatively static world of preindustrial society. It has ceased to work in our day. But the old idea lingers on to such an extent that it still turns our ways of dealing with marriage breakdown into a world of make-believe.[1]

---

1. The term "land of make-believe" is applied by Nelson M. Blake, in his book *The Road to Reno* (1962), to the situation that prevailed in the state of New York

We have not only not succeeded in curbing marriage breakdown but have aggravated its impact and magnified its consequences. Recently awareness of the inappropriateness of the traditional approach has begun to stir. The facts of the matter, which have been oddly obscured, have begun to be explored. New remedies are being discussed and tried. This book is meant to contribute to the discussion. What, indeed, are the facts? Why have they been disregarded? Why is the traditional approach ineffective? What have been the consequences? How could we do better? These are the questions. We do not pretend to have the final answers. They cannot be stated because we do not yet know enough about the facts of marriage breakdown and about its causes. The best we can do is state the problems. Once the right questions are asked, the way is open.

Marriage breakdown is no new phenomenon. It has occurred in the past. Christian society has not been able to prevent it. But in our time marriage breakdown has become a mass phenomenon. The number of marriages dissolved by divorce in 1967 was 62,835 in West Germany, 42,678 in England, 534,000 in the United States, and 83,243 in Japan.[2] These figures do not include the comparatively small number of marriages the end of which has been certified by a judicial decree of annulment or declaration of nullity or those cases where the factual breakdown of a marriage has not been followed by the formal act of divorce. The number of the latter is not known, but it is considerable even in countries where a divorce can be obtained as easily as in the United States. In Italy, where divorce until recently has been impossible, the number of marriages ending in separation or abandonment was in 1967 reliably estimated to be more than 100,000 a year.[3] Considering the minor children as well as the spouses of marriages terminated by divorce alone, the total number of persons involved in the United States was 1,588,000 in 1965.[4]

Concern about the problem is expressed in a mass of writing by law people, churchmen, educators, politicians, journalists, novelists, and what not. They all have contributed, mostly under the heading of divorce. Passions have been engendered, proposals, sensible or fantas-

---

before the divorce reform legislation of 1966. But the confusion described by Blake has been more general.

2. Statistisches Jahrbuch für die Bundesrepublik Deutschland 1969, at 44; Japan Statistical Yearbook 1968, table 15; United Kingdom, Annual Abstract of Statistics 1968, table 82; Statistical Abstract of the United States 1969, table 54.

3. See *infra* chap. 7.

4. National Center for Health Statistics, Divorce Statistics Analysis, U.S. 1964 and 1965, 1.

tic, presented. Every year usually produces legislation in quite a number of American states and foreign countries.

David R. Mace, then executive director of the American Association of Marriage Counselors, called the American divorce law "an absolutely ghastly, dreadful, deplorably messy situation" and the essay in *Time* magazine which quoted him remarks that nationwide there is an urgent, increasing cry "to reform and humanize the divorce system."[5]

Is the indictment justified? Is reform needed? How can the divorce system be humanized? What can be done about marriage breakdown?

An investigation of these problems will be undertaken in this book. If we may anticipate the answer, we shall find that the present state of American divorce law is not perfect, that it may justly be called messy, but that it is by no means deplorable; that something can be and is being done to humanize it, but that for a long time discussions have started from premises either unrelated or contrary to the facts of life, and consequently of little help.

A typical illustration of false premises was presented in the charge by Governor Edmund G. Brown of California to the commission which he convoked on 11 May 1966 to initiate "a concerted assault on the high incidence of divorce in our society and its often tragic consequences." In that charge he stated that "divorce produces not only broken homes but broken lives."

Even endless repetition cannot make true the proposition that lives or homes are destroyed by divorce. What may destroy homes or lives is something quite different: the breakdown of a marriage, an event in the realm of fact which is different from and regularly precedes that event in the realm of law which is called divorce, and which does no more than, ascertaining the fact that a marriage has broken down, restore the parties to the freedom of entering upon new relationships that will be recognized as legally effective marriages and thus as socially respectable.

The breakdown of a home often constitutes a catastrophe for the spouses and their children. If it occurs frequently, it can indeed be regarded as a social evil. But the restoration to the freedom of remarriage is by no means necessarily evil. In fact, it can be good for society as it reopens the way for the creation of new homes for the ex-spouses and their children, a home which is free from the taint of irregularity and which at least holds the possibility of being more harmonious than that which has broken down. If we are concerned about the good of society, we must focus our attention on the prevention or minimiza-

---

5. 87 TIME, no. 6 at 26 (1963).

tion of the incidence of factual marriage breakdown rather than upon stemming the tide of divorce. Reduction of the incidence of divorce may be a means toward the reduction of the frequency of factual marriage breakdown. But that effect cannot be taken for granted. It does not occur unless the availability of restoration to the freedom of remarriage encourages the readiness to yield to the temptation factually to break up an existing home. The existence of such a cause and effect relationship has frequently been asserted. Divorce, it has been said, breeds divorce. But does it? The proposition has been stated with as much fervor as the opposite that the unavailability of divorce breeds immorality. What evidence is there for either proposition? Even if it should be true, is the impossibility or difficulty of being restored to the freedom of legitimate remarriage the only device available to reduce the incidence of separation and family abandonment? Are there no other, perhaps more effective, devices to promote the stability of marriage? The traditional concentration of attention upon divorce has obscured the problem and impeded the search for effective remedies for marriage breakdown. So, what causal connection if any is there between a society's divorce law and the actual state of marriage stability? What devices are available for the effective protection and promotion of marriage stability? If we are concerned about the protection and promotion of the stability of marriages and the maintenance of the institutions of marriage, the family, and the home, we shall grope in the dark unless we formulate the problems in the manner just indicated. Insight into the true nature of the problem will help us to find an approach or, at least, to avoid approaches that are bound to fail.

Why has the American law of divorce reached a state that can properly be called messy? Why have the relevant problems been obscured? Why have the long disputes been so passionate and yet so sterile? History holds the explanation.

2
From Free to Indissoluble to Terminable Marriage

This book is not a "law book" but a book about law, about law, that is, in its impact on life. It is meant as an inquiry into the facts of life and an attempt to pave the way to an informed discussion of what, if anything, might or ought to be done. Among the facts of life, the law is one of importance even when it is flouted. The very practices designed to evade the law must take its existence into account. The practitioners of collusive and migratory divorce must know what the law is as much as the bad citizen who wishes to evade the tax laws or the criminal law. By this analogy I do not wish to indicate that the "divorce specialist" and the legal adviser of a would-be tax evader are equally reprehensible. Tax evasion is a crime and tends to be morally condemned; the lawyer who advises his client on how to obtain a migratory or even a collusive divorce faces a milder form of opprobrium, if any.

Fedya, engaging, chivalrous, but fickle, amorous, and susceptible to female charm, is married to Lisa, who, steadfast, loyal, and dutiful, is his very opposite in character. Fedya has repeatedly abandoned Lisa to carry on affairs with other women. His conscience impels him to set Lisa free so that she can marry Victor, a man of honor and duty. After long hesitation Lisa consents, but she shrinks from the necessity of having Fedya caught in the company of another woman. So Fedya decides to feign death. He arranges his clothes to be found at the shore of a lake in which some other man had drowned shortly before. When the body is found, it is believed to be Fedya's, who lives on, however, under an assumed name. But Lisa, believing herself to be free, now marries Victor.

But for the unusual ending, the story might have happened in New York or London. But the story is told by Leo Tolstoy in his drama *The Living Dead*, written in 1902.[1] The milieu is that of tsarist Russia,

1. The plot is taken from a case that was tried in 1897 before the District Court

where, as in New York of 1965 or England of 1937, adultery was practically the only ground for divorce for members of the Orthodox church.[2] Just as New York long paid respect to Christian tradition, so the tsar's government observed the teaching of the Orthodox church. As in New York and in other jurisdictions in which divorce is, or was, possible on adultery only, "hotel evidence" came to be concomitant with the strict law of divorce.

Let us now look at Scandinavia. In Sweden as in the other Nordic countries a marriage is terminated upon the mere application of either party, provided the parties have previously separated by mutual agreement and have lived apart from each other for, in Sweden, one year, or, in Denmark, eighteen months.[3] In Japan, divorce is even easier. A marriage is terminated by both parties notifying the registrar of their agreement to disagree.[4]

To the student of comparative law it is an impressive experience to realize how little the private law systems of the world differ from one another. Wide divergencies exist in public law, between democratic and authoritarian countries, between private enterprise countries and socialist countries. In the latter, the field of private law is narrower than in the former, but insofar as private law exists, it is of striking similarity, irrespective of whether the country is one of free enterprise or of socialist planning, whether it is democratic or authoritarian. Differences exist with respect to commercial and other contractual transactions; they can be annoying in international transactions, but they relate to matters of detail. In the field of property, especially property in land, the differences appear to be larger than they actually are. They lie more in the conceptual structure of the legal rules and institutions than in practical results. But in one field of private law diversity is glaring, namely, in that of divorce. No divorce at all is permitted in Andorra, Argentina, Brazil, Chile, Colombia, Eire, Paraguay, the Philippine Republic, or Spain; it is not available to Roman Catholics in Liechtenstein or Portugal. But in Japan it may be obtained upon mutual consent. Until 1970, in England, a divorce could be had only upon the grounds of adultery, cruelty, or desertion, i.e., of grave marital mis-

---

of Tula. Fedya, who was discovered to have feigned his death and then to have brought about a false entry on the register of civil status, was sentenced to one year's imprisonment. Lisa and Victor were found to have honestly believed in Fedya's death and, although their marriage was invalid, were acquitted of the charge of criminal bigamy.

2. SWOD ZAKONOV (Civil Code of 1833), arts. 45, 50, 54, 56.
3. See *infra* chap. 6.
4. See *infra* chap. 5.

conduct (and, in addition, upon the ground of the other spouse's incurable insanity), while in Switzerland a marriage may be terminated when it is found to be incurably disrupted for any reason.

We do not even have to go outside of the United States to find diversity of divorce laws, at least as they appear on the statute books. Until 1949, no divorce at all was obtainable in South Carolina. In New York, adultery was the only ground until 1967. But in Alaska, Kansas, Nevada, New Mexico, Oklahoma, and the Virgin Islands, a marriage may be terminated upon the mere ground of incompatibility of temperament,[5] in Illinois upon the ground of mental cruelty, whatever that may mean,[6] in over half the jurisdictions simply upon the fact that the parties have lived separate and apart from each other for a certain period of time, which varies from one year in the District of Columbia to ten years in Rhode Island.[7] But basically divorce law in the United States is similar to what it was in England until 1970: a divorce can be granted upon the ground of one spouse's grave marital misconduct, especially adultery, cruelty, or desertion for a certain length of time, provided the petitioner himself is not guilty too.

Variety also exists with respect to the mode in which a divorce is brought about. In the United States as in most other countries of Christian tradition, a marriage cannot be terminated, except by death, in any way other than by the decree of a court. In the Soviet Union, until 1968 even two courts had to act, first the people's court and then the appellate court.[8] In some Oriental countries the court is not, as with us, a secular court of the state, but it is, as it was in England and, into our own century, in eastern European countries, a religious body which applies the law of its faith rather than any secular law of the state. In Lebanon, for instance, the divorce law is different for every one of the nineteen religious groups, of which each has its own court.[9] In Denmark, Norway, and Iceland marriages are, at least normally, terminated by administrative agencies rather than by courts.[10] In countries which for Moslems still uphold the classical law of Islam, such as Afghanistan, Pakistan, or Saudi Arabia, a divorce, or we should rather say, a repudiation, is brought about by the extrajudicial, uni-

5. See H. H. CLARK, JR., THE LAW OF DOMESTIC RELATIONS IN THE UNITED STATES 349 (1968) (hereinafter cited as CLARK).
6. ILLINOIS LAWS 1967, 3087, § 1.
7. See CLARK 351.
8. See *infra* chap. 10.
9. P. CATALA & A. GERVAIS, 1 LE DROIT LIBANAIS 11, 33, 74 (1963); G. N. Sfeir, The Institution of Personal Status (University of Chicago Law School doctoral dissertation, typewritten), pp. 9–10 (1957).
10. See *infra* chap. 6.

lateral declaration of the husband.¹¹ In Japan, as we have seen, a marriage may be terminated by the mutual agreement of the parties and the notification of the registrar of civil status.¹² In ancient Rome at the period of the principate a marriage was dissolved simply by the parties' mutual consent or by the repudiation formlessly declared by one of them.¹³ Insofar as divorce is a judicial act to be brought about in proceedings in which one party figures as the plaintiff and the other as the defendant, wide variations exist in judicial attitudes. While in some places, for instance the Netherlands or certain counties of Wisconsin, the official law is taken more or less seriously, in most other places with an officially strict divorce law collusion is more or less openly condoned or encouraged, or strict laws are rendered ineffective through the recognition of migratory divorce. Following ancient tradition, as in Sweden, or new modern ideas as in Los Angeles County, California, Lucas County, Ohio, or in the state of New York, seekers of divorce may, as a more or less general rule, have to undergo efforts at reconciliation, which may, as in many places in France and Germany, be empty formalities or, as in some Swiss cantons, serious efforts to straighten out the parties' marital difficulties.

Truly, in the field of divorce, we find a bewildering variety, in the substantive laws, in procedures, and in actual practices. Why is it that here we do not find the measure of uniformity so conspicuous in other fields of private law?

The answer lies, of course, in the diversity of social factors by which the patterns of the various societies are determined. Among these factors ethical and religious value judgments are as important as, or even more than, objective facts of social, economic, and political development. These value judgments are widely held without conscious reflection or rational deliberation. They may be felt deeply or professed superficially. Upon the living they have been implanted in that process of acculturation which has shaped the civilization of those successive generations by which civilizations have been built and developed.

In Western civilizations two trends can be traced, two sets of drives, ideas, and ideals which have shaped our present institution of monogamous marriage including divorce. The struggle between and intermingling of these two trends has brought about results which have varied from time to time and which now vary from place to place. One of these

11. See J. N. D. Anderson, ISLAMIC LAW IN THE MODERN WORLD 40, 83 (1959).
12. See *infra* p. 109.
13. On divorce in Rome, see M. KASER, ROMAN PRIVATE LAW 247 (R. Dannenbring transl., Durban, 1965); E. LEVY, HERGANG DER RÖMISCHEN EHESCHEIDUNG (1925).

two trends has prevailed for centuries. In recent decades the pendulum has come to swing in the direction of the other, but there has not been a complete reversal of the ideas that have been dominant for the last fifteen hundred years.

The two competing ideologies may be called the Christian-conservative and the eudemonistic-liberal. When carried out consistently, the Christian-conservative principle implies that marriage is indissoluble save by death. Its consistent opposite implies that marriage may be terminated by either party at any time. The former principle is that of Roman Catholic canon law. The latter principle prevailed in ancient Rome in the time of the principate; in modern times it does not seem to have been fully adopted anywhere, at least not in official law.

Marriage as we know it is a product of centuries of Christianity.[14] From Judaism,[15] Christianity took over the commandment of strict premarital and extramarital chastity. Sexual intercourse is permitted only in marriage. It is by this commandment that Judaism differed from the other religions of the surrounding world. Time and again the Jews were reminded of it by the prophets, who were horrified by the constantly recurring temptation presented to God's people by the licentiousness of neighboring peoples with their orgiastic religious rites. Out of Jewish and older Roman ideals the Christian church fathers fashioned the rule of strict monogamy. Firm bounds were set to the sex drive. Intercourse was to be permissible only between one man and one woman, and between them only if they were united by the bond of Christian marriage.[16] Even then sexual activity was to be carried on only in the "natural" way apt to result in the procreation of issue.

Christianity's new idea was that marriage is to be indissoluble, that it is to last for the duration of the joint lives of the partners. Marriage is to be the fullest community of life. Sexual intercourse is to take place only between partners who are united in this complete union. It is not to be indulged for its own sake, not even between partners living together without the marital intent of permanency. Married partners, between whom alone intercourse is not sinful, ought to be able to rely upon each other in all ups and downs of life; and in past centuries,

14. On the history of marriage in general, see G. E. HOWARD, HISTORY OF MATRIMONIAL INSTITUTIONS (3 vols. 1904); E. A. WESTERMARCK, HISTORY OF HUMAN MARRIAGE (3 vols. 1891; 5th ed. 1922); same, SHORT HISTORY OF MARRIAGE (1926).

15. On postexilic Jewish sex morality, see C. M. EPSTEIN, SEX LAWS AND CUSTOMS IN JUDAISM 5, 152 (1967).

16. The classical exposition of the Christian ideal of marriage in the modern world is Pope Pius XI's encyclical *Casti connubii* [On Christian marriage], issued 31 December 1930.

especially in those of early Christianity, life was full of risk to a degree which it is hard for us today to imagine. Intercourse was also restricted to those who would be united not only by physical attraction or material considerations but by their common faith and the bond of common responsibility before God, a responsibility, above all, to raise their offspring in the faith in Christ and in the discipline of Christian morals. But even beyond this responsibility for the future generation and thus for the permanency of human society as God's creation, husband and wife themselves were to strengthen each other in the faith and thus to be *one* not only in the flesh but in spirit. In the symbolism of the time, this ideal was expressed through the doctrine of marriage being a sacrament, i.e., a vessel of divine grace. Significantly, this sacrament is not administered to the parties by the priest; it is mutually administered to each other by the parties. Man's most animalistic act is thus elevated to the highest bond of spirituality.[17] The idea is sublime. That the high demands of Christian sex morals have never been fulfilled completely, the church itself recognizes. It is aware of the sinful nature of man, and in the sacrament of penance, as combined with the institution of confession, the church has fashioned the way in which the commands of the morality of perfection can be combined with the imperfection of man.[18]

In the Christian sex morality the image of strictly monogamous indissoluble marriage is combined with the idea that the perfect chastity of the religious virtuoso is of even higher value. Such ideas were new in the ancient world, even though one or the other of the strands can be found in the cultures of Judaism, Hellenism, Rome, or the Near

---

17. Among theologians it was long controversial whether the spouses administered the sacrament to each other at the conclusion of the marital contract or at the first marital intercourse; *cf.* J. FREISEN, GESCHICHTE DES KANONISCHEN EHERECHTS 29 (Paderborn 1893, repr. 1963); E. FRIEDBERG, LEHRBUCH DES KATHOLISCHEN UND EVANGELISCHEN KIRCHENRECHTS 339 (3d ed. Leipzig 1889; 1 A. ESMEIN & R. GÉNÉSTAL, LE MARIAGE EN DROIT CANONIQUE 83 (2d ed. 1929); S. P. HANEY, THE DEVELOPMENT OF THE SACRAMENTALITY OF MARRIAGE FROM ANSELM OF LAON TO THOMAS AQUINAS (Catholic Univ. of America, Studies in Sacred Theology, 2d ser. 134, 1963). The former view constitutes the official doctrine of the Roman Catholic church, *cf.* T. L. BOUSCAREN, A. C. ELLIS & F. N. KORTH, CANON LAW 465 (4th ed. 1963); CODEX JURIS CANONICI, canon 1012 § 1, simply says: "Christ our Lord elevated the very contract of marriage between baptized persons to the dignity of a sacrament." The church nevertheless practices dissolution by the pope of marriages concluded by contract but not consummated by marital intercourse (*matrimonia rata non consumata*; canon 1119). This practice is justified by the idea that in dissolving such marriages the pope is not exercising human power but divine authority entrusted to the church by Christ. The existence of this delegation is derived from the long practice of the church, which has granted dispensations from the bond of nonconsummated marriage since the fifteenth century. BOUSCAREN, ELLIS & KORTH 614.

18. CODEX JURIS CANONICI, canon 870.

East which converged in Christianity. The new faith, its dogmas, and its institutions were fashioned by the church fathers of both the Greek and the Latin halves of the Roman empire and the schoolmen of the Middle Ages.[19]

Since Christianity was based upon the idea of Jesus of Nazareth being God, his word thus constituting divine revelation and the Gospels the true record of Jesus' life and words, the font of the new doctrine of Christian marriage had to be found in Holy Writ. The commandment of premarital and extramarital chastity was abundantly stated in the Old Testament, in Leviticus and Deuteronomy as well as in the books of the prophets.[20] The ideal of complete and chaste celibacy of the religious virtuoso was exemplified by Jesus himself, apart from the tradition of such Jewish sects as the Essenes. For the new dogma of indissolubility of marriage, the basis was found in several sayings of Jesus as reported in the Gospels.[21] Whether, as his words were later interpreted, Jesus meant to condemn the termination of a marriage by mutual consent of the spouses, as was possible and indeed frequent in the Hellenistic-Roman society of his day,[22] is open to doubt. Jesus moved in Jewish circles and addressed himself to Jews, where the only form of marriage termination was the repudiation of the wife by the husband.[23] It is understandable that Jesus, especially in the context of the Sermon on the Mount, might condemn the harshness of this law, which allowed a man to drive out his wife at any time.[24]

19. See 1 ESMEIN & GÉNESTAL, *supra* note 17; G. H. Joyce, CHRISTIAN MARRIAGE (1933); C. F. STAEUDLIN, GESCHICHTE DER VORSTELLUNGEN UND LEHREN VON DER EHE (1826).
20. Exod. 20:14 (Decalogue); Lev. 20:10–21; Deut. 22:13–29, 23:17, 18; Ezek. 16:15–18, 25 ff., 22:11, 23:1–49; Hos. 2:4–11, 4:2, 10; Isa. 3:9, 23:16.
21. Matt. 5:31–32; Mark 10:2–12; Luke 16:18. See also Rom. 7:2–3.
22. On divorce in Rome, see KASER, *supra* note 13, at 247; W. W. BUCKLAND, TEXT-BOOK OF ROMAN LAW 116 (3d ed. P. Stein 1963); LEVY, *supra* note 13; on the mores, see 2 W. E. LECKY, HISTORY OF EUROPEAN MORALS FROM AUGUSTUS TO CHARLEMAGNE 306 (3d ed. 1906); on the Hellenistic world, see 2 L. MITTEIS & U. WILCKEN, GRUNDZÜGE UND CHRESTOMATHIE DER PAPYRUSKUNDE 217 (1912); R. TAUBENSCHLAG, THE LAW OF GRECO-ROMAN EGYPT 91 (1944); on the Greeks, see W. G. BECKER, PLATONS GESETZE UND DAS GRIECHISCHE FAMILIENRECHT 145 (1932).
23. The basic scriptural passage is Deut. 24:1, 2; on marriage and divorce among the Hebrews, see D. W. AMRAM, JEWISH LAW OF DIVORCE 24 (2d ed. 1968); F. Horst, *Ehe im Alten Testament*, 2 DIE RELIGION IN GESCHICHTE UND GEGENWART 315 (3d ed. 1958); E. NEUFELD, ANCIENT HEBREW MARRIAGE LAWS (1944); D. R. MACE, HEBREW MARRIAGE (1953).
24. *Cf.* Mark 10:2–12: "The Pharisees came to him, and asked him, Is it lawful for a man to put away his wife? tempting him. And he answered and said unto them, What did Moses command you? And they said, Moses suffered to write a bill of divorcement, and to put her away. And Jesus answered and said unto them, For the hardness of your heart he wrote you this precept. But from the beginning of the creation God made them male and female. For this cause shall a man leave

The new ethics of sex and marriage constituted part and parcel of that reaction against the hedonistic latitude which had been characteristic of the Hellenistic society of imperial Rome. Austerity, strictness, and renunciation came to be the new values; asceticism, carried to extremes by the anchorites of the desert and the stylites of the East, became the ideal of the religious virtuosi.

Much time was needed for the new ideology to make its way in the core region of the Roman empire and in the lands of mission, inhabited by Germanic tribes who, in the storms of the great invasions, overran and conquered the western parts of the empire. Their conversion to Christianity did not imply the immediate acceptance of the Christian sex ethics, which were as new to them as they had been to the Hellenist and Oriental peoples of the eastern parts.[25]

The new order of ideas made necessary a far-reaching change in the method of social regulation of marriage. Nowhere, of course, were the matters of sex and marriage free of all social regulation. Incest taboos were universal and social norms were recognized everywhere as to propriety of marriage age, choice of partners, and the legitimacy of offspring. Mostly these norms belonged to the spheres of religion, convention, and morality. That means that the sanction of contrary behavior was expected to be supernatural retribution, or would consist in unorganized social disapproval or in the internal discomfort of pangs of conscience. The law, i.e., the norm structure enforced by politically organized society, had little concern for matters of marriage and the family. In Rome in particular the head of a "house," the *paterfamilias*, had, so to speak, sovereign power over all its members, except, in later

---

his father and mother and cleave to his wife; and they twain shall be one flesh: so then they are no more twain, but one flesh. What therefore God hath joined together, let not man put asunder. And in the house his disciples asked him again of the same matter. And he saith unto them, Whosoever shall put away his wife and marry another, committeth adultery against her. And if a woman shall put away her husband, and be married to another, she committeth adultery." It is difficult to see how, under Jewish law and in the Jewish community of the time of Jesus a woman could "put away her husband." That could be done in Roman-Hellenistic society. What reason should Jesus have to care about such foreign mores in a discourse with his disciples? On marriage and divorce in the New Testament, see H. Greeven, *Ehe im Neuen Testament*, 2 DIE RELIGION IN GESCHICHTE UND GEGENWART 318.

25. On marriage dissolution among the Germanic peoples, see R. HUEBNER, HISTORY OF GERMANIC PRIVATE LAW 613 (F. S. Philbrick transl. 1918); 1 H. BRUNNER, DEUTSCHE RECHTSGESCHICHTE 101 (2d ed. 1906); on the slow pace with which the Christian view of marriage was established, see H. PORTMANN, WESEN UND UNAUFLÖSLICHKEIT DER EHE IN DER KIRCHLICHEN WISSENSCHAFT UND GESETZGEBUNG DES 11. UND 12. JAHRHUNDERTS (1938); on England, see 2 F. POLLOCK & F. W. MAITLAND, THE HISTORY OF ENGLISH LAW 364 (2d ed. 1952 impression).

times, his wife.²⁶ Indeed, nobody but a *paterfamilias* could own any property or could be bound by contractual obligations. For torts committed by any member of the house, the head, and only the head, was financially responsible. The law, i.e., the regulatory power of the state, did not seek to penetrate into the internal structure of the houses of which the body politic was composed. Roman law, at least Roman private law, was a law dealing with relations between houses as represented by their heads. As for the houses themselves, the law could content itself with the establishment of rules determining membership. Such rules were, of course, indispensable. Strangely enough, however, for the determination of the initiation and termination of marriage, i.e., of that relationship which is basic for the creation of house membership, especially of offspring, Roman law contented itself with a reference to the norms of religion and convention. In early times marriage was, at least among the leading class of patricians, initiated by a religious ceremony (*confarretio*) or by *coemptio*. These rituals became obsolete in later republican times, when it became customary to marry simply by starting life in common, provided both parties had the intention thereby to become husband and wife. But no ritual, religious or secular, was prescribed by the law. The state simply accepted as a marriage what was recognized as such by the mores. In the same way, the state treated a marriage as dissolved when it was treated as such by the mores, under which it was sufficient that the parties separated, or that one terminated the community of marital life and so informed the other.²⁷ Attempts to limit freedom of divorce by such agreements as can still today be found in circles subject to Islamic or Jewish law were frustrated by the rule of their invalidity.²⁸

Initiation of a marriage presupposed, of course, that no taboo existed. In addition to the incest taboos, there were strictly religious ones, such as the one against marriage of a Vestal Virgin, and, above all, the political taboo against marriage outside the circle of *conubium*. A Roman citizen could not, and here the law entered, marry a non-citizen, unless the latter belonged to that privileged group of allies upon whom *conubium* had been expressly conferred. That no marriage was possible between a free person and a slave, or among slaves, was self-evident. Through legislation of Augustus, the scope of legal regu-

26. On marriage and family regulation in Rome, see *supra* note 22; also H. MAINE, ANCIENT LAW 91 (J. H. Morgan ed. 1917; 1st ed. 1861).
27. See *supra* note 22. The solemn declaration before seven witnesses was required by Augustus's *lex Julia* of 18 B.C. for a special situation rather than for divorce in general (see LEVY, *supra* note 13, at 46).
28. CODEX JUST. 5.4.14 (Diocletian) and 8.38.2 (Alexander Severus).

lation of marriage was somewhat extended by the attempt to reconfirm the old Roman virtues by discouraging hypogamy of members of senatorial and other upper-class houses.

Full freedom to terminate a marriage was a rule so firmly rooted in the mores that it took centuries of Christian effort to replace it by the new principle of indissolubility. Even when this new doctrine had begun to be settled in the teaching of the church,[29] and Christianity had become the established religion of the Roman state, the emperors, who were the heads of both the political and the religious side of the church-state empire, did no more than threaten with punishment a husband who would repudiate his wife without justification or a wife who would abandon the marital bond without good cause. The legislation, which started with Constantine, wavered a great deal.[30] Generally, repudiation by the husband was treated as justified in the case of a wife's behavior that would raise the suspicion of adultery, making an attempt upon the spouse's life, or committing such a serious crime as preparing poison, desecrating sepulchres, or treason. The punishment for unjustified repudiation or abandonment consisted in forfeiture of certain rights of marital property, confiscation of property, deportation, or imprisonment in a monastery.[31] Generally women were treated more harshly than men. They were also prohibited from remarrying before the expiration of five years so as to make sure that the repudiation would not be motivated by "cupidity."

Divorce by mutual consent did not fall under such prohibitions. The permissibility and effectiveness of such divorce were even confirmed by Justinian, who in 536 declared that "all that has been joined together by man can be separated by man."[32] Just six years later, Justinian at last took the fateful step of extending the penalties from unjustified repudiation to divorce by mutual consent.[33] Yet, this break with the tradition of centuries turned out to be so unpopular that in 566 is was repealed by Justinian's successor, Justinus II, shortly after his ascension to the throne (566).

29. See H. PREISKER, CHRISTENTUM UND EHE IN DEN ERSTEN DREI JAHRHUNDERTEN (1927); see also *supra* note 14.
30. 3 B. BIONDI, IL DIRITTO ROMANO CRISTIANO 171 ff. (1954); E. J. JONKERS, INVLOED VAN HET CHRISTENDOM OP DE ROMEINSCHE WETGEVING BETREFFENDE HET CONCUBINAAT EN DE ECHTSCHEIDING (Wageningen 1938).
31. Justinian in Novel 117 of 542, Novel 127 of 547, and Novel 134 of 556.
32. Novel 22.3. The proposition was obviously taken from Plato, Timaeus 13, see Biondi, *supra* note 30, at 185, a passage which in its structure is so analogous to it, as to that of the opposite expressed in Mark 10:9, that one is tempted to assume it was known to the unknown writer by whom it is ascribed to Christ.
33. Novel 117 of 542.

The enumeration in the imperial decrees of grounds for justifiable divorce foreshadows that doctrine of divorce as punishment for marital misconduct which in the sixteenth century reappeared in the ideas of the Protestant reformers and which has continued to dominate Western divorce law until the present. As in modern laws but unlike Protestant law, unilateral divorce was also justified in the case of a partner's grave infirmity of mind.[34]

Marriage did not become indissoluble until jurisdiction in marital causes was firmly established to lie with the courts of the church. The establishment of that jurisdiction extended over centuries of struggle between church and state, in the Byzantine empire and in the Germanic kingdoms of the west.[35] In matrimonial matters, exercise of jurisdiction by any kind of court, ecclesiastical or secular, constituted for the most part an innovation. Matters of marriage, as we have observed, had been largely outside the sphere of law. That the church, once it had organized itself on a bureaucratic-hierarchical pattern, headed by the Bishop of Rome, would develop lawlike norms on matters of internal organization and discipline and would establish for these matters a court system of its own, was but natural. But the church also claimed jurisdiction in those other matters which it denied to the state, i.e., the German kingdoms as they grew from primitive bands of conquering tribes into political organizations trying to emulate the Roman pattern and turning into that new form of political organization which was later to grow into the pattern of feudalism. The fields claimed for the jurisdiction of its courts by the church included all disciplinary, criminal, and civil jurisdiction over its members, the clergy. Since clerics were almost the only persons who could read and write, so that the king could not carry on his administration without them, he could not well give up his own jurisdiction over them without surrendering his power to the church. Nor could he yield to the church's claim of exclusive jurisdiction over all matters concerning church-owned land. The church was the largest landowner, and land was the essential form of wealth. By claiming jurisdiction over all matters of succession on death, the church sought to obtain a decisive voice over the distribution of wealth and thus of political power. If the church had succeeded in maintaining its claim to jurisdiction in matters of breach of contract, it would have obtained the power to regulate commerce according to its religious

---

34. The rule that repudiation of a spouse afflicted with "a most serious mental infirmity" was justified, was stated in Digest 24.3. 22.7, where it was ascribed to Ulpian 33 *ad edictum*.

35. On the following see ESMEIN & GÉNÉSTAL, *supra* note 17.

tenets and material interests. Besides, every exercise of jurisdiction involved the opportunity to levy fees and impose fines, two kinds of revenue of outstanding importance in an age of undeveloped methods of taxation. The struggle went back and forth for centuries.[36] In England, Henry II sought to consolidate the situation in the Constitutions of Clarendon (1164), but the quarrel continued and reached its culmination in the clash between the king and Thomas à Becket. The outcome varied from country to country. In England, in contrast to most other countries, the church succeeded in maintaining for its courts jurisdiction in matters of probate of testaments and of administration of personal estates of decedents, while descent of real property had to be left to the courts of the king for adjudication. Everywhere, including England, the church succeeded in maintaining jurisdiction in matters of marriage.[37] As these matters were regarded as essentially religious, the state did not claim jurisdiction over them. The idea that regulation of marriage and adjudication of matrimonial causes should lie with the political community was not seriously considered before the Reformation in the sixteenth century. Even today it is not fully accepted in all Catholic countries. In Spain marriage matters are still regarded as belonging to the church, and in Italy and parts of Latin America jurisdiction in matrimonial causes is still largely left to the courts of the church.[38]

With the establishment of a court system of its own, the church also had to develop a procedural and substantive law that could be applied in its courts. Thus there grew up that peculiar body of law known as canon law. It is law in the sense that its norms are formalized and expressed in that conceptualistic way in which Roman law came to be formalized in its later stage of development. It is "law" also in the sense that it is administered in courts, the structure and procedure of which are patterned on those of the late Roman empire. It is different from law in the strict sense of the word in that its sanction is not the action of some officer of politically organized society who inflicts upon the violator of the law some act of physical force such as imprisonment, death, or forced seizure of property. The sanction of canon law is the same as that of religion, namely, the fear of supranatural retribution. But in the framework of the church this sanction is set to work by the formal act of an officer of the church, ordinarily a bishop, such as excommunication or the imposition of penance. The fact that in the medieval

---

36. *Id.*
37. 1 W. HOLDSWORTH, HISTORY OF ENGLISH LAW 621 (7th ed. 1956).
38. See *infra* chap. 7.

framework of society the imposition by the ecclesiastical authority of spiritual punishment might be the occasion for the imposition by the secular authority of secular punishment strengthened the force of the canon law. Such cooperation was especially effective in the field of marriage, where ecclesiastical judgments of nullity or separation could be accompanied by property detriments to be suffered in the secular forum.

Canon law constitutes a unique case of juridification of religious tenets and commands. A close combination of law and religion exists in Judaism and Islam and, to some extent, in Hinduism.[39] But what has occurred there is the opposite of what occurred in Christianity. The law, instead of including religion, was swallowed up by religion. The sacred books, in Judaism the Torah as expounded in the Talmud, in Islam the Koran together, in Sunnite view, with the tradition of the Prophet, covers all and every aspect of life. But Christianity found itself compelled, besides the realm of the Lord, also to recognize that of Caesar. In its canon law the church has adopted the method of Caesar for the formulation and enforcement of the commands of its own realm. In the Jewish and Islamic view there is no realm of Caesar; there is only that of God, and that realm includes those affairs in which Caesar, i.e, the khalif, is interested. This view has resulted in the theologification of the law. Legal learning coincides with theological. This fact accounts for that peculiar climate of Jewish and Islamic law which Max Weber calls "material rationality" and which now tends to invade our secular law, since it has begun to be forged by the new religion of humanitarianism. The rules of law are developed so as to give expression to religious tenets and religiously inspired commands of ethics.

In that method of "formalistic rationality" which was characteristic of revived Roman law as well as of later nineteenth-century civil law and common law, the rules of law, which in the last resort constitute expressions of moral value judgments based to a considerable extent upon configurations of political power, have tended to be formalized and thus stabilized by the use of concepts of some abstract character. This tendency of secular law has invaded canon law in general and its marriage part in particular. What has been stated here in highly general terms will, we hope, become clearer in the following discussion and will simultaneously help us better to understand our present law of divorce. In fact, that law will remain incomprehensible or absurd if seen only outside its historical context. As absurd we would have to

39. On religious laws, see M. WEBER, LAW IN ECONOMY AND SOCIETY 224 (Rheinstein ed., paperback 1967).

judge in particular that feature of our law requiring that applications for restoration to the freedom of remarriage are to be prosecuted in basically the same kind of judicial procedure in which a court deals with claims for damages in a personal injury case, or with controversies between business firms litigating the validity or the interpretation of a commercial deal. A procedure of a seemingly similar kind made good sense when some private party or parties wanted in the ecclesiastical forum to establish the invalidity of a marriage against the opposition of the *defensor vinculi*,[40] or when a wife over the opposition of her husband, through proceedings in the ecclesiastical court, wished to lay the groundwork for claiming support from him without living with him. The translation of these procedural forms into the secular law concerning permission to remarry has been a source of incongruity and confusion, especially when, as in the United States, those features of the proceedings in matrimonial causes which distinguished them from civil litigation in matters of tort, contract, or property were dropped.[41]

Only the canon law background renders understandable also the present learning about nullity and voidability of marriages and about actions for declaration of nullity and annulment. Only the canon law background explains why a party's restoration to the freedom of remarriage depends on the spouse's having committed adultery or some other marital offense, and why, under the doctrine of recrimination, a marriage, while it may be dissolved when it has been disrupted by the misconduct of one party, may not be dissolved when it is so thoroughly confounded that both parties have been guilty of marital misconduct.

But we have run ahead of our story. We left it at the point when the church had ultimately established the jurisdiction of its courts in matrimonial causes and had thus been enabled consistently to enforce its doctrine of indissolubility of marriage. The effects of that doctrine were mitigated by the theological learning that was developed, in a manner of continuous refinement, about validity and invalidity of marriages and thus about the possibility of a marriage being declared null and void, with the resulting freedom of remarriage of the parties.[42]

Probably the development of such rules was due more to the necessity of intrinsic logic than to practical regard for human nature. When it became established that a marriage once concluded was to be indissoluble, it became necessary to work out clear criteria for determining

40. See *infra* p. 58.
41. See *infra* chap. 4, sec. II.
42. On the long history of this branch of canon law learning, see FREISEN, *supra* note 17, at 22 ff.; ESMEIN & GÉNÉSTAL, *supra* note 17, at 227 ff.

whether or not a marriage had been concluded. It was the merit of the canonists that they, following Roman tradition, made the conclusion of a marriage primarily dependent upon the will of the parties. *Consensus facit nuptias.* Their mutual consent, even without any ceremony, was to suffice for the conclusion of a marriage. But then it became necessary to prevent a marriage from being concluded without consent, and to see to it that consent, on general principle, be serious, real, and free of coercion or fraud. In the long run, it is true, the vitiating — or shall we rather say, the liberating — effects of coercion and fraud were restricted to the cases in which they would relate to "the essentials of the marriage relationship" and that concept was so considerably narrowed that a great many forced marriages or marriages induced by fraud have come to be held valid and so to be indissoluble.[43] In fact, the effect of fraud was limited to such an extent that one could justly say in France, "En mariage il trompe qui peut."

The concept of consent came to be so refined that it meant only the consent to enter upon a marriage in the sense of an indissoluble union including carnal knowledge apt to procreate issue. Mental reservation to maintain the relationship for a limited time only, for instance as long as love should persist, or a secret intention not to engage in marital intercourse, or not in "natural" intercourse, would prevent the conclusion of a valid marriage. There have been ups and downs as to the mode in which such a mental reservation might be proved. After a period of remarkable liberality around the turn of the last century, the requirements of proof have recently been tightened.[44]

Even when the consent was valid on the part of both spouses, a marriage could still be shown to be invalid because of the existence of such an objective impediment as holy orders, solemn vow of chastity, existing prior marriage, pre-contract, impotency, blood relationship, affinity, and spiritual relationship within the prohibited degrees. In the later Middle Ages these last-named concepts were broadened enormously. Considering the limited travel opportunities of the time and its rigid class structure — circumstances which very much limited the range of marriageable partners — it would seem that in any unsuccessful marriage the parties might well be proved to be related to each other in some way that would invalidate their marriage. To what extent nullity proceedings were actually used as a substitute for divorce, we do not

---

43. See *infra* p. 95. The canon law rules presently in force are those of the CODEX JURIS CANONICI, 27 May 1917. A revision of the code, initiated by Vatican Council II, is under way.

44. The present rules are stated in canons 1067–80 of the CODEX JURIS CANONICI.

know. The proceedings were lengthy and expensive, and resort to them may also have been discouraged by the mores for those who were anxious to maintain respectability. For those who were not, there was another substitute of which we shall still have to speak, namely, the ease with which one could disappear in a society without registration and without services for the tracing of missing persons.

In addition to nullity proceedings, canon law provided proceedings for judicial separation. Such a decree did not open up the possibility of remarriage. The marriage tie remained unaffected. But the concepts which were worked out for cases of separation and the procedural forms which were used continued to be applied when, beginning with the Protestant Reformation and steadily gaining impetus from the eighteenth century on, divorce, in the modern sense of dissolution of the tie of an existing marriage, began to be admitted, first in Protestant theology and then in the secular laws.

The resurrection of divorce marks the resurgence of that great trend which, since the days of Martin Luther, has been the antagonist of the Catholic doctrine of indissolubility of marriage and which has been constantly gaining ground at the expense of the latter. Martin Luther was the originator of a new idea which was to have far-reaching consequences. Marriage, he said, is not a sacrament but "a worldly thing." Its regulation belongs to the sphere of Caesar rather than that of God.[45] But Caesar, being under God, in shaping his law of marriage has to do it in the right Christian way, which means that he has to conform to the words of the Lord as reported in the Gospel. Taking Matthew more literally than the canonists of the Roman church, Luther found in it the permission for the secular lawgiver to permit a husband to put away his wife if she has committed adultery.

In the rejection of complete indissolubility Luther was joined by Zwingli[46] and Calvin.[47] They were equally anxious to condemn all kinds of lewdness and sexual impurity, but only Calvin expressly equated a married man's to a married woman's adultery as a ground for the other spouse to treat the marriage as broken. That only the innocent party was free to remarry was self-evident. Finding a scriptural basis in 1 Corinthians 7:15,[48] Zwingli and Calvin also regarded

45. VON EHESACHEN 205 (Weimar ed., vol. 30, part 3, 1910); on the Reformers and the subsequent course of Protestant ecclesiastical law of divorce, see 2 HOWARD, *supra* note 14, at 60; FRIEDBERG, *supra* note 17, at 415 ff.
46. J. C. MOERIKOFER, ULRICH ZWINGLÍ 261 (Leipzig 1867).
47. G. HARKNESS, JOHN CALVIN 147 (1931).
48. "If the unbelieving depart, let him depart. A brother or a sister is not under bondage in such cases: but God has called us to peace."

remarriage permissible for a spouse who had been definitely abandoned by his partner. Other grounds were added in practice.

The regulations were mostly contained in ordinances of the secular powers, but, as the bases were found in scripture, the resuscitated institution of divorce was conceived in analogy to the ancient institution of repudiation modified as it had been under the Christian emperors of Rome as retribution for grave marital misconduct. The new institution of divorce was thus started on the path of that principle of marital offense by which it is still dominated in the major part of the United States and in a great many other parts of the world of Christian tradition.

Soon the new institution also came to be burdened with that other feature which has fatefully determined the course of divorce law, namely, the idea that divorce was to be a matter of adversary civil procedure. In the early years of the Reformation, repudiation was a private act, as it had been in Rome. When the repudiating party wished to remarry, the minister had to determine whether the repudiation was so justified that the former marriage bond was dissolved. As this task turned out to be too difficult for ministers, judicial bodies were established, mostly by secular authority, to relieve the ministers of the delicate task.[49] If, following the practice of the Reformers, divorce was to be treated as a punishment of the guilty spouse and a privilege for the innocent, it was to be expected that a wife whose husband sought to put her away, conceivably without support, would resist, just as, later, a husband could be expected to resist his wife's attempt to put him away and simultaneously saddle him with a duty to pay alimony. It was no wonder either that the procedure to be followed in such cases would be patterned upon the model of separation and nullity proceedings of the ecclesiastical courts of the old church. After all, both institutions had been called divorce, limited or absolute.

The agencies to which the new proceedings were committed differed from place to place. In some of the Protestant principalities of Germany, matters of divorce were simply handed to the regular civil courts. In others, as well as in the kingdoms of Scandinavia, the prince kept the power to grant divorce in his own hands, frequently following the advice of his council or that special body through which he carried on his regime of the church, the consistory, or by special boards of citizens, or by the regular courts.[50] In Scotland, matters of divorce came to be

49. FRIEDBERG, *supra* note 17, at 416.
50. On the ideas developed by Protestant theologians and jurists, see A. L. RICHTER, BEITRÄGE ZUR GESCHICHTE DES EHESCHEIDUNGSRECHTS IN DER EVANGELISCHEN KIRCHE (1858).

handled by the commissary courts, ecclesiastical courts that frequently had secular lawyers among their members.[51]

The one country in which, in spite of its involvement in the Reformist movement, divorce did not take hold, was England. The Church of England never gave up its claim of continuing the Catholic tradition. Even today, it is an unsettled question whether the Church of England, seen as a whole, should be called Protestant or Catholic. In the time immediately following the breach with Rome it looked as if the Church of England might follow the example of the Protestants of the Continent and admit the possibility of divorce at least in the case of a wife's adultery. But in the reign of the Virgin Queen it was, after some hesitation, settled that marriage would remain indissoluble,[52] at least for the common man. Since the king in Parliament was the head of both the state and the church, he could, as a matter of special privilege, dissolve indissoluble marriages. From the late seventeenth century on, parliamentary divorce developed into a regular practice. But the proceedings were so cumbersome and expensive that they were available only to the most affluent. The number of parliamentary divorces thus remained low, one to three a year.[53] Under the general law of the land, marriage remained indissoluble, even though in the middle of the eighteenth century grounds and procedure came to be matters of settled routine. Not until 1858 was divorce admitted in the modern sense, as a dissolution of the tie of marriage obtainable in a secular court as a matter of law rather than of grace,[54] but even then adultery was to be the only ground, and that only if in the case of a husband's adultery it was accompanied by such aggravating circumstances as bigamy, rape, cruelty, or desertion for at least two years.

The reinterpretation of the Gospel by the Protestant Reformers started a movement that was in the long run to bear fruits which they had hardly desired and which were slow in ripening. For a century and a half the situation remained as it was shaped by Reformation and Counter-Reformation: no divorce at all in Roman Catholic re-

---

51. T. B. SMITH, SCOTLAND: THE DEVELOPMENT OF ITS LAWS AND CONSTITUTION 303 (1962); also 3 ENCYCLOPEDIA OF THE LAWS OF SCOTLAND 519 (1927).

52. C. E. P. Davis, in R. H. GRAVESON & F. R. CRANE, eds., A CENTURY OF FAMILY LAW 315 ff. (1957). No change was made even under the Commonwealth, in spite of the passionate criticism of John Milton (*The Doctrine and Discipline of Divorce Restored to the Good of Both Sexes*, 1 PROSE WORKS 198 [Philadelphia 1845]; *The Judgment of Martin Bucer concerning Divorce*, id. 256; *Tetrachordon*, id. 283; *Colasterion*, id. 356).

53. In the two centuries before 1850 the total number of parliamentary divorces did not exceed 250. R. H. Graveson, in GRAVESON & CRANE, *supra* note 52, at 5.

54. Matrimonial Causes Act 1857, 20 & 21 Vict. c. 85.

gions and in England, divorce available in comparatively rare cases and conceived as punishment for grave marital misconduct in Protestant territories. But with Reformation, Renaissance, and humanism new trains of thought had been set in motion, thought which moved away from the bases of scripture and church, which came to be secular and to find its sole base in human reason and nature. The intense concern of the educated with the documents of ancient Greece and Rome acquainted them with a social system in which marriage had been regarded as a secular affair, a contract, that, like any other, was concluded by the consent of the parties and that could be terminated even more easily than a commercial contract, namely, by the will of just one of the participants. Thinkers of the persuasion of rationalistic natural law and of the philosophy of the Enlightenment conceived of marriage as one of the avenues open to man in his pursuit of happiness, and man's right to pursue happiness was one of those inalienable rights which no government ought to be able to block.[55] What greater sources of happiness could be found than a harmonious marriage; what greater misery could there be than being caught in an unhappy one? If a marriage turned out to be unsuccessful, well, then each spouse ought to be free to put an end to it and seek happiness in a new marital venture.

This new notion of marriage, enthusiastically received by the sophisticated, was, of course, too radically opposed to tradition to be readily accepted by society in general or by legislators. But in an age in which legislation lay in the hands of absolute monarchs, the way was open to an enlightened prince to impose upon his people the new set of ideas, however strange they might appear to those who did not belong to the small but influential circle of the Illuminati. An eighteenth-century monarch took the lead, King Frederick II, later called the Great, of Prussia.

Frederick appears to have been the first European ruler to pour the new ideas about divorce into the mold of legislation, first by an edict of 1751,[56] and then in the great codification that was inspired by him but did not become law until 1794, eight years after his death. Under the Prussian General Code,[57] marriages could be dissolved, not

55. See M. ERLE, DIE EHE IM NATURRECHT DES 17. JAHRHUNDERTS (1952).
56. Circular Rescript of 27 September 1751: The authorities were admonished not to render divorce difficult in the case of marriages notoriously disturbed by violent enmity (*inimicitiae capitales*). In his cabinet order of 22 May 1783, the king ordered "that in matters of divorce one ought not to be so easygoing as to further abase; but one should not be too difficult either, because that would impede population." Apparently what the king meant was the number of births. See 3 H. DERNBURG, LEHRBUCH DES PREUSSISCHEN PRIVATRECHTS 56 (4th ed. 1896).
57. ALLGEMEINES LANDRECHT FÜR DIE PREUSSISCHEN STAATEN (ALR).

only for cause as under traditional Protestant law, but also by the mutual consent of both parties, provided the marriage was "utterly childless," or even upon the unilateral application of one party who would allege and prove "through relevant facts the existence of so violent and deeply rooted an aversion that no hope remains for a reconciliation and the achievement of the ends of the marital state." Those two new possibilities of divorce were, to be sure, hedged in by cumbersome and time-consuming formalities, but — and this was essential — they were given recognition in the legislative scheme of a leading prince of the time.[58]

The model of the Prussian General Code played a major role in future developments in Germany as well as in other countries, especially France and, it seems, in parts of the United States. In the seesawing struggle between the two orders of ideas about divorce, the liberal provisions of the Prussian Law of 1791/94 were later repealed by German legislation of 1896,[59] but the ideas expressed by them have continued to live and to combine with those of conservatism in the much criticized but inevitable compromise of judicial toleration of consent divorce brought about by the collusive allegation and "proof" of some official ground for divorce.

In France a spectacular course of events was set in motion by the revolutionary upheaval of 1789. Down to the very end of the *ancien régime* France, since the repeal of the Edict of Nantes in 1685 again a purely Catholic state, adhered to the traditional system of Catholic territories, save for some inroads into the idea of purely ecclesiastical regulation of marriage by that peculiar claim of limited secular jurisdiction in church matters known as Gallicanism. Apart from some royal ordinances concerning registration,[60] marriage remained a domain of ecclesiastical regulation and jurisdiction. Ecclesiastical decrees of nullity and separation from bed and board could thus be obtained, but a divorce *a vinculo* remained unobtainable, whatever the *philosophes* and the men of the *Encyclopédie* might say about the "irrationality, cruelty, and unnaturalness" of the system. But with the collapse of the old order came the triumph of the new ideas. In the sequel of the stormy events of 1789 many a Frenchman and many a French woman simply shook off the fetters of an unhappy marriage, walked out on, or sepa-

---

58. The provisions on divorce were contained in Part II, Title I, §§ 668 ff. The passage just quoted is from § 718a.
59. See *infra* p. 294.
60. Ordonnance de Blois, 1579; Ordonnance sur la procédure civile, 1667; Déclaration du Roi du 9 Avril 1736.

rated from, the old spouse and united with a new one in some form of secular ceremony or with no formality at all. Soon the situation became so confused that the new legislature, the National Convention, found it necessary to step in. The famous Law of 1792 anticipated later developments in France and elsewhere. Its intentions and its effects have been controversial among contemporaries and in later generations. We shall return to it in chapter 8. But first we shall observe the ways in which the clash of opinions made itself felt in the United States of America.

3
Divorce in the United States: Liberal Attack and Conservative Defense

[America has been famous for her love of liberty and her hatred of tyranny of every kind.] Therefore, it is hoped, the same spirit of indulgence will extend still further — to those unhappy individuals, mixed among every class of mankind, who are frequently united together in the worst of bondage. . . . Doth God require this sacrifice of our happiness?[1]

It is incomparably better that individuals should suffer than that an Institution, which is the basis of all human good, should be shaken, or endangered.[2]

> For ill-advised propriety
> Brings poverty with piety.[3]

These three quoted passages reflect the conflicting tendencies by which American laws of divorce have been shaped. One or the other tendency has prevailed at one time or another, or in one place or another. In its totality, the American law of divorce constitutes a compromise.

Among the many groups that have come together as the American nation, two have been conspicuous from early times: the religious believers and the men of adventure, the confessors of strict Christian morality and the seekers of unbridled liberty. American history might and ought to be written in terms of their conflict. The long trek from the Atlantic seaboard to the Pacific coast, from Plymouth Colony to

---

1. ANON., AN ESSAY ON MARRIAGE; OR, THE LAWFULNESS OF DIVORCE IN CERTAIN CASES CONSIDERED 3, 16 (1788), cited by N. M. BLAKE, THE ROAD TO RENO 48 (1962) (hereinafter cited as BLAKE; passages from Blake's volume are quoted with permission of the publisher, The Macmillan Company, New York).

2. TIMOTHY DWIGHT (president of Yale College), THEOLOGY, EXPLAINED AND DEFENDED IN A SERIES OF SERMONS (about 1816) 427 (5th ed. 1828), cited by BLAKE 58.

3. Anon., reproduced in LESLIE CURTIS, RENO REVERIES: IMPRESSIONS OF LOCAL LIFE (1912), cited by BLAKE 154.

Hollywood, the development from Puritan to hippie, the battles between outlaws and vigilantes, present these two sides. Law and order have been established, but the yearning for freedom and lawlessness has never been extinguished.

Shall the marriage bond be indissoluble, as demanded by Christian tradition? Identifying indissolubility of the marriage tie with actual stability of marriage, family, and society, the traditionalists have consistently opposed the never ending quest for marital freedom. In the United States the two antagonistic tendencies have found extreme expression. That easy divorce would inevitably result in the destruction of the institution of marriage and family has been as readily taken for granted as the opposite view that unavailability of easy divorce would inevitably promote vice, hypocrisy, and social unrest.

Institutionalist conservatism and individualist liberalism were not the only forces determining American attitudes toward divorce. The liberals found a not always welcome support in the feminist movement as well as from business interests anxious through easy divorce to promote the tourist trade. Conservatives have generally been united by the common Christian tradition, but the denominations have rarely worked together. In older times the fight against divorce was mainly conducted by Protestants. At the turn of the century the Catholic church became a potent force.

In France, Germany, Switzerland, the struggle between the opposing forces was fought in each country as a whole and the compromises were worked out on the central levels. Whatever differences exist between the various regions of France, Germany, or Switzerland, they constitute variations in the application of laws which are in force throughout each of these countries. Under the peculiar form in which the federal system works in the United States, the official laws differ from state to state, and above the level of fifty-seven separate jurisdictions the Supreme Court of the United States has erected a superstructure by which the state laws have been essentially modified.

Only in a few states is the law of the statutes applied by the courts as it is written. There are states in which, as in California, Nevada, New Mexico, or Florida, the official law expresses the idea of individualist liberalism. In the majority of the states the situation is similar to that which has developed in such "nonhomogenous" nations as France or Germany. A conservative law of the books has been turned by the courts into a different law in action in which the ideas of liberalism are given an outlet of an often extreme character. Officially or unofficially, liberalism has come to dominate the American practice of divorce. In American life, divorce has become a firmly accepted institution. In fact, among countries of Western tradition, the United States has long been that with the highest incidence of divorce (see table 1).

TABLE 1
DIVORCES PER 1,000 POPULATION, 1965 AND 1967*

	1965	1967
United States of America	2.47	2.64
United Arab Republic	2.17	1.85
Hungary	2.01	2.06
Romania	1.94	0.00†
U.S.S.R.	1.56	2.74
East Germany	1.44	1.55
Denmark	1.37	1.43
Czechoslovakia	1.32	1.39
Sweden	1.24	1.36
Austria	1.16	1.21
West Germany	0.93	1.00
Switzerland	0.84	not stated
Japan	0.79	0.83
England and Wales	0.78	0.88
Australia	0.75	0.82
France	0.72	0.75
Belgium	0.59	not stated
Mexico	0.58	0.72
Scotland	0.51	0.58
Netherlands	0.50	0.59
Canada	0.46	0.55
Venezuela	0.26	0.24
Faeroe Islands	0.19	0.16

Source: Demographic Yearbook of the United Nations 1968, table 34, Crude Divorce Rates.

* The rates stated indicate the number of divorces per 1,000 population. The more highly indicative rates of the number of divorces per 1,000 married women are not available for international comparison.

† The "low rate" is stated to be due to a change in the divorce law. In 1968 the rate is stated to have been 0.20. [Note in U.N. Yearbook.]

The United States rate in 1967 was 2.6 divorces per 1,000 population, and the provisional rate for 1968 was 2.9. This high incidence of divorce has come to be a cause of widespread alarm. Efforts to stem the tide have begun, based upon secular rather than religious motives.

Proposals to reduce the incidence of divorce by narrowing the grounds upon which a divorce may be granted have been suggested. A new, therapeutic approach seeks to help people overcome marital difficulties through counseling and conciliation. Education for family life aims at preventing marital discord by preparation for marriage. Family courts are being established in many parts of the country; each year brings legislation in one state or another. New answers are being sought continually. Divorce law is one of the liveliest parts of American law, and no one answer has yet been found which would satisfy everybody. In fact, how could one answer be found in a country as varied and as full of contrast as the United States? What has been found is a compromise. Like all compromises, it does not satisfy the advocates of consistent positions and firm convictions. But the American compromise works, as it has to work in a democratic, nonhomogenous society.

Like most of American law, the American law of divorce had its origin in the law of England. The English law of the early seventeenth century was simple: divorce was not available in the courts. While the Protestant reformers of the Continent reinterpreted the Gospel texts as permitting divorce in the case of adultery and even in that of persistent desertion and cruelty, the Church of England, after some initial hesitation, continued to adhere to the doctrine of indissolubility. By severely limiting the scope of annulment that had been available under Roman Catholic canon law, the Church of England became more popish than the pope. The only possibility of remarriage before the death of the spouse of a prior marriage consisted in the grant of a special privilege by the king in Parliament, i.e., in practice in a private bill enacted by Parliament. Grant of the privilege of remarriage by the Privy Council, the consistory, or some other body of supreme government power occurred in all countries in which the supremacy of a secular ruler had replaced that of the pope. In England, however, parliamentary divorces seem not to have occurred before the last part of the seventeenth century. Before 1669, when the first such bill was enacted, and 1715, a total of 5 parliamentary divorces was granted. Between 1715 and 1850, the number was 224,[4] with the rate slowly accelerating at the end of the period. Between 1801 and 1850 the yearly average was 2.2. With the exception of five, all the parliamentary divorces were granted to men.[5] The procedure, which was standardized in the eighteenth century, was time-consuming and so expensive that

4. 1 W. HOLDSWORTH, HISTORY OF ENGLISH LAW 623 (5th ed. 1931).
5. J. MACQUEEN, THE APPELLATE JURISDICTION OF THE HOUSE OF LORDS AND THE PRIVY COUNCIL TOGETHER WITH THE PRACTICE ON PARLIAMENTARY DIVORCE 482 (1842).

none but the wealthiest could avail themselves of this extraordinary remedy.[6]

Earlier in Presbyterian Scotland, divorce was recognized upon the grounds of adultery and desertion.[7] English Dissenters were not unanimous, however. The permissibility of divorce was argued vigorously by the Separatists and passionately advocated by John Milton. Under the Commonwealth, divorce was for a while available, only to be abolished again in the Restoration.

In the American colonies the Church of England doctrine was taken over without question in the southern plantations. Marriage there remained indissoluble until the time of the Revolution. But in the northern colonies trends came to the fore which owed their origin to the Puritan inclination to follow the doctrines of Calvin and the other Reformers.[8]

In New England, divorce was recognized and practiced from the beginning. The Separatists of Plymouth Colony, the Puritans of Massachusetts, and the colonies of New Hampshire and Rhode Island made provision for jurisdiction of regular civil courts, in Massachusetts after the repeal of the first charter by the governor and council. Occasionally, divorces were granted by the legislative assemblies. In the lists of statutory grounds, adultery and desertion, usually for at least five years, were thrown together with impotence, "fraudulent contract," premarital fornication with a relative of the spouse, and bigamy, i.e., acts which under a more technical legal approach would be treated as grounds for nullifying a marriage rather than as grounds for divorce. In general, only the innocent party was permitted to remarry.

The records, especially for the earlier period, are not complete. Yet the number of cases that can be ascertained is surprisingly high. In the small community of Plymouth Colony at least 6 divorces were granted between 1661 and 1692. In Massachusetts some 40 marriages were dissolved between 1639 and 1692. Between 1760 and 1786 the number of

---

6. The Royal Commission on Divorce of 1850 estimated the cost at approximately £ 700 to £ 800. Report, at 211 (1853).

7. When the Reformation took legal effect in Scotland on 24 August 1560, adultery was recognized as a ground for divorce immediately. Malicious desertion was recognized as a ground by Statute, 1573, c. 55. 1 P. Fraser, The Law of Scotland as Applicable to the Personal and Domestic Relations 655, 677 (1846).

8. The history of divorce in America is presented in detail in G. E. Howard, History of Matrimonial Institutions (3 vols. 2d ed. 1904), and A. W. Calhoun, Social History of the American Family from Colonial Times to the Present (3 vols. 1916; new ed., three vols. in one, 1945). A shorter, lively presentation is in Blake.

cases known to have been brought before the governor and council was 96. In only three of these cases was relief totally denied. In ten cases, which seem to have been initiated by wives upon the ground of the husbands' cruelty, the old canon law institution of separation from bed and board was revived, which generally seems to have been repudiated in New England. For Connecticut it was stated in 1788 that no less than 390 divorces had been granted in the preceding fifty years.[9] Considering the general spirit of the age and the sparsity of the population of the colony, that figure is astonishingly high.

In New York, a few divorces are known to have occurred during the Dutch period. Some divorces also were granted by English governors; more seem to have been issued after 1711. In New Jersey and Pennsylvania the inclination of the legislators to grant divorces resulted, in the latter part of the eighteenth century, in a conflict with the English government, which disallowed several of these private divorce acts. At the end of the colonial period, divorce was an established institution in New England, unknown to the laws of the southern colonies and of New York, and of occasional occurrence in Pennsylvania and New Jersey.

With the elimination of English domination American state legislatures were free to exercise that prerogative of divorce by private act which the Parliament in London had been wont to exercise for some time.[10] The trend was particularly strong in the southern states, especially in Georgia, where no less than 291 such acts were passed between 1798 and 1835. Both Georgia and Virginia attempted to follow the model of England, where Parliament would not pass a bill of divorce until the facts, i.e., in England the commission of adultery, had been found by a court actually to have occurred as alleged. In the ordinary case of a husband's petition for divorce because of his wife's adultery, under the rules followed by Parliament in the eighteenth century, the acceptance by Parliament of the petition for the enactment of a private bill of divorce had to be preceded by two judicial proceedings. First the petitioner had to obtain in the ecclesiastical court a decree of separation from bed and board, and then in a common law court a judgment holding the corespondent liable to the petitioner to pay damages for his criminal conversation with the petitioner's wife.

Among the earliest cases brought before southern legislatures were those in which a married white woman had given birth to a mulatto

9. BLAKE 39.
10. BLAKE 49.

child. In the first such case handled by the legislature of Maryland the wife and child were ordered to be sold into slavery.[11]

According to H. F. Page, by 1850 some 100 legislative divorces were granted in Ohio, over 100 in Pennsylvania between 1817 and 1849; in 1830–31 in one session of the Illinois legislature there were 24; in the Delaware session of 1848–49 the number of private divorces was 12, and in the Missouri legislature of the same year no fewer than 55.[12]

As legislative divorce became increasingly frequent, it began to be attacked as arbitrary, costly, and lacking in procedural safeguards. Following the model of New England, but involving various vicissitudes, one state after another enacted general laws on divorce giving jurisdiction to the courts and enumerating the grounds upon which a divorce was to be granted. Grounds for divorce were still thrown together with what might have been called grounds for annulment. Among the former, adultery figured as the most prominent and no differences were made between adultery committed by the wife and that committed by the husband, even though in the moral view of the times the former was regarded as more reprehensible than the latter. As Protestant Reformers had already done, desertion persisting for a certain minimum period of time was generally added as a ground for divorce. But as for cruelty, the legislatures were reluctant. If mentioned at all, it was generally treated as a situation that would entitle a wife to obtain a separation from bed and board. An abused wife might be regarded as deserving protection against her husband, but the idea that she might be allowed to enter upon a new marriage with another man was too shocking. Yet, in Rhode Island it was provided as early as 1798 that a judicial divorce should be granted to either party in cases of "gross misbehavior and wickedness repugnant to and in violation of the marriage covenant."

Even the most liberal laws were based upon the idea that divorce was to be a punishment for marital misconduct, especially the arch sin of adultery. The only situation in which guilt played no role was that of the married person who had disappeared and of whom for a number of years no news had been obtained, so that it was uncertain whether he was alive or dead. In several states the remarriage of the other spouse was to be valid even though the Enoch Arden might unexpectedly return.[13] But the idea that a marriage might be terminated

11. BLAKE 51.
12. PAGE, A VIEW OF THE LAW RELATIVE TO THE SUBJECT OF DIVORCE IN OHIO, INDIANA, AND MICHIGAN (1851), cited by BLAKE 56.
13. See H. H. CLARK, JR., THE LAW OF DOMESTIC RELATIONS IN THE UNITED STATES 63 (1968).

simply because it had broken down and without putting the blame on one party or the other did not find expression in any American statute of the first half of the nineteenth century.

In actual fact, escape divorce and divorce by mutual consent were by no means unknown. *Ex parte* divorces were granted by both courts and legislatures upon insufficient evidence, or no evidence, or even upon no statement of any specific facts at all. The existence of practices of "proving" fictitious facts by parties acting in mutual agreement was noted with alarm and occasional disapproval.

While reliable statistics are lacking, it is obvious that long before the Civil War divorce had become a common phenomenon of American life. By and large, legislation exhibited an attitude of growing liberalism, in a moderate form in New England, in more radical ways in the states of the frontier. With the westward march of settlement, divorce proneness and governmental willingness to accommodate a settler's desire to free himself from old bonds and start life anew moved westward, too. As the new states came to be consolidated, the conservative elements usually succeeded in ending the "excesses." The center of divorce thus moved from Ohio to Indiana, to Illinois, then to the Dakotas and farther west.[14]

While the incidence of divorce was high, it does not appear excessive if one considers the great extent of migration. Change of environment, often of an entire way of life, involves a temptation to be free of old ties of marriage and to establish new ones in the new community. Divorce was not the only device to open the door to remarriage. If communications are poor and registration of the populace is rudimentary or nonexistent, the male migrant who has left his wife behind may easily forget his intention to let her follow at a later time, and he may go through a new ceremony of marriage, or simply establish a common-law marriage with a new partner in his new place, without first having resorted to divorce. He is, of course, a bigamist. Nobody knows the number of undiscovered cases of bigamy. There is no doubt, however, that it is high, and that it was much higher in the nineteenth century when registration of civil status was rudimentary in the United States and disappearance was an easy substitute for divorce. Prosecutions for bigamy of a migrant who remarried in the United States while he was still technically married to a woman in Sicily, or on the eastern seaboard, were rare. How was the prosecution to prove that the prior marriage had not been terminated somehow somewhere? The reluctance of prosecutors to harass a migrant who had successfully estab-

14. See BLAKE 116.

lished himself in his new surroundings, and to destroy his new home and family, was matched by the disinclination of judges to favor the stay-at-home wife, in Europe or in the East, over the present wife and her children. The interests of the children of a bigamous marriage have come to be safeguarded by the almost universal enactment of so-called saving statutes, under which the children of an attempted but invalid marriage are to be treated as if they were legitimate. In many states this occurs whenever a ceremony of marriage has been gone through. In others, legitimacy does not take place if both parties to the attempted marriage knew that it would be invalid.[15] But if only one of the parties knew of a prior marriage, how is one to disprove the allegation of the other that he was not aware of the bigamous character of the new relationship?

If the migrant prospers in his new surroundings and dies with property left behind him, the stay-at-home wife may hear about it and claim a share in the estate for herself and her children. For disputes between the person with whom a decedent lived as his spouse at the time of his death and a spouse of an earlier marriage, most American courts have developed a device that enables them to favor the last spouse over the former.[16] The court presumes that some fact has occurred by which the prior marriage was dissolved before the latter was concluded. The former spouse who claims a share in the estate must prove not only that *she* never procured a divorce or annulment before the new marriage was concluded but also that no such divorce or annulment had been obtained by the decedent. While the former proof usually is easy, the latter may be next to impossible. The claimant has to trace all the movements of the decedent and then to search the records of all courts of all counties of each state of which the decedent was or might have been a resident.[17]

15. See CLARK, *supra* note 13, at 132.
16. See *id*. at 67.
17. In Spears v. Spears, 178 Ark. 720, 12 S.W.2d 875 (1928), the wife of the decedent's later marriage prevailed over that of his prior marriage even though the latter proved that no divorce had been obtained in any of the counties in which the decedent had resided. She should, the court held, have proved that no divorce had been obtained in any county in which the decedent might have sued without being a resident. The court emphasized the fact that the decedent had been a lawyer and was thus unlikely to commit bigamy. In the case of *In re* Biersack, 159 N.Y.S. 519, 96 Misc. 161, the surrogate, King's County, went so far as to uphold the legitimacy of a child of his mother's second marriage even though it was proved that neither the mother nor her first husband had obtained a divorce or an annulment before the mother had, without ceremony, concluded her marriage with the child's father. The surrogate was obviously impressed by the facts that at the time of her first marriage the mother had been only fifteen years old, that the first husband had

In fashioning this presumption of the validity of the last marriage, the American courts created a substitute for divorce that was flexible, convenient, and inconspicuous. While divorce has attracted attention and constituted a subject of controversy, the obscuration of bigamy through the almost irrebuttable presumption of validity of the last "marriage" has escaped the attention of the viewers-with-alarm. What American, indeed, would not approve of a device which protects the good, though perhaps bigamous, American wife and her children against the avarice of some woman in Poland?

In those states which have preserved common-law marriage, i.e., the possibility of entering a fully valid marriage without license and ceremony, a bigamous marriage can be transformed into a legally valid marriage.[18] If H marries W2 while his marriage bond to W1 still subsists, the new marriage is bigamous and invalid. But if H and W2 still live together as husband and wife when the marriage to W1 is terminated by her death or a divorce or an annulment, H and W2 are assumed at that time to conclude a common-law marriage, even though they may not even know of the termination of the prior marriage. In some states this assumption is not made in all circumstances, for instance, not if at the beginning of their cohabitation both parties know that their relation would be bigamous. But the preservation of the ancient possibility of informal marriage seems to some extent to have been motivated by the very desire to provide a cure for initially invalid marriages.

Resort to disappearance and bigamy or, as occurred occasionally, purchase of a bogus decree of divorce does not appeal to one who wishes to stay at home or to live in surroundings in which his status is likely to be known. These are the cases in which one is likely to turn to divorce or the acquisition of a mistress. The latter practice remains within the realm of semisecrecy and semirespectability. Divorce and remarriage are public events, attracting public attention, as individual cases and as institutions. As divorces became more frequent in nineteenth-century America, conservative criticism grew. In the two decades before the Civil War, divorce became the subject of passionate controversy,

---

abandoned her after six days, and that she had not had any news about his being alive or dead until after the death of her second husband.

In order to bastardize the child it should have been shown that neither of the parties to the first marriage had at the time not been bound by the bond of some prior marriage that had remained undissolved. "Where the legitimacy of a child . . . is assailed upon the allegation that one of the child's conceded parents was a party to an earlier marriage the presumption is in favor of legitimacy. This is one of the strongest presumptions known to the law" (169 N.Y.S. 523).

18. See CLARK, *supra* note 13, at 51.

especially in New York. In that state, political liberalism was in the ascendancy, but it had no success in the law of divorce. The statute of 30 March 1787,[19] under which adultery was the only ground for divorce, remained untouched. At the time of its enactment, this law constituted a liberal victory, as it substituted a legal right to divorce for the vagaries of discretionary divorce by the legislature, which seems to have been exercised rarely if at all. As the nineteenth century advanced, the narrowness of the New York statute came under increasingly severe criticism which, in turn, provoked heated replies from the conservative defenders of the traditional Christian view. For a long time these defenders were mostly Protestants; Roman Catholics did not exert a conspicuous influence in the continuing New York debate until the later decades of the century.

In the long debate in New York and in the country at large, every argument that can possibly be made for or against divorce has found vigorous expression. The chief argument of the advocates of divorce was, of course, derived from the liberal postulate of each individual's right to pursue his own happiness. It was with an argument of this kind that the committee on grievances of the assembly of the legislature of New York in 1840 recommended a liberalization of the state's law on divorce. In its report the committee quoted Bentham's postulate that the law ought to provide the greatest happiness to the greatest number and then concluded: "How inconceivably unwise is that severe policy which compels the continuance of a connection, where hatred and disgust is the predominant feeling, and where quarrels and criminations and often personal violence and brutal outrage make up the sum of everyday life."[20]

In the land of liberty it was natural to argue that the tyranny of an unhappy marriage was as detestable as that of despotism. So it was said, remembering the Revolution, that it is hoped that "the same spirit of indulgence will extend . . . to those unhappy individuals, mixed among every class of mankind, who are frequently united together in the worst of bondage to each other, occasioned by circumstances not in their power to foresee, or prevent, at the time of their union; which should entitle them to relief from humane legislators and the rest of mankind."[21]

The argument of commiseration was propounded with special reference to women. The possibility of divorce was urged as a means of

19. Laws of New York, chap. 69.
20. 63 Ass. Doc. No. 324 (18 April 1840), quoted by BLAKE 76.
21. Anon., *supra* note 1, at 3, cited by BLAKE 48.

protection for women abused by tyrannical, profligate or abusive husbands. Reform of divorce laws as "obsolete" as those of New York became a tenet of the aggressive feminist movement of the mid-nineteenth century. Arguing against the conservative views of Horace Greeley, Mrs. Elizabeth Cady Stanton referred to unhappy wives' suicides and wives' murders and asked: "What say you to facts like these? Now, do you believe . . . that all these wretched matches are made in heaven? that all these sad, miserable people are bound together by God?" [22]

Frequent also was the assertion that adultery and other forms of immorality are the inevitable concomitants of a strict divorce law. This argument was adduced, among others, by Joel Prentice Bishop in his *Commentaries on the Law of Marriage and Divorce*, the first major American treatise on the subject, where he wrote in 1852:

Nothing is more true than that "honest liberty is the greatest foe to dishonest license." If parties are married in law, but not in fact and therefore are forbidden to enter into connections which are real marriages, they will be liable, unless they are better — not worse — than the average of the community, to commit breaches of the rules of morality, either by promiscuous sexual indulgence, or by forming alliances in the similitude of matrimonial, from which a spurious issue may spring. Indeed, it is well known that, in England, where divorces from the bond of matrimony are only obtainable on application to Parliament, in rare instances and at enormous expense, rendering them a luxury quite beyond the reach of the mass of the people, second marriages without divorce, and adulteries and the birth of illegitimate children are of everyday occurrence, and the crime of polygamy is winked at.[23]

The same argument was used by Robert Dale Owen in his reply to Horace Greeley's charge that because of Owen's influence Indiana had made divorce so easy that the state had become "the paradise of free lovers." "You have," Owen replied, "elopements, adultery, which your law . . . virtually encourages; you have free-love, and that most terrible of all social evils, prostitution. You may feel disposed to thank God that you are not as other men, or even as these Indianians. I think that we are justified in His sight, rather than you. . . . God forgive you, Horace Greeley, the inhuman sentiment." [24]

Mrs. Stanton denounced existing laws as unequal. If the husband is the guilty party, he still retains the greater part of what she called the common property; if the wife is the guilty party, she goes out of the partnership penniless.[25]

22. 1 E. C. STANTON and others, HISTORY OF WOMAN SUFFRAGE 720 (1881), cited by BLAKE 93.
23. BISHOP § 285.
24. New York Tribune, 5 March 1860, cited by BLAKE 90.
25. 2 THE REVOLUTION 233–34 (15 October 1868), BLAKE 99.

The solution advocated by Mrs. Stanton and other radical feminists was complete freedom of either party at any time to terminate the marriage relationship. "The wisest possible reform," Mrs. Stanton wrote, "we could have on this whole question is to have no legislation whatever. The relations of the sexes are too delicate in their nature for statutes, lawyers, judges, jurors, or our public journals to take cognizance of, or regulate."[26]

Arguments like these made it easy to denounce the protagonists of divorce reform as advocates of free love,[27] especially since the demands of the supporters of unlimited or general sexual freedom necessarily included free choice of partners.

The dispute was acrimonious, but hardly ever were the arguments of either side supported by evidence. Only rarely did the liberals refer to foreign experiences. All the more remarkable is the following observation contained in a report presented to the assembly of the New York legislature by its judiciary committee:

> [The] pernicious effects [of unavailability of divorce] are visible in the social institutions and domestic manners of most of the countries of Catholic Europe. And a more forcible commentary can scarcely be made upon the subject under consideration than by a comparison of the manners and morals of two such countries . . . as Scotland and Holland, where not only adultery but desertion are causes of divorce with the morals and manners of Italy or Spain, where the marriage tie is indissoluble.[28]

The other side might then refer to "the Roman Republic, which under the sway of easy divorce, rotted away and perished, — blasted by the mildew of unchaste mothers and dissolute homes."[29]

In the sixteenth century discussion about divorce had been concerned with the interpretation of the words of Jesus as reported in the Gospels. While in the view steadfastly held by the Roman Catholic church, marriage is completely indissoluble, the Reformers and the Protestant theologians interpreted these passages as allowing divorce in the case of adultery and even of desertion. But even under the most extensive interpretation of the Gospel, divorce was to be kept within strict and narrow bounds. To the believer God's word was final. No debate could venture beyond the question of its right understanding. Reference to the Gospel was a natural ingredient in the debates about divorce reform and, quite naturally, the argument would mostly give expression

26. 2 THE REVOLUTION 36 (23 July 1868), BLAKE 99.
27. See BLAKE 97 ff.
28. 75 Ass. Doc. No. 73 (2 March 1852), BLAKE 77.
29. Horace Greeley in New York Tribune, 5 March 1860, BLAKE 91.

to the conservative point of view. The fight against such divorce mills as had arisen in Ohio, Indiana, Illinois, and South Dakota was spearheaded by Christian leaders like Bishop William H. Hare of the Episcopal church, a saintly man who had established a national reputation as the apostle to the Sioux. Attacks upon the divorce law of Connecticut, which had been among the most liberal in the early nineteenth century, was initiated by churchmen like Benjamin Trumbull and Timothy Dwight. Church groups were the moving forces in the conservative reaction to liberal divorce laws that arose after the Civil War and expressed themselves in the establishment, in 1885, of the National Divorce Reform League, which, in 1897, changed its name to National League for the Protection of the Family.

However, the interpretation of the Gospel words remained doubtful. Their authority was to be questioned by modern scholars who maintained that Jesus' strictures were not meant to be commands of universal and eternal validity but were addressed to the Jews of his own day. Criticism of the text began to throw doubt even upon the genuineness of the sayings attributed to Christ. Above all, simple resort to the Gospel bore no conviction to one who did not feel bound by scriptural command. In the secularized world it became necessary to support the traditionalist view by secular arguments. Even if monogamous marriage and the family grounded upon it were not divinely established institutions, their continued maintenance would be required as the basis of society, and their integrity was considered to be endangered by the possibility of easy divorce. An occasional individual might suffer under the yoke of an unhappy marriage; it would still be better to ignore such suffering, to maintain the stability of the institution. Marital unhappiness would be even less frequent if each person knew that marriage was indissoluble so that he would carefully ponder and choose before making the irreversible decision.

In a message vetoing one of the private divorce bills passed by the legislature of New York, the Council of Revision, of which Chancellor James Kent was an influential member, expressed itself in 1818 as follows:

> Anxiously aware of the evils which threaten the dearest interests of society, by increasing the causes or facility of divorces, the Council feel it to be their solemn and indispensable duty to oppose the dissolution of the marriage contract for any other than the single cause already provided by the general law of this state. . . . While the partial evils of indissoluble matrimony are sometimes witnessed and deplored, we ought to be consoled by the reflection that the peace and character of many thousands of families are preserved by the mutual forbearance and concessions between husband and wife, which are

induced by the ever impressive consideration that the voluntary tie which bound them, can never be dissolved.[30]

In its most radical form, the argument was expressed in 1816 by Timothy Dwight, president of Yale College: "[I]t is incomparably better that individuals should suffer than that an Institution, which is the basis of all human good, should be shaken, or endangered."[31]

A strict divorce law was necessary as a deterrent:

"It is very hard," said a culprit to the judge who sentenced him, "that I should be so severely punished for merely stealing a horse." "Man," replied the judge, "you are *not* so punished for merely stealing a horse, but *that horses may not be stolen.*" The distinction seems to me clear and vital.

Thus, Horace Greeley replied to those who emphasized the hardships which a strict law of divorce caused unhappy individuals.[32] Criminal punishment for stealing and the elimination of the possibility of legitimate remarriage were both seen as serving the same purpose of deterrence. *Punitur ne peccetur.*[33]

Just as criminal punishment through its deterrent effect is to protect society against being confounded by crime, so the law of marriage is to protect society against being confounded by laxity of morals, promiscuity, free love, and general profligacy. "Legitimately carried out," the *Woman's Journal* harangued against the liberal ideas of Mrs. Stanton, "these theories abrogate marriage, and we have then the hideous thing known as 'free love.' Be not deceived — *free love means free lust.* And let all women ponder well how they accept the specious arguments."[34]

In the view of the staunch conservative, Horace Greeley,

Marriage indissoluble may be an imperfect test of honorable and pure affection — as all things human are imperfect — but it is the best the State can devise; and its overthrow would result in a general profligacy and corruption such as this country has never known, and few of our people can adequately imagine.[35]

30. 41 Senate J. 98–101 (27 February 1818), Blake 72.
31. Dwight, *supra* note 2, cited Blake 58.
32. New York Tribune, 7 April 1860, Blake 92.
33. The parallel between criminal law and law of divorce also appears in that view under which, as in the view of the Protestant Reformers and the traditional American divorce statutes, divorce is admitted, not as an escape from a situation of unhappiness but as a punishment for marital misconduct. Under this notion of *Verschuldens-Prinzip* (or "divorce-sanction") one can say, as in the classical retributory theory of criminal law: "Punitur quia peccatum est." Under the view of *divorce-faillite*, no parallel between criminal law and divorce law appears to be justified.
34. Women's Journal 348 (5 November 1870), Blake 107.
35. New York Tribune, 18 December 1852, Blake 84.

If any evidence was necessary for this prediction, it was provided by ancient Rome, whose decline and fall was taken for granted to have been caused by the laxity of its law of divorce.[36]

In the debates of the nineteenth century, the interest of the children did not figure so prominently as it does today, but it was declared to be threatened by easy divorce, to be protected by strict laws on divorce.[37]

The radical views expressed by Stephen Pearl Andrews were thus answered by Horace Greeley:

> It is very clear, then, Mr. Andrews, that your path and mine will never meet. Your Socialism seems to me synonymous with Egotism, mine, on the contrary, contemplates and requires the subjection of individual desire and gratification to the highest good of the community — of the personal to the universal — the temporary to the everlasting. I utterly abhor what you term "the right of woman to choose the father of her child" — meaning her right to choose a dozen fathers for so many different children — seeing that it conflicts directly and fatally with the paramount right of each child through minority to protection, guardianship, and intimate daily counsel and training from both parents.[38]

That the strict rule of indissolubility of marriage combined with the traditional structure of marriage resulted in the subjection of wives to domination by their husbands was a frequently used argument of the feminist supporters of divorce reform. Less frequently was this aspect of the matter raised by the defenders of tradition. Only occasionally was reform openly opposed as jeopardizing male superiority. One of the few occasions on which that danger was explicitly evoked was in the final address to the jury by John Graham appearing for the defense in the murder trial of Daniel McFarland, who, in 1869, had shot Albert D. Richardson, the man whom his wife married after she had obtained an Indiana divorce from her tyrannical and alcoholic husband.

When this man Richardson [Graham pleaded], led this woman from her husband's house in Amity street, the husband had as much right to shoot him down as though Richardson had been guilty of her forcible abduction. That is the law of the Bible; for one of the two parties is superior and the other inferior. There is no absolute equality in the Bible between man and wife. As I understand the law of the Bible, it is that man was made for God and woman for man; that woman is the weaker vessel, and is meant to be under the protection of the stronger vessel, man; and that any attempt from any quarter to interfere with that supremacy, even though it be with the consent of the woman, is as much an infraction of the husband's rights as though it were the infliction of absolute violence upon her or upon him.[39]

36. See *supra* note 29.
37. New York Tribune, 28 January 1853, BLAKE 86.
38. *Id.*
39. THE RICHARDSON-MCFARLAND TRAGEDY 89–90 (1870), BLAKE 103.

McFarland was acquitted. The appeal to male superiority was as effective upon the jury of 1870 as it was later to be on the draftsmen of the Italian Penal Code of 1930.[40] Naturally, the McFarland case furnished ample ammunition to the feminist camp.[41]

During the Civil War and the political struggles of the Reconstruction, American minds were occupied by issues more tangible and more immediate than that of divorce. But it was not long before the increasingly upward trend of the divorce rate again appeared alarming.

The liberalism of the antebellum laws was expressed in the Connecticut law of 1849, which permitted divorce for "any such misconduct as permanently destroys the happiness of the petitioner and defeats the purpose of the marriage relation." [42] The attacks by conservative clergymen upon this "general misconduct clause" initiated a movement which from New England spread over the nation.

In the 1860s the Connecticut legislature found itself impelled to establish a committee to investigate the divorce situation. The collection of local statistics by the committee was followed by similar efforts in other parts of New England. They showed almost everywhere that the number of divorces had increased and the ratio between marriages concluded and marriages dissolved by divorce had decreased. The most spectacular change appeared in Massachusetts, where the ratio was 51:1 in 1860 and 21.4:1 in 1878. In Connecticut the ratio decreased from 14.1:1 to 10.6:1. Impressed by the statistics and the alarm spread by intellectual leaders like Theodore Woolsey, president of Yale, the Connecticut legislature did what western divorce mill states had done before; it repealed, in 1878, the general misconduct clause of its statute. Three years later, in 1881, the New England Divorce Reform League was founded with Dr. Woolsey as its first president and Samuel W. Dike, a Vermont Congregational minister, as its secretary. All during the next thirty years Dike was to play a prominent role in the movement. He remained the permanent full-time secretary of the organization and of those more comprehensive ones into which it was transformed, the National Divorce Reform League, established in 1885, and the National League for the Protection of the Family, as it has called itself since 1897. But during his long tenure of office Dike's role changed from that of ardent advocate of conservative reform into that of a doubter of its feasibility and efficacy. Impressed by the social science that had grown up toward the end of the century, Dike came to feel

40. See *infra* p. 186.
41. See BLAKE 101 ff.
42. Pub. Acts 1849.17, repealed by Pub. Acts 1878.305.

that no reform could be effectively undertaken without a comprehensive knowledge of the social facts, and the facts which he learned made him a skeptic toward the movement of which he himself was the leader and symbol. As a young minister, he had once refused to officiate at the remarriage of a divorced parishioner. In 1898, he openly opposed the proposal of a Congregationalist commission that ministers be urged not to marry divorced persons, and ten years later he took a stand against a similar proposal at a meeting of the Federal Council of Churches.

Dike's personal transformation exemplifies the transformation of the cultural climate. Both ended up in positions of compromise. In the end, Dike was able neither to give effective leadership to the conservatives nor clearly to embrace the liberal view. It was a position of compromise, unhappy for him and portentous for the law that came to prevail in the country for the long years preceding the presently emerging predominance of liberalism.

Owing to Dike's insistence upon the necessity of learning the facts, the federal government undertook the collection of statistical and legal data. A comprehensive inquiry by Carroll D. Wright, commissioner of labor, resulted in the monumental *Report on Marriage and Divorce, 1867–1886*.[43] When the conservative reformers later succeeded in gaining for their cause the support of President Theodore Roosevelt, a continuation report was compiled and published in 1908–9.[44]

The statistical data and their interpretation by the social scientists made Dike waver in his conviction. But it took time to put the brakes on the conservative reaction against divorce.

Secular combined with ecclesiastical forces in a drive to abolish or at least limit divorce through legislation. State legislatures were besieged to stiffen laws that were, like those of Connecticut or of western divorce mill states, regarded as overly liberal. Conservative states like New York or South Carolina were pressured not to yield to liberalizing tendencies. But conservative state legislation was not enough. Migratory divorce in Ohio, Indiana, Illinois, the Dakotas, or Nevada was recognized as a means to evade the strict laws of a divorce seeker's home state. Few or no statistics were available on the incidence of migratory divorce. The sporadic evidence available indicates that it occurred frequently, but not quite so frequently as the public believed it to occur. Out of that belief, efforts were directed toward uniform divorce legis-

43. 1889, rev. ed. 1891, 2d ed. 1897.
44. BUREAU OF THE CENSUS, MARRIAGE AND DIVORCE 1887–1906.

lation for the whole nation. Enactment by the Congress of a federal law on marriage and divorce would have required an amendment to the Constitution enabling Congress to legislate on the subject. Three amendments had been added to the Constitution after the Civil War. Four others were adopted in the following decades. But the Congress could not be moved to propose an amendment to extend federal legislative power to the field of family life. Between 1884 and 1947 motions were introduced in every new Congress, variously striving to achieve uniform federal legislation on marriage and divorce, or on divorce alone, or at least to inhibit migratory divorce. None of these proposals ever came to a vote. Only a single one reached the stage of committee discussion.[45] Opposition united liberals with southern defenders of states' rights and racists who would not be satisfied with a federal law that would not also forbid interracial marriages. But the principal cause of the failure was the politicians' feeling that the issue was not only not urgent but that it was too emotional to be publicly debated. Democracy requires compromise. How could a legislature compromise on an issue ultimately depending on religious and philosophical convictions? Besides, a compromise was in the process of being worked out by the courts. So, why should the comfortably sleeping dogs of religious conviction and of emotionalism be awakened?

Recognizing the difficulties of obtaining a federal divorce law, the conservative reformers embarked on the parallel effort of bringing about uniform divorce restriction by coordinated legislation of the states.

Toward the turn of the century, the center of the anti-divorce movement shifted from New England to New York. On the initiative of William C. Doane, Episcopal bishop of Albany, twenty-five Protestant denominations united in 1903 in the Interchurch Conference on Marriage and Divorce. In January 1905 a delegation of this organization called on President Theodore Roosevelt, who had repeatedly used strong language to warn the nation against the threatening collapse of its moral traditions. He was easily moved to present a message to Congress. But, heeding Samuel Dike's insistence on factual knowledge as a necessary preliminary to action, he merely requested the authorization of funds for a new statistical inquiry to bring up to date the Wright report of 1897. So the only fruit of the presidential intervention was the compilation and publication of the Bureau of the Census report of 1908–9.

New York also was the starting point of the movement paralleling

---

45. BLAKE 145 ff.

that for federal legislation, namely, for obtaining uniformity through coordinated legislation by the states. It was New York's special interest in the problem of migratory divorce that prompted Governor David B. Hill in 1889 and 1890 to exhort the legislature to take the initiative in organizing coordinated state action on marriage and divorce. The initiative resulted in the creation of the National Conference of Commissioners on Uniform State Laws, a body composed of delegates of the states, usually appointees of the governor. The first session was held in Saratoga in 1892. During the almost eighty years the conference has now been in existence, it has drafted and recommended for enactment by the states some 185 statutes on a great variety of topics. Few, however, have been enacted into law by all, or substantially all, the states. The greatest achievement has been the Uniform Commercial Code, which was drafted by the conference in collaboration with the American Law Institute, published in 1956 and again, in revised versions, in 1957 and 1967. By 1968, the code had been adopted by all states except Louisiana, and also by the District of Columbia and the Virgin Islands. As to marriage and divorce, the topics which engendered the National Conference of Commissioners on Uniform State Laws and which figured prominently on the agenda of the conference during the early years of its existence, the outcome has been negligible. An Act Regulating Annulment of Marriage and Divorce was approved in 1907 and adopted in just three states: Delaware, New Jersey and Wisconsin. It was so unsatisfactory that the endorsement by the conference was withdrawn in 1927. A Divorce Jurisdiction Act, approved in 1930 and adopted in just one state, Vermont, was rendered obsolete in 1943 by a decision of the Supreme Court of the United States. After another long interval, the conference in 1947 approved a Uniform Divorce Recognition Act, which, more modest than its predecessors, was adopted in California, Louisiana, Montana, Nebraska, New Hampshire, North Dakota, Rhode Island, South Carolina, Washington, and Wisconsin.[46]

In 1965 a new effort was initiated apparently in connection with the divorce law reform that was at long last under way in New York. The report submitted by the special committee on uniform divorce and marriage laws of the National Conference indicates a new spirit and states new aims. No longer is divorce presented as an evil that must be repressed in order to save the home, society and civilization.

It is singularly appropriate [the committee stated] that the whole subject be evaluated anew, due to the great sociological changes which are being daily

46. 1969 HANDBOOK OF THE NATIONAL CONFERENCE OF COMMISSIONERS ON UNIFORM STATE LAWS 193.

effected in day-to-day living. This is particularly true in the home, in marriage contracts, in the raising and custody of children, in religious circles and in the rapidly developing fields of social work. The Ecumenical spirit pervades the world. The sole emphasis in the past upon the religious and the moral in divorce and marriage, is now affected by the social and economic problems of contemporary life.[47]

A law as proposed by the committee was to eliminate the traditional grounds for divorce and adapt to contemporary conditions laws that are based upon misconceived ideas of a past age.

But we have anticipated the course of events, and we had better return to those events which followed the failure of the conservative effort at the turn of the century.

Was the conservative effort a failure? William L. O'Neill seems to believe that it was. In his book *Divorce in the Progressive Era*,[48] he uses the issue of divorce to illustrate how the advocates of the New Morality of individual freedom clashed with the defenders of the Victorian order of society. The topic is well chosen. The issue of divorce was, indeed, a focal point in the ideological struggle of the period between 1880 and 1940. Easy divorce figured among the postulates of libertarian individualists, freethinkers, socialists, feminists, and hedonists. The certainty of the belief in the universal necessity of traditional Christian morals was shaken by social scientists like William E. Lecky, comparatists like Henry Maine, and literary men like Henrik Ibsen, G. B. Shaw, or H. G. Wells. Doubts as to the effectiveness of legislative efforts to repress divorce were raised by the findings of social science, which was coming to maturity. The data presented in Carroll D. Wright's comprehensive statistical inquiry and their evaluation by Walter F. Willcox[49] apparently contributed to paralyzing the fighting spirit of Samuel Dike, the occupant of the key position in the organized wing of the conservatives. O'Neill also ascribed weight to the conservatives' lack of unity and a gradual loss of conviction. The center of opposition shifted to Roman Catholics, who now blocked all attempts to liberalize the divorce laws of New York. Among Protestant ecclesiastics as well as among lay defenders of the old order were advocates of limitation of the grounds for divorce to the traditional marital offenses of adultery, desertion, and cruelty. Some were willing to add habitual drunkenness, while still opposing such general misconduct clauses as that of the old Connecticut statute. Unwilling to break with the notion of divorce as

---

47. 1965 HANDBOOK 181.
48. 1967.
49. THE DIVORCE PROBLEM: A STUDY IN STATISTICS (Columbia College Studies in History, Economics, and Public Law, vol. 1, no. 1, 1st ed. 1891, 2d ed. 1897).

a punishment for guilt, they also tried to prevent divorce for such objective grounds as incurable insanity, not to speak of such omnibus terms as incompatibility or marriage breakdown. Toward the end of the period, when hopes of a nationwide strict divorce law had faded, a last stand was made to insure effectiveness of strict laws of at least those states which, like New York or the Carolinas, tried to remain bulwarks in the defense of the American home. Attempts to induce the states to agree on a uniform law barring recognition of migratory divorce of residents continued to be made into the 1940s and a similar tendency reappeared in New York's otherwise liberalizing law of 1965. They have to a large extent been made ineffective by the Supreme Court of the United States.

O'Neill does not maintain that the state of the law of divorce was directly determined by the arguments made for or against its availability. He rather uses the problem of divorce as a means to illustrate the development of the intellectual and moral climate which was determining the totality of American life of the period. It was the period which is widely called the Progressive Era, an era of belief in progress and of profound change in all aspects of society, the economic, the technical, the political, the intellectual, the moral, the religious. But it was still an era in which traditions were strong, in which millions were church members not merely in name, and in which Christian dogma and Christian morals were still forces to be reckoned with. Sexual freedom was not only postulated but practiced, by women and by men, but sex had not yet become the daily topic of the novel, the screen, or the advertising media. Obscenity laws were still enforced, education had not yet become fully progressive, racial inequality was still taken for granted, the old religion was firm and not only in the Bible belt. In the last decades of the period patriotism was expressed first in the War to Make the World Safe for Democracy and then in isolationism and anticommunism of the postwar years, culminating in the Palmer raids. The ethics of strict Protestant tradition brought about the noble experiment of Prohibition.

But the Prohibitionists' victory was limited to the law of the books. In action, Prohibition was made ineffective by the resistance of the individualist libertarians who were unwilling to live by the rigor of the Prohibitionist morality. The result was a compromise between the pious law of the books and the licentious flourishing of the bootleggers and the speakeasy. It required the shock of the Depression and the liberals' political victory in the New Deal to adjust to the law of reality. The sub rosa institution of tolerated flouting of the Prohibition law is a parallel to the flouting of the divorce laws in actual practice, and the breakthrough of realism that swept away the Volstead Act in 1933 has its counterpart in the present movement in the divorce field.

But in the 1920s and for many years to come, both conservatism and liberalism were more or less evenly balanced. Only for the intellectuals was it *de rigueur* to be liberal, and liberalism meant not only partiality for labor but also search for new values. Above all, it was the time of irresistible growth of industry, of urbanization, of the shift of the political, moral, and intellectual center from the farm to the city. In short, the Progressive Era was an era of contrasts, of transition, and thus of dispute. It was the era of increasing demands for social reform, especially of laws protecting labor and establishing social security. But the legislative reform would not come to easy fruition. What was not already blocked in the legislature ran the risk of being declared unconstitutional by the courts. Government in all its branches was still dominated by those groups which demanded freedom of economic activity, and they were supported by public opinion which was anxious to see the resources of the country developed and which believed that economic freedom was the system best suited to that end and thus to benefit all. This belief was under attack, but it needed the Great Depression to open the way for the New Deal and the new period of governmental intervention in favor of those groups which under the system of noninterference had been unable to obtain their "just" share. The successive beneficiaries have been the farmers, labor, and now the Negro. The farmers had to carry on their struggle essentially through their own organizations. Labor and the Negro have had the support of the intellectuals. But while the New Deal brought the economic restructuring of American society, it did not also imply the victory of the New Morality. That breakthrough seems to have occurred during only the past few years, the years following Barry Goldwater's defeat at the polls. During the years of the New Deal and after, the restructuring of the moral fabric was still undecided; in the Progressive Era it had been in preparation. During all these decades moral conservatism and the New Morality were in the state of precarious balance. Both traditionalists and innovators had to live together in the same society. They had to come to terms, to work out a compromise.

4
Our Dual Law of Divorce: The Law of the Books and the Law in Action

Perhaps there is no statute in Ohio more abused than the statute concerning divorce and alimony. Perhaps, there is no statute with which greater imposition is practiced upon the court. — Hitchcock, J., in Harter v. Harter, 5 Ohio 319 (1832).

In our survey of the course of American views on divorce, we stopped at the 1930s. All through the preceding one hundred years and at an even earlier time, divorce had been a subject of controversy. In fact, it was a subject about which holders of divergent philosophies of life clashed passionately. In contrast to England, the American states, with hardly an exception, had long ceased to treat marriage as completely indissoluble. The Protestant tradition of America had induced practically all the states to admit divorce, but to a limited extent only and as a punishment for grave marital misconduct. The idea that the law should provide freedom of remarriage simply because the existing marriage had failed to bring happiness had turned up every now and then, but by 1920 it had almost vanished from American law. Or so it seemed, at least when one identifies law with the wording of the statutes, the law of the books. The law actually applied in the courts was different. Divorce for misconduct had been turned into divorce by consent. How this result came to pass will now be our subject.

I. THE LAW OF THE BOOKS

When Chester G. Vernier's *Survey of the Divorce Laws of the Forty-eight American States, Alaska, the District of Columbia, and Hawaii*[1] was closed in October of 1931, the statutory grounds for divorce were distributed as shown in table 2. All those grounds of divorce which were enumerated in the statutes of a significant number of jurisdictions were forms of marital misconduct, as they were stated by Martin Luther and his successors in their interpretation of the New Testament. Divorce

---

1. 2 AMERICAN FAMILY LAWS (1932) (hereinafter cited as VERNIER).

TABLE 2
STATUTORY GROUNDS FOR DIVORCE IN THE UNITED STATES, 1931

Grounds	Number of Jurisdictions
Adultery	50
Desertion	47
Cruelty	43
Imprisonment or conviction of crime	43
Drunkenness	40
Nonsupport	15
Drug addiction	6
Gross neglect of duty	3
Vagrancy of husband (Missouri, Wyoming)	2
Fugitive from justice (Louisiana, Virginia)	2
Committing crime against nature (Alabama)	1
Infecting wife with venereal disease (Illinois)	1
Public defamation of other spouse (Louisiana)	1
Refusal to cohabit with other spouse for three years (New Hampshire)	1
Husband leaves U.S. with intent to become citizen of a foreign country and has not supported wife who is an alien or citizen of another state (New Hampshire)	1
Gross misbehavior or wickedness (Rhode Island)	1
Lewd bevahior of wife (Kentucky)	1

Source: VERNIER, 3–4, 70 71.

was regarded as repudiation of a guilty spouse by the innocent as punishment for misconduct. Those grounds which were found in the statutes of only a few states were but variations of the same theme. The comparatively frequent mentioning of drunkenness stemmed from the belief that alcoholism was not a disease but a vice. Other less frequently mentioned grounds were variations of the general theme of cruelty and were listed separately because cruelty happened to be interpreted narrowly by the courts of the jurisdiction or for some other accidental reason.

The idea that a divorce might be granted where a marriage had failed without the fault of either of the spouses was, where it was expressed at all, limited to the special case of incurable insanity, which was mentioned in the statutes of seventeen jurisdictions.[2] In a broader sense this idea was expressed in the statutes of those seven states under which a divorce was obtainable without proof of an offense simply when the parties had lived separate and apart from each other for a stated

2. *Id.* 3–4, 61.

period of years. The statutory periods were long: ten years in Rhode Island and Texas, seven years in Louisiana, and five years in Kentucky, North Carolina, Washington, and Wisconsin.

No less than forty-three states also declared impotency at the time of marriage to be a ground of divorce, and nine did so for bigamy. These situations — as well as those of fraud in bringing about the marriage, nine states; duress in obtaining marriage, five states; consanguinity and affinity, four states; conviction of crime before marriage, two states; antenuptial unchastity, two states; nonage at marriage, one state; leprosy, one jurisdiction (Hawaii); loathsome disease at time of marriage, 1 state — are, strictly speaking, grounds for invalidity or voidability of marriage rather than grounds for divorce. So was, of course, invalidity or voidability in general, which was expressly stated as ground for divorce in two states (Maryland [void] and Rhode Island [voidable]). Such terms were included in divorce laws either out of the desire to give alimony to the wife or because of insufficient clarity about the difference between divorce on the one side and annulment and declaration of nullity on the other.[3] In one state, South Carolina, divorce did not exist at all. Its introduction into the law of the state was even expressly prohibited in the state constitution.[4] In New York adultery was the only ground for divorce.

The idea that divorce was to be a punishment of a party guilty of marital misconduct and a privilege for the innocent was expressed not only in the statutory lists of grounds for divorce but also in the catalog of so-called defenses that had been developed by the courts and had found a frequently incomplete and bewildering expression in the statutes.

First of all, there was the "defense" of condonation, which it had been found appropriate expressly to mention in the statutes of twenty-nine jurisdictions.[5] Even a guilty spouse was not to be cast away once the offense had been condoned by the innocent one. Much learning and judicial diversity developed about what constituted condonation, and whether it was definite or given only under the condition that the guilty spouse would be permanently penitent so that the old offense could be "revived" as a ground for divorce if it, or some other offense, were committed again. All courts also seemed to agree in the view that a husband's act of marital intercourse performed in knowledge of the wife's misconduct was to be irrefutably presumed to indicate the

3. See *infra* p. 91.
4. Art. 17, § 3.
5. For the data on this and the following, see VERNIER 72–73.

mental state of forgiveness. A wife's act could be regarded as excusable because of economic necessity.

Furthermore, divorce would not be granted on the ground of adultery to the pimp-husband of a prostitute or to anyone else who had "connived" at his or her spouse's adultery. Twenty-eight states said so expressly in their statutes. In the others the idea was generally applied by the courts. After all, it followed with logical necessity from the principle of marital offense. On details, the courts were, of course, not in full agreement. Is it necessary for the "defense" that the plaintiff had actively arranged the adultery, or does it suffice that he knowingly allowed it to occur?

The third "defense" appearing in the statutes, in those of twenty-nine jurisdictions, was "recrimination." It, too, was widely, although not universally, practiced by the courts even in the absence of express statutory reference. If divorce is conceived as a reward for a blameless spouse, it can, of course, not be granted to one who has himself been guilty of misconduct. But of this basic idea the courts failed to be universally conscious. In fact, the judicial mind was not everywhere aware of the very notion that divorce was to be a punishment for guilt and a reward for virtue. After all, the notion had been the product of historical accident rather than of deliberate policy.[6] The doctrine of recrimination was developed some two thousand years ago in connection with the problem under what circumstances a divorcing Roman husband would be allowed to retain his wife's dowry. When recrimination found entry, via England, into America, that origin had long been forgotten. But there it was. Various rationalizations was excogitated, among them not only the idea that the privilege of divorce should be withheld from a misbehaving spouse but also that beloved idea that "he who comes into equity must come with clean hands." As judicial divorce had not existed in England before 1858, it could, of course, not constitute a part of Equity. But in the United States divorce was generally entrusted to the Equity courts, where the clean hands doctrine was routine. Besides, uneasiness was growing about a rule which allowed divorce to a marriage that had been confounded through the misconduct of one spouse but not to one that had been confounded even more by the misconduct of both. The idea of divorce because of objective failure of the marriage was in the air. No wonder that the doctrine of recrimination was expressed in a variety of statutory terms and, even more so, of judicial practice. Was it to apply whenever the

6. J. G. Beamer, *The Doctrine of Recrimination in Divorce Proceedings*, 10 KANS. CITY L. REV. 213 (1942).

plaintiff had been guilty of any marital misconduct, or only of misconduct falling into the same statutory pigeonhole as that of the defendant, or only if the plaintiff's misconduct was that most serious ground of all: adultery? Or was the plaintiff's rectitude to be compared with that of the defendant? Would recrimination bar divorce applied for on any ground, or only for some, or exclusively in the case of adultery? The topic was full of doubts and of fine-spun theories upon which much learning was expended but little thought of reasoned policy.[7] Finally, there was the "defense" of collusion.

II. COLLUSION

Where, as in Japan, freedom of remarriage can be brought about by the free agreement of the parties,[8] or, as in Muslim tradition, by the unfettered desire of the husband, no governmental controls are needed. But in our law restoration to the freedom of remarriage can be obtained only through the issuance of a governmental license called a decree of divorce, and no such license is to be issued unless there exists one of those situations in which the law permits it. The facts constituting a ground for divorce must have actually occurred and none of the "defenses" to divorce must be present. The issuance of a license to remarry requires that the situation be investigated by an agency of the government, just as it is in the case of an application for a license to drive an automobile, to practice law or medicine, or to build a dwelling house. In all such cases the license is issued by an administrative agency which makes sure that a license is not issued unless all the conditions which the law prescribes are really present. But licenses to remarry are issued by the courts which generally deal with litigious matters so that in their procedure they can properly expect that evidence upon which their decisions must be based will be presented by the parties litigant. Of course, a defendant may choose not to litigate and not to present any evidence by which plaintiff's allegations of fact might be contradicted. In such a case the court will usually accept the plaintiff's allegations and decide against the defendant by a default judgment irrespective of whether or not the plaintiff's factual allegations are true. But can that simple technique be applied in cases of divorce? The statute law prescribes that a divorce ought to be granted if, and only if, there have really occurred those facts which the legislature has established as grounds for divorce and if there is present

---

7. See VERNIER 82; H. H. CLARK, JR., THE LAW OF DOMESTIC RELATIONS IN THE UNITED STATES (1968) (hereinafter cited as CLARK).

8. *Infra* chap. 5.

none of those facts which the law has established as a bar to divorce. Obviously, if the law is to be observed, the adversary procedure which works in cases of ordinary civil litigation cannot be fully relied on in matters of divorce. In such cases there may be no litigation. The divorce may be desired by both parties, or one has acquiesced in the other's desire and chooses not to contradict the petitioner's allegations or not to reveal facts which would constitute a bar to divorce. The court may be deceived by the uncontradicted allegation of untrue facts, or by the nonrevelation of facts which it ought to know if its decision is to conform to the law. A divorce might thus be obtained collusively.

In its basic sense collusion means fraud on the court, the imposition upon it of untrue facts.[9] In a broader sense, collusion means the deliberate withholding from the court of information about facts which it ought to know in order to decide the case in strict accordance with the law, such as the fact that adultery that has really occurred was committed with the connivance of the petitioner or that the petitioner has also committed adultery. In a more technical sense, collusion is the "corrupt bargain" of the parties in which they agree to cooperate so that a divorce may be obtained. Under a strict view any such bargain constitutes collusion, while, under another, the bargain is not corrupt unless it is agreed that false facts are to be imposed upon the court or that relevant true facts are to be withheld from it.

If the collusive evasion of the divorce law is to be avoided, the adversary procedure, which works so well in ordinary civil litigation, has to be modified by means designed to safeguard the public interest in the proper enforcement of the law. In every case of divorce, the state, so it has been said innumerable times, is the third party. For the same reason the church is the third party in all cases of nullity of marriage, and from ancient times it has established an elaborate system of safeguards designed to make sure that the principle of indissolubility of marriage is not evaded by collusive conduct of nullity cases. The grounds of nullity — coercion, fraud, mental reservation, consanguinity, affinity, nonage, impotency, clerical status, etc. — are narrowly defined.[10] Thus no remarriage may take place without special permission, and permission is not to be granted unless the proper ecclesiastical authority has found that there indeed exists one of those situations in which a marriage is regarded as invalid under canon law.[11] The proper ecclesiastical

9. On the meanings of collusion in Anglo-American law, see CLARK 361.
10. CODEX JURIS CANONICI, canons 1067–80.
11. Even where the prior marriage was valid, remarriage can be permitted in two special situations. Under canon 1119 a marriage which has not been consummated, i.e., one in which no marital intercourse has taken place, may for good cause (*ex*

agency is the ordinary,[12] i.e., as a general rule, the bishop of the diocese. Since investigations require time and experience, bishops have placed them in the hands of tribunals. The practice has been regularized and formalized, so that inquiry through an ecclesiastical tribunal has become an indispensable part of canon law procedure.[13] If it is to perform its task, the ecclesiastical tribunal can, of course, not simply rely upon the petitioner and his "spouse." The latter may be as anxious to get his freedom as the petitioner, or he may acquiesce in the petitioner's desire and support, or choose not to deny, the petition's allegations. For those cases in which the facts are not proved by clear and indisputable documentary evidence (*Codex juris canonici*, canon 1990), canon law developed a battery of devices to make sure that the tribunal would learn the true state of fact. In their present form they are stated in the *Codex juris canonici* of 1917, Book IV, Part I, especially Title 20 (*De causis matrimonialibus*) and in the Instruction for the Diocesan Tribunals concerning the Procedure in Cases of Nullity of Marriage (*Instructio servanda a tribunalibus dioecesanis in pertractandis causis de nullitate matrimoniorum*) of 15 August 1936.[14]

The safeguards are elaborate. Venue is determined unalterably in the diocese in which the marriage was concluded or where the defendant or, in the case of a mixed marriage, the Catholic party, has his domicile.[15] Shopping for a forum reputed to be "easy" is thus excluded. The tribunal is staffed with three judges rather than one, as it is in other ecclesiastical matters.[16] The grounds of nullity and the absence of bars to a declaration of nullity must be proved to the "moral certitude" of the judges.[17] A declaration of nullity may never be based exclusively upon statements of the parties. Their testimony must be corroborated by other witnesses or by authentic documentary proof or by physical examination. In case of alleged impotency or non-

---

iusta causa) be dissolved by the Holy See. By virtue of the so-called *Privilegium Paulinum* a marriage validly existing between nonbaptized parties may be dissolved when one party becomes converted to and is baptized in the Christian faith while the other remains unbaptized (canons 1120–27). The basis is 1 Corinthians 7:12–15: "If any brother hath a wife that believeth not, and she consent to dwell with him, let him not put her away. And the woman which hath a husband that believeth not, and if he be pleased to dwell with her, let her not leave him. . . . But if the unbelieving depart, let him depart. A brother or a sister is not under bondage in such cases: but God hath called us to peace."

12. CODEX JURIS CANONICI, canons 1966, 1570 § 1, 1572.
13. *Id.*, canons 1573 ff.
14. 28 ACTA APOSTOLICAE SEDIS 313–61; English transl. at 2 S. WOYWOD, PRACTICAL COMMENTARY ON THE CODE OF CANON LAW 739 (1952).
15. Canon 1964.
16. Canon 1576 § 1.
17. Instruction (*supra* note 14), art. 197.

consummation the testimony of each party may have to be supported by seven reliable persons' testimony on the party's probity and veracity.[18] Most important of all, the conduct of the case does not lie in the hands of the parties. The church itself participates as the third party, represented by the *defensor vinculi* (defender of the bond), who is to make investigations, introduce evidence of his own, and bring to the notice of the court all facts which may stand in the way of a declaration of nullity.[19] If the tribunal declares the marriage invalid, the *defensor vinculi must* enter an appeal so that the case can be tried all over again before the appellate tribunal.[20] If on appeal the decision is again in favor of nullity, the *defensor may* again appeal so that the case can be tried, a third time, in the Sacra Romana Rota in Rome.[21] Except those cases in which the nullity of the marriage appears from authentic documentary evidence of certain impediments enumerated in canon 1990 of the *Codex iuris canonici*, a declaration of nullity always requires the corresponding judgments of at least two tribunals and at both steps the search for the full and true state of facts is guaranteed elaborately.[22]

Many, although not all, of the safeguards of the canon law also appear in the secular laws of foreign countries as well as of American states.[23] Shopping for an "easy" forum is discouraged by prescribing that suits for divorce must be brought in the state and, frequently, also in the judicial district in which both parties or one of them resides, or where they had their last common habitation.[24] Frequently, it is even necessary that residence be established for a certain minimum period immediately preceding the commencement of the suit. Although it is generally provided that procedure in cases of divorce is to be, as in other civil cases, either general or as in equity or at law,[25] excep-

18. Witnesses *septimae manus*. Instruction, art. 137. See also Instruction of the Congregation of the Sacraments, on the Institution of Cases of Ratified and Nonconsummated Marriages, of 7 May 1923, 15 ACTA APOSTOLICAE SEDIS 389.
19. CODEX JURIS CANONICI, canons 1967, 1587, 1968, 1969.
20. *Id.*, canon 1986.
21. *Id.*, canons 1987, 1598, 1599.
22. In spite of all the safeguards, collusion cannot be prevented completely. In a case decided in an English court in 1537 (1 Dyer 13a, 73 Eng. Rep. 29) it was alleged that a "divorce," i.e., a declaration of nullity, was obtained in the ecclesiastical court by perjury. The same allegation was made in Bury's Case, decided in 1560 (2 Dyer 179a, 73 Eng. Rep. 394); see D. Engdahl, *Full Faith and Credit in Merrie Olde England*, 5 VALPARAISO U. L. REV. 1, notes 67, 68 (1970). Complaints about fraudulent practices in ecclesiastical courts are common in present-day Italy.
23. The details vary greatly. For the American laws as they stood in October 1931, see VERNIER 92 ff.
24. See CLARK 384.
25. See VERNIER 130; CLARK 379.

tions are established exactly to see to it that the state of facts is truthfully and completely presented to the court. In contrast to ordinary civil cases the defendant's failure to appear or to contest the plaintiff's allegations may not result in the assumption that the facts alleged by the plaintiff are true. Judgment may thus not be rendered by default. Where the defendant fails to appear or to plead, proceedings are *ex parte*, which means that the plaintiff has to prove those facts which he alleges to constitute the ground for divorce.[26] Generally, neither the plaintiff's own sworn testimony nor the defendant's admission of the facts is sufficient to prove the ground for divorce or to disprove a defense. There must be corroboration by testimony or other evidence.[27] The absence of facts that might amount to a defense must in many states be averred in the complaint, the truth of which must be verified by the plaintiff's oath. He must swear, for instance, that he has at all times behaved himself as a true and loyal spouse,[28] or that he is not guilty of collusion. A number of states provide for the participation in divorce cases of a *defensor vinculi*.[29] In order to give the court opportunity in a suspicious-looking case to call for the investigatory activity of the defender of the bond, the court, adjourns the case, as it may do in Scotland, or, as England provided from 1860 to 1970, the divorce decree has the provisional effect of a decree nisi or, as it is called in the United States, an interlocutory decree,[30] so that the bond is not terminated until, after a certain minimum period, the court issues its "decree absolute." The latter method serves the additional purpose of slowing up the judicial termination of marriages. Contrary to the practice generally observed in civil litigation, examination of the parties and the witnesses is not to be conducted by the parties' attorneys but by the judge, and the court may even summon witnesses that have not been presented by the parties or *ex officio* induce independent investigations.

If all these safeguards were observed, a divorce would be as difficult to obtain as it is supposed to be under statute law. But they are not observed.[31] The laws of those few states which provide for the possi-

26. See CLARK 395.
27. CLARK 399.
28. VERNIER 131.
29. CLARK 381; VERNIER 92; C. S. Connolly, *Divorce Proctors*, 34 BOSTON U.L. REV. 1, 11 (1954).
30. *Interlocutory Decrees of Divorce*, 56 COLUM. L. REV. 228; CLARK 402.
31. Well-chosen items from the vast literature on how divorce cases are handled in the courts are presented in C. FOOTE, R. J. LEVY & F. E. A. SANDERS, CASES AND MATERIALS ON FAMILY LAW 631–769 (1966). The results of an intensive field study of divorce courts are presented in M. B. VIRTUE, FAMILY CASES IN COURT (1956). See

bility of participation in the proceedings of a defender of the bond are generally regarded as ineffective.[32] The topic has met with so little interest that factual investigations are lacking almost completely.[33] The only data that could be found are from Michigan, where a statute of 1897 [34] created the possibility of the court's calling on the public prosecutor to enter an appearance for the protection of minor children as well as of the public interest. In 1919, Public Act No. 412 enabled counties to create the new office of Friend of the Court, who, under the statute now in force,[35] is charged with the protection of the interests of minor children. In some counties it seems that he is also to act as divorce proctor in the public interest. But in that capacity he seems to act but rarely. In 1949, several thousand divorce cases, of which at least 90 percent were uncontested, were pending in Wayne County, Michigan (Detroit), but in only twenty-eight cases did the Friend of the Court enter an appearance "in the public interest" as contrasted to the vast number of cases in which he went into action to safeguard the proper custody and support of minor children.[36] On the basis of field studies carried on in 1952 and 1953, M. B. Virtue found the facilities provided by Michigan to have been inadequate.[37] Even in England, the King's or, as the case may be, the Queen's, Proctor hardly ever undertakes any investigation of his own. He does not appear unless it is suggested to him by some member of the public or by the court that the evidence presented in a divorce case is suspect.[38]

furthermore Note, *Collusive and Consensual Divorce and the New York Anomaly*, 36 COLUM. L. REV. 1121 (1936); L. C. MARSHALL & G. MAY, THE DIVORCE COURT — MARYLAND (1932), and same, THE DIVORCE COURT — OHIO (1933).

32. P. A. RYAN & D. GRANFIELD, DOMESTIC RELATIONS 311 (1963); FOOTE *et al.*, *supra* note 31, at 679.

33. The few American cases dealing with the right of a representative of the state to intervene in a divorce suit, are collected in 22 A.L.R. 1112 (1923).

34. Pub. L. No. 315, § 45; now Mich. Stat. Ann. 25.120–21.

35. Mich. Stat. Ann. 25.171–75.

36. G. Squire, *Divorce and the Friend of the Court*, 29 MICH. ST. B.J. 15, 19 (April 1950).

37. *What Is a Family Court*, 37 MICH. ST. B.J. 14, 16 (July 1958).

38. In the version of the Matrimonial Causes Act, 1965, the relevant provision reads as follows:

Sec. 6. Intervention of Queen's Proctor. — (1) In the case of a petition for divorce —
   (a) the court may, if it thinks fit, direct all necessary papers in the matter to be sent to Her Majesty's Proctor (hereafter in this and the next following section referred to as "the Proctor"), who shall under the directions of the Attorney General instruct counsel to argue before the court any question in relation to the matter which the court deems it necessary or expedient to have fully argued;
   (b) any person may at any time during the progress of the proceedings or before the decree nisi is made absolute give information to the Proctor on any

In his testimony before the Gorell Commission, Sir Bargrave Deane, justice of the Probate, Divorce, and Admiralty Division of the High Court, stated that collusion was practiced in an enormous number of cases but that it would not be detected by the court or by the King's Proctor. "You hardly ever get a case of collusion established, perhaps two in the case of the year; not more, certainly." [39]

Before the same commission the Earl of Desart, who, as the Treasury Solicitor, had been the King's Proctor for fourteen and a half years, testified that during his term of office the annual number of inquiries varied from 306 to 631, but the actual intervention was no more than 11 to 34 a year. Of these about 1 or 2 were cases of "collusion," apparently in the sense of collusion agreements, while the others were cases in which the petitioner had failed to reveal his own adultery.[40] After all, the six-week period required between the decree nisi and the decree absolute was too short to allow meaningful investigation.[41]

The idea that the state, as the third party, is represented by the

---

matter material to the due decision of the case, and the Proctor may thereupon take such steps as the Attorney General considers necessary or expedient;

(c) if in consequence of any such information or otherwise the Proctor considers that any parties to the petition are or have been acting in collusion for the purpose of obtaining a decree contrary to the justice of the case, he may, under the direction of the Attorney General and ofter obtaining the leave of the court, intervene and retain counsel and subpoena witnesses to prove the alleged collusion.

(2) Where the Proctor intervenes or shows cause against a decree nisi in any proceedings for divorce, the court may make such order as may be just as to the payment by other parties to the proceedings of the costs incurred by him in so doing or as to the payment by him of any costs incurred by any of those parties by reason of his so doing.

(3) The Proctor shall be entitled to charge as part of the expenses of his office —
(a) the costs of any proceedings under subsection (1) (a) of this section;
(b) where his reasonable costs of intervening or showing cause as mentioned in subsection (2) of this section are not fully satisfied by any order under that subsection, the amount of the difference;
(c)If the Treasury so directs, any costs which he pays to any parties under an order made under the said subsection.

Subsection (1) (c), i.e., the provision meant to inhibit collusion, was repealed by the Divorce Reform Act of 1969, Sec. 9.

In addition to his duties as Treasury Solicitor and to his now defunct duties in divorce cases, the Queen's Proctor also represents the crown in certain admiralty matters. 7 HALSBURY, THE LAWS OF ENGLAND 388 (3d ed. 1954).

39. ROYAL COMMISSION ON DIVORCE AND MATRIMONIAL CAUSES, 1 MINUTES OF EVIDENCE, no. 1144, CD. 6479 (1912).

40. ROYAL COMMISSION ON DIVORCE AND MATRIMONIAL CAUSES, 2 MINUTES OF EVIDENCE, nos. 15,995–16,003, CD. 6480 (1912–13).

41. When introduced in 1860, the period was fixed at three months. In 1866 it was extended to six months and in 1946 shortened to six weeks. See MORTON COMMISSION REPORT, CMD. 9678, at 249 (1956).

judge, is dead. American judges are not accustomed to taking the examination of parties and witnesses out of the hands of the attorneys, and even less to conducting investigations *ex officio*. In some states it has even been held to be inappropriate for a judge to exercise such functions, and where a judge or a master conducts the examination of parties and witnesses it is rarely done in a manner likely to reach the truth.[42]

Prevention of collusion is furthermore impeded by the narrow definition which the courts have come to give to the term.[43] If collusion is defined as a corrupt bargain, two questions arise: what is a bargain, and when is it corrupt?

Nobody is under any duty to put up a defense in a lawsuit. This principle is as fully recognized in suits for divorce as it is in suits for debt or for damages, for eviction, or for contesting a will. But if in a formal agreement a husband promises to pay his wife so many dollars if she will sue for divorce, collusion exists. But what of a mere "understanding" that so and so many dollars will be paid as monthly alimony and that the husband will, of course, not defend against the divorce which he is anxious to obtain and for which he supplies the wife with the necessary true evidence? Courts have come predominantly to deny the collusive character of such an understanding, and lawyers will, of course, be careful to avoid its formalization. But cases in which courts have an opportunity to pronounce any views about what exactly constitutes collusion are infrequent. Occasionally a party may regret the financial terms of the understanding that has been reached and reveal the bargain to the court in order to preserve the financial benefits connected with the continued existence of the marital bond. Somewhat more frequently, but still rarely, after the divorce one party tries to back out of the bargain, and applies to the court to set aside the divorce because of its having been obtained collusively. Then the court is faced with a dilemma.[44] Shall it vindicate the integrity of the judicial process, reinstate the marriage, and thus invalidate a subsequent marriage, or perhaps marriages, concluded by parties who believed themselves to be free? Shall it reward a party who has been a participant to the corrupt bargain? Or shall it resort to the doctrines of *in pari delicto* or of

---

42. For an illustration, see Note, *The Administration of Divorce: A Philadelphia Study*, 101 U. PA. L. REV. 1204 (1953), repr. in FOOTE et al., *supra* note 31, at 683. This reprint is followed, at 692, by the passage from VIRTUE (*supra* note 31, at 86–91) which presents specimens of the perfunctory examination conducted by petitioners' attorneys in the courts in which divorce cases were handled in Chicago in 1952–53.

43. See *supra* p. 60.

44. CLARK 419.

clean hands and leave matters as they are? More and more courts are inclined to take the second position.

The husband has been found in a hotel room, partly undressed, together with a woman other than his wife. Who knows whether he has really committed adultery with her, or that the "discovery" was not prearranged? How is a court to check on the truth of the sworn testimony that a husband has committed cruelty by slapping his wife over the face twice? How is the court to ascertain that a husband's leaving the marital home occurred against his wife's intention and thus constitutes desertion rather than an agreed-upon separation? And if he "deserted" his wife, was he really away from her the entire period required by the statute? Was the wife willing to receive him back during all that time? Is it true that they never met and had intercourse? Has the petitioner been completely truthful when she swore that she has at all times been a good and faithful wife, or that there is no collusion between the parties? Does she even know what collusion means? Are people likely to tell the sad and possibly sordid story of their marriage?

In spite of the elaborate procedural precautions established by canon law, collusion has not been completely prevented in the tribunals of the Roman Catholic church. In secular courts it reigns practically unchecked. The number of uncontested divorces is estimated to amount to at least 90 percent of all divorces pronounced by American courts. Nobody knows in how many of these cases the true facts are not, or not fully, revealed to the court. But all experienced observers agree that their number is high. Dressed up as a divorce for misconduct, consent divorce, abhorred in the official law of all states, is an established institution of American law.

III. MIGRATORY DIVORCE

"Migration" within the United States

The courts' failure to combat collusion allows one set of devices by which the strict statutory scheme is frustrated. Another method has been made possible by the judicial sanctioning of migratory divorce.

By migratory divorce we mean the case in which a divorce seeker living in a place in which divorce cannot be obtained at all, or only under difficulty, resorts to the court of another place in which a divorce can be obtained more easily or, perhaps, just more discreetly. If a restrictive divorce law is to be effective, the state must see to it that it applies to all those persons in whose marital life the state is interested, and that to these persons all avenues of easier divorce are closed.

For the majority of the countries of the so-called civil law the persons in whom the state takes such an interest are its nationals. Italy, for instance, which has until recently refused to admit divorce at all, does not regard as divorced an Italian national who has obtained a divorce in some foreign country. Other countries under whose statutes a divorce is supposed not to be obtained easily are disinclined to recognize as divorced a national who has obtained an easy divorce abroad.[45]

In the United States and the British Commonwealth nationality cannot be used to determine the circle of persons in whose family affairs a state is interested. British nationality does not determine the relation between an individual and any one of those numerous parts of the Commonwealth or even of the United Kingdom having legal systems of their own. English, Scottish, Australian, etc., laws of divorce are not the same. In the United States each state and territory has its own law of divorce. "Belongingness" of an individual to any particular British or American jurisdiction is thus determined by domicile or residence rather than nationality. In common-law countries it has long been regarded as settled that jurisdiction to pronounce a divorce rests exclusively with the state of the domicile.[46] It is furthermore regarded as self-evident that in matters of divorce the courts of the state of the domicile will apply no law other than that of their own state.[47]

The common-law rule of applying in divorce cases the law of the forum or the necessary coincidence of the forum with the domicile constitutes a major difference from the attitude of the Continental countries where forum and applicable law do not necessarily have to coincide but where the substantive law applicable is, as a general rule, the law of the country of which the parties, or at least one of them, are nationals, irrespective of the place where the suit occurs.[48]

45. See, for example, the complicated rules of the Federal Republic of Germany contained in §§ 328, 606, 606a, and 606b of the Code of Civil Procedure as amended by Law of 18 June 1957 (BGBl.I 609), and art. 7 of Law of 11 August 1961 (BGBl.I 1221). Surveys of the situations in which foreign divorces will or will not be recognized in other countries are R. MOSER, DAS EUROPÄISCHE EHESCHEIDUNGS-UND EHETRENNUNGSRECHT (1948); V. HOYER, ANERKENNUNG VON ENTSCHEIDUNGEN IN EHESACHEN IM AUSLAND (1951); 1 E. RABEL, THE CONFLICT OF LAWS 497 (2d ed. U. Drobnig, 1958). As to France, see Cass. civ. soc. 7 janv. 1964, REV. CRIT. DROIT INT. PRIVÉ 345 (1964).

46. AMERICAN LAW INSTITUTE, RESTATEMENT SECOND: CONFLICT OF LAWS, PROPOSED OFFICIAL DRAFT, Part I, §§ 70, 71 (1967); 1 RABEL, *supra* note 45, at 428; A. EHRENZWEIG, CONFLICT OF LAWS 238 (1962).

47. RESTATEMENT SEC. 285; 1 RABEL 428.

48. Under the Hague Convention on Divorce of 1902, of which in 1964 the following countries were participants: Hungary, Italy, Luxembourg, Netherlands, Poland, Portugal, and Romania (P. Paone, *Divorzio, Diritto internazionale privato*, in 13 ENCICLOPEDIA DEL DIRITTO 526 [1964]), as well as under the laws of conflict of laws of the Federal Republic of Germany, Austria, Switzerland, and others, a divorce is not

In the United States, the Constitution provides in article IV, section 1, that

Full Faith and Credit shall be given in each state to the public Acts, Records, and judicial Proceedings of every other State.

The constitutional command was implemented by the Act of Congress of 26 March 1790, which, in the version of 1948, provides that

Such Acts, records and judicial proceedings . . . shall have the same full faith and credit in every court within the United States and its Territories and Possessions as they have by law or usage in the courts of such State, Territory or Possession from which they are taken.[49]

If the Full Faith and Credit Clause were applied literally, every judgment, including every decree of divorce, that is rendered in one state would have to be recognized as effective in every other state of the Union. Such an absurd result has been prevented by the Supreme Court of the United States when it read into the clause the limitation that no state is required to recognize a judicial decision rendered by the court of another state unless such other state had jurisdiction to entertain the proceedings.[50] An elaborate set of rules determining the circumstances under which a state has jurisdiction to entertain lawsuits of one kind or another has been worked out by the Supreme Court of the United States. Jurisdiction to terminate a marriage has been ascribed to the state of the domicile. At the turn of the century, Sioux Falls, South Dakota, occupied the position which is now held by Reno, Nevada, as the haven for divorce seekers living in states with strict divorce laws. But a divorce obtained there was held not to be entitled to full faith and credit if neither party was domiciled there, even though the defendant had participated in the South Dakota proceedings.[51]

But which state is that of the domicile? That question presents spe-

---

to be granted unless the facts constitute a ground for divorce under both the laws of nationality and the law of the forum. See 1 RABEL 459.

49. 28 U.S.C. § 1738.

50. Thompson v. Whitman, 85 U.S. (18 Wall.) 457 (1873).

51. Andrews v. Andrews, 188 U.S. 14, 23 S.Ct. 237, 47 L.Ed. 366 (1903). Andrews and his first wife had lived in Massachusetts. He went to South Dakota there to obtain a divorce. The wife appeared by counsel, denied Andrews's South Dakota residence as well as her desertion, and counterclaimed, alleging cruelty. Later, upon receiving a sum of money, she withdrew her appearance. The divorce was granted to Andrews, who returned to Massachusetts and there married wife no. 2. Upon Andrews's death litigation between the two wives was decided by the Massachusetts court in favor of wife no. 1. This decision was upheld by the Supreme Court of the United States. In 1901, the Court had held in Bell v. Bell, 181 U.S. 175, 21 S.Ct. 551, 45 L.Ed. 804, that recognition need not be given to the divorce decree rendered *ex parte* in a state in which neither party was domiciled.

cial difficulties in divorce cases when husband and wife have separated and are living in different states. As early as 1856 it was held by the Supreme Court of Rhode Island that a married woman could have a domicile different from that of her husband and that she could bring a suit for divorce in the state of her domicile if she had left the state of the marital home because of a fault of her husband's.[52] Conversely it was held by the Supreme Court of the United States that New York was bound to recognize a divorce obtained by the husband in Kentucky, where the parties had lived together as husband and wife until the wife left the state and resumed her former New York domicile.[53] Kentucky was said to have continued to be the "matrimonial domicile" and this concept of matrimonial domicile was given special significance five years later in *Haddock* v. *Haddock*,[54] the leading case in the matter for the next thirty-six years. Mr. and Mrs. Haddock married in New York, but did not live together there. Immediately after the marriage ceremony the husband left the state and, after wandering for several years, established himself in Connecticut. In that state he obtained an *ex parte* decree of divorce, which he pleaded as a defense when his wife subsequently sued him in New York for maintenance. The Supreme Court of the United States held that the decision depended upon whether or not the husband's divorce had been obtained in the state of the matrimonial domicile. The answer was negative. The matrimonial domicile was said to have remained in New York, the state where the wife had continued to live when her husband had left her wrongfully. The determination of the matrimonial domicile was thus made to depend upon whether that party who had left the other had done so with or without just ground. A deserter should not be able to rid himself of his spouse by moving to a state of easy divorce. Hence, whenever the question arose whether or not faith and credit were due to an *ex parte* divorce obtained in a state in which only one of the spouses was domiciled, the court had to investigate whether the plaintiff had brought about the separation with or without just cause. Conceivably the Supreme Court of the United States might have to dig into that issue. In fact, that august tribunal was never bothered with such a vexed question during all the thirty-six years the *Haddock* rule was the law of the land. It was abolished when *Haddock* v. *Haddock* was overruled in 1942.

O. B. Williams was a storekeeper in the village of Granite Falls, Cald-

---

52. Ditson v. Ditson, 4 R.I. 87.
53. Atherton v. Atherton, 181 U.S. 155, 21 S.Ct. 544, 45 L.Ed. 794 (1901).
54. 201 U.S. 562, 26 S.Ct. 525, 50 L.Ed. 867, 5 Am.Cas. 1 (1906).

well County, North Carolina. George Thomas Hendrix worked in his store. Since 30 May 1916 Williams had been married to Carrie W. Williams, with whom he had reared a family of four children. Hendrix had been married for about twenty years to Lillie S. Hendrix. O. B. Williams and Lillie fell in love with each other and on 7 May 1940 left their homes for Las Vegas, Nevada, where they appeared at the Alamo Court, a motel. After a stay of exactly six weeks both filed suits for divorce in the Las Vegas court. The divorce of O. B. was granted on 26 August, that of Lillie on 4 October. Their respective spouses had received only constructive notice of the proceedings and had not participated in them. On the same day the second divorce, that of Lillie, was granted, she and O. B. went through a ceremony of marriage in Las Vegas. After a total absence of six months, they returned to North Carolina and settled down to live together as husband and wife in Pineola, Avery County. The state's attorney felt impelled to prosecute O. B. and Lillie for the crime of bigamous cohabitation.[55] The prosecution based its case on *Haddock v. Haddock*. The matri-

---

55. In his article entitled *And Repent at Leisure: An Inquiry into the Unhappy Lot of Those Whom Nevada Hath Joined Together and North Carolina Hath Put Asunder*, 58 HARV. L. REV. 930 (1945), at p. 933, Thomas Reed Powell states that in 1930 the population of Granite Falls was 2,147 and that of Pineola 306. The two villages are but a short distance from each other in the hill region near the Great Smoky Mountains. Their mores were not those of Peyton Place.

The statute under which O. B. and Lillie were prosecuted, North Carolina Code § 4342 (N.C.G.S. 14–183), deals with two crimes, viz. (1) bigamy, i.e., the act of going through a bigamous ceremony of marriage in North Carolina, and (2) bigamous cohabitation, i.e., the living together in North Carolina as husband and wife of two persons who have gone through a bigamous marriage outside of North Carolina.

It should be noted that Mr. Hendrix, the husband of Lillie, might also have been punishable for bigamy. In the second state trial against Lillie he testified that in North Carolina he had initiated a divorce suit against Lillie and had remarried. Nothing was said, however, about his actually obtaining a divorce before his remarriage. Whatever interest the first Mrs. Williams may have had in having O. B. sent to jail came to an end when she died before the second state trial. See Powell, *supra*, at 962 n. 92.

Criminal prosecution for bigamy or bigamous cohabitation based upon nonrecognition of an out-of state divorce seems to have been rare. In his article, which was published in 1945, Powell mentions only four cases decided in the twentieth century by higher state courts and published. Of these, two occurred in Vermont (State v. Woods, 107 Vt. 354, 179 Atl. 1 [1935], and State v. Shufelt, 107 Vt. 358, 179 Atl. 3 [1935], one in California (People v. Harlow, 9 Cal. App. 2d 643, 50 P.2d 1052 [1935], and one in North Carolina (State v. Herron, 175 N.C. 754, 94 S.E. 698 [1917]), The "divorce" involved in the California case was an over-the-counter divorce unilaterally obtained by the husband in Chihuahua, Mexico.

Of older cases, Powell, at 974 n. 124, cites the following from the concurring opinion of Mr. Justice Murphy (65 S.Ct. 1101): People v. Dawell, 25 Mich. 247 (1872); State v Armington, 25 Minn. 29 (1878); People v. Baker, 76 N.Y. 78 (1879); State v. Westmoreland, 76 S.C. 145 (1906).

monial domicile of both couples, the Williamses and the Hendrixes, had been North Carolina. Both O. B. and Lillie had left their matrimonial homes without just cause. Divorces obtained by them outside of North Carolina were thus not entitled to faith and credit in North Carolina. Only secondarily was it alleged that the accused's stay in Nevada did not constitute a bona fide domicile because during all that stay they intended to return to North Carolina once the divorces were obtained. North Carolina thus appeared justified in treating the Nevada divorces as ineffective not only under the rule of *Haddock* v. *Haddock* but also under that of *Bell* v. *Bell*.[56] The jury returned a general verdict of guilty. O. B. was sentenced to imprisonment with hard labor for not less than three and not more than ten years, Lillie to imprisonment with hard labor for not less than three nor more than five years. The judgments of conviction were affirmed by the Supreme Court of North Carolina[57] but reversed by the Supreme Court of the United States.[58] That Court, speaking through Mr. Justice Douglas, found that it was not possible to know on which ground the jury had found the defendants guilty: on the ground that they had left their matrimonial domiciles without just cause and were thus, under the *Haddock* rule, incapable of establishing in any other state domiciles that could give that state jurisdiction to terminate their marriages, or whether the domiciles which the Nevada court had found them to have established in Nevada were a sham. As to that possible second ground, the Supreme Court of the United States found it unnecessary to express any opinion, because, holding the first ground insufficient to justify the refusal of North Carolina to recognize the Nevada divorce, its decision had to be reversed. The case was remanded to the courts of North Carolina so as to give that state an opportunity to make its own decision on the reality of the Nevada domicile.

In holding North Carolina to be unjustified in denying faith and credit to the Nevada divorces upon the ground of the parties having left the matrimonial domicile without just cause, the rule of the *Haddock* case was expressly overruled. The Court declared that each state has the power to determine the marital status of its own domiciliaries even if in so doing it indirectly terminates the marital status of a nondomiciliary.

Each state as a sovereign has a rightful and legitimate concern in the marital status of persons domiciled within its borders. The marriage relation creates problems of great social importance. Protection of offspring, property inter-

---

56. *Supra* note 51.
57. State v. Williams, 220 N.C. 445, 17 S.E. 2d 769 (1940).
58. Williams v. North Carolina, 317 U.S. 287, 63 S.Ct. 207, 87 L.Ed. 279, 143 A.L.R. 1273 (1942).

ests, and the enforcement of marital responsibilities are but a few of the commanding problems in the field of domestic relations with which the state must deal. Thus it is plain that each state by virtue of its command over its domiciliaries and its large interest in the institution of marriage, can alter *within its own borders* the marriage status of the spouse domiciled there, even though the other spouse is absent. There is no constitutional barrier if the form and nature of the substituted service . . . meet the requirements of due process.[59]

If Nevada has the power within its borders to terminate the marriage of a person domiciled within that state, the command of full faith and credit renders it necessary to treat that marriage as terminated for all other states including that in which the other spouse is domiciled. Otherwise the same person might be regarded as married to one spouse in one state and treated as single or as married to another spouse in another state. The resulting confusion would be intolerable.

For O. B. Williams and Lillie Hendrix the decision was only a temporary victory. The North Carolina prosecutor was adamant. The accused were tried again and this time the jury was instructed merely to decide whether or not O. B. and Lillie had actually abandoned their domiciles in North Carolina and established new domiciles in Nevada. On the evidence the jury found them guilty as charged. The verdict implied that the jury had found that the accused had at all times intended to go to Nevada merely for the purpose of staying there long enough to obtain their divorces and then to return home to North Carolina immediately. The domicile which the Las Vegas court had found to exist in Nevada was thus a mere sham, the accused had never become domiciliaries of Nevada, their Nevada divorces were not entitled to faith and credit, their Nevada marriage was bigamous, and their living together in North Carolina constituted the crime of bigamous cohabitation. This time, the sentence was for the male defendant imprisonment for not less than one nor more than three years, and for the female imprisonment for not less than eight nor more than twenty-four months. Hard labor was no longer mentioned. The judgments were affirmed by both the Supreme Court of North Carolina[60] and the Supreme Court of the United States.[61]

The rule of *Bell* v. *Bell*[62] was thus restored, its complication by the *Haddock* rule eliminated. "Under our system of law," Mr. Justice

---

59. 317 U.S. 398, 63 S.Ct. 213, 87 L.Ed. 286, 145 A.L.R. 1280 (my italics).
60. State v. Williams, 224 N.C. 183, 29 S.E. 2d 744 (1944).
61. Williams v. State of North Carolina, 325 U.S. 226, 65 S.Ct. 1092, 89 L.Ed. 1577, 157 A.L.R. 1366 (1945).
62. *Supra* note 51.

Frankfurter declared, "judicial power to grant a divorce — jurisdiction strictly speaking — is founded on domicile." [63]

But domicile was from now on the domicile of the plaintiff only. If a married person actually moves away from a state with a strict divorce law and actually establishes his domicile in the state where divorce is easy, he can effectively free himself from the tie of his marriage and thereby terminate the marital relationship for both himself and the spouse that has stayed at home. Under the *Haddock* rule the state with the strict divorce law prevailed over that of the state with easy divorce. Under the rule of *Williams I* the relationship is reversed. The state with easy divorce prevails over that with the strict law. But, under *Williams II*, it was still necessary that one or the other of the parties actually establish his domicile in the state with easy divorce. This pronouncement does not mean that he has to live in his new state permanently. But it is necessary that at the time of moving into the divorce state, or at least at some point before the initiation of the divorce suit, he has actually intended to remain in that state for some indefinite period. If he has had such an intention, he has become a domiciliary, even though he might change his intention after the initiation of the divorce suit and decide to move back to the state of his former domicile. But the divorce would not be entitled to faith and credit if the plaintiff had the intention of staying in the divorce state for a temporary purpose only, for instance to stay in Nevada just for the six weeks required by Nevada law and immediately upon obtaining the divorce to use the return ticket that he had brought with him. Recognition by other states of a Nevada, Idaho, Florida, or similar divorce is thus to depend upon a person's state of mind, a fact which is said not to be known to anybody but the devil. But the difficulty of proving was facilitated by the Supreme Court of the United States when it held in *Williams II* that a finding of domicile by the divorce court is entitled to be taken for true until it has been disproved by strong and clear evidence.

The fact that the Nevada court found that they were domiciled there is entitled to respect, and more. The burden of undermining the verity which the Nevada decrees import rests heavily upon the assailant.[64]

The Nevada divorce of a party who carefully followed the advice of experienced counsel was thus endowed with a presumption of nation-wide effectiveness that is difficult to disprove. But there still remained the necessity of creating at least the appearance of a true change of

63. 325 U.S. 226, at 229.
64. 325 U.S. 233, 65 S.Ct. 1097, 89 L.Ed. 1583, 157 A.L.R. 1371.

domicile by one or the other party. It was removed three years later for those cases in which the parties were willing to cooperate, a willingness that might be purchased by one party's concessions to the other in matters of alimony, property settlement, or child custody.

This result was achieved in two cases which were decided by the Supreme Court of the United States on the same day, 7 June 1948. The parties of *Sherrer* v. *Sherrer*,[65] Edward E. and Margaret C. Sherrer, had long lived together as husband and wife in Massachusetts. On 3 April 1944 the wife, accompanied by the two children of the marriage, left for Florida, where she instituted proceedings of divorce on 6 July, shortly after the end of the period of ninety days of residence required by Florida law. The husband retained Florida counsel, entered a general appearance, and denied all allegations of his wife including the allegations as to her Florida residence. The hearing was held on 14 November. The husband appeared personally to testify with respect to a stipulation entered into by the parties relating to the custody of the children. The wife introduced evidence to establish her Florida residence. Counsel for the husband neither cross-examined nor introduced evidence in rebuttal. On 29 November the Florida court entered a decree of divorce after specifically finding that "petitioner is a bona fide resident of the State of Florida." No appeal was filed by the husband. Two days after the decree of divorce had been entered, the wife was married in Florida to Henry A. Phelps, a former Massachusetts neighbor, who had come to Florida shortly after Mrs. Sherrer's arrival in that state. On 5 February 1945, the newlyweds returned to Massachusetts. In the Florida proceedings, Mr. Sherrer had apparently promised to turn over some real estate to his wife. This promise he now regretted. So in June, Mr. Sherrer started proceedings in Berkshire County, Massachusetts, praying for permission to convey his real estate and file a judicial declaration that he was still married to Margaret because her Florida divorce and her marriage to Phelps were invalid. The Massachusetts court heard evidence, found that Margaret had never obtained a domicile in Florida, and granted Edward the relief he had requested. That decree was affirmed by the Supreme Judicial Court of Massachusetts but reversed by the Supreme Court of the United States, speaking through Chief Justice Vinson.

On the same day the Court decided in the same sense the case of *Coe* v. *Coe*.[66] In that case the effectiveness of a Nevada divorce was contested by the wife; she alleged that her husband, who had initiated the

65. 334 U.S. 343, 68 S.Ct. 1087, 92 L.Ed. 1429.
66. 334 U.S. 378, 68 S.Ct. 1094, 92 L.Ed. 1451.

Nevada proceedings and to whom the Nevada divorce had been granted, had not obtained a domicile in that state. Upon the evidence presented by her the Massachusetts court decided in her favor. The decision was reversed by the Supreme Court of the United States. In the Nevada proceedings the wife had not only not contested the husband's allegations of domicile but had even filed a counterclaim. She had had "full opportunity to contest the jurisdictional issues." As she had not availed herself of the opportunity, she could not be allowed to do so in new proceedings. All issues determined in the Nevada decree including that of jurisdiction had matured into *res judicata*. The Nevada court's decision was thus entitled to be given full faith and credit in all other states.

In both *Sherrer* and *Coe*, the Supreme Court of the United States referred to a case it had decided ten years earlier, *Davis* v. *Davis*.[67] That case dealt with a situation in which a husband had left the matrimonial home in the District of Columbia and established himself in Virginia. In the divorce proceedings which he started there his wife appeared, contested the husband's allegation that he had obtained a Virginia domicile, and presented evidence to rebut this allegation. The Virginia court decided against the wife and granted the husband a decree of divorce. The wife thereupon started a suit in the District of Columbia to obtain maintenance from the husband, claiming that the Virginia divorce was invalid because the husband had not been domiciled there, so that Virginia lacked jurisdiction. The court in the District of Columbia heard evidence on the issue of the husband's domicile, found that he had never been domiciled in Virginia, and rendered judgment in favor of the wife. This decision was reversed by the Supreme Court of the United States on the ground that the District of Columbia had failed to give full faith and credit to the decision of Virginia. The issue of domicile, the court held, had been litigated there and the decision on that issue participated in the *res judicata* effect of the Virginia judgment.

> She may not say that he was not entitled to sue for divorce in the state court, for she appeared there and by plea put in issue his allegation as to domicile, introduced evidence to show it false, took exceptions to the commissioner's report, and sought to have the court sustain them and uphold her plea. Plainly, the determination of the decree upon that point is effective for all purposes in this litigation.[68]

In the *Davis* case, the issue of domicile had been actually litigated;

67. 305 U.S. 32, 59 S.Ct. 3, 83 L.Ed. 26, 118 A.L.R. 1518 (1938).
68. 305 U.S. 32, 40, 59 S.Ct. 3, 6, 83 L.Ed. 26, 29, 118 A.L.R. 1518, 1522.

in *Sherrer* and *Coe* it had not. In the *Sherrer* case, the Court quoted what it had said in *Stoll* v. *Gottlieb*,[69] a case which had nothing to do with divorce but which had been concerned with a money claim alleged to have arisen out of a business transaction. There the court declared:

> It is just as important that there should be a place to end as that there should be a place to begin litigation. After a party has had his day in court, with opportunity to present his evidence and his view of the law, a collateral attack upon the decision as to jurisdiction there rendered merely retries the issue previously determined.[70]

In both *Sherrer* and *Coe*, the party who had his day in court was the spouse who had lost on the divorce issue. But what about the state, which courts have innumerable times said to be the third party to every suit of divorce? Has the commonwealth of Massachusetts had its day in the courts of Florida or Nevada in litigations of which a Massachusetts state agency neither had nor could have had any knowledge? Apparently, the commonwealth was not meant to be precluded from denying that Mrs. Sherrer or Mr. Coe had been domiciliaries of the divorce-granting states if an officer of the commonwealth should start proceedings in the name of the commonwealth to have Mrs. Sherrer-Phelps convicted of the crime of bigamy or to deny to the Phelps couple advantages to which married people might be entitled under the tax or welfare laws of Massachusetts.[71] But nothing has been heard about a bigamy prosecution of Mr. and Mrs. Phelps or of any other couple, in Massachusetts or, with the apparent exception of New Jersey, anywhere else, ever since the spectacle of the *Williams-Hendrix* case.[72] State prosecutors simply do not prosecute, and nothing has been heard from tax, welfare, or other offices, state or federal, which might have

---

69. 305 U.S. 165, 172, 59 S.Ct. 134, 138 (1938).

70. Some state courts have indicated that a foreign bilateral divorce might not be given faith and credit if it was clearly obtained in a collusive attempt to evade the law of the state of the domicile. A few courts have held so. But, as Professor Clark aptly observes, "the issue is largely academic, since well instructed divorce litigants are generally careful to behave like adversaries even though they are not" (CLARK 293).

71. On the problem of whether or not the state of the domincile is precluded from attacking a bilateral foreign divorce, see *id.*

72. John de Meo, a resident of New Jersey, having unilaterally obtained a Mexican mail order divorce, in New Jersey entered upon a new marriage. Charged with bigamy he did not plead that his Mexican divorce was valid, but solely that he believed it to be valid and that he had entered upon his remarriage in good faith. His conviction of the crime of bigamy was upheld by the New Jersey Supreme Court, State of New Jersey v. John de Meo, 20 N.J. 1, 118 Atl. 2d 1, 56 A.L.R. 2d 905. A conviction upon a similar state of fact was sustained in State v. Najjar, 1 N.J. Super. 208, 63 Atl. 2d 807. After the death of Chief Justice Vanderbilt even New Jersey seems to have ceased to prosecute victims of the belief in the effectiveness of Mexican mail order divorces.

collaterally attacked the effectiveness of a divorce decree rendered upon an allegation of divorce state domicile by one party and not contested by the other. So the door has now been opened to unlimited migratory consent divorce.

But there still existed some risk. The effectiveness of a divorce might be attacked by private persons who have not been parties to the divorce proceedings and who might thus be regarded as not being bound by the *res judicata* effect of the divorce decree. Such an attack might be made by the new spouse of a divorced person or by a blood relation of one of the parties. If the new marriage does not work out, either spouse might try simply to walk out on it, claiming that the spouse's divorce is void and that consequently the remarriage is bigamous and invalid. Such attempts are generally stopped by state courts, which hold that not only the spouse who has brought about the divorce or who has allowed it to be brought against him is estopped from later denying its effectiveness, but that the estoppel also extends to a new spouse who has helped to bring about the divorce or who has availed himself of the divorce by marrying the divorced person with knowledge of the latter's previous marriage.[73] Children of the new marriage are widely protected by so-called saving statutes, which apply not only to marriages void because of bigamy but to all or many types of invalid marriages, and which ascribe legitimacy to the offspring of such marriages if at least one of the parties to the marriage was ignorant of the facts causing it to be invalid or, even more generously, if the parties have gone through a ceremony of marriage even in full knowledge of its invalidity.[74] Finally, there is the risk that the validity of a divorced person's migratory divorce and remarriage may be questioned by a blood relation. The situation is illustrated by the case in which this risk was barred by the Supreme Court of the United States, the case of *Johnson* v. *Muelberger*.[75]

E. Bruce Johnson was married three times. After the death of his first wife in 1939, he married Madoline, with whom he established a common residence in New York. The marriage turned out to be unhappy. In June 1942, Madoline went to Florida, where she filed her bill of divorce on 29 July. Under Florida law no divorce is to be granted to any person who has not resided in Florida for at least ninety days im-

---

73. See *infra* p. 89; Cook v. Cook, 342 U.S. 126, 72 S.Ct. 157, 96 L.Ed. 164 (1951).
74. See CLARK 132.
75. 340 U.S. 581, 71 S.Ct. 474, 95 L.Ed. 552 (1951); see also Aldrich v. Aldrich, 378 U.S. 540, 84 S.Ct. 1687, 12 L.Ed. 2d 1020 (1964).

mediately preceding the filing date.[76] Madoline's allegation of having resided in Florida for the required time was not contested by her husband, who, as it was later stated by the New York surrogate, "had full opportunity to contest the jurisdictional issues." The Florida divorce was granted to the wife, and in 1944 Mr. Johnson entered upon his third marriage, with Genevieve. In 1945 he died, leaving a will in which he gave his entire estate to Eleanor Muelberger, the daughter of his first marriage. Under New York law a husband cannot completely exclude his wife from sharing in his estate. Under § 18 of the New York Decedents' Estate Law, the surviving spouse is entitled to one-third of the estate of the predeceasing spouse even if the latter has tried to disinherit her. Genevieve thus claimed a one-third share in the Johnson estate. This claim was contested by Eleanor, who maintained that the Florida divorce obtained by her father's second wife was ineffective and that, consequently, his purported third marriage had been bigamous and void. The lower New York courts held in favor of Genevieve, but were reversed by the New York Court of Appeals.[77] The Florida decree, that court held, was binding on both parties to the Florida proceedings. If under Florida law the decree were also binding upon the daughter, the Full Faith and Credit Clause, together with the Act of Congress by which it is implemented, requires that such binding effect also be recognized in New York. However, Florida law was interpreted by New York's highest court so as not to bind the daughter, who had been a stranger to the Florida proceedings. But Florida law was read differently by the Supreme Court of the United States. The Florida decree was found under Florida law to bind not only the parties who had participated in the divorce proceedings but also a third party where there exists a relationship to the parties such as in the case of Mrs. Muelberger. The court did not find any Florida decision which had ever held so. It found it sufficient that no Florida case had been brought to its attention holding that in Florida a child may contest its parent's divorce where the parent has been barred from contesting by *res judicata*. Under this decision it is left to the divorcing state to determine whether or not the divorce can be attacked by third parties. Obviously, no state in which divorcing has been developed into a tourist industry is likely to expose its divorces to third-party attack.[78] There remains the question whether a third party might

76. Fla.Stat.Ann. § 65.02, as construed in Curley v. Curley, 144 Fla. 728, 198 So. 584 (1940).
77. 301 N.Y. 13, 92 N.E. 2d 44 (1950).
78. Nevada has expressly taken care of the matter in Nevada Rev. Stat. § 125.185:

not have to be regarded as being deprived of property without due process of law if property rights of his can be affected by proceedings in which he neither did nor could participate. But it was intimated in *Johnson* v. *Muelberger* that a person who at the time of the divorce was just an expectant heir of one of the divorcing parties did at that time not have a "right" of which he might be deprived. The door to collateral attack by a third party thus seems to be effectively shut.

States like Nevada, Florida, Idaho, or Arkansas owe their popularity to the ease with which divorces can be obtained in their courts. This ease does not necessarily appear from the wording of their divorce laws.[79] The text of the Nevada statute is not much different from that of other states. For a long time divorce appeared to be firmly grounded on marital misconduct. But one of the acts of misconduct listed in the statute is "extreme cruelty"[80] and this concept is given the widest possible meaning of mental cruelty. How broadly it is understood cannot be ascertained owing to those features of Nevada divorce procedure which constitute the main reason for Nevada's attractiveness. The facts upon which the divorce is demanded need not be spelled out unless the defendant asks for a bill of particulars and in the trial court divorce cases may be heard in chambers and the record is impounded and thus kept away from public inspection.[81] Consent divorces are, of course, not appealed. Thus, it is impossible to know any more about Nevada grounds for divorce than the fact that no uncontested petition for divorce seems ever to have been denied.

A slight inconvenience is constituted by the requirement that the divorce plaintiff has to allege under oath that he is, and for at least six weeks prior to the filing of the complaint has been, a resident of Nevada.[82] By decision of the Nevada Supreme Court the term "residence" as used in the divorce act has been interpreted to be equivalent

---

"No divorce from the bonds of matrimony heretofore or hereafter granted by a court of competent jurisdiction of the State of Nevada, which divorce is valid and binding upon each of the parties thereto, may be contested or attacked by third persons not parties thereto" (added by Laws 30 March 1959, c. 361, at 554).

79. F. W. Ingram & G. A. Ballard, *The Business of Migratory Divorce in Nevada*, 2 LAW & CONTEMP. PROB. 302 (1935); N. M. BLAKE, THE ROAD TO RENO 152 (1962).

80. Nev. Rev. Stat. § 125.010, no. 6. The more genteel ground of the parties' having lived separate and apart without cohabitation is also available under no. 9 of the section stated. The discretion given to the court in such case does not seem to be exercised in consent cases to withhold the divorce. Shortly after the enactment of the New York divorce reform act of 1966, the minimum period required by Nevada law was reduced from two years to one year by Nevada Law 5 April 1967, c. 278, at 805. For good measure the same law added the new ground of "incompatibility."

81. §§ 125.030, 125.110.

82. § 125.022.

to domicile.[83] That means that a Nevada residence cannot be established by anyone who does not intend to live in Nevada for more than the limited time necessary to obtain a divorce. A divorce seeker who has come to Nevada with the intention of leaving the state as soon as he has filed his petition for divorce would seem not to be a bona fide resident of the state. But the only state that could prosecute for perjury would be Nevada, and that state will hardly choose to spoil an important domestic industry.

In the 1930s the territory of the Virgin Islands tried to compete with Nevada. Its substantive law of divorce looked even more attractive. When the islands were acquired by the United States from Denmark in 1917, the Danish divorce law remained in effect there, and that law had provided for many years that divorce might be granted not only because of marital misconduct but also upon the simple ground of incompatibility of temperament.[84] So as to make this convenient law easily available to tourists who would spend money in the tropical paradise, the divorce law of 1944 was made to provide in § 9 that a divorce suit might be commenced after a six-week residence in the territory. The U.S. Circuit Court of Appeals for the 3d Circuit, which sits in Philadelphia and which hears appeals from the District Court for the Virgin Islands, held that residence within the meaning of the Virgin Islands act was equivalent to "domicile" and thus implied the intention of living in the Virgin Islands for an indefinite period of time.[85] To this inconvenient interpretation of its law, the legislature of the Virgin Islands replied in 1953 by adding to § 9 of the divorce law a new paragraph which reads as follows:

> ... If the plaintiff is within the district at the time of the filing of the complaint and has been continuously for six weeks immediately prior thereto, this shall be prima facie evidence of domicile, and where the defendant has been personally served within the district or enters a general appearance in the action, then the court shall have jurisdiction of the action and of the parties thereto without further reference to domicile. ...

The purpose of this amendment was to do away with the necessity of committing perjury. Sworn testimony of the plaintiff's physical presence for six weeks was to suffice. No evidence would be required of the plaintiff's intention. But this effort to take the vestige of dishonesty out of migratory divorce was not permitted to stand. Judge Her-

---

83. Walker v. Walker, 45 Nev. 105, 198 P. 433 (1921); Latterner v. Latterner, 51 Nev. 285, 274 P. 194 (1929). The residence, these cases held, must be "bona fide."
84. See *infra*, chap. 6.
85. Burch v. Burch, 195 F.2d 799 (1952).

man Moore of the District Court refused to cooperate. In a case in which the defendant husband had entered a general appearance, but did not contest the plaintiff wife's allegation of six-week "residence," the judge on his own initiative asked for proof of intention. When no such proof was furnished, he denied the divorce. On appeal he was upheld by the court in Philadelphia, the majority of which held that domicile in the technical sense was a requirement of divorce jurisdiction indispensable under the Due Process Clause of the Constitution of the United States.[86] In the following year another case of the same type was taken all the way to the Supreme Court of the United States. Its decision was against the validity of the 1944 Amendment, but the court took care to base this holding upon the Organic Act for the Territory of the Virgin Islands, which it interpreted to limit the jurisdiction of the territory to persons who are actually its domiciliaries. The question whether or not the jurisdiction of states was similarly limited by the Fourteenth Amendment to the Constitution of the United States was left open.[87] But judicial reversals have not destroyed the availability of the Virgin Islands. In 1962, 1963, 1964, and 1965, the divorce rates per 1,000 population were 2.2, 2.3, 2.4, and 2.5 for the United States. They were 5.2, 4.3, 4.9, and 5.7 for the Virgin Islands. As stated in the *United Nations Demographic Yearbook, 1967* (table 26), the number of divorces granted in the Virgin Islands in the period 1962–66 (180, 171, 200, 247, and 294) includes annulments and divorces among "non-permanent residents."

Obviously, in dealing with the Virgin Islands, the Supreme Court of the United States did not wish to cast doubts upon those cases by which it had made easy divorce generally available to migrants and pseudo-migrants. Under these cases, the present state of the law can be summarized as follows:

1. If both parties cooperate so that the defendant enters a general appearance and then fails to deny the plaintiff's allegation of residence or domicile, a consent divorce may be obtained in any state which is willing to pass off consent divorces under some such heading as divorce for mental cruelty and which does not require that the plaintiff be present and pay hotel bills for an inconveniently long time. Such a divorce must be given full faith and credit in all states of the Union.[88]

2. An *ex parte* divorce, i.e., a divorce obtained by one party without

---

86. Alton v. Alton, 207 F.2d 667 (1953).
87. Granville-Smith v. Granville-Smith, 349 U.S. 1, 75 S.Ct. 553, 99 L.Ed. 773 (1955).
88. Sherrer v. Sherrer; Coe v. Coe; Johnson v. Muelberger.

the other's having entered an appearance, may not be denied full faith and credit in any state unless the party who has not participated in the divorce proceedings cares to attack the divorce and is able to overcome the presumption of correctness of the divorce court's finding that the divorce plaintiff was truly a resident-domiciliary of the divorce state at the time when the suit for divorce was commenced.[89] Full faith and credit must be denied when the party who was the defendant in the divorce proceedings proves that he had no knowledge of the pendency of these proceedings because the divorce plaintiff had failed to notify him in a way that would be consistent with the requirements of due process of law.

In *Haddock* v. *Haddock* the Supreme Court held that a husband who obtained an *ex parte* divorce in a state of which he had actually become a domiciliary could not deprive his wife of maintenance if he had left the matrimonial home without just cause. The court achieved this result by declaring that a decree of divorce thus obtained was not entitled to full faith and credit. *Haddock* v. *Haddock* was overruled by *Williams* v. *North Carolina*. However, the protection of the wife against loss of monetary claims or property rights was restored through a different technique.

Jurisdiction to terminate a marriage by a decree of divorce depends on the domicile of one or the other of the parties, which means in practice the domicile — genuine or fictitious — of the plaintiff. But jurisdiction to order a person to make payments or to deprive him of a right to claim payments depends traditionally on jurisdiction over the person of the defendant.[90] If the defendant is an individual (rather than a corporation), he must, roughly speaking, either have been personally served with process in the state in which the proceedings are instituted against him, or he must have voluntarily entered an appearance in the proceedings or have otherwise submitted to the jurisdiction of the state, or he must be a domiciliary of the state. This principle of long standing was made applicable to matters of divorce in a decision rendered by the Supreme Court of the United States on the same day it decided the cases of *Sherrer* v. *Sherrer* and *Coe* v. *Coe*.

Up to that time it had been taken for granted that a decree of divorce terminated not only the bond of a marriage but also all its incidents, including a wife's right to maintenance. If before the divorce the wife had obtained a decree ordering her husband to pay her separate maintenance, he could have it terminated as soon as he obtained

---

89. Williams v. North Carolina; Williams v. State of North Carolina.
90. The leading case is Pennoyer v. Neff, 95 U.S. 714, 24 L.Ed. 565 (1877).

a divorce. It was irrelevant that the decree of separate maintenance had been obtained in a court of one state and that of divorce in another, provided only the decree of divorce was entitled to full faith and credit. The right to maintenance belonged only to a wife. An ex-wife might have a right to receive alimony from her husband, but this right must be specifically created by judicial decree and traditionally it was taken for granted that such creation could occur exclusively through the same decree by which the marriage was terminated. Unless an order to pay alimony was contained in the decree of divorce, the ex-wife's right to support was gone forever, and a hostile husband could hardly be expected in his own bill for divorce to ask that he be ordered to pay alimony to his wife. An *ex parte* divorce obtained by a husband was likely to be a decree depriving the wife forever of all right to support. The complicated rule of the *Haddock* case was developed by the Supreme Court of the United States exactly as a means to avoid depriving the wife of support when the husband left her without just cause. When, in *Williams I, Haddock* v. *Haddock* was overruled, the Supreme Court had to break with the traditional idea under which all incidents of marriage were automatically terminated with the divorce. The jurisdiction rules that were newly established for *ex parte* divorce were held to be limited to the termination of the marriage tie. Jurisdiction on matters of dollars and cents and also on matters of child custody were held to be subject to rules of their own. The idea that jurisdiction for determining the right of support need not coincide with jurisdiction to terminate the bond of a marriage was first expressed in the separate concurrent opinion of Mr. Justice Douglas in the case of *Esenwein* v. *Esenwein*.[91] A husband who had left the marital home in Pennsylvania and had obtained an *ex parte* divorce in Nevada applied to the court in Pennsylvania for the termination of his duty to pay separate maintenance to his wife, which had been established by decree of the Pennsylvania court. The Supreme Court of the United States affirmed the Pennsylvania denial of the petition, finding that upon carefully weighing the evidence presented to it, the Pennsylvania court had regarded as refuted the Nevada court's finding of a Nevada domicile in that state. In his concurring opinion Mr. Justice Douglas pointed out that the Pennsylvania court's refusal to regard the wife's right to separate maintenance as terminated might have been proper even if the husband had actually established a domicile in Nevada.

91. 325 U.S. 279, 281, 65 S.Ct. 1118, 89 L.Ed. 1609, 157 A.L.R. 1396 (1944).

It is not apparent [Mr. Justice Douglas wrote] that the spouse who obtained the decree can defeat an action for maintenance or support in another state by showing that he was domiciled in the State which awarded him the divorce decree. It is one thing if the spouse from whom the decree of divorce is obtained appears or is personally served. . . . But I am not convinced that in absence of an appearance or personal service the decree need be given full faith and credit when it comes to maintenance or support of the other spouse or the children.[92]

This idea found support in the concurring opinion of Mr. Justice Rutledge. It became the law of the Court in its opinion rendered in the case of *Estin* v. *Estin*[93] and delivered by Mr. Justice Douglas. In 1943 a decree of separation and maintenance had been granted to Mrs. Estin by a court of New York, where the parties had lived together until 1942 and where the wife continued to be domiciled. In May 1945, the husband obtained a Nevada *ex parte* divorce. He thereupon ceased paying maintenance to his wife. In the New York proceedings instituted by the wife, the husband pleaded the Nevada divorce. His plea was overruled, the New York court holding that even if the husband had been domiciled in Nevada and while the Nevada divorce might thus be entitled to full faith and credit as to the termination of the marriage, New York was not obliged also to recognize it as terminating a property right of a resident of New York. This view of the New York court was upheld by the Supreme Court of the United States, which thus established in American law the doctrine which has come to be called that of divisible divorce.

A husband who has obtained an *ex parte* divorce is thus free to remarry, but he may be sued for support by his ex-wife in any state which provides such a remedy and which has personal jurisdiction over him.[94] Ready restoration to the freedom of remarriage has thus been elegantly combined with protection of the stay-at-home spouse.

Migratory Divorce in a Foreign Country

Using the Full Faith and Credit Clause of the Constitution of the United States and the act of Congress by which it is implemented, the Supreme Court has developed the duty of each state to treat as effective the bilateral divorces of every state, and those *ex parte* divorces decreed by the state of which the plaintiff was a domiciliary at the time he instituted the divorce proceedings, irrespective of how long or how short a time that domicile may have existed. But what about an *ex*

---

92. 325 U.S. 279, 282, 65 S.Ct. 1118, 1119, 89 L.Ed. 1609, 1611, 157 A.L.R. 1396, 1398.
93. 334 U.S. 541, 68 S.Ct. 1213, 92 L.Ed. 1561 (1948).
94. Vanderbilt v. Vanderbilt, 354 U.S. 416, 77 S.Ct. 1360, 1 L.Ed. 2d 1456 (1957). On other possible consequences of the doctrine of divisible divorce, see CLARK 314.

parte divorce granted by a sister state of which the plaintiff was not a domiciliary? And what about a divorce obtained in Mexico, France, or somewhere else outside of the United States?

The problem of recognition of divorces granted in a state other than that in which one party is domiciled or which is at least stated in the decree as that of the domicile has been much discussed in recent years. Several states have shown willingness to free from the shackles of marriage military personnel stationed in a state without being domiciled there. If the term domicile is understood in the traditional sense, it does not make a serviceman a domiciliary of the state into which he is ordered by superior command and which he can at any time be ordered to leave. Like a student registering in an out-of-state university, or a federal civil servant subject to transfer from one place to another, the serviceman enters the state without the intention of remaining there indefinitely. Since such *animus manendi* is indispensable for the establishment of a new domicile, the serviceman retains the domicile in which he was settled before he entered the military service. He is not a domiciliary of the state in which he is stationed unless he decides that he wishes to live there indefinitely after separation from the military establishment. Proof that such an intention has been formed and, even more so, of the exact moment at which it was formed, is, to put it mildly, difficult. Alabama, Alaska, Arkansas, Texas, and other states have thus enacted statutes allowing the granting of a decree of divorce to a serviceman who is simply stationed in the state, or has been stationed there for some minimum period of time. The courts of these states held their statutes to be all right. The Supreme Court of the United States, which has the last word, has not yet had any occasion to express its view.[95] No one, it seems, has so far felt the urge to carry a case to Washington. In the context of a discussion of migratory divorce the problem can be left alone. The lawyer-advisers of parties agreeing to seek a divorce will advise them to pick a forum that can be expected to insert in the decree a finding of domicile and thus to render it safe against attack. For this reason we can also forget about the puzzling opinion rendered by Judge Goodrich in *Alton* v. *Alton*, in which he declared a Virgin Islands divorce invalid because, in accordance with the statute, the decree said nothing about domicile and, so it was held, a divorce rendered outside of the domicile is invalid under the Due Process Clause of the Fifth and, conceivably, also under that of the Fourteenth Amendment to the Constitution of the United

---

95. On the problem, see R. A. Leflar, *Conflict of Laws and Family Law*, 14 ARK. L. REV. 47 (1960).

States.⁹⁶ Which person would in the case of a consent divorce be deprived of his liberty or property, the court did not disclose. Another consideration that may be omitted from discussion here is the rule that no divorce can have any validity, not even in the state in which it is rendered, if such minimal requirements of fairness — indispensable to procedural due process — as giving notice to the defendant have been disregarded.⁹⁷ As long as procedural due process has been observed, no provision of the Constitution of the United States and no other rule of federal law prevents a state from ascribing effect to an out-of-state divorce, even though it need not be given full faith and credit under article IV, section 1, of the federal Constitution. This freedom of the states applies to United States divorces rendered bilaterally without a finding of domicile or rendered *ex parte* outside of the domicile. It also applies to French, Mexican, and other divorces obtained outside of the United States.

A decree of divorce rendered by a court or other agency of a foreign country is a special kind of the broader category of "foreign judgment." It is not self-evident that the act of a foreign court by which a marriage is terminated is regarded as having that effect in American courts and agencies. Some countries are reluctant to recognize foreign decrees of divorce.⁹⁸ In many countries the requirements for recognition are expressed in statutes. In all American states it seems that the problem has been left to the courts, and, traditionally, the courts of countries of Anglo-American law have been remarkably willing to recognize foreign judgments in general and decrees of divorce in particular.⁹⁹ A foreign judgment is, in general, "recognized" when it is final, when the minimum requirements of due process have been observed in the foreign proceeding, when there has been no fraud, and when the country by whose court the judgment was rendered has jurisdiction in concordance with the notions held in the American state in which the effectiveness of the foreign judgment is pleaded.¹⁰⁰ These requirements are basically the same as those under which an American state is obliged to give faith and credit to judgments of American sister states. But, contrary to the latter situation, an American court may refuse

96. 207 F.2d 667 (1953).
97. See R. A. LEFLAR, AMERICAN CONFLICTS LAW 35 (1968); A. T. VON MEHREN & D. T. TRAUTMAN, THE LAW OF MULTISTATE PROBLEMS 877 (1965).
98. See 1 RABEL, *supra* note 45, at 497.
99. See A. A. EHRENZWEIG, CONFLICT OF LAWS, 161 (1962); LEFLAR, *supra* note 97, at 171; C. Peterson, *Res Judicata and Foreign Country Judgments*, 24 OHIO ST.L.J. 291 (1963).
100. See the numerous cases listed in 13 A.L.R. 3d 1425.

faith and credit to a foreign-nation judgment which in some way appears to be incompatible with the public policy of the American state where the question of recognition is raised. The concept of public policy is vague. It varies from place to place and from time to time. With respect to a foreign-nation judgment's effect of terminating a marriage, it has rarely played any role. But it may be of significance with respect to custody, alimony, property, and support terms.

With respect to jurisdiction, a difference exists between sister state and foreign-nation divorce decrees insofar as in the former the meaning of the term jurisdiction is regarded as being implied in the Full Faith and Credit Clause of the Constitution of the United States, which signifies that in the last resort this meaning is to be determined by the Supreme Court of the United States. As we have seen, jurisdiction has been predicated by the Court on the domicile of the divorce plaintiff.[101] So far the determination of what the term exactly means within the context has been avoided by the Court. Also, the recognition of domicile as a basis of divorce jurisdiction does not necessarily exclude the possibility that some day the Court may also regard it as sufficient that the party or parties have some other tie with the divorce-granting state. As we have seen above, the plaintiff's domicile in the divorce state must not necessarily have existed in fact. It suffices that the divorce decree contains a finding of domicile and that the decree has been rendered in bilateral proceedings. Even if the finding were incorrect, it is *res judicata* and may thus not be questioned in the court of any other American state.[102] It is through this binding effect of the finding of domicile in bilateral cases that the Supreme Court of the United States has imposed consent divorce upon the states of the Union.

If a divorce has been pronounced by a court of a foreign country in which at the commencement of the proceedings both parties were domiciled, in the sense in which the term is understood in the general parlance of American law, every American state is likely to recognize it. If, for instance, at the time of the divorce proceedings both parties were nationals of Mexico, had been born in the state of Chihuahua and had lived there all their lives, a divorce decree of a court of Chihuahua rendered in bilateral proceedings free of unfair dealing will almost certainly be recognized everywhere in the United States. If an American moves to the Côte d'Azur, there purchases a home, lives under circumstances making it clear that he intends to remain in France indefi-

---

101. Williams v. North Carolina, 317 U.S. 287, 63 S.Ct. 207, 87 L.Ed. 279 (1942).
102. Sherrer v. Sherrer, 334 U.S. 343, 68 S.Ct. 1087, 97 L.Ed. 1429 (1948). On the possibilities of collateral attack by a third person or the state, see *supra* p. 74.

nitely, and obtains a divorce in the court of Nice, he can be practically certain that his marriage will be regarded as terminated everywhere in the United States. We use weasel words because there is a faint chance that some American state may feel its public policy violated if the Chihuahua decree was rendered upon the basis of the parties' mutual agreement to have their marriage terminated, or because of incompatibility or some other ground unrecognized by the official divorce law of the American state in question. If somebody wishes to make trouble, he might also say that the domiciliary divorce was pronounced not by a court but, as may be done in Denmark, by an administrative agency or, as is done in Lebanon, by a religious tribunal or, as in Afghanistan, by the unilateral declaration of the husband or, as in Japan, by the extrajudicial private agreement of the parties. Even in such cases a truly domiciliary divorce can be regarded as reasonably safe against attack.

But what about the American who has gone to Paris, or to Ciudad Juárez, just for the purpose of obtaining a divorce and who goes home to Chicago, New York, or Denver as soon as he has the decree in his pocket? How about the intermediate situation in which the establishment of a domicile is dubious?

Irrespective of doubts that may have existed about the effectiveness of migratory divorces obtained in foreign countries, Americans, acting like citizens of so many other countries, have tried, and their attempts have been more successful than those of Italians, Spaniards, or Argentinians.

In the 1920s, France was the favorite country,[103] and for a while the French courts were accommodating. *Injures graves* could be produced for American clients as easily as for French, and proof of a French domicile, which is usually required by French courts, was not difficult to satisfy either. It is reported that between 1919 and 1927 the number of American couples divorced in France rose from a very few to several hundred a year. In 1927 an American newspaper published in Paris compiled a list of about three hundred American couples known to have obtained a French divorce in 1926. Of them, many were certainly not domiciliaries of France. They came to Paris for a stay sufficient to get a fast divorce, and went back home right away, as they had intended from the outset. In fact, the same apartment figured repeatedly as the alleged place of residence. The newspaper publicity resulted in action by French authorities who did not wish their country to become a

---

103. See L. T. Bates, *The Divorce of Americans in France*, 2 LAW & CONTEMP. PROB. 323 (1935); on the French law of divorce, see *infra* chap. 8.

divorce mill for Americans. Disciplinary measures were taken against several lawyers. Above all, the minister of justice approached the president of the fourth civil chamber of the Paris court, the Tribunal de la Seine, where were centered the compulsory conciliation proceedings that must precede the filing of an action for divorce in Paris. The ministry advised him to apply a six-month residence test before issuing permission to start proceedings. The district attorneys were admonished to make use of their statutory standing to act as defenders of the bond in cases of aliens who would not have actually resided in France for at least six months. This admonition did not find much response. The business load of the French state's attorneys is too extensive to allow them to make use of their capacity to intervene in civil cases. There also was no longer much need. The atmosphere changed. Americans found it increasingly difficult to obtain divorces in French courts. In 1934, the number of French divorces granted to Americans was estimated not to have exceeded twenty-five.

As French divorces went out of fashion, Mexican ones came into vogue.[104] When the Mexican revolution broke out in 1910, marriage was indissoluble throughout the Republic. A decree enacted by the federal congress on 14 December 1874[105] had expressly declared marriage to be indissoluble in any way other than by the death of one of the spouses. Ecclesiastical influence was swept away by the revolution. On 29 December 1914, Carranza, first chief of the constitutionalist armies, issued a decree authorizing the governors of the states to admit divorces for valid cause or on mutual consent, provided the parties had been married at least three years. The decree was meant to counteract the tendency of the poorer classes to prefer illegitimate unions to indissoluble marriages. Legislation for the Federal District and the federal territories of Baja California and Quintana Roo soon followed. The present version is contained in the Civil Code for the Federal District and the territories of 30 August 1928.[106] Its substantive law of divorce is liberal.[107] It lists no fewer than seventeen grounds for divorce, among them mutual consent, provided the marriage has existed for at least one year.[108] If the couple is childless and if they agree on

---

104. M. Summers, *The Divorce Laws of Mexico*, 2 LAW & CONTEMP. PROB. 310 (1935); CLARK 294.

105. Art. 23, para. 9.

106. The Code took effect on 1 October 1932 (decree of 29 August 1932).

107. Art. 267. R. GALLARDO, DIVORCIO, SEPARACIÓN DE CUERPOS Y NULIDAD DEL MATRIMONIO EN LAS NACIONES LATINO-AMERICANAS 387 (Madrid 1957); see also V. C. GARCÍA MORENO, LA LEY DE DIVORCIO DE CHIHUAHUA 73 (1966); A. Aguilar Gutierrez, in 2 INSTITUTO DE DERECHO COMPARADO, PANORAMA DEL DERECHO MEXICANO 53 (1965).

108. Arts. 274.

the liquidation of their community property, no court intervention is needed. Similar to the law of Japan, where a marriage is terminated upon the notification of the registrar that the parties are in agreement to do so, under the Mexican federal law the bond is cut upon the registration of the childless parties' agreement. However, both parties must appear individually and in person before the registrar, and fifteen days must elapse between their appearances.[109] Proceedings before the registrar or in court must be in the district of the parties' residence. As is usual in Mexico, the legislation of the states follows the federal law more or less closely.[110] As far as the substantive law is concerned, the state of Chihuahua is also in general accord,[111] except that it offers the additional divorce ground of incompatibility of character [112] and provides that all divorces including those based on mutual consent must be pronounced by a court. What is, or until November 1970 was, unique in Chihuahua is the regulation of jurisdiction. The basic provision, article 22, looks innocent enough. Venue, and, by implication, jurisdiction, lies with the court of the plaintiff's place of residence (*lugar de la residencia del actor*) or, in cases of divorce by mutual consent, with the court of the place of residence of either party. Section 24 continues: "The residence within the meaning of article 22 of this statute is proved by the entry in the municipal register of the place." [113]

Entry in the municipal register of the border town of Ciudad Juárez is simple. You drive up to the city hall, sign your name in the register, and pay the fee of 150 pesos. No questions will be asked, no documents are required, no oath needs to be sworn. You then receive a certificate stating that you have registered. You are now a resident of Ciudad Juárez, State of Chihuahua, Mexico, within the meaning of article 22 of the divorce law, and right away you file with the court your petition for divorce on the ground of incompatibility. As shown by the *Rosenstiel* case,[114] if proper preparations have been made by correspondence with the gentleman who is to be your attorney, the procedure can be gone through in about one hour. Then you drive back over the bridge to El Paso, and you can be back home in New York the same day you left. A Mexican lunch may be had over there or in the airport

109. Arts. 272, 273.
110. On the state laws see the survey in GARCIA MORENO, *supra* note 107.
111. Ley de divorcio, of 15 July 1933, as amended by decree of 20 June 1946.
112. Art. 3, XIX.
113. "La residencia para los efectos del articulo 22 de la presente ley se acreditará con la constancia respectiva del registro municipal del lugar."
114. Rosenstiel v. Rosenstiel; Wood v. Wood, 16 N.Y.2d 64, 209 N.Y.2d 709, 13 A.L.R.3d 1401 (1965); see also Comment, *Mexican Bilateral Divorce: A Catalyst in Divorce Jurisdiction Theory*, 61 Nw. U.L. REV. 584 (1966).

restaurant on the Texas side of the Rio Grande. Your spouse has already sent the necessary power of attorney to the Mexican lawyer who is to appear in court for him. Your attorney alleges incompatibility of character; your spouse's attorney has no objections. The divorce is pronounced immediately, and a few days later the mailman will deliver your decree together with the English translation. If you wish to enjoy the attractions of Ciudad Juárez or the good hotel accommodations available in El Paso, you may dispense with registration in the municipal register and accompany your Mexican attorney to the court. If the other party's duly constituted attorney declares that his client does not object to the proceedings, the court's jurisdiction is established under article 23 of the Chihuahua divorce law. As far as the Chihuahua law is concerned, it is not even necessary to make the trip. The parties may appoint their attorneys by mail. If the attorneys thus designated appear before the court in Ciudad Juárez and each declares that his client submits to the proceedings, jurisdiction is also established. Finally, if you can establish that in spite of a diligent search you have failed to discover your spouse's whereabouts, you may have the summons published twice in the *Periodico Oficial del Estado de Chihuahua* and then obtain a decree *ex parte*.[115]

Of what value is a French or Chihuahua divorce to an American? If the law of the books were enforced in the traditional sense, all such divorces would be worthless except in those rare cases in which an honest-to-goodness domicile actually existed in France or Chihuahua. Americans who settle down in France are not numerous; the number of those choosing to live in Ciudad Juárez is likely to be small. According to the law of the books, i.e., here the law of conflict of laws as it was once recognized generally, no marriage bond of an American domiciliary could be cut by a court in France, Chihuahua, or anywhere else. But who cares? Having obtained the divorce in Paris or Ciudad Juárez, people consider themselves rid of the shackles of the old and free to enter upon a new marriage. Where the parties have acted in mutual agreement, the dollar-and-cent matters have been settled in advance. As long as the contractual obligations are fulfilled and neither party chooses to renege on the settlement, nobody has any reason to worry. Under the law of the books, the parties may be liable to be sent to the penitentiary for the crime of bigamy, but apart

---

115. In 1970 the Chihuahua law was changed to make it more closely correspond to the general type of Mexican divorce law. Apparently, in consequence of the liberalization of the divorce laws of New York and other American states, the divorce business of Chihuahua had fallen off so that the desire for respectability could overcome that for revenue.

from, perhaps, New Jersey,[116] the risk of a public prosecutor's starting trouble is practically nonexistent. The law in action relegates him to nonaction.

Only where someone tries to renege, or where a third party seeks to invoke the law of the books, is there any reason for a court to look into the matter. But for parties who have had experienced legal counsel, the courts have worked out a law in action that is almost, although not entirely, free of pitfalls.

The first point to consider is the old-fashioned toughness that can still be found in a few states. Decisions of New Mexico, New Jersey, and Ohio have declared Mexican divorces on fictitious residence to be worthless.[117] Until 1 January 1967, New Yorkers could not have consent divorces at home unless they were willing to go through the distasteful rigmarole of hotel evidence. The courts of New York have been anxious to protect their people from such indignity. In almost every one of the surprisingly high number of cases in which the effects of bilateral foreign divorces were involved, the lower courts of the state have found a way to avoid the consequences that might have followed if these divorces had been held to be ineffective. Where one party had actually appeared before the divorcing court and the other had participated in the proceedings in person or through an attorney, the New York courts either treated the foreign divorce simply as effective, or they resorted to a special device through which the "invalid" divorce was to almost all practical effects made equal with a valid divorce. That device is the so-called doctrine of estoppel.[118] Building upon bases that had their origin in Roman law, canonists and civilians of Europe developed the idea that a person who by his conduct had induced another person to believe that he would consistently hold to a certain position should not be allowed suddenly to turn around.[119]

116. State v. DeMeo, 20 N.J. 1; 118 A.2d 1; 56 A.L.R.2d 905 (1955).
117. Golden v. Golden, 41 N.M. 356, 68 P.2d 928 (1937); Warrender v. Warrender, 42 N.J. 287, 200 A.2d 123 (1964); Bobala v. Bobala, 68 Ohio App. 63, 33 N.E.2d 845 (1940); Mountbatten v. Mountbatten, 1 All E.R. 99 (1959). In all these cases the plaintiff had personally appeared in Mexico and the defendant appeared through an attorney. See also Du Quesnay v. Henderson, 24 Calif. App. 2d 11, 74 P. 2d 294 (1937); Bergeron v. Bergeron, 287 Mass. 524, 192 N.E. 86 (1934); State v. Najjar, 1 N.J. Super. 208, 63 A.2d 807, aff'd 2 N.J. 208, 66 A.2d 37 (1949); Reik v. Reik, 109 N.J.Eq. 615, 158 A. 519, aff'd. 112 N.J. Eq. 234, 163 A. 907; for a detailed discussion of cases of nationwide scope see R. F. Chase, *Domestic Recognition of Divorce Decree Obtained in Foreign Country and Attacked for Lack of Domicil or Jurisdiction of Parties*, 13 A.L.R. 3d 1419 (1967).
118. CLARK 295.
119. E. RIEZLER, VENIRE CONTRA FACTUM PROPRIUM (1912); B. Staehelin, *Estoppel und Vertrauensprinzip*, in FESTSCHRIFT FÜR SIMONIUS 381 (1953).

Popularly speaking, estoppel means that you may not blow both hot and cold. No one who has obtained a divorce on his own motion, or has acted in a way that presupposes the validity of a divorce obtained by someone else, will be allowed to take advantage of the possible invalidity of the divorce. If Anne has procured a divorce from Henry, or has cooperated with him in bringing it about, she will not be allowed later on to turn around and, alleging that the divorce is invalid, claim from him separate maintenance or, after his death, a share in his estate. If Henry has procured the divorce and thereupon marries Betty, he will not be allowed later on to deny the validity of the new marriage if it turns out to be disappointing. If Betty sues him for maintenance or for divorce and alimony, he may not plead that the divorce from Anne was invalid. If at the time of her marriage to Henry, Betty knew of his divorce from Anne, she too will not be allowed to plead invalidity in a divorce suit brought against her by Henry, nor may she claim a legacy left to her by an uncle on the condition that she be unmarried.

The estoppel device is flexible. It is not uniformly applied in all states. It cannot well be used to cut off claims of third parties who are not in privity with a person who has either himself obtained the invalid divorce or has put it to his advantage. The widest use has been made in the state of New York, where it was sanctioned by the highest court, the Court of Appeals.[120] Of course, that decision is a precedent only in cases with the same factual setup, but estoppel has been used by the lower courts so widely that it is fully justified to speak of the "myth of the invalid divorce." [121] Through the combination of recognizing as valid bilateral divorces obtained in Chihuahua or anywhere else and by means of estoppel rendering harmless the invalidity of foreign divorces obtained under circumstances that would still let them appear "invalid," a situation was created in New York which, together with the judicial toleration of hotel evidence and the liberal practice of annulment,[122] practically emasculated that state's strict divorce law of the books. The law received its death blow in 1965, when the Court of Appeals sanctioned the lower courts' constant practice of treating as valid not only — as required under the command of the Supreme Court of the United States — bilateral divorces obtained in Nevada,

---

120. Krause v. Krause, 282 N.Y. 355, 26 N.E.2d 290 (1940).
121. F. V. Harper, *The Myth of the Void Divorce*, 2 LAW & CONTEMP. PROB. 335 (1935); A. C. Jacobs, *Attack on Decrees of Divorce*, 34 MICH. L. REV. 749 (1936), reprinted in ASS'N OF AMERICAN LAW SCHOOLS, SELECTED ESSAYS ON FAMILY LAW 987 (1950).
122. *Infra* p. 96.

Idaho, Florida, or elsewhere in the United States but also the bilateral divorces obtained in Ciudad Juárez. New York's highest court openly confessed that the state's divorce law of the books had become so ineffective that it would no longer even be regarded as the expression of the state's public policy. That policy had come to be determined by the United States Supreme Court's command to give full faith and credit to bilateral Reno or Florida divorces. What difference should it make whether the party acting as plaintiff had spent six weeks or just one day in the divorce mill place? As long as he had troubled to go there at all and the other party had in some way participated in the proceedings, the New York couple's marriage bond would be treated as cut.[123] Consent divorce was recognized by the law in action. The law of the books was buried for all those who were willing to go on a one-day round-trip flight to El Paso–Ciudad Juárez.

IV. ANNULMENT

Judicial blindness to collusion and judicial countenance of law evasion through migratory divorce have been the devices for transforming the strict divorce law of the books into the indulgent law in action. In addition, the courts, especially those of New York and California, have resorted to a third device, that of easy annulment.

In New York, before its law was amended in 1966, annulment was resorted to as a means of evading the strictness of the divorce law, under which adultery was the sole ground and which prohibited remarriage by the guilty party.[124] In California annulment afforded short-

---

123. Rosenstiel v. Rosenstiel; Wood v. Wood, 16 N.Y.2d 64, 209 N.E.2d 709 (1965).

"Bergan, J.: The duration of domicile in sister States providing by statute for a minimal time to acquire domicile as necessary to matrimonial action jurisdiction is in actual practice complied with by a mere formal gesture having no more actual relation to the situs of the marriage or to true domicile than the formality of signing the Juárez city register. The difference in time is not truly significant of a difference in intent or purpose or in effect.

"The State or country of true domicile has the closest real public interest in a marriage, but, where a New York spouse goes elsewhere to establish a synthetic domicile to meet technical acceptance of a matrimonial suit, our public interest is not affected differently by a formality of one day than by a formality of six weeks.

"Nevada gets no closer to the real public concern with the marriage than Chihuahua. . . .

"A balanced public policy now requires that recognizing of the bilateral Mexican divorce be given rather than withheld and such a recognition as a matter of comity offends no public policy of this State."

On the case, the practice preceding it, and its consequences, see H. H. Foster, Jr., *Recognition of Migratory Divorces: Rosenstiel v. Section 250*, 43 Nw. U. L. REV. 429 (1968).

124. For the evasion of the prohibition of remarriage of the guilty party through the lifetime of the former spouse, the courts of New York opened another easy way by

road termination of marriage to get around a law which stretched the length of divorce proceedings by interposing an interlocutory decree, after a delay which until 1970 was at least one year, before the final termination of the marriage.[125]

Like other features of the American law of marriage, annulment was taken over from English ecclesiastical law, which, in turn, continued the canon law of the Catholic church. In canon law the elaboration of rules on the validity of marriages had become necessary as a consequence of the principle of indissolubility. Even though the conjugal community of life might have ceased to function, the legal bond of matrimony would continue to exist and thus prevent remarriage of either spouse as long as the other were alive. But the *impedimentum vinculi* presupposed that a *vinculum*, a marriage bond, had been effectively created. The creation of the bond required that the parties had actually intended to create it and that its emergence was not inhibited by some mandatory rule of divine or human canon law. Among these rules those defining the prohibited degrees of consanguinity, affinity, and spiritual relationship were given a wide meaning, so wide that they could allow a declaration of nullity in a good many cases of marriages that turned out unhappy.[126] In the English Reformation this escape hatch was so drastically narrowed that it lost its significance as a substitute for divorce. The rules on reality and freedom of marital consent, which became available in later Roman Catholic canon law,[127] also remained strict in the practice of the courts of the Church of England as well as in the American courts, by which they were taken over. The two principal grounds which were recognized as possibly vitiating the free consent indispensable for the creation of the marriage bond were coercion and error, especially error induced by fraud. In

---

holding that the statutory provision of Domestic Relations Law, § 8, meant solely to prohibit the celebration of a remarriage within the state of New York. Fisher v. Fisher, 250 N.Y. 313, 165 N.E. 460, 61 A.L.R. 1523 (1929) and numerous decisions of lower courts. After the expiration of three years, permission to remarry in New York could be granted by the New York court. The courts of other states having similar statutes tend to hold invalid the marriage concluded by a resident when the celebration at an out-of-state location was chosen for the very purpose of evading the prohibitory law. See CLARK 405.

125. Calif. Civil Code, § 132.

126. See *supra* p. 21.

127. On the history: J. FREISEN, GESCHICHTE DES KANONISCHEN EHERECHTS BIS ZUM VERFALL DER GLOSSATORENLITERATUR 227 (1887, repr. 1963); on modern canon law: CODEX JURIS CANONICI, canons 1081–93; T. L. BOUSCAREN, A. C. ELLIS & F. N. KORTH, CANON LAW 565 (4th ed. 1963); S. WOYWOD & C. SMITH, PRACTICAL COMMENTARY ON THE CODE OF CANON LAW 749 (1952); bibliography at U. MOSIEK, KIRCHLICHES EHERECHT 175, 180, 186, 194, 202, 208 (1968).

dealing with attacks upon the validity of a marriage based on one of these grounds, the courts in both England and the United States were guided by the tendency not to allow annulment to become a substitute for divorce. The principle of indissolubility of marriage was not to be subverted by indirection.

Attacks based on the ground of coercion seem never to have been frequent, even though the law did not constitute a major obstacle. Bishop,[128] whose work is the first American treatise on the subject, states that the legal principles which govern the question of duress as applied to marriage do not appear to differ essentially from those which govern its application to other contracts. He disagrees with Ayliff,[129] who in 1726 said that in order to avoid a marriage contracted through fear, it must be such fear as may happen to a man or a woman of good courage and resolution, and such as imparts danger, either of death or of bodily harm. The few reported cases seem to indicate that if a woman devoid of courage and resolution be in such a state of mental terror as not to know what she is about to do, the marriage is subject to being declared invalid.[130] The cases generally present a combination of fraud and duress, such as appeared in *Harford* v. *Morris*.[131] One of the guardians of a young school girl, having great influence and authority over her, took her away to the Continent, there hurried her from place to place, and married her off against her will.[132] The decision in *Scott* v. *Sebright*, the leading modern English case[133] on the subject, also applies the general contractual standard. Through financial machinations of Sebright, Miss Scott's health had been so seriously affected that she was reduced to a state of bodily and mental prostration. She was thus incapable of resisting threats of false accusation of unchastity and of being driven into bankruptcy unless she married Sebright. The unconsummated marriage was declared invalid.

In cases of consent effected by error, the English ecclesiastical courts took the same position as that taken by canon law. The only errors said to vitiate consent are those of error as to the identity of the partner and so-called error of condition.[134] Declarations of nullity were

---

128. J. P. Bishop, Commentaries on the Law of Marriage and Divorce §§ 119–23 (1852).
129. Parergon Iuris Canonici Anglicani 362.
130. See Fulwood's Case, Cro.Car. 482, 488, 493 (1638).
131. 2 Hagg. Cons. Rep. 423, 161 Eng.Rep. 792 (1776).
132. See also Wakefield v. Turner; Turner's Nullity of Marriage Bill, 17 Hans. Parl. Deb. N.S. 1133. Miss Turner's friends resorted to a bill in Parliament, because her testimony would have been inadmissible in the ecclesiastical tribunal.
133. (1886) 12 P.D. 21.
134. Error of condition means error as to the formalized social status of the partner,

granted in a few cases in which girls of just about twelve years of age had by a combination of pressure and deception been so terrorized that they had no clear idea of what they were doing when in confusion they uttered words of consent to marry fortune-hunting adventurers.[135] But generally the law was said to be determined by the special nature of the marriage contract, in which the parties take each other "for better, for worse, for richer, for poorer, in sickness and in health, to love and to cherish" until death. No mistake resulting from lies or fraudulent practices in respect to the character, the fortune, the health, or the social position of the partner would be allowed to affect the validity of the marriage.[136] Marriage was, indeed, to be indissoluble. The principle was not to be weakened by allowing dissolution under the name of annulment. In England this position of utmost strictness was expressed by the president of the Probate, Divorce and Admiralty Division as late as 1897 [137] and it took forty years before the harsh rule was mitigated enough even to admit annulment where the fact that the wife at the time of the marriage had been pregnant by another man had been concealed from her partner in marriage.[138] In making such slight concession, England reluctantly began to follow the course American courts had entered earlier, although cautiously.

Contracts of a business nature are generally annulled by courts of Equity when the petitioner has proved that the other party intentionally misled him as to some facts and that he would not have made the contract if he had known the true state of facts. For an annulment of such a contract it suffices that there has been a fraud, and that the fraud was "material." [139] In the United States, where ecclesiastical tribunals were never established as courts of the state, and where marital causes have been handled by Equity courts, the ideas by which these courts were guided in nonmarriage cases easily came to influence the handling of marriage cases. But, the ideal of indissoluble marriage was still rooted too deeply to allow the adoption of a rule that might open

---

such as the erroneous belief that the partner is the successor to the throne of a monarchy (H. JONE, 2 COMMENTARIUM IN CODICEM IURIS CANONICI 306 [1954]), or that he is a free person rather than a serf, or that he is the person entitled to succeed to undivided farm property under such laws as the Hereditary Farm Law, of 29 September 1933, of National Socialist Germany (A. RETZBACH, DAS RECHT DER KATHOLISCHEN KIRCHE 232 3d ed. [1963]).

135. See the cases cited by Bishop, *supra* note 128, at §§ 103 ff.

136. In France, the situation was neatly expressed by the adage reported by A. LOISEL, INSTITUTES (1758 ed.): "En mariage il trompe qui peut."

137. Moss v. Moss, [1897] P. 263.

138. Matrimonial Causes Act, 1937, § 7. The Matrimonial Causes Act, 1950, § 8, added affliction with venereal disease unknown to the other party.

139. AMERICAN LAW INSTITUTE, RESTATEMENT OF THE LAW OF CONTRACTS §§ 470, 474.

the way to weaken a marriage even in states in which statutes expressly provided that a marriage might be annulled on the ground of fraud. The compromise formula that suggested itself was to require for an annulment not only that the fraud be "material" but that it also relate to a fact "essential to the nature of marriage." That formula became current in the United States when it had been adopted in 1862 by so influential a court as the Supreme Judicial Court of Massachusetts speaking through Chief Justice Bigelow.[140] Five months after her marriage to Reynolds, a young man of seventeen, the bride, a woman of thirty, gave birth to a child. Prior to the marriage the parties had known each other for only six weeks. In his suit for sentence of nullity Reynolds alleged and proved to the satisfaction of the court that he was induced to marry the woman by her fraudulent representation that she was chaste and virtuous. What the court held to be essential for the nature of marriage was the woman's ability at the time of the marriage to conceive by her groom and to bear his child. Being at the time pregnant by another man, the bride lacked that ability. How this reasoning might be squared with the firmly established rule that impotence does not constitute a ground of nullity unless it is permanent and incurable, remained unexplained. The real motive of the court is more likely to have been the desire to spare the husband the dilemma in which he would find himself if annulment were denied. As the court expressly stated, he would have either to repudiate the stranger's child and thus pronounce to the world the shame of his wife or to accept the bastard child as his.

The formula of fraud concerning a fact essential to the nature of marriage has the advantage of vagueness. The courts have been able to employ it without the necessity of clearly defining what facts are essential. The tendency has been to be reluctant and to limit essentiality to those facts which relate to the sex aspects of marriage, such as affliction with venereal disease, false representation by the woman that she is pregnant by her partner, concealed intent not to consummate the marriage or not to have intercourse likely to produce progeny, also concealed intent not to go through with a promise to follow the secular conclusion of the marriage with a religious ceremony considered by the other party essential to relieve intercourse from the stigma of sin. Annulments have been rarely granted for fraudulent misrepresentations of character, past life, or social standing and hardly ever for misrepresentation on matters of property or income.[141]

---

140. Reynolds v. Reynolds, 3 Allen (85 Mass.) 605.
141. On the present American law and the tendencies of the judicial decisions, see

Why, indeed, should a court open the door of annulment with its retroactivity and possible inequities in matters of property settlement, support, and legitimacy of children, if divorce is available? (For the ratio of divorces to annulments in the country as a whole, see table 3.) But in New York until 1966 divorce was not available except in the case of proved or staged adultery. Naturally, New York lawyers looked to annulment, especially annulment on the ground of fraud, and the courts were willing to accommodate them (see table 4).

TABLE 3
RATIO OF DIVORCES TO ANNULMENTS IN THE UNITED STATES

Year	Divorces	Annulments	Ratio
1922	148,815	2,795	49:1
1930	191,591	4,228	45:1
1940	256,692	7,440	34:1
1950	371,309	13,200	27:1
1962	413,000	12,692	31:1
1963	428,000	12,701	31:1

Sources: H. JACOBSON, AMERICAN MARRIAGE AND DIVORCE 90, 113, (1959); for 1962, NAT'L CENTER FOR HEALTH STATISTICS, DIVORCE STATISTICS ANALYSIS 1962, at 5.

TABLE 4
MARRIAGE TERMINATION IN NEW YORK STATE
("Provisional" Figures)

Year	Absolute Divorce	Dissolution*	Annulment	Separation
1951	6,350	400	4,500	950
1952	6,150	400	4,500	950
1953	5,800	400	4,300	900
1954	5,400	400	3,950	900
1955	4,800	350	3,750	900
1956	4,750	300	3,600	850

Source: JACOBSON, *supra* table 3, at 113.
* Enoch Arden decrees.

In 1962 about two-thirds of all American annulment decrees (8,315) were granted in the states of New York and California. There they constituted respectively 35.6 and 11.1 percent of the state total of decrees terminating marriage. In the nation as a whole, annulments con-

---

CLARK 100; R. Kingsley, *Fraud as a Ground for Annulment of Marriage*, 18 S. CALIF. L. REV. 213 (1945).

stituted 3.1 percent of the total.[142] In 1963, the number of annulments granted and their percentage of the total number of decrees were in New York, 2,284 or 36.2 percent; in California, 6,134 or 10.9 percent.[143]

It is impossible to say at exactly what date the lower courts of New York began to shift from the traditional essentiality test to the new test of materiality. The official sanction of the Court of Appeals was pronounced first in 1903 in *Di Lorenzo* v. *Di Lorenzo*[144] and repeated in 1933 in *Shonfeld* v. *Shonfeld*.[145] Di Lorenzo, a young man, had broken up an affair he had had with a middle-aged woman. He was induced to return to New York when she wrote to him that she was pregnant, and to marry her when she presented the baby to him. Some considerable time later Di Lorenzo discovered that the child was not only not his but not even hers. The action for annulment was vigorously contested. The case was tried to a jury. The trial court's decision for the plaintiff was reversed by the Appellate Division, but upheld by the Court of Appeals. Judge Gray declared that there was no reason why the contract of marriage should be excepted from the general rule that every misrepresentation of a "material fact, i.e., any fact made with the intention to induce another to enter into an agreement and without which he would not have done so, justifies the court in voiding the agreement."

Di Lorenzo was still concerned with a matter of progeny. In *Shonfeld* the misrepresentation referred to dollars and cents, a matter which so far had been treated as not relevant to marriage causes even in New York. For several years Shonfeld had been keeping company with a girl. But whenever the question of marriage was brought up, he declared that he had not yet so established himself in life that he could support a wife and family. In May 1930, when the subject again came up between them, she told him she had enough money to establish him in business. Shortly thereafter Shonfeld was offered a partnership in a jewelry store, provided he could contribute $7,000. The lady offered to make this sum available and participated in the negotiations with the prospective partner. But in the negotiations with Shonfeld as to what should come first, the money or the marriage, she won out. The marriage was celebrated, but there was no money. She had none. The marriage was not consummated. Shonfeld sued for an annulment, but, although the action was not contested, the annulment was denied by

142. NAT'L CENTER FOR HEALTH STATISTICS, DIVORCE STATISTICS ANALYSIS 1962, at 5.
143. *Id.* 1963, at 10.
144. 174 N.Y. 467, 67 N.E. 63, 63 L.R.A. 92, 95 Am.St.R. 609.
145. 260 N.Y. 477, 184 N.E. 60.

both the trial court and the Appellate Division. It was ultimately granted by the Court of Appeals, which held that any fraud that had actually induced a party to enter upon a marriage sufficed to entitle that party to a decree of annulment. "The fraud need not," it was stated, "necessarily concern what is commonly called the essentials of the marriage relation — the rights and duties connected with cohabitation and consortium attached by law to the marital status."

In relation to the facts of the case, Judge Crouch said:

> The obligation of a husband to support his wife is no less lightly to be entered than the other obligations of the marital relation. The ability to support is correspondingly important. While the plaintiff's attitude may have been something less than heroic, realization of the responsibilities of marriage need not be condemned as sordidly mercenary. . . . No public policy demands that prudent consideration of ability to fulfill the duty of support shall not have a legitimate place in the determination by a party of whether or not to marry.

In *Di Lorenzo*, the Court of Appeals had been unanimous. In *Shonfeld*, three judges — Lehman, O'Brian, and Crane, dissented. The lengthy dissenting opinion, written by Judge Crane, opened with these lapidary sentences:

> The marriage in thise case was a mere matter of bargain and sale. The woman bought the man for $6,000, and because she failed to have the money, the man seeks to have the marriage annulled. The question really is whether the marriage ceremony in this state is of any binding force or whether it is an empty ceremony.

The clash between the two competing philosophies of life is neatly illustrated by the two opinions delivered in the case.

Judge Crane's dissent presaged a change of attitude in New York's highest court. This was to find expression in the case of *Woronzoff-Daschkoff* v. *Woronzoff-Daschkoff*.[146] On 24 March 1947, an American lady, thirty-two years old, born in India and possessed of great wealth, was married to Woronzoff-Daschkoff, an impoverished Russian nobleman émigré, forty-five years of age. A European honeymoon, paid for by the lady, continued until August, when the lady went to India on matters of business. The husband sailed to New York to await her return. When she came back in November, she lived with him in her home for about a month, when a quarrel took place in which he upbraided her "for her meanness in money matters," and told her that he had not married her for love but solely for her money. She threw him out of the house and brought action for annulment. She alleged that he had induced her to marry him by the fraudulent asser-

---

146. 303 N.Y. 506, 104 N.E. 2d 877 (1952).

tions that he loved her, that he had always earned his own living, and that he had never taken money from any woman. The defendant contested the action, but the annulment was granted by the trial court, which found that defendant had indeed married the plaintiff solely for money, that he had rarely, if ever, worked for a living, and that he had received from his first wife a large amount of money as the price for a divorce. The decision was affirmed by the Appellate Division, but reversed by a unanimous Court of Appeals. The opinion, written by Judge Desmond, reads as if the court wished to return to that test of "essentiality for the marriage relation" which it had so explicitly repudiated in *Di Lorenzo* and *Shonfeld*. Said Judge Desmond:

> Defendant was no model of chivalry or propriety. . . . [The] proof, believed by the trier of the fact, was enough, we will assume, to expose him as a fortune hunter, a sluggard, a hypochondriac, and a man who took his promises lightly. But this is a suit to annul a marriage for fraud and while we have, for better or worse retreated (Di Lorenzo v. Di Lorenzo, 174 N.Y. 467; Shonfeld v. Shonfeld, 260 N.Y. 477, 481) from the old idea that marriages can be voided only for frauds going to the essentials of marriage, that is, consortium and cohabitation, it is, nonetheless, still the law in New York that annulments are granted, not for any and every kind of fraud . . . but for fraud as to matters "vital" to the marriage relationship only. . . . Premarital falsehoods as to love and affection are not enough nor disclosure that one partner "married for money." . . . Lack of robust health is not enough. . . . Of course, a husband is under a legal duty to support even a well-to-do wife . . . and, in ordinary cases the man's intent premaritally formed, not to support his wife, might perhaps be enough to nullify a marriage. But this husband never promised his wife to support her, and, obviously, was never expected to.

After that decision, the number of New York annulments went down.[147] In 1961 the number was 2,310; in 1962, 2,331. By 1963 it was down to 2,284.[148]

It is difficult to say to what extent, if any, this considerable drop was due to a stiffening of the attitude of the New York courts. In uncontested cases which, as in divorce, contribute the overwhelming majority of annulments, it should not have been difficult for the lawyer so to arrange the allegations and the evidence that a decree of annulment could be justified under the *Woronzoff-Daschkoff* rule or under any other. Strangely, during the period of declining annulments, the number of New York adultery divorces dropped from 5,253 in 1958, to 4,084 in 1961.[149] The number of Nevada, Florida, and Mexican divorces

---

147. See table 4, above.
148. NAT'L CENTER FOR HEALTH STATISTICS, DIVORCE STATISTICS ANALYSIS 1963, at 10.
149. Compiled from 3 VITAL STATISTICS OF THE UNITED STATES 1961 § 3, at 3–17–18 (1965).

obtained by New Yorkers since 1952 is not known. But in 1965, Judge Bergan, in the opinion rendered in *Rosenstiel* v. *Rosenstiel*, mentioned that "it has been estimated that many thousands of persons have been affected in their family and property status by" decisions of lower New York courts recognizing Mexican divorces.[150] In the *Woronzoff* case the Court of Appeals did not overrule the proposition it had expressed two years earlier in *de Baillet-Latour* v. *de Baillet-Latour*:[151]

[The Court of Appeals] is without any power to review the weight of the evidence or to pass on the truthfulness of the witnesses. . . . If the evidence makes out a prima facie case for annulment under New York law, we must affirm.[152]

The Court of Appeals will thus do no more than say whether or not a marriage is voidable if the plaintiff was induced to enter upon it by the kind of fraud of which the plaintiff's attorney has presented the constituent facts and which the trial court has accepted as having been proved. In an uncontested case the trial court, if it is inclined to do so, will grant the annulment even in a fact situation that would not satisfy the requirements of the Court of Appeals. The decisive power rests with the trial court judges. Their attitudes have differed widely. Some have been ready to grant an annulment in a case where

150. 16 N.Y.2d 64, 71, 209 N.E. 2d 709, 711.
151. 301 N.Y. 428, 94 N.E. 2d 715 (1950).
152. The facts are stated in detail in the dissenting opinion of Justice Froessel, in which Justices Conway and Dye concurred. A wealthy New York lady, when she was fifty-nine years of age, took as her third husband a gentleman, six years younger, member of the New York bar, born in the Netherlands and pretending to be a member of a prominent European family with a château in France. The parties lived together for several months in a bedroom with twin beds. When the lady gained the impression that the baron had married her for her money, she separated from him and brought an action for annulment alleging and testifying that the defendant by his premarital conduct had by implication promised that he would have marital intercourse with her, that the marriage had not been consummated during all the time the parties had shared the same bedroom, and that plaintiff at the time of the marriage had intended not to have intercourse with her. The plaintiff's son, an associate of his mother's attorney, testified in corroboration, stating that the defendant had told him that the marriage had not been consummated. All this testimony was denied by the defendant, according to whose testimony he had had regular marital relations with the plaintiff. The trial court observed that the two parties' testimony was equally "forthright" and that it was induced to give greater credence to that of the wife because of the corroborating testimony of a physician who had seen the plaintiff two years after she had separated from the defendant and who had on that occasion observed four scars on the lady's body. This testimony was regarded as decisive over the defendant's statement that he had never seen any scars on the lady's body. "No court would hesitate for a moment," Judge Froessel said, "to grant a divorce on the ground of adultery to a spouse of either of these parties, if they were not husband and wife. But here they are, with every right to engage in marital relations and yet it is said they did not."

the fraud consisted in nothing more than untrue expressions of love;[153] others have been hard-boiled traditionalists anxious to prevent New York's unique divorce law from being subverted.[154] It would be interesting to know to what extent the divorce specialists elaborated that particular science which flourished in Germany under the name of divorce geography and under which cases tend to accumulate in the courts known to be soft and to stay away from those known to be tough.

V. "CRUELTY"

Collusion by definition requires cooperation. A collusive divorce is a consent divorce dressed up as a divorce for cause. Migratory divorce does not necessarily require consent, but cooperation of the parties is advisable to forestall later attacks. Annulment may be obtained *ex parte* or against the other party's active opposition; but proceedings in American courts, especially in New York and California, are eased and shortened when the parties are in agreement. By closing their eyes and neglecting procedural safeguards, the courts have created an American divorce law in action that differs widely from the divorce law of the books.

But the judicial readiness of "no see, no hear, no speak" has not been the only way. In several states, easy divorce even in contested cases has been brought about by benign interpretation of "cruelty."

---

153. So, for instance, in the case of Ryan v. Wurmbrand-Stuppach Ryan, 156 Misc. 251, 281 N.Y.S. 709 (1935). In romantic Vienna young Baroness von Wurmbrand-Stuppach and young Baron Wolff were ardently in love. Unfortunately, both families were impoverished. The baroness's mother knew a ready remedy. Ravishingly beautiful Marianne was sent to New York; there she was to induce some American millionaire to fall in love with her and to marry her. In a quick divorce the fortune should then be obtained from him which would restore the wealth of the two Old World families. The plan seemed to work. Marianne had barely arrived in New York when John Ryan, son of a wealthy building contractor, impressed by her beauty and her expressions of ardent love, proposed to her. The marriage was a social event, but the denouement followed quickly. On the wedding night, before the marriage could be consummated, Marianne broke down and confessed the plot. The uncontested annulment was readily obtained by John on the ground that Marianne had deceived him about her feelings.

154. Compare the following utterances of Judge Walsh, quoted in Comment, *Annulments for Fraud — New York's Answer to Reno?* 48 COLUM.L.REV. 900, 914: "Marriage is a sacred institution . . . vital to the state . . ."; plaintiff's unfortunate plight "the result of her own folly . . . truly an example of the adage, 'Mary in haste, repent at leisure'" (Smith v. Smith, 44 N.Y.S.2d 826, 827 [S. Ct. 1943]).

"Some shallow and thoughtless attorneys and some interested parties argue 'if parties cannot live together, let them have a divorce or annulment.' That is not the law of his State nor of civilized people. Experience has shown that those who do not make a success of the first marriage rarely do any better in the second or third. That alone is good reason why the parties and the States should try to preserve the first marriage" (Hafner v. Hafner, 66 N.Y.S.2d 442, 444 [S.Ct. 1946]).

Ecclesiastical practice has long recognized that a wife need not live with a husband whose abusive conduct threatens to result in her death or in serious impairment of her health, and has treated cruelty of such gravity as a ground for separation from bed and board. Under the authority of the Reformers, Protestant states came to treat such extreme cruelty as a ground of divorce *quoad vinculum*. Women were not only to be protected against dangerous husbands but allowed to find a new home and family rather than being condemned to remain in the sad position of a person without a place in society.[155] American statutes early recognized cruelty as a ground for judicial separation and for divorce.[156] But the term was meant to be understood in that tradition sense in which it was applied by the English ecclesiastical courts in suits for separation from bed and board, a sense which found its classical expression in the opinion delivered by Sir William Scott, later Lord Stowell, in *Evans* v. *Evans*.[157] In that sense cruelty is "conduct in one of the married parties, which furnishes reasonable apprehension that the continuance of the cohabitation would be attended with bodily harm to the other."[158]

> This must be understood, [the judge declared] that it is the duty of the courts, and consequently the inclination of courts, to keep the rule extremely strict. The causes must be grave and weighty, and such as show an absolute impossibility that the duties of the married life can be discharged. In a state of personal danger no duties can be discharged. . . . What merely wounds the mental feelings is in few cases to be admitted, where not accompanied with bodily injury, either actual or menaced. Mere austerity of temper, petulance of manners, rudeness of language, a want of civil attention, even occasional sallies of passion, if they do not threaten bodily harm, do not amount to legal cruelty. They are high moral offences in the marriage state undoubtedly, not innocent surely in any state of life, but still they are not that cruelty against which the law can relieve. Under such misconduct of either of the parties, for it may exist on one side as well as on the other, the suffering party must bear in some degree the consequences of an injudicious connection, must subdue by decent resistance or by prudent conciliation, and if this cannot be done, both must suffer in silence.[159]

These words aptly expressed the spirit of the times as it reigned not only in England. In 1852 as liberal an author as Joel P. Bishop called Lord Stowell's opinion "one of the master-productions of that luminous intellect" and observed that "it has been ever since regarded as

155. See *supra* chap. 2.
156. See BISHOP, *supra* note 128, at §§ 454 ff.
157. 1 Hagg. Cons. Rep. 35; 161 Eng. Rep. 460 (1790).
158. Bishop § 454.
159. 1 Hagg. Cons. Rep. 35, 37; 161 Eng. Rep. 466, 467.

the leading authority on this subject." His words were said to have "gained almost the weight of the statute law."[160] The way in which the American statutes were, and in large measure still are, phrased indicates that American legislatures agreed with the judge of the English ecclesiastical court.

In order to constitute a ground of divorce or even of separation, cruelty has to be "intolerable,"[161] or "extreme and repeated,"[162] or it must be "intolerable severity,"[163] or "actual violence attended with danger to life or health, or reasonable apprehension of such violence,"[164] or such "inhuman treatment as to endanger life."[165] All these and similar formulas could be found in American statutes as of 1968.[166] It is a far cry from these words to the practice of numerous courts which regard general marital unkindness as cruelty constituting a ground for divorce.

The transformation of the concept of cruelty did not come about all at once. It proceeded along two avenues. One way of denaturing the original meaning of the statutory provisions is illustrated by the practice of Illinois. Until mental cruelty was expressly added to the statute by an amendment of 1967,[167] not only the state supreme court but the trial courts too insisted upon requiring that the "extreme and repeated cruelty" consisted of at least two acts of physical violence. In order to be extreme the acts also had to result in serious discomfort to the plaintiff. So the plaintiff would be asked by her attorney: "When your husband slapped you in the face, did it cause you great pain and suffering?" "Yes." Or the plaintiff's corroborating witness, frequently her mother or her sister, could be asked: "Did you see any physical marks in the plaintiff's face?" "Yes."[168] Rarely would any effort be made to ascertain whether the defendant had actually performed the ritual of at least two slaps.

A more effective way to dispense with perjury is opened where, under the wording of the statute or by judicial interpretation, mental cruelty suffices to constitute a ground for divorce. The first step was the observation that health can be impaired, even seriously, by con-

160. BISHOP § 454 n.
161. Conn. G.St.S. § 46–13.
162. Ill. Stat. ch. 40, § 1.
163. 15 Vt. Stat. A, § 551.
164. Ala. Code 1959, titl. 34, § 29.
165. Iowa Code Ann. §§ 5988, 5989.
166. See CLARK 341–42.
167. Laws 1967, at 3087, § 1.
168. VIRTUE, *supra* note 31, at 90.

duct having no physical impact. But, why require proof, true or ritualistic, of an impairment of physical health? Why not be satisfied with an impairment of mental well-being caused by truly abusive conduct? Or simply asking for "proof" of such physical difficulties as loss of sleep, loss of weight, nervousness, and other such symptoms as are generally produced by marital tension or general dissatisfaction with life. In that way cruelty has become a catch-all term rendering it possible to obtain a divorce for the asking even under the statutory formula of the Field Code, which requires cruelty to consist in "the infliction of grievous bodily injury, or grievous mental suffering." [169] The next stage is reached when the courts accept as sufficient the standardized allegation and "proof" of such acts as nagging, neglect of household duties, moodiness, or use of offensive language. Perhaps the eating of crackers in bed is not so generally accepted as it is made to appear by the standard phrase used in conversation by California lawyers. But the phrase correctly symbolizes the situation. The ultimate is reached under the law of Nevada, where it suffices for the plaintiff simply to allege that she has been treated cruelly by the defendant, and no spelling out of concrete facts is required unless the defendant asks for a bill of particulars which, of course, cannot occur in an uncontested case.[170]

Every now and then appellate courts have stuck to a more serious interpretation of cruelty. Every now and then even a trial judge or referee insists upon a more literal interpretation of the statutory words. Not in all states has cruelty been reduced to a meaningless catch-phrase. But in the United States the general trend is in this direction. Here, as in France,[171] Germany, Switzerland,[172] and other countries,[173] cruelty has become a convenient tool for emasculating a strict law of the books and for turning it into an easy divorce law in action.[174]

The cooperation of the courts has made it possible for the great

169. Wording of California Civil Code §§ 92, 94, before the amendment act of 1969.
170. *Supra* p. 76.
171. See *infra* chap. 8.
172. See J. STREBEL, DIVORZI 18 (1944); H. HINDERLING, DAS SCHWEIZERISCHE EHESCHEIDUNGSRECHT 15, 20 (3d ed. 1967).
173. See Report of the Law Commission, § 22, Putting Asunder, § 50 (see *infra* pp. 328, 349).
174. On the troublesome problems of professional ethics with which divorce lawyers are confronted, see H. S. Drinker, *Problems of Professional Ethics in Matrimonial Litigation*, 66 HARV. L. REV. 443; H. J. O'GORMAN, LAWYERS AND MATRIMONIAL CASES (1963); Note, *The Role of the Lawyer in Divorce*, 21 U. PITT. L. REV. 720 (1960); L. C. Di Stasi, Annotation, *Participation in Allegedly Collusive or Connived Divorce Proceedings as Subjecting Attorney to Disciplinary Action*, 13 A.L.R. 3d 1010 (1967).

bulk of divorces to be obtained upon the ground of mutual consent, which is frowned upon by the official law of every state of the Union. How has it been possible for this discrepancy to develop between the law of the books and the law in action? We shall postpone the attempt to find an answer until we have examined the divorce situation of a number of other parts of the world.

II

DIVORCE IN THE CULTURAL CONTEXT

5
A Non-Christian Country: Japan

In two parts of the world, widely distant from each other, there is little discrepancy in the matter of divorce between the law of the books and the law in action. Both Japan and the countries which are frequently, although not quite correctly, called Scandinavian have unitary laws of divorce. To be sure, in neither of these regions does the divorce law of the statutes completely reflect the law by which people actually live. But what divergencies exist are of minor importance. By and large the statute laws of Japan and of the Scandinavian countries are applied as they are written. They can be so applied because they recognize divorce by mutual agreement as the normal form of divorce. In the Scandinavian statutes this decisive fact is bashfully hidden behind a façade of divorce for marriage breakdown; in Japan it is openly expressed in the statute.

The present *Japanese* law of divorce is stated in section IV (arts. 763–71) of Book IV (Family Law) of the Civil Code, in the version of law no. 61 of 1947. Subsection I (arts. 763–69) deals with divorce by agreement, subsection II (arts. 770–71) with judicial divorce.

Divorce by agreement is the normal form. In each year from 1948 to 1959 over 90 percent of all Japanese divorces were obtained this way.[1] Divorce by agreement is the counterpart of marriage. A marriage becomes legally effective when the agreement of the parties is communicated to the registrar of civil status.[2] A divorce becomes effective in the same way, i.e., by communicating the agreement of the parties to the registrar. No court or judge or other public officer participates. The agreement does not require any formality. It may be made in writing or orally. The communication to the registrar may also be

---

1. Tatsuo Sameshima, *The Japanese Family Court*, 9 ANNALES DE LA FACULTÉ DE DROIT D'ISTANBUL (8e année, no. 13), 131, 146 (1960) (hereinafter cited as Sameshima); ICHIRO KATO, ZUSETSU KAZOKUKO [Graphic family law] 37 (1963) (hereinafter cited as KATO).
2. Civil Code, art. 739, para. 1.

made orally by both parties or by an instrument signed by them. In both cases two witnesses are required.[3] The communication will not be accepted by the registrar unless the parties have agreed upon which of them is to have the parental power over their minor children.[4] The agreement must also determine who is to take actual custody of the children and decide matters pertaining thereto. But the agreement need not precede the divorce and, if it has been made, it may be changed by the Family Court if such a change is necessary for the benefit of the children.[5]

Ordinarily, when parties agree to terminate their marriage, they also agree about child custody and *zaisen-bunyo*, i.e., the payment to be made by one party to the other, usually by the husband to the wife, and constituting a combination of property settlement and support for a usually short period of transition. If the parties have agreed that the marriage be terminated and who is to have parental power over the minor children, but have not reached agreement on all or some of the side issues, either party may apply to the Family Court to bring about a settlement.

Failure to reach an agreement upon one spouse's desire to obtain a divorce may be due either to the other party's opposition to being divorced or, more frequently, to the other party's refusal to agree to the divorce upon the terms proposed. In such situations the party anxious to have the marriage terminated must bring the matter before the Family Court, which through its conciliation committee will seek to effect either a reconciliation and continuation of the marriage or, more frequently, an agreement concerning terms on which the marriage may be ended. If no agreement is reached on the question of

3. Civil Code, arts. 764, 739, para. 2.
4. Civil Code, art. 765, para. 1; art. 819, para. 1.
5. Civil Code, art. 766. Japanese law distinguishes between parental power and custody. The former term is the more comprehensive. The terminology is taken from the laws of Germany. In general, the Japanese Civil Code of 1898 constitutes a simplified version of the draft of the German Civil Code. Book IV, Family Law, enacted by Law No. 9 of 1898, diverged considerably from the German model, because the Japanese government of the time was anxious to maintain the traditional structure of the Japanese family and, through it, of Japanese society. However, technical concepts for which traditional Japanese law had no counterpart were taken over from Germany. Simplifying the model of what is now § 1626 of the German Civil Code, art. 820 of the Japanese code provides that "the person who exercises parental power has the rights and incurs the duty of providing for the custody and education of his or her child." Without his permission the child may not carry on an occupation (art. 823). Finally, he manages the property of the child and represents the child in transactions concerning his property (art. 824). Custody seems to correspond to the German term "Care of the child's person" as distinguished from "care of the child's property" (see German Civil Code, § 1626).

whether or not the marriage is to be terminated, either party may file a suit in the District Court to have a divorce pronounced on one of the grounds enumerated in article 770 of the Civil Code, which is as follows:

> Husband or wife can bring an action for divorce only in the following cases:
> 1. if the other spouse has committed an act of unchastity;
> 2. if he or she has been deserted maliciously by the other spouse;
> 3. if it is unknown for three years or more whether the other spouse is alive or dead;
> 4. if the other spouse is attached [afflicted] with severe mental disease and recovery therefrom is hopeless;
> 5. if there exists any other grave reason for which it is difficult for him or for her to continue the marriage.
>
> Even in cases where any or all of the grounds mentioned in items numbered 1 to 4 inclusive of the preceding paragraph exist, the Court may dismiss the action for divorce, if it deems the continuance of the marriage proper in view of all the circumstances.[6]

As table 5 shows, in the overwhelming majority of cases, divorce is effected by extrajudicial agreement of the parties. Cases in which the courts must intervene are rare.

TABLE 5
DIVORCES BY TYPE
(Percent)

| Year | Agreement | Family Court | | District or Higher Court Judgment |
		Conciliation	Judgment	
1948	98.2	1.5	0.1	0.2
1949	96.9	2.7	...	0.4
1950	95.5	3.9	...	0.5
1951	94.3	4.9	...	0.8
1952	93.8	5.4	...	0.8
1953	93.7	5.7	...	0.8
1954	93.2	6.0	...	0.7
1955	92.8	6.4	...	0.8
1959	91.5	7.5	0.1	0.9

Source: Sameshima 131, 146; KATO 37.

The Family Court, which plays an active role in a small, but constantly increasing, fraction of divorce cases, is a modern institution. In both function and structure it differs from those courts which are

---

6. The translation of this article and of all other articles of the Civil Code quoted here is that of the Ministry of Justice, 1962. It is to be assumed that under charges 2, 3, and 4 prior proceedings in the Family Court are unnecessary.

called "family" courts in the United States. It combines within it the functions of a juvenile court, probate court, trial court in matters of family support, and conciliation agency in all kinds of family disputes. Cases of delinquency of juveniles and of crimes committed against juveniles are handled in the court's Juvenile Adjudgment Division, all other matters in the Domestic Relations Division.[7] The jurisdiction of the Domestic Relations Division covers matters of guardianship, adoption, probate, administration of estates, family support, disputes between husbands and wives, parental discipline over children, and conciliation in matters of divorce and in any case concerning personal affairs or relating to the family.[8]

The Family Courts are courts of first instance, of equal rank with the District Courts, which have jurisdiction in all civil and criminal matters that do not belong to the Family Courts. The importance and dignity of the Family Courts has been emphasized by the frequency by which Family Court judges have been promoted to positions of high rank. Matters of juvenile delinquency and of family affairs are combined in one court because they are considered to be related to each other. The judge dealing with a case of juvenile delinquency is believed to be able to spot general family troubles, and vice versa. Timely intervention is thus regarded as possible. Experience, I have been told, does not fully bear out this expectation. In the major Family Courts, juvenile cases and family matters are handled by different judges, frequently in different parts of the Family Court building. Cooperation between the two sections of the court does not always seem to be close.

The combination of the two fields of jurisdiction also seems to be due to the similarities of procedure. It is informal, paternalistic, and inexpensive. Juvenile cases are handled according to ideas similar to those held by the fathers of the American juvenile court movement. A procedure corresponding to the due process requirements laid down

---

7. Law for the Determination of Family Affairs (Family Court Law), Law No. 152, of 6 December 1947, as amended by Law No. 260, of 21 December 1948; Law No. 123, of 1 May 1950, Law No. 222, of 9 June 1951, and Law No. 91, of 2 May 1956. A concise description, in English, of the Family Courts, their organization and their function, is GUIDE TO THE FAMILY COURT OF JAPAN, published in 1959 by the General Secretariat of the Supreme Court of Japan. Details of procedure are spelled out in Supreme Court Rule No. 15, of 29 December 1947, as amended by Rule No. 38, of 28 December 1948, Rule No. 12, of 11 July 1949, Rule No. 14, of 8 May 1950, Rule No. 4, of 31 March 1951, Rule No. 10, of 15 September 1951, Rule No. 5, of 29 May 1954, and Rule No. 8, of 2 May 1956.

8. Family Court Law, arts. 9, 17.

by the Supreme Court of the United States in *In re* Gault,[9] would be regarded in Japan as a perversion of the juvenile court idea.

On the family affairs side many issues are handled by way of adjudication, although of a particularly informal one. But personal disputes between spouses, particularly disputes concerning divorce and its consequences, are handled by way of conciliation rather than adjudication. In the conciliation proceedings, the judge is assisted by probation officers and by councillors and conciliation commissioners. In appropriate cases the judge can also draw upon a physician or a nurse, both of whom are members of the staff of the court. The probation officers are university graduates in sociology, psychology, or education who have passed the examination held by the Supreme Court and who have received specialized training in the Training and Research Institute of the Supreme Court.[10]

In general, three to four probation officers are attached to each Family Court judge. The councillors and conciliation commissioners are members of the public, usually persons of experience who enjoy social respect. Physicians and lawyers are frequently among them. They serve without pay. In 1953, there were 6,068 councillors (5,181 men and 887 women) and 17,823 conciliation commissioners (14,523 men and 3,300 women).[11]

In matters of divorce which, it may be repeated, do not come up before the Family Court unless the parties fail to agree either on the termination of their marriage or on the terms of the divorce, the conciliation proceedings are conducted by a conciliation committee, which is normally composed of one judge and two conciliation commissioners, one of whom is usually a woman. The session may have been prepared by an investigation conducted on the judge's order by a probation officer or a medical member of the staff. Investigations may also be carried on in the course of the conciliation proceedings, which may extend over a number of sessions. These sessions are held in a pleasant room, frequently in a modern building specially designed as a Family Court. In good Japanese fashion, the friendliness of the atmosphere is enhanced by a flower arrangement upon the table around which the participants are seated.

The effort to induce the parties to reach an intelligent and just set-

9. 387 U.S. 1, 78 S.Ct. 1428, 18 L.Ed.2d 527 (1967).
10. See JUNSHIRO UDAGAWA, OUTLINE OF THE RESEARCH AND TRAINING INSTITUTE FOR FAMILY COURT PROBATION OFFICERS IN JAPAN (1961).
11. Sameshima 132.

tlement of their dispute is taken seriously. The committee seeks to help them understand their difficulties, see the facts as they are, and deal with each other in a mature manner. (In those cases which I had the opportunity to observe in 1962, investigation of the problems was conducted; in-laws, paramours, or other third parties were called in; and time-consuming talks were patiently being carried on with both parties, either together or separately.) The conciliation committee tries to induce the parties to reach an agreement, but the agreement — and this is important — need not necessarily be to continue the marriage. It may just as well be an agreement to terminate the marriage upon specific terms of custody and support of children and of *zaisen-bunyo*. In fact, agreements of the latter kind are more frequent than "conciliations" in the sense of continuing the marriage (see table 6).

TABLE 6
DIVORCE CASES — MODES OF DISPOSITION IN FAMILY COURTS, 1959

	Number		Percent	
Total number of divorces	72,455		100	
Total number of cases brought in Family Court	15,057			
1. Agreement reached: total	7,191		48	
to continue marriage		803		5
to separate		240		2
to terminate marriage		6,148		41
2. Settlement failed	1,851		12	
3. Settlement not attempted	247		2	
4. Decided by judgment of Family Court	54			
5. Application withdrawn	5,674		38	
6. Disposed of in other way	40			

Sources: KATO 36; JAPAN STATISTICAL YEARBOOK 1968, table 15.

Of the divorce cases brought before the Family Courts, a considerable number are withdrawn before the proceedings have been completed. How many of these are cases of resumed marital relation cannot be ascertained. Sameshima estimates that about one-third of the cases withdrawn are reconciled. But, as stated earlier, reconciliation in the Japanese sense of the term, does not mean resumption of the marital relation but simply the reaching of an agreement, which may be to resume the marriage or to terminate it under arrangements agreed upon.

What is primarily of interest in the present context is the fact that of the number of agreements reached through the efforts of the Family Court, the number of agreements to terminate the marriage is about six times higher than that of the agreements to continue the marriage. These figures impressively illustrate the difference between "conciliation" Japanese style and conciliation European-American style. The Japanese system cannot be used, as it is by Müller-Freienfels,[12] as an example of how to prevent divorces. But it does serve as an example of how to deal with the problem of marriage breakdown in a straightforward way, aiming at the adjustment of conflicting interests of private individuals so that individual freedom is combined with flexibility.

Both of the Japanese institutions, divorce by agreement and the Family Court, are adaptations of ancient Japanese traditions to modern conditions. Divorce by private act and without intervention of public authority historically constituted an integral part of that type of social organization which has been called the "family system"[13] and which continued substantially the same until the end of World War II. The state was composed not of individuals but of groups: the warrior-vassals (*samurai*) grouped around their lord (*daimyo*), the guilds and, above all, the families. The order of society was hierarchic rather than egalitarian: the parents were superior to their children, the older brother to the younger brothers and sisters, the husband to his wife, the landlord to his tenants, the master to his servants, the teacher (*sensai*) to his pupils and, above all, the emperor to his subjects. The ethics was that of Confucianism: the same piety that was to bind son to father was to prevail in all relations of superior-inferior and quite particularly in that of the emperor or, more realistically, the *shogun*, and the people. The basic cell of society, the family, was not the nuclear family of husband-wife and minor children but the extended family, the house (*Ye*) potentially consisting of several generations and lorded over by its head, in whom all the property was vested. This organization resembled that of ancient Rome; the position of the head of the house was similar to that of the Roman *paterfamilias*. But, different from the Roman system, upon the death or the abdication of the head of the house, property and position were not divided among the children but passed on undivided to the eldest son. If there was

---

12. EHE UND RECHT 307 (1962).
13. On modern Japanese family law and its historic development see Yozo Watanabe, *The Family and the Law: The Individualistic Premise and Modern Japanese Family Law*, in ARTHUR T. VON MEHREN, LAW IN JAPAN 364 (1963); Rex L. Coleman, *Japanese Family Law*, 9 STAN. L. REV. 132 (1956). For a comparison of Japanese and Western divorce laws, see M. Rheinstein, Tokyo Lectures, Judicial Research and Training Institute, Tokyo, 1962.

no son, continuity of the home and, with it, of the worship of the ancestors, was brought about through adoption, which was not conceived, as it is today, as an institution of child welfare.

Marriage was concluded in a Shinto ceremony in which the partners indicated their union by drinking three cups of sake (*san-san-kudo*) three times, but this ceremony was preceded by an agreement made between the heads of the two houses and regularly brought about by a go-between (*nakodo*). Future spouses had little to say in the choice of their partners. Marriage was not supposed to require mutual love but dutiful obedience of the wife, first to the head of her own house and, after the ceremony, to her husband, to the head of the new home she had now entered, and to her mother-in-law and the wife of the head of the house. A husband would find mental and sentimental stimulation in the company of geishas, or sexual satisfaction through concubines or prostitutes. The wife was to bear children and obediently to accept her lot whatever it might be. If it turned out that the wife displeased her husband, the head of his house, or her mother-in-law, the husband would hand her a letter of divorcement (*mikudari-han*) and the marriage and her membership in the husband's house would be ended. In form the divorce was a bilateral transaction. However, as the inferior, the wife was in duty bound to cooperate, so that, in fact, divorce was the unilateral privilege of the male. The only way by which a wife could terminate an intolerable marriage was by taking refuge in one of the two divorce temples (*Engiridera*), the nunnery of Tokei in Kamakura or that of Mantoku in Nitta. The children always remained in the home of the husband. Alimony did not exist.

To what extent this system of family organization was common to all classes of the population is not clear. In the period of the Tokugawa shoguns (1615–1867) it was the system that prevailed among the warrior class, the *samurai*. It was the system which, slightly revised, the reformers of the Meiji era sought to secure as the general system in all of Japan. It did ideally fit into the system of Confucianism which the restored imperial regime sought to preserve as the ethical basis of the modern nation Japan was to become after the breaking of the isolation long fostered by the Tokugawa shoguns. When, after thirty years of study and hesitation, a simplified version of the German draft Civil Code was enacted as the Civil Code of Japan (so-called Meiji Code), Books IV (Family Law) and V (Succession)[14] deviated from the German model to become a modernized version of the traditional family system of the

---

14. Law No. 9 of 1898.

samurai. The "house" as lorded over by its head was to be the basic unit of society,[15] but concessions had to be made to the changing spirit of the times. Marriage was supposed to be a contract between the spouses, but if a member of a house married without the consent of the head of the house, he could be expelled by the head and thus excluded from his right to be supported by the head.[16] In addition, the registrar was not to accept the notification of marriage of a male person below the age of thirty or of a female below the age of twenty-five who sought to conclude a marriage without the consent of parents belonging to the same house as the son or daughter.[17] The Western idea that no marriage ought to become effective without participation of, or at least registration by, an officer of the government fitted in well with Meiji ideology. Thus it was provided that no marriage was "to take effect" before notification of the registrar of civil status.[18] A kind of governmental control was achieved by forbidding the registrar to accept the notification of a marriage prohibited by law.[19] The Code stated clearly that divorce required the mutual consent of both husband and wife and the notification of the registrar.[20] It thus became necessary, for cases in which consent was not given, to establish the possibility of divorce for cause, to be effected by judicial decree. The principal grounds [21] were desertion and such ill-treatment or insult that further living together would be impracticable. Significantly, ill-treatment or insult was a ground for judicial divorce if it was practiced by an ascendant of the other party, or if an ascendant of the other party was the victim. Adultery as a ground for divorce was treated in the same way as it was in the contemporary laws of England and France. The husband was entitled to divorce upon a single act of adultery committed by the wife, but the husband's adultery was to be a ground for divorce only if it was accompanied by aggravating circumstances.

The family system of the Meiji Civil Code, with its basis in Confucian ethics, its emphasis on authority, and its pattern of a society of "houses," fitted in well with the ideology dominant in the period of the China Incident and World War II. But the military dictatorship also engendered resentment and abhorrence. With defeat and surren-

15. Meiji Code, arts. 732 ff.
16. Meiji Code, arts. 750, 742.
17. Meiji Code, art. 772.
18. Meiji Code, art. 775.
19. Meiji Code, art. 776.
20. Meiji Code, arts. 808, 810.
21. Meiji Code, art. 813.

der, long-smoldering resentment flared up. Willingly, or even eagerly, Japanese believers in democracy cooperated with the Allied Occupation authorities in sweeping away the hierarchical order and its base, the family system. Along with the abandonment of the idea of godship of the emperor and the constitutional structure, the land reform did away with the power of the landlords, and the enactment of a new family law destroyed the home structure and all family relations of subordination. The new family law [22] took the place of the former Book IV of the Civil Code and is commonly referred to as the New Civil Code. Parents and adult children, elder brothers and siblings, husband and wife, are now on levels of legal equality. The office of head of the house has been swept away, along with the institution of the house. While the changes were radical in respect to the structure of the family and the relations among its members, they were only minor with respect to divorce. Among the grounds for judicial divorce simple adultery of the husband was declared to constitute a ground entitling the wife to a decree, and the clauses of the Meiji Code referring to ill-treatment of, or by, an ascendant of one spouse as a ground for divorce for the other were deleted. Also inserted was a new clause entitling a spouse to a judicial divorce "if the other spouse is attached [afflicted] with severe mental disease and recovery therefrom is hopeless." [23] Divorce by agreement remained unchanged.[24]

But an innovation of far-reaching importance was the establishment of the network of Family Courts through Law No. 152 of 6 December 1947, with its comprehensive jurisdiction in matters of family life, succession, and juvenile delinquency, and with its elaborate scheme of mediation in matters of divorce and other family disputes. In some sense this new system continued, in a new shape, traditions of long standing. Family disputes should, as far as possible, be shielded from the gaze of the public. Matters of divorce should be discussed primarily among the parties themselves and the circle of their relatives. Where such private handling does not result in agreement, the dispute should be handled in the intimacy of the conciliation committee, from which the public is excluded and where lawyers rarely, if ever, participate in the negotiations. Only in those rare instances in which no agreement can be reached should the case be handled in a public courtroom. Quite generally, the normal way of dispute settlement in Japan is that of negotiation or mediation. Confucian ethics abhors the rigidity of law.

22. Law No. 222 of 1947.
23. New Civil Code, art. 770, no. 4.
24. New Civil Code, arts. 763–69.

Gentlemen do not litigate. They deal with one another fairly and justly. If there be need, they will be helped by a mediator, but they do not go to court.

American business people dealing with the Japanese wonder at their reluctance to spell out in detail the terms of a deal. Even in complex matters, a Japanese contract tends to be brief, to be limited to the principal terms. The foreign partner's insistence on detailed provision for every conceivable contingency is regarded as an offensive expression of distrust. If any dispute should ever arise, gentlemen will know how to handle it in accordance with fairness and decency. These traditions have begun to weaken in recent times, but they are far from dead.

The Japanese are still a nonlitigious people. The number of judges and lawyers is amazingly small. Until just a few years ago the number of graduates of the Judicial Training and Research Institute was 135 a year, and graduation from that institute is indispensable for being a judge, a prosecutor, or member of the bar. Even if one considers that the functions of the Japanese bar are much narrower than those of the American, the figures are amazingly low for a nation of ninety million people constituting one of the world's leaders in commerce and industry.

In spite of the ease with which a marriage can be terminated under Japanese law, the divorce rate is by no means high (see table 7). Since

TABLE 7
Divorce Rate in Japan, the United States, and Germany, Selected Years, 1912 to 1967

	Japan		U.S.	German Empire	Federal Republic of Germany
	Number	Rate		Rates	
1912	59,143	1.17	1.0	0.25	
1926	50,119	0.83	1.6	0.54	
1938	44,656	0.63	1.9	0.72	
1940	48,556	0.68	2.0	0.75	
1947	79,551	1.02	4.4 (1946)		1.68
1955	75,267	0.84	2.3		0.92
1959	72,455	0.78	2.1		0.89
1961	69,323	0.74	2.2		0.88
1965	77,195	0.79	2.5		1.00
1967	83,242*	0.83*	2.6		1.05

Sources: Japan Statistical Yearbook 1968, table 15; U.S. Department of Commerce, The American Almanac for 1971, table 53; E. Wolf, G. Lüke & H. Hax, Scheidung und Scheidungsrecht 465, 467; Statistisches Jahrbuch für die Bundesrepublik Deutschland 1969, at 45.
* Provisional.

1938, the rate per 1,000 population has consistently been about one-third of that of the United States, slightly lower than that of the German Reich. It should also be noted that the divorce rate of rural regions is not, as in Western countries, consistently lower than that of urban. This surprising phenomenon can probably be explained by the fact that under the old family system a wife was likely to be thrown out when she failed to get along with her mother-in-law, and that the wife's readiness to accept the divorce was more a formality than a reality. The old way of life is in decline; it disappears more rapidly in the cities than in the country.[25] However, as urbanization and industrialization increase, they begin to have the same influence in Japan as they have in Western countries and to drive the divorce rate upward.[26]

But the increase of marriages in which the partners have freely chosen each other as against marriages arranged by elders has not resulted in major differences in the incidence of divorce.[27] On the other hand, in the period between 1951 and 1959 displeasure of the husband's parents or grandparents with the son's or grandson's wife decreased as a cause of divorce from 25 to 5 percent, while incompatibility increased as a cause of divorces sought by husbands from 32 to 48 percent.[28]

The number of divorces shown in the official statistics does not fully correspond to that of actual divorces. There can be no divorce unless there is a marriage. But in Japan the term "marriage" has two different meanings. As stated in article 775 of the Meiji Code and article 739 of the New Civil Code, a marriage does not become legally effective before the registrar has been properly notified of it. But, in the popular view, a couple is married and treated as respectable as soon as the parties have gone through the ceremony of *san-san-kudo*.[29] Such an unregistered marriage is known as *nayen*-marriage. Notification of the registrar may be delayed or never occur at all. Under the old family system *nayen*-marriage would be used to evade the requirement of

25. T. Fueto, *Japan: Revision of the New Civil Code*, 6 AM. J. COMP. L. 559, 565 (1957).

26. The complex interplay between the disappearance of tradition, reducing old-style divorce, and modernization, increasing divorce new-style, has been investigated in detail by Takeyoshi Kawashima and Kurt Steiner, *Modernization and Divorce Rate Trends in Japan*, 9 ECON. DEVELOPMENT AND CULTURAL CHANGE 213, 228 (1960).

27. See KATO, table 6.3 at 83. The only major difference appeared in 1959 in divorces applied for by the wife because of infidelity of the husband. In this category the number of divorces terminating "love marriages" was about one-third higher than that terminating "arranged marriages." Women marrying for love seem to take a misstep of the husband more seriously.

28. KATO, table 6.2 at 81.

29. See *supra* p. 116.

consent of parents or of the head of the house. It would be, and still is, used as a trial marriage. The marriage is not recorded as long as it is uncertain whether the wife will bear a son to continue the lineage, or whether or not she fits in with the husband's family, especially with his mother. If the wife is found unsatisfactory, she can be dismissed, without her consent and without *zaisen-bunyo*.[30] When the wife is approved, the marriage is registered and becomes formal.[31]

While we do not know how many *nayen*-marriages there are and how many of these are terminated informally, in 1959, according to Kato, the dissolution of 1,906 of them resulted in conciliation proceedings concerning damages for breach of promise of marriage.[32] The number of marriages registered in 1959 was 553,665.[33] Perhaps we may conclude that the number of *nayen*-marriages informally terminated, while perhaps not negligible, is not so high as significantly to increase the Japanese divorce rate. Investigations also indicate that "delay of registration for the purpose of facilitating a repudiation of the bride" in the interests of the family is becoming less prevalent.[34]

In Japan, the present law of divorce is criticized in two respects. The wife's consent, which is necessary for a divorce by agreement, is suspected as not always freely given. There is even, it is said, the possibility that every now and then the wife's seal is affixed without her knowledge to the notification sent to the registrar.[35] But the proposals

---

30. But a *nayen*-wife may, under certain circumstances be entitled to damages for breach of promise of marriage.

31. On analogous practices in Turkey and the resulting legal problems, see K. Lipstein, *The Reception of Western Law in Turkey*, ANNALES DE LA FACULTÉ DE DROIT D'ISTANBUL (5e année, no. 6), 11, 17 (1956); H. V. VELIDEDEOGLU, *De certains problèmes provenant de la réception du Code Civil Suisse en Turquie*, id. 99, 111; Z. F. Findikoglu, *Special Aspects of the Turkish Reception of Law*, id. 155; H. Timur, *De la publication et de la célébration du mariage en Turquie*, id. 166; Rheinstein, *Note*, 5 AM. J. COMP. L. 266 (1956).

In Japan it was found necessary to extend to *nayen*-spouses the protection of a number of laws on social security. See Watanabe, *supra* note 13, at 366.

32. KATO 109.
33. KATO 15.
34. Kawashima & Steiner, *supra* note 26, at 219. As indicated by an investigation of the Department of Welfare, the interval between inception and registration of marriages in 1947 was 9.6 percent within one month; 39.9 percent from one month one day to six months; 28.2 percent from six months one day to one year; and 22.3 percent over one year. Detailed figures for Yamaguchi prefecture in southern Honsho are given in the article by T. Fueto, *The Discrepancy between Marriage Law and Mores in Japan*, 5 AM. J. COMP. L. 256, 260–64 (1956); see also Watanabe, *supra* note 13, at 389.

35. Fueto, *supra* note 25, at 564; Coleman, *supra* note 13, at 132, 150; Watanabe, *supra* note 13, at 367.

to subject the wife's written consent to scrutiny by the registrar or the Family Court have not been acted upon. Such control, it is feared, might increase the reluctance to have marriages registered and might thus prevent the publicizing of marital status and frustrate the very purpose of protecting wives. Besides, women generally are said to be satisfied with the present state of affairs.[36]

The second subject of criticism is the absence of permanent alimony. *Zaisen-bunyo*, of which the New Civil Code speaks in article 768,[37] is officially designated as "property settlement" or "property distribution." This definition may be misleading. The marital property regulation of the New Civil Code is the same as that in most of the United States: the husband owns his property, the wife hers. Any asset about which there is doubt whether it belongs to the husband or the wife is presumed to be owned by them in common.[38] Upon divorce, each spouse takes his assets; property actually or presumptively owned in common is divided. But under the heading of *zaisen-bunyo* one spouse, in the overwhelming majority of cases the wife, may receive property, usually in the form of a money payment, that may be meant to serve two purposes: to allow the wife a share in those assets which the husband has accumulated during the time in which the wife co-operated with him in his business or on his farm, or during which she conducted his household and brought up his children. The second purpose is that of facilitating the wife's adjustment to her new situation, to serve as a kind of severance pay. As shown by table 8, the amounts awarded in Family Court proceedings are modest. The *zaisen-bunyo* amounts include the so-called solatium, i.e., damages that may be assessed for objectionable conduct destroying the marriage, but not the support for children which the husband has to pay when the children are not in his custody.

Proposals to provide for divorced wives more generously have not,

---

36. Watanabe, *supra* note 13, at 382.

37. Art. 768 reads as follows: "Husband or wife who has effected divorce by agreement may demand the distribution of property from the other spouse. If no agreement is reached or possible between the parties with respect to the distribution of property in accordance with the provisions of the foregoing paragraph, any of the parties may apply to the Family Court for measures to take the place of such agreement, except, however, after the lapse of two years from the time of the divorce.

"In the case mentioned in the preceding paragraph, the Family Court shall determine whether any such distribution is to be made or not and if it is to be made, the sum as well as the mode of the distribution, taking into account the sum of such property as is acquired by cooperation of the parties and all other circumstances."

38. New Civil Code, art. 762.

TABLE 8
AMOUNT OF ZAISEN-BUNYO AWARDED, 1956

Yen*	Number	Percent
None	2,201	38
Up to 10,000	259	4
Up to 30,000	695	12
Up to 50,000	644	11
Up to 100,000	801	14
Up to 200,000	470	8
Up to 300,000	251	4
Up to 500,000	155	3
Up to 1,000,000	69	1
Over 1,000,000	29	1
Others	205	4
Total decided	5,805	100
Undecided	7,928	
Total applications	13,733	

Source: Statistical data of the Family Courts for 1956. Reprinted from Watanabe, *supra* note 13, at 391 (table 4) with permission of the publisher, Harvard University Press. See also KATO 100–101.
* In 1956, 10,000 yen = approx. $27.77.

or not yet, met with success. The present system is a compromise. Under the old family system a wife that was divorced by her husband or his head of house, would return to her former house, where she would be maintained like all other members. The children that she had borne her husband belonged to his house and would be maintained there. Now, while the house system survives in fact among a considerable part of the population,[39] it is no longer universal. Thus a divorced wife cannot necessarily find refuge in the house whence she came. She is, instead, forced into the labor market, and this effect may be as welcome in Japan as it is in East Germany. But for a good many divorcees the labor market seems to be limited to the dance halls and massage parlors, which are numerous, and to the places of prostitution, which are also numerous although not officially permitted. The decrease in the significance of the traditional house system may well compel the Japanese lawmakers to enlarge *zaisen-bunyo* in the direction of permanent alimony. But it must also be noted that in the United States, where permanent alimony has long been recognized, the courts show a marked tendency to refuse alimony to a woman who is able to support herself and whose marriage has been of short dura-

39. Watanabe, *supra* note 13; Kawashima & Steiner, *supra* note 32.

tion. Such a system has another advantage of far-reaching importance. If an ex-husband is saddled with an obligation to pay alimony to an ex-wife until she dies or remarries, he is likely to be prevented, and she is likely to be discouraged, from remarrying. The system thus jeopardizes the very purpose of a divorce law ought to pursue, namely, that of facilitating remarriage. By its very essence a divorce is a restoration of the parties to the freedom of remarriage. Early remarriage creates the chance of marital satisfaction for both parties and a new home for the children that will be presumably more harmonious than the former one. A divorce law which discourages remarriage or saddles the husband's new family with unbearable burdens is self-defeating. In spite of the criticisms of some of its features, however, the divorce law of Japan appears to be regarded as well designed and functional. Its basic features, mutual agreement as the normal form of divorce and mediation through a judge assisted by *honoratiores*, are firmly accepted.

Western divorce laws have grown up against the background of the Christian tradition of indissolubility of marriage. Indeed, marriage has been regarded as a sacred institution, ordained by the Lord to be indissoluble. Western divorce law has developed in the atmosphere of that tradition, reluctantly admitting the termination of the marriage tie in exceptional situations of serious marital misconduct. In Japan, the sacred institution has been patrilineal succession, the permanency of the male line maintaining the tradition of the house and the worship of the ancestors. Marriage supplemented by adoption, has been the device by which the continuance of the male line is secured. The wife, it is true, entered the house of the husband, but there was no reason why she should be kept in it if she turned out to be barren or otherwise unsatisfactory. To replace her in the interest of the house involved no moral stigma.[40] As the old adage said: "The womb is only borrowed." In such a system it was self-evident that a marriage could be unilaterally terminated by the husband.

The old family system is on its way out. Western ideas have taken a firm hold in industrialized and urbanized Japan, but not the ideas of the Christian tradition, which is rapidly losing ground in the West. What has taken hold in Japan is that factual Western system in which individualist liberalism has established a belief in the existence of a fundamental right to the pursuit of individual happiness. Unlike those Western countries where Christian conservatism with its emphasis upon the priority of the community's interests over those of the individual is

---

40. Kawashima & Steiner, *supra* note 26, at 217.

not yet moribund, Japan has not had to hide, behind a Christian façade, the reality of its divorce practices, namely, divorce as normally the result of agreement, and freely available whenever the parties have agreed to disagree. In effect, the Japanese system is the same as that of the industrialized West. But, it dispenses with hypocrisy and thus provides straightforward mediation for that minority of cases in which agreement about termination of a marriage and the accompanying terms cannot be reached by the parties involved.

6
Liberalism Dominant: Sweden

1. The family is the basic cell of society. It is based upon monogamous marriage. Marriage is a relationship meant to be exclusive and to last for the joint lives of the spouses.

2. Attempts to enforce the ideal of permanency of marriage or to curb extramarital sex activity by means of law are futile.

3. The breakdown of a marriage regularly results in serious mental and economic consequences for the parties and their children. The main task of the law of divorce is that of mitigating as much as possible the damaging consequences.

4. It is not the task of the law to bar the establishment of new family homes for the parties and their children.

These are the principles of a society which, starting from the common Western tradition of Christianity, has traveled the full way to dominance of liberal individualism. They have found expression in the laws of the five Nordic countries. The principal ground upon which a divorce, i.e., restoration to the freedom of remarriage, can be obtained, is the factual breakdown of the marriage, proved by separation of a certain period of time and the mutual consent of the parties. If the termination of the marriage tie is sought by one party alone, divorce is on general principle also obtainable without much difficulty.

Although the great majority of divorces is obtained upon the mutual consent of the parties, it is nevertheless justified to emphasize that officially the Scandinavian laws are based upon the principle of *Zerrüt-*

Portions of this chapter were published in 1970 as chapter 7 of the book edited by Paul Bohannan under the title *Divorce and After* and published by Doubleday & Company, Inc., Garden City, New York.

In the presentation of the Swedish law of divorce the author was able to draw upon an extensive report prepared at the University of Chicago Comparative Law Research Center by Mr. Sven Beckman of Stockholm. Other principal sources are: Johan Thorsten Sellin, Marriage and Divorce Legislation in Sweden (doctoral dissertation, University of Pennsylvania, 1922) (English translation of the Swedish statute, with explanation); FOLKE SCHMIDT, ÄKTENSKAPSRÄTT (1964); Folke Schmidt, *The "Leniency" of the Scandinavian Divorce Laws*, 7 SCANDINAVIAN STUDIES IN LAW 167 (1963); IVAR NYLANDER, STUDIER RÖRANDE DEN SVENSKA ÄKTENSKAPSRÄTTENS HISTORIA (1961).

Sweden

tung" (deep, permanent discord) rather than that of simple agreement. Consent is important as evidence of marital discord rather than in itself. Marriage is still regarded as being concluded for life.[1] Divorce, however easily it may be obtained, still constitutes the exception. The Scandinavian laws resemble the law of California, as it stood until 1970, under which, in fact though not in theory, a divorce could always be obtained when the parties were in agreement or when one party exhibited the serious desire to be free, but under which one year had to elapse between the interlocutory and the final decree. Compared with such American jurisdictions as Nevada, Idaho, Arkansas, or even such states as Illinois, where the officially professed principle of guilt is in fact turned into that of mutual consent, the Scandinavian laws with their waiting periods are strict.

Even though the persuasion of individualism is the official rather than the hidden basis of Scandinavian divorce law, the divorce rates are, as shown in table 9, considerably lower than those of the United States. The data on divorce can be assumed closely to approximate those of factual marriage breakdown. Once a marriage has ceased to exist in fact, Scandinavians, especially Danes and Finns, appear to be inclined to have it also terminated at law. Suits for separate maintenance[2] seem to be used almost exclusively as preliminaries to divorce. The number of Roman Catholics, to whom divorce is religious anathema, is negligible. The population almost solidly belongs, at least nominally, to the Lutheran State Church.[3]

The Scandinavian situation indicates that a divorce law clearly based upon the individual view of live and let live has, at least so far, been compatible with the maintenance of the institution of marriage, even

---

1. This idea is neatly expressed in the formula prescribed for the use of the pastor or the secular official by whom the marriage is performed. As prescribed by the royal proclamation of 3 December 1915, the secular officiant must address the parties as follows:

"The end of marriage is the welfare of the individuals who desire to enter matrimony. Do you, A.B., take C.D. as your wife for better or for worse? Do you, C.D., take A.B. as your husband for better or for worse? Take each other's hands in confirmation. By virtue of my office, I declare you husband and wife. Never forget the promise of lifelong faith, which you have now made. Live together in mutual love, confidence, and respect, and consider your responsibility to future generations. May happiness and unity be yours and bless your home."

Two ends of marriage are stated in this formula, the welfare of the individual and the maintenance of society, but, significantly, the first place is given to the individual.

2. The determination of what right of maintenance, if any, one party has against the other, is an incident of the action for judicial separation.

3. In Sweden 99 percent.

TABLE 9
RATES OF DIVORCE PER 1,000 POPULATION, NORDIC COUNTRIES AND UNITED STATES, 1951–68

	51–55 average	56	57	58	59	60	61	62	63	64	65	66	67	1968
Denmark	1.53	1.46	1.43	1.46	1.42	1.46	1.43	1.38	1.38	1.37	1.37	1.40	1.43	
Finland	0.85	0.85	0.81	0.83	0.83	0.82	0.88	0.89	0.92	0.97	0.99	1.04		
Iceland	0.75	0.62	0.70	0.85	0.88	0.71	0.90	0.69	1.08	0.92	0.85	0.98	0.93	
Norway	0.65	0.62	0.58	0.58	0.62	0.66	0.68	0.67	0.67	0.60	0.69	0.71	0.76	
Sweden	1.18	1.18	1.20	1.17	1.17	1.20	1.16	1.17	1.12	1.20	1.24	1.32	1.36	1.39
United States	2.4	2.3	2.2	2.2	2.2	2.2	2.3	2.2	2.3	2.4	2.5	2.5	2.6	2.9

SOURCES: HELVI SIPILÄ, BÖR LAGSTIFTNINGEN OM ÄKTENSKAPSSKILLNAD REFORMERAS? 41 (Vammala, Finland, 1957); DEMOGRAPHIC YEARBOOK OF THE UNITED NATIONS 1968, table 34; U.S. DEPARTMENT OF HEALTH, EDUCATION AND WELFARE, INCREASES IN DIVORCES 4 (1970); P. H. JACOBSON, AMERICAN MARRIAGE AND DIVORCE 90 (1959).

if it is accompanied by a far-reaching alleviation of traditional sex taboos.[4]

In the Scandinavian countries, especially Denmark and Sweden, the sexual revolution which has taken place in association with modern industrialization, urbanization, female emancipation, and birth control techniques has probably gone farther than in other parts of the once Christian world. The change in the sex mores is a part of that general liberalization of life that has been characteristic of the countries of Henrik Ibsen, August Strindberg, Ellen Key, and Edward Westermarck.

The starting point of the Scandinavian development was the same as that of all non-Orthodox Europe: the medieval principle of indissolubility of marriage. As in other Lutheran and Reformed countries, the reinterpretation of the Gospel by the Reformers brought slight inroads. Adultery and certain cases of desertion[5] were recognized as grounds entitling the innocent spouse to repudiate the guilty so as to be set free to remarry by ecclesiastical authority. In Sweden this practice was formalized in the Ecclesiastical Ordinance of 1572, which explicitly ordered the clergy to watch over the marital lives of the people. In their sermons the pastors were assiduously to admonish the people to preserve harmony in their homes. In particular it was declared to be the churchman's duty, through individual warning and appropriate means of ecclesiastical discipline, to prevent a marriage from being broken up by discord. The rules concerning this ecclesiastical duty to deal with "quarrelsome couples," which in the long run was to have important consequences for the development of divorce, was elaborated by the Church Law of 1686. A quarrelsome couple should first be admonished by its pastor and then, if necessary, by the chapter of the diocesan cathedral. If they failed to reform, the case was to be reported to the secular authority, which should resort to imprisonment or "other appropriate punishment," meaning flogging, fine, prison, or

---

4. On Swedish attitudes toward sex, see the article *L'amour en liberté*, L'EXPRESS, no. 708, 1, 34 (January 1965).

5. In seventeenth-century Sweden a letter of divorcement would be issued to a married person if his or her spouse had left the realm with the intent permanently to terminate the marital community of life. A letter of divorcement would also be issued if a party to a marriage had left the home for a legitimate reason but had not been heard of for seven years. No divorce was available if a spouse willfully deserted the home and remained inside the realm at a known address or drove the other spouse out of the home. In such cases the procedure was to be that applicable to "quarrelsome couples." Through the means of church discipline the clergy had to reconcile the parties. If they refused to follow the clergy's efforts, punishment would be meted out by the secular court.

the stock. If that would not help, the scandalous quarreling was to be stopped by forcibly separating the parties from each other for a limited period of time, during which the congregation were to pray for their reformation. Ultimate punishment, after futile public admonition from the pulpit, could be the Great Bann, which meant not only exclusion from participation in worship but social boycott in secular affairs as well, possibly leading to banishment from the realm. The same extreme punishment was to be meted out to a married man or woman who had deserted the home or driven out his or her spouse, and stubbornly refused to resume a peaceful marital life.

It is a far cry from such ecclesiastical coercion of marital harmony to the present law. The intervening steps reflect the growing secularization of the state and society and the concomitant transformation of the basic morals. A first step was taken in the Church Law of 1686 itself, which transferred to the secular courts the investigation of the facts in cases of application for marriage bond termination on the grounds of adultery, flight from the realm, or disappearance. The issuance of letters of divorcement remained with the cathedral chapters. But they were not to issue letters until so ordered by the secular authority.

No major change was made by Sweden's great codification of the law, *Sveriges Rikes Lag*, of 1734, which, preceding Napoleon's codes by seventy years, constitutes the second oldest of the great codifications of European law.[6] Significantly, however, quarrelsome couples were henceforth to be punished exclusively by fine which, it is true, could be transformed into flogging or imprisonment in the case of nonpayment. The ultimate punishment of the bann was not formally abolished, but it became obsolete. The authorities came to prefer to drag out the case until one party might provide the other with the divorce ground of adultery or flight from the realm or seven years' disappearance, or until the matter found a natural end through one party's death. Or, and this device was to assume increasing significance, the innocent party would receive a royal dispensation freeing him from the bond of the marriage that had become a sham, thus restoring him to the freedom of remarriage.

The practice of granting freedom of remarriage by special governmental dispensation was not peculiar to Sweden. It was indeed common to, it seems, all those countries which broke with Rome in the course

---

6. The first was the King Christian V Law, enacted for Denmark in 1683 and for Norway in 1687. The Swedish Code, profoundly amended many times is, in form, still in effect in Sweden as well as in Finland, which at the time of the Code's enactment was a part of the Swedish realm.

of the Reformation. In territories of monarchical rule, the power of dispensation was exercised by, or in the name of, the monarch. In England, the grant of divorces by the king in Parliament, which meant by private act of Parliament, was the only way in which a divorce could be obtained until 1858. Until 1971 it also was the only way for residents of the Canadian Province of Quebec, who could not obtain a divorce in any way other than by private act of the Parliament of the Dominion.[7] The practice long prevailing in numerous states of the United States, to have divorces granted by the legislature, also derived from the English tradition.[8] In Denmark, Norway, and Iceland, the majority of divorces is still granted by administrative agencies in a well-established, inexpensive procedure (see table 10). In fact, from a theoretical point

TABLE 10
Divorces Granted by Administrative Agencies and Courts in Denmark, 1954–66

	Local Admin. Authority	Ministry of Justice	The Courts
1948	6,777		549
1954	6,193	15	478
1955	6,290	19	462
1956	5,997	10	492
1957	5,978	8	450
1958	6,069	15	487
1959	5,937	9	511
1963	5,935	3	522
1964	5,970	0	513
1965	6,013	1	513
1966	6,223	0	503

Sources: Denmarks Statistisk Årbog 1960; 1966, table 24; 1968, table 26; 1969, table 28.

of view, no reason exists why restoration to the freedom of remarriage should not belong to the domain of the executive, at least in all those cases — and they are the overwhelming majority everywhere, including the United States — in which the parties are not in dispute at all or have been able to settle whatever dispute there may have been on child

---

7. The jurisdiction belonged to the Parliament of the Dominion rather than that of the province, because under the British North America Act, 1867, which still operates as Canada's constitution, jurisdiction to legislate on matters of marriage and divorce belongs to the Dominion rather than to the provinces (see art. 91).
8. See NELSON M. BLAKE, THE ROAD TO RENO 48 ff. (1962).

custody, alimony, or property settlement. It is the courts' function to decide controversies. The reason why courts have been charged with jurisdiction to grant freedom of remarriage is an accident of history.

In Sweden, divorce by governmental dispensation first occurred about the same time as in England, the late seventeenth century. As in England, it long remained rare. Two to four cases long constituted the annual average. The earliest dispensations were granted in cases in which the commission of adultery had been made highly probable but was not proved with that strict certainty under which alone the courts would grant a divorce. Other early instances were cases of quarrel and dissension in which the measures of ecclesiastical discipline as well as the fine imposed by the secular authority had failed to reunite the couple. Since flight from the realm was considered recognized by Holy Writ as a ground for judicial divorce, the government found it appropriate to grant dispensations also in the case of a spouse being banished from the realm by way of punishment. To these grounds were added a senstence to life imprisonment and, in the late eighteenth century, punishment for a crime involving moral turpitude. Following ancient tradition, spouses of lepers were occasionally granted dispensation in early times. In the fourth decade of the eighteenth century spouses of persons found to be incurably insane were allowed to remarry when the circumstances made it necessary to provide a new mother for minor children, or a new provider for a woman. As the eighteenth century progressed, dispensations were granted in other cases of special merit or hardship, such as one spouse's attempt upon the life of the other; violence of character threatening the petitioner's life or safety; habitual abuse of intoxicating liquor; persistent refusal of marital intercourse; infectious disease; habitual wastefulness in matters of property; and, finally, such deep and lasting discord as would preclude any hope of resumption of a normal marital life.

The government, before it would grant a petition, regularly requested a statement of opinion from the diocesan chapter. The liberal attitude of these ecclesiastical authorities is remarkable. From the early eighteenth century on, liberalism was potent in Swedish theology. In the latter part of the century ideas of rationalist natural law had come to be popular among the intelligentsia, especially the urban clergy. Governmental practice of dispensation was particularly liberal during the regency period between the assassination of King Gustavus III (1792) and the accession to the throne of Gustavus IV Adolphus (1796), when the screws were tightened again. The reactionary regime was ended with the king's deposition on 13 March 1809. Bernadotte, later King

Karl Johann, was imposed as crown prince upon the new king and with the arrival of this son of the French Revolution, Swedish liberalism was revitalized. Among the demands for reform of many traditional institutions marriage and divorce occupied a prominent place.

A committee of the four estates of the Diet proposed a reform of the law of divorce that, as the report expressed it, should be based upon the idea "that marriage, as a moral union, is founded upon the mutual respect of the spouses, so that, once that mutual respect has vanished, the marriage has ceased to exist in their sentiments and in their conscience, even though there may still exist the appearance of the bond that had once been established."

This expression of individualist liberalism was approved by all four houses of the Diet, including the clergy. But the new law that was promulgated as the Royal Edict of 27 April 1810 was a cautious document that left many doors open. The list of grounds for judicial divorce was slightly extended by the addition of those situations in which the granting of a governmental dispensation had become customary: banishment from the realm; attempt upon the plaintiff's life; sentence to imprisonment for life; and incurable insanity that has existed for at least three years. In a conservative vein there was added the proviso that the divorce was to be refused where the plaintiff had provoked, or participated in, the commission of the crime for which the defendant had been sentenced, or if the defendant's insanity had been caused or accelerated by the plaintiff's conduct. For the rest, the government should remain authorized to grant dispensation for special reasons. By way of example, but without intent to bind the government, the following were stated: sentence of death or of loss of honor, or of dishonoring punishment, or sentence of honorable detention for two years or more; wasteful management of property; alcoholism; cruel temperament; and, finally, in elaboration of earlier practice, the situation in which "the sentiments and thoughts of the spouses so manifest themselves in mutual hostility that, breaking out at every occasion, they ultimately turn into aversion and hatred." As to the last ground, mutual aversion and hatred, it was apparently expected, although it was not clearly prescribed, that the ancient procedure of admonition and fine should have remained without success. It was clearly stated, however, that the government was to examine the spouse of the petitioner and that it should obtain the report of the pastor of the parish, as well as the advisory opinion of the cathedral chapter of the diocese and of the Supreme Court of the realm.

The dispensation was a strictly personal matter. It authorized the person to whom it was granted to receive from the cathedral chapter of his diocese the letter of divorcement which he needed if he wished a pastor of the church to perform a ceremony of remarriage for him. On general principle, no such authorization would result for the spouse of the grantee. As for him, the impediment of existing marriage continued until that marriage would find its natural end through the death of his partner. Gradually, this original theory seems to be obscured. Remarriage of the partner became permissible first, it seems, upon the grantee's remarriage, then upon the grantee's consent. Besides, the government could always grant the dispensation to the petition's spouse, too. In the nineteenth century such permission came to be regarded as a matter of course. A prohibition of remarriage of the grantee's spouse had to be expressly stated in the decree of dispensation.

The proceedings were cumbersome and time-consuming; they remained so even under the comparatively liberal practice of the later nineteenth century. They were commonly referred to as "the long road to divorce," in contrast to the "short road" that developed out of the ancient institution of judicial divorce for desertion beyond the borders of the realm, that had figured as a ground for divorce as early as the Ecclesiastical Ordinance of 1572. Also known as Copenhagen divorce, this institution was simply a consent divorce, disguised as divorce for misconduct and tolerated by the courts. One spouse would take the train to some city beyond the Swedish border, usually Copenhagen, and would obligingly write from there that he, or she, had left the marital home without intention to return. Action for divorce upon the ground of desertion could be started in the Swedish court the next day and, being uncontested, could be decided quickly. Appeal would be waived. The "deserter" could return and both parties were free to remarry.[9]

Compared with present figures, the number of divorces was modest even in the early years of the twentieth century (see table 11). But it was sufficiently high to provoke some viewing with alarm. The judicial farce of the short road was criticized not only because, as a law inviting migratory divorce always does, it results in advantage of the affluent over the poor, but also because of its inherent hypocrisy. That kind of critique was bound to be strong in Scandinavia, where literature, theology, and philosophy united in calling for truthfulness and sincerity in all walks of life.

Sweden, which had long been an agrarian corner of Europe, had

9. A typical consent divorce is described by August Strindberg in his play *The Bond (Bandet)* 1893–97.

TABLE 11
DIVORCE IN SWEDEN, 1831–1968

	Number of Divorces	Divorces per 1,000 Population
1831–40	106	
1841–50	108	
1851–60	121	0.03
1861–70	130	0.03
1871–80	193	0.04
1881–90	234	0.05
1891–1900	538	0.07
1901–10	474	0.09
1911–20	911	0.16
1921–30	1,813	0.30
1931–40	2,925	0.45
1941–45	4,876	0.75
1947	7,058	0.97
1948	6,782	1.09
1949	7,602	1.14
1950	7,991	1.19
1951	8,431	1.19
1952	8,185	1.14
1953	8,393	1.17
1954	8,676	1.20
1957	8,858	1.20
1960	8,958	1.20
1965	9,563	1.24
1968	11,011	1.39

Source: STATISTISK ÅRSBOK FÖR SVERIGE, 1951, table 49; 1955, table 45; 1969, table 40.

started upon its economic and social transformation. Industry began to grow to impressive size (see table 12). A laboring class appeared and organized itself into a powerful political party. The cities expanded from small towns into large centers of industry, shipping and commerce. Women entered the institutions of higher learning and the of-

TABLE 12
COMPARISON OF POPULATION EMPLOYED IN AGRICULTURE
AND INDUSTRY, SWEDEN, 1870–1950
(Percent)

	1870	1920	1945	1950
Agriculture	51.6	38.4	28.2	23.4
Industry, commerce, and communications	12.5	44.2	57.0	63.0

Source: 9 HANDWÖRTERBUCH DER SOZIALWISSENSCHAFTEN 162 (1956).

fices of business and government. They began to demand equality with men, politically, socially, and sexually. The double morality of the nineteenth-century bourgeois came under attack. The sexual freedom that was in fact enjoyed by men was postulated for women too. In plays that were to stir the world, Henrik Ibsen gave expression to the new spirit. The tragedy of unhappy marriage was presented by August Strindberg with an as yet unheard-of realism. The traditional taboos of sex were passionately attacked.

In 1905 the new spirit found expression at the polls. The Agrarian party, which had dominated the political scene, was defeated. In 1909 a new constitution was made. A total revision of the code of early eighteenth-century vintage was one of the reforms demanded. The pain felt over Norway's secession from the union with the crown of Sweden (1905) eventually gave way to a strong feeling of Scandinavian solidarity which resulted in the establishment of a scheme for Scandinavian cooperation in legal reform.[10] In both Norway and Denmark transformations similar to those of Sweden had provoked plans to adapt to the new spirit the laws on family relations, especially the relation of husband and wife.

The revision of that part of the Swedish General Code which deals with land (*Jordabalken*) had already been initiated under the old political regime.[11] For the new cabinet of the liberals, family law was naturally chosen as the next field of reform rather than the obsolete scheme of civil and criminal procedure, where modernization was regarded as more urgent by the conservatives. In the family law they demanded only one change, the abolition of the Copenhagen divorces. But a much more comprehensive reform was demanded by the liberal element that had now assumed the leading role in intellectual and political life. Their most urgent demand was female emancipation, above all abolition of the wife's subordination to the husband in matters of family management, education of the children, and marital property. As to divorce, the demand was for a clean break with the remnants of a religious dogma that had lost its spell even in the leading circles of the church. The demand was for a law that would no longer favor the rich over the poor, that would no longer expose the parties to the "humiliating indignity" of public admonition in church, that would instate truthfulness in place of the hypocrisy of feigning desertion to

---

10. See Birger Ekeberg, *The Scandinavian Cooperation in the Field of Legislation*, in 1 INSTITUT INTERNATIONAL POUR L'UNIFICATION DU DROIT PRIVÉ, UNIFICATION OF LAW 321 (1948); Algot Bagge, *The Uniform Laws of the Nordic Countries*, in the same publication, YEAR-BOOK 1961, at 179.

11. The *Nya Jordabalk* was promulgated as the Law of 14 June 1907.

foreign parts. Above all, the new divorce law should no longer aggravate the emotional and economic shock of divorce but should rather make it easier for all persons concerned — spouses, children, and even a paramour — to reestablish new, happier homes. Also, the new law should abolish the anomalies and hardships resulting from the haphazard way in which the old divorce law had grown up, such as the lack of adequate provision for the needs of a spouse, especially a wife, that might arise in consequence of the divorce. The unbending rule of property forfeiture which accompanied judicial divorce for adultery was to be replaced by a flexible scheme of damages that would apply in all appropriate cases.

Reform was also demanded with respect to the rules on the conclusion of marriage. Obsolete institutions should go, such as the effect of a formal betrothal to one person to prevent the conclusion of a marriage with another person. Abolition was also demanded of the ancient institution of "incomplete marriage." That counterpart to American common-law marriage had been developed by ecclesiastics as a means to reduce illegitimacy. By subsequent sexual intercourse a promise of marriage was transformed into a marriage which, although valid, would not have the full status and property effects of a marriage celebrated in church. In Sweden, this once general notion of medieval churchmen was preserved into the twentieth century. It was defended as necessary in view of the custom widely followed among the peasantry, that a betrothed pair would have sexual intercourse but would wait with the ceremony of marriage until pregnancy was apparent. "Incomplete marriage" was thought to be apt to prevent a man from reneging on his promise after intercourse. Generally more appropriate ways were demanded to improve the situation of illegitimate children without forcing anyone into an unwanted and prospectively unfortunate marriage.

High on the list of the reformers' postulates was the equalization of secular and religious marriage ceremonies, and the removal of anomalies that had arisen in consequence of the hesitant and unsystematic way in which secular marriage had come to be accepted.[12]

The list of reformist demands was long. But they were all expressions

12. Until 1781 marriage could not be celebrated in any way other than by ceremony in the Lutheran State Church. By Royal Decree of 24 January 1781 Catholics and members of other "alien faiths" were granted the freedom to form congregations and with it the privilege of concluding marriages in accordance with their rites. In 1782, Jews were given the same privilege; but not until 1863 was intermarriage permitted between Jews and Christians. It was for such marriages that the possibility of a nonreligious ceremony was for the first time provided in Sweden. For other persons, the possibility of secular marriage was opened through the Dissenter Law of 1873 (Royal Decree of 31 October) and a Law of 1908.

of the same spirit of secular liberalism that was dominating the intellectuals of Scandinavia, including theologians, as well as the growing numbers of working people united in the Social-Democratic party, whose leadership was no less individualistic in matters of life and culture than the bourgeois leaders of cultural and spiritual life. Sweden, like Denmark and Norway, had turned into a country of firmly established liberalism. All three countries were ready resolutely to reshape their laws in accordance with the new spirit. A clear insight into the key role of the family resulted in the choice of family law as the first topic to be reformed, just as family law, together with the land law, was to be the first field to be reshaped in post–World War II Japan, or as it is now being reshaped in the countries of Africa and Asia.

The task of remaking the entire body of family law turned out to be so extensive that it was undertaken in stages rather than all at once. But so pervading has been the effect of the new spirit that the several parts constitute a coherent whole, a consistent legal embodiment of individualist liberalism. The community of this spirit also made it possible that in its essential parts the work could be carried on cooperatively by Sweden, Denmark, and Norway, whose scheme of uniform legislation was later joined by Finland and Iceland shortly after these countries obtained national independence. The greatest urgency was for reform of the laws on concluding marriages and terminating them. Statutes dealing with these topics were enacted in Sweden in 1915, in Denmark in 1922, in Norway in 1918, in Iceland in 1923, and in Finland in 1929. Of the later laws, the most important are those on the incidents of marital relationships, especially marital property (Sweden, 1920, Denmark 1925, Norway 1927, Finland 1929, Iceland 1923) and on illegitimate children (Norway 1915, Sweden 1917, Finland 1922, Denmark 1908–37, Iceland 1921).

The concern about human rights and individual welfare which inspired these laws has found further expression in the comprehensive legislation on social security and public welfare through which the Scandinavian countries have established themselves as models of the welfare state. In Sweden this vast body of legislation has been enlarged by a number of laws designed to reverse the falling birth rate by encouraging child birth and favoring large families.[13] This policy, however, has not prevented the continued implementation of the liberal tradition through legislative legalization of birth control and of abortion.[14]

13. See G. Karlsson, *Social Policies and Marriage Stability in Sweden*, 9 ANNALES DE LA FACULTÉ DE DROIT DE L'UNIVERSITÉ D'ISTANBUL, (no. 13) 240 (1960).
14. Swedish Law of 17 June 1938.

Acts of Swedish legislation are prepared with great care. The preparation of legislative drafts of importance is usually entrusted to a permanent board of legal experts of high standing, the so-called Law Commission (*Lagberedningen*). That institution played a long and important role in preconstitutional days. In 1842, it was abolished, but, with the awakening of reformist zeal, it was reconstituted in 1902. Among its members were Hjalmar Westring and Birger Ekeberg, jurists of the highest standing. Their draft of the law of marriage and divorce met with high praise by the committee of four Supreme Court justices to whom, in accordance with general Swedish practice, it was submitted next. Although Hasselrot, the minister of justice, by whom the draft was introduced in the Upper House of Parliament, was a Conservative, the cabinet was as much aware as the country of the fact that it had been brought into office for the sole job of preserving the country's neutrality in the European war that had broken out in August 1914. Hasselrot did not hesitate to recommend the adoption of the new provisions on divorce. They were needed, he observed, because the old law had become obsolete; it was inconsistent and it challenged citizens to undergo, as he called it, humiliating formalities. A new law was needed that would correspond to the views that then prevailed in society. "Otherwise people might come to prefer other forms of sex relationship to that of marriage." This remark referred to those irregular unions commonly called "Stockholm marriages" and believed to be frequent among the working-class population of the cities.

The need for both Copenhagen divorces and Stockholm marriages was to be equally eliminated by frank recognition of the futility of efforts to prevent marriage breakdown by impeding divorce. In its report the Law Commission pointed at the experience generally observed abroad, especially in Germany, that most couples desiring a divorce seem to be willing to produce the necessary "evidence."

It is in general useless to try to maintain the formal tie between spouses whose inner relationship has deteriorated so thoroughly that no happy marital life can be expected any more. To require the parties to prove their discord to a court means to impose upon them hardship and discomfort. Very rarely would a judge find himself induced by such evidence to refuse the decree of separation. Dropping the requirement of such proof in cases of the parties' mutual consent simply means that their consensus is accepted as sufficient proof.

With these words the Law Commission justified the crucial provision of the draft under which a judicial separation and, upon the expiration of one year, a divorce would be pronounced whenever both parties to the marriage had agreed in the statement to the court that "they had found themselves unable to continue their relationship."

It was on this provision that conservative opposition concentrated, but all that the passionate critics within the Parliament and its ecclesiastical components could achieve was a modification of the words which did not affect the substance. As it now reads § 1 of chapter 11 makes it clear that the reason for the marriage termination is "deep and permanent discord which has rendered the parties unable to continue their marital life," but the existence of such discord is conclusively presumed from the fact that both spouses have agreed to apply for the separation. The principle of breakdown is thus made to appear the guiding policy, but in fact consent divorce is the legislative basis. Of a slightly more than merely rhetorical significance is the modification the opposition was able to achieve with respect to procedure. Under the draft it was not required that parties to a joint petition had previously submitted to an attempt at reconciliation. If no such attempt had been made prior to the filing of the joint petition, the draft provided that the proceedings be adjourned so as to give the parties an opportunity to see their pastor or a secular conciliator. But if they failed to avail themselves of that opportunity, the case would proceed to the decrees of separation and divorce. Upon conservative insistence the provision was altered so as to make it a condition for the court's accepting the parties' joint petition that they file with it a certificate from the pastor or the conciliator to the effect that an effort at conciliation had been made and failed. A motion to require a second conciliation attempt before a decree of separation was transformed into a final divorce, was defeated. Potentially, this change could be of practical significance. What it would actually amount to would depend on how seriously the conciliators took their tasks. In the course of events diversities turned out to exist in this respect, and diverging evaluations have been expressed. Expert opinion seems to incline to the view that the requirement of compusory attempts at conciliation has not resulted in hardship but has rather helped to inhibit hasty and insufficiently considered divorces. Present opinion also tends to observe, however, that a single attempt at a time when the decision jointly to approach the court has already been made is bound to have little effect. Marriage counseling, available at any time and carried on by experts, if necessary over long periods of time, is now regarded as more promising, provided it is not geared to persuading parties to continue or resume patently unsuccessful marriages.

The law was enacted on 11 November 1915 and re-enacted with slight modifications as the Marriage Law (*Giftermalsbalken*) of 11 June 1920, of which the provisions on divorce constitute the eleventh chapter. Its most prominent feature is the possibility of a marriage being terminated upon the joint petition of both parties. But the case must proceed in two steps. Upon their joint petition the parties must obtain a decree of separation which presupposes that they have agreed on the monetary aspects. Then, when a year has passed, the decree of divorce may be obtained as of right upon the unilateral petition of either party (§§ 1 and 3). The long-road tradition has thus been preserved.

The statute refrains from speaking of divorce by mutual consent. The divorce is rather made to appear as one granted upon the ground of deep and permanent discord, irrefutably proved by the parties' joint petition and their one-year factual separation following the first judicial decree.

The two-step procedure is also available to obtain a breakdown divorce upon one party's unilateral petition. The party who unilaterally applies for the decree of separation must prove that "in consequence of difference in temper and ideas, or of other circumstances, a deep and permanent discord has arisen between the parties." The text (§ 2, para. 2) goes on to provide that even where such proof is made, the court *must* refuse to grant the decree of separation where the petitioner "can reasonably be required to continue the marital relationship in view of his own conduct or because of other special circumstances."

Under § 2, para. 1, judicial separation upon unilateral petition and the subsequent termination of the marriage may be obtained by a party who proves that the other is guilty of flagrant neglect of his duty to support the petitioner or their children, or that he otherwise ignores his duties toward the petitioner or their children in a palpable manner, or that he is following a dissolute way of life. In such a case the court is given discretion to refuse the decree of separation for the same reasons for which it is ordered to refuse it in the case of § 2, para. 2.

In addition, the statute provides a list of grounds for divorce obtainable by a spouse upon his unilateral petition and without previous judicial separation.

Under § 4 either party may obtain a divorce, "where husband and wife have without decree of separation actually lived apart from each other on account of discord for at least three years." But if in such a case the termination of the marriage is contested by the other spouse, the court is given discretion to refuse the divorce if it deems it fit to do so "because of the petitioner's conduct or because of other special circumstances." As it has turned out, in Sweden such a refusal is almost unheard of, but in Denmark and Norway the proviso seems not to be entirely dead letter.

No judicial discretion to refuse a unilateral petition for divorce exists where the defendant has "willfully and without just cause kept himself away from the marital relationship for two years or more" (§ 5), or "where a spouse has been absent for three years or more under such circumstances that it is not known whether or not he is alive" (§ 6). An immediate divorce, i.e., termination of the bond without preceding decree of separation, may furthermore be obtained upon one party's unilateral petition where the other has exposed him to infection with venereal disease (§ 3) or where the other has been plotting against his life or has committed against him acts of severe physical cruelty (§ 10), or if the other spouse has been sentenced to serious punishment (§ 11). If one spouse is addicted to the immoderate use of alcoholic beverages or narcotics the court may grant the other an immediate divorce "if it finds some special reason for so doing" (§ 12). A divorce may be granted to a petitioner whose spouse has been insane for three years and there is no hope of permanent recovery (§ 13). Of course, there is also the old standby, adultery, to which there have been added "other punishable sexual acts" (§ 8) and the conclusion of a bigamous marriage (§ 7).

As shown in table 13, by far the largest number of Swedish divorces is obtained under § 3 as a sequel to a judicial separation obtained at least one year earlier either bilaterally or unilaterally. The number of

TABLE 13
MARRIAGE TERMINATIONS IN SWEDEN, 1956–68

	Judicial Separations	§ 3	Adultery	§ 4	Others
1956	9,248	6,809	1,096	487	216
1957	9,048	7,091	1.097	441	229
1958	9,233	6,913	1,081	454	209
1959	9,657	6,928	1,173	437	223
1960	9,221	7,242	1,117	412	181
1961	9,113	6,884	1,201	427	181
1962	9,428	7,056	1,186	426	181
1963	9,640	6,679	1,238	386	193
1964	10,537	7,276	1,311	391	191
1965	10,942	7,644	1,381	373	165
1966	11,537	8,293	1,424	424	127
1967	12,201	8,656	1,483	431	152
1968	13,622	9,029	1,413	420	149

Source: STATISTIK ÅRSBOK FÖR SVERIGE, ÅRGANG 53, 1966, table 39; 56, 1969, table 40.

short-road divorces obtained upon the ground of adultery is also considerable. The statistics do, of course, not indicate in how many cases adultery was the true psychological motive, or in how many it was staged or altogether fictitious. In the third place of frequency stands the divorce unilaterally obtained after three years of factual separation (§ 4).

The impression that discretion is not used to deny a decree is based upon information by Swedish experts. Decisions of trial courts are not published and matters of divorce are hardly ever carried up to the Supreme Court. During the entire period from 1915 to 1955, it seems that in only one case the Supreme Court held justified the judicial refusal of a separation. A man wished to legitimate his child by marrying its mother. But his petition to be separated from the wife to whom he had been married for some forty years was denied because through a divorce the wife would have lost the right after the petitioner's death to receive a widow's pension. Today the divorce would in all probability be granted because under more recent legislation survivor's benefits are no longer necessarily lost by divorce from the person through whom they are acquired. In certain circumstances the benefits may now be awarded to the former spouse or split between a former spouse and the spouse to whom the employee or civil servant is married at the time of his death.[15] In this way Sweden has remedied a situation in which other countries' judges find themselves faced with the distasteful dilemma of either depriving a deserving woman of what constitutes her sole or main support in old age, or refusing to regularize an irregular union of possibly long standing and to legitimate its offspring.

The Law of 1915–20 has retained, although in a significantly modified form, the old distinction between the short and the long roads to divorce. For the wide scope of discretion that once rested with the administration, firm legal rights to obtain a divorce have been substituted, although some measure of evaluation or even discretion has been given to the courts. If the courts had wished to do so, they might have used this power to reinforce the ancient doctrine of recrimination and to give the defendant spouse an effective veto. Under their corresponding statutes, the courts of Denmark and Norway are said occasionally to use their power to deny unilateral petitions for a divorce or separation, but in Sweden this power seems to have been relinquished. Swedish courts also tend to accept the fact that one party petitioned for judi-

---

15. Law of 28 May 1959 (SFS No. 287) 13 § 2.

cial separation as sufficient proof of the marriage being as profoundly and permanently disrupted as required by § 2 para. 2.

The courts are making so little use of their discretionary power because apparently most, or all, of the members of the judiciary are convinced that it is not possible for a court to obtain helpful information about imponderable aspects and matters of an intimate personal nature. Observation of life and literature seems to have convinced the judges that it is inane to search for guilt in matters of marital discord and that it is futile to attempt by governmental coercion to restore harmony among spouses who, by actually living apart from each other, have demonstrated that their marriage has become a failure. The individualist Swedish attitude is characterized by the absence of considerations of *praeventio generalis*. History, so it is believed, has disproved the thesis that people with marital difficulties might be induced to overcome them by the knowledge that freedom of remarriage is not easily obtainable. Examples illustrating the unreality of such a thesis were contained in the Law Commission's report. The conviction that marriage breakdown is caused by factors other than easy availability of divorce, and that it cannot be prevented by a strict divorce law, seems to have come to be generally accepted.

The view just stated is confirmed by the development of divorce practice in Denmark. While the law of that country coincides with that of Sweden in most respects, a few different features have been worked into Denmark's Marriage and Divorce Law of 30 June 1922. While administrative divorce has been abolished in Sweden, it has been retained as the normal procedure in Denmark. Petitions for separation and subsequent divorce are normally filed with an administrative office or with the Ministry of Justice, where all declarations and allegations of the parties are submitted in writing. If there is a dispute of fact or law that cannot be settled by the parties, the case is handled by a court, where an oral hearing may take place, usually in chambers.[16]

Almost always such disputes are concerned with child custody, alimony, child support, or property settlement. Even where resistance is allegedly made to the termination of the marriage, it is almost invariably a means to induce the party moving for the divorce to agree to the other party's terms on the custody and money issues. In those few cases which reach the courts, it is said that every now and then the divorce is denied either because the marriage is found not to be incurably disrupted or because special circumstances are thought to render ap-

---

16. See *supra* p. 131.

propriate the maintenance of the bond of a marriage that is concededly disrupted beyond repair.[17]

Another special feature of Denmark's law is the longer duration of the period between the first and second decrees. In Sweden that interval is one year, in Denmark a year and a half. It is regarded as probable that this difference in the laws is at least to some extent responsible for a conspicuous difference of statistical data (see table 14). In Sweden

TABLE 14
COMPARISON BETWEEN DISCORD AND ADULTERY AS GROUNDS FOR DIVORCE IN SWEDEN AND DENMARK
(Percent)

Years	Sweden		Denmark	
	Discord	Adultery	Discord	Adultery
1921–25	89	4	62	21
1926–30	91	3	69	21
1931–35	92	2	66	24
1936–40	93	2	62	31
1941–45	89	7	60	44
1946–50	88	9	48	46
1951–55	89	11	51	45

Source: Sipilä, *supra* table 9, at 40.
Note: Figures represent percent of all marriage terminations, except by death.

the overwhelming majority of divorces is based on the ground of deep and permanent discord. The percentage of adultery divorces has, although slightly rising, remained small. In Denmark, however, it has been both high and rising. In both countries divorce for discord has to follow the long road, which is longer in Denmark, while adultery divorce is obtainable by the short road, which in the case of an uncontested petition may be very short indeed. The data can hardly be regarded as indicating that adultery is more prevalent in Denmark than in Sweden. What they do seem to indicate is a greater readiness of Danes to resort to the short road even if it involves the admission of adultery. Perhaps this tendency is connected with the greater directness of the Danish administrative procedure. It is doubtful, however, that the difference also indicates a lessening of the disrepute of adultery in Denmark as compared with an increasing respectability in Sweden of those irregular unions which must wait a year after the first decree before they can be regularized.

17. See O. A. BORUM, FAMILIERETTEN 112 (2d ed. 1946).

Other differences have appeared in the statistical data. In Denmark, the divorce rate has been consistently higher than in Sweden, and there it has been higher than in either Norway or Finland.[18]

In contrast to the official law of the majority of American states, in the laws of the Scandinavian countries judicial investigation of guilt has been limited to that insignificant minority of cases in which a divorce is sought neither in mutual agreement of the parties nor upon immediate admission by the defendant in proceedings commenced unilaterally. Discussion of guilt has also been reduced to a minimum in the decision of the issue of child custody. As in the United States, the dominant formula declares the best interest of the children to be decisive. Only in cases of equal fitness of both parents is the court directed to consider the comparative guilt of the parties.[19] In actual practice, little, if any, application seems to be made of this provision. The courts read the statute as referring to "real" guilt rather than to formal guilt in the sense of concrete acts of cruelty, adultery, or desertion. They are convinced that it is next to impossible in a case of marriage breakdown to find out by which party's guilt it was "really" caused. Like American courts those of Sweden are thus inclined to follow the rules of thumb that custody of children of tender age be awarded to the mother and that weight should be attached to the wishes of older children.

Greater weight is ascribed to guilt in the statutory language on the problem of alimony. In deciding whether alimony should be granted to a wife and, if so, how much, the courts are ordered to consider both the wife's needs and the husband's capacity, as well as "other circumstances."[20] But then the statute adds: "However, no alimony shall be granted to the spouse who bears the principal guilt for the divorce." Again, the courts are reluctant to make use of the provision which would expose dirty linen to public view. Besides, how is a court to determine not only who is guilty in the real sense of the term, but *principally* guilty? Being less chivalrous than American judges have been for a long time, Swedish courts do not hesitate to refuse alimony

---

18. See *supra* p. 128.
19. Marriage Law, ch. 11, § 24.
20. § 29. A different standard is stated for the wife's separate maintenance before divorce. Since she is still his wife, the husband has to maintain her on the same standard on which she could live if there were no separation. But allowance is to be made for the increase in cost due to the necessity of supporting two separate households. It would be interesting to know how this provision works out in the case of a man whose income just suffices to maintain one household.

to a woman able to support herself. The chances for gold diggers are minimal.

The only context in which the Swedish courts pay attention to guilt is that of damages. Under § 24 of the statute, a spouse may be ordered to pay damages "when the decree of divorce is based upon conduct which has inflicted grave harm upon the marriage or where a previous decree of separation was based upon a serious breach of his duties toward the other spouse." By its wording, the provision eliminates the great mass of divorces obtained upon joint application. But in cases of divorce for cause damages are occasionally awarded to a wife if the court feels that in the property settlement she should receive more than one-half of the community property to which she is normally entitled. The provision is compatible with the general tendency to avoid painful and extended investigation into "real" guilt, because in cases of divorce for cause guilt must be ascertained at any rate. In evaluating the Swedish law on custody, property settlement, and alimony it is important to keep in mind that a judicial determination is made only in that minority of cases in which the parties have failed to settle their differences by their own agreement.

All the Scandinavian laws pay much attention to the possibility of avoiding divorce by means of compelling the parties to submit to attempts at conciliation. Conciliation must be resorted to before a joint petition for a first decree based upon "deep and permanent discord" will be accepted. In the comparatively rare cases of unilateral petition for divorce for cause, the failure of one party to appear before the conciliator can of course not be allowed to inhibit further proceedings. It suffices for the petitioner to prove that he has appeared before the conciliator and the other party had been properly summoned. If the defendant fails to heed the summons, a second attempt may be ordered by the court after the institution of the proceedings. If that summons again remains unheeded, the case will proceed.

This conciliation procedure is the modernized version of the ancient ecclesiastical admonition and warning procedure which once had to precede a petition to the king for dispensation to remarry. The law is thus framed upon the assumption that the pastor of the parties' parish is still the natural conciliator. But concessions had to be made to those alienated from the church, whose number was considerable as early as 1915. Cities and districts must provide secular conciliators for those who do not wish to appear before a pastor. In the major cities, conciliators are appointed by the city administration. They are usually lawyers, frequently appellate court judges, who act as conciliators in their spare time. Usually, at least one-half of the nonclerical conciliators are women. Not many conciliators are required; in Stockholm there were only six in 1955. For each case they receive a modest fee from the city — U.S. $3.00 — in 1955; to the parties in a case the services are gratuitous.

Upon the express application of a party, the court may appoint a mediator specially to act in an individual case. Such applications seem to be rare and, when they are made at all, to be limited to communities in which no general nonclerical conciliator is available. The great bulk of the cases is still handled by the ministers of the Lutheran State Church.[21]

The lay conciliators are appointed for three-year terms, and how carefully they are selected is indicated by the fact that from 1942 to 1949 the office of conciliator in Stockholm was held by a man who later became chief justice of Sweden.[22] But however eminent the official conciliator may be as lawyer and citizen, like most pastors of the church he lacks special training.

Under the law [23] married people may turn to the conciliator not only as a preliminary to judicial separation and divorce but also for the adjustment of disputes and quarrels they may wish to have settled just for the purpose of preserving their marriage. But as little use seems to be made of this opportunity as of its Swiss counterpart, where adjustment of marital quarrels belongs to the judge unless the canton or the municipality has a conciliator available. Parishioners may, of course, as of old, turn to their pastor for advice and counsel, but then they look upon him as their spiritual adviser rather than as conciliator within the meaning of the state's law. The law describes the functions of the conciliator rather vaguely. All it says is that "he shall try in a suitable manner to discover the cause of the discord or quarrel and to bring about a reconciliation." [24]

This vague statement is significant in that it does not charge the conciliator with the task of advising people on how to handle problems of child custody, property settlement, and support in the event the conciliator cannot bring about a reconciliation in the sense of persuading the party or parties to desist from the plan to terminate the

21. For parties belonging to some other religious denomination the minister of their congregation is the regular conciliator.
22. Mr. Nils Beckman.
23. Ch. 14, § 1.
24. Ch. 13, § 3. The law also expressly provides that the conciliator is bound to keep secret whatever is revealed to him by the parties and that he cannot be compelled to testify about communications made to him.

marriage. In this respect the Swedish system of conciliation, like that of France or Germany, essentially differs from that of Japan. One of the criticisms of the Swedish system of conciliation is to the effect that it embodies the view that the preservation of a marriage is good and its termination evil. This view, which was still potent in Sweden when the present law was enacted, is now widely regarded there as obsolete.

If one believes the purpose of the conciliation proceedings to be to dissuade divorce seekers from carrying out their intention, one may be induced to emphasize the fact that in the city of Stockholm the ratio between conciliation cases handled and petitions for separation/divorce filed annually has consistently been 5:4. This proportion cannot simply be regarded as indicating that 20 percent of all Stockholm conciliations have been "successful." It is not known in how many cases of these 20 percent the commencement of court proceedings in Stockholm has been omitted because of true reconciliations in the sense of the parties' actually reuniting, in how many cases such reconciliation has lasted beyond the three months before the expiration of which the conciliation effort must be followed by the filing of the petition with the court, and in how many cases no action was filed within that period because of death, removal from the city, or the parties' decision simply to continue to live separately without formalization by a judicial decree.

In a resolution adopted by the Association of Country Judges, conciliation proceedings were declared to be hardly more than an empty formality. This view seems to be shared by those lawyers, most of them women, by whom the bulk of divorce cases is handled and whose clients are said mostly to be impoverished, neglected, and overworked women. Typical in this respect is the following statement by a lawyer, Mrs. Sonja Branting Westerstrahl. In her work with legal aid clients she remembers seeing "nothing but a gray, hopeless, tragic sequence of marriages, for which divorce was the best or indeed the only possible solution." In this connection it seems to be significant that in Sweden alcoholism seems to be one of the most frequent causes of marriage breakdown. In a lecture summarizing his experience as a conciliator, Chief Justice Beckman stated that alcoholic husbands typically exhibit two diverse attitudes before the conciliator, either truculent obstinacy or abject contrition, both appearing in the same individual at different times. If the man happens to be in his pangs-of-conscience phase while he is with the conciliator, the wife may be open to persuasion to make another try. How long the penitent stage will last is another question.

How seriously a conciliator will take his task, what ideas he has about its usefulness, how persuasive he wishes to be, how much or how little he will be inclined to regard desistance from a plan of divorce as desirable, and how much understanding he will have for the parties' psychological, ethical, economic, social, or medical problems, all depend entirely on him. Clerical conciliators are or were regarded as being more generally inclined toward the traditional view of marriage as good and divorce as bad. However, the liberal-individualist view, which has come to permeate all walks of Swedish life, is by no means infrequent among the clergy of the Lutheran State Church, whose members are also seeking to be better prepared for those counseling activities which are now occupying a considerable part of their professional time. A handbook on marriage counseling, containing contributions by representatives of various disciplines, was published by Dean A. Anderberg of Uppsala Cathedral,[25] and counseling has begun to appear in the curriculums of the theological faculties of Swedish universities.

To supplement the system of conciliation with one of marriage counseling, or even to substitute counseling for conciliation, has thus come to be a postulate. Counseling is regarded as superior to conciliation in several respects. The marriage counselor helps his client in each case to find that adjustment which appears best to suit his individual situation. Rather than to aim at patching up marital troubles regardless of circumstances, the marriage counselor may well regard other solutions as preferable. But the counselor's chances of curing a sick marriage are better than those of the conciliator. The latter is rarely approached before the legal papers have all been prepared by the lawyers, who may have gone through lengthy negotiations to bring about the agreement between the parties about child custody, support, and property matters without which the court cannot treat the petition for separation. At that stage the parties' decision is not likely to be reversed by the often perfunctory effort of the conciliator. The parties are also likely to have obtained from their lawyers the impression that the conciliation attempt is just a formality to be got through as quickly and painlessly as possible. Another criticism of old-style conciliation points at the fact that a personal meeting before the conciliator may at that late stage be painful for hostile or estranged spouses. For this reason, or in order to save a party the expenses and the loss of time connected

25. MEDLING I ÄKTENSKAP (1950).

with a journey to a place different from that of a new home, a conciliator may occasionally find it sufficient to communicate with one of the parties over the telephone or by correspondence. Nowhere in the statute is it expressly prescribed that the conciliator see the parties simultaneously or even that he see them at all,

Of particular importance is the fact that the marriage counselor has gone through a special course of training to enable him to spot each client's particular problems, to recognize which course of action is most suitable for the case, and, as is so often necessary, to refer the client to a psychotherapist or other expert for special advice or possibly for extended treatment.

Sweden has not yet developed marriage counseling as a recognized and organized profession. But some projects started in Stockholm have begun to emerge from the experimental stage into maturity. An important step was taken in 1960, when the Swedish Parliament passed an ordinance authorizing state-subsidized family counseling bureaus.[26] Under this ordinance, a municipality or town can receive financial assistance from the government for the establishment of centers for counseling in matrimonial and family problems which may engage comprehensively in all kinds of family counseling or specialize in counseling on family planning and abortion or marital and premarital counseling, and which have on their staff such experts as social workers, psychiatrists, or other physicians. Their services are to be rendered free of charge and all members of the staff are bound to treat as confidential all matters coming to their knowledge in the course of their activities. The large number of trained personnel that is needed is not yet fully available. The advisability of uniting in one office counseling on abortion and marriage counseling has met with some doubts.

Denmark also requires that an attempt at reconciliation be made as a preliminary to the filing of a petition for separation on the ground of "deep and permanent discord," be it, as is usual, jointly made by both spouses or by only one of them. Conciliators are pastors of the Lutheran State Church or special officials on the staff of the administrative agency by which the majority of Danish divorces is handled. The latter, being specialists, tend to be more experienced than the nonecclesiastical conciliators of Sweden. The system has nevertheless been widely criticized. Marriage counseling is regarded as better adapted to present needs than the conciliation system, which, after all, is a relic from the preindividualistic age. Marriage counseling services are carried on extensively by a branch of the comprehensive service system of the

26. Royal Decree of 2 December 1960 (SFS No. 710).

Danish welfare state, the Mother's Aid Centers. First established in 1939, these centers were initially meant to give advice and assistance to pregnant women, wed and unwed, and to mothers of newborn children. The offices which presently exist in the country as agencies of the Ministry of Social Welfare have gradually expanded their activities so as to cover matters of abortion, birth control, paternity, adoption, educational counseling, premarital counseling, and marriage counseling. Plans to overhaul the ancient system of conciliation and, eventually, to merge it with the work of the Mother's Aid Centers are under consideration.

As a by-product, the system of conciliation has provided opportunities of observation not easily available to a judge. The courts rarely if ever try to search for the true causes of the marital discord on the basis of which they pronounce their decrees. A conscientious and thoughtful conciliator can obtain glimpses or even insights into what really lies behind marriage breakdown. Mr. Nils Beckman took good advantage of this opportunity when he was one of the conciliators of Stockholm. His impressions are presented in an as yet unpublished lecture, a summary of which may be given here. The main points are:

> Contrary to widely held opinion, divorce is more common among working-class people than among the upper class. Among the latter frequent divorce is characteristic only of a small clique.
>
> The initiative for putting an end to a marriage rests to a large extent with the woman. She takes the step when hopes have faded for a change in the character of an alcoholic, an intemperate, or in a man who turns out incapable of holding a steady job.
>
> Trouble with in-laws figures prominently among the causes of marriage breakdown.

In this survey of foreign countries, Scandinavia, especially Sweden, has been chosen because of the opportunity to observe the changes in the law and practice of divorce which are concomitant with a shift of social climate from Christian traditionalism to fully established individualist liberalism. Scandinavia was a comparative latecomer in Europe's rise of civilization. Not until the end of the first millennium A.D. was Christianity fully established there. With the possible exception of Denmark, Scandinavia long played a role in history more through the Norsemen's depredations in other lands, the establishment of new nations in Normandy, England, Russia, and Sicily, and the poetic preservation of ancient Germanic myths. But the Scandinavian countries were among the first to accept the Reformation and the only ones to remain almost totally unaffected by the Counter-Reformation. Through Gustavus Adolphus's intervention in the Thirty Years War,

Sweden became a Continental power with possessions on what are now the Soviet, the Polish, and the German coasts of the Baltic Sea. The ideas of humanism and the Enlightenment found early entrance into Sweden and ready acceptance among the intellectuals. All through the eighteenth century English and French influences vied with each other for predominance in the political scene and, through and with it, in the intellectual life of the country. French influence became dominant in Scandinavia just when the new, liberal ideas had reached the height of their influence in France. The firmly established Lutheran State Church was, of course, committed to the traditional morals of Christianity, but even in the clergy liberalism achieved an early foothold among the theologians of Uppsala.

This general development of Sweden's intellectual climate is reflected in its law of divorce. Save for the exceptions admitted by Luther, marriage was on principle indissoluble. Matters of marriage, as of old, belonged to the sphere of religion. The clergy was the guardian of the sex morals and the marital life of the people. It exercised its function by means of church discipline, if necessary with the help of the secular arm of the government. But secularization of rules regarding sex morals and marriage was imperceptible by virtue of the fact that the king was the head of the church, which itself was but a part of the total government of the country. The king would grant dispensation on the basis of which the cathedral chapters of the church would issue letters of divorcement, which, in turn, would authorize the clergy to engage in that ceremony without which a fully recognized remarriage would not be possible. The royal practice of granting dispensation was never extensive, but in view of the smallness of the population it was by no means insignificant. Its importance was enhanced by the fact that practically no people other than those of the socially and politically significant classes would ever resort to the device. To be divorced was not exactly praiseworthy, but the fact that dispensation came from the king gave the institution of divorce a certain aura of respectability. While liberalism became influential in the Swedish bourgeoisie at an early time, it did not obtain political dominance until the twentieth century, which broke the political predominance in the Parliament of the nobility in the first and the peasants in the second chamber.

The Swedish divorce law of the turn of the century was typical of a country in which an intellectually and morally potent liberalism had not yet succeeded in overcoming the political power of traditionalism. Inevitably such a society develops a dualist divorce law: a strict law of the books and a lenient law in action. Inevitably, in circles to which divorce is not easily available, a tendency will grow up to resort to unions other than legitimate marriage. The Swedish species were the Copenhagen divorce of the well-to-do and the Stockholm marriage of those who could not afford the cost of divorce.

In the Law of 1915, the shift of political dominance from traditionalism to liberalism found official expression. The Law and its counterparts in the other Scandinavian countries were typical products of liberalism. But, in keeping with the temper of the time of enactment, these laws did not go the full way. Concessions were made to the traditionalist view, which was still of some influence in 1915. The Law contains a long list of causes of divorce in the ancient sense of the *principle of offense*; divorce on the ground of *breakdown* proceeds through two stages with a minimum interval of one year or, in Denmark, one year and a half; consent divorce is dressed up as divorce based upon "deep and permanent discord"; all separation-divorces other than for cause must be preceded by an official attempt at reconciliation; discretion is given to the diverse granting agencies to refuse restoration to the freedom of marriage because of special circumstances or, in reminiscence of the old doctrine of recrimination, because of the petitioner's own conduct; except in the case of a petition filed in mutual agreement of the parties, the ground alleged by the petitioner must be proved by him, and the court is supposed not to be satisfied with the mere allegations or admissions of the parties.

Most of these concessions to traditionalism have been reduced to a mere paper existence. As in other parts of the world the courts simply make no use of their investigatory powers. As in France, Germany, or California, the concept of cruelty has been so broadened as to cover all behavior of a spouse that is alleged by the other to be obnoxious to him, and evidence of such behavior is readily accepted. In Scandinavia the wording of the statute indicates a duty of the divorce-granting agency to investigate, if necessary *proprio motu*, whether the marriage is really disrupted deeply and permanently. Danish and Norwegian executive agencies occasionally engage in such investigation. In Sweden one party's unilateral allegation of deep and permanent discord is given by the court more or less the same conclusive effect that by the text of the law is ascribed to the fact that the parties have petitioned jointly.

The deterrent effect of the statutory waiting period is widely eliminated, at least in Denmark, by resorting to adultery as the ground predominantly alleged. Conciliation tends to be regarded as a superfluous formality. To all practical effects, Scandinavia has made available that combination of consent divorce and possibility of unilateral divorce which constitutes fulfillment of the demands of individualist liberalism. In accordance with these postulates, the attention of lawmakers and law appliers has shifted to the handling of the consequences of marriage breakdown. The understanding that the law in general, and the divorce law in particular, does not effectively deter the realization of a desire to terminate a distasteful marriage, is now generally accepted. It is regarded as the function of the law to mitigate the consequences, and the possibility of a new life through a legal remarriage is believed to be among the most effective remedies, and to benefit the parties themselves as well as their children. If the causes of marriage breakdown are to be kept within bounds, marriage counseling and family-life education are regarded as effective means, together with a comprehensive scheme of measures designed to relieve the individual citizen of those disruptive catastrophes of the economy or of health which experience has shown release a chain of events likely to end in the breakdown of personalities, of marriages, and of homes. The steadiness of the Swedish divorce rate over the two decades from 1945 to 1965 seems to indicate that these efforts have not been without success. Consistently the Swedish divorce rate of 1.2 per 1,000 population has been just slightly above one-half of the divorce rate of the United States, where the law, at least of the books, has by no means been a consistent expression of liberalist individualism.

In Sweden liberalism seems to have been helped in its ascendancy to official expression in the law by special characteristics of the social and political structure of the country which constitutes a marked difference to that of the United States. Both Sweden and the United States are fully established democracies, but Sweden is not a mass democracy. Traditionalist elements are still conspicuous in Sweden, among the upper classes and, even more so, among the peasantry. In a country of mass democracy such elements may be able to prevent the liberalization of the divorce law of the books. If in such a country liberalism is strong, the compromise will be worked out in the courts rather than the legislature and the law in action will cease to correspond to the law of the books. This is what has happened in Germany, in France, and in the United States. In Sweden, political life is determined by a *valentior pars* which is almost uniformly liberal and whose foothold on political leadership is so firm that it can disregard nonliberal views held by even sizable segments of the public. Divisions between political parties are determined more by notions of economic policy than of *Weltanschauung*. The candidates presented to even the traditionalist voters are likely to be liberals in their basic value attitudes, irrespective of whether they are labeled Social Democrat or People's party or even Right Wing party. The leaders of the Social Democrats may be collectivist in economic matters; in matters of personal life in general, and of sex and family life in particular, they have been faithful to Engels's postulate of a society in which a strong family life grows in and through marriages which are based upon mutual love and affection and upon full equality of the sexes. The leaders of the "bourgeois" parties tend to be intellectuals whose views on matters of freedom of personality, equality of the sexes, and the ideal of marriage based on love and affection are unlikely to differ from those of the Social Democrats. Fundamentalists, of whom there are quite a few in Sweden, have little chance to find political expressions of their views on sex.

The intellectuals who represent the Swedish counterpart of the New Left are the originators of the project of radical family law reform now (i.e., in 1970) under consideration in Sweden. A report of the minister of justice, Mr. Kling, was placed before the cabinet on 15 August 1969. As published by the newspapers, its key part is as follows:

The new legislation should as far as possible be neutral in its relationship to various forms of cohabitation and different moral ideas. Marriage has, and ought to have, a centred place in family law, but one should attempt to see that the family legislation does not contain any provisions which create unnecessary difficulties for, or burden upon, those who beget children or start a family without marrying.

To some extent, nonmarital relationships have already been assimilated to marriage. Under social security laws a concubine's position is not much different from that of a lawfully wedded wife. In the practice of inheritance taxation a concubine is not subject to the high tax levied upon a stranger to the decedent, but only to the lower tax levied upon the share in an estate passing to an unpaid servant, and a lawsuit is now pending in which it is claimed that the concubine's share be subject to the still lower tax payable out of the share passing to the decedent's widow. The equation of concubinage with marriage in the views of society is strikingly illustrated by the fact that Mr. Per Albin Hansson, who was Sweden's prime minister from 1932 to 1946, was never married to the woman with whom he lived, but she was without question treated as the lady ranking right after the members of the royal house, in the official government directory she is listed as his widow, and she has the unquestioned right to receive the pension due a prime minister's widow.

Whether a Swedish attempt to free sexual unions from the bonds of governmental regulation and to treat them purely as affairs of free individual love will be more successful than the analogous attempt made in the early years of the Russian Revolution will have to await the future.

7
Marriage Breakdown in a Divorceless Country: Italy

Even though divorce is easy in Japan and the Scandinavian countries, its incidence is not identical with that of marriage breakdown. Divorce is neither necessary nor even possible in the case of failure of a Japanese *nayen*-marriage. In both Japan and Scandinavia, Roman Catholics, whose numbers are small, may content themselves with legal or factual separation rather than resort to severing the bond. One couple or another may just forget about divorce because there is no desire for remarriage, or out of protest against the sociopolitical system of which marriage and divorce are parts, or for financial reasons, or just out of indifference. But by and large we can assume that in Japan and Scandinavia the number of divorces approximates that of the cases of marriage breakdown.

The opposite situation prevails in Italy. Until 1 December 1970, the institution of divorce did not exist, and whether it exists now is a question of Italian constitutional law not yet settled. So the number of divorces has been zero; that of cases of factual marriage breakdown amounts to several hundred thousand. In the report accompanying the draft divorce law introduced in the Senate on 12 June 1958 by Senators Luigi Renato Sansone and Giuliana Nenni, it was estimated that the number of married couples living in Italy at the time whose life in common has been permanently ended by separation or abandonment was about 600,000.[1] Alfredo Todisca estimated that in 1954 about 70,000–80,000 inhabitants of Milan, and about 1,000,000 inhabitants of Italy as a whole lived in so-called irregular unions, i.e., relations of

---

1. See reprints of the report in MARIO BERUTTI, IL DIVORZIO IN ITALIA 151, 159 (1964) (hereinafter cited as BERUTTI); and in 7 I PROBLEMI DI ULISSE (anno 13), 67, at 68 (June 1960).

concubinage in which one party, or both of them, were married to persons other than the de facto companion.[2]

In his report on the two draft bills introduced in 1958 into the Chamber of Deputies by Messrs. Fortuna and Spagnioli respectively and combined into one bill by the Fourth Permanent Commission, the reporter for the majority, Deputy Lenoci, conceding that statistics are not always reliable, expressed himself as follows:

Just by way of approximation, we may remember that in 1964, Mr. Sansone, when he presented his bill on the so-called "little divorce," indicated that the number of separated couples in Italy amounted to about 600,000. Since then numbers of applications for judicial separations filed every year have been 14,000, and of judgments rendered 10,000. To the 600,000 one thus has to add another 140,000 so that the total is 740,000. According to reliable estimates, each case of judicial separation corresponds to three cases of factual separation. To the 740,000 one has then to add about another 420,000. We thus have in Italy some 1,160,000 separated couples, which means some 2,300,000 separated persons.

However, one has to make some subtractions from, and some additions to, these figures. One must subtract the number of approximately 400,000 who have died since 1964, and add the approximately 500,000 "white widows," i.e., the wives of those emigrants who have established for themselves new families abroad. No doubt can exist about that last figure. It has been established on the basis of a census of governmental inspiration and is accepted by the National Catholic Association for Emigrant Families.

We thus have in Italy a total of 2,500,000 separated persons. About one-third of them have established new illegal families. The new "spouse" and the offspring participate in the situation of being "outsiders of the law of marriage" [fuorilegge del matrimonio]. No less than 5,000,000 people are thus involved in the tragedy of indissolubility and have to suffer its consequences. . . .

If one compares statistics, one finds that in Italy the number of separations is higher than that of divorces in other countries.

In Great Britain the divorce rate is 0.52 per 1,000 population, in France 0.59, in Poland 0.53, in Belgium 0.40. In Italy the rate of separations is 0.70; one person of every 1,400 resorts to separation.

These figures are reported by Gabriella Parca, who recently conducted an inquiry of a limited, but representative sample of 250 separated persons, in which she considered the social composition of the Italian population, its geographical distribution as well as the groupment by age (*I separati, inchiesta sul matrimonio in Italy*, ed. Rizzoli).[3]

As in other parts of Catholic Europe, the regulation of the incidents of marriage was regarded as a task of secular government in the con-

---

2. Article published in LA STAMPA of 4 April 1954, noted by BERUTTI 75.
3. Camera dei Deputati, V. Legislatura, N. 1-467-A, presented on 30 April 1969, pp. 12, 13.

geries of states which in the eighteenth century covered the area of the present Republic of Italy. But the bond of marriage being regarded as a matter of religious concern, its regulation was left to the church, its laws and its courts. Marriage being indissoluble in the view of the church, divorce could, of course, not exist. In those cases in which a marriage might be found to have been incurably defective in its inception, it might be declared null and void by an ecclesiastical court. But once a marriage had been validly concluded, no court of the church could terminate it,[4] no other court had anything to do with the matter, and the old Roman way of terminating a marriage, by the parties' own act and without necessity of intervention of any court or other public agency, had long been outlawed.

In France, the incipient secularization of marriage while prompted by the Gallicanist desire to establish a minimum influence of royal government upon society's most basic relationship, was completed by the Revolution and confirmed by Napoleon's legislation. With the secularization of marriage came the possibility of its termination by divorce, as it had been postulated by the *philosophes* of the Enlightenment and their revolutionary followers.[5] The victorious armies of the French Republic and of Napoleon brought the new secular law to Italy. After 1795, compulsory civil marriage and the possibility of divorce were introduced in practically all parts of Italy. However, not much use seems to have been made of divorce. For the kingdom of Naples, which covered the southern part of the peninsula and the island of Sicily, Benedetto Croce could find evidence of no more than three divorces, of which only one seems to have been followed by the remarriage of one of the parties.[6] The official law of marriage was of little concern to the masses. Among the upper classes the men had easy ways to find satisfactory pleasures outside of marriage, and the women were accustomed to suffering in silence.

As soon as the Napoleonic rule was broken, the unpopular institution of divorce was abolished. In most of the Italian states the secularization of marriage was undone and the rule of the church's law and the church's courts was restored. In those parts of northern Italy which were incorporated in the Austrian monarchy and where thus the Austrian General Civil Code of 1811 was in effect,[7] the system of regulat-

4. Except in the rare cases of *matrimonium ratum sed non consumatum* and of the *privilegium Paulinum*. See *supra* chap. 2.
5. See *infra* chap. 8.
6. ANEDDOTI E PROFILI SETTECENTESCHI (Naples, 1914) 315 ff., cited by BERUTTI 20.
7. I.e., the present regions of Lombardy, Vento, Venezia Giulia, and Trentino-Alto Adige.

ing marriage by the secular power was retained, but, as to divorce, the government of his Apostolic Majesty, the Emperor of Austria, adapted its secular law to the religious ideas of the principal denominations of the empire. Divorce remained available to a limited extent to non-Catholic Christians, of whom there were practically none in the Italian provinces. Jews could terminate their marriages by mutual agreement, and a Jewish man could repudiate his adulterous wife.[8] For Catholics, marriage was to be as indissoluble under the secular law as it would be under the canon law of the church;[9] and practically all the people of the Italian provinces were Catholic.[10]

In the struggles of the Revolution of 1848 and the wars of the Risorgimento, Austrian rule and domination were broken, and in 1861 Italy was united under the king of the house of Savoy. Even before the unification was completed in 1870 with the annexation of the Papal States and the transfer to Rome of the seat of the government, a new Civil Code was promulgated in 1865 for the then kingdom of Italy.[11] Through it, secular regulation of marriage by the state was established. Civil marriage became compulsory, as in France, so that no relation that was to be regarded as a marriage could henceforth be concluded in any way other than that of a secular ceremony before the mayor of the municipality or his delegate. If parties wished to do so, they might still go through a marriage ceremony in church, but that ceremony was to have no effect within the realm of the law of the state.[12] Yet, as the

---

8. Austrian General Civil Code of 1811, § 115.
9. *Id.* §§ 133–35.
10. *Id.* § 111. When the Republic of Austria joined Germany in 1938, the marriage law of the Austrian civil code of 1811 was replaced by the marriage law for Greater Germany (*Grossdeutsches Ehegesetz*), of 6 July 1938 (RGBl. I 807). It established a uniform law for all denominations, with liberal rules on divorce. With slight modification, the law is still in effect in Austria, which in 1949 had the highest divorce rate (1.8 per 1,000 population) of those European countries which published statistics on divorce. The Austrian divorce rate was 1.12 in 1962, 1.14 in 1963, 1.16 in 1964–65, and 1.19 in 1966 (U.N. DEMOGRAPHIC YEARBOOK 1966, table 26). In the parts of Italy which were ceded by Austria after World War I (South Tyrol, Trento, Venezia Giulia), Italian marriage law was introduced by the Decree of 4 November 1928, no. 2325.
11. In 1870, the Code was extended to the province of Rome and in 1871 to the provinces of Mantua and Venice. On the unification of the private law of Italy, see A. AQUARONE, L'UNIFICATIONE LEGISLATIVA DEI CODICI DEL 1865 (1960); M. CAPPELLETTI, J. H. MERRYMAN & J. M. PERILLO, THE ITALIAN LEGAL SYSTEM 45 (1967).
12. Cf. Civil Code of 1865, arts. 93, 117. Unlike the laws of Germany or other countries requiring a secular ceremony as an indispensable requirement of a legally valid marriage, Italian law did not prohibit the clergy from performing a religious marriage ceremony before the performance of the secular. Various later efforts to establish such a prohibition met with failure. See ARTURO CARLO JEMOLO, IL MATRIMONIO 33 (3d ed. 1957). For Italians who were satisfied with their marriage being valid within the religious realm, it thus remained possible to enter upon unions which,

Austrian Code had done for Catholics, the new Italian Code declared the tie of marriage to be indissoluble.[13] Indeed, going beyond the Austrian precedent, marriage was henceforth to be indissoluble for all Italians, including the small group of non-Catholics. The principle of indissolubility seems to have corresponded with the spirit of the times. There was no powerful public demand to introduce an institution which was alien to the tradition of the Catholic nation and which could be dispensed with by those who made use of the traditionally available substitutes for divorce: keeping a mistress; resort to prostitutes; separation with or without establishing an "irregular union"; emigration or other disappearance combined with bigamy.

Italy's unification through the house of Savoy and its prime minister, Cavour, had been achieved in conflict with the pope, who lost his sovereignty over the Papal States and objected to the substitution of Cavour's principle of a free church in a free state for the hitherto prevailing supremacy of the church.[14] The pope withdrew into self-imposed imprisonment at the Vatican. Church and state remained in a state of enmity that made it troublesome for Catholic believers to participate in the life of the new nation, provoked disputes between secular and ecclesiastical authorities, and continued to poison the political life of the country. But no liberal government could pay the price demanded by the church for reconciliation, within which restoration of the pope as a territorial sovereign and return of marriage to ecclesiastical regulation occupied prominent positions. Benito Mussolini was willing to pay the price and able to reduce it in at least the first-named respect.[15] The pope was restored to sovereign rule over a territory of his own, but that territory was to be limited to the tiny state of Vatican City,

---

while constituting marriages from the point of view of the church, were mere concubinage from the point of view of the state and its law. The occurrence of such relationships seems to have been frequent, especially among people to whom questions of title to property were of little concern.

The arguments which were made at the time for the system of compulsory civil marriage are summarized by JEMOLO, *supra*, at 29 ff. They make interesting reading at the present time in which the system, regarded as indispensable in the 1860s, has been abandoned in favor of a system under which religious marriage is normal.

Three significant newspaper articles of the time are reprinted in AQUARONE, *supra* note 11, at 314 ff.

13. Civil Code of 1865, art. 148.
14. See G. D'AMELIO, STATO E CHIESA: LA LEGISLAZIONE ECCLESIASTICA FINO AL 1867 (1961).
15. On the "reconciliation" in general, see E. P. Y. HALES, PIO NONO (1954); M. FALCO, THE LEGAL POSITION OF THE HOLY SEE BEFORE AND AFTER THE LATERAN AGREEMENTS (1935); A. Bertola, *Accordi Lateranensi*, 1 NOVISSIMO DIGESTO ITALIANO 149 (1957), and the extensive literature listed there.

i.e., the palace of the Vatican, its gardens, Saint Peter's Church, and the square in front of it, together with a few noncontiguous churches in Rome and the country estate of Castel Gandolfo.

Whether, in the field of marriage, the price was paid fully or not, is a matter of controversy. Within the complex and extensive body of the Lateran Treaties of 11 February 1929, a central position is occupied by article 34 of the Concordat, the first paragraph of which reads as follows:

> The Italian State wishes to restore to the institution of marriage, which is the foundation of the family, that dignity which corresponds to the Catholic traditions of the people. It therefore attributes the civil effects of the sacrament of marriage as it is regulated by the Canon Law.

The position of the church, maintained for Italy as well as the world at large, then and until the Second Vatican Council and, perhaps, still today, had been firmly expressed by Pope Pius IX in the Syllabus of Errors attached to his encyclical *Quanta cura*, of 8 December 1864:

> It is an error and it is not permissible for a Catholic to believe that the sacrament of marriage is a mere accessory to, and is separable from, the contract or that marriage can occur between Christians by virtue of a mere civil contract or that controversies concerning marriage or promise of marriage [*sponsalia*] belong by their nature to the secular jurisdiction.

Under this view, the secularization of marriage that was performed by the Code of 1865 was heretical. But not even Mussolini was willing to concede a complete reversal. In the course of the lengthy negotiations by which the Lateran Treaties were prepared, the church had to make a concession, which must be regarded as of little importance in view of the fact that non-Catholics constitute but a minority in Italy and that Italian Catholics are accustomed to celebrating their marriages in church even if in their political views they are opposed to clericalism in the sense of political power aspirations of the clergy. Under the compromise thus worked out an Italian may choose between concluding his marriage in religious or in civil form.[16] Civil marriage remained possible in Italy, but, under the new scheme, it is no longer compulsory. Any Italian belonging to a denomination recognized by the state may celebrate his marriage in the form made available by

---

16. On the Italian law of marriage under the Concordat and the Civil Code of 1942, see JEMOLO, *supra* note 12; M. LUZZATI, IL MATRIMONIO IN ITALIA (1967); A. Bertola, *Matrimonio-diritto civile*, 10 NOVISSIMO DIGESTO ITALIANO 340 (1964); M. Miele, *Matrimonio-diritto internazionale privato, ibid.* 403; M. Piacentini, *Matrimonio degli acattolici, ibid.* 429; A. Bertola, *Matrimonio religioso, ibid.* 439; see also the extensive bibliographies contained in these articles.

that denomination. Valdensians and Protestants may thus be married by their ministers, Jews may marry in the Jewish form, and Catholics in the Catholic — and Catholics are 98.8 percent of the Italian population.[17]

Under the basic rule as stated in article 34 of the Concordat, the civil effects automatically attach to the sacrament of marriage as regulated by canon law, and the sacrament of marriage as regulated by canon law requires the conclusion of marriage in the form prescribed by canon law, i.e., according to *Codex juris canonici*, canon 1094, celebration before a priest of the church. As soon as concluded in this way, the relationship is a marriage not only in the contemplation of the church but also in that of the state. It is not only that intercourse between the parties is legitimate rather than sinful, as it would be if the parties were not united in religiously lawful wedlock. It also means the rise of those incidents which together constitute marriage in the sense of the secular law of the Italian state: legitimacy of the offspring, mutual rights and duties of support, rights of social security, rights of succession upon death, etc.[18]

The coordination of the principle of the Concordat with the legal order of the Italian state presented thorny problems. The state was unwilling to let the church create marriages that would contradict principles of public policy regarded as fundamental. It was also anxious to maintain the integrity, unity, and reliability of its registers of civil status. The fact that a person has gone through a civil ceremony of marriage with one person does not constitute a canon law impediment to a Catholic marriage with another person, even if the partner of the prior ceremony is still alive. In the church's view the relation created by the civil ceremony is in the case of a baptized person not a marriage at all. From the church's point of view, such a person is free to enter upon a true marriage, i.e., one concluded before a priest in accordance with canon law. But from the state's point of view the act of going

---

17. 1970 CATHOLIC ALMANAC 442.

18. According to article 8 of the Law of 27 May 1929, no. 847 (Gaz. Uff. 8 June, no. 133), the priest has to read before the parties the following articles of the Civil Code:

Art. 143. Marriage imposes upon the parties the duties of living together, of fidelity and of mutual assistance.

Art. 144. The husband is the head of the family; the wife follows his civil status, takes his family name, and is bound to accompany him to whatever place he regards as appropriate for establishing his residence.

Art. 145. The husband is bound to protect his wife, to keep her with him and to provide her with all that is necessary for those needs of life which correspond to his means.

The wife must contribute to the support of her husband when his means are insufficient.

through a second ceremony cannot initiate a valid marriage but constitutes the crime of bigamy.[19]

Discrepancies also exist between the state's and the church's law concerning mental capacity to marry. Under the state's law a person judicially declared to be mentally incompetent is incapable of marrying.[20] Under canon law, the judicial declaration of mental incompetence is as such irrelevant with respect to marriage. A person judicially declared to be mentally incompetent can enter upon a marriage valid under canon law if at the moment of the ceremony he knows what he is doing and understands the meaning of the institution of marriage.

The Italian state law of marriage and canon law differ in other respects, but only the two features just mentioned appeared sufficiently important to the state for it to deny the civil effects to a marriage affected with either one of them, even though the marriage was valid under canon law. The mechanism for denying "civil effects," is the system of registration of civil status, in the integrity of which the Italian state has expressed a paramount interest.

If a couple wishes to enter upon marriage before a priest of the Catholic church, they must not only fulfill all the formal and substantive requirements of the canon law, which regularly include the publication of bans at the parish church,[21] but they are also supposed to obtain from the state's registrar of civil status a certificate showing that the two impediments of state law just mentioned are absent.[22] Before the certificate is issued the registrar must place the banns at the door of the city or village hall for ten days, including two Sundays, and if he learns that a party to the intended marriage has previously gone through a civil or a non-Catholic religious marriage which has not yet been effectively terminated, he must refuse the issuance of the certificate. The same situation prevails if a party is a person judicially declared incompetent.

Immediately upon the performance of a ceremony of marriage the priest must send to the registrar of civil status a copy of the certificate, which is to be recorded by the registrar. But recordation is to be refused if the registrar now learns that a party is a person judicially declared incompetent or still bound by a civilly valid prior marriage. Without registration upon the state's register no marriage concluded before a

19. Civil Code, art. 86; Criminal Code, art. 556.
20. Civil Code, art. 85.
21. CODEX JURIS CANONICI, canons 1022 ff.
22. Law for the implementation of the Concordat, of 27 May 1929, no. 847, art. 7.

Catholic priest can be effective within the sphere of the state's law. Only when it is registered does it have these effects retroactively, as of the day of the ceremony.[23] This denial of the civil effects to certain marriages which under the church's view fulfill all the sacrament may not be in full accordance with the terms of the Concordat, but the church has not seen fit to protest.

With respect to the two kinds of marriage disapproved by the state in spite of their constituting the sacrament of the church, the state's law of implementation of the Concordat also establishes an exception from the Concordat's principle that matters of nullity concerning marriages celebrated before a Catholic priest be handled exclusively by the courts of the church. The annihilation of a marriage of a person judicially declared to be mentally incompetent, and of a marriage which is bigamous under the law of the state but not under that of the church, belongs to the jurisdiction of the courts of the state.

Just as the secular validity of a marriage celebrated before a Catholic priest depends upon an act of the state, namely, its registration, an ecclesiastical judgment or decree of nullity or of dispensation from an unconsummated marriage does not become effective in the sphere of the state's law until it has been declared to have such effect by the state's appellate court having jurisdiction *ratione loci*. An ecclesiastical judgment or decree is thus treated like a judgment of a court of a foreign country, which also can have no effect in Italy until it has been declared effective by the proper Italian appellate court.[24] In order to facilitate the task of the Italian state's court the Concordat provides that the judgments and decrees of the courts and authorities of the church are to be submitted to the highest tribunal of the Holy See, the Supreme Court of the Signatura, which is to certify the proper observation of canon law rules on jurisdiction, service of process, and default.

Prima facie the situation seems not to be much different from that existing under the laws of all American states, the United Kingdom, Scandinavia, and a good many other countries under which parties may also choose between civil and religious conclusion of their marriages. However, there are weighty differences.

First, under the Italian scheme, the validity of a marriage concluded before a Catholic priest is determined for the spheres of both church

23. Civil Code of 1942, art. 2; Law of 27 May 1929, no. 143 (Gaz. Uff. 8 June, no. 133).
24. Code of Civil Procedure, arts. 796 ff.

and state by the law of the church.[25] Under the American scheme, the validity of a marriage for the sphere of the state's law is always determined by the state's courts and under the state's law, even though the marriage was concluded in religious form.

If the marriage ceremony has been performed before a priest of the Roman Catholic church and the validity of the marriage is subsequently drawn into question by one of the parties or a third person, in the United States the issue must be decided under the state's law by a court of the state if the decision is to have significance within the sphere of the law, for instance in connection with a matter of support, succession on death, or immigrant status. In Italy the state desists from interference with a marriage concluded before a Catholic priest. The decision of whether or not the ceremony has resulted in the sacrament is left to the exclusive determination of the ecclesiastical court, whose decision is relevant in both fields, religious and secular law.[26] If a religiously concluded marriage has been declared invalid by the court of the church, and if that decision has been declared civilly effective by the state's court, which must do so if the ecclesiastical judgment is formally regular, the marriage will be treated as invalid not only by the church but also by the state.[27]

In the United States, Catholics and other religious believers may, of course, turn to their ecclesiastical authority for the determination of the religious validity of a marriage; but the decision of the ecclesiastical authority is without effect in the sphere of secular law. If legal consequences are intended, nullity or annulment must be rendered by the secular court.

In the United States divorce is available in the secular court and with the secular consequences of restoration to the freedom of remarriage, irrespective of whether the marriage was celebrated secularly or religiously. Divorce is available in the state court to non-Catholics and Catholics alike and to the latter without regard to whether they were married before a justice of the peace or before the parish priest. If a Roman Catholic avails himself of divorce in the secular court, he may be regarded as a sinner by the church and incur ecclesiastical censure or punishment, possibly excommunication. But, as far as the state is concerned and its law, he is no longer bound by the bond of marriage and is free to enter upon a new one. In Italy, the state has

25. Law of 27 May 1929, no. 847 (Gaz. Uff. 8 June, no. 133), § 5.
26. Concordat of 11 February 1929, Italian Law of 27 May 1929 (Gaz. Uff. 5 June 1929, no. 130) § 34, para. 4.
27. Law of 21 May 1929, § 17.

adopted the indissolubility of the marriage bond of Catholics and by its own law the state has seen fit to apply this same rule to non-Catholics as well.

In the United States the marriage relation has been secularized; in its inception, its incidents, and its termination it has been subjected to the law of the state as applied in the state's courts. The only concession that has been made to religion is the possibility opened to parties to have their marriage relationship initiated by a religious ceremony. In Italy, marriage was secularized by the Code of 1865 so thoroughly that the religious ceremony was deprived of its effectiveness to initiate a marriage that would be valid before the state's law. As to termination, death was declared to be the only ground; all possibility of divorce was excluded. This norm was in accordance with the principle of the Catholic church, but it was the state's law rather than that of the church. By the Concordat of 1929 and its implementing legislation, the secularization of marriage was undone. The regulation of the marriage relation of Italians who chose to marry in religious form was handed to the religious communities, i.e., for Roman Catholics to the Catholic church and its courts. That no room was to be given to divorce, even for non-Catholics, was clear to both parties to the Lateran Treaties, the church and the Fascist government. Both fascism and the monarchy of the house of Savoy, which believed itself forced to allow fascism to take power in 1922, broke down in World War II. The Constituent Assembly of the new Republic of Italy had to decide whether to accept or to repudiate the Lateran Treaties. For the dominant party of the time, the Christian Democrats, acceptance was self-evident. Disturbance of the reestablished peace between state and church at that time appeared undesirable also to the second largest party, the Communists. The treaties, including the Concordat, were thus continued with an overwhelming majority in the Republic's constitution.[28]

For non-Catholics the situation in Italy is similar to that existing in the United States. Provided they belong to a denomination which is recognized by the state, such persons may have their marriages celebrated before a secular official, the registrar of civil status, or before a minister of their denomination. In the latter case the ceremony may not be performed, however, without a license, which will not be issued if the intended marriage is not permissible under the law of the state.

28. Constitution of the Italian Republic (Gaz. Uff. 27 December 1947, no. 298), art. 7.

Cases of nullity and annulment are within the exclusive jurisdiction of the courts of the state, which will apply the state's law, i.e., the same that applies to marriages concluded in the secular form.[29]

The nonavailability to Italians of the possibility of liberation from the bond of lifelong marriage, i,e., practically of the possibility of legally recognized remarriage during the lifetime of the other spouse, has resulted in apparently widespread efforts at evasion.

One way was, and still is, that of permanent emigration into a country in which divorce and remarriage are available. Such a decision is not lightly taken. Besides, it is not easy to find the right country.[30] If one chooses to emigrate into a European country other than one of the Communist group,[31] he must not only give up life in Italy but also his Italian citizenship and must acquire the nationality of his new country which, if possible at all, may take many years.[32]

Acquisition of nationality is not necessary to obtain a divorce in the United Kingdom, Denmark, Norway, and Iceland. But at least so far the divorce laws of England and Scotland have been strict and to acquire the necessary "domicile" there may take as many years as, or more than, it takes to acquire nationality in a Continental country.[33]

In Denmark, Norway, and Iceland the divorce laws are less strict [34] and the courts are not quite so reluctant as the British to find a change of domicile, but none of these countries seems to have attracted Italians in search of divorce. Besides, unless the divorce was preceded by the loss of Italian nationality and the acquisition of that of the new country, the divorce will not be recognized as having any effect in Italy or any other country following in its conflicts law the principle of nationality.

The obvious country to go to is the United States, provided one can get in. American courts universally apply to a person's divorce problems the law of their own state, and they take jurisdiction if the

---

29. Civil Code, art. 83; Law of 24 June 1929, no. 1159 (Gaz. Uff. 10 July 1929, no. 164); Decree of 24 February 1930, no. 2891 (Gaz. Uff. 12 April, no. 87).

30. On the problems of the law of conflict of laws which are involved in matters of divorce, see 1 RABEL, THE CONFLICT OF LAWS 441 ff. (2d ed. 1958).

31. In matters of marriage and divorce, the courts in the USSR follow the same method as that used in American courts: each court applies the law of its own state, but as a general rule it will not take jurisdiction unless the plaintiff resides in the state. See L. A. LUNZ, 2 INTERNATIONALES PRIVATRECHT 327 (1964).

32. An Italian national automatically loses his Italian citizenship when he lives outside of Italy and, upon his voluntary application, is naturalized in a foreign country. Italian Citizenship Law of 18 June 1912, no. 555 (Gaz. Uff. 30 June, no. 153), art. 8, no. 1.

33. See RABEL, *supra* note 30, at 150 ff.

34. See *supra* chap. 6.

petitioner has resided in that state for a certain period of time, but the periods are not long [35] and in finding the establishment of a residence most American courts are lenient. Having obtained an American divorce in the state of his residence,[36] the Italian is free to remarry in the United States, even before he is naturalized as an American citizen. But as far as Italy and most of Europe is concerned, he is still treated as married to the spouse from whom he was divorced by the American court.[37] Even later naturalization in the United States will not, for Italy and other "nationality countries," validate a remarriage previously concluded.

In a French, German, Swiss, or other European court, an Italian cannot obtain a divorce as long as he is an Italian.[38] In their laws of conflict

35. E.g., six weeks in Nevada or one year in California or Illinois.
36. Or, with his spouse's cooperation, in that of a fictitious residence; see *supra* chap. 4.
37. Each of the two marriages is a so-called limping marriage (*matrimonium claudicans*), i.e., a marriage regarded as existing under the law of one state and as nonexistent under the law of the other. If all relations with the old country are severed, including matters of property, the fact that Italian courts and agencies do not recognize his new marriage will be a matter of indifference to the immigrant. But if he returns to, or simply visits, Italy or if property is located there, the consequences may be embarrassing. On limping marriages in general, see RABEL, *supra* note 30, at 451, 478, 558, 607, and literature indicated there.
38. In France, cases of speedy acquisition of citizenship have become known in recent years, the best known being that of Carlo Ponti. When he and his wife were naturalized in France in 1966, they could quickly obtain a divorce in France, and he was then free to marry Sofia Loren. The ceremony, celebrated on 9 April 1966 after the French divorce, resulted in a relationship recognized as a valid marriage in France, in Italy, and elsewhere. From the Italian point of view, the Mexican divorce obtained by Ponti before he became a national of France and was thus still a national of Italy was ineffective in terminating his marriage to his prior wife, and so the following ceremony of marriage between him and Sofia Loren was also ineffective. Such a marriage could be concluded only by a new ceremony celebrated after the acquisition of French nationality and the French divorce. Also, under French law the acquisition of French nationality by Ponti did not imply the acquisition of French nationality by his prior wife, Giuliana Flastri (French Nationality Code, Ordinance of 19 October 1945, art. 64, no. 4). If she had remained a national of Italy, her husband's French divorce would, from the Italian point of view, not have been effective for her. Under Italian law, Ponti would then have been married to Giuliana, and under French law to Sofia.

Under the French Nationality Code of 19 October 1945, as amended by Ordinance no. 59-64 of 7 January 1959, and Law no. 61-1408, of 22 December 1961, art. 69, no foreigner may be naturalized unless he justifies it by his assimilation to the French community. Ordinarily, the foreigner must have resided in France for five years (art. 62). A two-year residence may be treated as sufficient in the case of one who has rendered important services to France by contributing distinguished artistic, scholarly, or literary talent, by introducing a new industry or some useful invention, or by establishing in France an industrial or agricultural enterprise (art. 63, n. 3). The waiting period can be entirely waived in the case of a foreigner who has rendered exceptional services to France or whose naturalization presents an exceptional interest of laws these countries apply in matters of personal status the law of the country of which the person concerned is a national. To a national of Italy these courts will apply the law of Italy, and under that law divorce does not exist. Exceptions are made in some countries for women who have married an Italian national; under Italian law such women automatically acquire Italian nationality,[39] but those who had before marriage been nationals of the country to whose court they now turn for a divorce, may benefit from the law of their former nationality, which they may indeed have preserved, in addition to that of Italy, or which they may be able to reacquire.[40]

If an Italian acquires the nationality of another country and also loses that of Italy, he can obtain a divorce under the law of his new country. But naturalization in a European country takes many years, if it can be obtained at all. If it is, and if Italian nationality is lost, the divorce could be expected to be recognized in Italy so that remarriage in Italy is possible even after reestablishment of residence there.[41]

---

to France (art. 64, n. 9). Ponti and his first wife obtained their naturalization under this provision.
39. Italian Citizenship Law, *supra* note 32, art. 10, para. 2.
40. *Cf.*, for instance, German Introductory Law to the Civil Code, of 18 August 1896 (RGBl. I 896.604), art. 17, para. 3. and Nationality Law of 19 May 1957 (BGBl. I 1251) § 6, now repealed by Law of 8 September 1969 (RGBl. I 1581).
41. But see *infra* note 43. If only one of the spouses is a national of Italy while the other is a national of another country, a French divorce can be obtained if both parties are residents of France, since French courts now apply French law to the case of spouses of different nationalities residing in France. Affaire Lewandowski, Cass. 15 March 1955, Recueil Dalloz 1955.540 (ann. Chavrier), Juris-Classeur Périodique 1955. II.8771 (ann. Ponsard), REV. CRITIQUE DE DROIT INTERNATIONAL PRIVÉ 1955, 320.

In its decisions in the Affaire Ferrari, of 6 July 1922 (Recueil Dalloz 1922.1.137, Recueil Sirey 1923.1.5, ann. by Lyon-Caën) and of 14 March 1928, Dalloz hebdomadaire 1928.253, Recueil Sirey 1929.1.92), the French Court of Cassation held that a woman of French nationality may obtain a divorce from her Italian husband. As far as Italian law is concerned, such French divorces are of no effect. As to certain problems that may arise under French law, see H. BATIFFOL, DROIT INTERNATIONAL PRIVÉ 514 (3d ed. 1959).

The implications of a limping marriage are illustrated by the case of an Italian painter whose American wife obtained an easy divorce in Nevada and thereupon went through two subsequent marriages and divorces. The husband, unable to emigrate from Italy, at long last obtained an Italian judgment declaring the Nevada divorce effective in Italy (App. Torino, 28 June 1948, [1948] Foro Ital. I, 909). This decision was one of those in which the Appellate Court in Turin, under the vigorous presidency of Judge D. R. Peretti-Griva, tried to bring about a more liberal recognition of foreign divorces in Italy. Upon appeal by the procurator-general, the decision was declared erroneous by the Italian Court of Cassation (16 March 1950, no. 563, [1950] Foro Ital. I. 388). From the Italian point of view, the Italian husband had to remain married to the American lady and was the legal father of the children born by her to her new husbands (BERUTTI 101). Fortunately, in the concrete case the decision of the Court of Cassation had theoretical significance only. An appeal taken by the procura-

This possibility was used, before World War I, by some Italians, whose number was small, but who attracted attention among the public and in legal circles. In the major part of the Hungarian half of the Austro-Hungarian monarchy, including the Italian speaking city of Fiume,[42] a liberal divorce law was in effect. For a while, it was also comparatively easy to be naturalized as a national of the kingdom of Hungary. The speediest way was that of being adopted by a Hungarian national, and upon appropriate payment it was not too difficult to find a Hungarian who would adopt as his son an unhappily married Italian. After divorce in Hungary, a remarriage could then be celebrated. The practice of Fiume divorces assumed major proportions when, after World War I, Fiume was severed from Yugoslavia, to which the Allies intended to give it, and occupied by the band of Italian patriot-adventurers led by the poet Gabriele d'Annunzio. From 1921 to 1924, when it was annexed to Italy, d'Annunzio ruled the place as a free city and liberally granted Fiuman citizenship to divorce-seeking Italians, even if they established a merely fleeting residence in his realm. After an initial period of bafflement, the practice of Fiume divorces was stopped when the Italian Court of Cassation held that a foreign divorce would not be recognized if the foreign nationality had been acquired for no purpose other than that of obtaining a divorce.[43]

Recently cases of people of such prominence as Sofia Loren and Carlo Ponti have attracted attention to divorces obtained in Mexico, the country of easiest divorce.[44] From the point of view of traditional Italian law such divorces are worthless. If the party to such a divorce later goes through a ceremony of marriage with a new partner, he may, under Italian law, be imprisoned for bigamy, a risk from which he is saved if before remarriage he acquires the nationality of another country under whose law the Mexican divorce is recognized.[45]

Since the Concordat the liberating effect of bona fide acquisition of a foreign nationality and subsequent foreign divorce has become limited to the small number of Italian marriages concluded in non-Catho-

---

tor-general "in the interest of the law," does not destroy the effect of the decision appealed from as between the parties.

42. The city now belongs to Yugoslavia and is called Rijeka.

43. See P. Paone, *Divorzio-diritto internazionale privato*, 13 ENCICLOPEDIA DEL DIRITTO 529 (1964).

44. See *supra* note 38.

45. Carlo Ponti is said to have been saved from punishment for bigamy committed by his Mexican proxy marriage of 1957 to Sofia Loren which followed his Mexican divorce, by having declared this new marriage invalid for a happily discovered formal defect.

lic form. If the Italian marriage was concluded in the Catholic rite, no foreign divorce will be recognized even if at the time of the divorce both parties are foreigners. Such at any rate is the situation if at the time of the Italian church marriage at least one party was an Italian national.[46] The leading case [47] contains dicta that no foreign divorce can be recognized in Italy even if at the time of the Italian church marriage both parties were foreigners, or even if the foreign parties went through a Catholic marriage anywhere in the world.[48]

Under both the secular law of Italy and the canon law of the Catholic church, a marriage once validly concluded is indissoluble during the joint lives of the parties. But the mere fact that the parties have gone through a ceremony of marriage does not necessarily mean that they are tied by the bond of matrimony. The marriage may be "invalid." If an Italian national has married in the civil form or in the religious form of a denomination other than the Roman Catholic, the decision concerning validity belongs to the secular courts and the grounds of invalidity are determined by the secular law. But if the marriage was celebrated according to the rite of the Roman Catholic church, jurisdiction in matters of validity belongs to the ecclesiastical authorities of the church, whose decision is determined by the canon law.[49]

The invalidity grounds of the secular law of Italy are narrowly de-

46. JEMOLO, *supra* note 12, at 377.
47. Cass., Sez. unite, 6 August 1949, no. 2241 [1949] Foro Ital. I. 908. On later decisions, see M. Stella Richter, *Recentissime di giurisprudenza*, 15 RIV. TRIM. DI DIRITTO E PROCEDURA CIVILE 1030, 1035 (1961); M. CAPPELLETTI & J. M. PERILLO, CIVIL PROCEDURE IN ITALY 380 (1966).

Recognition of a foreign divorce of foreigners does not even seem to be guaranteed by the existence of a treaty providing for the mutual recognition of judgments between Italy and the country whose court pronounced the divorce. In the case in question (Cass. civ., Sez. unite, 12 March 1970, no. 635, [1970] Giur. Ital. I. 1. 1019) one spouse, it is true, had been an Italian national at the time of the marriage. But the opinion contains dicta indicating that the decision would be the same if both parties had been foreigners at the time of their Italian church marriage.

48. For criticism see JEMOLO, *supra* note 12, at 379.
49. Concordat, art. 34, para. 4

The grounds by which a marriage is invalidated by the canon law are stated exclusively in *Codex juris canonici*, Book III, Title 7: . . . As to the exceptional situation in which a marriage concluded before a priest of the Catholic church may, for reasons of secular law be declared invalid by a secular court, see *supra* p. 165.

Before the Concordat took effect in 1929, many marriages were celebrated in Italy in both forms, the secular and the Catholic. For such cases art. 22 of the Implementation Law of 27 May 1929 provides that the ecclesiastical judgment of nullity is by the proper appellate court of the state to be made effective for the sphere of the secular law when it finds that the nullity was pronounced by the church's court — for a ground that is also admitted by the civil code. As to the numerous controversies to which this provision has given rise, see JEMOLO, *supra* note 12, at 357 ff.

fined.[50] The drafters of the "Codice Mussolini" were careful not to let nullity proceedings become a substitute for divorce. Hence, the number of secular judgments of nullity or annulment is exceedingly small. Impotence is said occasionally to be used as an escape. It is rumored that in such cases, as well as in petitions for papal dispensation from the impediment to remarriage created by an unconsummated valid church marriage, there has been occasional resort to a physician's testimony as to the virginity of the wife.

Ecclesiastical judgments of nullity cannot be easily obtained either. In modern canon law the scope of the prohibited degrees, which once opened a substitute for divorce, has been limited drastically. Declarations of nullity because of fear (*metus*)[51] or error[52] are much more difficult to obtain than New York or California annulments on the ground of fraud.[53] But still, canon law is not quite so consistent as the secular law of Italy. The elaborate canon law learning on marital consent can by skillful handling be used to provide an avenue of escape.

To create a valid marriage, the consent of both parties is indispensable. "Consent cannot be supplied by any other human power."[54] Around this fundamental principle canonist learning has developed a complex structure of refinements. Consent can be modified by giving it under a condition, precedent or subsequent. "I take you as my spouse provided you are not afflicted with tuberculosis," or "provided you have always been chaste," or "your property is worth more than $1,000,000," or "under the condition that you shall have no right to engage with me in sexual intercourse apt to result in the procreation of issue," or "so that our marriage shall be ended when I cease to feel love for you." Of course, no priest will assist in the ceremony of marriage if a party openly declares his consent illegally or immorally conditioned or under a condition which excludes the essentials of the sacrament, i.e., either party's exclusive right to engage with him in sexual intercourse apt to procreate issue, or the indissoluble character of the parties' relationship. But the conditions need not be stated openly. The party's consent is not of proper marital character if the condition by which the sacrament is excluded seriously and clearly exists in the party's mind at the moment in which he makes his marital declaration. The apparently valid declaration does not express the

50. Civil Code, arts. 117–29.
51. CODEX JURIS CANONICI, canon 1087.
52. *Id.* canons 1082–1084; see *supra* p. 92.
53. *Supra* chap. 4.
54. Canon 1081, para. 1, "Consensus . . . nulla humana potestate suppleri valet."

party's true consent. The mental reservation deprives the consent of its true marital character. A party's consent is, of course, presumed to be correctly expressed by the words or signs he used in the marriage ceremony.[55] But this presumption is rebuttable, especially through documentary evidence created in advance. Parties who are cautious, competently advised, and not bothered by conscience for being sinners in the contemplation of the church deposit with a notary a carefully worded document expressing a condition incompatible with the sacramental character of marriage and making it clear that this mental reservation exists at the very time in which they would express their apparently unconditional vows. If at some later time a party wishes to free himself of the bond of the apparent marriage, he is likely to obtain an ecclesiastical decree of nullity which, under the Italian Concordat, also eradicates the civil effects. In the contemplation of the church the relationship never was a marriage.[56] The parties have committed the sin of concubinage, but the church may grant them absolution. Since the canonist doctrines are subtle and subject to occasional variations in the practice of the Sacra Romana Rota,[57] the necessary document must be composed by a skilled expert in canon law. Successful conduct of the case in the ecclesiastical forum also requires the services of an expert whose fee is likely to be considerable. Besides, the case will be time-consuming. So it is no wonder that in Italy it is widely believed that ecclesiastical judgments of nullity and papal dispensation from the impediment of a nonconsummated valid marriage constitute a privilege of the wealthy and well-connected and that the occasional success of less well-to-do persons in winning such a privilege is regarded as mere accident.[58]

55. Canon 1086, para. 1, "Interni animi consensus semper praesumitur conformis verbis vel signis in celebrando matrimonio adhibitis."
56. The most famous case of this kind is that of Gulielmo Marconi, the inventor of wireless telecommunication, whose marriage of thirty-three years was declared invalid when he proved that at the time of the marriage he and his bride had agreed to obtain a divorce if aversion should develop between them. Another prominent case is that of Caroline Lee Radziwill, the sister of Jacqueline Kennedy, and of the Italian movie star Renato Rascel. The latter's eleven-year-old marriage was declared invalid when he convinced the tribunal that he and his bride had agreed never to procreate children. Gratefully Rascel dedicated funds for a chapel.
57. See JEMOLO, *supra* note 12 at 212 ff. and the canonist literature there cited.
58. Data indicative of the size of the activity of the ecclesiastical tribunals in matrimonial causes were given on 16 January 1969 at the opening of the judicial year of 1969 for the tribunals of the Vicariate of Rome, i.e., the Tribunale Ordinario with jurisdiction for cases of dispensation from the impediment of subsisting unconsummated marriage, the Tribunal of First Instance with jurisdiction of matrimonial cases of the district of the Vicariate of Rome, and the Appellate Tribunal with jurisdic-

Under the Italian law of conflict of laws, the secular court by which an Italian's secular marriage is declared invalid or annulled, need not be an Italian court. The decree may be rendered by a foreign court. Like any other foreign judgment, such a decision, if it concerns an Italian, has no effect in Italy until it is declared valid by an Italian appellate court.[59] As a general rule, an Italian court, when asked to declare a foreign judgment effective, does not enter upon a reexamination of the merits of the case. Even if wrongly decided, in fact or in law, a foreign judgment will be declared effective in Italy if it satisfies the following requirements.[60]

1. The foreign court by which the judgment was rendered must have had jurisdiction as determined by Italian notions. In matters of nullity of marriage or annulment this means that the party who figured as the defendant must have truly had his residence in the district of the court.

2. The defendant must have been properly summoned.

3. Either the defendant must have entered an appearance or certain procedural rules must have been observed before judgment by default was rendered against him.

4. The foreign judgment must be final in the sense of having matured into *res judicata*.

5. Judgment must not be inconsistent with another judgment rendered by an Italian court.

6. There is not pending before an Italian court any lawsuit between the same parties concerning the same subject and instituted before the foreign judgment became final.

7. The foreign judgment must not be contrary to the public order of Italy.

The first six requirements are purely formal. The seventh has been generally understood to imply that in a case of nullity or annulment of the marriage of an Italian national the foreign court must have

---

tion of matrimonial decisions rendered by the Tribunals of the Vicariates of Naples and Cagliari.

In 1968, the tribunals of first instance had to deal with 1,106 cases, the appellate tribunal with 558. The tribunals of first instance rendered 315 decisions, the appellate tribunal 255. Nullity was decreed by the tribunals of first instance in 250 cases and by the appellate tribunal in 199. Appeals were filed against 216 decisions of the tribunals of first instance and against 50 decisions of the appellate tribunal. The total number of cases pending in 1968 was 1,664. Of these 395 were conducted in *forma pauperis* or of *spese vive* (24 EPHEMERIS JURIS CANONICI 420 [1969]).

59. Code of Civil Procedure of 28 October 1940, art. 796; see CAPPELLETTI & PERILLO, *supra* note 47, at 367 ff.

60. Code of Civil Procedure, art. 797.

based its decision upon a ground recognized by Italian law.[61] Thus, if an Italian seeks to have his marriage declared invalid or annulled in, let us say, a Swiss court, the judgment will be worthless in Italy unless the Swiss court has applied Italian law. Since the Swiss, like most other European courts, apply the law of the country of nationality in matrimonial causes, that requirement of Italian recognition would be fulfilled. But, so one will ask, why should an Italian then be particularly interested in seeking a declaration of nullity or an annulment in a foreign court rather than in one of his own country? The answer lies in the realm of evidence. Under Italian law a party may have his marriage annulled if he can prove that at the time of the conclusion of the marriage the other party was impotent.[62] If an annulment on the ground of impotency is sought in an Italian court, a physician, or several physicians, will be appointed by the court to undertake the necessary examination and to report the result to the court.[63] Being "auxiliary officials of the court,"[64] the doctors will take their task seriously. No annulment will thus be pronounced in any case other than one of actual *impotentia* strictly proved through court-appointed physicians to have existed at the time of the marriage. But if the case comes up in a court of Switzerland, that court may follow the procedural rules of its own cantonal law and allow proof of impotency to be made by a physician chosen and paid by the parties. Apparently, it is not too difficult for parties to find a doctor who would certify the necessary impotency. Besides, in the canton of Ticino they speak Italian, Lugano is a lovely place, one can conveniently transact business in Milan, even while having a real or fictitious residence in Lugano or Chiasso. The number of annulments thus obtained in Swiss, especially Ticino, courts, while small, was large enough to make this practice not insignificant as a technique for providing a divorce substitute for the affluent.[65] But the practice was stopped by the Court of

61. Corte di Cassazione, sez. unite, 27 October 1953, no. 3504, Repertorio Gius. Civ., heading: Delibazione, nos. 47, 49 (1960); CAPPELLETTI & PERILLO, *supra* note 47, at 379; 71 DIRITTO ECCLESIASTICO II. 214 (1960).

62. Italian Civil Code, art. 123: Continuous (*perpetua*) impotence, irrespective of whether it is absolute or relative, may be adduced by either spouse as a ground of nullity, provided it already existed prior to the marriage. Inability to procreate may not be adduced as a ground of nullity unless one of the spouses lacks the organs necessary for procreation. The action is open to the other party provided he had no knowledge of the defect prior to the marriage and provided further that no more than three months have elapsed since he obtained such knowledge.

63. Experts are normally to be selected from a list of names permanently maintained by the court. Code of Civil Procedure, art. 61.

64. *Cf.* CAPPELLETTI & PERILLO, *supra* note 47, at 230.

65. BERUTTI 83.

Cassation in 1959 when it held that the public order of Italy required that the foreign court not only apply the substantive law of Italy but also observe the rules of Italian procedural law on the taking of evidence.[66]

The great majority of marriages of Italians are concluded in church. Under the Concordat, jurisdiction to declare such marriages invalid belongs exclusively to the courts of the church. But does that provision of the Concordat also apply to church marriages celebrated by an Italian outside of Italy. Neither the Concordat nor the Italian Implementation Law expressly addressed itself to that problem. Italians who had entered upon church marriages outside of Italy used this silence to have their marriages annulled by the secular court of the country in which they resided, especially Switzerland, and such foreign judgments were declared effective in Italy by several appellate courts, especially that of Turin.[67] That court continued its practice even after the Court of Cassation held that foreign secular courts had no jurisdiction to declare invalid an Italian's marriage celebrated in the Catholic rite irrespective of whether the ceremony had taken place in Italy or abroad and irrespective of whether at the time of the marriage residence had been in Italy or abroad.[68] That avenue too was closed with the enactment of an innocent looking law that allowed appeals to be presented by the public prosecutor in matrimonial causes, other than separations, and in proceedings to have foreign judgments rendered in such cases declared effective in Italy.[69]

Another place for nullity and annulment suits was San Marino, the tiny sovereign republic of minute population,[70] high up in the Apennines and surrounded on all sides by the Republic of Italy. This miniature country and Italy have a treaty of mutual recognition and en-

66. Corte di Cassazione, 16 April 1959, no. 1138, [1959] Foro Ital. I. 1301; 42 RIV. DIRITTO INTERNAZ., with note by Morelli, 626 (1959).

67. JEMOLO, *supra* note 12.

68. These principles were pronounced in a series of decisions beginning with that of 11 June 1934, [1934] Giur. Ital. I. 1.745, and culminating in that of the United Sections of 25 July 1949, [1949] Foro Ital. I.801. As to more recent cases, see *Richter, supra* note 47, at 1034, and A. PALMIERI, IL MATRIMONIO CONCORDATARIO DEGLI ITALIANI ALL'ESTERO E DEGLI STRANIERI IN ITALIA 121–22 (1968). On the role of case law in Italy, see J. Merryman, *The Italian Style*, 18 STAN. L. REV. 396, 398 (1966); CAPPELLETTI & PERILLO, *supra* note 47, at 49.

69. Law of 30 July 1950 (amending art. 72 of the Code of Civil Procedure) no. 534 (Gaz. Uff. 1 August 1950, no. 174). Expecting that the public prosecutor of Turin might not be eager to prosecute such appeals, the law provides that the appeal may be prosecuted not only by the prosecutor attached to the *iudex a quo* but also by that attached to the *iudex ad quem*.

70. In 1969, the resident population was 18,627; in addition there were 7,500 San Marinesi living outside of the state, but entitled to vote.

forcement of judgments.[71] In contrast to the ordinarily necessary judgment of *exequatur* to be rendered by a full panel of five appellate court judges, a San Marino judgment is rendered effective in Italy by the simple decree of the court's president, acting without his colleagues. If he finds in a nullity suit that the defendant had been an actual resident of San Marino, the San Marino decision must be declared effective in Italy. But who wants actually to reside in San Marino for the required period of one year? Who can find a place to stay there other than a hotel or a tourist home — places unlikely to be recognized as a residence? The trick was checked by the simple expedient of posting Italian carabinieri at the border who would monitor the comings and goings of Italians.[72]

As matters have stood, the only way open for the mass of unhappily married was that of separation, formal or informal. Formal separation may be by court decree or by agreement of the parties judicially certified.[73] Judicial separation belongs completely to the jurisdiction of the secular courts, even if the marriage in question was concluded religiously. As separation does not affect the marriage bond, the church is not interested in the matter. In form, it constitutes the secular version of the ancient separation from bed and board. In fact, the Italian action for judicial separation, like that of New York, serves to provide maintenance for the wife, custody of and support for the children, and the adjustment of the property relations of the spouses.[74] The parties'

71. Treaty of 31 March 1939 (Gaz. Uff. 16 September 1939, no. 217) amended by the Accords of 28 February 1946 (Gaz. Uff. 13 May 1946, no. 110) and 29 April 1953 (Gaz. Uff. 25 August 1954, no. 194). Under Italian pressure San Marino, on 27 May 1943, enacted a law (No. 20 of 1943) intended to stop the practice by which the secular court of San Marino assumed jurisdiction in cases concerning the validity of a marriage irrespective of where the marriage had been concluded and irrespective of whether it had been concluded in secular or religious form. Article 2 of the law of 1943 prohibited the introduction before the court of San Marino of any complaint concerning the validity of any marriage concluded anywhere before a Catholic priest. But the law does not exclude jurisdiction when both parties have subjected themselves to it. In those cases in which, under the San Marino law of conflict of laws, the substantive law of San Marino is applicable, the secular court of San Marino applies the provisions of the canon law of the Catholic church. The substantive law of San Marino is the Roman law in the form in which it once was the common law of Europe and under that law matters concerning the validity of marriages are to be determined by the laws of the church. See G. PRADER, IL MATRIMONIO NEL MONDO 452–53 (1970).

72. P. Pavolini, *Vari metodi per divorziare*, 7 I PROBLEMI DI ULISSE (anno 13), 79, 82 (June 1960).

73. Civil Code, arts. 150 ff., 158.

74. Civil Code, arts. 155, 156. Judicial separation may have grave consequences for the guilty party. He loses all benefits to which he would have been entitled under an antenuptial settlement; he may be deprived, totally or in part, of the enjoyment of the rents and profits of the property of minor children to which an Italian parent may

life in common is ended, but the bond of their marriage continues. Not only may neither marry while the other spouse lives; they also continue to be bound by the duty of marital fidelity. Sexual intercourse of the wife with a third person and the husband's openly living in concubinage with another woman constituted offenses punishable under the Criminal Code until the relevant provisions were recently held by the constitutional court unduly to discriminate between the sexes and thus to be unconstitutional.[75] In both cases, the wife's adultery and the husband's living in concubinage, prosecution had to be initiated by the aggrieved spouse. Although such prosecutions increasingly met with moral blame, they were not infrequent.[76] The number of cases in which the threat of prosecution was used as a means of blackmail is, of course, not known.

If separating parties can agree upon the terms of the separation, they may, within certain limits, adjust them by their own agreement, which, upon being judicially certified, becomes a basis for compulsory enforcement.[77] The bond of marriage continues in the same manner as in the case of a separation by decree. According to official statistics, the figures for the periods from 1933 to 1941 and from 1947 to 1968 are shown in table 15.

If maintenance of the wife or support for the children is not claimed or not expected to be enforceable, and if the parties are not interested in the clarification of the property incidents of their relationship, the separation or the abandonment remains unformalized. There is also the possibility of an agreement being made by the parties without its being submitted to the court for authorization. Such an agreement is not legally binding,[78] but it may be voluntarily observed.

The number of nonformalized separations is not known. High estimates have been published in recent years. The figures mentioned for Italy as a whole reach into the millions.[79] The figure stated in the Comasco Report for the decade from 1946 to 1956 is 431 for the two

---

otherwise be entitled; in short, he loses all property benefits of marriage, except the right to receive support. The wife may be prohibited from further using her husband's name.

75. Corte Costituzionale, 19 December 1968, no. 126, [1969] Foro Ital. 1.4, and 3 December 1969, no. 147, [1970] Foro Ital. I.17.

76. Prosecutions for adultery and concubinage in 1963 numbered 2,141; in 1964, 2,286; in 1965, 2,198; in 1966, 2,131; and in 1967, 2,054 (ISTITUTO CENTRALE DI STATISTICA, COMPENDIO STATISTICO ITALIANO, 1964, table 88; 1965, table 82; 1966, table 90; 1967, table 95; 1968, table 75).

77. Civil Code, art. 158; Code of Civil Procedure, art. 711.

78. Civil Code, art. 158.

79. See *supra* p. 158.

TABLE 15
MATRIMONIAL ACTIONS IN ITALIAN COURTS,
1933–41 AND 1947–68

Year	Actions for Separation	Annulments
1933	4,523	
1934	4,329	
1935	3,982	70
1936	4,377	86
1937	5,041	57
1938	5,432	97
1939	5,286	133
1940	5,151	122
1941	5,149	155
1947	10,465	
1948	9,418	91
1949	8,928	96
1950	8,883	84
1951	7,711	77
1952	7,862	44
1964	11,536	66
1965	11,383	56
1966	12,401	
1967	13,995	
1968	15,420	

Sources: ISTITUTO CENTRAL DI STATISTICA, ANNUARIO DI STATISTICA GIUDIZIARIA, vol. 15, table 4 (1965); 19, table 16 (1969).
Note: No statistics available for the war years 1942–46.

provinces of Como and Varese (population 993,000 in 1950). The number of separations formalized in the two provinces during the same period was said to have been 232.[80] As indicated in my discussion of the Ticino-Comasco inquiry, the number of informal separations is likely to be higher than 431.[81] How high it actually was, is unknown.

The fact that an Italian could not gain the freedom of remarriage during the lifetime of a spouse has not prevented separated people from engaging in sexual intercourse with persons other than their spouses and from establishing relations with them ranging all the way from occasional contacts to homes with the stability which marriage is supposed to have. The number of such "free unions" (*unioni libere*) and of the "outlaws" (*fuorilegge del matrimonio*) is not known. It is common knowledge that it is considerable. According to views widely held

80. See FESTSCHRIFT FÜR HANS G. FICKER (1967) 385.
81. *Infra* p. 306.

in Italy, the number and the percentage of broken marriages and of irregular unions go into the millions.[82]

The position of separated spouses under Italian law is precarious if the separation has been formalized and even more so if, as in the majority of cases, it has remained informal. The marital community of life has ceased to exist, but the legal bond of marriage continues. This fact implies first of all for each party the impossibility of remarriage during the lifetime of the partner. The system of registration of civil status[83] is so strict and all-pervading, and the requirements of documentary proof to be presented by an applicant for a marriage license are so stringent,[84] that it is next to impossible in Italy to go through a ceremony of marriage if a prior marriage still exists. If one should overcome all the obstacles or if he has gone through a remarriage ceremony abroad, he and his partner are guilty of the crime of bigamy punishable with imprisonment of up to five years.

The bigamous marriage is, of course, civilly invalid. But even the bigamous marriage may not be treated as invalid until it has been declared to be so by the proper court.[85] The ancient doctrine of putative marriage, which is maintained in the Italian Civil Code for all types of invalid marriages, protects a party that has entered upon the "marriage" in good faith as well as the children.[86] The latter are treated as legitimate if at least one of the parties to the marriage was in good faith.

The fact that the new marriage may be treated as valid under the law of some other country is irrelevant for Italian law as long as the party in question is a national of Italy. Under the rules of the Italian law of conflict of laws an Italian remains subject to Italian marriage law even if he has established himself in another country.[87] Italian

---

82. See *supra* p. 158 and BERUTTI, 159. Assuming, somewhat arbitrarily, that all the persons affected have entered irregular unions and that two children have been born to each such union, the total number of *fuorilegge* is estimated to have been 4,000,000 in 1954. In the same year the total population of Italy was 48,768,000. In the census of 1951, the number of married resident males was stated to have been 9,928,640 and that of married resident females 10,020,651 (ISTITUTO CENTRAL DI STATISTICA, COMPENDIO STATISTICO ITALIANO, 1956, table 15). The corresponding figures of the census of 1961 were 11,390,988 and 11,402,514 (IST. CENTR. STAT., X CENSIMENTI GENERALI DELLA POPULAZIONE, vol. 5, table 2-A. If the estimate by Sansone and Nenni is correct, about 5 percent of the marriages were broken.

83. Decree-Law of 9 July 1939, no. 1238, on registration of civil status (Gaz. Uff. 8 August, no. 180).

84. *Id.*, arts. 95–106.

85. Arg. Civil Code, arts. 117 ff.

86. Civil Code, art. 128.

87. Civil Code, Provisions on the Law in General, art. 17; Civil Code, art. 115.

law ceases to be applicable to him when he ceases to be an Italian national.

The consequences following a separation in the field of private law are well defined if the separation has been formalized by judicial decree,[88] but even then awkward situations can arise if the separation is followed by the establishment of an irregular union. The situation is even more awkward if, as occurs much more frequently, the separation has remained informal.

For present purposes it is not necessary to set out the details of the problems of property that may arise between the parties or in their relations to outsiders. Suffice it to say that in theory the relations normally existing in a functioning family are not altered. If, as still happens in Italy, a dowry has been given to the husband by the wife or her family, it will not be easy for her to get it back from the husband and to use it for her own purposes.[89] In an irregular union established subsequent to the separation, the property relationships between the partners are simple. They are strangers to each other. Strangers they also remain, in that either partner may break up the relationship at any time, that there are no duties of support, no social security benefits for the survivor, no claims against third parties by whose fault the breadwinner has been killed or incapacitated, and no mutual rights of intestate succession. Even gifts or testamentary dispositions made by one partner in favor of the other or of the children may to a considerable extent be defeated by the legal husband or wife's right to a life estate in a portion of the estate of the predeceasing spouse.[90]

While in France the mass phenomenon of free unions has begun to find some, although wavering, attention in the law,[91] Italian law does not, or not yet, tolerate any inroad into the principle that any sex relationship other than that of lawful wedlock cannot have any legal consequences that would even remotely approximate those of marriage.

This principle is applied inexorably to the children procreated in an irregular union. If the mother is married, her husband is treated as the child's father, even though he has been separated from the mother for years.[92] He may contest his paternity by proving that be-

---

88. Civil Code, art. 156.
89. Civil Code, art. 202.
90. Civil Code, arts. 540, 542–43, 581–85.
91. See G. MARTY & P. RAYNAUD, DROIT CIVIL, II-1 (*Les Obligations*) 356 ff. (1962). For a judicial opinion enforcing the concubine's right to recovery of damages under article 1382 of the Civil Code, see Cour d'Appel de Riom, 5 July 1965, [1966] Recueil Dalloz 549.
92. Civil Code, arts. 231–32.

cause of distance or other reasons it was objectively impossible for him to have had intercourse with his wife during the period of possible conception,[93] or that during that entire period he was legally separated from his wife.[94] In contrast to American law, Italian law does not permit that the legitimacy of the child be contested collaterally as an incident to a suit concerned with such matters as succession on death. As a general rule legitimacy cannot be contested by anyone other than the mother's husband, and he cannot do so except by commencing a lawsuit aiming specifically at the negation of his paternity; an action which must be commenced within three months of, generally speaking, the date of obtaining knowledge of the child's birth.[95] If the mother's husband fails to act within the period, the child is irreparably *his* child for all purposes of the law. The child bears *his* name rather than that of the mother's male companion; *he* has the parental power over the child. He is thus entitled to have the child taken away from the home of its factual parents and have it handed over to his custody.[96] If in some way the child should acquire property, it may turn out that during the time of the child's minority the rents and profits from that property may legally belong to the mother's husband, with whom she may not have lived for many years.[97] If any legal transaction is to be made for the child, it is, as a general rule, to be represented by his "father," i.e., the mother's legal husband. Mutual rights of indefeasible intestate succession exist between the child and him. But no legal relationship whatsoever exists between the child and his actual progenitor.

If the mother's husband has brought suit in time and has succeeded in refuting the presumption of his paternity, the child is illegitimate. So also is the child born to an unmarried woman who lives in an irregular union with a married man. But the child of the married woman is not just simply an illegitimate person but one belonging to the special category of adulterine children, which fact has serious consequences for him. In the common law a child born out of wedlock was once regarded as *filius nullius*; he had ties of legally relevant relationship with neither his father nor his mother. Present-day Italian law, like French law, still retains this once generally held principle. But legal relationships can ordinarily be established through "recognition" of the child by his mother or his father or both. In general, recognition

---

93. Civil Code, art. 235, nos. 1–2.
94. Civil Code, art. 235, no. 3.
95. Civil Code, art. 244.
96. This is the general principle established in art. 316 of the Civil Code.
97. Civil Code, art. 324.

is frequent, especially by the mother,[98] but an adulterine illegitimate cannot be legally recognized by a parent who was married at the time of the child's conception.[99] Thus if the male companion of the mother was married, recognition by him is excluded. By an informal declaration he may subject himself to a duty to support the child, but he cannot be compelled to do so.[100] Neither is there a possibility for the child to bear the man's family name. If the mother is unmarried she may by recognition confer her name upon the child,[101] but if an illegitimate child remains unrecognized, he has the name neither of his mother nor of his progenitor. The officer of civil status then assigns some name to him.[102]

If the mother's husband has succeeded in overcoming the presumption of his paternity, the child is an adulterine bastard and thus nobody's child. The fact of his illegitimate birth appears not only on his birth certificate but on every one of those innumerable documents on which in Italy an individual's father's name has to be indicated. By the Law of 31 October 1955,[103] the indication of the names of father and mother was prohibited on birth certificates, other certificates of civil status, and all other official documents in which such indication was formerly required by law and in which the person in question is to be identified for purposes other than those connected with the exercise of rights or the performance of duties derived from legitimacy of filiation. Once this law is generally observed,[104] it will avoid some degree of embarrassment.

The awkward consequences of the legal rules on the name of the offspring of irregular unions make for frequent temptation to misstate the facts in reporting the birth of the child to the registrar of civil status, especially to hide the existence of a marriage of one or the other of the parents or of both. If the child is simply illegitimate rather than an adulterine illegitimate, he can be entitled to bear the name of the mother or even the father.[105] However, false statements made

---

98. Civil Code, art. 250.
99. Civil Code, art. 252.
100. On the adulterine child's limited right of support and succession, see A. TORRENTE, MANUALE DI DIRITTO PRIVATO §§ 484, 506, 509, 514, at 722, 759, 764, 774 (6th ed. 1965).
101. Civil Code, art. 262.
102. Decree-Law of 9 July 1939, no. 1238, *supra* note 83, art. 71.
103. No. 1064, Gaz. Uff. 19 November 1955, no. 267; its *Regolamento di attuazione*, the *Decreto Presidente della Repubblica*, 2 May 1957, no. 432, was published in Gaz. Uff. 24 June 1957, no. 156.
104. But see BERUTTI 77.
105. Civil Code, arts. 250, 262.

to the officer of civil status constitute the crime of alteration of status, which is punishable more severely than the killing of a wife by her husband when he has discovered that she has committed adultery, namely, with imprisonment of at least five years and up to fifteen years.[106] The much criticized rigor of this provision has been mitigated in part by a decision of the Court of Cassation which held not punishable an unmarried man who, upon reporting the birth of a child of whom he admits to being the father, refuses to state not only the name of the mother but also to indicate whether she is married or not.[107] All the unmarried man or widower need say is that the child was born of his illegitimate relationship with a woman "who does not wish to be named." Upon such registration of the child's birth, the father may recognize it and then confer upon it his name. This way is not open to a man who is married to a woman other than the mother of the child. If upon reporting the child's birth, the married father declares himself unmarried, he is guilty of the crime of alteration of status.

While remarriage is not possible in Italy during the lifetime of one's spouse, nothing stands in the way after the spouse's death. The way to remarriage can be opened by uxoricide and the completion of the comparatively short-term punishment which is likely to follow.[108] In his delightful movie comedy *Divorce Italian Style* Pietro Germi has illustrated this substitute for divorce. The annual number of convictions for the crime of honor killing is high. According to Berutti, it amounts to several hundred a year.[109] But the figures cover a variety of real situations. Besides, one may have doubts about how many of these crimes are committed after adultery contrived for the very purpose of justifying the killing that might open the way to remarriage. *Divorce Italian Style* has proved to be a strong device of political propaganda through an artistic director supported by a cast of comic actors.[110] Satire does not necessarily reflect reality. But the existence in Italian law of the very notion of crime of honor is significant.[111] It

---

106. Penal Code, art. 567.

107. Cass. Sez. unite, 19 April 1963, no. 963, [1963] Giur. Ital. I. 1. 965 ff.; BERUTTI 80–82.

108. Penal Code, arts. 578 (*Infanticidio per causa di onore*), 587 (*Omicidio e lesione personale a causa di onore*).

109. BERUTTI 62–72.

110. The actors were Marcello Mastroianni, Stefania Sandrelli, Daniela Rocca.

111. The efforts of the minister of justice of 1966, Orenzo Reale, to bring about the repeal of the privileged treatment of homicide for honor has not yet succeeded. The Reale bill was prompted by the case of Gaetano Furnari, schoolteacher, 44, who in 1964 shot to death, before his students, the professor of geography, Francesco Speranza, seducer of Furnari's 19-year-old daughter. "I am a Sicilian," Furnari declared. "In my

expresses in a typical way that spirit which is dominant in Italy and which has so long prevented the introduction in that country of the institution of divorce.

We have been dealing with the Italian situation so extensively because Italy serves well as an illustration of a country in which traditionalist Christian conservatism has so far been dominant. This statement has a variety of implications.

The unification of Italy was brought about by statesmen and intellectual leaders who were liberal and anticlerical. But their liberalism was of a special variety. They attacked national disunity, foreign domination, political preponderance of the clergy, princely aspirations toward absolute rule, efforts to shackle freedom of thought, of speech, or of the press. But their liberalism did not cover the family. They were not interested in female emancipation, in breaking the husband-father's domination in the home, or in loosening the close ties of Italian family life.

Divorce was no acute problem even for the liberal intellectuals who constituted the *valentior pars* of Italy, and still less to the masses, irrespective of whether they were good Catholics or anticlerical socialists. Italian men did not need legalized remarriage if their marriages turned out to be unsatisfactory. Besides, the great majority of marriage expectations were likely to be modest and disappointment consequently rare. The age at marriage was high, especially for men. One ought to be able to support a family. Mate selection was a family affair rather than the outcome of falling in love. The latter was the privilege of the heroes of opera, who would dramatically illustrate the evil consequences of such folly. Marriage was one thing and love another, and nothing but mischief would result if the two happened to be mixed. But there were the substitutes, at least for the men: houses of prostitution and the mistress system. The wives were expected to be virtuous and to find satisfaction in the children and in the constant contacts with cousins, aunts, grandparents, etc. If consolation was necessary, it could be found through the church.

---

veins flows blood rather than dirty water. I just had to do it." He was sentenced to two years and eleven months in prison. Other widely known cases are the following:

Concetta Benigno, Siciliana, together with her father, killed her fiancé because, when asked when the marriage would be celebrated, he had answered: "Why such a hurry?"

Giovanni Perla, Sicilian vendor of ice cream, killed his wife with twenty-eight stabs of his knife because she had accepted a cigarette from a widower.

Franco Angeleri, office clerk of Lucca in Tuscany, killed his wife with his dagger when he found her at the house door engaged in conversation with the mailman (DER SPIEGEL, 1966, no. 8, at 94).

Liberalism lost its dominant role in Italian politics with World War I. The Fascists, who ruled the country for twenty years, had no inclination to change that pattern of family life which fitted in so well with their system of a hierarchically ordered, strictly disciplined, masculine society. Besides, Mussolini was anxious to maintain the peace with the church which he had brought to the country through the Lateran Treaties of 1929.

In post–World War II Italy the Christian Democratic party has been the ruling party ever since the collapse of the Fascist system and the establishment of the Republic. The party has close ties with the church, and for the church indissolubility of marriage has been axiomatic. The church has also firmly maintained the traditional image of the family within which the principle of indissolubility is tenable: that of the closely knit patriarchal unit whose primary purpose is the procreation and education of issue and in which, as in society in general, the roles and rights of men and women are unequal. This image was not only an ideal but also a widely accepted reality. It has now begun to be shaken by the socioeconomic transformation of Italy from a predominantly agricultural and craftsmen's society into one of urbanized large-scale industry. The transformation has been more rapid, more extensive, and more complete in the north than in the south. The old difference in economic development between the two parts of the country has been aggravated. While the old family pattern still dominates in the south, in the north, a new type of family formation, family size, and family structure has developed rapidly, without, however, having so far eliminated the old. In the new family pattern the relation between husband and wife has assumed those traits to which we have become accustomed in other countries of high urbanization and industrialization, a pattern in which women are no longer content with a position of submission, silent suffering, and consolation in religion; and the men, too, are no longer willing, or financially able, to keep a mistress or to consort with prostitutes; indeed the prostitute's role, too, has changed with the abolition of organized houses,[112] and the girls now being streetwalkers or road drivers.

The demand for the possibility of legalized remarriage has correspondingly increased, but until 1969 none of the several bills introduced in the legislature received even a hearing. The modest attempt undertaken in 1954–58 to introduce what was called "little divorce" for causes of extreme hardship, failed as had all earlier attempts. The forces of tradition rightly understood that divorce on the large scale

---

112. Law of 20 February 1958, no. 75, Gaz. Uff. 4 March 1958, no. 55.

would follow inevitably once the door was opened to the tabooed institution. The introduction of a new bill in the spring of 1965 was immediately answered by the call from leaders of Catholicism to all believers in tradition to come to the defense of indissoluble marriage. The modernization of the church for which the Second Vatican Council was convened has not yet resulted in a softening of the traditional doctrine. But the pressure has increased, especially through the rapid expansion of the number of irregular unions and their growing respectability. For a long time such unions have been common among Italy's lower classes. Now, they have penetrated into the upper and middle classes and the participants no longer expect to be treated as outcasts. High members of the judicial service, like Peretti-Griva or Berutti, have assiduously agitated for admitting divorce.

Yet, deep as the changes are in Italy and strong as the demand for legalized remarriage has grown, it is not certain whether the country is ready to break with its long tradition. No break was possible as long as the Christian Democratic party was dominant. Its long-time rule was weakened in 1962 when the government coalition, by including the Socialists, was opened toward the left (*apertura a sinistra*). In 1965 the Socialist deputy Loris Fortuna introduced a new divorce bill which, after elections, was reintroduced in 1968. Inside and outside the Chamber of Deputies, the bill was discussed passionately. Divorce has become a national issue of prime importance. The nation has split into *divorzisti* and *anti-divorzisti*. The dailies, the popular illustrated weeklies, the media, the periodicals of serious cultural and political discussion have been flooded with items; marchers have demonstrated in the streets for freedom and against clericalism, or for the preservation of the sacred values of the Italian family and the protection of Italy's women seen to be endangered by mass abandonment. The church has mobilized its forces; repeatedly, the pope himself has fervently warned that legislators should "venerate, honor and defend" the indissolubility of marriage.[113] But neither the prayers, sermons, and admonitions nor the filibuster of one hundred Christian Democratic deputies was of any avail. In November 1969, the Fortuna bill was adopted in the Chamber of Deputies by a vote of 325 to 283, and on 9 October 1970 the Senate followed with a vote of 164 for and 150 against the bill. Because the Senate had made some changes, the bill had to go back to the Chamber of Deputies. There the vote, taken on 1 December 1970, was favorable again (322 to 278 on one and 371 to 277 on a second tally), and on the same day the law was signed by

---

113. Time Magazine, 5 December 1969, at 52.

the president of the Republic, Signor Saragat.[114] In both chambers the bill was supported by the Communists, who in 1946 had voted for the continuance of the Mussolini Concordat and thus of the church's domination over marriage.

First, the new law is meant to render possible the regulation of the vast number of irregular unions formed under the old regime and to reduce the incentive to the formation of such unions in the future. But the conditions under which one can obtain the divorce that must precede remarriage are not easy. Marriage partners who seek to terminate the bond must have lived separate from each other for at least five years. But if one of them, the defendant, objects, the minimum period of separation is six years, and seven if the plaintiff is the party declared the exclusively guilty one in the decree by which the separation was judicially pronounced. The period begins with the day on which the parties appear before the presiding judge of the tribunal dealing with the petition for judicial separation or judicial approval of the parties' separation agreement. A purely factual separation will be insufficient in the future. It can be a basis for a divorce only if it began on or before 1 December 1968. Instead of the separation ground which in 1970 existed in twenty-four American states and in England, the Italian law, like that of New York, has adopted the conversion ground. But the Italian law is stricter than the New York law of 1966, under which it suffices that a separation agreement be filed with the county clerk. In Italy it must be presented to and certified (*omologato*) by the court. Expenses must thus be incurred and a judicial attempt at reconciliation must be made at the time of the separation. The exclusion of future informal separation as a basis for divorce has, of course, not made such arrangements disappear. But it means that in order to lay the basis for a future divorce it is necessary either that both parties agree on a separation or that one party go to court and prove the other guilty of a matrimonial offense. Under articles 151–53 of the Civil Code a spouse can obtain a judgment of judicial separation if he proves that the other has been guilty of abandonment or cruelty, or, if the defendant is the wife, of adultery; but if the defendant is the husband, the proof must be of adultery "constituting a grave injury to the wife."[115] The preliminary of judicial separation may also be obtained where the other spouse has been sentenced to long-term

---

114. Law of 1 December 1970, no. 898, Gaz. Uff. 3 December 1970 no. 306.
115. Civil Code, art. 151, para. 2.

imprisonment or declared to be permanently unworthy to hold public office[116] or, by the wife, when the husband fails to establish a home or, although he has the necessary means, refuses to establish one that would be commensurate with his circumstances.[117]

Against an "innocent" spouse who is unwilling to make a separation agreement as well as to sue for judicial separation, the conversion ground of article 3(2)(b) is thus not available. The other grounds enumerated in the new law in the main deal with the rare hardship situations described in the last of the unsuccessful bills that preceded the new law. The "little divorce" (*piccolo divorzio*) had been meant to constitute the wedge to open the door for divorce on a more generous scale. Under the law as enacted, a divorce can thus be obtained by a spouse where the other has been sentenced to the penitentiary or to imprisonment for more than fifteen years. But an exception is made for the case of political crimes and crimes committed for motives of special moral or social value.[118] Italy thus preserves a trace of the once common special treatment of the "honorable crime," such as killing a daughter caught in fornication. A divorce will also be granted a spouse if the other has been judicially found to have committed against his spouse or against a child certain crimes of violence, sexual abuse, fraudulent abuse of fiduciary position, or has obstinately violated his duties of family support.[119] A divorce can be obtained furthermore by an Italian whose spouse is a foreign citizen, has obtained a divorce or an annulment abroad, and has entered upon a remarriage abroad.[120] Finally, it is provided that a divorce be obtainable where a marriage has remained unconsummated.[121]

In all cases an attempt at reconciliation has to be made by the presiding judge of the divorce court and in certain cases also by the judge in charge of the preparation of the case for trial.[122] In cases of conversion divorce there will thus be two or even three attempts at reconciliation, the first of which is to be made in the proceedings for the judicial separation of the parties or the judicial certification of their separation agreement. In order to counteract attempts at collusion, the judge in charge of the preparation of the case is authorized to take evidence

116. Civil Code, art. 152.
117. Civil Code, art. 153.
118. Art. 3 (1) (a).
119. Art. 3 (1) (b), (c), and (d).
120. Art. 3 (2) (e).
121. Art. 3 (2) (f).
122. Art. 4, paras. 4 and 6.

ex officio, and the participation in the proceedings of the state's attorney is obligatory.[123]

It will be possible but not easy to obtain a divorce in Italy if the Act of 1970 is effective as a part of the law of Italy. But is it? The embattled defenders of tradition will probably challenge in the constitutional court the constitutionality of the Divorce Act. In the text a distinction is made between "dissolution of a marriage contracted in accordance with (*a norma del*) the Civil Code (art. 1), and "pronouncement of the cessation of the civil effects following from the registration" on the state's register of civil status of a marriage "celebrated in religious rite and properly registered" (art. 2). The word "divorce" is carefully avoided, but the conditions for the two measures as well as their secular consequences are exactly the same. In its title the law is simply called Regulation of the Cases of Dissolution of Marriage. Is such a law compatible with the Concordat of 1929, the continued validity of which has been anchored in the Constitution of 1946?[124] If, as expected, the constitutionality of the Act is upheld, the Christian Democrats are planning to bring about its early repeal through a referendum.[125] Apparently they believe that the attack upon the traditional pattern of the Christian family will be disapproved by a majority of the voters, especially the women. The crusade can be expected to use all the instruments of political propaganda and clerical pressure. Whether it will succeed is an open question. If all hurdles can be overcome, the peace that was restored between Italy and the church in 1942 may be endangered. In formal protests the pope has stated his view that the introduction of divorce for marriages concluded in the church would violate the obligation Italy undertook in the Concordat. The government has entered upon diplomatic negotiations with the Holy See, and the pope may indeed find it advisable to be less intransigent. The battle about divorce has ceased to be centered upon divorce. It is a part of the battle over restructuring Italian society. A victory of the *divorzisti* will be a decisive step. By its intervention, the Vatican has turned divorce into a symbol. If the defense is lost, the church's traditional power position will be shaken. Laicism and with it all the forces aiming at

123. Art. 4, para. 8, and art. 5, para. 1.
124. For a recent survey of the arguments in favor and against the constitutionality of a divorce law, see G. Pugliese, *Aspetti constituzionali del problema*, in IL DIVORZIO IN ITALIA 105 (1969).
125. The implementation of article 138 of the Constitution of 1947, which demands that the institution of referendum be established, was prevented by the Christian-Democratic party until it was prompted by its resistance to divorce to promote the implementation law of 25 May 1970, no. 352 (Gaz. Uff. 15 June 1970, no. 147).

fundamental social, economic and political reform will have won a decisive success. But victory of the *anti-divorzisti* would be likely to spell out the hopelessness of the efforts to transform Italy's social structure by orderly means and powerfully strengthen the forces of revolution. The church may thus find it expedient to agree on a more flexible interpretation of the Concordat and, in the long run, even to adopt that softened version of the dogma of indissolubility that is propounded already by some Catholic theologians.[126]

126. Ignace Lepp in 1966 MARRIAGE (magazine), June–July 1966 (see Time Magazine, 22 July 1966, at 54); Bernhard Häring, S.J., professor at the Alphonsian Academy in Rome, in DER SPIEGEL, 1970, no. 15, at 188.

8
Divorce in a Split Society: Les Deux Frances

The Protestant reformers initiated two movements, which, although expressing ideas that were not identical, became closely related to each other in the development of events: the secularization of marriage, and the opening of an escape from unhappy marriages. The secularization of marriage has not yet been fully carried out in all Catholic countries. In Spain, Eire, Malta, Argentina, Brazil, Chile, Colombia, Paraguay, the Philippines, and, in the main, Portugal, the state has, it is true, assumed the task of enacting laws of marriage, but it has shaped its laws so that they conform to the church's dogmas of the sacramental nature of marriage and its indissolubility. Conformity of the secular law or, as in Italy and Spain, official recognition of the church's law and jurisdiction has persisted in those countries in which the Catholic faith and through it the Catholic approach to life and society have remained dominant. Time and again different approaches have been tried. For short periods the opposing forces have brought about laws permitting divorce, but these laws have been short-lived. In Italy, divorce was available during the brief period of Napoleonic domination, in Spain for a few years preceding the destruction of the Spanish Republic by Francisco Franco, in Argentina in the last year of the regime of Juan Perón. But Catholicism has remained the religion of almost the entire population of these countries and what anticlerical or liberal movements have arisen, and however influential these movements have come to be, political circumstances have prevented them from achieving so deep a break with tradition as the introduction of divorce.

France, too, is a country in which Catholicism is the religion of the vast majority of the population. But there political events have made

In collecting the materials for this chapter, I was greatly helped by Dr. Samuel Stoljar, now member of the faculty of the National University of Australia, Canberra.

it possible for liberal individualism to break the hold of tradition, to achieve the full secularization of marriage, and to establish divorce firmly in the law and the mores of the country. However, if we except the short spell of the great Revolution of 1789, liberal individualism never obtained so complete a hold over France as it has in Sweden. Ever since the Revolution there have been the two Frances, that of the ideas of 1789 and that of prerevolutionary conservative Catholic tradition.

Ever since the ebb of revolutionary enthusiasm that set in with the establishment of the directorate in October 1795 and gained impetus with Bonaparte's ascent to power, French history has been characterized by the struggle between the two camps. Not that the line between them could always be neatly drawn. Often enough the split has gone right through the souls of individual Frenchmen. But with varying acerbity the two philosophies have struggled with each other, and with varying results. The vagaries of the struggle have found expression in the successive changes of political regimes and constitutions; they have found corresponding expression in the successive changes of the French law of divorce.

The two basic philosophies, which we have called the conservative-Christian and the liberal-individualist, are complex bodies of ideas and sentiments. Each of the two presents many variations, and the two tend to shade into each other. It is often not possible to say to which camp an individual belongs. He himself may not know, or he may belong to both, at alternate times or at the same time. But in the realm of ideas the contrast exists, and so it does in the realm of politics and, consequently, in that of the law. Later on we shall try to define it more closely. For present purposes it will suffice to say that in the conservative view, insofar as it not simply hearkens to the word of God, the community interest is dominant, and in the liberal the interests of individuals. In the words of one of the most powerful and most influential statements of the liberal position, the American Declaration of Independence, of 4 July 1776, men have an inalienable right to the pursuit of happiness. Society and its political embodiment, the state, exist for the sake of the individual human beings. The state is not to interfere with the sphere of individual liberty beyond the measure absolutely necessary to safeguard the maximum of liberty of each citizen that is compatible with the liberty of all the others. Opinions have varied on the question of how great a liberty of the one is compatible with that of all. Today's liberal regards as necessary a much wider scope of state interference with individual liberty than did his eighteenth- or nineteenth-century forebears. He has come to believe that certainly in the economic sphere, the safeguarding of the maximum liberty of all requires a very large measure of governmental curtailment of the liberty of each. But for him, as for Thomas Jefferson, Wilhelm von Humboldt, or Voltaire, the happiness of the individual is the basic value. What greater source of unhappiness can there be than a failing marriage, what greater happiness than marital bliss? So if a marriage turns out to be unhappy, the way must be open to shake off the yoke and to seek happiness in a new union with another partner. What right has the state to prevent its citizens from pursuing such happiness? Why should it make impossible or cumbersome the exercise of the natural right of divorce?

For the "conservative," the basic value is the community rather than the individual, the family, the race, the nation, or mankind. Marriage is regarded not, or not so much, as an avenue to individual satisfaction and happiness but as an institution that is to serve society, above all the institution to provide the cradle for successive generations. That institution has to be firm if it is to fulfill its purpose. Better that an individual suffer from the consequences of a poor choice of partner or from the harshness of fate than that he undermine the firmness of the institution. Marriage, if it is to serve its function for the community, is to be indissoluble; divorce is not to have a place if the community is to be secure. This conservative position is powerfully strengthened when its supporters believe that it has been ordained by the Lord himself. However, the institutional approach to marriage also occurs in the officially atheistic surrounding of the Soviet Union, where divorce, while permitted, was for many years not easy to obtain.

The two views do not necessarily have to be so uncompromising as these extreme positions suggest. The liberal postulate of free and easy divorce can be supported by the argument that society's interest requires a certain measure of individual happiness which must not be prevented by the impossibility of escaping from an unhappy into a hopefully happier marriage, and that the very welfare of society's children is jeopardized when they grow up in homes torn by dissension. Justification for the conservative position, in turn, can be sought in the argument that individuals' awareness of the indissolubility of marriage will render them cautious in the choice of a mate and will thus tend to promote marital harmony and happy homes. Such views have not always been rationalizations of preconceived positions, but experience seems to indicate that human beings differ in their basic attitudes and that it has been due to their divergency that laws of divorce have so often been expressions of compromise rather than of the consistently rational implementation of a clearly conceived policy. As we have indicated, a high measure of consistency can be found in the divorce laws of those countries where history has allowed one or the other of the two basic views to gain dominance: the steadfast rejection of divorce in the countries of predominantly Catholic tradition, and, on the other hand, the free admission of divorce in Japan or, to a lesser degree, the Scandinavian countries. In other countries, among them the United States, the two views coexist and a compromise has had to be worked out between them. So it has also been in France. In neither country has the compromise been easy, in neither does it seem to be fully satisfactory or final. But in both it appears the best that could be achieved in the circumstances. In the United States the result is more complex, and the way in which it has been brought about has been tortuous. After all, we have fifty states, each with its own law of marriage and divorce. In France, the law has been uniform, the development has been easier to observe, and the compromise nature of the present state of affairs is more apparent. To the understanding of the American scene an understanding of the French may thus be of help.

France, solidly Catholic in the eighteenth century, had at one time been hospitable to Calvin's French version of Protestantism. In the religious wars of the sixteenth century the spread of Protestantism was stopped by the alliance between the crown and the Counter-Reformation. The massacre of Saint Bartholomew's Day (24 August 1572) ended the growth of Protestantism. The revocation of the Edict of Nantes (1685) terminated toleration of it. But for almost two centuries France had its community of Protestants whose members seem to have practiced divorce within the narrow limits permitted by Calvin. As divorce was not permitted to Catholics, tensions apparently developed, especially as the privileges of the Edict of Nantes were gradually curtailed by Louis XIV.[1]

Down to the end of the *ancien régime*, Catholicism was not only the established but the only permitted religion of the French kingdom. The canon law of marriage was the law of France. In accordance with

---

1. In the *Journal de jurisprudence*, Lebrun mentions a case in which Protestants, after having obtained a divorce from their ecclesiastical authority and having both entered upon new marriages, were arrested, tortured, and ordered, under threat of punishment of death, to separate from their new partners and to resume their marital life together. See 1 H. COULON, LE DIVORCE ET LA SÉPARATION DE CORPS 164 (1890).

the canon law a marriage could be declared null and void with the consequence of the parties' being free to enter upon other marriages. Also in accordance with the canon law, a married person could under narrowly defined circumstances obtain a judicial divorce from bed and board. But divorce in the sense of restoration to the freedom of remarriage after conclusion of a canonically valid marriage and prior to the death of the partner was unobtainable. Yet, however Catholic the law was in its content, steps were taken in the direction of its secularization in the sense of the state's substituting its regulatory power for that of the church. In the sixteenth century causes of separation had come to be determined by the secular courts of the king rather than those of the church. In the eighteenth century the royal courts ousted the ecclesiastical courts also from their jurisdiction in cases of nullity of marriage.[2]

By the Ordinance of Blois, of 1579, the state ordained formalities to be observed in the ecclesiastical conclusion of marriage. By that ordinance and one of 1629, it established rules of its own for the registration of births, marriages, and deaths. The registers were still to be kept by the parish priests, but under supervision of officers of the royal government.[3] Marriages, of course, continued to require conclusion in church. The encroachments of royal power over that of the church were incidents of the movement of Gallicanism in which the royal aspirations were supported by the French clergy against the claims of the papacy.[4]

While the state had obtained a measure of control over the institution of marriage, it by no means touched upon the content of Catholic doctrine and canon law, the sacramental nature of marriage and the indissolubility of the marriage bond. But this foundation was undermined by the laxity of the sex morals of the upper class and by the constantly mounting ideological attack of the intellectuals.

Christian marriage certainly was a living reality in the bourgeois

---

2. A. ESMEIN, HISTOIRE DE DROIT FRANÇAIS 644 ff. (1901). The result was achieved by means of the *appel comme d'abus*, a remedy resembling the means by which the royal courts of England obtained control of, and finally substituted themselves for, the ecclesiastical courts of the Church of England. However, in England the latter kept jurisdiction over matters of nullity until the court reform of 1857.

3. H. Conrad, *Die Grundlegung der modernen Zivilehe durch die französische Revolution*, 67 ZEITSCHRIFT DER SAVIGNY-STIFTUNG FÜR RECHTSGESCHICHTE, GERMANISTISCHE ABTEILUNG 336, 342 (1950).

4. The most famous expression of the movement was in the Declaration on the Gallican Liberties, of 1692, drafted by Bossuet. It ought to be remembered that the modern doctrine of state sovereignty was first expressed in France (JEAN BODIN, DE LA RÉPUBLIQUE, 1586).

middle class that was steadily increasing in number, wealth, and national importance. Its demands for political rights commensurate with its contribution to the national life, especially its financial contribution, constituted the most conspicuous impetus for the Revolution. The life of the peasants also seems on the whole to have corresponded to the precepts of the church. But, following the model set by the kings, especially Louis XV, the usufructuaries of the major part of the nation's wealth engaged in conspicuous orgies of consumptive luxury and of sex. The Christian command against seeking carnal pleasures outside the lawful wedlock was disregarded by the men, unmarried and married, and widely loosened for the women. Marriage might be indissoluble, but it was far from being the *remedium concupiscentiae*. The public display of disregard for the Christian command of purity of marriage could not fail to reinforce the attack upon the doctrines of sacramental character and indissolubility that had been launched by the intellectuals.

The Protestant reformers had reduced the indissolubility of the bond of marriage from a sacred dogma to a command of Christian living that would allow of exceptions in special situations. With the renewal of Greek and Roman learning, memories of the dissolubility of marriage among the ancients were rekindled. With the growing emancipation of thought from religious dogma and precept, new ideas about man and his role in society and in the universe began to develop. Nature, along with Holy Writ and, later on, without or against it, came to be consulted as to what would be the natural system of law by which men were to live.

To think new ideas about marriage and divorce was natural for Montesquieu, the observer of laws and mores the world over. He recognized that divorce is generally of the greatest political utility.[5] Divorce, this means, is of interest not just to the church but to the state. The postulate of secularization, together with that of dissolubility by mutual consent, was implied in that legalistic formula which emphasized the contractual nature of marriage. As a contract, marriage is an institution of universal natural law. It was only by the Catholic church that the notion of sacrament was added, so it was proclaimed by Voltaire,[6] who was obviously acquainted with the thoughts of King Frederick II (the Great) of Prussia that found expression in Prussia's marriage edict of 1754, and after Frederick's death in that most liberal

---

5. L'ESPRIT DES LOIS, liv. 16, chap. 15; see also the ironical remark in LETTRES PERSANES, 1. cxvii.
6. DICTIONNAIRE PHILOSOPHIQUE, v. Mariage.

of all modern codifications of marriage law, the Prussian General Code of 1791–94.

The conclusion that the state ought to emancipate itself from the notion of marriage as a sacrament and treat it exclusively as a civil and, of course, dissoluble, contract was drawn by Rousseau.[7] Diderot injected into the discussion the argument that indissolubility of marriage necessarily resulted in the tyranny of men over their wives and that the escape of divorce had to be available if women were not to be objects of ownership.[8]

How well the soil was prepared at the eve of the Revolution is indicated by such publications as those of Jacques Lescène des Maisons,[9] or the anonymous body who uttered the *Cri d'une honnête femme qui réclame le divorce*.[10] The former anticipates the argument that was later on so strongly emphasized in Engels's attack on bourgeois marriage,[11] that marriage had become a game of mutual deception subject to the rule of caveat emptor.[12] Once divorce was available, the author hoped, a candidate for marriage would no longer dare to deceive the other about his character or other qualities, because discovery would be followed by repudiation. Once divorce was available, marriage would be a matter of "taste and genuine mutual affection" rather than a bargain in the market place. About the anonymous lady who uttered her cry for divorce, we are told by her editor that she was of distinguished family and that she found herself compelled to demand the availability of divorce as the only escape from the horrible secrets of her marriage which she would describe in her tract.

When the storm broke in 1789, France was ready to follow the example of Prussia and Denmark, to shake off ecclesiastical dominance over marriage and to initiate a new era of free pursuit of individual happiness as it had been postulated by the intellectual leaders of rationalist natural law and the Enlightenment. Reason itself demanded the opportunity of remarriage before the death of the spouse of an

7. CONTRAT SOCIAL, liv. 4, chap. 8.
8. SUPPLEMENT AU VOYAGE DE BOUGAINVILLE; see also LA RÊVE D'ALEMBERT (conversation between Mlle. de L'Espinasse and Bordeu, MÉMOIRES DE DIDEROT [LETTRES À MLLE. VOLAND]). That Diderot was aware of the potential danger of his emancipatory views is indicated by his warning that these ideas should not be preached to children or to "grandes personnes." He obviously thought the latters' ideas about marriage morality were already more than sufficiently easy.
9. CONTRAT CONJUGAL; OU, LOIX DU MARIAGE, DE LA RÉPUDIATION ET DU DIVORCE 179 ff. (Paris, 1781).
10. Paris and London, 1770.
11. Der URSPRUNG DER FAMILIE, DES PRIVATEIGENTUMS UND DES STAATES (1884).
12. Popular wisdom expressed this sad truth in the proverb: "Quant au mariage, il trompe qui peut" ("As to marriage, everybody cheats").

insufferable marriage. It seems that quite a few Frenchmen and women availed themselves of such a possibility even before it was officially sanctioned by law more than three years after the storming of the Bastille. The enactment of the famous Law of 20 September 1792 appears, indeed, to a considerable extent to have been motivated by the need to regularize a situation of fact that had arisen spontaneously, and to control what appeared to be excesses of the newly won freedom of divorce.[13] The old idea of marriage as a social institution, to be maintained for the common good, was not dead,[14] even though it was to be further weakened in the heyday of Jacobinism.

The enactment of the Law of 1792 had been preceded by the solemn pronouncement in the revolutionary Constitution of 1791, that the law regarded marriage merely as a civil contract.[15] The principal features of the new law were these:

1. Divorce in the sense of termination of the bond of marriage was to be permitted only upon those grounds which were enumerated in the statute. Two of these grounds were broad enough: mutual consent and incompatibility of temper. But the two grounds were hedged in by cumbersome and time-consuming formalities.

In addition the Act enumerated eight specific situations in which the termination of a marriage might be procured. Five were formulated upon the model of the ancient institution of judicial separation, which, it will be remembered, was obtainable in cases of grave misconduct of one spouse against the other. Slightly broadened in the new secular law, these grounds were cruelty,[16] desertion for two years

---

13. In the preamble to the law of 1792, it is said expressly that "Numerous married couples did not wait to enjoy the benefits of the constitutional provision declaring marriage to be a private contract." In the Assembly, M.-E. Guadet observed that the tribunals — apparently the family tribunals established in 1790 (see Sirey, vol. 1789–1830, at 49 ff.) — had already decreed divorces and that he himself had participated in such judicial activity (Moniteur, 1 September 1792). The number of people actually divorcing before the Law of 1792 was sufficiently large to prompt the retroactive validation of such divorces by a law enacted on 6 Floréal an II (1794), art. 6. Aubert du Bayet demanded the law on the ground that it would reestablish public morality, tighten the marriage bond, and reduce the number of divorces (2 Moniteur, no. 245, at 1039 [1792]).

14. Robin, reporter of the committee charged with the preparation of the Law, stated in the Assembly that even though the greatest latitude should be given to divorce, it was still necessary "to protect such a very important institution as marriage from the *bizarreries* of instability of character and affection" (2 Moniteur, no. 252, at 1072 [1792]).

15. Title II, art. 7.

16. The phrase used — *excès, sévices et injures graves* — is the same as that of the Napoleonic Code, art. 231, and of the present law of France, Civil Code, art. 232. These terms cover what may be roughly rendered as both physical and mental cruelty.

or more, notoriously dissolute conduct of life.[17] The idea of guilt and misconduct was also implied in the ground of conviction of infamous crime. A political note underlay the provision under which a divorce was to be available to persons whose spouse had emigrated from France. In the time of internal revolution and external war, an emigrant was, of course, an enemy of the people. The spirit of individualistic enlightenment found expression in the availability of divorce in the case of a spouse's absence without news for at least two years, and in that of a spouse's incurable insanity. In contrast to modern laws, adultery, it will be observed, was not separately cited as a ground for divorce. Apparently, a man's simple adultery was not regarded as sufficiently serious, and that of a woman to be so delicate as to require it to be hidden behind the façade of a less scandalous ground.

2. The ancient remedy of judicial separation, with its characteristic feature of continuance of the marriage bond and thus of continuing disability to remarry, was abolished. In cases in which a judicial separation had been pronounced prior to the Law of 1792, either party could unilaterally have it transformed into a divorce.

3. As a general rule matters of divorce did not have to be brought before a judicial tribunal. The marriage bond was ended when, upon proof of observance of the formalities and delays prescribed by the Law, the divorce was registered by an administrative officer.

4. Disputed matters of partition of property, alimony, child custody, and child support were to be adjusted by family arbitrators.

The Law of 1792 clearly constituted a radical break with the pre-revolutionary past. In accordance with the postulates of the Enlightenment, marriage was proclaimed a secular institution designed to serve individual human beings in their pursuit of happiness. But the ancient notion of marriage and the family as the basic unit of society was too strong to be discarded completely. The bond of an existing marriage was not to be terminated lightly. Serious efforts were to be undertaken in each case to test the firmness of the parties' intention and to bring about a reconciliation. The enormous role the family continued to play in French life in spite of revolutionary upheaval and Jacobin rhetoric is illustrated by the way in which the family was used as the instrument of delay and of reconciliative efforts. The machinery was, indeed, cleverly adapted to the fact that in eighteenth-century France a marriage was a union not only, or, perhaps, not so much, of the individuals as of two family clans. Just as the families had played

---

17. *Dérèglement des moeurs notoire*, art. 1 no. 4.

their roles when the bond of marriage was bound, the families also were to play their roles in its untying.

When parties sought to terminate their marriage by mutual consent, a public officer had to convene a family council, which was to consist of three close relatives of each spouse. Only in those exceptional cases where no relatives were available was it sufficient to resort to friends. At the meeting of the council, which was to take place no earlier than one month after it had been summoned, the spouses had to explain their reasons for their desire to terminate their marriage. The members were expected to dissuade the spouses from their intention. Failure to effectuate a reconciliation was to be recorded by an officer of the municipality and signed by all participants. Upon proper deposit of this record at the municipality, the divorce could then be effected by the registration of the parties' agreement by the registrar of civil status. However, application for such registration could not be made earlier than one month and not later than six months after the meeting.

When a divorce was sought unilaterally upon the ground of alleged incompatibility of temperament, the family council had to be convened three times; first, one month after summons, then two months after the first meeting, and again three months after the second meeting. Again, application for registration of the failure of conciliation had to be made at the earliest one month and at the latest six months after the last meeting.

Upon registration the marriage was terminated in all respects except one: The parties had to wait another full year before they were free to remarry anyone except each other if the divorce had occurred upon the ground of consent or incompatibility. In all other cases the husband was free to remarry immediately, but the wife had to wait one year, except where there was no risk of *perturbatio sanguinis*, i.e., the case of the other spouse's unexplained absence for five years or more. This concern about the clarity of blood lines was maintained even at the height of Jacobinism. When the waiting period was abolished for the male by the Law of 8 Nivôse an II (28 December 1793), it was maintained for the female, although abbreviated to ten months, i.e., the length of a possible period of gestation that could have followed a last intercourse of the parties on the very day of their divorce. By the Law of 4 Floréal an II (23 April 1794) it was made possible to shorten the female's waiting period if she gave birth after the divorce.

In the cases of mutual consent and incompatibility, the divorce could be brought about without the invocation of any judicial authority. No such necessity existed either in cases of divorce because of a party's conviction for an infamous crime or because of unexplained absence for five years or more. Only in the case of other specific grounds, especially that of cruelty, was it necessary that the ground be proved to, and ascertained by, a judicial authority, namely, the proper family arbitration tribunal as established by the Law of 1790.

In later times, the Law of 1792 was denounced as a permit of licentiousness and an attack upon the sanctity of marriage, family, house, and society. To an American today, it does appear a sensible and forthright effort to deal with one of society's least tractable problems. In the Jacobin period immediately following the enactment, a few tries were made in the direction of further permissiveness, only to be replaced, in 1804, by the less permissive scheme of the Code Napoléon.

Before contemplating legislation subsequent to the Law of 17 September 1792, we must take notice of a law that was enacted together with it, the Decree of 20–25 September 1792 "determining the manner of ascertaining the civil status of the citizens."[18] In France, as in all Christian Europe, baptisms, marriages, and funerals had long been recorded in church registers. In France, the royal government asserted its interest in the accuracy, completeness, and preservation of the entries and issued regulations binding upon the ecclesiastical authorities. With the introduction of civil marriage and of divorce as events by which civil status would be changed, the registration of which could not be expected, however, to be carried out by parish priests, the time had come to carry out the demand for full secularization of the regulation of civil status, i.e., of family matters. Registration of births, marriages, divorces, deaths, and such other changes in civil status as legitimation was entrusted to secular authority, the municipalities. It was to be uniform in all France under the supervision of the government. There was thus born the first system of complete registration of those events which determine a citizen's legal position in society and concerning which it is of vital interest, to the citizen and the community, to have an accurate and generally accessible method of proof. The system thus established by France, elaborated and perfected by later French legislation, has spread all over the world, although not always in that degree of perfection to which it was developed in its home country. In the United States in particular, state systems of registration are still in many respects defective.

French authors have widely presented the legislation immediately

18. Décret qui détermine le mode de constater l'état civil des citoyens (SIREY, LOIS ANNOTÉES 1789–1850, at 207).

following the Law of 1792 as the expression of Jacobin radicalism and revolutionary hybris. An observer more remote from the still smoldering French disputes may find more valid reasons. Two major measures were contained in the Law of 4 Floréal an II. All divorces that had been obtained in the period between the adoption of the Constitution of 1791 and the enactment of the Law of 17 September 1792 were retroactively validated. That measure was obviously meant to clarify the status of those apparently numerous persons who had regarded the pronouncement of the Constitution as self-executing and had not waited for a more detailed law to bring about the termination of their, preponderantly prerevolutionary, marriages.

The second measure related to the future. Marriage termination through registration by the registrar of civil status was henceforth to be obtainable upon proof of actual separation of the spouses for a period of at least six months.

In the Convention this measure was stated to be necessary because it had turned out that parties anxious to have a marriage terminated had found the periods required in the cases of consent and incompatibility too long, or had been unable to convene a family council, and thus had simply resorted to de facto separation and the formation of a new, although irregular union. France, in other words, had experienced what happens regularly whenever pressure for easy and quick relief from marital dissatisfaction is strong and the law tries to stem the tide. As in all such cases, the dam broke. The legislators of revolutionary France saw no reason why the obvious popular pressure ought to be compelled to flow into the channel of irregularity. To make sure that the law might not be sabotaged by conservative public officers, a registrar's refusal to cooperate in the legal prescribed ways was threatened with punishment. For the same reason of reducing the pressure toward the formation of irregular unions, the law also simplified and abbreviated the procedure in cases of divorce upon the ground of desertion.

This Law of 23 April 1794 marks the high tide of liberalism in French divorce legislation. Shortly after its enactment the Jacobin rule was broken, Robespierre was executed, the Convention dissolved. Under the new directorate Constitution of 1795, conservative France could again raise its voice, and the revolutionary legislation on divorce became one of its principal targets. As early as 3 August 1795 (15 Thermidor an V), both amendments to the Law of 1792 were repealed. As before the Law of 1793, remarriage was not to be possible before the expiration of one full year after the divorce was registered. Termination of the marriage bond upon the ground of six months' de facto separation was no longer possible. The Law of 1792, thus restored in its original shape, began to come under increasingly heavy attack. Prime target of the critics was the dissolution of marriage upon one party's allegation of incompatibility. As in the Prussian Law of 1791, the use of the term "incompatibility of temperament" was apparently due to the influence of Montesquieu, who a century earlier had pointed out that it was indeed due to incompatibility that marriage might end in failure and require the remedy of divorce. To the draftsmen of the Law of 1792, the term recommended itself for the additional reason that it would render it unnecessary for the seeker of divorce to reveal those intimate details by which incompatibility expressed itself. Solicitude to avoid public scandal, we shall see, also played a role in the formulation of the provision of the Napoleonic Code by which the Law of 1792 was ultimately replaced. To what extent the end could be achieved under a scheme that invited incisive debate in three successive meetings of members of two different families appears doubtful. But what invited attack was the vagueness of the term that seemed to allow the unilateral repudiation of marriage from unrevealed and possibly fanciful, whimsical or evil reasons. Particularly shocking seemed the fact that under the cloak of unsubstantiated allegation of incompatibility a faithful spouse might be repudiated by one who had subverted the marriage by his own misconduct. The powerful nature of this argument is testified to by the tenacity with which the doctrine of recrimination has survived in American law as well as in provisions of the divorce laws of the Federal Republic of Germany, Switzerland, socialist Poland, and Czechoslovakia, which all allow a defendant to prevent the termination of a concededly collapsed marriage upon proof of the plaintiff's having caused the collapse by his own misconduct. Upon the force of such argument, unilateral allegation of incompatibility disappeared from the law of France in 1804 and, a century later, from that of Prussia.

The Law of 1792, especially as amended by the laws of 1793 and 1794, constituted an embodiment of the individualist approach to marriage that was by no means so radical as it has been presented by French critics or as this approach has found expression in present divorce laws of some states of the United States or of Mexico. While its Prussian counterpart survived for nearly a century, it turned out to be too individualist for France, whose people were not ready to subscribe to the idea that had found temporary victory in the days of Jacobin dominance.

How little the Law corresponded to the feelings of the French masses is shown by the statistics. While extensive use was made of divorce in Paris, the Law remained a dead letter for wide districts of rural France, and of the French population of 28 million, 80 percent lived in the country and in small towns.

In Paris, to be sure, figures were at a level that easily appeared alarming to observers not yet familiar with American divorce rates of the mid-twentieth century. In the first quarter of 1793, the number of divorces, while it did not, as recently in Napa County, California, surpass the number of marriage ceremonies, at least came close to that number. At other times, the ratio between divorces and marriages concluded was 1:5 or even 1:3. Just as it is not justified today to say that in the United States every fifth marriage ends in divorce, it is not justified to make corresponding statements for revolutionary France. The overwhelming number of marriages terminated by divorce shortly after 1792 had been concluded in prerevolutionary days. Many of these marriages must have been "dead" before their parties were at last restored to the freedom of legitimate remarriage. In addition to this backlog, which appears to have constituted the majority of cases, there were the marriages whose viability was destroyed by the physical and emotional upheavals of a tumultuous era, war, and general reordering of values. Leaders and followers of these events as well as victims tended to congregate in that one city, Paris, which in those days was more than ever the heart of France.

The short eras of the directorate and the consulate brought respite from the upheavals of the Revolution. They were eras characterized simultaneously by a consolidation of the revolutionary ideology of liberal individualism and a resurgence of the ideology of conservative traditionalism that had been temporarily submerged but never destroyed. All through the years of turmoil the family had continued to function as the stable basis of French society. All the other groupings that had stood between the citizen and the state had been merged in the newly hammered "Nation — One and Indivisible." Feudal groupings, the trade and craft guilds, the class organizations of the nobility, the clergy, and the Third Estate, all were broken up. State and citizen found each other directly rather than obliquely, as before, through the ancient intermediate bodies. But, was it really the individual citizen who now faced the state? Was it not rather the individual as the member of a family? While all other groupings had lost their significance, the family had gained importance for both the citizen and the state. In the Napoleonic consolidation of the coexistence of the two

Frances, the family was thus ascribed a prominent role. The family, and that meant, above all, marriage, had to be firm and stable. But was it possible, after the experiences of the Enlightenment and the Revolution to return completely to the concept of the indissolubility of the marriage bond? Was it necessary? The revolutionary idea of liberal-individualist France had not yet so fully abated that one could dismiss its demand for a marriage law that would leave open an escape from unhappiness.

In each of the successive drafts of a civil code that were submitted to the legislative bodies, the scheme of the Law of 1792 was preserved even though the draftsmen of the first three had personal doubts about the matter. Prerevolutionary France did not have a uniform system of private law. In the north, each province had its own body of local customs, among which the "Custom of Paris" (*Coutume de Paris*) occupied a position of eminence. Like the other customs, it had been officially restated in several successive versions, the latest being that of 1580. In the south, Roman law had escaped the oblivion into which it had generally fallen with the barbarian invasions of the western half of the Roman empire. The revival it had experienced, after the twelfth century, first in Italian and then in French universities, extended in some measure to the north, without, however, eliminating the autonomously developed customs of the area. In a few matters of private law royal legislation of the seventeenth and eighteenth centuries established uniform rules throughout the kingdom. A common tradition of legal learning was strengthened by the great, comprehensive treatises of the jurists Jean Domat (1625–96) and Robert Pothier (1699–1772). But no truly uniform body of private law could grow up in a judicial system that lacked a common supreme court for the country as a whole. The seventeen courts of last resort, called *parlements*, were of equal rank, and there was no higher court that could have brought about uniformity in legal practice.

Unification of the law and establishment of one single supreme court for the entire country was a major demand of the revolutionary movement. The old customs were felt to be incompatible with the principle of equality, because they embodied privileges of the nobility and the clergy. There was also the feeling that the nation could not be "une et indivisible" as long as its law constituted a crazy quilt. Codification as the means toward unification was demanded in the hope that it would render the law so simple and intelligible to the citizen that he could not only understand and obey it in the conduct of his affairs, but that he could follow and control its application by the judiciary that was suspected of having little sympathy for the new order. Finally, and this was decisive, codification was demanded in order to secure the attainments of the Revolution, to safeguard and define the newly won freedom of economic activity and of personal life.

As early as 5 July 1790, it was resolved by the Constituent Assembly that "the civil laws should be reviewed and reformed by the legislators, and that there should be produced a code of laws that would be simple, clear, and appropriate to the Constitution." In the Constitution of 1791, it was accordingly provided that "a code of private law will be made, uniform for the entire kingdom." In the turbulent years immediately following, this point of the program could not be carried out. But a first draft of a civil code was presented to the directorate in 1793 and revised versions, all prepared by Cambacérès, in 1794 and 1796. When he had become one of the consuls of the French Republic, the next draft, submitted in 1799, was prepared by Jacqueminot.[19] They all failed of adoption. The more consolidated atmosphere of Bonaparte's consulate was needed to carry to completion the long effort at codification.

In the commission which acted under the chairmanship and with the active participation of Bonaparte, the topic of divorce constituted a subject of extensive discussion.[20] The criticism of revolutionary law in general and of divorce law in particular that was being voiced with increasing intensity, also found expression in the Conseil d'Etat and the Code Commission. Portalis, the most influential of the four principal draftsmen, openly expressed his aversion against the institution of divorce; he recognized, however, that it was too late to deprive Frenchmen of it, since they had had it for ten years. Bonaparte was convinced that divorce could not be completely abolished. Repeatedly it has been surmised that his position was influenced by incipient plans to terminate his marriage to Josephine de Beauharnais. Certainly, as a statesman he knew the temper of his time.

A basic argument in favor of divorce was that freedom of divorce was a necessary concomitant of freedom of religion. What this meant was that the notion of indissolubility was not a characteristic of marriage as an institution of natural law but a doctrine of the Catholic church, so that with the disestablishment of Catholicism as the official religion of the state, its peculiar doctrine no longer had a place in secular law.

---

19. As to divorce, the scheme of the Law of 1792 was followed, but through simplification of procedures and shortening of delays, divorce would have been made easier.

20. The materials preparatory to the code are fully presented by A. FENET, RECUEIL COMPLET DES TRAVAUX PREPARATOIRES AU CODE CIVIL (Paris, 1836).

What emerged from the discussions first as the Divorce Law of 30 Ventôse an XI (21 March 1803) and then as title VI of Book I of the Civil Code of 30 Ventôse an XII (21 March 1804) was a law much less liberal than that of 1792. That law had been based upon the idea that divorce was the natural concomitant of marriage.[21] While at its beginning marriage was still regarded as being concluded forever, the possibility of its premature termination was nevertheless to be reckoned with. In the Code, divorce was relegated to an exception, a privilege that might be granted by the state in exceptional situations. In contrast to the law of the Revolution in which divorce could be brought about by a married party himself whenever, after mature deliberation as ascertained by the observance of the statutory formalities and delays, he found that his marriage had failed to produce the expected happiness, the Code made divorce a punishment for grave misconduct. If we apply the terminology that has become current in modern French usage, the shift was from *divorce faillite* to *divorce sanction*, from the possibility of escape from a marriage that has become bankrupt to punishment for guilt. Divorce thus came to be assimilated to the ancient ecclesiastical institution of judicial separation or, as it was often called, limited divorce. In that context, the idea of punishment for guilt had been justified. When granted to a husband, judicial separation entitled him to throw his wife out of the house, with a minimum of support or no support at all, and with his continued enjoyment of her fortune. When granted to a wife, judicial separation meant that her husband had to support her on a generous level, that he might have to give up the enjoyment of all or some of her property, but that he would be deprived of her company and comfort. But did the idea of punishment make sense in the different framework of restoration to the freedom of remarriage? The transfer of an idea from a framework in which it made good sense to one in which it did not, was a fateful mistake. Neither in France nor anywhere else where the same mistake was made has it worked out as planned. Universally, it can be said, statutory schemes of *divorce sanction* have been transformed into schemes, in actual practice, of *divorce faillite*, in England, in the United States, in Germany and elsewhere. Because of the fact that in France the system of the Civil Code was in effect for just fourteen years, the transformation did not become apparent until its reestablishment shortly before the end of the century. About these developments we shall speak later.

21. *Cf.* Voltaire's bon mot that divorce must have been invented, at the latest, two weeks after the invention of marriage.

The influence of the *ancient droit* of judicial separation was made obvious by the list of types of misconduct for which a divorce was to be obtainable. They were:

1. Adultery of the wife, i.e., any single act of infidelity committed by her (art. 229).

2. The husband's open and notorious living with a mistress in the marital home (art. 230).

3. The conviction of either spouse to criminal punishment involving infamy (art. 231).

4. Maltreatment, excesses, or grave injury committed by one spouse against the other (art. 232).

There had disappeared from the list the ground of desertion, as well as the grounds of unexplained disappearance and of insanity. Disappearance was, rather poorly, taken care of in a different part of the Code (art. 139), which provided a rebuttable presumption of death for the case of an unexplained absence of a person for a certain minimum period that as a general rule, was fixed at four years (art. 115). The recognition of insanity as a ground for divorce was regarded as incompatible with the character of marriage as a union "for better or for worse, in sickness and in health."

That incompatibility of temper and, even more, the unilateral allegation of incompatibility, had to be eliminated as a ground for divorce, was self-evident in the new political climate. It had constituted the chief target for the attacks of the conservatives by whom this ground for divorce was presented as the opening of the door to licentiousness and depravity. But, strangely enough, the Code did retain as a cause for divorce the other chief target of criticism: divorce upon the ground of mutual consent. Its preservation was due to Bonaparte, who strenuously argued that in the interest of avoiding scandals it was necessary to provide the possibility of obtaining the termination of a marriage without revelation of its true, sordid cause. This was the argument that had already been made in favor of those provisions of the Law of 1792 which allowed divorce upon the ground of mutual consent as well as of that of alleged incompatibility. Frenchmen should be allowed to keep their family skeletons in the closet.

Obviously, the idea was not easy to implement within a system of *divorce sanction* that would seem to require full revelation of the facts to the court so that it could ascertain whether they fell within the limited catalog of misconduct constituting a cause for divorce. Unlimited admission of consent divorce would have been equally undesirable. The outcome was a complex scheme which, pretending to be a method of genteel divorce, amounted to admission of consent divorce, but under such difficult and unattractive conditions that it is hard to see how anyone who had a "real" ground for divorce would ever resort to it simply to avoid publicity.

The provision (art. 233) was finally worded as follows:

The mutual and lasting consent of the spouses, expressed in the manner prescribed by law, and subject to the conditions and according to the tests set out by law, is considered to be sufficient proof that life in common has become unbearable to the spouses, and that there exists a peremptory cause for divorce.

The Scandinavian laws hide consent behind marriage breakdown; Napoleon's Code hid breakdown behind consent.

Among the conditions set out by the law was, first of all, the necessity of adding to the consent of the husband and his wife that of the parents of each, or, if the parents were dead, that of the grandparents. This requirement continued the tradition of regarding matters of marriage as affecting not just the individual partners but their families. Under the Law of 1792 this idea had found expression in the requirement of convening a council of members of the two families concerned. It is interesting to note that in the discussion of the Code the family council was declared to have turned out to be ineffective. Relatives other than parents were said to be uninterested; family ties were no longer felt to imply obligations. The decay of the "great family," which in American sociology is so generally regarded as a phenomenon typical of recent industrialization and urbanization, was observed, and deplored, in France of 1804.

The other requirement was the necessity for each party to divest himself of one-half of his property and to settle it upon the children of the marriage. Such a measure may have been regarded as a safeguard for the children against the hazard of their parents's remarrying. It could not be other than a deterrent against preferring genteel consent divorce to open divorce for cause.

In addition, there were the following limitations:

1. Consent divorce was not admitted unless the husband was above the age of twenty-five, and the wife above that of twenty-one. Only mature persons should be able to avail themselves of the dangerous institution (art. 275).

2. The marriage must have lasted at least two years (art. 276). There must have been a genuine effort, but it was not required that the parties actually have lived together for the two years.

3. Consent divorce was not possible where the marriage had lasted

forty-five years or more, or where the wife was forty-five or more years of age (art. 277).

4. Finally the parties had to be in agreement on the amount of alimony payable by the husband to the wife, on the wife's place of future residence, and on the custody of the children (art. 280).

Consent divorce hedged in by such cumbersome requirements was unlikely to become a popular institution. In contrast to France, where this peculiar sort of consent divorce was abolished in 1818, along with all other kinds of divorce, the institution has remained in effect in Belgium, where the French Civil Code was introduced under Napoleon's rule. Of 61,168 divorces obtained in Belgium in the period from 1925 to 1966, 10,674, i.e., ca. 17 percent, were obtained on the ground of consent.[22]

The divorce system of the Napoleonic Code has been criticized for lacking consistency, for being a compromise. Of course it was. What else could it have been in a period of compromise? That was exactly what France needed and what she was given by Napoleon. Under him the two Frances were united, politically and socially, through military glory and through wise efforts to preserve what was necessary of the Revolution's achievements in a climate of return to the traditionalism of the eternal France of religious, industrious living, *joie de vivre*, and family. It was for the restored royal regime to upset the balance, reestablish the dominance of the conservatives and the church, and abolish divorce. Article 6 of the Charter of 4 June 1814, proclaimed Catholicism again to be the official religion of the state.

The church also succeeded in its struggle against divorce, in which it had never ceased and which it voiced in public ever since the ebbing of the revolutionary fever had allowed it openly to speak out again. As early as 1797, the Gallican church had proclaimed that it remained "unalterably attached to the doctrine of the Gospel and the teaching of the Church Universal concerning the exclusiveness, the perpetuity, and the indissolubility of marriage."[23] The Catholic ideal of marriage was propagated with particular vigor through the Marquis de Bonnald,[24] who at the earliest possible occasion introduced in the Chambers the law abolishing divorce that has remained known under his name. By this law, of 8 May 1816, title VI of Book I was deleted

22. 88 ANNUAIRE STATISTIQUE DE BELGIQUE 96 (1967).
23. *Décret du Concile national de France*, reprinted in COLLECTION DES PIÈCES IMPRIMÉES PAR ORDRE DU CONCILE NATIONAL DE FRANCE 8 (Paris, 1797).
24. DU DIVORCE CONSIDÉRÉ AU 19e SIÈCLE RELATIVEMENT À L'ÉTAT DOMESTIQUE ET À L'ÉTAT PUBLIC DE LA SOCIÉTÉ (Paris, 1801); RÉSUMÉ SUR LA QUESTION DE DIVORCE PAR L'AUTEUR DU DIVORCE AU 19e SIÈCLE (Paris, 1801).

from the Civil Code.[25] For the next seventy years, judicial separation was to be the sole remedy for marital failure. Along with other freedoms, the freedom of remarriage remained suppressed.

The following decades resemble the situation that prevailed in Italy, except that in France the liberal influence not only was stronger but also received repeated encouragement in the revolutionary movements of 1830, 1848, and 1870–71. But passionate propaganda for the reestablishment of divorce met with equally passionate counterattacks. As in Italy, prostitution, the mistress system, and irregular unions flourished, but none of the numerous bills succeeded until the dominance of conservatism was again broken in the failure of MacMahonism in the Third Republic. The renaissance of divorce in 1884 would have been short-lived if that new onslaught of conservatism that occurred in the strange form of the Dreyfus scandal had not been overcome. In the resulting victory, laicist liberalism emerged so strong that the institution of divorce could even survive the Vichy regime. In de Gaulle's Fifth Republic its availability is not questioned. In judicial practice, the statutory scheme of *divorce sanction* has been replaced by that of *divorce faillite*.

But we have anticipated the outcome of a turbulent development. Under the regime of the restored Bourbon kings, no attempt was made to reintroduce divorce. Conservatism was too strongly in the saddle. But when the July Revolution of 1830 had initiated the reascendancy of liberalism, four bills were not only moved in the legislature, in the first four years, but actually adopted in the Chamber of Deputies, only to be defeated, however, in the Chamber of Peers. The Republic that was reestablished by the March Revolution of 1848 was too short-lived to undertake lasting reforms, as to divorce or as to other matters. The Second Empire owed its existence to the fears of the bourgeois that a revival of the ideas of 1789 might again bring to a reign of terror or, worse, dictatorship of the proletariat. The era was not very likely to allow social reforms. Besides, prosperity offered enough byways to men to render divorce unnecessary, and as for women, as in Victorian England they were supposed to suffer in silence, provided they did not find consolation with a lover. The era, after all, was the classical era of the triangle, of Moulin Rouge, and of Madame Bovary. As in the *ancien régime*, liberal France had to express itself through the intellectuals, to many of whom the reestablishment of divorce became a cause.

---

25. All pending actions for divorce by mutual consent were stopped; all other actions for divorce were transformed into actions for judicial separation.

The Third Republic came into being as the result of the debacle of 1870. It was accompanied by the Paris Commune, an event so thoroughly frightening to the French bourgeois that the hankering for security again gave an uplift to conservatism, represented by military leaders like MacMahon and Boulanger. But laicist liberalism was in the ascendancy, reaching dominance after the violent struggle centered upon the person of Captain Dreyfus. A stage in this resurgence of liberal France was marked by the reintroduction of divorce.

The ground had been prepared by intellectual leaders like Alexandre Dumas *fils*.[26] The legislative change was brought about through the incessant activities of Alfred Naquet. In 1876, he published a powerful appeal for the reestablishment of divorce.[27] In the same year he submitted his first proposal, which closely resembled the scheme of the Divorce Law of 1792. For such a decided expression of liberalism, the time was not yet ripe again. So he reduced his ambition in his new bill, which simply aimed at restoring those sections of the Civil Code that had been repealed in 1816.[28] After initial rejection, this bill was passed in 1884, after the Senate had removed the article that would again have allowed divorce by mutual consent.[29] Divorce, as it was restored by the *loi Naquet*, was clearly conceived as *divorce sanction*.

26. LA QUESTION DE DIVORCE (Paris, 1879).   27. LE DIVORCE (Paris, 1876).
28. A change was made, however, with respect to adultery. For the wife to obtain a divorce, it was no longer necessary to prove that the husband had a mistress living in the marital home. As in the case of the husband's action for divorce, one single act of infidelity by the husband would suffice to entitle the wife to a divorce. The change had been foreshadowed by the judicial practice in actions for judicial separation, which had come in appropriate cases to treat even a single act of adultery by the husband as a "grave injury" to the wife that could entitle her to a judicial separation. See 1 A. COLIN & H. CAPITANT, DROIT CIVIL 201–02, 280 (11th ed. 1947). The change is indicative of the growing strength of the demand for equality of the sexes which, in France probably even more than elsewhere, was voiced more by male intellectuals than by female feminists. Remarkable also is the weakening of the sentiment of the importance of blood lines of which the change constitutes an expression. Curiously enough, this sentiment continued to survive in the provisions of arts. 337–39 of the Criminal Code, which continued to threaten with punishment the adultery of a married woman, but not that of a man unless committed with a mistress brought to live in the marital home. This survival of the differentiation in the criminal law resulted in factual inequality in divorce proceedings. Since a wife's adultery always constituted a criminal offense, the police could be requested to furnish a record (*procès-verbal de constat*), which would then be used as evidence in the husband's action for divorce.

Conviction of crime was held to be a ground for divorce when it occurred during marriage, through a French court, and resulted in a sentence of death, penal servitude, transportation, or solitary confinement, but not in the case of simple imprisonment or fine. Concealment of a conviction that had occurred before a marriage, could be regarded as a case of *injure grave*.

29. On the struggle of the nineteenth century, see J. BONNECASE, PHILOSOPHIE DU CODE NAPOLÉON AU DROIT DE FAMILLE 268 (1928); H. Lalou, *Histoire du divorce en France*, NOTES DU CONGRÈS DE DROIT CANONIQUE (1947).

Adultery, conviction of infamous crime, and "maltreatment, excesses, and grave injury" were to be the only grounds for divorce. For good measure it was added that no action for divorce was to be received on any ground before the marriage in question had lasted three years.[30] It was the last-named of the three grounds which in later development was seized to bring about the transformation of the statutory scheme of *divorce sanction* into the actually practiced pattern of *divorce faillite*. This development had been prepared by the practice of the courts in connection with judicial separation. The Law of 1816 had left intact the statutory catalog of grounds for divorce; only it had transformed them into grounds for judicial separation. The husband's forcible detention of his wife,[31] the husband's depriving his wife of food,[32] infection with venereal disease,[33] refusal to follow up the civil ceremony of marriage with a religious one,[34] the husband's desertion of the wife,[35] his refusal to consummate the marriage,[36] all these and other similar acts had been found to constitute maltreatment, excesses, or grave injury within the meaning of article 232 of the Civil Code.

This broadminded approach to judicial separation stands in contrast to the extreme reluctance of the courts to grant annulments, which seems to have been caused not only by the narrowness of the statutory provisions [37] but also by a judicial zeal not to jeopardize that indissolubility of the marriage bond which had at last been vindicated against the onslaught of the Revolution. In this respect their attitude was similar to that of the English ecclesiastical courts after the rejection of the ideas of the Protestant reformers, and to that of the courts of Italy.

The Third Republic was the longest era of political stability in post-revolutionary French history. Not that this period, from 1870 to 1940, lacked political movement. Like other periods, it was filled with the competing aspirations of the two Frances, but, after the initial onslaught of conservatism, and after the Conservatives' debacle in the Dreyfus affair, the liberal wing was dominant. Divorce, retintroduced in 1884, not only remained firmly established but became more and more socially accepted and legally broadened. Just as in the major

30. Art. 233, repealed by Law of 2 April 1941.
31. Cass. 16 November 1825, Sirey, Rec. gén. 1re série, t. 8, at 213.
32. Bruxelles, 14 August 1834 (divorce), Pas. belge 1834, 2.238.
33. Lyon, 4 April 1818, Sirey, Rec. gén. 1re série, t. 5, at 370.
34. Angers, 29 January 1859, D.1860, 2.97, S.1859, 2.77.
35. Dijon, 30 July 1868, D.1868, 2.247.
36. Metz, 25 May 1869, D.1869, 2.202, *cf.* on this case, the preceding ones, and the French and Belgian practice of the courts in general, 3 Coulon, *supra* note 1, at 14–15.
37. Civil Code, arts. 180 ff.

part of the United States and in other countries of statutory *divorce sanction*, increasing liberalization of the law was brought about by judicial practice rather than by legislation. The judicial practice followed two lines of convergent development. The meaning of the term "maltreatment, excesses, and grave injury" (art. 232), and the rules of procedure which were meant to prevent parties from obtaining a divorce on fictitious facts mutually agreed upon came to be disregarded. Consent divorce, while officially outlawed, has become not only possible but, just as in the United States, the normal case. Neither the conservatives of Vichy with their motto "Fatherland, Work, and Family" nor General de Gaulle managed to change this state of affairs. Just as in the United States, the transformation of *divorce sanction* into *divorce faillite* had its source in the courts of the big cities, especially Paris, whose overburdened judges have neither the time to determine what true facts may be hidden behind the testimony of the parties' witnesses nor the inclination to stand up against the demands of the *vox populi* and the appeal for sympathy for the victims of domestic misery. If the French divorce rate is still considerably lower than that of the United States, this is due to a combination of still strong Christian conservatism and a low degree of reluctance to establish irregular unions after the de facto breakup of a legally continuing marriage. Here we find not only two, but three, Frances: the left-wingers who regard formalized marriage and divorce as unnecessary bourgeois rigmarole; on the right, the followers of tradition; and, in between, the liberal Frenchman who has emancipated himself from clericalism but still cherishes respectability. We have no statistics showing the strength of these groups. Comparison of the divorce rate of France with that of a country of different socio-political climate is therefore of little use.

Again, we have anticipated a result. A brief survey of the process by which it was brought about will throw some light on the parallel development in the United States. Among the three statutory grounds for divorce in France that of *injure grave* came to outweigh adultery and conviction of crime. The latter two were saved from obliteration only because they were treated as "peremptory causes." Once the adultery or the conviction is proved, the divorce follows automatically, while in the case of *injure*, the court is, at least in theory, required to determine whether it is sufficiently *grave* to justify the divorce. Proof of conviction of crime is, of course, easy. Proof of adultery was, at least for a husband, facilitated by the obtainability of a police report or, for both partners, through prearrangement. Divorce on the ground of adultery would also give a vindictive plaintiff the satisfaction of preventing the defendant's remarriage to his or her paramour and, for a period of three years, to anybody. Nothing, however, prevents a plaintiff from calling adultery an *injure grave* and thus saving the defendant from being labeled an adulterer or an adulteress.

The term "maltreatment, excesses, or grave injury," as used in both the Napoleonic Code and the present Code, was taken from the judicial practice developed in prerevolutionary France in matters of judicial separation. Following canon law tradition a separation would be declared justified in cases of conduct of one spouse, usually the husband, that would endanger the life and limb of the other. As in England, "moderate chastisement" of his wife was permissible to a French husband. It was in the nineteenth century practice of the time in which divorce was abolished, as well in the Belgian practice in divorce cases, that the scope was broadened to cover, first, acts, which, even though not physical, would endanger the partner's physical health. Next came impairment of mental equilibrium and well-being, and finally every act that could be regarded as a violation of the marital duties of "fidelity, succor, and assistance," as established in article 212 of the Civil Code. In the process, the terms "maltreatment" and "excesses," which originally were understood to have meanings of their own, were swallowed up by the term "injury," which was taken to cover any and all conduct that would so seriously hurt the feelings of the partner as to make it unfair to expect him to continue life in common. In actual practice, especially in the courts of the big cities, the requirement of seriousness or gravity of the "injury" came to be neglected. Ultimately, the term *injure grave* covered as wide a range of situations as the term "cruelty" or "mental cruelty" in the practice of the courts in California or other American states, or as the similarly vague formula of § 1568 of the German Civil Code of 1896 [38] or of art. 49 (now 43) of the German Marriage Act of 1938–45.[39]

In France, the term *injure grave* is now interpreted not only as covering desertion without any minimum limit of time but also as supplementing the meager provisions of the Civil Code on annulment. Deception about personal characteristics that might be expected to be

---

38. A divorce shall be granted to the party of a marriage if "the other party has so seriously violated his or her marital duties that the other cannot in fairness be expected to continue the marriage."

39. "A spouse may sue for divorce if the other spouse, through grave marital misconduct or through dissolute or immoral conduct has been guilty of so gravely confounding the marriage that one can no longer expect the restoration of such a community of life as would correspond to the essence of marriage."

relevant to the other party, or even lack of communication concerning such characteristics, is treated as grave injury justifying divorce.

When Naquet's bill for the restoration of divorce was before the Parliament, it contained, along with the other grounds for divorce of the Napoleonic Code, also that of mutual consent. Whatever progress the renaissance of liberal views had made in France, the time was not yet ripe for such a step. While the Chamber of Deputies agreed with Naquet, divorce by consent was removed from the law in the Senate. At the turn of the century, when conservatism seemed to have suffered a decisive defeat in the Dreyfus affair, and anticlerical liberalism had reached a height of fervor, new efforts were made to reintroduce consent divorce as an institution of official French law.[40] That effort also failed, but not so much because of conservative resistance as because it no longer appeared necessary. In a different way, so to speak through the back door, consent divorce had made its entry without any of the delays, formalities, and deterrents which the Napoleonic Code and, consequently, Naquet's draft had provided. If parties are in agreement that their marriage be terminated, they have to do no more than present to a big city court a statement indicating a situation traditionally treated as *injure grave,* no matter whether or not it is true, or whether or not it has in fact influenced the well-being or feelings of the party who has agreed to act as the plaintiff. A common device consists in the presentation to the court of a letter — previously prepared jointly by the parties or their advisers — containing insulting remarks concerning the plaintiff. Upon the presentation of such a letter the divorce follows as a matter of course. This result is reached even though French law provides that in all cases of divorce the state's attorney must be notified so as to give him the opportunity to enter the case as the defender of the marriage bond and to reveal the result of his investigation to the court. Actual intervention by the state's at-

---

40. In 1903, the indefatigable Naquet called consent "the most natural ground for divorce" (LA LOI DU DIVORCE 241). COULON, LE DIVORCE PAR CONSISTEMENT MUTUEL (1902), admonished the legislators not to insist on a law that would inevitably be disregarded. The same argument was made by COLONDRE, LE DIVORCE PAR CONSENTEMENT MUTUEL (1904). Of the numerous additional publications, we ought to mention P. & V. Margueritte, *Mariage et divorce,* REVUE ET REVUE DES REVUES 449 (1900); LES DEUX VIES (1902); COULON & DE CHAVAGNES, LE MARIAGE ET LE DIVORCE DE DEMAIN (1908). Numerous doctoral theses have been written on the subject, largely using the argument that marriage, being a contract, should, like any other contract, be capable of dissolution by the agreement of those parties by whose agreement it had been created. This legalistic argument has, of course, no persuasive effect on anyone who regards marriage as an institution in the maintenance of which society is interested and who is then likely to express this view by, or to hide it behind, the legalistic slogan that marriage is a status rather than a contract.

torney simply does not occur, nor do the courts, except perhaps in remote, conservative, rural regions, ever attempt to go behind the evidence presented by the parties. As in the United States the *divorce sanction* of the official law of the books has effectively been transformed into *divorce faillite* of the law in action. As in the United States this state of affairs is much deplored as jeopardizing the public's respect for law and lawyers and as corrupting morality.

Divorce cases rarely reach the higher courts. As in the United States, the overwhelming majority of French actions for divorce are uncontested. When the action is commenced, the parties are already in agreement that the marriage bond be terminated. Any controversy that may have existed about child custody, property partition, or alimony has been settled by negotiation. The state's attorney does not make use of his chance to intervene. If the divorce is granted, who will appeal? A refusal of the tribunal to grant the divorce hardly ever occurs. The parties have wisely picked a court known to be overburdened and to be accommodating. In the rare case that is pushed up to an appellate court, even if the litigation seemingly turns about the grant of the divorce, the real issue is who is to be labeled "guilty" and thus to be disadvantaged in respect to property settlement, alimony, damages, and child custody. The appellate court's determination of who has been guilty of grave injury against whom, is final. The point does not reach the highest court of France, the Court of Cassation. Quite generally, the supervision exercised by that illustrious tribunal over the lower courts is less strict than that exercised by American state supreme courts or by the supreme courts of Germany, Switzerland, and other countries. The application of such standards as fault in matters of tort or, in contracts, of good faith is generally left to the "sovereign evaluation by the trier of fact," i.e., the bench of the trial court of first or second instance. One of these standards is that of a grave injury as used in article 232 of the Civil Code.[41] Free reign is thus given to an overburdened, liberal-minded court like the trial court of Paris, the Tribunal de la Seine, and the court above it, the Cour d'Appel de Paris. All the Court of Cassation requires is that the lower court's decision contain express statements concerning what specific acts the court regards as constituting the "injury," why it regards them as "grave," and that they have made the continuation of mar-

---

41. For illustrations of these practices see Req. 17 November 1902, D. 1903.1.405; 2 June 1904, D.1904.1.474; Civ. 2 March 1926, D.H.1926.282; Req. 12 March 1945, D.1945.220.

ried life intolerable.⁴² Published opinions indicate that acts of the following kinds have been regarded as "grave injury" within the meaning of article 232:

Persistent voluntary refusal of the husband to engage in marital intercourse.⁴³
The wife's failure to take proper care of a child.⁴⁴
The husband's unproven charge of adultery raised against the wife.⁴⁵
The husband's abandonment of the marital home.⁴⁶
The wife's unjustified refusal to live at the home chosen by the husband.⁴⁷
Commission of a punishable act that directly affects the spouse in his or her honor or marital rights, even if it has not resulted in conviction of the kind stated in article 231 of the Civil Code.⁴⁸

Constantly, the courts have insisted, however, on the necessity that in order to constitute grave injury conduct must be voluntary. Infection with disease not contracted by the person's own voluntary act⁴⁹ or conduct caused by mental disease cannot constitute a ground for divorce.⁵⁰ Up to this point the notion of *divorce sanction* is still maintained.

42. See, for instance, Civ., sect. civ. 26 April and 8 May 1950, D.1950.452 and 430; 7 March 1951, D.1951.331; 9 January 1952, D.1952.194; 5 May 1952, D.1952, Somm.58; Civ.2d sect.civ. 6 May 1953, D.1953.479; 6,7, and 11 May 1953, D.1953.495.
43. Req.12 November 1900, D.P.1901.1.21.
44. Civ.2d sect. civ., 2 May 1963, D.1963, Somm.113.
45. Req.10 January 1906, D.P.1906.1.136.
46. Req.3 January 1893, D.P.1893.1.517 (case of judicial separation).
47. Civ.2d sect. civ. 9 January 1957, D.1958, Somm.21.
48. Toulouse, 31 December 1888, D.P.1890.2.104 (case of judicial separation).
49. Lyon, 20 November 1903, D.P.1904.2.136.
50. See Civ., 2d sect. civ., 2 May 1958, D.1958.509. On the present state of the case law, see J. PATARIN, CAUSES DU DIVORCE, JURIS-CLASSEUR CIVIL, ART. 216–230 DU CODE CIVIL (1965); 1 (2) A. MARTY & P. RAYNAUD, DROIT CIVIL 303 (2d ed. 1967).

9
Land of Socialist Experimentation: The Soviet Union

In the matter of marriage and divorce, the Union of Soviet Socialist Republics has been a laboratory of experimentation. In the half-century since the Revolution of 1917, the law of marriage and divorce has veered between positions that at least seem to constitute opposite poles.[1]

The position of the revolutionaries of 1917 was determined by the socialist classics, especially the writings of Friedrich Engels[2] and August Bebel.[3] To them the family of capitalist society appeared to be an instrument of exploitation. Women were subjected to male domination; children were the subjects of tyrannical fathers. Marriage was a treaty between the capitalist who gave away his daughter together with her dowry and the member of another capitalist group that would pool the dowry with its own funds. Marriage was arranged by the families. Love and mutual attraction were to play no role. Under the

---

1. As sources for this chapter, the following were used: H. J. BERMAN, JUSTICE IN THE U.S.S.R. (1963); A Bilinsky, *Die sowjetische Scheidungspolitik*, 13 ZEITSCHRIFT FÜR DAS GESAMTE FAMILIENRECHT (FAMRZ) 521, 648 (1966); A. I. Pergament, *Familienrecht*, in 2 S. N. BRATUS, ed., SOWJETISCHES ZIVILRECHT 433 (1951, 1953); R. DAVID & J. N. HAZARD, LE DROIT SOVIÉTIQUE (1954); A. FEIFER, JUSTICE IN MOSCOW (1964); E. FLORKOWSKI, DAS SOWJETISCHE EHESCHEIDUNGSRECHT (1967) (hereinafter cited as FLORKOWSKI); H. K. GEIGER, THE FAMILY IN SOVIET RUSSIA (1968); V. GSOVSKI, SOVIET CIVIL LAW (1948); J. N. HAZARD, SETTLING DISPUTES IN SOVIET SOCIETY (1960); J. N. HAZARD, LAW AND SOCIAL CHANGE IN THE U.S.S.R. (1953); J. N. HAZARD, J. SHAPIRO, & P. B. MAGGS, THE SOVIET LEGAL SYSTEM (1969); D. MACE & V. MACE, THE SOVIET FAMILY (1963); O. M. Stone, *The New Fundamental Principles of Soviet Family Law and Their Social Background*, 18 INT'L & COMP. L.Q. 393 (1969); W. Müller-Freienfels, *Zur revolutionären Familiengesetzgebung*, 2 JUS PRIVATUM GENTIUM: FESTSCHRIFT FÜR MAX RHEINSTEIN 842 (1969).

2. DER URSPRUNG DER FAMILIE, DES PRIVATEIGENTUMS UND DES STAATES (1884; English ed. THE ORIGIN OF THE FAMILY, PRIVATE PROPERTY AND THE STATE, 1942).

3. DIE FRAU UND DER SOZIALISMUS (1892).

double standard of bourgeois morality, the men were free to find satisfaction with mistresses or prostitutes — other victims of exploitation — while all extramarital ventures were strictly forbidden to women. Women were also deprived of the opportunities of education and thus prevented from being independent. They were confined to the area of the household and the children; they had no chance to escape and had to suffer in silence even the worst abuse by their husbands. Only in the exploited class of the proletariat, according to the revolutionaries, would marriage be founded on its true basis, love and affection. The proletarian had no property; for him marriage was thus free of the taint of bargain. Among the workers, unions between men and women were concluded freely and, as they were free of the fetters of private property, they could also end these unions freely once love and affection ceased. This pattern of proletarian marriage was to be the universal of the new socialist society, in which the free termination of a marriage would not be impeded by any worry about children, as the care of the young would be the task of the state rather than of the parents.

To what extent the Marxist view of the bourgeois family in general, and of the Russian family in particular, corresponded to reality is irrelevant. It was taken to be true as much as the alleged ideal of proletarian marriage. To such leaders of the Revolution as Alexandra Kollontai and perhaps even to Lenin, it seemed obvious that the state, in itself a tool of capitalist exploitation, would have to keep its hands off marriage even before it had fully withered away in the new communist society. In a social order in which religion was regarded as opium for the masses, it was equally clear that marriage had to be freed of all religious bonds and ceremonies by which it had been dominated in tsarist Russia. No longer would it be necessary to initiate a marriage with an ecclesiastical ceremony. No longer would anyone be prevented from entering upon a new pursuit of marital happiness when he had failed to find it in an existing union. Barely a month after the assumption of power, the Bolshevik government promulgated two decrees by which legal force was given to the new creed.[4] In the following year, the new rules were consolidated and amplified in the Code of the RSFSR, of 16 September 1918, on marriage, family and guardianship. Codes of essentially similar content were promulgated

---

4. Decree of the All-Russian Central Executive Committee and of the Council of People's Commissars of the Russian Socialist Federal Soviet Republik (RSFSR), of 18 December 1917, on civil marriage, on children, and on the registers of civil status; Decree (of the same authorities), of 19 December 1917, on divorce.

in the other Soviet republics.⁵ Divorce was to be freely obtainable upon the simple expression of both partners to a marriage or of one alone. This radical rule not only expressed the new proletarian ideal; it also opened the way out of marriage for believers in the new creed who found it intolerable to live with a spouse who was a reactionary, a conservative, or a counter-revolutionary. But as the state had not yet withered away, minimum cooperation with its organs was felt to be necessary. The conclusion of a marriage had to be registered with the new state agency that was to take over from the church the registration of births, deaths, and other events affecting the civil status of the citizens of the Soviet state. A divorce was not to be effective until it was either registered by the registrar of civil status or pronounced by a court. If the divorce was desired by both parties they would either appear before the registrar or turn to the people's court. The former method was cheaper than the latter, but in neither case was the cost more than the modest sum of about 10 rubles. The court procedure had the advantage of providing a judicial order susceptible of enforcement concerning the monetary and other effects of the divorce. If the divorce was sought by one party only, he had to turn to the people's court. But in no case was the court to engage in any inquiry. The expression of the wish to be divorced was in itself the ground for divorce. The requirement of cooperation with a governmental agency did not fully correspond with the official doctrine of the time, under which the function of the family was destined to be taken over by the new collectives, and matters of love and comradeship between the sexes were to be of concern to no one but the participants, who would be guided by the new socialist morality rather than by the heavy hand of the law. But the requirement of formalization of marriage and divorce resulted also in practical difficulties. It was incompatible with the revolutionary doctrine which continued to be pronounced passionately and incessantly. Just as the belief in the ultimate disappearance of the state, the doctrine of love and companionship as a completely private affair was in contradiction to the continued existence and the continuous expansion and intensification of the power machinery of the government. But the anarchist element of Marxism was attractive. If it was no longer necessary, in order to get married, to go before and pay the priest, why should one go to and pay the registrar? Why should one travel from the village to the seat of the office, why expose oneself to dangers in the troubled times of

---

5. A survey of the differences is given in FLORKOWSKI 292 nn. 78–81.

civil war? So there developed in the Soviet land what had developed in Turkey, Japan, or Latin America when official registration was established as a requirement for marriage by a government whose views were not understood by the masses: de facto marriage became a mass phenomenon. What difference would it make for a couple whether their marriage was or was not registered? In the revolutionary atmosphere public opinion did not require registration as a condition of respectablity. In Marxist doctrine, illegitimacy did not carry a stigma. Indeed, the distinction between legitimate and illegitimate birth would no longer make sense in a society in which children were to be brought up in collectives rather than parental homes and in which marriage would no longer have any function other than that of providing a framework for the exercise of the new morality of pure love and affection untainted by materialist motives. Even apart from the idealistic image, considerations of property, support claims, or inheritance carried little weight in the impoverished Russian world of the 1920s. Under a strict legalistic view an unregistered union might be a concubinage, the offspring might be illegitimate, but what true revolutionary would take such a legalistic view? In the popular view the distinction between registered and unregistered marriages was obliterated. A man and a woman who had begun to live together in the manner of husband and wife would regard themselves as married and would be so regarded irrespective of whether or not they had bothered to visit the registry office and to pay the fee. Just as the American term "common-law marriage" came to be ambiguous, so did the Russian term "brak." The difference between registered and unregistered, between "legal" and "factual" marriage was obscured.

After the years of external and civil war, conditions were more peaceful in 1921. In the work of reconstruction even private enterprise had to be used, at least temporarily, and government had to be reorganized and consolidated. In these years of the New Economic Policy it was also felt necessary to reconstruct the law and its machinery. Comprehensive codifications were promulgated in 1922 and 1923.[6] Along with them the law of marriage, family, and guardianship, which, in the socialist view, constitutes an autonomous field of the law rather than a branch of private law, was also to be revised. The old Code of 1918 now appearing to be too fragmentary, a draft was completed,

---

6. In the RSFSR, the following codes were enacted: Civil Code of 31 October, 1922; Labor Code, of 30 October 1922; Agrarian Code, of 30 October 1922; Criminal Code, of 1 June 1922; Code of Criminal Procedure, of 25 May 1923; Code of Civil Procedure, of 7 July 1923; Code on the Organization of the Courts, of 31 October 1922.

but it became the subject of intensive and passionate discussion within government and party circles as well as in plants, kolkhozy, and other collectives. The focus of these debates was the problem of informal marriage and informal divorce. Should the new code follow classical Marxist doctrine and thus sanction the popular practice, or should the renascent state power continue to insist on reaffirming the state's concern in marriage? In party theory, orthodoxy was still dominant. Under the leadership of Pashukanis, the legal writers still maintained that law and state were remnants of the bourgeois past that would soon disappear so that the government of men would yield to the administration of things. In the legislation of 1917 and 1918, registration of marriage and divorce was meant to be the device to eliminate the jurisdiction of the church. That purpose had been achieved. So why not go the whole way now and abolish the requirement of governmental cooperation in matters of noneconomic personal life? The debate went on for four years until in the RSFSR the new code on marriage, family, and guardianship was promulgated on 19 November 1926, to take effect on 1 January 1927.[7]

The new law did not fully abolish all governmental participation in the matter of conclusion and termination of the man-woman relationship, but it substantially embraced the orthodox doctrine and thus also sanctioned the popular practice. Under the theory of the Code of 1926 the conclusion and the termination of a marriage are purely private transactions. In that respect the Soviet law corresponded to the pre-Tridentine law of the Catholic church, *consensus facit nuptias*, adding that divorce is not only possible but is brought about by the private act either of both parties or of one party alone. If it is desired, a marriage or a divorce may be registered by the government's registrar of civil status. But such registration does not bring about the change in the parties' status. Its effect is merely that of providing evidence. In the absence of registration, the proof of the conclusion or the termination of a marriage soon presented the same difficulties that arise in the United States in connection with common-law marriage. If the existence of a purely factual marriage were to be judicially decided, the court had to find in favor of its existence if the parties had mutually recognized each other as husband and wife, or if the parties in fact lived in such a way that the existence of a marriage

7. The Code, usually referred to as the Family Code of 19 November 1926, was published in the Official Gazette of the RSFSR, Sobranie Uzakonenii (S.U.), no. 82, art. 612 (1926); Similar, but not fully identical codes were enacted in the other republics.

was to be assumed.[8] As indicia for the existence of a marriage the courts were to consider such facts as the actual common life of the parties, the common conduct of their household, written expressions made toward third persons in letters or other writings, giving of support by one party to the other, or cooperation in the care of the children.[9] But writers insisted that the courts had to disregard one fact that would have allowed them with certainty to assume the existence of the *animus maritalis*, namely, the performance of a religious marriage ceremony.[10]

The situation created by the Code of 1926 resembled that of English law of the time preceding Lord Hardwick's Act of 1753. A marriage would be valid irrespective of whether or not its conclusion was accompanied by a formal act, but the formalized marriage presented certain advantages over the informal. In England the purely common-law marriage failed to create rights of dower or courtesy. In Soviet law parties to an unregistered marriage were disadvantaged with respect to pension, social security benefits, taxes, and membership in building cooperatives. Besides they were not allowed to have a common surname. In a registered marriage the parties could either keep their different surnames or assume as their common surname that of the husband or of the wife.

Registration of a divorce was possible only if the marriage had been registered, but for the registration of the marriage no time limit was established. It could be applied for even months or years after the factual conclusion of the marriage, but the evidentiary effect of the registration extended to the date of the factual conclusion of the marriage as stated on the register. As the registration of a marriage that of the divorce had only evidentiary significance. The marriage, and with it its incidents, was terminated at the moment the parties, or one of them, walked out on the other or in other ways manifested his intention to terminate the relationship. If desired, the event would then be recorded upon the written or oral application of both parties or one of them. In the latter case the fact that the divorce had been registered was communicated three days later to the other party, provided his or her address was known. Popularly, the procedure came to be called "divorce by postcard." If the divorce was not registered, the burden of proving that the marriage had in fact been terminated lay with the party who alleged that it had.

8. Code of 1926, art. 11.
9. Code, art. 12.
10. See Florkowski 311 n. 287.

The government apparently preferred the clarity of registration of marriage and divorce to the vagueness of purely factual relationships. But the theory demanded freedom from state interference. The developing socialist morality was expected to free the man-woman relationship from the dependence on religion and government that had resulted from mankind's corruption by private property. But what actually occurred was a violent swing in the opposite direction.

In 1924 Lenin died. In 1929 Trotzki was exiled. Stalin established his dictatorship and his policy of rapid industrialization. The purges, the collectivization, the scarcity of consumer goods caused by emphasis upon the development of heavy industry, the preparation for the defense of the Soviet land against the expected fascist onslaught, they all required obedience of the people, discipline, patience, an overpowering police force, an omnipotent government. No longer would the people be allowed to expect law and the state to wither away immediately. That hope was not abandoned but it was removed to the eschatological future. Pashukanis, up to then the leading jurist, had misread the classics when he foretold the early advent of the stateless society and pronounced the ephemeral character of law a remnant of bourgeois society. Such a theory was now declared to be that of an enemy of the people. Leadership in juristic thought was assumed by Vishinsky, the prosecutor in the great purge trials. The classics had been equally misread by those who, like Goichbarg, expected the family soon to become superfluous and to be replaced by the collective. The family was rediscovered as the basic cell of the community and as being based upon marriage in the sense of a lasting, monogamous community of life of equal partners, in which the younger generation was to be raised to useful, responsible citizenship in the communist state. Freedom of divorce as it had been postulated by Engels, and more cautiously by Lenin, was reinterpreted to mean freedom to escape from a relationship that, in spite of serious effort, had failed to be useful for society; it thus excluded the freedom to flit recklessly from one sexual venture to another. In the changed atmosphere permissiveness had to yield to regulation. Purity of sexual behavior was no longer expected to be achieved only by the free influence of socialist morality. Supplementation by governmental force appeared to be called for. The revolutionary tradition was still strong enough to preclude attempts to regulate sexual conduct by means of the criminal law. But the law was used to establish the new image of marriage. The first major step was taken by the promulgation, on 27 June 1936, of the decree of the Central Executive Committee and the Council of People's Commissars of the USSR, concerning the "prohibition of abortion, the increase of allowances to women after childbirth and to large families, the enlargement of the network of lying-in clinics, nurseries, and kindergartens, the greater severity of punishment for violation of duties of support, and some changes in the law of divorce."[11] This new family protection law was a federal enactment, effective throughout the Soviet Union. It did not abolish de facto marriage nor did it openly do away with freedom of divorce. In fact, nothing was changed concerning the termination of purely factual marriages. But the termination of a registered marriage was to be all but worthless unless the divorce was also registered, and in order to obtain registration it was required that, except in certain special circumstances, both parties had personally to appear before the registrar and the divorce was to be entered in the personal passports of both parties. Besides, the fees for registration were drastically increased: 50 rubles for the first divorce, 150 for the second, and 300 for the third and every following divorce. For the majority of the population these sums were formidable. The number of registered divorces consequently dropped considerably. In the RSFSR the number of divorces registered in 1938 was 42.3 percent smaller than that of 1936. In the Ukrainian SSR the decrease was 34.7 percent; in the Bielorussian SSR, 44.1 percent; in the total territory of the USSR it was 35.8 percent.[12]

The decisive step was taken eight years later, when the Soviet Union was at war and its armies had almost succeeded in liberating the Soviet territory. On 8 July 1944 the Presidium of the Supreme Soviet of the USSR issued its "decree concerning allowances for pregnant women and mothers living alone with several children, the increased protection of motherhood and childhood, the establishment of the honorary title of Heroic Mother, and the decoration of Motherhood Glory and Motherhood Medal.[13] Unregistered marriage and unregistered divorce were abolished. The distinction between legitimate and illegitimate children, which the enactments of 1917 and 1918 had sought to wipe out, was reestablished. The reciprocal rights of support between legitimate children and their parents were strengthened, but an illegitimate child had no claim of support at all against his father. In fact all inquiry into the fatherhood of an illegitimate child was prohibited, and so

---

11. Sobranie Zakonov (S.Z.) USSR, 1936, no. 34, art. 309.
12. A. M. Sverdlov, *K voprosy o kodifikacii brachno — semeinogo zakonadelstva*, in V. M. CHKHIKVADZE & A. N. YODKOVSKII, eds., VOPROSY KODIFIKACII 105 (1957), cited in FLORKOWSKI 327 n. 448.
13. Vedomosti Verkhovnogo Sovieta USSR (VVS.USSR), 1944, No. 37.

in that respect Soviet law came to be what the Code Napoléon had been in France in 1804. Mothers were to receive an allowance from the government for each illegitimate child until the child completed his twelfth year of age. The decision to terminate a marriage was no longer left to the unfettered discretion of the parties. No divorce was to occur unless a court had, "after investigating the motives for the initiation of the petition and after having resorted to measures to reconcile the parties, found the divorce to be necessary."[14] In reaching a decision the courts were to be guided by "concern for the children and the mother and the strengthening of the institution of the family as one of the most important tasks of the Soviet State."[15] The proceedings required the activity of two courts. The petition was to be brought up at the local people's court, whose judge, sitting alone, was to hear the parties, investigate the facts, and attempt to bring about a reconciliation. A new petition was then to be made at the next higher court in the republic or autonomous region. These courts, which bear different names in the different parts of the USSR, are usually referred to as district courts. In the large republics they are intermediate appellate courts; in the smaller ones they may be the supreme courts. This higher court was again to hear the case, again to attempt reconciliation, and ultimately to decide about the granting or denial of the divorce. The marriage was not terminated, however, until, upon petition of the parties or one of them, the divorce was registered by the Office of Civil Status. A fee of 10 rubles was to be paid at the commencement of the proceedings in the people's court, but the court would not hear the case until the petitioner had, at his expense, given public notice of his intention in a local newspaper. At the end of the proceedings, another fee was payable, the amount to be fixed by the court between the limits of 50 and 200 rubles.

The new regulation of marriage, divorce, and illegitimacy differed from those ideas which were professed as Marxist doctrine in the days of the Revolution. The principal reason for this sharp turn was, of course, the change in the political climate of the USSR. But other, more concrete reasons were at work both to bring about the changes and to preserve some of the ideas of 1917. In the Stalinist era, the true motives of the new legislation were not published. But much has become known through later discussions, especially those extensive debates by which the reforms of 1965–67 were preceded. Conclusions can

---

14. Decree of 8 July 1944, arts. 25, 26.
15. Preamble.

also be drawn from the circumstances of the times which provoked the legislation of 1936–44.

To a considerable extent Stalinist family legislation was motivated by considerations of population policy. For some time the population increase had stagnated. The death rate had fallen spectacularly. By 1958 it was one-fourth of what it had been in 1913. But the birth rate had decreased as well. By 1958 it was only one-half the rate of 1913. The decrease was particularly marked between 1926 and 1955. The population increased, but not as much as seemed desirable. Also the increase appeared seriously threatened by the enormous number of men lost in the war. In 1944, there were 50 percent more women of child-bearing age than men of a comparable age. The surplus should not be wasted by the state. But if marriage and the family were both to be strengthened, the men had to be encouraged not only to marry but also to produce offspring with the unmarried women. If their marriages were not to be threatened by jealousy and scandal, they would have to be protected against their extramarital ventures becoming known to their wives. Just as in Napoleon's France the bourgeois family had to be protected against the scandal of intrusion by the offspring of proletarian mistresses, so there was also in the Soviet Union the prohibition of 'recherche de la paternité" and, in the USSR, the assumption by the state of the financial care of illegitimate children. The strengthening of the family, on the other hand, had become necessary because of the communist state's interest in the welfare of the nation's offspring as well as its fear that the national strength and vigor might be sapped by laxity of morals, sexual and otherwise. The public institutions for child care had been developed vigorously. To a considerable extent they freed women for work outside of the home, but they were far from totally replacing the home, as classical Marxist theory had expected them rapidly to do. The home was still the cradle of Soviet youth. Its preservation and strengthening were demanded by the national interest. In the nation's interest it was also necessary to stop the relaxation of morals that had set in with the Revolution. Lenin himself had expressed concern about the attitude of regarding sexual intercourse as a mere satisfaction of physical need akin to the quenching of thirst by drinking a glass of water. The great tasks of industrialization and collectivization, not to speak of national defense and war, required discipline, self-mastery, patience, comradeship, courage, the same virtues which are required for a stable home life, a harmonious marriage, and education for useful citizenship. Purity of morals and marriage stability were thus to be emphasized in education, in public propaganda, through hortative activity in the home, the plant, and the farm collectives, through public administration as well as through the law. Divorce was not eliminated. Such a step would have been too radical a departure from the ideology of the Revolution. To impede remarriage after an unsuccessful venture would have been contrary to the aim of promoting happy, well-functioning families. But divorce was to be discouraged. It was to be an ultimate way out of a marriage which responsible state organs had found to have failed in its social function. The aim was the same as that expressed in England in the report of the group convoked by the Archbishop of Canterbury, and as announced many a time in Western countries. Have the Soviets been more successful in reaching it than Western countries?

In judicial practice the Soviet courts have found themselves faced with the same difficulties which have arisen in other countries under the statutes in which divorce is based upon the principle of breakdown. When indeed is a court to hold that a "divorce is necessary"?

In order to give some guidance to the courts, the Supreme Court of the USSR, on 16 September 1949, pronounced a set of directives.[16] They were meant to counteract the liberal tendency that was exhibited by many courts and to emphasize the policy of protecting and promoting family stability. But the court was reluctant to speak in concrete, unambiguous terms. It elaborated the vague formula of the statute by announcing a set of principles which were expressed in part positively and in part negatively. The guiding principle was stated as follows: "A marriage is to be terminated only when on the basis of the concrete circumstances, the court has become convinced that the initiation of the suit for divorce was based on deeply considered serious motives, that the preservation of the marriage would be contrary to socialist morality, and that it could not create normal conditions for a common life of the spouses and the education of the children."

The court furthermore stated that the parties' agreement to have their marriage dissolved did not by itself constitute a sufficient reason to grant a divorce. "The events," so it was said, "must be so serious

16. Directive No. 12/814, of 16 September 1949 (SBORNIK DEISTVUYUSHCHICH POSTANO-VIENII PLENUM VERKHOVNOGO SUDA SSSR 1924–1957 GG. 164 [1958]). Directives are frequently issued by the Supreme Court of the USSR and the supreme courts of the several republics and autonomous regions. The institution existed in tsarist Russia and resembles the *arrêts de règlement* of the highest courts of prerevolutionary France. They are universally followed by the lower courts. On the present legal bases see FLORKOWSKI 65–66.

that neither a fortuitous conflict between the spouses caused by a temporary circumstance nor a desire of one spouse or both to terminate the marriage which is not justified by serious reasons can be regarded as a sufficient ground for divorce."

Rather than enumerating precisely defined grounds for divorce, the directive of the federal Supreme Court again formulated an omnibus clause. But that clause made clear at least enough to indicate that the new Soviet law of divorce was based upon the principle of breakdown.

The principle of breakdown has also found expression in the wording given to article 25 by the decree of the Presidium of the Supreme Soviet of the USSR of 10 December 1965,[17] which was obviously meant to consolidate rather than modify the substantive law of divorce as it had been established in 1944. But in article 14 of the All-Union Fundamental Principles of the Law of Marriage and the Family, of the Supreme Soviet of the USSR, of 27 June 1968,[18] the latest act of Union legislation, the necessity of judicial inquiry has been limited to contested divorces and to uncontested divorces of spouses having minor children. By a new about-face parties having no minor children can obtain a divorce through simple registration by the registrar of civil status of their agreement. In the same simple way a divorce may now be obtained when there has been a judicial declaration that a spouse is missing and cannot be traced, or has been judicially found to be of unsound mind or an imbecile; or where a spouse has been sentenced to deprivation of liberty for not less than three years. But a divorce by simple registration becomes effective, and the certificate of divorce is issued, only after the expiration of three months from the date of application.[19]

Another innovation is the rule that a husband may not apply for a contested divorce while his wife is pregnant or before the expiration of one year after she has given birth to a child. A far-reaching procedural change had already been made by the Decree of 10 December 1965. The division of the proceedings into two judicial stages was abolished. Jurisdiction to grant divorce was vested in the people's courts,

17. VVS.USSR, 1965, No. 49, at 1084.
18. VVS.USSR, 1968, No. 27/241, at 401; English text by Novosti Press Agency Publishing House, Moscow (n.d.), also in the appendix to the article by Stone, *supra* note 1, at 410; a French translation follows the article by C. Kourilsky, *La loi de 1968 et l'évolution du droit soviétique de la famille*, ANNUAIRE DE L'U.R.S.S. 251, 270 (1969); an English translation of article 14 (divorce) is given in HAZARD, SHAPIRO & MAGGS, *supra* note 1, at 522.
19. Art. 14, para. 9.

where procedure is simpler than in the district courts and which can be reached more easily than the district court, whose territory is often extensive, especially in as yet thinly settled regions. The principle of breakdown has thus found twofold expression. Apparently breakdown is assumed to exist in all cases in which both parties have agreed to have their marriage terminated. In contested cases its existence must be ascertained by a court which must inquire whether further common life for the spouses and preservation of the family have become impossible. In that inquiry the courts are still to be guided by the Supreme Court directive of 1949.

Although the judicial determination of breakdown is now limited to the small number of contested cases, and, perhaps, to the larger number of uncontested cases of parents of minor children, it is still of interest to see how the omnibus clauses of the decrees and the Supreme Court directives were understood by the courts, to which they left a wide range of interpretation and thus of discretion. What motives for the initiation of a divorce suit are "profoundly considered and serious"? When exactly would "the preservation of the marriage be contradictory to the principles of socialist morality"? When is it that the preservation of the marriage "cannot create moral conditions for common life of the spouses and the education of the children"? The last-named formula is the one for which it is most possible to find a determinable meaning, provided the formula is read so as to signify that in a given situation the restoration of the common life of the spouses and of wholesome conditions for the education of the children is improbable. But there still remains the job of determining the degree of improbability.

What is meant by "impossibility of a continued common life of the spouses and of preservation of the family"? If that term were to be applied literally, no divorce would ever be granted. As long as both spouses are alive their life in common is never "impossible," except perhaps where one of the parties is institutionalized because of a mental disease for which it can be predicted with certainty that no progress in the medical art will ever devise a cure. Furthermore, what is meant by "preservation of the family" and by "impossibility" of such preservation? The terms had to be given more concrete meaning by the courts and the legal scholars, whose activities have come to assume increasing importance in the USSR.

The practice of the courts and the views expressed in the voluminous body of legal writing are analyzed in detail by Florkowski.[20] It appears that although the formulas of the decrees of 1944 and the directive of 1949 have been cited time and again, no one has rendered them concrete enough to constitute unbending rules in neatly defined situations.

As seems inevitable in any system of divorce based on the principle of breakdown, the tendency to consider one party guilty also appeared in the USSR. Every now and then a petitioner tried to allege and prove some kind of marital misconduct of the respondent, or a respondent was allowed to bar a divorce by proving that the breakdown of the marriage had been caused by the marital misconduct of the petitioner. Even courts inclined to deny a divorce to a petitioner who had brought about the breakdown of the marriage by abandoning the spouse and living in an irregular union with another partner. But such tendencies never prevailed. They would have subverted that policy which, in the welter of divergent views, seems to have emerged as dominant: Where a marriage has so thoroughly ceased to function that nothing is left but the empty hull of the legal bond, a way ought to be opened for the creation or regularization of a new union holding the prospect of a happier and more harmonious home. This idea is now regarded as one of the demands of the new, specifically socialist morality. Soviet writers, not to speak of Soviet judges, still lack acquaintance with the social structure of Western countries and the ways in which moral values have developed there.

A controversy developed about the cases in which the parties are agreed in their desire to obtain a divorce. Strict adherence to the policy of 1944 would seem to have forbidden the grant of a divorce in any case in which it was not certain that the marriage had so degenerated that nothing was left of it but the formal bond. Could such a state of fact be presumed from the parties' agreement to have their marriage ended? Would the presumption be permissible in at least those cases in which a new, irregular union had been established by one of the spouses or perhaps by both? Except in Bielorussia and to some extent in the Ukraine the courts inclined toward granting a divorce in such cases in the early years of the 1944 law. Possibly the courts were reluctant too abruptly to impose upon the populace a legal system which repudiated the one under which people had lived for thirty years and which had been hailed as a major achievement of the Revolution.

20. At 95–163.

It was exactly to check this trend that the Supreme Court of the USSR issued its directive in 1949. For a time the judicial attitudes stiffened, only to revert soon to the more accommodating attitude.

Under the basic statutory provision a marriage is to be terminated when it has broken down and its restoration is impossible. From this formula one could conclude that marriage breakdown might assume various degrees of severity ranging from slight temporary disturbance of marital harmony all the way to complete and irremediable disruption, and that no divorce should be granted unless the breakdown has reached that ultimate degree of severity. The courts have refrained from taking such a view. They have preferred to regard the statutory formula as a unit ordering them in every case to determine whether "the marriage had broken down and its restoration was impossible." In that way they have reserved to themselves a wide range of discretion to invest the formula with meaning corresponding to basic attitudes that might differ from time to time and from place to place. The basic attitudes that have been contending with each other are the same in the USSR as in other countries undergoing industrialization and social transformation. There as here the individualist-liberal and the collectivist-conservative views oppose each other. In the early years of Sovietism, the individualist-liberal view of marriage assumed extreme forms and established itself as the doctrine officially approved by the government and the party. The opposite view was adopted by the Stalinist regime. Marriage and family were again to be stabilized as the basic cells of society. Conservatism in matters of marriage was thus demonstrated to be not simply a survival of Christian tradition but also a desideratum of purely secular statism. The case of the USSR also indicates that discrepancy between the law of the books and the law in action is not limited to the "bourgeois" part of the world. But in the USSR it was less conspicuous because the policy of strictness was not expressed with full definiteness in the law of the books. The texts were so formulated as openly to leave the courts the possibility of pursuing a policy which hardly ever fully responded to the policy of the Stalinist government. In the post-Stalinist era the official policy has been modified so as to make it conform to the popular views, which had never ceased to exercise their influence in the courts.

Just as the enactment of the Family Law Code of 1926 had constituted a part of the effort to codify Soviet law in general, the divorce law reforms of 1965 and 1968 occurred within the framework of a general revision of Soviet law. Under the Constitution of 1936, legislation in matters of private law, family law, criminal law, civil procedure, criminal procedure and certain other matters belongs to the sphere of the Union republics. But the legislative organs of the USSR are empowered to establish basic principles, by which each of the republics is to abide. In the 1960s, such federal principles have been enacted in all the fields just mentioned, in many cases going into much detail. As in the 1920s, the codification of the law of marriage and divorce took longer than that of the other fields. The basic questions are controversial and the government wished them to be discussed publicly and thoroughly. In 1963, the publication of the draft had been announced; but the decree that was promulgated by the Presidium of the Supreme Soviet of the USSR on 10 December 1965 and ratified by the Supreme Soviet in August 1966 dealt with only a small part of the topic, namely, procedure in matters of divorce. Comprehensive reform of the substantive law of marriage, the family, and guardianship was not completed until 1968. The new basic principles were promulgated by the Presidium of the Supreme Soviet of the USSR on 27 June 1968.[21]

The act of 1965 modified that feature of the Stalin law of 1944 which had been most widely criticized — the necessity of proceeding in two courts in order to obtain a divorce. One court was now to be enough and that court was to be the easily accessible people's court rather than the often remote and more formalistic district court. That step also speeded up the proceedings and had the further effect of reducing the scope of appellate review exercisable in matters of divorce by supreme courts. Under the Soviet system of procedure a party can appeal as a matter of right from the trial court to the court next higher to it in the judicial hierarchy. As long as divorces were handled by the district courts, an appeal could have been carried to the supreme court of the Union republic in question.[22] Now the courts to which appeals must be brought are the district courts, which are numerous in the larger Union republics and whose decisions are rarely if ever published. Divorce cases can now reach a supreme court only where a "protest" against the decision of a district court is raised by a public prosecutor or the president or vice-president of the supreme court or the district court. Such a protest is to be raised *ex officio* against a decision which appears flagrantly contrary to the law. Frequently, however, the initiative is taken by the losing party, who requests the ap-

21. *Supra* p. 233.
22. Or even to the Supreme Court of the USSR, if, as in the smaller republics and autonomous regions, their Supreme Court is the court directly superior to the people's courts.

propriate officer to raise the protest. The informal procedure in which the decision is scrutinized by the official resembles the way in which petitions for certiorari are handled in American courts, where the decision of whether or not a judgment is to be brought before the full court is, however, always made by a judge. In Western countries local courts, especially busy ones, are generally more inclined to comply with petitions for divorce than supreme courts, which are infrequently confronted with the realities of marital failure, which never see an uncontested case, and which are more likely to heed antidivorce attitudes expressed in the law of the books. No reason appears to justify the view that the situation might be different in the USSR. The Law of 1965 was meant to facilitate judicial divorce, but it did not remove the deterrent of high costs. Even though the judicial proceedings were now concentrated in the people's court, and even though it was no longer necessary to incur the expense of publishing the announcement of a divorce suit in a newspaper, a high fee of at least 50 and at most 200 rubles was still to be paid for the registration of the divorce which had to follow the decision of the court and without which the marriage would not be terminated. This formidable deterrent was abolished by the Law of 1968 for all cases in which there is no dispute and in which the parties have no minor children, i.e., for at least one-half of all divorces. Contested cases are as rare in the USSR as they are in the United States or anywhere else. In fact they may be even rarer in view of the reluctance of Soviet law to provide alimony for any person longer than one year. As in Japan, alimony thus is more like severance pay intended to facilitate transition than a means of permament support. The realm of possible dispute is thus likely to be limited to the determination of custody and support of minor children, a problem that does not arise in the 50 percent of cases in which no minor children are involved, and to the problem of property settlement, a question which presupposes the existence of property to be divided. Objection to the termination of the marriage as such is exceedingly infrequent anywhere. In the USSR any such objection has little chance to be considered and is therefore seldom raised. Socialist morality disapproves not only of hate and spite but also of such materialistic motives as the desire to prevent the loss of a pension right.[23] A large percentage of the divorces will be effected without judicial proceedings, thus without officially attempted conciliation proceedings, and at the minimal cost of simple registration. Consent divorce has been

---

23. See the cases related in FLORKOWSKI 137–38.

recognized by the law of the books, at least for cases in which no minor children are involved. For the safeguarding of children's interests judicial control is still considered necessary. To what extent the control will be effective remains to be seen. Soviet society is greatly concerned about the welfare of its youth. It would be interesting to explore whether that concern has developed any devices more effective than the elaborate institutions of West Germany or England or the primitive techniques of the major part of the United States.

The reform of 1965–68 appears to be a radical reversal of the Stalinist ideas of 1944. But it should be regarded rather as an acknowledgment that the law of divorce is not only needed to achieve the end of promoting family stability but can actually constitute an obstacle to it. The Soviet family has been consolidated as Soviet society was consolidated. The cultural climate of the country is no longer that of the revolutionary era nor of the years of Stalinism. Excesses of sexual license are disapproved not only by officialdom but by society. Stability of marital and family life is the ideal demanded by socialist morality. The schools, the Komsomol, the armed forces, the party, the collectives, all the forces and organizations by which the individual is molded guide him in this direction. Informal marriage is no longer possible. More and more marriages are concluded not in the perfunctory way and the dingy rooms of the registrar of civil status, but in an impressive, although simple, ceremony conducted in the cheerful atmosphere of a "marriage palace." Abuse of alcohol, which has been one of the most potent sources of family discord, may induce the intervention of some organs of the collective community of the plant, the office, the bloc of dwellings, or the kolkhoz, organs which may also step in as censors or conciliators in other cases of domestic trouble or irregularity. It would be interesting to know more about their role as well as about that of the comrades' courts, which, favored in the Khrushchev era, were meant to act as semiofficial guardians of socialist morality. Devastation of sexual morals and family life was largely the result of the upheavals of the Revolution, the preceding external war, and the subsequent civil war. The confusion was heightened by the unrealistic doctrine of the classic communist writers and their early disciples. Their expectations of an immediate socialist elysium could not be fulfilled, and the disappointment helped to confound the anomie created by the collapse of the old society, its institutions, and its moral code. Consolidation had hardly set in when Soviet society was again shaken by the forced pace of industrialization, the destruction of the kulaks, the collectivization of the farms, the terror of the

Stalinist persecutions, and, most profoundly, by the German invasion, the devastation of open and partisan warfare, and the decimation of the country's male population. Only since the death of Stalin in 1953 has consolidation had a new chance. It seems to have gone far, but not yet to be complete. But the USSR has come to resemble those countries in the West in which unrest and uncertainty about moral values is principally the result of the industrialization and the continuing waves in which that process has been going on. The old-type American family with its strong ties among even remote relatives and its domination by the patriarch has disappeared. It produced its own stresses and tensions, but women rarely rebelled, the men could indulge in extramarital ventures, and divorce was frowned upon, conceived of as repudiation of an unfaithful wife by an outraged husband, and rarely resorted to.

In the Soviet Union, as elsewhere, it took time for the new system of the nuclear family to establish itself and to reach a state of stability. The intermediate stage of the transitional family was peculiarly open to disruption. The old ideas of right and wrong had lost validity, the new ones had not yet taken hold. Perhaps the type of the transitional family has not yet fully disappeared in the Soviet Union. But the new type has achieved predominance and this new type is basically the same as that of the family in the industrialized, urbanized society of Western countries. If there are differences, they may be of two kinds, operating in opposite directions. Through its collective organs Soviet society seems more powerfully to impose conformity than Western society, which has grown steadily more permissive. On the other side, in the aftermath of repeated upheaval, terror, and scarcity, a comparatively large proportion of the Soviet people is said to have given up hope, to have ceased to strive, to live from day to day without belief and without values. This "Nychyevo man," with his attitude of "so what" is unlikely or unable to hold to a steady course in work, in personal life, in marriage. The type is by no means absent in the West, where it in fact seems to have increased in recent years. In the Soviet Union it may perhaps be on its way out. Of course, stresses exist in the new-type Soviet family. They are of the same kind as those by which Western families are shaken, the stresses of change in social status or geographic location, of disappointed expectations, of psychopathic personality, immaturity, personality clashes. In the Soviet Union they may be heightened by the greater involvement of the women in production and the still existing shortage of material goods, especially housing. Serious as these factors may be, they have not prevented the increasing consolidation of marriage and family life. In this process of consolidation the law of divorce seems to have played a minor role. It must be doubted whether the difficulty of obtaining a divorce under the law of 1944 has prevented the breakdown of any single marriage. If it has had any share in bringing about the stabilization of family life, it has been indirectly through its significance as a symbol of the new morality, i.e., as a factor in the transformation of the cultural climate. Quite obviously, however, the difficulty of obtaining a legal divorce, and thus having the way opened to legitimate remarriage, has had the negative effect of not only not reducing but of rather increasing the incidence of irregular unions or, as they are called in the USSR, of informal marriages.

The number and the rate of judicial, i.e., of legally effective, divorces was sharply reduced by the legislation of 1944. In 1940 the rate of judicial divorces was 1.1 per 1,000 population. In 1945 it fell to 0.6. In 1950, it was 0.4, but the average for 1960–64 again rose to 1.34.[24]

The Family Protection Law of 1936, by which registration was made necessary for the termination of a registered marriage, and by which the fees for the registration of a divorce were fixed at 50 rubles for the first, 100 rubles for the second, and 300 rubles for every further divorce, is said to have reduced the number of registered divorces between 1935 and 1938 by 66.6 percent in Kazakhstan, by 44.1 percent in Bielorussia, by 42.3 percent in RSFSR, and by 34.7 percent in the Ukraine.[25]

The reforms of 1965–68 are the result of a long, intensive debate in which legal writers played a major role but which was also carried on in the collectives in which Soviet public opinion is formed.[26] Many of the arguments are reminiscent of those which have inevitably appeared wherever the problem of divorce has been discussed: The law ought to discourage ill-considered and ill-justified divorces;[27] it ought to prevent arbitrary attempts to shake off marital responsibilities.[28] People ought to be careful not to exercise corrupting influence upon youth,[29]

---

24. DEMOGRAPHIC YEARBOOK OF THE UNITED NATIONS 1968, table 34; see also A. Bilinsky *Die sowjetische Scheidungspolitik*, 13 FAM.R.Z. 521, 522 (1966), citing M. G. Sverdlov, *Zakon vrazvode i statistika*, SOVIETKOIE GOSUDARSTVO I PRAVO, no. 10, 1964, at 33. The figures given there are said to be not fully reliable because it was not yet clear in the 1950s that a judicially allowed divorce would not be effective until its registration at the registrar's office. Many parties are said to have failed to register so that the data on registration of divorces lag behind those on judicial decrees.
25. FLORKOWSKI 327, n. 448.
26. See FLORKOWSKI 255 ff.
27. Sverdlov as cited in FLORKOWSKI 273.
28. Sverdlov and Orlova, as cited *ibid*.
29. Orlova, as cited *id*.

to protect the family, society's smallest cell, and thus to perform one of the most important tasks of the state.[30] Some argue that a law allowing easy divorce breeds divorce;[31] others maintain that it is none of the state's business to inject itself into the marriage life of its citizens and thus to interfere with personal freedom, that a happy family life cannot be brought about by force, that the incidence of marriage breakup depends on the socioeconomic circumstances rather than statutory norms.[32]

The decisive reason for the reform of the 1960s seems to have been the recognition that the legislation of 1936–44 had turned out to be of little effect. After the initial drop in the rate of judicial divorces it began to rise again from 0.6 in 1955 to 1.3 in 1961[33] and 1.7 in 1965.[34] The courts are said to have been eventually less reluctant to allow divorces. In 1959 only 3 percent of all divorce suits brought in the USSR are said to have ended in refusal.[35] The conciliation attempts of the people's courts are reported frequently to have been perfunctory and meaningless.[36] The uncontested cases are said to have been disposed of by the courts in "trials" lasting from three to five minutes.[37]

The decisive motive for the reform seems to have been the continued flourishing of factual divorce and, consequently, of factual, i.e., unregistered, marriage. The high cost of a registered divorce was prohibitive, but if it had a deterrent effect, it was not that of preventing family breakdown but simply that of having it formalized by judicial decision and registration. Another inconvenience was provided by the rule that judicial proceedings had to be instituted at the place of residence of the defendant.

Informal marriage and informal divorce had been hailed as great achievements of the Revolution. They had become part and parcel of the social fabric. In the process of consolidation these institutions have become less respectable, but the social pressure has not achieved that strength which in the United States has made common-law marriage a lower-class institution. In Italy a law that is lacking universal approval has achieved for the irregular union a measure of respecta-

30. Rabinovic, as cited *id.* 274.
31. Sverdlov, as cited *id.* 275.
32. See FLORKOWSKI 270–73.
33. FLORKOWSKI 438 n. 89.
34. U.N. DEMOGRAPHIC YEARBOOK 1967, table 26.
35. Sverdlov, as cited in FLORKOWSKI 379, n. 47, where data from various localities are also reported.
36. See FLORKOWSKI 170.
37. FLORKOWSKI 154.

bility. In the Soviet Union the respectability which the Revolution attempted to bestow upon such relationships has not been fully destroyed. Of course, exact figures are as little available in the USSR as elsewhere. But they are believed to be high, so high that the desire to reduce their number is regarded as a prime motive of the reform legislation of the 1960s.[38] Sverdlov, who for many years was the leading Soviet scholar of family law, was inclined to place a low estimate upon the number of factual divorces and irregular unions, but other observers have reached different conclusions. Yurkević reports that in the period of the law of 1944 the spouses had been separated at the commencement of the proceedings in the people's court for more than one year in 72.2 percent of all cases, for more than three years in about 40 percent, and that at the commencement of the proceedings in the district court about 50 percent of all parties lived in relations of factual marriage with new partners.[39] In 1958 S. Kurylev wrote in *Izvestia*:

> The existing divorce procedure . . . results in a situation in which many registered marriages exist on paper only. The fact is that the parties to such marriages have long since entered into informal marital relations with other mates, relations they are unable to formalize because of the unduly complex divorce procedure.[40]

Much other material is cited by Geiger.[41] The best evidence is supplied by the statistical data about official divorce. In 1965, the last year under the 1944 law, the divorce rate for the USSR was 1.7 per 1,000 population. In 1966, the first year of the 1965 law, it jumped to 3.1, i.e., about 25 percent above the 2.5 rate of the United States. The backlog of cases in which use was made of the relatively slight reduction in the difficulty of regularizing an irregular situation, must have been enormous.

38. Bilinsky, *supra* note 24, at 522.
39. FLORKOWSKI 378, n. 37.
40. 22 May 1958, cited in GEIGER *supra* note 1, at 259.
41. See GEIGER 257–58.

III

THE PROBLEM RESTATED

10
The Democratic Compromise

Our survey has shown that the dualism of the law of divorce is not peculiar to the United States. We find it just as well in France, Germany, and, as we shall see, in England, and to a lesser extent in Switzerland and even in Scandinavia. If we look to reality rather than form, dualism exists in an extreme way in Italy. The only country in which the law in action almost fully coincides with the law of the books is Japan. There consent divorce is openly admitted as an institution of official law. With us, consent divorce is a flourishing institution of the law in action, but has hardly found a place in the law of the books.

The existence of collusive practices and of migratory divorce has, of course, been widely observed in the United States and abroad. But that these practices amount to divorce by consent, is rarely admitted. Practitioners know that a divorce as such is rarely contested, and where there is no contest there is either agreement on the termination of the bond or at least acquiescence, i.e., consent divorce. Whether in these cases the termination of the marriage is truly justified under the rules of the books, or whether grounds are fabricated or bars to divorce are concealed, the court does not know. While not every uncontested divorce is collusive, it is always a consent divorce except in those infrequent cases of *ex parte* divorce in which the defendant did not know of the proceedings and was thus unable to defend.

Controversy between parting spouses is, of course, not infrequent with respect to the dollar-and-cents matters of property settlement, alimony, and child support and also with respect to child custody and visitation rights. But in the overwhelming majority of cases these matters are settled between the parties either before the case goes to court or while the proceedings are pending. In scarcely 10 percent of all cases in which a divorce is granted is there any controversy left for judicial decision. Among these there are some in which the defendant resists the termination of the marriage bond. But it is hard to know whether such resistance is due to desire to preserve the marriage bond or to spiteful reluctance to let the partner be free or to dissatisfaction with the property or custody terms which the partner is willing or, perhaps, unwilling to concede.

Statistical data are scarce and spotty. The only extensive data are from Japan, where consent divorce is an officially recognized institution. In 1948, no less than 98.2 percent of all Japanese divorces were achieved by the parties' notification of the registrar, and in 1.5 percent the agreement was brought about through negotiation in the Family Court, so that in effect 99.7 percent of all divorces were of the consent type and a mere 0.3 percent were obtained in litigious procedure. Ten years later, in 1959, notification of the registrar accounted for 91.5 percent and mediation of the Family Court for 7.5 percent, bringing consent divorces to 99.0 percent of the total; litigated divorces accounted for the remaining 1.0 percent.[1] Even in that 1 percent of cases to be decided in the District Court, the litigation seems to be concerned more with *zaisen-bunyo* and child support than with the termination of the marriage bond.

The Japanese are a notoriously nonlitigious people, generally preferring amicable settlement to legal contests. But the information we have from Western countries indicates that the situation is no different there. Data about undefended divorces in the United States were collected by the Bureau of the Census for the years from 1887 through 1932, except 1907 to 1915 and 1917 to 1921. Estimates from statistics for selected areas were made for 1933 to 1950 by Jacobson, who compiled a table showing the proportion of contested divorces (see table 16).

The data show startlingly large geographic differences. For the year 1929, the percentages of contested cases is reported to have been as high as 62.2 in Nevada, 39.1 in the District of Columbia, and 31.5 in Maryland, and as low as 6.9 in New York, 6.5 in Illinois, 2.3 in Delaware, and 2.0 in North Carolina.[2] The percentage for the entire country was thus figured to have been 11.8. But these differences are apparent rather than real. They do not indicate the percentage of cases in which the termination of a marriage was applied for by one party and resisted by the other, but merely the percentage of those in which a case was "contested" in the formal sense in which the term was defined by the Bureau of the Census. In that sense, a case was supposed to be

---

1. See J. KATO, GRAPHIC FAMILY LAW 37 (1963). The decrease in the percentage of agreements reached without official intervention and the corresponding increase of divorces settled in the Family Court seems to be due to the increased familiarity of the populace with the novel institution of the Family Court.

2. BUREAU OF THE CENSUS, MARRIAGE AND DIVORCE 1929, at 56.

reported as contested "if the defendant filed an answer, or if any evidence was offered in opposition to the divorce. . . . If no defense was made against the granting of the divorce, the answer will be 'No.' "[3]

The bureau regretted that the sources placed at its disposal did not permit it to penetrate the formal screen. How little the figures reflect reality is demonstrated by the study of the Maryland cases of 1929 undertaken by L. C. Marshall and G. May and so far the only incisive investigation.[4] The high percentage of defended cases in Maryland is shown to be

TABLE 16
FINAL DECREES OF ABSOLUTE DIVORCE AND ANNULMENT CONTESTED IN THE UNITED STATES, 1887–1950

Period	Percent Contested
1887–91	14.6
1892–96	15.0
1897–1901	15.4
1902–6	15.9
1916	13.6
1922–25	14.0
1926–30	12.1
1931–35	13.0
1936–40	13.4
1941–45	15.7
1946–50	14.8

Source: P. H. JACOBSON, AMERICAN MARRIAGE AND DIVORCE 120 (1959).

due, first, to the fact that it constitutes a percentage not just of those cases in which the action was for divorce in the sense of termination of the bond of marriage, but of the combined number of actions for divorce *a vinculo*, annulment, divorce *a mensa et thoro*, and separate maintenance. In the two last-named actions, which are concerned with dollars and cents, the incidence of real contest is, of course, higher than in actions for divorce *a vinculo* and for annulment. But in these cases, too, contest is practically limited to property questions, alimony, child custody, and child support. In their detailed analysis Marshall and May established that these matters are settled by agreement even in the overwhelming majority of those cases in which an answer has been

3. *Id.* 30.
4. THE DIVORCE COURT — MARYLAND 198 (1932).

filed. Defendants take this step either, as they can in Maryland, to expedite the case or to make sure that the divorce will have nationwide validity or to exert pressure for negotiations about the financial aspects. At the final hearing contests are shown to have dwindled to 4–5 percent of the cases in which a divorce *a vinculo* is granted, and that small percentage includes few cases in which the defendant is opposed to the termination of the marriage rather than to the financial or custody terms. The pertinent chapter in Marshall and May's book is thus aptly titled "The Mirage of Judicial Controversy."

There is no reason to believe that true controversy about the termination of a marriage is anywhere more frequent than it is in Maryland. In Cook County, Illinois, which contains Chicago and some of its suburbs, 97 percent of the 16,068 divorces granted in 1967 were apparently uncontested.[5]

In New York, the number of matrimonial actions called undefended and disposed of during the judicial years 1942–43 through 1953–54 are shown in table 17. Undefended cases range from a high of 94 percent of all cases in 1943 to a low of 76 percent in 1948, with the other years falling in between.

In California in the fiscal year 1963–64 the superior courts disposed

TABLE 17
UNDEFENDED MATRIMONIAL ACTIONS, NEW YORK, 1942–54

Judicial Year	Total Dispositions	Undefended Cases (without Separations)*
1942–43	9,630	9,487
1943–44	10,766	10,591
1944–45	12,289	12,103
1945–46	18,848	18,619
1946–47	18,747	18,507
1947–48	14,236	13,950
1948–49	11,518	11,242
1949–50	11,080	10,780
1950–51	10,742	10,457
1951–52	10,630	10,341
1952–53	10,553	10,291
1953–54	9,566	9,337

Source: STATE OF NEW YORK, TWENTIETH ANNUAL REPORT OF THE JUDICIAL COUNCIL 36 (1954); TWENTY-FIRST ANNUAL REPORT 39 (1955).
* The number of separations which are excluded here was never more than about 350 per judicial year.

5. U.S. DEPARTMENT OF COMMERCE, RECORDS OF CHIEF JUDGE, DIVORCE DIVISION, STATISTICAL BULLETIN, no. 53, at 79 (1968).

of 82,083 cases of divorce, separate maintenance, and annulment, and in 1964–65 of 99,827. The modes of disposition of these cases were 15.3 percent before trial in 1963–64 and 17.3 percent in 1964–65. With a trial, 78.9 percent were uncontested and 5.8 percent contested in the first year, and 77.5 percent uncontested and 5.2 contested for the second.[6]

For the Federal Republic of Germany, Austria, France, and England undefended divorces have been estimated consistently to be about 90 percent of all divorces.[7] The Law Commission said the English undefended petitions amounted to 93 percent.[8] In Canada, uncontested divorces are also said to be 90 percent of the total.[9] If these figures, as is probable, refer to merely technical rather than real contests, the incidence of the latter would be as rare in those countries as it is in the United States.

If a legislature were to enact a statute providing that the partners to a marriage be restored to the freedom of remarriage simply upon the expression of their mutual agreement, it would do no more than recognize the actual state of affairs. In the United States as elsewhere consent divorce is freely available, in spite of the efforts of the official law to exclude or prevent it. Perjury may have to be committed, expensive travel may have to be undertaken, procedural safeguards against collusion may have to be disregarded, but we have consent divorce, and attempts of legislatures to exclude it will remain ineffective unless the machinery of the secular courts is made equal to that of the tribunals of the Roman Catholic church with their watchdog, the defender of the bond. But wherever a secular legislature has sought to establish a counterpart, the attempt has been ineffective. The legislative schemes have been half-hearted, designed to look good on paper and not to function in practice.[10] Contrast between paper scheme

---

6. JUDICIAL COUNCIL OF CALIFORNIA, TWENTIETH BIENNIAL REPORT 115 (1965); JUDICIAL COUNCIL OF CALIFORNIA, ANNUAL REPORT OF THE ADMINISTRATIVE OFFICE OF THE CALIFORNIA COURTS, JUDICIAL STATISTICS FOR THE FISCAL YEAR 1964–65, at 22, 27 (1966).

7. W. MÜLLER-FREIENFELS, EHE UND RECHT 239 (1962), citing for Germany, SCHIFFER, DIE DEUTSCHE JUSTIZ 140 (2d ed. 1949); for Austria, SCHWIND, 1948 OESTERREICHISCHE JURISTENZEITUNG 123; for France, M. ANCEL, in 3 TRAVAUX DE LA COMMISSION DE RÉFORME DU CODE CIVIL 604 (1947–48); and for England J. Gower's testimony before the Royal Commission on Marriage and Divorce, Minutes of Evidence 18 (1952–56).

8. The Law Commission, Reform of the Grounds of Divorce 12 (Cmnd. 3123, 1966, repr. 1967).

9. Report of the Special Joint Committee of the Senate and the House of Commons on Divorce 98 (1967).

10. See *supra* p. 60.

The Problem Restated

and actuality is the very characteristic of the entire system of divorce. It has to be. It is the only system that can function in a democratic country where the social climate is as diffuse as it has so far been in the United States, France, or Germany.

Democracy does not simply mean rule by majority. Such a belief has resulted in the repeated failures of democratic government in France and Germany. In the United States, democracy could endure because the system of government contains elaborate safeguards for minorities. The federal scheme guarantees political influence to groups which, while they are in the minority in the nation at large, can muster majorities locally. The bills of rights of the constitutions of the United States and the states protect individuals and minorities against infringement by majorities on both the national and the local levels. The judiciary is to see to it that these guarantees are observed. Bicameralism, executive veto, and staggered terms of senators are apt to prevent sudden shifts of voters' preference from overriding views where permanent majority character has not yet become certain. The custom which allows one single senator to block the majority will gives power to a minority view held so strongly that it expresses itself in a filibuster. Above all, the two great parties are not monolithic blocs uniting all their voters by identity of economic interest or philosophic world view. Either party is a congeries of constantly shifting groupings of diverse, or even divergent, economic, social, idealistic, or religious interests which are held together by a constant process of fluid compromises. Compromise has been the heart of the political process in the United States as in Great Britain. There the process has functioned with lesser formal safeguards than in the United States. British minorities have been traditionally patient and British majorities have been sensitive to minority interests and sufficiently prudent not to ride roughshod over the minority views of the day, which may be the majority views of tomorrow.

In a system of representative democracy the political compromises are supposed to be worked out in the legislative bodies, in whose committees constant efforts are made to achieve the widest accommodation to minority interests that is possible in the circumstances. At times, certain minorities, especially ethnic, have not been sufficiently organized to express themselves in the legislatures and other policy-making organs. Such minorities, as at one time labor and now the Negroes and sectors of student youth, have long been quiescent. When they awoke to political consciousness, they resorted to spectacular devices to strengthen their own solidarity, to attract attention, and to demonstrate the dangers that might follow continued neglect of their demands. Once the street parades, strikes and acts of violence have served their purpose, the group is incorporated in the body politic and participates in the never-ending process of working out compromises. Such, at least, has so far been the course of American political life. The question of whether it will continue thus to function is not pursued in this book.

In France and Germany, too, democracy, as long as it works, means compromise. Only, the structure has not been sufficiently resilient. The political parties have been organized along inflexible lines of economic interest or religious-philosophical world view. Minorities have been unable to exert sufficient influence; majorities have been unwilling to accommodate minority interests. Violent upheavals have thus been inevitable. But their systems have not been completely inflexible. Compromises have been worked out on many matters, but the process has at times had to work outside of the legislature. And so it was at times in the United States.

Compromise means discussion followed by give and take. Compromise means that each participant yields to some extent from his initial demands, that neither group puts its demands on the table with a simple take it or leave it. But the possibility of yielding, or of at least public, open yielding, does not always exist. A political group can yield on matters of dollars and cents. But it is hard to yield on matters of basic conviction, on matters involving ultimate values, not to speak of eternal salvation or damnation. Of exactly this kind is the issue of divorce. The controversy about divorce has been one between basic philosophies and ultimate religious convictions. In Christian tradition the indissolubility or near-indissolubility of marriage is a tenet of faith. It is a divine command. Man cannot abrogate the word of Christ. Violation of the command is sin, the sanction is eternal damnation. With the growing secularization of life the religious basis of the belief in the necessity of indissoluble marriage has lost ground. But it is still a powerful force in the minds of millions of believers, not only of the Roman Catholic faith. And the religious basis has been supplemented by secular convictions about the indispensability of family stability for the stability of society and civilization. Such views have been powerful also in the Soviet Union, where family discipline has come to be regarded as a necessary basis for military and labor discipline and of socialist solidarity. Such convictions, religious or secular, combine with the identification of divorce with marriage breakup, or with the belief that a strict law of divorce is an effective deterrent to marriage breakup.

Religious faith does not need evidence. A tenet of faith cannot and need not be proved. Its force is beyond and above reason. So, too, is a secular faith held as a basic world view. In spite of all references to the fall of the Roman empire, nobody has proved and nobody can prove what connection there is between marriage stability and social stability. And nobody has proved or can prove the faith of Friedrich Engels and other socialist classics that the bourgeois family is, like property, the source of all social evil and that no good society can exist before both these institutions have been eradicated.[11]

What can be proved, however, is the ineffectiveness of a strict divorce law as a deterrent to family breakup and as a guarantee of family stability. How shall we explain the indifference toward the ineffectiveness of strict divorce laws in societies in which the desire for individual freedom and equality of the sexes has become strong? Why is it that the prevalence of consent divorce is hidden behind the façade of divorce for misconduct or for marriage breakdown? Why have statistical data about uncontested divorce hardly ever been collected? Is not all this make-believe a part, probably an indispensable one, of the compromise that has been worked out silently, one might even say surreptitiously, in the courts rather than openly in the legislatures? As any good compromise should, the compromise on divorce satisfied, although not fully, both sides. The conservatives are made happy by the strictness of the law of the books. Those who are liberal to the extent of seeking freedom of remarriage for themselves, are satisfied by the ease with which their desire is accommodated in practice. Those who are not directly concerned as divorce seekers or protectors of the faith have little need for considering the problem at all. The only ones who feel troubled are those occasional academics who view with alarm the hypocrisy of the system, the light-hearted way in which perjuries are committed and condoned, and who fear for the integrity of the law and the respect in which the law and its priests should be held by the public. At one time I was a member of this band. With advancing age I have come not only to accept but to admire the compromise. It has preserved peace in respect of an explosive issue, explosive just because it is an issue between beliefs deeply felt and thus unshakable by discussion and incapable of open adjustment. An assemblyman who is a convinced Catholic can hardly yield on an issue that affects salvation

---

11. F. ENGELS, DER URSPRUNG DER FAMILIE, DES PRIVATEIGENTUMS UND DES STAATES (1884) (English transl.: THE ORIGIN OF THE FAMILY, PRIVATE PROPERTY AND THE STATE; Moscow: Foreign Languages Publishing House, n.d.); A. BEBEL, DIE FRAU UND DER SOZIALISMUS (English transl.: WOMAN IN THE PAST, PRESENT AND FUTURE, London, 1894).

and, in his belief, plunge into sin those for whose welfare he feels responsible. Even less is open yielding possible for the assemblyman who does not hold such belief himself but whose political fortune depends on voters guided by the Catholic hierarchy. The state of New York presents a striking illustration. For decades the two political parties have found themselves in precarious balance. Neither could afford to alienate the voters in the nineteenth century of strict Protestant faith, in the twentieth of Catholic persuasion. Rarely is an assemblyman inclined to risk political suicide. The issue of divorce has been a hot potato which nobody in New York politics dared to touch. Until 1964 none of the few attempts to induce study of the divorce issue even reached the floor of the New York legislature. But not only in New York was the watchword "Let sleeping dogs lie." With few exceptions it prevailed in the legislatures of the United States as well as of France, Germany, and England. It long prevailed in Italy, although the form and the effects have been different there.

Debates of legislatures are public. Many, perhaps most, of the decisions are, it is true, scarcely noticed by the press. But a motion to change the law of divorce, or merely to study its functioning, attracts attention. Almost inevitably it will be taken up by the press and will result in public discussions spiced with venom. A contested divorce case, too, will attract the attention of the press, especially when the issues are salacious and the parties prominent. But what interest does the press take in the monotonous mass of uncontested divorces? They are dull and no news reporter is likely to waste his time in the courtroom in which they are handled on the assembly line. Nobody knows of the tragedies and the misery except the parties and the judge. He cannot avoid being aware of all the sadness, the disappointed hopes and expectations, the yearning for freedom. He hears the testimony. He knows that it may be false. But it may be true. It often is. Why should he go behind it? Even if he wanted to, he has neither the tools nor the time. The devices which statutes and procedural history have given him, have been whittled away by nonuse. Here is the plaintiff, mostly the woman,[12] from the working class in the majority of cases,

12. In 1939 the figures of decrees of divorce and annulment granted in suits brought by husbands were 65,740, and in suits brought by wives 185,260; the figures for 1948 were 125,749 and 297,464 (JACOBSON, *supra* table 16, at 120). The data on plaintiffs to whom divorces or annulments were granted in the divorce registration area in 1961 were husbands, 33,856; wives, 87,357; not stated, 3,915. Of decrees granted in the divorce registration area in 1962, 26.5 percent were to husbands; 70.9 percent to wives; and 6.6 percent not stated. In 1963, 28.0 percent of the plaintiffs in the divorce registration area were husbands and 72.0 percent were wives

visibly miserable and unhappy. She has told her story, corroborated by the necessary number of witnesses. The husband has been properly served with process, but he has not come to court. So why not grant the divorce? A judge new in the divorce court may care, may order the husband to appear, may ask questions and attempt conciliation. Once divorcing has become routine, the judge is not likely to continue wasting such time and effort. So the divorce court becomes Siberia. The judge is anxious to escape into less distasteful divisions of the court, and the mill grinds on. Marriages are terminated upon this or that kind of misconduct which may or may not have occurred.

Some judges may have been aware that they were modifying the law, especially in cases where migratory divorces were recognized. We can assume that Mr. Justice Douglas knew what he was doing in *Williams* v. *North Carolina*. Judge Bergan makes it clear in his opinion in the *Rosenstiel* case that the court was knowingly and intentionally emasculating the official law of New York, in order to bring about its long overdue reform. But in innumerable cases the law of collusion has been eroded simply by nonuse, and the divorce monopoly of the domicile by mechanically following precedent. Judges have just plodded along the beaten path, hardly knowing that they were bringing about results contrary to what they had undertaken when they had sworn to uphold the law. In a sense, they have even done exactly that: followed practices which have matured into customary law. The same assumption can be made for the members of the divorce bar, although not for the attorneys of the legal aid societies who have shied away from divorce cases in which clients or witnesses would have to perjure themselves. But significantly legislation has been enacted that is designed to free them from at least one set of scruples. In Illinois and in other places the bar of recrimination has been officially changed into a defense.[13] So it is no longer necessary for a plaintiff to assert under oath that she has always conducted herself as a true and faithful wife. If a defendant wishes to use a plaintiff's misconduct as a threat, let him do so. But where there is no contest, the issue need no longer be raised by the plaintiff herself.

Apart from such statutes of recent vintage, the transformation of the strict divorce law of the books into the consent divorce law of judicial practice has been brought about without fanfare. The process

---

(U.S. DEPT. OF HEALTH, EDUCATION AND WELFARE, VITAL STATISTICS OF THE UNITED STATES, MARRIAGE AND DIVORCE 1961, table 4-10; DIVORCE STATISTICS ANALYSIS 1962, at 29; 1963, at 39).

13. Illinois Laws 1967, at 2979, § 1 adding section 8 a to the Divorce Act.

would not have unrolled in the limelight of publicity. The public has hardly been aware of what has been going on. The cognoscenti have kept quiet so generally that one might well speak of a conspiracy of silence. In the shadow world of practice, consent divorce has become an established institution in the United States and elsewhere.

In the United States the transformation has been radical, thanks to the multiplicity of state laws and thanks also to the liberals' fear of rekindling the weakening flame of conservatism as well as to the insight into the futility of their efforts of such conservative leaders as Samuel Dike. The duality of the law of divorce is a species of the broader genus of sub rosa institution. Laws are placed or kept on the statute book although they are not enforced and are unenforceable. The most famous example was the "noble experiment" of Prohibition. The production, importation, and sale of alcoholic beverages was prohibited, but they were generally obtainable from the bootlegger and at the speakeasy. The compromise between high-minded prohibitionists and thirsty souls resulted in such pernicious corruption that the federal prohibition act had to be repealed in 1933. But in a few states prohibition lingered on as an uneasy compromise of generally available liquor and official prohibition maintained on the statute book by a coalition of fundamentalist clergy and bootleggers. Blue laws are still in the statute books, not only in some states in New England, and are flouted in practice. Laws against fornication or the "unspeakable and detestable crime against nature" are hardly ever applied. But they remain on the statute book available in an unpredictable way as *brutum fulmen*. Connecticut's famous law against birth control remained in force officially, although a dead letter, until it was buried in 1965 by the Supreme Court of the United States.[14] The broad wording of the Mann Act [15] has never been modified even though it is no longer used to prosecute anyone but a genuine "white slaver." Broadly worded vice laws and gambling laws are kept on the books although those who are entrusted with their enforcement use them almost exclusively for extraneous purposes. For decades the antitrust laws were part of the official law of the United States without being enforced as they were meant to be.[16]

Sub rosa latitat serpens. Below the surface of an official law of high-minded moral purposes hides the "snake" of nonenforcement. Of this

---

14. Griswold v. Connecticut, 381 U.S. 479, 85 S.Ct. 1678, 14 L.Ed. 2d 516.
15. 18 U.S. Code. § 2421; Note, *Interstate Immorality, the Mann Act and the Supreme Court*, 56 YALE L.J. 718 (1947).
16. THURMAN ARNOLD, SYMBOLS OF GOVERNMENT (1935; repr. 1962).

phenomenon, common to many parts of the world and rampant in the United States, but one example is consent divorce hidden under the façade of divorce as punishment of misconduct or as an escape hatch open solely in cases of complete and irremediable marriage breakdown. The institution had to be developed as the inevitable compromise between conservatives able to keep statute makers in fear and liberal pursuers of individual happiness. Like other kinds of sub rosa institutions, that of unofficial consent divorce cannot grow in the publicity of the legislature. The compromise has, as in the other cases, to be worked out where there is little or no public attention, in executive offices or, in our case, in the courts and the offices of the divorce specialists of the bar. The compromise has not been reached in the ways of officially professed democratic ideology. But it has been necessary. It has been elaborated in a process which is as much a part of democracy as that of official lawmaking in the legislatures. It has resulted in satisfaction of almost everyone concerned. It has been inevitable wherever liberalism has reached significance without being sufficiently strong to eliminate those views of tradition which dominated Christian society for a millennium. No such compromise has been necessary in non-Christian Japan. It has appeared in a much attenuated form in Scandinavia, where liberalism has come to be the dominant ideology. The compromise has not been prevented in Italy where the dominant political position is held by a party devoted to maintaining Christian tradition. The compromise had even appeared in tsarist Russia, where the liberalism of wide circles of intellectuals had to face the orthodoxy of the Holy Synod. In countries so deeply split in ideology as Germany and France, the compromise is almost as comprehensive as in the United States. In the Soviet Union the compromise has assumed the form of governmental vacillation between utmost liberality and rigorous strictness. In the United States the compromise of legal duality must be maintained as long as conservatism is sufficiently powerful to prevent liberalism from coming to the fore. Does that situation still exist today, in 1971? Much seems to indicate that conservatism has weakened to the point of allowing the liberalism of the law in action to be recognized and find expression in the law of the books. For the advance of liberalism and the retreat of conservatism evidence can be found in both the life of the country in general and in recent developments of official divorce law in particular. But the recent developments in the divorce field also indicate that conservatism is still a power to be reckoned with.

The course of the law of divorce has been characterized by another feature: the consistent ignoring of the possibility and the frequent use of factual separation. Divorce is not identical with marriage breakdown. The alternatives are not family cohesion and formal divorce. A married couple may split up without resorting to divorce. Where divorce is impossible or difficult or expensive, informal marriage breakup becomes a mass phenomenon when the cultural climate changes from traditionalism to industrialism and urbanization. But it has taken a long time for this fact to be perceived and accentuated in the discussions about divorce. In this respect the American arguments of Horace Greeley and his companion defenders of indissolubility are as characteristic as the Soviet tendencies of the Stalin period or, quite recently, the report submitted to the Italian Chambers of Deputies by the minority of the Committee on Legal Affairs,[17] i.e., primarily the Christian Democrats. In this remarkable document one finds all those traditional arguments for indissolubility which one finds the world over, together with allegations about incompatibility of a law allowing divorce with the Italian Concordat of 1929 and the constitution of 1946. One also finds statistical data tending to show that in "divorce countries" the incidence of illegitimacy is higher than in divorceless Italy or Spain, and allegations that the existence of divorce has not prevented such evils as adultery, sex crime, uxoricide, or irregular unions.[18] But otherwise this last-named phenomenon, which figures prominently in the report of the majority of the committee,[19] is hardly mentioned at all. The report simply states:

> In Italy one is continuously faced with uncontrollable figures about factual separation and concubinous people who are just waiting to be divorced. Nobody has so far succeeded in looking at these statistics. The reason is quite simple: they do not exist. . . . The advocates of divorce . . . have found it necessary to talk about the "outsiders of the law of marriage" and to resort to figures with many zeros.[20]

The existence of the compromise is simply denied or overlooked by the reporters, who are certainly sincere in their allegation of freedom from clerical influence and of their endeavor solely to argue on the basis of reason in a matter the discussion of which is said to be

17. Camera dei Deputati, Relazione della IV Commissione Permanente (Giustizia), N. 1-467-A-bi5, submitted on 7 October 1968, Castelli and Maria Eletta Martini reporters. In the same vein is F. LIGI, DIVORZIO DIBATTITO IN ITALY (1968).
18. At 5–6.
19. Camera dei Deputati, Relazione della IV Commissione Permanente, N. 1-467, submitted on 30 April 1969, Lenoci reporter, at 12; see *supra* p. 159.
20. At 6, 12.

dominated by passion and prejudice.[21] Statistics about factual marriage breakup and irregular unions do, of course, not exist in Italy. The figures with the many zeros may be exaggerated, but they are based on the observation of facts which are conspicuous. The incidence is not insignificant either in England, France, or Germany; and the other form of the compromise, discrepancy between the divorce law of the books and that in action has been equally obvious in all places where divorce, while it is available, is not obtainable as freely as it is demanded in the given cultural climate.

21. At 2–3.

11
What Is the Evil: Divorce or Marriage Breakdown?

A long way back, in chapter 1, we stated that our inquiries about divorce were prompted by the efforts of the Interprofessional Commission on Marriage and Divorce. The commission's mandate was to draft a model law that would stem the rising tide of divorce and restore the stability of the American home and family. The effort failed. No model law was produced by the commission. Why? In retrospect after manifold inquiries, I believe, I can see why we failed or, indeed, why we had to fail.

First of all, the commission was as split about the problem as the people at large and we were as vague about the split as the public. In the privacy of the courtrooms, a compromise had been reached that satisfied everyone and no one. The conservatives had their strict laws and the liberals had easy divorce. The democratic compromise had been reached. Some insiders who knew what was going on felt uneasy about the hypocrisy of the system. But if the system worked, why should one provoke public discussions about it? We never articulated the problem in this way, but we felt it. So we shied away from producing an open split in our commission and in the public.

Another reason why discussions, insofar as we had any, never reached beyond preliminaries, was that some of us had doubts about the solution that was self-evident to the chairman, Paul Alexander, Judge of the Court of Domestic Relations of Lucas County, Ohio., i.e., of Toledo. He was the country's most ardent protagonist of the Family Court Plan and the therapeutic approach. But, while he was "Mister Therapeutic Approach," he was a gentleman who would never think of forcing upon others his own ideas, however deeply he was convinced of their truth. The Family Court Plan appeared attractive. Judge Alexander's court in Toledo was a model of effectiveness. But would the plan work equally well under other judges? Was its success due to

Paul Alexander's unique personality or to the general features of the plan? We did not know.

Third, the Interprofessional Commisison failed in its task because it had no clear insight into the problem which it was supposed to solve. The high divorce rate and its seemingly continuous growth had created the impression that something was wrong in society, that there was some evil that was to be fought. Naïvely we took it for granted that the evil was divorce. In that we shared the belief of almost everyone who had ever thought about divorce legislation in the United States and elsewhere. But is the belief true?

If it were, the solution of the problem would be easy. Abolish divorce. Then there would be no divorces at all, the divorce rate would be zero, and everything would be perfect. But would it? Would marriage, home, and family be safe and stable if there were no divorce? Are they safe and stable in Italy? Were they stable in England before the judicial divorce was introduced in 1857 or before it was made readily available in 1937? Are these institutions more stable in Canada where the divorce rate is lower than in the United States, or in New York as compared with Oklahoma?[1] One needs but a fleeting acquaintance with Italy to see that marriage stability is not perfect in that divorceless country. Considerable numbers of Italian marriages are broken, husbands leave their wives and families, wives run away, couples separate more or less amicably, not to speak of prostitution or the mistresses kept by married men. It was this observation which prompted our inquiries. If they allow any conclusion it is to the effect that if there is any evil one might think to eliminate or reduce, it is not divorce, but the factual breakdown of marriages, the factual events of abandonment and separation.

Factual marriage breakdown is not easy to define. In one sense we may regard every marriage as having broken down that has failed to give the spouses the degree of happiness or satisfaction they hoped for when they took the fateful step of matrimony. Frequent quarrels or mere disharmony may sap the energies of spouses and adversely affect their happiness and their effectiveness as citizens. If there are children, their mental and physical well-being is likely to be impaired. Hostility between the parents, frequent or even occasional domestic quarrels, not to speak of physical violence, alcoholism, or drug addiction,

---

1. The divorce rate in 1940 was 0.9 per 1,000 population in New York and 4.2 in Oklahoma (P. H. JACOBSON, AMERICAN MARRIAGE AND DIVORCE 100 [1959]). In 1965 the New York rate was 0.5 and the Oklahoma rate 4.8 (DIVORCE STATISTICS ANALYSIS, U.S. 1964 AND 1965, at 20–21).

are bound to stunt the children's sound development. From society's point of view such situations are evil; they have attracted the attention of moralists, psychiatrists, and reformers bent upon the improvement of the human lot. But they concern us here only when they result in abandonment or separation. It is in this sense that marriage breakdown is linked to divorce. Besides, situations of internal dissension are not susceptible to exact observation and statistical comprehension. We are concerned with marriage breakdown as a mass phenomenon and the problem of how, if at all, its incidence might be reduced. It is for this compelling reason of statistical observability that we shall limit ourselves to inquiry concerning marriage breakdown in the sense of physical cessation of the spouses' life in common, i.e., of abandonment and separation.

Statistical comprehension of even these phenomena is not easy. Divorce is a formalized event which, in our society, is embodied in a formal act, the decree of a court. It is not easy to achieve an exact count of even such formalized events. The correctness of official statistics of divorce depends upon the reliability and regularity of the court records and of the reports to be made by local officials to central offices of vital statistics. In the United States neither completeness nor correctness is guaranteed.[2]

How much more difficult is it to count such nonformalized events as separation or abandonment? No state or country has so far prescribed the duty of informing a public agency of a separation or an abandonment so that it might be officially recorded. It is possible, to be sure, to count the judicial decrees rendered between married persons and presuppose that these persons do not live together, i.e., support orders, decrees of separate maintenance, or decrees of judicial separation. However, not all separated or abandoned wives initiate such suits or carry them on to a decree. The husband may pay voluntarily, or the wife knows that he is so irresponsible or impecunious that a suit would be useless, or she has means of her own and does not choose to be supported by an estranged husband, or she believes that, as the party guilty of the breakdown, she has no chance to win, or she does not know the husband's whereabouts. Besides, suits for support may be brought more than once between the same parties. Finally, a decree or a series of decrees of maintenance, affecting a particular couple

2. M. Rheinstein and A. Plateris, *The Importance of Central Files of Divorce Records*, 46 A.B.A.J. 1285 (1960), repr. in 26 NEVADA STATE BAR J. 116 (1961); A. Plateris, *Statistical Data on Marriage Stability*, 9 ANNALES DE LA FACULTÉ DE DROIT D'ISTANBUL 258, 272 (8e année, no. 13); JACOBSON, *supra* note 1, at 5, 8.

may be, and frequently is, followed by a decree of divorce. Counting suits or decrees of maintenance is not equivalent to counting separations and abandonments. Yet, if they existed, as they do not, comprehensive counts of such suits or decrees could, with caution, be used as circumstantial evidence affording some approximation of the incidence of marriage breakdown.

On the occasion of a census or a field study of limited scope, one may make an effort to count the number of married persons who do not live together with their spouses. Such efforts have been undertaken, but only in a few places and solely in recent years.[3] Comparisons in time and place are thus hardly possible. Besides, the difficulties standing in the way of an exact count are formidable. A census taker may be expected, more or less exactly, to count in how many cases both spouses of a married couple are "present" and in how many one spouse is "absent." But these terms need closer definition. Is a spouse present or absent, if, because of a housing shortage, he or she lives in a room in the attic, while the other spouse and the children live in an apartment in the same building? At what moment must a spouse be "present" in the other spouse's home in order so to be counted.[4]

If we define the term "married person — spouse absent" so as to include a merely temporary interruption of a normal life in common, we must consider that in a comprehensive census the same couple will appear twice: the husband will be listed in one place, with the indication that his wife is absent, and vice versa. If we wish to enumerate the number of married couples which are not together, we would then have to divide by two the total number of "married persons — spouse absent." But will that result be correct? On the day of the census one spouse may be in a district covered by the census, while the other is not. If, as in the Federal Republic of Germany, the count of "married person — spouse absent" is nationwide, one member may be abroad and thus not covered by the census. The problem is even more acute in the United States, where counts of "married person — spouse absent" are limited to small, regionally defined samples, which are then used for projection for the nation as a whole.[5]

3. See Plateris, *supra* note 2, at 261. Detailed data are given in W. M. Kephart & T. P. Monahan, *Desertion and Divorce in Philadelphia*, 17 AM. SOCIOL. REV. 719 (1952).
4. This aspect is relevant where, as in Belgium, France, and Great Britain, the census counts de facto population; it is less relevant in Canada, Germany, and the United States, where the census counts the de jure population.
5. In the United States in the census of 1940, 1950, and 1960, but not in that of 1970, a distinction was made between persons "married, spouse present," and persons "married, spouse absent." A person was classified as "married, spouse present,"

Even if we know the exact number of couples who do not live together for a certain minimum period of time, the number is not identical with that of broken marriages. Spouses may not live together for a great variety of reasons. The husband may be a ship captain or a traveling salesman or an explorer or an oil engineer working in Arabia; or he may be off to war or one spouse may be institutionalized in a hospital, an asylum, or a prison; or the wife may be away, perhaps for months, to nurse a sick parent, or what not. In all such cases we have a "married person — spouse absent" without the marriage necessarily having broken down. That situation does not exist unless the absence is due to discord between the spouses. How does the census taker know the reasons for the absence? Can the technique of asking the "present" spouse be trusted to yield uniformly truthful answers? Are there any other techniques available? Perhaps the investigator asks neighbors, the postman, or other people who may be regarded as knowledgeable. A census taker can hardly resort to that device. It may be available to the investigator in a small-scale field study, but the results cannot be accurate.[6]

While accurate statistical data about factual marriage breakdown are lacking, we have an abundance of experiential observations by psychiatrists, psychologists, social workers, and sociologists. While lawyers and lawmakers have concentrated their attention upon divorce and neglected factual marriage breakdown, behavioral scientists have looked upon family disintegration as a unitary phenomenon paying scant attention or no attention at all to the law in general and the law of divorce in particular. A few observations have been made on the influence of divorce legislation in connection with statistical inquiries,[7]

---

if the husband or wife was reported as a member of the household, even though he or she may have been temporarily absent on business or on vacation, visiting, in a hospital, etc., at the time of the enumeration. The group "married, spouse absent" included married persons employed and living for several months at a considerable distance from their homes, those whose spouses were absent in the armed forces, separated persons (those living apart because of marital discord but not divorced), migrants whose spouses remained in other areas, husbands or wives of inmates of institutions, and all other married persons whose place of residence was not the same as that of their spouses. U.S. PUBLIC HEALTH SERVICE, DEPT. OF HEALTH, EDUCATION, AND WELFARE, VITAL STATISTICS — SPECIAL REPORTS vol. 39, no. 3, DEMOGRAPHIC CHARACTERISTICS OF RECENTLY MARRIED PERSONS 104 (1954). The figures can thus not serve as a basis for propositions on marriage breakdown. For the same reason, the statistical data collected in the Federal Republic of Germany cannot be used for our purposes, although they, too, distinguish between married persons whose spouses are present and those whose spouses are not present.

6. See *infra* p. 306.

7. [L. Bodio] *Le separazioni personali di coniugi e i divorzi in Italia e in alcuni altri stati*, 1 ANNALI DI STATISTICA, Ser. 3 (1882); J. BERTILLON, ETUDE DÉMOGRAPHIQUE

but they have failed to attract the attention of lawmakers. Besides, they were concerned with the relation between divorce laws and divorce rather than that between the laws and marriage breakdown followed or not followed by divorce. But no insight into the effectiveness of legislation can be obtained if we neglect those cases of factual marriage breakdown which are not followed by divorce. It is exactly the lack of accurate data about these situations which has stood in the way of rational treatment of marriage instability.

Not divorce but the factual breakup of a marriage constitutes the social evil which has been decried so often and so passionately.[8] It is this situation which turns the children into "orphans," which is likely to throw them and perhaps the wife too as a charge on the taxpayers, which creates the psychological problems of loneliness, and which injects a general element of instability into the fabric of social life. But none of these effects is produced by divorce, which is an event occurring not in the world of social living but in the universe of formal law. Divorce can be varyingly defined as the pronouncement of a court, the paper on which this pronouncement is recorded, or the legal situation which arises from the pronouncement. In this situation the parties, or occasionally only one of them, are free to do something which they could not do before: they are now free to enter upon new relationships capable of being recognized as legally valid marriages.[9] Apart from that one aspect the decree of divorce does not bring about any significant change in the position of the parties resulting from the factual breakup of their marriage, a factual event which by legal necessity must precede the legal event of the divorce. The decree of divorce may, of course, contain judicial dispositions concerning the payment of alimony to the wife and support for the children, the settlement of the parties' relations with respect to property, and the custody of the children. But all such dispositions could also be, and frequently will have been, made prior to and independent of divorce proceedings. The problem of maintenance can be raised in a suit for separate mainte-

---

DU DIVORCE ET DE LA SÉPARATION DE CORPS DANS LES DIFFÉRENTS PAYS DE L'EUROPE (1883); W. F. WILLCOX, THE DIVORCE PROBLEM (2d ed. 1897); C. D. Wright, MARRIAGE AND DIVORCE IN THE UNITED STATES: FIRST SPECIAL REPORT OF THE COMMISSIONER OF LABOR 150 (1889, rev. 1891, 2d ed. 1897); A. CAHEN, STATISTICAL ANALYSIS OF AMERICAN DIVORCE (1932).

8. What follows in this chapter is substantially a reprint of parts of the author's article *The Law of Divorce and the Problem of Marriage Stability*, 9 VAND. L. REV. 633 (1956).

9. On state laws restricting freedom of remarriage after divorce, see Note, 56 COLUM. L. REV. 228 (1956), and literature cited therein; also H. H. CLARK, JR., LAW OF DOMESTIC RELATIONS 405 (1968).

nance, a prosecution for nonsupport, or an action upon a separation agreement or for the payment of the value of necessaries. A property settlement can be brought about by means of such proceedings as a suit for partition, or for a declaratory judgment, or to clear title, or an action of trespass or ejectment.

If a person, without being divorced, lives together with a companion other than his spouse, the irregularity of the relationship, if it becomes known, may expose the parties to social ostracism and, in some states, to punishment for some such crime as "living in open adultery." But the social stigma does not apply in all groups of the population, and prosecution for crimes of the kind is rare. Of course, the irregular relationship will mean that the children are illegitimate and that none of the property and other legal effects of marriage applies between the parties or to their issue. But if there is no issue or no property, the parties may not care. Only if they care about the social, religious, or legal characteristics of their status will it be indispensable that the new relationship be initiated by a proper marriage ceremony, and for that purpose it is necessary that a divorce be obtained by one or both of the parties who are bound by the bond of an earlier marriage.

As long as the bond of marriage exists, the parties also remain subject to the duty of marital fidelity. Any act of intercourse with a third party constitutes adultery. Either party is then exposed to the risk of giving the other a ground for divorce under which the wife may be deprived of her claim for support, or the husband may become subject to the duty of supporting the wife. There may also exist the threat of criminal punishment. But these risks have not deterred hundreds of thousands of Italians, English people, Germans, French, and, so one can safely assume, considerable numbers of Americans, from informally breaking out of their marriages and living in new, though irregular, unions.

Restoration to the freedom of the marriage market is an effect within the realm of law and, perhaps, also of religion and morals, but the decree of divorce is not that event which turns a woman into an abandoned wife, or a couple into one whose home is broken. While we may legitimately speak of orphans of separation or abandonment, it is misleading to speak of orphans of divorce. No decree of a divorce court has ever thrown a child into a position in which he is deprived of a home and of the love and care of his two parents. That deprivation is the effect of the factual breakdown of the parents' marriage, but not of the decree of the divorce court by which the factual breakdown of the marriage may or may not be followed. If we are interested in family stability, the trends in its development, and the ways by which it might be protected or promoted, we must, therefore, look at the cases of actual marriage breakdown rather than at decrees of divorce.

The widespread feeling that something ought to be done about divorce originates in the widely, if not generally, held opinion that the number of cases of marriage breakdown has greatly increased in recent times and that correspondingly the stability of marriage has seriously declined. Is this opinion correct? It is probably true that the incidence of marriage breakdown has increased. But does that mean that marriage stability has declined so considerably that the institution of marriage is in serious danger? Besides, to what extent the incidence of marriage breakdown has increased, we do not know. All we know is that the rate of divorce has steadily and considerably increased — increased, that is, not only in absolute numbers but in a proportion greater than the increase of the population. But this increase does not necessarily allow the conclusion that there has also occurred a corresponding, or even any, increase in the number of cases of marriage breakdown.

Theoretically it would be possible that the large increase in the divorce rate since 1850 does not reflect any increase in the rate of marriage breakdown. It is conceivable that the rate of the latter has remained unchanged or has even decreased, and that the increase in the divorce rate is due solely to an increase in the number of those cases in which the factual marriage breakdown has been subsequently formalized by the taking out of a divorce decree by one of the parties or the other. It is not probable that the true state of affairs actually corresponds to this theoretical possibility. For reasons still to be discussed it is probable that the rate of marriage breakdown has indeed increased, although we do not know how much. Just as improbable as that the marriage breakdown rate has not increased at all, is that it has increased in exactly the same measure as the divorce rate. With the general rise of the common man from lower-lower to upper-lower or middle-class standards, which has been so characteristic of at least the past fifty years in the United States and in other industrial countries, we know that middle-class mores are now observed by a portion of the population larger than that by which they were observed in 1850. This fact implies that a larger portion of those whose marriages have been broken down factually must now find it necessary to formalize such breakdown by the taking out of a decree of divorce. How large that section is today and how large it was in

1850 or at any time between these dates, we do not know, just as we do not know how many marriages in fact are broken up today or were broken up in 1850. It would be wrong, however, to assume that in 1850, or at any time before or after, that number would have been insignificant. On the contrary, we have good evidence that the nineteenth century, or the eighteenth, were not at all the "good old days" as they seem so often to be regarded by romanticists. In those days marriage breakdown did occur and it seems to have occurred in a significantly high number of cases in this country, in England, and elsewhere.

The situation in England is instructive because the institution of judicial divorce did not exist there before 1858. The fact that family breakup occurred there before that date, just as it occurs today in Spain, Italy, and other divorceless countries, should be an additional warning against that identification of family breakup and divorce which is so common in present-day discussions. Just as we have no contemporary statistics of factual marriage breakdown, we have, of course, none for eighteenth- or nineteenth-century England. We have other evidence, however, which, while it does not give exact figures, indicates that marriage breakdown actually occurred on a significant scale. This evidence is contained in the documents which have been left behind by contemporaries as well as in writings in which use of such documents has been made. Strangely enough, nobody seems as yet to have expressly investigated the problem of the stability of the English family of the eighteenth and nineteenth centuries. When we became interested in this problem at the University of Chicago Comparative Law Research Center, we had to cull information from modern biographies and historical works as well as from such contemporary sources as diaries, autobiographies, parliamentary debates, letters, and reports of foreign travelers.[10] The mass of the material that ought to be explored is immense. It is necessary that attention be paid particularly to such sources as court records, reports of factory inspectors, newspapers, police and court records, moral tracts, and also to plays, novels, and popular literature. Although we could do no more than look over a small fraction of the material that should be explored, we believe that the investigation has been sufficiently extensive to allow at least some tentative conclusions.

The impression which emerges from this study of some of the sources

---

10. The research was conducted by Gerhard O. W. Mueller. See his study *Inquiry into the State of a Divorceless Society: Domestic Relations Law and Morals in England from 1660 to 1857*, 18 U. PITT. L. REV. 545 (1957).

is, first of all, that the mores of the various groups and layers of English society differed greatly. The image of monogamous, lifelong, and faithful marriage appears to have approximated reality most closely among the middle class, especially insofar as its members belonged to dissenter churches. Significantly different mores are found, however, both in the top and the bottom layers of society. Among the former the number of separations seems not to have been insignificant. Even more frequent, however, seems to have been the marriage in which the outside façade of a common home was maintained and, perhaps, a measure of common marital life, too, although the husband kept a mistress or frequented prostitutes. Among the bottom groups irregular unions, abandonment, and informal switching were anything but unknown. In all layers of society, except, perhaps, the very top, the maritally dissatisfied male and, to a considerably lesser extent, the female, could avail himself of a freedom which has been greatly reduced in present society, the freedom of disappearance. The police were poorly organized and services for the tracing of missing persons were all but unknown. For a workman, a rural laborer, an industrial "mechanic," or an impoverished clerk it was easy, under a newly assumed name, to submerge himself in the teeming proletarian masses of the East End of London or in the slums of Lancashire. If a man, or a woman, could disappear in these crowds, he could also establish a new union there with or without ceremony of marriage. If he wanted to have a ceremony, it was not difficult to find a Fleet parson, at least before the enactment of Lord Hardwick's Act in 1753. That the new "marriage" might be bigamous was no serious threat in a society in which discovery was improbable.

If Whitechapel or Manchester were too close to home, there were the wilds of Australia, New Zealand, and, above all, America, where a new life could be started not only in the economic but also the marital sense. Immigration to the United States was unrestricted until 1917 and the chance of punishment or other embarrassment because of bigamy was small for the man who had run away, with or without his mistress, from his European wife and family. It was minimal, too, for the American husband, who had run away from his family in the East and established a new one at the frontier. For the protection of such men and their new "wives" and children American courts fashioned the all but irrebuttable presumption of the legal validity of a person's last marriage.[11] To this protection of the American "family"

---

11. See *supra* p. 35; Note, *The Conflict of Presumptions on Successive Marriages by the Same Person*, 30 HARV. L. REV. 500 (1917), repr. in ASS'N AM. LAW SCHOOLS, SELECTED ESSAYS ON FAMILY LAW 287 (1950).

of the runaway husband was added the protection of the husband himself against claims of support that might be brought against him by his abandoned wife and children. The rules on jurisdiction for claims of family support and on the enforcement of foreign judgments of support were fashioned so as to render it practically impossible that an immigrant husband, or one who had migrated within the United States, could be seriously embarrassed by his abandoned family.[12] Why should a man in such circumstances bother with taking out a divorce which might be either entirely unobtainable in his home country or at least involve him in considerable expense? Figures of immigration into such countries as Australia, Canada, or the United States ran into the hundreds of thousands per year. Internal migration was and still is high in the United States. Nobody knows to what extent migration has been the substitute for divorce. It is no farfetched speculation, however, to suspect that it served this end more frequently in 1850 than in 1950 and that in 1850 the number of such cases was anything but insignificant. There are no statistics of undiscovered cases of bigamy or even of migration-abandonment followed by neither a divorce nor a bigamous marriage. There is only circumstantial evidence.

In the 1950s, a million persons were said to disappear annually. According to a breakdown prepared by Tracers Company of New York, among the cases they handled in thirty-two years, there were 79,620 husbands, of whom 51,205 were wanted for support, 17,222 had departed because of mother-in-law trouble, and 11,193 had left with other women. Of the 4,806 wives, 216 were wanted because they had abandoned their children, 4,437 had left because of mother-in-law trouble, and 153 had run away with other men.[13]

The point we are trying to make here is not that the incidence of factual marriage breakdown was higher in 1850 or 1900 than it is today, or that it was the same, but only that we do not know the number and that a possible increase cannot be deduced from the statistically ascertainable increase in the divorce rate. It is possible, or indeed probable, that since people can no longer disappear as freely as once they could, they are more likely to seek a formal divorce and thus a legalization of a subsequent marriage. Also, in the earlier years a larger percentage of the population belonged to those bottom layers of society

---

12. On the difficulties encountered under traditional American law by one who attempts to prosecute a claim for family support from abroad or across a state line, see W. H. Baldwin, *The Present Status of Family Desertion and Non-Support Laws*, 38 PROCEEDINGS OF THE NATIONAL CONFERENCE OF CHARITIES AND CORRECTIONS 406 (1911). See also J. C. Colcord, *Family Desertion and Non-Support*, 6 ENC. SOC. SCI. 78 (1931).

13. Chicago Daily News, 3 March 1956.

in which the lack of a formal divorce and remarriage constitutes less of a stigma than it does among the middle classes. In the absence of statistics we simply cannot know to what extent the rise of the divorce rate indicates a rise in marriage instability, or a shift from the informal to formalized marriage termination due to changed social conditions and mores.

That such a shift from informal to formalized marriage breakup has been responsible for at least a part of the increase in the divorce rate, appears to be highly probable in view of the facts just stated. It also can be regarded as certain that there has occurred a considerable increase in the cases of factual marriage breakdown. In the countries of full industrialization, the cultural climate of the present differs profoundly from that of the mid-nineteenth century. In the new society many factors cooperate to increase the desire to break out of an existing marriage and to reduce the institutions by which such a desire may be held in check.[14] Two lines of development appear to have played a particularly important role: the decreased financial and personal dependence of women upon their husbands, and, in partial connection with this phenomenon, the changed image of the institution of marriage.[15]

In the premodern world the possibility of escaping from a distasteful or intolerable marriage situation was very unlikely for a woman. It was difficult enough for a spinster to find her place in society; there simply was no place for the woman who had left her husband. Unless she had parents living who were willing to receive her, or a lover with whom she might run away and disappear, the wife of even the most tyrannical, cruel, or profligate husband had little choice but to bear her lot in patience, or to enter a house of prostitution. The law made it impossible for a married woman to have an income of her own, unless her family had the means and the foresight to make her and her children the beneficiaries of a settlement in equity. Society had but few places for an unattached woman to earn a decent living. To eke out a living was difficult enough for the widow of a husband who did not leave her assets sufficient to yield a comfortable income. If loneliness and lack of income were combined with the stigma of being a deserter, a woman's fate was intolerable. The economic and social facts which stood in the way of a wife's shaking off even the worst abuse were aggravated by the educational system which, insofar as it

---

14. See *infra* chap. 13.
15. The literature is immense. For a good survey, see C. KIRKPATRICK, THE FAMILY: AS PROCESS AND INSTITUTION, chap. 7 (1955).

provided any education at all for a woman, did not aim at endowing her with a training that would enable her to live a life of independence.

We need not relate here the details of the profound change which has taken place. Perhaps in the United States women have not yet attained that almost full position of equality with men which they now occupy in the Scandinavian countries or Germany, but it certainly has become possible for an American woman to live her own life and to occupy a respected place in society if she remains unmarried, if she is a widow, or if she has factually broken off a marriage which has become intolerable to her or simply distasteful. The law not only allows her to have her own property and income, but also is ready in most cases to give her and her children claims for maintenance or alimony and support. The economy provides her with ample opportunity to find an independent place of work and an income of her own. The schools have prepared her for such a role; and the social stigma that once attached to the situation has all but disappeared.

It would have been miraculous had the newly won freedom of onehalf of the population not been used to terminate unwanted marriages. Although we do not know the figures, we can and must assume that the great event of female emancipation has brought with it an increase in the number and rate of cases of factual marriage breakdown. Since it is probable that at least some of these cases have been followed by formalization through divorce, we are justified in assuming that to some extent the rise in the rate of divorce is connected with the change in the social position of the female half of the population.

The other development which we are justified to assume has brought about an increase in the number and rate of factual marriage breakdown and, consequently, of divorce too, is that transformation of the image and pattern of marriage which has taken place during the past two or three generations. It has been intensively observed and extensively described by the sociologists.[16] Ernest Burgess has called this development one from institutional to companionship marriage. These terms describe the situation well, although they have sometimes been misinterpreted. The terminology does not mean to say that "modern" marriage is not an institution in the sense of a configuration of set patterns and expectations of social behavior. It also does not imply

16. See especially E. BURGESS & H. J. LOCKE, THE FAMILY: FROM INSTITUTION TO COMPANIONSHIP 483 ff. (2d ed. 1953), and literature cited therein; R. S. CAVAN, THE AMERICAN FAMILY (1953); K. N. Llewellyn, *Behind the Law of Divorce*, 32 COLUM. L. REV. 1281 (1932), 33 COLUM. L. REV. 249 (1933); F. R. KLUCKHORN, THE AMERICAN FAMILY: PAST AND PRESENT AND AMERICA'S WOMEN (1952).

that companionship and love would not have played important roles in "old-time" marriage. What is meant is a short-hand reference to the fact that in our present society of urban living and industrial mass production the institution of marriage has lost some of the functions which it had to fulfill in "old-time" society and has assumed certain new ones which it did not have to fulfill to the same extent before. Marriage has, of course, retained that function which may be called its basic one, that of providing the cradle and home for the newly born members of society. In a large measure, marriage has also remained the basic unit of consumption, although it has to share this role with the plant canteen, the school lunchroom, the luncheon club, and the cafeteria. But the roles the family once played in education and recreation have been largely, although not entirely, transferred to the schools and the public places of entertainment. The role of constituting an important unit of production is still played in some measure by the family on the farm or the corner grocery store, but it has disappeared for the overwhelming mass of the population. But in inverse ratio to this change has been the increased significance of marriage as the haven of rest in which the city dweller hopes to find the understanding and companionship which he craves. He craves it more, indeed, than his forebears, who lived in closer proximity with nature, had closer contacts with brothers, uncles, nephews, or sisters, aunts, and grandmothers, and who could find more easily congenial friends in the more homogenous small towns and villages of the past. Above all, his more extensive education has made modern man more aware of his psychological needs and has, perhaps, increased their intensity. In consequence, finding the mate by whom the new needs will be satisfied has become more difficult. It is easier to find a wife who is a good housekeeper, an efficient helper on the farm, and a good mother to a flock of children, or a husband who is a good provider, than a mate who is an ever ready congenial companion, who shares not only sorrows and troubles, but also tastes, interests, and circle of acquaintances, and who remains congenial in all these respects and many more, not only in the youthful years of early love and bliss but through all the vicissitudes and transformations of a lifetime with its growth in body, mind, and soul. In all these more subtle aspects of marriage we need more, we expect more, and we are more easily disappointed. Of course, this transformation has not taken place in an equal measure in all groups of the population. The old patterns continue to exist alongside the new ones and the innumerable transitions which are possible in between. The image and pattern of marriage is not the same among farmers, college professors, automobile workers, recent immigrants from Sicily, big-city white-collar employees, southern Baptist clergymen, or Hollywood stars, not to speak of Hopi Indians, Mexican fruit pickers, and poor southern Negroes. But there has been a transformation of the marriage pattern among what we may call the great American middle class, that class which represents America to us as well as to the world at large. This transformation has been one of refinement, of greater emphasis upon the spiritual as against the physiological and economic aspects of the marriage relation.[17] Its concomitant has been a greater risk of failure and disappointment which, in conjunction with the newly won freedom of the female half of the population, is likely to constitute a cause of marriage breakdown that would not have occurred in the older days. Again we must emphasize, however, that we have no figures.

To what extent we are inclined to regard these changes as improvement depends largely upon the place on which we stand in the kaleidoscope of the social structure and upon the extent to which we are free from the tendency to idealize the past. Possibly the transformation of marriage appears as an improvement, especially if one considers that it has been accompanied by a decline in America of not only the mistress system, which at one time played a significant role here, too, as well as of what was once called *the* social vice, prostitution. These developments may be worth the price of an increased incidence of marriage breakdown. One may also believe that the very development of industrialization and urbanization which seems to have brought about that not exactly determinable increase of cases of family breakup may well carry within itself the possibility that in the long run the incidence of marriage breakdown may decrease. This possibility is indicated by investigations which point in the direction that among all groups of the population the rate of family breakup is smallest among that group which appears most typically to represent the new age, i.e., that of the college and university graduates. If the facts found by Goode and other investigators[18] justify this conclusion, it might indicate that the top level of that kind of education which our society has elaborated may develop not only the new demands on marriage but also the abilities to fulfill them.[19]

17. *Cf.* Llewellyn, *supra* note 16, at 1281.
18. W. J. GOODE, AFTER DIVORCE 33 ff. (1956); Hajnal, *Analysis of Changes in the Marriage Pattern by Economic Groups*, 19 AM. SOCIOL. REV. 295 (1954).
19. See N. Foote, *Matching of Husband and Wife in Phases of Development*, 4 TRANSACTIONS OF THE THIRD WORLD CONGRESS OF SOCIOLOGY 24 (1956).

If we regard family stability as a social good, a situation of high incidence of marriage breakdown constitutes a social evil. Its reduction deserves to be an aim of social policy. But what about divorce? It does not occur by itself but only as a sequel of marriage breakdown. Insofar as divorce opens the door to legitimate remarriage and thus to the creation of new homes free of any taint of illegitimacy, it is a social good rather than an evil. But if the easy availability of divorce is conducive toward a high incidence of marriage breakdown, good social policy requires that the incidence of divorce ought also to be reduced. Is it? This is the question to which we shall now turn.

12
Does Divorce Breed Breakdown?

"Divorce breeds divorce." This assertion has been made time and again, with deep conviction and without evidence. In its terse form, the proposition is misleading. It does not mean to suggest that easy availability of divorce induces those whose marriages have already collapsed to formalize the breakdown. The assertion is that easy availability of divorce encourages marriage breakdown. Is this true?

In the absence of statistical data on factual marriage breakdown, how can one inquire whether there exists a cause and effect relationship between a society's law of divorce and its state of marriage stability? Before presenting the fragmentary empirical data we shall try theoretically to determine what kinds of relationship may conceivably exist.

If a married couple does not wish to live together, they cannot be compelled to do so. The law can preclude divorce, but it cannot prevent factual marriage breakdown. The law can deny freedom of remarriage, but it cannot thereby prevent a man and a woman from living together in a union which may be called irregular but which may resemble matrimony in every respect except the absence of the legal bond. All the divorce law can do is prevent the transformation of the factual relationship of concubinage into a legitimate marriage. In some parts of the world, especially in a good many states of the United States, the statute books contain provisions threatening with criminal punishment such acts as concubinage, adulterous concubinage, adultery, or even fornication, i.e., extramarital sexual intercourse. Unless the marital bond has been terminated, the duty of marital fidelity binds even parties who have long ceased to live together. He who breaches that duty is punishable, apart from the fact that he is guilty of sin and of morally reprehensible conduct. But the religious opprobrium does not impair the indifferent, and fear of moral blame is of no effect in circles in which it does not work. The fear of prosecution for crime is no deterrent, because the statutory provisions are limited to a paper existence modified by unpredictable occasional prosecution.[1] As long as adultery was punishable in Italy or Germany no prosecution could be initiated except upon the application of the legitimate spouse.[2] The provisions thus helped to cool feelings of hatred or served as tools of blackmail. But application to the courts was rare. The number of convictions for adultery was insignificant.[3] As a threat against the breakup of a marriage such laws, if they are ever considered at all, may perhaps deter one who is considering breaking up his marriage because he is infatuated with another sex partner and intends to engage in sexual intercourse with him or her. Only remotely may such a law be regarded as a bar to a possible future relationship which is not yet concretely contemplated. In the United States laws of the kind under discussion are known to be unenforced and are therefore irrelevant as devices of deterrence. To all practical effects a strict divorce law can thus do little more than prevent the creation of a legitimate marriage relationship with a new partner. This fact has no deterrent effect at all in the case of a person who is not only dissatisfied with his existing marriage but feels fed up with marriage generally and does not contemplate remarriage. To one who contemplates either the general possibility of some future sex relationship or a definite relationship with a new partner already known, the impossibility or difficulty of establishing the new relationship as a legitimate marriage is no deterrent if he does not care about legitimacy. Concern about the legitimacy of a new relationship may have its source in religion, in moral conviction, in thoughts about social respectability, in worries

---

1. A. C. KINSEY, W. B. POMEROY & C. E. MARTIN, SEXUAL BEHAVIOR IN THE HUMAN MALE 389 (1945); H. L. A. HART, LAW, LIBERTY, AND MORALITY 27 (1963); H. H. Foster, Jr. & D. J. Freed, *Les infractions contre la famille et les mœurs en droit des Etats-Unis d'Amérique*, 35 REV. INTERNATIONALE DE DROIT PÉNAL 611, 631, 690, 703 (1964); M. PLOSCOWE, SEX AND THE LAW 148 (1962); G. O. W. MUELLER, LEGAL REGULATION OF SEXUAL CONDUCT 16 (1961).

2. German Criminal Code, § 172; Italian Criminal Code, arts. 559 (adultery of a married woman; punishable on husband's application), 560 (married man living with a concubine; punishable on wife's application).

3. In the Federal Republic of Germany, the number of persons convicted of adultery was 144 in 1954, 162 in 1955, and 176 in 1956 (R. Sturm, *Les infractions contre la famille et les moeurs en droit allemand*, 35 REV. INTERNAT. DE DROIT PÉNAL 445, 453 (1964). The numbers of divorces obtained on the ground of adultery were 2,739 in 1954, 2,422 in 1955, and 2,610 in 1956 (E. Wolf, G. Lüke & H. Hax, SCHEIDUNG UND SCHEIDUNGSRECHT 471 [1959]). As in a case of adultery usually two persons are convicted, the portion resulting in criminal punishment was exceedingly small. See W. MÜLLER-FREIENFELS, EHE UND RECHT 109 (1962). Section 172 of the Criminal Code was repealed by the Law of 25 June 1969 ([1969] BGBl. I 645). In Italy prosecutions for adultery or concubinage are said to have been very rare. The relevant provisions of the Criminal Code were declared unconstitutional in 1968–69.

about the legitimacy of offspring, or in the consideration of the advantages of legitimate marriage under laws concerning such matters as succession to property, income, estate or inheritance taxes, life insurance, pensions, or the like.

Religious scruples in mid-twentieth-century America no longer have the force they had in Puritan Massachusetts Bay Colony, although they are still powerful for the millions of believers. How large their number is, cannot be estimated. It does not coincide with the number of members of churches. One may be motivated by religious scruples even though he does not belong to a church, or he may be a member of a church and yet have few religious scruples. The person who is strongly motivated by religion or ethics is not likely to break up his marriage relationship or to ponder the legitimacy of a new relationship which might follow his existing marriage. This strong motivational effect of religion or ethics is likely to act at a stage prior to that at which the consideration of the divorce laws is likely to play any role.

The motivational force of the consideration of social respectability of a new relationship varies among different groups of the population. It tends to be weakest in the bottom economic group. In the present-day United States this group is to some extent characterized by color. In nineteenth-century America to disregard the lack of respectability of a sex relation was common among large groups of the white population, just as it was in England until, in 1951, divorce was made financially accessible to the less affluent. Generally, observation indicates that disregard for social respectability tends to be more common the more difficult or the more costly it is to obtain a divorce and thus to conclude a legitimate remarriage.

Even where a new relationship is not officially a legitimate marriage, it may be passed off as such so that the appearance of respectability is created. In countries like Italy, the Federal Republic of Germany, or France it is not easy for anyone to use a name other than the one which is ascribed to him by strict rules of the law. Where everybody must be registered with the police and where no change of name is possible without the approval of a governmental agency, it is next to impossible for Signora Bianchi to pass herself off as Signora Rossi, and so to appear as the wife of the man with whom she lives. But in the United States, what prevents Mrs. Short from calling herself Mrs. Long?

The appearance of the name may be thought to be strengthened by a marriage certificate obtained in a marriage ceremony. Of course, if the partner to that ceremony is still married to another person, the ceremony does not result in a legitimate marriage. The relationship is bigamous and the act of going through the ceremony constitutes the crime of bigamy, which is threatened with serious punishment in the United States as well as elsewhere. However, in the United States this crime can be committed more easily than anywhere else and its detection is more difficult. In Continental countries anybody who wishes to go through a ceremony of marriage must provide strict documentary proof that he is legally free to do so. Any marriage is noted on the birth record and nobody whose birth record shows such an entry is able to go through a new ceremony until he proves by official document that his prior marriage has been dissolved by death of the partner, divorce, or annulment. The commission of bigamy would be next to impossible, were it not for the destruction of records and the upheaval of war and mass migrations.[4] The number of such convictions is also negligible in the United States, but for a different reason. Strict proof of the dissolution of a prior marriage is rarely required of anyone who applies for a marriage license. Commonly an applicant is simply asked whether he has ever been married before and, if so, how and when this marriage was terminated. Usually the answer must be verified by oath. Documentary proof is hardly ever required.[5] The detection of bigamy is a matter of chance and accident, especially when the new place of residence is remote from the old. To some extent the fear of a later discovery, punishment, and disgrace is likely to have a deterrent effect. However, this fear is far from universal. How large the number of bigamous relationships is, can, of course, not be determined. It can, however, be said with certainty that in the United States it is considerably higher than in Continental countries.

The motivational force of the desire to protect the offspring from the stigma of illegitimacy is likely to diminish with the availability of devices of birth control. Where the birth of children is not prevented, or is even desired, the force of the fear of illegitimacy depends upon the strength of the desire for respectability. It is highest among the middle classes, to whom respectability is a matter of vital concern, but the higher the concern about respectability, the lower is the like-

4. In Germany before World War II, there were 60 convictions for bigamy in 1934, 50 in 1935, and 52 in 1936. After the war the numbers were 541 in 1950, 330 in 1951, 272 in 1952, 203 in 1953, 155 in 1954, 105 in 1955, and 184 in 1956. 8 NIEDERSCHRIFTEN ÜBER DIE SITZUNGEN DER GROSSEN STRAFRECHTSKOMMISSION (76th–90th meetings), 628 (1959).

In England and Wales 28 persons were "apprehended" for bigamy in 1968, but not a single one was found guilty. HOME OFFICE CRIMINAL STATISTICS, ENGLAND AND WALES 1968, table 1(a) Cmnd. 4098 (1969).

5. M. E. RICHMOND & F. S. HALL, MARRIAGE AND THE STATE 42 (1929).

lihood of family breakup. In the Victorian age, when concern about respectability was high, the façade of a functioning marriage was likely to be preserved even though the marriage was dead in the feelings of the partners. The husband was more likely to seek satisfaction with a mistress than to go through the disgrace of divorce and remarriage. In present-day America divorce as such is disreputable only in constantly shrinking groups of the population. Illegitimacy is still regarded as serious. However, the stigma can be avoided not only through birth control and abortion, but also by passing off the new relationship, and its offspring, as legitimate.

While the effect of the criminal law as a deterrent against concubinage or adulterous relationships must be regarded as next to zero, with respect to other kinds of law it may make a difference whether a certain relationship is or is not a legitimate marriage. At the death of one partner the legitimate spouse is entitled to a major share in the estate. In the United States, this share cannot be defeated by a will attempting disinheritance. A concubine has no rights of intestate succession. Of course, each partner may institute the other as a legatee under his or her last will, conceivably for the totality of the estate. But if at the time of his death the predeceased spouse was still married to another person, that person, the legitimate spouse, may step forward and claim her or his indefeasible share in the estate. The concubine and her children may find themselves in a precarious situation. Even where nobody interferes with testamentary claims of the concubine and the children of the concubinous relationship, a larger share of the estate will be consumed by taxation than in the case of succession by a legitimate spouse or legitimate children, provided, of course, the tax collector knows that the relationship was irregular.

Consideration of rights of succession to property or of death duties will play no role unless there is property. The motivational force is of no effect among the propertyless. But even among those who have property and may give consideration to the course of inheritance and to inheritance taxation, the difference between marriage and concubinage has to a considerable extent been wiped out by that peculiar device of American law, the presumption of validity of the last relationship that outwardly had the appearance of marriage.[6] If a man and a woman live, or have lived, together in a relationship which outwardly presents the appearance of marriage, the courts presume that the relationship was initiated by a transaction suitable to result in marriage.

6. *Supra*, chap. 4.

Of greater weight may be the apprehension of the loss of pension rights to which a surviving spouse may be entitled under social security laws or under private arrangements. With the growing importance of such rights the fear of their loss has probably become stronger as a deterrent from the transformation of a separation into a divorce than the incentive through a divorce to escape from the duty of marital fidelity. A separated or abandoned wife is likely to know or to believe that the commission of "adultery" will no longer automatically deprive her of the custody of her children or of her claim to be supported by her husband, and the male partner is likely to know that "adultery" committed by him will no longer automatically subject him to more cumbersome duties of support.

Where, as in France ordinarily,[7] or on the basis of special agreement as in Italy,[8] income earned by either spouse is community property, it regularly continues to be so even when the partners have separated. Only a judicial decree puts an end to this potentially awkward situation.[9] Neither in Italy nor in France has this rule prevented the mass incidence of purely factual separations.[10]

Custody of the children can always be regulated by a court of law in an action for habeas corpus or by the chancellor in proceedings in equity or, in certain cases, by the juvenile court. The wife may even assume her maiden name without going through the divorce court. At least factually each party may also find it possible to establish a new relationship and a new home with another partner without benefit of formal divorce and remarriage.

More important than the legal advantages which divorce may provide over mere separation, appears to be the psychological satisfaction of reacquisition of freedom. The freedom need not necessarily be that of immediate remarriage. Only a comparatively small percentage of divorcees has a prospective new partner waiting around the corner (see table 18).[11] The freedom desired will often be simply the feeling of no longer being tied to a partner who has come to be hated or despised or, perhaps, with lingering loyalty regarded as a psychological impediment to adventure. But even in those cases the freedom of re-

7. Civil Code, arts. 1400, 1401.
8. Civil Code, arts. 217, 210.
9. French Civil Code, art. 1441; Italian Civil Code, art. 225.
10. On the legal situation in the American community property states, see W. G. DE FUNIAK, PRINCIPLES OF COMMUNITY PROPERTY (1943).
11. A table compiled by Jacobson on the basis of samplings indicates that in 1934 only 21.8 percent of the male divorcees, and 23.9 percent of the females remarried within one year after the divorce; the percentages of all those remarried within two years were 30.6 of the males and 33.8 of the females (JACOBSON, *supra* Table 18, at 70).

marriage, potential rather than actual, to be sure, is likely to be the decisive motive.[12]

Contemplation of the difficulties a strict divorce law places in the way of establishing a new legitimate marriage may, as we have seen, act as a deterrent to family breakdown in various ways. As the threat of punishment may act as a deterrent not only on the person who is actually about to commit theft, murder, or treason, so a strict law of divorce may act not only by way of *praeventio specialis* but also of *praeventio generalis*. The threat of criminal punishment is established *ne peccetur*, not only by the one deliberating whether or not to go ahead with a criminal design but also by the public at large. The stigmatization of certain conduct as criminal can, in some circumstances, have the general educational effect of bringing moral and religious considerations into play. It becomes a part of the cultural climate and indirectly acts as a deterrent. A similar effect may come from a strict law of divorce. Awareness of the difficulty or impossibility of obtaining a divorce may have a stabilizing effect upon married life when divorce and marriage breakdown are not neatly distinguished from each other. In lower income groups, people, especially women, are likely to be well aware of the possibility of obtaining a judicial decree of support and maintenance without a divorce. To what extent people of higher income are aware of such possibilities, we do not know. Some of them, men and women, have certainly heard of the possibility of obtaining decrees of separate maintenance or of concluding separation agreements to be followed, if necessary, by actions for breach of contract.

TABLE 18
AVERAGE NUMBER OF YEARS, FOLLOWING DIVORCE, BEFORE REMARRIAGE OR DEATH, UNITED STATES, 1948

At Attained Age	Males	Females
20	2.5	1.6
30	2.0	3.5
35	2.7	5.9
40	4.0	9.3
45	5.6	12.3
50	6.9	13.8
55	7.9	14.0

Source: P. H. JACOBSON, AMERICAN MARRIAGE AND DIVORCE, table 40, at 84 (1959).

12. Ultimately, the majority of divorcees remarry, but the length of the interval indicates that a search for a new partner is necessary in a great many cases. *Cf.* JACOBSON, *supra* table 18, at 82; W. J. GOODE, AFTER DIVORCE 269 (1956).

Apart from financial considerations, identification of marriage breakdown and divorce may have a stabilizing influence upon marriage life if divorce is regarded as religiously sinful, morally wrong, or socially disreputable. However, whether such views exist in a given society and, quite particularly, whether they are sufficiently widespread to influence the incidence of marriage breakdown, is difficult, if not impossible to determine. The existence and the extent of such views depend on the cultural climate of the society in question. The stabilizing effect of religious, moral, or social views concerning marriage as such must be distinguished from the stabilizing effect of the divorce laws as such, i.e., the stabilizing effect of the awareness that the creation of a new legitimate marriage relationship may be difficult or impossible. Such a deterrent effect is likely to be small. On the other hand the stabilizing effect of religious, moral, and social views may be powerful, especially if they are combined with such objective circumstances as the impossibility or difficulty existing for a divorced, a separated, or an abandoned woman to reestablish an economic existence for herself and her children. As the example of the Prussian Code demonstrates, the influence of such views and circumstances may be so powerful that the incidence of marriage breakdown is at a minimum even though the divorce law is liberal in the extreme. But the opposite may occur too. As demonstrated by present-day Italy, the inclination to break up a marriage and to yield to such temptation is, like the opposite attitude, a result of those views and circumstances which in their totality make up the cultural climate of a given society. The divorce law, too, tends to be influenced by the cultural climate. However, the degree of strictness or liberality of the law does not always or necessarily have fully to correspond with the actual behavior. The cultural climate may be so complex that it affects actual marriage stability in one way and the configuration of the law in another. Actual attitudes and law tend to coincide in a society of considerable homogeneity. They tend to diverge in a society exhibiting some considerable degree of pluralism.

A society's cultural climate is composed of a great variety of factors. What are they? How do they operate?,

A region's meteorological climate is the product of a considerable number of factors, such as maximum, minimum, and average temperatures, distribution of temperature changes, the amount and distribution of precipitation, direction and velocity of wind, duration and distribution of sunshine, etc. The meteorological phenomena in turn are caused by a complex of circumstances such as geographic latitude, elevation above sea level, distance from the ocean, topographic structure of the surface, etc. The term "cultural climate" is used here as a shorthand reference to the totality of subjective and objective phenomena by which the culture of a society, its style of living, are determined. The cultural climate of medieval Europe was different from that of the mid-twentieth century. The cultural climate of Communist China differs from that of Western Europe or North America. To lesser degrees, the cultural climate of Sweden differs from that of Italy, that of Maine from that of California.

Theoretical analysis of the concept of cultural climate belongs to the field of social psychology. What we mean by the cultural climate as related to marriage stability and the divorce law is demonstrated by the concrete illustrations presented in the preceding chapters.

When Italy was unified in the middle of the nineteenth century, the cultural climate was characterized by an interplay of Roman Catholicism and liberalism. The latter played a significant role in the political and intellectual life of the country. But the former was dominant, especially in the regions of the center and the south. Catholicism was of the traditionalist, antimodernistic kind of Leo X and Pius IX, of the Syllabus of Errors [13] and the Anti-Modernist Oath,[14] and the pope's voluntary captivity in the Vatican. To the church, Cavour was the enemy. For the state it was an urgent task to prepare a reconciliation with the church or at least not to deepen the rift. After all, Catholicism not only held an almost unlimited sway over the minds of the center and the south but was also a profound influence in the north, including Piedmont, the home region of the house of Savoy and of Cavour. In Catholicism, especially the traditionalist Catholicism of mid-nineteenth-century Italy, individual happiness in this world is not the goal of human existence. Rather, the goal is the next world, for which the world of the living is but a preparatory stage. Whether the soul is to find perpetual bliss or eternal damnation depends on how the man has lived in this world. Here, too, happiness can be obtained, but only in the consciousness of devotion and obedience to God and his church, and in the fulfillment of the duties of the status into which one has been placed by God. Happiness can be achieved not in the pursuit of secular pleasure but in the fulfillment of duty, in obedience and discipline. The greatest happiness can be found in that state which consists in the full dedication to God and the complete obedience to his and the church's commands, the state of the religious. But happiness can also be attained in the faithful performance of the duties

13. Pius IX's encyclical *Quanta cura*, of 8 December 1864.
14. Pius X's encyclical *Pascendi*, of September 1907.

of secular life as described in the church's interpretation of the Word of God. A state of man which the church has applied particular care in describing, is that of marriage. Its end is not the pursuit of sexual pleasure, of human love or companionship, but the perpetuation of the race for the glorification of God. Marriage has to be strictly monogamous. It is indissoluble, and what love and pleasure it presents is the reward of devotion to God and the fulfillment of the duties of the Christian. The Augustinian doctrine of marriage as a sacrament, a vessel of Divine Grace, symbolizes and summarizes this ideal. Since man is sinful he cannot fully live up to the duties of the marital state or to any other of the commands of God and his church. However, forgiveness of sin will be found through the church for the one who faithfully submits to its divinely established authority. In the cultural atmosphere of Italy in the 1850s and 1860s, the Catholic view of marriage was firmly established, together with the complementary institutions of prostitution and the mistress system. These were concessions to the flesh for which the church would provide forgiveness. For the state it was not only politically advisable but natural to formulate its marriage law in accordance with the view which held almost exclusive sway over the people, including its leading classes. To allow divorce would have been as shocking and as meaningless as it had been in the period of Napoleonic domination, in which divorce had been officially obtainable. The new Italian Civil Code of 1865 simply followed the pattern of the Austrian Code of 1811, which had been in effect in Lombardy and Veneto. Marriage was to be regulated by secular law, but the secular law was essentially to coincide with that of the church. For the initiation of a marriage, it is true, a civil ceremony was necessary. However, once marriage had been concluded it was to be indissoluble.

Since the time of unification, Italy, especially northern Italy, has undergone profound social change. The country has become a democracy. Secularism has grown. It is represented not only as it was in the nineteenth century, by the Liberal party, but more powerfully by the Social Democrats, the Socialists, and the Communists. Yet, the dominant party has long been the *Democrazia Christiana*, which, although not externally, is ideologically tied to the Vatican. So the divorce law remained unchanged until the Catholicism of the Italian pattern has loosened its dominant position. The Catholic view is challenged by secularism. Italy is no longer a country with a homogenous cultural climate. The plurality of basic attitudes, as in other, similar parts of the world, finds expression in the discrepancy that has developed between the law of the books and the law in action. In Italy, where the law of the books proscribed divorce completely, the discrepancy was more pronounced than anywhere else, more than in Eire or in those Latin American countries where divorce is also not admitted but where the countertendencies have not yet gathered so much force as in Italy.

The development of the cultural climate in Sweden has been the reverse of that of Italy, where high conservative traditionalist homogeneity has changed into plurality. In Sweden, the course of events has been from an almost completely traditionalist conservative homogeneity to an individualist liberalism which has become so dominant that it can almost be called homogenous. After a long period of sub rosa development of substitute institutions, such as the Copenhagen divorce, the official law was changed in 1905 and those remnants of traditionalism which it contained have become an almost completely dead letter in the practice of the courts and in social reality. In 1970, the government was even planning the adaptation of the law to that radically individualist view under which marriage ceases to be a public concern and loses its monopoly of respectability. Perhaps that view will turn out to be more appropriate than it was in the Soviet Union, where it was tried, abandoned, and retried.

Pluralism characterizes the situation in both France and the Federal Republic of Germany. The contrast between the two Frances still exists, between the conservative Catholic tradition and the ideas of 1789. The appearance of the third element, the hammer and sickle, has further complicated the situation. In matters concerning personal life, including marriage and divorce, liberal leanings have been more outstanding in French communism than they have been in the ambiguous attitudes of Soviet communism.

In Germany, the contrasts have been even more marked. The law of the books, uniform since 1 January 1900, expressed the principle of marital offense. In 1938, a provision was added which, based upon the principle of breakdown, embodied a somewhat qualified separation ground. In judicial practice and by the statutory amendment of 1961,[15] the door was opened to reintroduce consideration of guilt in cases in which a contested divorce is applied for upon the objective ground of breakdown. During all these vicissitudes of the law of the books, the law in action has been fairly consistent in allowing consent divorce disguised as divorce for offense or breakdown. Official statistics about uncontested divorce are not available, but good evidence indi-

---

15. Law of 11 August 1961, [1961] BGBl. I 1221.

cates that the incidence is not lower than the 90 percent or more in which it consistently occurs in the United States, England, France, and Japan. The cultural climate is not homogenous. The conservatives have been strong enough to keep on the books a law of a fair degree of strictness. The law in action is different. As in other places, where the democratic compromise could not be worked out in the legislature, it was brought about in the trial courts, especially those of the big cities, where the court calendars are overcrowded and the judges are every day confronted with the harsh facts of life. But an adaptation of the law of the books to the law in action is in the offing. As in the United States, the cultural climate has changed so considerably and individualist liberalism has become so prominent in the Federal Republic of Germany that it may well succeed in having enacted into law those radical proposals which are presently under discussion and to which even prominent representatives of traditionalism seem to have resigned themselves.

Our theoretical conclusions are fortified by statistical inquiries of the past and by those which were undertaken at the University of Chicago Comparative Law Research Center. The number of earlier inquiries is small. The earliest survey of laws and judicial decrees of divorce and judicial separation was undertaken in Italy in connection with one of the abortive attempts to introduce divorce into the legal system of that country. The comparison of such countries as Sweden, where the law was permissive but the rate of decrees low, with countries like France, where the rate of decrees (of separation) was higher in spite of a restrictive law, induced the author of the survey to state that "the frequency of divorces and of separations in relation to the population or to marriage does not appear to be greater in countries where legal regulations make it easier for spouses to obtain them. Therefore it is necessary to find other motives for explaining a stronger or weaker tendency to break marriage bonds in different countries." [16]

A more elaborate inquiry was published one year later. It was undertaken in France in connection with the dispute about the reintroduction of divorce that agitated France in the early 1880s and resulted in 1884 in the adoption of the *loi Naquet,* which, with the exception of divorce by mutual agreement, restored to the Civil Code the provisions about divorce of the original version of 1804 that had been repealed in 1816 in the course of the politico-social reaction against

---

16. [L. Bodio,] *Le separazioni personali di coniugi e i divorzi in Italia e in alcuni altri stati,* 1 ANNALI DI STATISTICA, Ser. 3, at 92 (1882).

the ideology of the Revolution of 1789.[17] The author of the incisive inquiry was Jacques Bertillon, the great pioneer of modern demography.[18] The work is remarkable in method and in insight. Incisively Bertillon correlated data about judicial separation, which was the only relief at the time available in France, and on divorce as it existed in other European countries, with data on nuptiality, illegitimate births, suicide, occupation, religion, age at time of marriage, age at time of divorce or separation, number of children, etc. In his exploration of the respective influence of the law and of the mores, he compared the incidence of divorce or judicial separation or both in different parts of a country with a uniform law, such as France, Switzerland, Bavaria, Belgium, or Hungary; in different countries having different laws; and in places where law has undergone changes in time. The startling differences he discovered between different parts of a country with a uniform law and the equally startling uniformities among regions with different laws or between periods of changing law, Bertillon explained by the overwhelming preponderance of mores over official law. As it is impossible to regulate love by such laws as that of Bavaria which prohibited paupers from marrying, so it is futile to try to prevent spouses from parting if they are determined to end their life in common.

The aim of his work was stated by Bertillon to be an effort "to establish the statistical laws of divorce," and he asserted that he had searched for them "with the impartiality of the physicist who is searching for the laws governing inanimate matter."[19] The conclusion is succinctly stated:

What exercises the predominant influence on the frequency [of divorce and judicial separation] is the state of the mores, especially of religious attitudes. Legislative dispositions have little to do with it.[20]

If a law introducing the possibility of divorce hardly changes the number [of judicial separations], is it not certain that a law by which the number of grounds is increased has even less influence? If two spouses have seriously decided to quit, they will always find in the law some means to achieve their end. Irrespective of whether the law is mild or harsh, they invariably find a tool to serve their end. But if the text of the laws is of such doubtful influence on the number of suits, another text is of noted influence, viz. the schedule of fees and costs. . . . One may compare, although with some caution, the statistics of judicial decrees of two countries having different laws. . . . But

17. See *supra* p. 215.
18. ETUDE DÉMOGRAPHIQUE DU DIVORCE ET DE LA SÉPARATION DE CORPS DANS LES DIFFÉRENTS PAYS DE L'EUROPE (1883).
19. *Id.* 10.
20. *Id.* 9.

one must distrust comparison between two countries with highly different legal expenses.[21]

The inquiry of Walter F. Willcox, member of the faculty of social science and statistics of Cornell University,[22] was stimulated by, and based upon, the vast collection of statistical data contained in the Wright report of 1889.[23] In the preface to this book, Willcox expressed himself as follows:

> The study of divorce of which this pamphlet is the result was commenced when fresh from the reading of philosophy in Germany, and a month or more passed in turning the leaves of Trendelenburg, Bluntschli, Stahl and the whole line of "Naturrecht" theorists. Nothing was found to shake my conviction that the policy of the Catholic church, refusing divorce in all cases, is the ideal one for a state to adopt. Then I chanced upon M. Bertillon's *Etude Démographique de divorce* and, undeterred by the columns of figures, read and reread it. It convinced me that his method was sound and, deserting the *a priori* road of laying down what marriage and divorce ought to be, I applied myself to a patient examination of Mr. Wright's Report in the effort to understand what they are. My conclusions are contained in the following pages. In their present form, therefore, they are based on two books: the method is derived from Bertillon, and the data from Wright. A critic must have a keen eye to detect in them any influence of the first six weeks' reading. If a similar revolution should be started in the mind of any reader by the facts here recorded, I shall be most amply repaid.[24]

Having computed divorce rates for all forty-eight states, Willcox found that they could be grouped in three geographical belts: the lowest rates, 5 to 130 divorces to 100,000 married couples, in the states of the eastern seaboard exclusive of Maine, New Hampshire and Florida, and, without geographic contiguity, in Louisiana and New Mexico; the highest rates, 390 to 800, were found in the states of the Pacific Coast and the Rocky Mountains, excluding Arizona and New Mexico, but also in Maine; and an intermediate rate of 140 to 380 in the states between the Alleghenies and the Rocky Mountains, but excluding Louisiana.[25]

In a chapter entitled "Influence of Legislation on Divorce" (2d ed. 41–61), Willcox tries to correlate the differences in the divorce rates with the statutory lists of grounds of divorce and also changes in the statutory lists with changes in the divorce rates of the states in which

---

21. *Id.* 13–14.
22. THE DIVORCE PROBLEM: A STUDY IN STATISTICS (Columbia College Studies in History, Economics, and Public Law, vol. 1, no. 1) (1st ed. 1891, 2d ed. 1897).
23. CARROLL D. WRIGHT (Commissioner of Labor), A REPORT ON MARRIAGE AND DIVORCE IN THE UNITED STATES, 1867–1886 (Washington, 1889); on the role of this famous document in American thinking about divorce, see *supra* chap. 3.
24. 2d ed. at iii.
25. 2d ed. at 37–40.

such changes had been made in recent times. The statutory formulas are taken at face value. No effort is made to find out whether different meanings have been judicially given to such recurring terms as cruelty or desertion. Eliminating those which are, properly speaking, grounds for annulment rather than divorce and among the grounds for divorce those which could be found in the statutes of no more than two states, Willcox did not find any clear correlation between a state's divorce rate and the number of grounds for divorce listed in its statute. Nor did he find that within a state or country a significant correlation existed between changes in its list of statutory grounds and in its rates of divorce, or between divorce rates and legal restrictions on marriage or remarriage.

The fact that in all states of the eastern belt from New York to Georgia low divorce rates coincide with small numbers of grounds for divorce is explained by

> these large and old states [being] very conservative and averse to radical changes of the law. Their social and economic conditions have probably changed less than those of the other two groups. Certainly this is true of the southern half of the belt, where divorce is least frequent. . . . The three belts of states do not in any way conform to the differences in the legal grounds for divorce. . . . The clear tendency of states in geographical proximity to stand in juxtaposition in the table is equally unexplained by any similarity in their divorce law.[26]

Restrictions on divorce are thus found to exert but a minor influence on the incidence of divorce.

> The single efficient means of reducing divorce by law, neglecting as unadvisable and impracticable the South Carolina method,[27] is to make it expensive. . . . The conclusion of the whole matter is that law can do little. Agitation for the change of law may educate public opinion. It may even be the most efficient and powerful means of education. Such effects no statistics can measure, and, therefore, in a paper like this the educative influence of law must be neglected, but the immediate, direct and measurable influence of legislation is subsidiary, unimportant, almost imperceptible.[28]

If there is to be a remedy against the rising incidence of divorce, it must be sought in the realm of morals.

> Moral education . . . in our schools is sadly lacking. Obviously it should relate, not directly to divorce, but to all the relations and duties of home life

---

26. 2d ed. at 45, 47.
27. At the time of Willcox's writing, South Carolina did not have the institution of divorce at all.
28. 2d ed. at 61.

so constantly and sadly misunderstood. The neglect of these is the seed, and divorce only the fruit.[29]

In connection with the long dispute about advisability of introducing divorce in Italy, a new study of foreign laws and statistics of divorce and judicial separation was undertaken by Augusto Bosco.[30] Observing that the incidence of divorce and judicial separation was different in states of identical or similar legislation, and that the influence of legislative changes appeared to be observable for only short periods, he concluded that legislative formulas do not have much effect and are just a minor factor among those which determine a people's inclination to resort to divorce and judicial separation.[31]

Where there are no causes so to disturb family life as to render conjugal community impossible or difficult, or where citizens are disinclined to take their matrimonial troubles to court, the law is used but little even though it may facilitate divorce or judicial separation. But where such causes exist or where the mores favor the judicial resolution of marital controversies, such marriages will be dissolved even though the code may forbid it, and where the grounds are limited to a small number, they will be used irrespective of the rigor of the wording.[32]

The view of the small role of the law in stopping the rising trend of divorce rates is confirmed in the writings of James P. Lichtenberger[33] and Alfred Cahen.[34] In fact, so thoroughly are social scientists convinced of the irrelevancy of divorce laws that in recent writing the legal aspects of family breakdown are more or less neglected. They are unaware of the socially important problem of how to regularize purely factual separations and irregular unions.

The impression that strict divorce legislation is ineffective in checking the rising demand for freedom of remarriage has been confirmed by the study of the relationship between changes of German legislation and incidence of divorce in Germany that was undertaken at the University of Chicago Comparative Law Research Center. In 1953, a seminar made possible by the Chicago-Frankfurt Academic Exchange

---

29. 2d ed. at 73. In the present days of discontent with the establishment, the following passage may not be without interest: "The discontent which Mr. Bryce finds characteristic of the age is, perhaps, in part explicable as the discouragement resulting from the failure to regenerate the world on either side of the Atlantic by any sort of legislation."
30. DIVORZI E SEPARAZIONI PERSONALI DI CONIUGI: STUDIO DI DEMOGRAFIA COMPARATA (1908).
31. *Id.* 450 ff.
32. *Id.* 458.
33. DIVORCE: A STUDY IN SOCIAL CAUSATION, esp. at 108–9 (1909).
34. STATISTICAL ANALYSIS OF AMERICAN DIVORCE, esp. at 79–80 (1932).

Scheme was conducted in Frankfurt jointly by Professor M. Horkheimer, director of the Frankfurt Institute of Social Research, Professor Ernst Wolf of the Faculty of Law of the Johann Wolgang Goethe University in Frankfurt, Professor Everett C. Hughes of the Department of Sociology of the University of Chicago, and Professor Max Rheinstein of the University of Chicago Law School. In 1954–55 Professor Ernst Wolf spent a semester at the Law School of the University of Chicago. He brought with him Dr. Gerhard Lüke, now professor at the University of Saarbrücken, Dr. Gerhard Baumert, sociologist, and Mr. Herbert Hax, statistician. In Chicago the visitors participated in a seminar on family stability that was jointly conducted by Professors Karl N. Llewellyn and Max Rheinstein of the Law School and Professor Nelson Foote of the Department of Sociology. The investigation of the German situation was continued in Germany after the visitors' return. The work and its results are described in detail in the book by E. Wolf, G. Lüke, and H. Hax entitled *Scheidung und Scheidungsrecht*.[35]

The idea of using statistical material from Germany was conceived because in that country the divorce laws were changed twice within a period for which ample and detailed statistical materials are available. The first change occurred on 1 January 1900, when the new Civil Code for the German empire, of 18 August 1896, replaced the numerous different laws which had been in effect in the country up to that day. The second change occurred under the National-Socialist regime, in 1938, when the marriage and divorce law of the Civil Code was replaced by the new marriage law for Greater Germany. With slight modifications brought about in 1945 by Control Council Law No. 16, the provisions of the law of 1938 are still in effect in the Federal Republic of Germany.

Because of the diversity of the divorce laws preceding the Code of 1896 the effects of the change had to be investigated separately for each of the different parts of the Reich. In the pre-Code law of divorce, three major groups of districts could be distinguished: (1) those of the Prussian General Code of 1791–94, (2) those of the Code Napoléon; and (3) those of the so-called common law of Germany.

The Prussian General Code, which was in effect in the state of Prussia in about one-half of its territory, and in a few small territories outside of Prussia, was the most liberal of these laws. As a product of the Enlightenment and decisively influenced by the secular thought of

---

35. *Supra* note 3. The following pp. 293–303 reproduce substantial parts of my review of this book published in 65 AM. J. SOCIOL. Notes 36–44 refer to this book.

Frederick the Great, it allowed divorce not only on the ground of misconduct but also, at least as a general rule, upon mutual agreement, and even upon the unilateral petition of one spouse based upon "insuperable aversion" to the other. The Prussian Code thus clearly followed the notion that a marriage might be terminated not only because of one party's guilt and misconduct but also where, without any party's fault, the marriage had become thoroughly disrupted beyond hope of repair. The Prussian Code was, indeed, the earliest of modern divorce laws which embodied this "principle of breakdown" that had been postulated by the thinkers of the Enlightenment as a necessary concomitant of every individual's inalienable right to the pursuit of happiness, but which has been consistently condemned by religious, especially Roman Catholic, conservatives as being incompatible with the ideal of Christian marriage.

The traditional Christian notions had found expression in the common law of Germany, which was, indeed, as far as marriage and divorce were concerned, identical with ecclesiastical law. It was, however, not the same for Catholics and Protestants. For Catholics the rule was that of the canon law as modified by the Civil Status Law of 6 February 1875. Marriage was indissoluble except for adultery. In Protestant ecclesiastical law, too, marriage was, on general principle, regarded as concluded for life, but the concession was made that a marriage would be dissolved in certain cases of grave misconduct, namely, adultery, desertion, and cruelty of a particularly serious character. In contrast to the breakdown principle of the Prussian Code, the Protestant common law thus strictly followed the principle of misconduct, while the Catholic common law adhered to the principle of indissolubility.

Similar to the position of the Protestant common law was that of the Code Napoléon. On general principles, divorce was to be granted only in cases of guilt, but the definition of what might be called cruelty was less strict. Furthermore, in addition to divorce for guilt, the code provided for divorce on the ground of mutual agreement of the spouses. However, the procedure provided for the expression of the agreement was so cumbersome and time-consuming that divorces based on it were rare.

In the new Civil Code it was not easy to find a solution acceptable to the whole country. The final result was similar to that of the Code Napoléon. Any possibility of divorce on the ground of mutual agreement was abolished, however. All traces of the breakdown principle were deleted. Divorce was to be granted exclusively in the case of guilty misconduct. The general tendency of the draftsmen was one of hostility toward divorce. In their report they stated that it was their intention to stem the rising tide of divorce and firmly to establish the principle of stability of marriage.

The changes brought about by the new Code were considerable for the regions under the Prussian Code and those of the common law. In the former, divorce became considerably more difficult; in the latter it was made somewhat easier for Protestants and much easier for Catholics.

What were the actual effects of the legislative change in the various parts of the country? To what extent, if any, was the hope of the draftsmen of the Code that it might stem the rising tide of divorce realized?

Three sets of statistics were used by the investigators: those of petitions for the initiation of the conciliation proceedings which under German law must precede the filing of an action for divorce; those of decrees of divorce granted as related to the total figure of divorce proceedings; and those of divorces granted per each 100,000 population. Each set of figures was subdivided by appellate court districts, so as to correlate them to the different regions of pre-Code law. A further correlation was undertaken, relating the figures to the religious composition of the populace by region. All three sets of statistics cover the period from 1881 to 1915, that is, nineteen years before and sixteen years after the new law went into effect. The number of petitions for the initiation of conciliation proceedings was computed for each 100,000 population. Changes in the figures indicate changes in the extent of the desire for divorce. The authors are aware that, for the sake of reliability, the number of petitions should have been figured per 10,000 marriages rather than per 100,000 inhabitants. They believed, however, that the latter correlation might be used just as well because the percentage of married people among the total population not only was remarkably stable during the period of investigation but also showed no great differences between different regions of the Reich. In 1880 the married people in the total population amounted to 34 percent; in 1910, 35.8 percent. In 1880 the regional differences varied between 38.1 percent and 31.2 percent; in 1910 between 40.8 percent and 32.8 percent. The authors also state that, to learn the extent of the desire for divorce, it might be helpful to know the number of approaches made to lawyers by persons considering divorce. No such figures are available, however, and thus the next best index is provided by the figures for petitions for the initiation of conciliation proceedings.

Throughout the country the figures increased during the period under observation. For the country as a whole the figure for 1880 was 34.5 petitions for every 10,000 of the population; in 1913, the last normal year before World War I, it had risen to 61.5. The figures, however, indicate regional differences. In one region the upward trend does not show any increase or decrease at the time of the introduction of the new law; in a second region the upward trend is somewhat increased; and, in a third, the curve shows a downward break in 1900, which is reversed after a very few years. These three regions respectively coincide more or less with the region of the Code Napoléon and the predominantly Protestant parts of the North German region of the common law; the South German regions of the common law, which have both a predominantly Catholic and a predominantly Protestant population; and the region of the Prussian Code.

The authors draw the following conclusions:

The introduction of the Civil Code has not slowed the increase of the number of petitions for conciliation proceedings and has thus not reduced the extent of the desire for divorce. Especially in this respect did the new law have no effect. In some of those regions in which the divorce law was liberalized one can even observe a certain increase in the trend. It is by no means certain, however, whether this increase would not have occurred independently of the change in the law. But nowhere was the upward trend broken. Even in the regions of the Prussian law, where the divorce law was tightened, the trend did not change appreciably.[36]

The authors properly observe that the increase in the years after 1900 was even greater than that shown by the figures of petitions for conciliation proceedings, because in these years the courts showed a steadily increasing willingness to grant permission to file an action for divorce without preceding conciliation proceedings. The authors are certainly justified in concluding that the draftsmen of the new code failed in their expectation of reducing the desire for divorce. They do recognize, however, that the differences from the pre-Code law may have had a certain influence insofar as in the regions of difficult divorce the increase in the trend began somewhat later than in those of easy divorce. This difference tends to be minimized by the fact that in those regions where the increase started earlier the curve also tended to flatten out earlier.

36. At 139.

Does Divorce Breed Breakdown? 297

The second set of figures indicates the numbers of decrees of divorce per 100 proceedings terminated, data regarded as indicative of the attitude of the courts. Has the introduction of the Civil Code rendered the courts more inclined to deny divorces? For the Reich as a whole the change in the law is hardly reflected at all in the figures. During the nineteen years preceding the change the number of divorces granted per 100 proceedings terminated was 72.2; for the fourteen years after the change it was 71.0.[37] The almost stable average, however, results from changes in opposite directions in different parts of the country: in certain districts the figure rose by more than four points; in others it dropped by more than four points; and in a third group little change was observable at all. The first group is composed preponderantly, although not exclusively, of districts of the common law, especially of Catholic law; in the second, one finds, among others, a considerable number of districts of Prussian law and the Code Napoléon; the third group consists primarily of districts of Protestant common law. More pronounced is another correlation: before the change of the law, the percentage among terminated divorce cases of those terminated by a decree of divorce varied between the districts of different appellate courts by a surprisingly large margin. In Munich it was as low as 47.1 percent; in Dresden, as high as 77.9 percent. After 1900 the percentages dropped most in those court districts where they had been extraordinarily high and rose most in those in which they had been extraordinarily low. In the pre-Code period percentages had varied 30.8 points; in the Code period the variance was reduced to 18.5 points.[38] It seems as if there had occurred not only a unification of the substantive law but also a reduction of differences in judicial attitudes.

As the authors point out, however, the figures cannot be regarded as direct evidence of changes of judicial strictness or liberalism. They might be so regarded if the percentage of cases terminated other than by a decree of divorce all referred to judicial denials of divorce. But the figures also cover cases terminated either by dismissal by the plaintiff or by the death of one of the parties. While the number of the latter can safely be regarded as negligible, that of the former has been comparatively high. It was lowest (15.9 percent) in 1881–85 and highest (25 percent) in 1915. Surprisingly, the authors have not attempted to obtain the percentage of decrees denying divorce by subtracting from the total of cases terminated the sum of the cases terminated by

37. At 156.
38. *Ibid.*

decree of divorce and those terminated without decree. These figures are as given here in table 19.

These figures indicate that in the first four years of the new law the courts seem indeed to have been somewhat stricter than before; but, from 1904 on, the percentage of judicial denials of divorce dropped again to the level of the last years preceding the change in the law and continued to drop, although slowly, until the outbreak of World War I in August 1914 resulted in a considerable increase in terminations by dismissal or death.

The percentage of decrees refusing divorce may appear astonishingly high, even at its lowest point of 7.6 in 1908 and 1909. However, this figure does not indicate the percentage of marriages whose dissolution was denied by the courts. The figures refer to actions dismissed, and the dissolution of one and the same marriage may well be, and often is, applied for in two actions, one brought by the husband and

TABLE 19
TERMINATION OF DIVORCE CASES
(Percent)

	By Decree of Divorce	Without Decree	By Decree Denying Divorce
1881–85	71.7	15.9	12.4
1886–90	71.7	17.1	12.2
1891–95	70.9	17.9	11.2
1896	73.3	17.0	9.7
1897	73.3	17.1	9.6
1898	73.5	17.1	9.4
1899	73.2	17.3	9.5
1900	66.8	20.2	11.0
1901	66.7	20.1	13.2
1902	70.5	18.1	11.4
1903	70.8	18.7	11.5
1904	72.3	18.5	9.5
1905	71.8	18.8	9.4
1906	72.6	18.5	9.1
1907	71.0	19.7	9.3
1908	69.6	22.7	7.6
1909	73.8	18.5	7.6
1910	72.0	19.9	8.1
1911	71.2	19.4	8.6
1912	72.1	19.3	9.4
1913	72.5	19.5	8.0
1914	73.2	19.1	7.7
1915	64.7	25.0	10.3

one by the wife. In case of such action and cross-action, German law provides the possibility of divorce being pronounced upon the action of both parties. However, the court also may dismiss one party's action and allow only that of the other. It is certain that the figures on actions dismissed contain cases in which the marriage in question was, notwithstanding, terminated upon the action of the other party. To obtain a more reliable impression of possible changes of judicial attitudes, it would thus be necessary to have figures showing judicial refusal of termination of marriage (i.e., cases in which the court dismissed both action and cross-action) — figures which are not available. The figures must thus be treated with caution insofar as judicial attitudes are concerned. In no circumstances would it be permissible to treat the figures of terminations of cases without decree as coinciding with the number of reconciliations occurring after the commencement of the suit.

The third set of figures, the number of divorces per 100,000 population, refers to what is commonly known as the divorce rate, changes in which are regarded as indicative of the divorce trend of any given country. It was the professed intention of the makers of the new Civil Code to stop the increase which the divorce rate had shown continuously over the past decades. It was even more their intention to stop the upward trend in those parts of the Reich where divorce had so far been comparatively easy. Did they succeed? The trend of the divorce rate gives the answer. To ascertain the trend with greater certainty than is obtainable from the raw figures, and particularly to find out whether in 1900 the trends of the several districts were upward or downward, the authors computed for each year the median height of the curve and the median rate of change, using the method of least squares.

The figures thus computed demonstrate that before 1900 the trend was rising in the districts of most and, since 1900, in those of all appellate courts. In a few court districts the trend shows a slight downward break in 1900. The majority of the latter districts belongs to the region of the Prussian Code, but there are among them also two districts of Protestant common law. In all these districts the break is small, and the trend rose continuously after 1900. While the break in the Prussian law districts may be attributed to the change of the law, it did not last. Nowhere did the change prevent the continued rise. In many districts the curve was even steeper after 1900 than before.

The authors thus conclude:
The shape of the law of divorce was neither the cause of the divorce

wave nor even one of its essential conditions. In the main, the influence of the law did not make itself felt as against that of other circumstances. Some kind of effect is observable only where basic peculiarities of content had been in effect for decades. This means that the basic view by which the authors of the Civil Code had allowed themselves to be guided, was wrong. Neither was it possible upon a broad scope to prevent spouses who were ready to resort to divorce from doing it, nor could the new Code influence their moral or religious attitudes with respect to their marital relation to each other.[39] The rising trend is rather regarded as having been the result of changes in the structure of society, especially of what is called the change of the "old society" into modern mass society.

The unimportance of the factor "divorce law" is also indicated by the figures for the period after 1914. The outbreak of World War I resulted in a drop of the divorce rate of almost one-third. In 1916 and 1917 it began to rise again. In 1919 it reached twice the height of 1913. The total increase within the seven-year period from 1913 to 1919 was indeed twice that of the thirty-five years from 1881 to 1915. A small drop during the 1920s was reversed again in 1928. The rate of divorce per 100,000 population was 59.1 in 1920, 62.2 in 1921, 63.3 in 1930, and 65.0 in 1932.[40] In 1933, the first year of the Nationalist Socialist regime, the rate per 100,000 population was 65.1; in 1934, it was 81.9, i.e., three times that of 1913, when it had been 26.6.

In 1939, the first year after the liberalization of the divorce law by the statute of 1938, the rate reached 89.1. The drop to 70.5 in 1940, which followed the outbreak of World War II, was proportionately smaller than the drop that had accompanied the outbreak of World War I. For the war years no divorce statistics were collected. In 1946, the first postwar year, the rate already surpassed that of 1939; in 1948 it climbed up steeply; and in 1949 it reached the all-time peak of 188 (i.e., twice the figure of 1939 and seven times that of 1913). From 1949 to 1956 the rate steeply dropped to 82 in 1956.[41]

From these figures the authors again draw the conclusion that the effect of the factor "law" was unimportant in comparison with other factors by which the structure of society was influenced. Neither the strictness of the Civil Code of 1896 nor the liberalizing of the National Socialists' divorce law appears to have influenced behavior in any ap-

39. At 175–76.
40. At 465.
41. At 467–68.

preciable way. The vast changes which did occur must be regarded as the results of social circumstances other than the law.

This result is remarkable even though the analysis is concerned with the legal event divorce rather than with the ultimately relevant event of marriage breakdown. Theoretically, it is possible that the rise of the divorce rate reflects an increase not in breakdown but only in the frequency of its being made official by a decree of divorce. Perhaps the rate of breakdown was already 188 in 1881 and has remained static ever since, so that in 1881 only 8.7 divorces were sought for every 188 separations, in 1948 divorces were obtained in all cases of separation, and in 1956 in only 82, so that in every 102 separations no divorces were obtained. Such a situation, while theoretically possible, is improbable. Upon the basis of other observations it can be assumed, to be sure, that the number of separations made official by divorce has increased, especially in consequence of the change of workers' attitudes from proletarian to bourgeois respectability. That proportion of the German population in which it is socially feasible, after the breakup of a marriage, to establish a new "free" union without divorce seems to have decreased among the lower classes. It may well have increased, however, at higher levels. However that may be, it is improbable that the changes in the divorce rate are due exclusively, or even preponderantly, to shifts from nonofficialization toward increasingly official recognition of actual breakdowns of marriages. Even though divorce statistics do not directly reflect changes in actual breakdowns, the German statistics seem to allow the conclusion that changes in the number of breakdowns are to some extent reflected in the changes of the divorce rate. It is highly probable that, if the change in the law made in 1900 has failed to stop the increase of divorce, it has certainly failed to reverse the trend in the breakdown of marriages.

The authors, nevertheless, believe that in one special respect the law has not been ineffective. Before and after the changes of 1900 and 1938, German law provided that, as a general rule, no action for divorce may be commenced until a conciliation of the parties has been attempted by a judge. In addition to their analysis of the statistics of divorce in general, the authors have also analyzed the statistics of conciliation proceedings. By ascertaining the number of actions commenced per 100 conciliation proceedings, they believe that they are able to learn the percentage of cases in which conciliation proceedings were successful in effecting reconciliations. The authors are, of course, aware that the figures do not allow any direct conclusions. On the one hand, parties may fail to follow up the conciliation proceedings with an action for divorce though remaining unreconciled and thus continuing to live apart. On the other hand, the courts may allow the commencement of an action for divorce without prior conciliation proceeding, where such a proceeding appears to be hopeless, and the courts have shown a steadily increasing readiness to make use of this power of dispensation.

Even if these and other sources of possible error are considered, the figures throw some light upon the effectiveness of conciliation proceedings when carried on in a serious manner. In the period before World War I the percentage of cases in which conciliation proceedings were not followed by action for divorce was remarkably high. During the period from 1881 to 1899 it was 41.3 percent for the country as a whole; in the districts of five courts it was above 50 percent; in one-third of the districts it was above 40 percent; and in one-half of the districts it was above 30 percent. However, in other districts the figures were much lower: in one, conciliations not followed by an action for divorce were as low as 3.1 percent.[42] These wide differences seem to indicate that the manner in which the conciliation proceedings were conducted varied greatly within the Reich and that they were generally conducted in a more serious manner in the eastern districts, with their traditionally paternalistic government, than in the western districts, where the tradition is liberal-democratic.

The period from 1900 to 1913 showed a slight drop in the rate of success of conciliation proceedings. For the Reich as a whole it was 34.6 percent; in the district with the highest rate, Königsberg, it changed imperceptibly, from 60.9 percent to 59.1 percent, but in the district which now had the lowest rate, Munich, it was −1.2 percent. The negative figure indicates that the courts granted dispensations from the requirement of reconciliation proceedings in more cases than those in which such proceedings had taken place and had not been followed by an action for divorce.[43]

After World War I the proportion of actions to conciliation proceedings increased rapidly. The figures, available for Prussia only, are as follows: 1917, 100.3 percent; 1919, 87.5 percent; and after 1920, continuously above 100 percent.[44] Owing to a number of circumstances conciliation proceedings had ceased to be taken so seriously as they had been before the war.

42. At 147.
43. At 148.
44. At 152. The number of actions could exceed that of conciliation proceedings because the courts could allow an action to be commenced without previous conciliation proceedings when it appeared that such proceedings would be futile.

Two conclusions may be derived from these figures: (1) conciliation activities can be helpful if conducted seriously, and (2) the mere legislative command that an action for divorce must be preceded by conciliation proceedings does not guarantee their being carried on seriously and competently.

At the time of the inquiry, reform of the divorce law was vividly discussed in Germany. While it was widely demanded that a marriage might be more easily dissolved upon the objective ground of breakdown, Roman Catholic writers were demanding, if not complete abolition of divorce, at least its limitation to cases of guilty misconduct, that is, in other words, that the principle of breakdown in the Marriage Law of 1938 be abolished and the guilt principle of the Civil Code of 1896 be restored. In their book the authors have analyzed these proposals, in the light of the statistical data. Their conclusion is that a return to the principle of guilt could not be expected to reduce the divorce rate in any appreciable way, to say nothing of promoting the stability of marriage. The influence of social factors other than law they found to be so much stronger that a statutory return to the principle of guilt would be of hardly appreciable influence.

The attempt undertaken by the makers of the Civil Code to stem the divorce tide by strictly adhering to the guilt principle not only ended in failure but actually helped to promote time-conditioned dangerous tendencies in the society in general and in the administration of justice in particular. The limitation of the catalog of statutory grounds for divorce could as little protect marriage as it was possible to stop inflation by the pronouncement of statutory maximum prices.

In the decisive points, namely, that of the attitude of spouses toward their marriage and toward each other, the statutory compulsion failed to have effect. By far the largest number of persons desiring divorce were influenced neither in their marital conduct nor in their resolution to obtain the desired divorce. In large groups of the population, especially among parties to marriages disrupted without fault, the statutory limitation of the grounds for divorce was felt to be unjust. The authority of the law was thus weakened, and the parties and their attorneys were made to feel they were in a situation of morally justified self-defense. The rise and growth of collusive practices and the courts' acquiescence therein appear to have been essentially caused by this factual situation.

The validity of the conclusions has been contested by statisticians who applied to the German data the Box-Tiao method developed for the interpretation of time-series-quasi-experiments.[45] In an as yet unpublished paper,[46] the authors regard it as "unfortunate" that I used the word "insignificant" in my review and was as unjustified to regard the German investigation as a confirmation of Willcox's conclusion that "the immediate influence of legislation is subsidiary, unimportant, almost imperceptible."

In the parlance of statisticians, the word "significant" has a technical meaning. If one investigates the probability that differences between some groups are due to chance and finds that such probability is very low, then the characteristic according to which a universe was divided into subgroups is assumed to be significantly associated with that universe. But if one finds a higher probability that differences are due to characteristics other than the one by which the universe is divided into subgroups, one holds the latter difference to be statistically insignificant. For the determination of the degree of probability that differences between two subgroups are due to characteristics other than the one by which the universe is divided into subgroups, various methods can be used. In using the Box-Tiao test, Glass, Tiao and Maguire found that "the effect of the introduction of the new Civil Code in 1900 is reflected in both the divorce rate and the petition for reconciliation rate."

The critics mean that the data do not allow an unequivocal answer to the question of what the post-1900 trend of the divorce and petition for reconciliation rates would have been if the divorce laws had remained unchanged. That unanswerable question was not asked by the German team. What they wished to know was whether or not the Civil Code had reached the result desired by its draftsmen who, emphasizing indissolubility as an essential characteristic of marriage and calling divorce an anomaly, had intended through rendering divorce difficult to discourage the conclusion of ill-considered marriages and to induce spouses to conduct their married lives in a manner corresponding to the nature of marriage.[47]

45. G. E. P. Box and G. C. Tiao, *A Change in Level of a Non-Stationary Time Series*, 52 BIOMETRIKA 181 (1965). The Box-Tiao method of statistical analysis was developed on the basis of the studies by Donald T. Campbell: D. T. Campbell, *From Description to Experimentations: Interpreting Trends as Quasi-Experiments*, chap. 12 in C. W. HARRIS, ed., PROBLEMS IN MEASURING CHANGE (1963); D. T. Campbell & J. C. STANLEY, *Experimental and Quasi-Experimental Design for Research on Teaching*, chap. 5 in N. L. GAGE, ed., HANDBOOK OF RESEARCH ON TEACHING (1963).

46. G. V. Glass, G. C. Tiao & T. O. Maguire, Analysis of Data on the 1900 Revision of German Divorce Laws as a Time-Series-Quasi-Experiment.

47. 4 MOTIVE ZU DEM ENTWURF EINES BÜRGERLICHEN GESETZBUCHES FÜR DAS DEUTSCHE REICH 563 ff. (1888).

The investigations of the past as well as the German research of the University of Chicago Comparative Law Research Center were based on statistical data concerning decrees of divorce and of judicial separation. These matters can be counted with some accuracy, but their incidence is not indicative of a society's state of marriage stability unless one also considers the incidence of factual marriage breakdown, a matter not easily ascertainable or countable. If conclusions are to be drawn as to the relationship between divorce law and marriage stability, it is necessary to obtain data about factual marriage breakdown not expressed in judicial decrees of divorce or separation. Attempts to obtain such data were made at the University of Chicago Comparative Law Research Center in the inquiries about the Italian-Swiss border region and about the United States.

The Comasco-Ticino research is described in the present author's article entitled "Marriage Breakdown in Ticino and Comasco, and published in *Festschrift für Hans G. Ficker* 385–409 (1967). The plan was to compare for the decade of 1947 to 1956 the cases of marriage breakdown that had occurred in the easy-divorce Swiss canton of Ticino and the divorceless Italian provinces of Como and Varese (Comasco), i.e., a region of comparatively homogenous ethnicity, religion, and socioeconomic structure (see table 20).

The Swiss count of judicial decrees and of the relatively small number of nonformalized separations, made by a team of young Swiss law-

TABLE 20
MARRIAGE BREAKDOWN IN TICINO AND COMASCO, 1947–56

Ticino	
Divorces	730
Judicial separations	200
Annulments	19
Informal separations	161
Total marriage breakdown	1,110
Rate of marriage breakdown per 1,000 population	0.6285

Comasco	
Judicial separations	142
Judicially certified separations	90
Secular annulments	21
Ecclesiastical annulments	11
Foreign divorces judicially declared effective	16
Informal separations	431
Total marriage breakdown	711
Rate of marriage breakdown per 1,000 population	0.14

The Problem Restated

yers, seems to have been fairly accurate. The count of nonformalized Italian separations was made for each parish by its priest, a great many of whom seem to have misunderstood the meaning of the term "factual separation" and to have engaged in estimates based upon the limited circle of their acquaintances. Besides, the Comasco classification is particularly difficult because it is a region of considerable male migration. Traditionally a sizable number of Comaschi have been engaged in the building trades, as simple masons or as highly skilled decorators or sculptors. They exercise their trade all over Italy and many migrate to other countries. The women stay at home and wait for their husbands' return, which may never occur. When is such a "white widow" deserted? When is the marriage to be regarded as broken down? A control count carried on in a part of the Province of Como yielded separation figures three times higher than those reported for the same part by the priests. The Italian figures are thus open to doubt. Certainly the rate of Ticino is less than 4.5 times that of Comasco.

The number of cases of purely factual breakdown seems to be higher than 431 and that of all cases of breakdown higher than 711. But even if these figures were correct, they would be considerable for a society in which the institution of divorce does not exist.

The third of the Chicago inquiries was concerned with the United States, where divorce is regulated by state law and the statutes of the fifty states differ widely from one another. Some statutes are strict, others permissive. Differences are also certain to exist in the incidence of marriage breakdown. What relationship is there between the degree of legal strictness or permissiveness on the one side and the incidence of marriage breakdown on the other?

The inquiry was made by Alexander Broel-Plateris, at the time a candidate for the degree of Doctor of Philosophy in the Sociology Department of the University of Chicago and now a member of the staff of the National Center for Health Statistics in the U.S. Department of Health, Education, and Welfare. Using the statistical method of analysis of variance the investigator sought to find out the relationships not merely between strictness of the law and incidence of marriage breakdown but also between these phenomena and other variables of presumed social significance.

The complex course of the investigation is described in the Appendix below. The results can be summarized as follows:

1. Great permissiveness of the law, while it may be associated with comparatively high incidence of marriage breakdown and of divorce, is also associated with a lower incidence of separation without divorce.

2. Differences in the incidence of marriage breakdown between residence areas of the same state are even greater than those between different states. The incidence of marriage breakdown, as well as the inclination to transform a separation into a divorce, is considerably greater in urban, especially metropolitan, than in rural areas.

3. Variations in the incidence of marriage breakdown and the permissiveness of divorce laws are positively correlated with variations in a number of nonlegal variables indicating degree of industrialization, economic position of women, religion, and what may be called the degree of comparative settledness or restlessness of an area.

IV

THE LIBERAL BREAKTHROUGH

13
A Change of Climate

That Western society is undergoing profound change is generally recognized today, with or without approval, with or without misgivings. A conspicuous feature of this change in cultural climate is the greater permissiveness of society toward once proscribed lines of individual conduct. In reaction to the pressure toward conformity of conduct and thought exercised by totalitarian regimes, the apprehension of social collapse through pluralism has been waning in the democratic nations. Freedom from restraints is postulated for every kind of conduct that is not scientifically proved to be socially harmful. Along with freedom from restraint for open expression of social dissent, homosexuality, pornography, abortion, etc., freedom of remarriage is sought ever more insistently and more successfully. So the change in social climate is finding expression in a new rise in the rates of divorce, indicating a rise in marriage breakdown, as well as in a set of laws and legislative drafts of liberal or even radical character.

The parallelism demonstrates again that both the divorce laws and the incidence of marriage breakdown are dependent upon cultural climate. Again it is also demonstrated that incidence of marriage breakdown increases in times of accelerating social change with the unsettling tendencies toward anomie.

Divorce rates, after reaching a peak in the wake of World War II, leveled off in the 1950s. Table 21 shows the course of the divorce rates in seventeen countries. In the industrial countries of the Western world the course is roughly parallel. The rates were at a peak shortly after World War II. Around 1951 they uniformly fell and leveled off. Around 1963, they began to rise again. The new rise of the divorce rates coincides with the emergence of other elements of the new social climate, such as the New Left, youth culture, social protest, women's liberation, the new attitudes toward sex, hippiedom, drug use, and crime in the streets.

In earlier chapters we have indicated that the sway of the compro-

TABLE 21
RATE OF DIVORCES PER 1,000 POPULATION

	1950	1955	1960	1962	1963	1964	1965	1966
Austria	1.52	1.16	1.13	1.12	*1.14*	1.16	1.16	1.19
Belgium	0.59	0.50		*0.51*	0.56	0.58	0.59	
Canada	0.39	0.39	0.39	0.36	*0.41*	0.45	0.46	0.46
Denmark	1.61	1.53	1.46	1.38	1.38	1.37	1.37	1.36
Finland	0.91	0.85	0.82	0.89	*0.93*	0.97	0.99	1.05
France	0.85	0.67	0.66	0.65	0.63	*0.69*	0.71	0.71
Germany-East	2.7		1.40	1.36	1.33	*1.51*	1.56	1.72
Germany-West	1.69	0.92	0.88	0.82	*0.92*	0.99	0.93	0.98
Japan	1.01		0.97	0.74	0.75	0.73	*0.79*	0.80
Netherlands	0.64	0.51	0.49	0.48	*0.49*	0.51	0.50	0.50
Norway	0.71	0.59	*0.66*	0.67	0.67	0.69	0.69	
Poland	0.44	0.49	0.50	0.59	0.64	0.67	0.75	
Sweden	1.14	1.21	1.20	1.17	1.12	*1.20*	1.24	1.32
Switzerland	0.90	0.89	0.87	0.83	0.82	0.83	0.83	
United Kingdom (England and Wales)	0.69	0.59	0.51	0.61	*0.67*	0.72		0.73
USSR		...	1.3	1.3	*1.5*	1.6	1.6	
United States	2.6	2.30	2.18	2.22	2.27	2.35	2.4	2.4

Sources: UNITED NATIONS, DEMOGRAPHIC YEARBOOK 1967, table 26; STATISTISCHES HANDBUCH FÜR DIE REPUBLIK ÖSTERREICH 1968, table 3.01; CANADA YEAR BOOK 1968, table 30; STATISTICAL YEARBOOK OF FINLAND 1968, table 39; STATISTISCHES JAHRBUCH DER DEUTSCHEN DEMOKRATISCHEN REPUBLIK 1969, table 9; STATISTISCHES JAHRBUCH FÜR DIE BUNDESREPUBLIK DEUTSCHLAND 1969, tables 11, 14, and International 4; JAPAN STATISTICAL YEARBOOK 1968, table 15; JAARCIJFERS VOOR NEDERLAND, 1965–66, table 42; STATISTICAL ABSTRACT OF SWEDEN, 1969, table 40; UNITED KINGDOM, ANNUAL ABSTRACT OF STATISTICS, table 82.

Note: Italic numbers indicate years in which the rates began to rise.

mise of having a strict divorce law on the books and an easy one in action may be near its end. Liberalism seems to be about to achieve a breakthrough or has perhaps achieved it already. Conservatism seems to have lost much of its former influence. At least for the time being, individualist liberalism has become so influential that divorce laws have begun to be adapted to its tenets ever more closely.[1]

In the course of this evolution recognition is given to the fact that divorce or continuation of the marital community of life are not the only alternatives available to people dissatisfied with their marital situation. Increasing attention is now given to the intermediate alternatives of factual breakup and forming irregular unions. The realization that these solutions are widely used where divorce is impossible or hard to obtain and the belief that proliferation of such situations may be unwholesome for society constitute one of the considerations which are resulting in the liberalization of the official laws of divorce.

For the liberalization of the divorce law several techniques are available. One technique could be the open admission of consent divorce without such cumbersome and time-consuming formalities as are required in Belgium, where the divorce chapter of the Napoleonic Code is still in effect in essentially the original version.[2] That method is available in Japan, in Mexican states, and, for childless couples, in the Soviet Union. It is planned in Sweden, but it has not yet been adopted in any West European or Anglo-American jurisdiction. In those areas liberalization is achieved either through adding to the traditional offense grounds the so-called separation ground, or through the replacement of the offense grounds by the breakdown ground, or through some combination of these methods.

Permitting divorce without proof of a marital offense simply because the parties have lived separate from each other for a certain period of time does not constitute an appreciable liberalization of the divorce law unless the period is short. But adding to the offense grounds the separation ground with long, or very long, periods has constituted an opening wedge. It was the means for the moderate liberalization of the German law through the statute of 1938,[3] the earlier, but more radical Scandinavian laws of the first decade of the twentieth century[4]

---

1. On types of modern divorce laws and the underlying ideologies, see O. BRUSIIN, ZUM EHESCHEIDUNGSPROBLEM (Helsinki, 1959); W. G. FRIEDMANN, LAW IN A CHANGING SOCIETY 205 (1959).
2. Arts. 233, 275 ff.
3. *Supra* p. 301.
4. *Supra* pp. 139 ff.

and the liberalization of the divorce laws of a considerable number of jurisdictions in the United States.[5]

As so often in the United States, a precursor appeared at a surprisingly early date. In 1850, the separation ground was admitted in the divorce law of Kentucky.[6] The time for which the parties were required to "have separated and lived apart, without any communication whatever" was five years. It took sixteen years for Wisconsin to follow, also requiring five years of "voluntary living separate."[7] Then it took twenty-seven years for Rhode Island, where, in tune with the divorce conservatism dominant at the time, the period of separation was fixed at no less than ten years.[8] The real movement for the enactment of "living separate lives" had to wait until the wave of conservatism had abated. In 1955, such laws were in effect in eighteen states. By 1968, the number had increased to twenty-two. In Rhode Island ten years are still required. But generally the periods for living separate have been reduced. The shortest, those of the District of Columbia, Nevada, and North Carolina, are now one year, the longest, five years, are those of Arizona, Idaho, Kentucky, and Wisconsin.

The living-apart laws differ in details. Does factual separation suffice to start the period, or is it necessary, as in Scandinavia, to obtain a judicial decree of separation or, as required under the New York law of 1966, either a decree or a private separation agreement filed with a public agency? Where, as in Arizona, Idaho, Kentucky, Louisiana, Nevada, North Carolina, Rhode Island, and Washington, it is sufficient that the parties simply have lived separate for the required period, the door is open to collusion. The requirement of the Virginia statute, that the parties must have resided in the state at the time of the separation presents unnecessary hardship if it is enforced, but does not necessarily exclude perjured evidence in uncontested cases.

What is meant by living separate? Must it have its origin in a voluntary act of the parties, or of at least one of them? What about a separation due to one party's imprisonment or hospitalization or military service? Or what about the marriage of the oil engineer who has gone

---

5. On the separation ground in American law, see W. E. McCurdy, *Divorce — a Suggested Approach with Particular Reference to Dissolution for Living Separate and Apart*, 9 VAND. L. REV. 685 (1956); W. Wadlington, *Divorce without Fault, without Perjury*, 52 VA. L. REV. 32 (1966); H. H. FOSTER, JR., & D. J. FREED, LIVING APART AS A GROUND FOR DIVORCE (Monograph No. 4, Am. Bar Assoc. Section of Family Law, 1966); H. H. CLARK, JR., THE LAW OF DOMESTIC RELATIONS IN THE UNITED STATES 351 (1968).

6. Laws of 1850, C. 498, at 55.

7. Laws of 1866, ch. 37, at 40.

8. 1893 Pub. Laws, ch. 1187, at 313.

to Arabia? Does it make a difference whether he has parted from his wife amicably or in a huff? Or whether he has determined never to return to his wife, initially or at some time while she was a grass widow? Some of the American living-apart statutes have sought in various ways to overcome such difficulties of interpretation, others are silent and have left the answer to the courts.

The second method of changing repudiation of a marriage partner because of marital offense into simple restoration to the freedom of remarriage has been the admission of divorce upon the objective ground of breakdown. This method cannot be clearly distinguished from the separation ground because in many statutes separation for a certain period of time is stated to constitute evidence of marriage breakdown, refutable as in the German law of 1938, or irrefutable as in the Swedish law of 1905.

Marriage breakdown for one special reason, namely, that of incurable insanity of a marriage partner, has frequently been admitted as a ground for divorce long before breakdown in general was so recognized. So insanity appeared in the German Civil Code of 1896, the English Act of 1937, as well as in the laws of a good many American states.[9] Although the incurable insanity of one spouse can impose severe hardship upon his marriage partner, the idea that a spouse might repudiate a mate that needs special care and support appears to contradict the traditional marriage vow "to cherish, in sickness and in health, for better or for worse." It is remarkable that in 1970 statutes allowing the dissolution of a marriage because of one spouse's insanity were in effect in no less than thirty-four American jurisdictions. The release from the bond of marriage is surrounded with safeguards. The insanity of the "defendant" must be ascertained with certainty; the insanity must be so serious that it requires institutionalization. It must have lasted for a certain minimum period of time, which may be as short as eighteen months in Alaska, or as long as five years in sixteen states. Frequently it is also said that the insanity must be "incurable" which, of course, means incurable under the state of the medical art as of the time of the proceedings.

The general idea that the door to remarriage ought as a rule to be opened whenever a marriage has turned out to be dead, irrespective of any misconduct of a spouse, found expression in the Prussian Code of 1791–94, as well as in the early statutes of a few American states. In the course of the nineteenth century such laws allowing divorce on

---

9. W. E. McCurdy, *Insanity as a Ground for Annulment or Divorce in English and American Laws*, 29 VA. L. REV. 771 (1943); CLARK, *supra* note 5, at 356.

the ground of "insuperable aversion" or of "incompatibility of temperament" or "of character" became targets of conservative attack. In the 1960s, no such laws existed any longer outside of Mexico and three American jurisdictions: Alaska, New Mexico, and the Virgin Islands. But these have now been joined by Kansas, Nevada, and Oklahoma, and in 1969 the ground of breakdown pure and simple found open recognition in the California statute allowing the dissolution of a marriage whenever an "irretrievable breakdown" has been caused by "irreconcilable differences" existing between the spouses, and this provision became the model for the Uniform Act put forward by the National Conference of Commissioners on Uniform State Laws in 1970. If this radical proposal is followed, the liberal breakthrough will be complete. But it has not yet been adopted so far. The new laws enacted or proposed in the 1960s are still compromises, different, to be sure, from the compromise that resulted in the long-lasting contrast between divorce laws of the books and divorce laws in action. The new compromises are no longer worked out between legislatures and courts but within the legislatures. Conservative forces have not yielded to the new move without resistance. Provisions meant to stem the tide of divorce are still being worked into the new laws. To what extent, if any, they will achieve the intended effect, is doubtful. The conservative ingredient is strongest in the new statutes of England and New York, weak in those of California, Iowa, and Texas [10] and in the proposals brought forward in West Germany, the Netherlands,[11] Sweden,[12] and in the American draft of the Commissioners on Uniform State Laws.

10. California Statutes 1969, ch. 1608, adding Part 5 to Division 4 of the Civil Code; Iowa Acts 1970 (63 G.A.), ch. 1266, amending Iowa Code, ch. 598; Texas H.B. No. 53 of 1969, ch. 888, revising Family Code, Title 1.

11. Herziening van het echtscheidingsrecht, Koninklijke Boodschap aan de Tweede Kamer der Staten-Generaal, Zitting 1968–1969, 10213, nos. 1–5.

12. *Supra* p. 156.

14

The Liberal Breakthrough, I: England and New York

ENGLAND

In England the worldwide trend toward secularizing the regulation of marriage began later than in continental western Europe. Before the Reformation the regulation of marriage in England was, as on the Continent, a concern of the church. During the Reformation the Church of England was united with the state in somewhat the same way as was the Orthodox Church with the Russian state. Regulation of marriage remained with the ecclesiastical side of the establishment. Matrimonial causes of nullity and separation were heard in the ecclesiastical courts.[1] The Church of England maintained its monopoly over assisting in the creation of marriage relationships,[2] until 1836, when civil marriage before a registrar was at last permitted. Matrimonial causes of separation and nullity continued to be heard in the ecclesiastical courts and, after some initial hesitation, the doctrine of indissolubility of marriage was continued. As the grounds for nullity, which had so generously been available before, were limited, the rigor of the law came to be even more pronounced. To be sure, the highest authority for both state and church, the king in Parliament, pronounced divorces in individual cases. But their number was small, the proceedings took years, and the cost was prohibitive to all but the wealthiest.[3]

The indissolubility of the legal tie of marriage was not equivalent to factual indissolubility of married life. Especially in the days of

---

1. *Supra* p. 24.
2. No ceremonial assistance to the conclusion of a marriage had been necessary at all until 1754. Until that year in accordance with the ancient law of the Church of Rome as it had been continued by the Church of England, a marriage could be concluded without any ceremony by the mere informal agreement of the parties to take each other as husband and wife.
3. *Supra* p. 24.

George III and the Regency, sex morals were lax, irregular unions were frequent, disappearance was a ready substitute for divorce, prostitution and the mistress system flourished.[4] It was perhaps this availability of substitutes which stood in the way of the rising demand for judicial divorce. At last, in 1857, the Divorce Act[5] was passed, over the passionate opposition of those who predicted the most catastrophic consequences, even though the innovation was modest enough. In effect the change simply amounted to a reinterpretation of the Gospel, which was now read as permitting divorce in the case of adultery. From 1 January 1858 on, a man was to be judicially authorized to rid himself of a wife who had committed one single act of adultery. In doubtful accord with scripture but under the influence of the incipient movement for the protection of women, a woman was also to be entitled to divorce, but only if the husband's adultery was accompanied by some outrage such as severe physical cruelty, desertion, or rape.[6] Simultaneously with the admission of judicial divorce, jurisdiction in matrimonial causes was transferred from the ecclesiastical tribunals to a new secular court, the Court for Divorce and Matrimonial Causes, that was merged with the new Supreme Court of Judicature in the course of the sweeping judicial reforms of the 1870s.[7] Divorces were no longer so prohibitively expensive as they had been under the system of parliamentary divorce. But they were still inaccessible to people of modest means, not to speak of the poor. Besides, divorce brought social stigma even more severe, perhaps, than did infidelity. As recently as 1936, an English king was compelled to abdicate because he insisted on marrying a divorcee. So the number of divorces remained small in the early decades of the new law. After an initial backlog of 244 petitions filed in 1858 had been disposed of,[8] the number of divorces dropped to 187 in 1861. Between 1876 and 1880 the number slowly increased to an

4. G. O. W. Mueller, *Inquiry into the State of a Divorceless Society: Domestic Relations Law and Morals in England from 1660 to 1857*, 18 U. PITT. L. REV. 545 (1957).

5. Matrimonial Causes Act, 1857, 20 & 21 Vict. c. 85. On the Act of 1857, its background and the divorce law of the century following its enactment, see R. H. Graveson in GRAVESON & F. R. CRANE, eds., A CENTURY OF FAMILY LAW (1957).

6. A wife might obtain a divorce if "the husband had been guilty of incestuous adultery, or of bigamy with adultery, or of rape, or of sodomy or bestiality, or of adultery coupled with such cruelty as without adultery would have entitled her to a divorce *a mensa et thoro*, or of adultery coupled with desertion, without reasonable excuse, for two years or upwards" (§ 27).

7. By the Judicature Act 1873, all jurisdiction formerly exercised by the Court for Divorce and Matrimonial Causes was assigned to the High Court of Justice, where it was exercised in the Probate, Divorce and Admiralty Division.

8. Morton Commission Report 355 (Cmd. 9678, 1956).

annual average of 277; between 1881 and 1886 the annual average was 335; between 1895 and 1900 it rose to an annual average of about 500.[9] Of course, there had also been an increase in the population of England and Wales from 20,066,000 in 1861 to 32,528,000 in 1901.[10]

Divorce law, nevertheless, remained a topic of interest, indeed so much so that in 1909 a royal commission was appointed, with Lord Gorrell as chairman, to investigate and report upon the subject. The report was published in 1912.[11] The recommendations of the majority were remarkably liberal. Like a man, a woman should be entitled to a decree of divorce upon the partner's single act of adultery. In addition, the following new grounds for divorce should be added: (1) willful desertion for three years and upward; (2) cruelty; (3) incurable insanity, after five years' confinement; (4) habitual drunkenness found incurable after three years from the first order of separation; and (5) imprisonment under commuted death sentence. The minority, among them Cosmo Gordon Lang, the then Archbishop of York, regarded such broadening of the grounds of divorce as too dangerous for the stability of marriage, the home, and society.

The outbreak of World War I diverted attention to problems more urgent and less divisive than reform of the divorce law. The only change that was made in the aftermath of the war was part of the movement for female emancipation and equality of the sexes. Under the Matrimonial Causes Act, 1923, a woman was to be entitled to a decree of divorce upon her husband's single act of adultery and without the necessity of aggravating circumstances. However, as in other belligerent countries, the English divorce rate turned sharply upward with World War I. In 1915 the rate of divorces per 1,000 population had been 0.02, and in 1920 it was 0.08. The rise that followed World War II was even more spectacular. In 1938 the rate was 0.15, in 1947 it was 1.36.[12]

Two years before the outbreak of World War II, the first major reform occurred in the divorce law of England. The Matrimonial Causes Act, 1937, generally konwn as Herbert's Act, was sponsored by A. P. (later Sir Alan) Herbert, the well-known contributor to *Punch*. In his book *Holy Deadlock* (1934) he had held up to ridicule the law and the collusive practices which it invited. When he had himself elected to Parliament from Oxford University, he introduced the private member's bill

---

9. GRAVESON & CRANE, *supra* note 5, at 12.
10. WHITAKER'S ALMANAC 1969, at 607.
11. Report of the Royal Commission on Divorce and Matrimonial Causes, Cd. 6478.
12. Morton Commission Report 368.

which, enacted into law, added to adultery the following new grounds for divorce: (1) willful desertion for three years and upward; (2) cruelty; (3) incurable insanity, after five years' confinement. Also introduced were the following new grounds of nullity: (1) insanity or incipient insanity at the time of marriage; (2) concealment of epilepsy; (3) recurrent insanity or communicable venereal disease, and (4) pregnancy by another man at the time of marriage.[13]

The unsettling consequences of World War II were compounded by the social revolution which followed it. Not only was there a profound change in the cultural climate but, as an incident thereof, the divorce court was opened to the masses, to whom free legal aid was made available in 1950.[14]

As in other industrialized countries the divorce rate in England rose continuously, less, it is true, than in the United States or Germany, but sufficient to cause alarm every now and then. Between 1857 and 1888 the number of petitions for divorce filed annually was more than doubled from 244 to 529 in 1887. In 1900 the number was 609; in 1910, 755; in 1919, 5,085; in 1920, 4,481; in 1930, 4,159; and in 1940, 6,915. The number of decrees nisi rose from 494 in 1900 to 2,610 in 1919, 2,985 in 1920; and 7,691 in 1938 (first year after Herbert's Act).[15]

"The effect of the First World War had been to cause 15 *hundred* more petitions to be filed each year and of the Second World War to cause 20 *thousand* more petitions to be filed each year."[16] (See table 22.)

It is known that in England irregular unions are numerous, that marriages dissolved factually but not legally are even more numerous, and that the overwhelming majority of applications for divorce are uncontested.[17] Before Herbert's Act was passed, hotel evidence was known to be used widely. England had become a land of compromise, of discrepancy between the law of the books and the law in action.

The prevalence of uncontested and collusive divorces is all the more remarkable in that England, following the ecclesiastical model, provided built-in safeguards in its law. Under the law of 1857 no divorce could be granted unless the defendant was proved to have committed the offense of adultery. But even if adultery had been committed, divorce was barred if the act had been condoned; and if the plaintiff

---

13. Various minor changes were made by subsequent acts. A consolidated text was enacted as the Matrimonial Causes Act 1950.
14. Legal Aid and Advice Act 1949. It went into effect on 2 October 1950.
15. Morton Commission Report, App. II, 354–55.
16. The Registrar General's Statistical Review for England and Wales for the Five Years 1946–50, Text, Civil, 57, as cited in Morton Report 8.
17. Law Commission Report 8, 18, Cmnd. 3123, 1966 (repr. 1967).

The Liberal Breakthrough, I   321

was also guilty of adultery, the granting or refusal of the divorce rested, as it still does, in the discretion of the judge. In order to make sure that the statutory scheme was followed strictly and that no divorces were granted that would not be clearly permissible, the English legislature followed the model of canon law procedure. A public officer, called the King's (Queen's) Proctor, was to act as defender of the bond.[18] In order to give him a chance to investigate and also to slow up the proceedings, the system of the interlocutory decree was established in 1860.[19] If the court held that a divorce was justified, it would issue a decree nisi. But the marriage would not be terminated until the issuance of the decree absolute, which could not be applied for until three months, or after 1866,[20] six months, had elapsed.

TABLE 22
DIVORCE IN ENGLAND FOLLOWING WORLD WAR II

Year	Number (Decrees Absolute)	Rate per 1,000 Population
1946	29,100	0.68
1947	58,444	1.36
1948	42,711	0.98
1949	34,217	0.78
1950	30,331	0.69
1951	28,265	0.65
1952	33,274	0.76
1953	29,736	0.67

Source: Morton Commission Report 268.

The attempt to keep the granting of divorces strictly within the narrow limits of the law may perhaps have worked in the early years. But the number of cases has grown so that effective control by the King's Proctor is not possible. The great bulk of cases go undefended. Hotel evidence has been resorted to as much as it has in New York. The high incidence of divorce resulted in criticism of the expansion of the grounds for divorce that had been introduced by the Act of 1937. But continuation of the system of the marital offense also provoked criticism, and change to the system of marital breakdown was advocated.

In 1951, a new royal commission was appointed to investigate the

---

18. See *supra* p. 60.
19. Matrimonial Causes Act 1860, 23 & 24 Vict. c. 144, §§ 5–7.
20. Matrimonial Causes Act 1866, 29 Vict. c. 32, § 3.

problem of divorce and to consider what changes, if any, should be made in the law. This commission, presided over by Lord Morton of Henryton and thus usually referred to as the Morton Commission, held 102 meetings and received evidence from 67 organizations and 48 individual witnesses. The report (Cmd. 9678), published in 1956, is a formidable document of 405 pages. The task of the commission was comprehensive. It was

> to inquire into the law of England and the law of Scotland concerning divorce and the matrimonial causes and into the powers of courts of inferior jurisdiction in matters affecting relations between husband and wife, and to consider whether any changes should be made in the law or its administration, including the law relating to the property rights of husband and wife, both during marriage and after its termination (except by death) bearing in mind the need to promote and maintain a healthy and happy married life and to safeguard the interests and the well-being of children; and to consider whether any alteration should be made in the law prohibing marriage with certain relatives by kindred or affinity.

On matters contained in this large assignment the commission made 149 recommendations for England and 81 for Scotland. But on the issue of the grounds on which a divorce should be granted, the nineteen members of the commission could not give a unanimous answer. All but one, it is true, agreed that the principle of marital offense should remain the basis of the law. Indeed, they recommended that a new offense should be added to the list — acceptance by a wife of artificial insemination without the husband's consent. They furthermore recommended that divorce should remain available where a spouse is a mental defective provided he has been confined in an institution for at least five years on account of his or her dangerous or violent propensities and where recovery from such propensities is highly improbable. Another recommendation was that willful refusal by a spouse to consummate the marriage be transformed from a ground of nullity into a ground of divorce. Beyond this, the commission was split. Nine members stated that

> the principle that a marriage should be dissolved if it has irretrievably broken down (as exemplified by divorce by consent, divorce at the option of either spouse after a period of separation, or divorce on a comprehensive ground of breakdown of marriage) should not be introduced into the law.

But nine other members declared that

> there should be provision for divorce in cases where, quite apart from the commission of a marital offence, the marriage has broken down completely; accordingly, where husband and wife have lived separate and apart for a period of at least seven years immediately preceding the application, it should

be possible for either spouse to obtain a decree dissolving the marriage, provided that the other spouse does not object.

Four of these nine members wished to go further and permit either spouse to obtain a dissolution of marriage on this ground, notwithstanding the other spouse's objection, if he or she could satisfy the court that the separation was in part due to the unreasonable conduct of the other spouse.

One member, Lord Walker, dissenting from the view that the principle of marital offense be retained, recommended:

A marriage should be indissoluble unless, the spouses having lived apart for no less than three years, either spouse shows that the facts and circumstances affecting the lives of the parties adversely to one another are such that it is improbable that an ordinary husband and wife could ever resume cohabitation.

Failing the adoption of this proposal, Lord Walker considered that the doctrine of matrimonial offense should be retained without the new ground of complete marriage breakdown.[21] Among the witnesses whose conservative views seem to have carried weight were clerics of various denominations, among them Geoffrey F. Fisher, Lord Archbishop of Canterbury.[22] It is largely due to his successor, Arthur M. Ramsey, that the problems for which the Morton Commission could not find unanimous answers were again brought up for public consideration. In 1963, a Labor Member of Parliament, Mr. Leo Abse, introduced in the Commons a bill which resumed what Mrs. Eirene White had proposed ten years earlier in a bill she introduced that would add to the existing grounds for divorce the new ground of living apart for seven years. It was this proposal that was specifically considered by the Morton Commission. Mr. Abse's bill contained measures to promote reconciliation. To ensure the passage of these he withdrew the controversial clauses. Subsequently, an amendment aiming at restoring them was moved in the House of Lords, but was disagreed. In the course of a debate on that amendment, on 21 June 1963, the Archbishop of Canterbury, while opposing divorce on the ground of seven years' living apart, stated his dissatisfaction with the existing law of divorce and, as he expressed it, the operation of the divorce court, meaning, apparently, the existing practice of collusive consent divorce. "If it were possible," His Grace remarked, "to find a principle at law of breakdown of marriage which was free from any trace of the idea of consent, which conserved the point that offences and not only wishes are the basis of the breakdown and which was protected by a far more

21. Morton Report 310.
22. Minutes of Evidence, 6th Day (28 May 1952).

thorough insistence on reconciliation procedure first, then I would wish to consider it." [23]

Obviously, what Archbishop Ramsey had in mind was a system under which the practice of the divorce court would be tightened: no divorce unless there has been a true breakdown of the marriage, provided the breakdown was caused by a marital offense; no divorce unless reconciliation had been attempted; and, by implication, no divorce until the fact of complete breakdown of the marriage was fully proved to the court. The archbishop had discovered that adoption of the principle of marriage breakdown would by no means facilitate divorce, least of all if a marital offense had to be proved to have been the cause of the breakdown. The aim was similar to that pursued in 1965 by the Catholic bishops in New York.[24]

How should, how could, this novel idea be implemented? In order to elaborate it, the archbishop appointed a group of experts of high standing. Of its thirteen members only the chairman, the Bishop of Exeter, and two others were churchmen, six belonged to the legal profession, among them Professor J. N. D. Anderson, director of the Institute of Advanced Legal Studies in the University of London, Lord Devlin and Mr. Justice Phillimore; there were furthermore a sociologist, a psychiatrist, a writer on Christian ethics, and a Labor member of Parliament. In January 1964 they were invited by the archbishop to review the law of England concerning divorce and,

> recognizing that there is a difference in the attitudes of the Church and State towards the further marriage of a divorced person whose former partner is living, to consider whether the inclusion of any new principle or procedure in the law of the State would be likely to operate
>
> (1) more justly and with greater assistance to the stability of marriage and the happiness of all concerned, including children, than at present; and
>
> (2) in such a way as to do nothing to undermine the approach of couples to marriage as a lifelong covenant.

The report was published in 1966 under the title *Putting Asunder: A Divorce Law for Contemporary Society*. It is a remarkable document, written in a clear style that avoids the stilted phraseology so typical of ecclesiastical pronouncements. In a lively way the authors tell the readers how they reached their conclusions and by what considerations they were guided. They did not regard it as their task to discuss what should be the marriage teachings of the church. Their concern was the secular law of the state applicable alike to believers and non-

---

23. PUTTING ASUNDER: A DIVORCE LAW FOR CONTEMPORARY SOCIETY 5 (1966).
24. *Infra* p. 358.

believers. Any attempt to impose on a secularized society a marriage law identical with the dogma of a particular religious community was repudiated. Similar to the position taken in the Roman Catholic church at Vatican Council II and applied by the organization of Catholic laymen in its assent to divorce law reform in New York, the Archbishop's Group recognized that the law of the land providing for the dissolution of legal marriage is of but secondary importance to those whose loyalty to Christ does not depend upon human law.[25] Nevertheless, the Group declared the problem of divorce and remarriage not to be outside the church's concern. Data of social life were taken into consideration, but they were observed in the context of Christian value judgments. The Group never lost sight of their terms of reference as stated by the archbishop and as requiring any reform law "to do nothing to undermine the approach of couples to marriage as a lifelong covenant."

When taken literally, this reference would seem to exclude all possibility of divorce. As soon as divorce is available, even if on the narrowest ground, one must regard it as possible that upon entering marriage a party might think of the possibility of divorce and might thus not regard the assent to the marriage as a lifelong covenant. Obviously, this was not what was meant by the archbishop or his group. Apparently, what they meant was that the law should not induce couples to enter marriage with the intention that it be no more than a temporary affair. Marriage should continue to be intended for life even though the parties might be aware of the possibility that it could be terminated in the unexpected event of ultimate failure. What was to be guarded against was official approval of trial or time marriage or a system that would allow the dissolution of a marriage upon a fleeting whim or outburst of temper.

If understood in that sense, the possibility of consent divorce would not have been totally outside the permissible scope of the Group's consideration. Nor would it seem that the Group was prevented from inquiring whether it was within the power of any law to prevent consent divorce however undesirable that institution might appear. But the Group neither could nor wished to sever themselves from the Christian tradition. "The fatal defect of the consensual principle," said the authors, "is that it subjects marriage absolutely to the joint will of the parties, so making it in essence a private contract."[26]

Discussions of whether marriage is a status or a contract have been

---

25. PUTTING ASUNDER 12.
26. *Id.* 34.

as frequent as they are inane. Their principal result has been to obscure the fact that marriage in the sense of community of life is, indeed, subject to the joint will of the parties and that the law can do no more than prevent legitimate remarriage. The Archbishop's Group simply allowed themselves to be stifled by the bad odor of the term "civil contract," a term which has much emotional force but is devoid of ascertainable content. Had they looked behind the façade, the Group would most likely have come up with a solution more workable than that proposed in their report.

The Group acknowledged that the principle of the marital offense is out of date, conceding, of course, that the Church of England had contributed to the development of this doctrine. But they firmly asserted that the Church of England "is very far from being committed to treating that shape as sacrosanct." It was, as it is pointed out, developed in the context of proceedings for separation from bed and board, where "the matrimonial offence remains the appropriate and, indeed, the indispensable basis for the law." [27]

The aptness of the principle to divorce was "found to be open to formidable objections, not only on moral and legal grounds, but on social and psychological grounds as well. [28]

The present legal doctrine [it is said] commits the courts to a superficial conception of the relationship between husband and wife. From a moral point of view, first of all, the mere fact that one spouse has, as the Morton Commission puts it, done something "fundamentally incompatible with the undertakings entered into a marriage" does not in itself make a case for dissolving the marriage.

There are all sorts of other ways in which the situation created by (say) an act of adultery might be dealt with by the two persons concerned. So in reality it is only if they fail to deal with it in any of those other ways that there is a case for divorce.

So the Group concludes that the real ground for the divorce is the marital failure which may or may not follow the commission of the offense. "The concentration of judicial attention upon the offences defined by the law invokes a false sense of values." [29]

The Group then proceeds to denounce the hypocrisy of the accusatorial procedure with its superficiality and remoteness from reality.

If the parties are agreed that there is no solution to their problem except divorce, they must not tell the court so. . . . Sometimes a suitable offence can be conjured up from the history of the marriage; sometimes, if those

27. *Id.* 27.
28. *Id.* 28–29.
29. *Id.* 29.

concerned are not too scrupulous, one will be contrived; in either case a nonsense is made of the law. Reduction to absurdity is achieved with the possibility that the court may refuse a decree because there are faults on both sides.[30]

The Group cannot but acknowledge that "the law in effect admits 'divorce by consent', since, if the offense is proved and any collusion successfully concealed, the court is bound to grant a decree without further inquiry into the actual state of the marriage."[31] This passage indicates the Group's agreement with the archbishop's desire to do away with that system which in practice allows divorce by consent, and to substitute for it a system of such strict procedural safeguards that divorce by consent will be precluded not only in theory but also in fact.

In order to achieve this aim the Group was ready to jettison the time-honored principle of marital offense. In order to make that step more palatable they continued to point out what has often been stated by earlier critics, namely, that the distinction between an "innocent" and "guilty" spouse is "preposterous." The once influential view that a spouse who has committed adultery was to be prevented from remarrying by being regarded as spiritually dead and so without rights, was said to be "much weaker than it used to be," even though it might not altogether have disappeared.[32]

Finally the Group pointed out the inconsistency of the present law of England: "If, as many defenders of the present law have insisted, the moral principle underlying the doctrine of the matrimonial offense is right and necessary to be maintained, then divorce on the ground of a spouse's insanity must surely be immoral."[33]

What now is the "new basis for divorce" that the Group recommends after this emphatic condemnation of the principle of marital offense and the admission that the present law in effect admits divorce by consent?

Observing judicial practice, the Group concluded that the principle of the matrimonial offense had all but been abandoned and that a new principle, that of "the intolerable situation" had taken its place. The Group first speaks of those cases where the plaintiff, in obedience to the statute, reveals to the court that he too has committed adultery and thus invokes the discretion of the court. In such

30. *Id.* 29–30.
31. *Id.* 30.
32. *Id.* 31.
33. *Id.* 33.

cases, the group states, the court exercises distributive justice by taking into consideration the interests of all concerned: the parties to the suit; the petitioner's partner in adultery, especially if there is a desire for remarriage; any children involved, whether of the marriage or of adulterous cohabitation; and the community at large. No evidence is adduced as to the extent, if any, to which the interest of the community at large is considered and, if so, how this interest is defined. But, significantly, another factor is added: "The court is expected to come to some conclusion about the prospects of reconciliation if a decree were to be refused."[34] In a footnote it is stated that discretion is asked for in 30 percent of all petitions for divorce. "We are advised that the instances in which it is refused are 'relatively few.'"

Another sign of change is seen in the transformation of the concept of cruelty from one referring to conduct intended to hurt, into one signifying a situation which, created through the conduct of the respondent, the petitioner ought not to be called upon to endure. Since under this practice a divorce can be obtained on the ground of cruelty where the acts have been those of an insane person,[35] the doctrine of the matrimonial offense has been transformed "out of all recognition."[36]

Obviously assuming that a marital situation intolerable to one spouse is equivalent to one in which marital cohabitation has ceased beyond any hope of repair, the Group endorsed the view that was expressed in 1956 by Lord Walker, who as a minority member of the Morton Commission had said:

The true significance of marriage as I see it, is life by cohabitation in the home for the family. But when the prospect of continuing cohabitation has ceased the true view as to the significance of marriage seems to require that the legal tie be dissolved. Each empty tie — as empty ties accumulate — adds increasing harm to the community and injury to the ideal of marriage.[37]

The view expressed by Lord Walker is said by the Group to be shared "by a great many thoughtful and conscientious persons."[38] As the name best suited, the Group chose the term "breakdown of marriage" and recommended that the law of England be changed so as to adopt this principle. The fundamental question to be answered by the divorce court should thus be:

34. *Id.* 35.
35. Williams v. Williams, [1963] 3 W.L.R. 215, [1963] 2 All E.R. 994. The idea was first recommended in 1912 by the Gorell Commission and repeated in 1956 by the Morton Commission, para. 256.
36. PUTTING ASUNDER 36.
37. Morton Commission Report 341, cited in PUTTING ASUNDER 38.
38. PUTTING ASUNDER 38.

Does the evidence before the court present such failure in the matrimonial relationship, or such circumstances adverse to that relationship, that no reasonable probability remains of the spouses again living together as husband and wife for mutual comfort and support?[39]

The question thus arises, what evidence suffices and how is it to be obtained? As the Group says:

> The primary and fundamental question would be: Does the evidence before the court reveal such failure in the matrimonial relationship, or such circumstances adverse to that relationship, that no reasonable probability remains of the spouses again living together as husband and wife for mutual comfort and support?[40]

The standard seems to be a subjective one. Is there a reasonable probability that the individual couple before the court may again come to live together as husband and wife for mutual comfort and support? This test differs from the definition by Lord Walker, who is cited as regarding as decisive in the matter whether or not it is "improbable that *an ordinary husband and wife* would ever resume cohabitation."[41]

In order to make the necessary finding, the court would have to consider in evidence "all the relevant facts in the history of the marriage."[42] A considerable period of time of the parties' having lived apart from each other would be important but not in itself conclusive proof of breakdown.[43]

Evidence received by the Group suggested that judges might be reluctant to be put in the position of having to make predictions about the future of individual marriages. But the Group believed that the issue of irremediable breakdown would be no less justiciable than that of whether the proved conduct of a spouse would, if continued, cause injury to the health of the other spouse, or the decision on which of the parties is guilty of desertion where the decision, as it often does, depends on the skill of the tactical maneuvers.[44] But, if really *all* the relevant facts in the history of the marriage are to be brought to the knowledge of the court, and if the court is really to consider the whole truth and nothing but the truth, then new attitudes and procedures will be called for. Indeed, such new attitudes and procedures constitute the very gist of the proposals of the Archbishop's Group. They

39. *Id.* 38–39.
40. *Ibid.*
41. *Id.* 39. The italics are mine.
42. *Ibid.*
43. *Ibid.*
44. *Id.* 43.

constitute the application of modern casework techniques to the canon law system of *ex officio* investigation by a defender of the bond. No explanation is given why the task should not be performed by the Queen's Proctor on whom it has been incumbent so long. In fact, this officer is not mentioned in the report. Perhaps the Group had given up hope that Parliament would appropriate the funds necessary to make that office effective. Or the Group wished perhaps to avoid that criticism which specific reference to the proctor system could be expected to provoke. So the proposal is rather to create a new body of officers attractively named "forensic social workers." They should "when required to do so, verify attempts at reconciliation, test the reliability of assertions made to the court and investigate other matters on which the court wished to be informed." [45] Provisions should also be made for the intervention, when needed, of counsel representing the public interest or the interests of children of the family. While the requirement of both parties' personal appearance before the court in all cases is dismissed as potentially oppressive, attendance of both parties should be encouraged, and it should be compelled when the court considered it to be necessary.[46]

The Group recognized that the full adoption of the inquest device in all, or at least in all uncontested, cases would be so expensive as to render such a suggestion utopian. One can but wonder to what extent the proposed scheme would be different or less expensive. If the scheme were adopted, one would, indeed, have to agree with the Group that the change from the principle of marital offense to the principle of breakdown would not increase the number of divorces.[47] A decrease, indeed a considerable one, would be inevitable, if the new law of divorce were to contain two additional features which the Group declared to be indispensable parts of its proposal.

(1) [The court should] refuse to render a decree where the conduct of the petitioner in regard to the marriage was found to be such that in the court's judgment making a decree would be against the public interest; and
(2) where the maintenance proposed would not in the court's judgment be just to the dependent spouse or the children of the family.[48]

The Group also wished

to check the tendency, prompted no doubt by considerations of expense and judicial time, to draw too sharp a line between contested and uncontested

---

45. *Id.* 70.
46. *Id.* 69–70.
47. *Id.* 43.
48. *Id.* 74–75.

suits. It would go far to frustrate the purpose of basing divorce on breakdown if . . . people got the impression that uncontested cases were less important in the law's eyes than those that are contested, and could therefore be expected to go through automatically, without serious inquiry into the reality of the breakdown alleged.[49]

It is for this reason that the group disapproved of bringing uncontested cases into the jurisdiction of the county courts.[50]

A scheme like that proposed in *Putting Asunder* might effectively stem the rising tide of divorce. But would it also put an end to factual marriage breakdown? Was it acceptable to English people of the 1960s? The answer turned out to be negative.

The postulate that the distinction between contested and uncontested divorce be deemphasized and that jurisdiction in all matters of divorce should remain in the High Court was repudiated with the Matrimonial Causes Act, 1967,[51] which gave county courts power to deal with matrimonial causes that are undefended. The Act only formalized what had been actual practice for some time. But because of the Act an undefended divorce case may now be handled by a solicitor from start to finish, and it is no longer necessary to call in a barrister in addition to the solicitor. The Act is unlikely substantially to change the perfunctory handling of uncontested divorces. The congestion of the county courts is being increased by the extension of their jurisdiction in cases of contract and tort,[52] but it may result in lowering the cost and thus in savings for the Legal Aid Fund, where divorce proceedings account for by far the largest number of legal aid certificates issued.[53]

The inquest system, which constitutes the heart of the scheme proposed by the Archbishop's Group, was found to be unworkable and unacceptable by the body which is now the fountainhead of English law reform, the Law Commission. That body, established under the Law Commission Act of 1965,[54] constitutes a *novum* in legislation and law reform. It consists of five members. In the 1969 composition the chairman, Sir Leslie Scarman, was a judge, two members, L. C. B. Gower and Norman S. Marsh, were academic teachers of law, Neil Lawson and Andrew Martin were barristers. A solicitor, Arthur Stapleton

49. *Id.* 77.
50. *Ibid.*
51. 1967 c. 56, in force since 11 April 1968, 47 Halsbury Statutes of England 775 (1968).
52. Administration of Justice Act 1969, c. 58.
53. 119 NEW LAW JOURNAL 794 (1969).
54. 1965, c. 22.

Gotham, had been appointed special consultant. Another commission of similar composition was established for Scotland. In contrast to its predecessor, the Lord Chancellor's Law Reform Committee, the work of the Law Commission occupies the full time of the members, who are also aided by a full-time professional staff. The duties of the commission are extensive; it is "to take and keep under review all the law with a view towards its systematic development and reform, including in particular the codification of such law, the elimination of anomalies, the repeal of obsolete and unnecessary enactments, the reduction of the number of separate enactments and, generally, the simplification and modernization of the law." Significantly, the commission is directed "to obtain such information as to the legal systems of other countries as appears to the Commission likely to facilitate the performance of any of their functions." [55]

The establishment of the two British law commissions was spurred by the existence of such organizations as the New York Law Revision Commission and the Louisiana Law Institute. But, in contrast to them, the British commissioners are to devote their full time to their tasks. The British law commissions differ from the legislative staffs of Continental ministries of justice in that they constitute the independent voice of the legal profession rather than arms of the executive branch of the government.

The report of the Archbishop's Group was scarcely published when the Lord Chancellor, Lord Gardiner, who, as a member of the House of Lords had initiated the establishment of the law commissions, referred the matter for advice to the English commission. Its report was presented to Parliament in November 1966.[56]

The members of the commission regarded it as their duty to consider not only the report of the Archbishop's Group but also other proposals for reform of the existing grounds of divorce. They hesitated, however, to recommend a particular course of action. Such a decision was felt to touch upon controversial issues the settlement of which belonged to Parliament. Their own function, the commission held, was to point out the implications of various possible courses of action and to mark the boundaries of choice. The analysis of the various possible approaches is preceded by a brief inquiry meant to create the atmosphere necessary for calm discussion. Should the rise of the divorce rate cause alarm? The answer, a reassuring no, is based upon those arguments which have

---

55. Law Commissions Act 1965, § 3.
56. The Law Commission, Reform of the Grounds for Divorce — the Field of Choice, Cmnd. 3123 (repr. 1967).

been propounded in recent American and British discussions. An increased number of divorces is alarming only if it indicates an increase in the number of broken homes. Even an increase in the number of broken homes might merely indicate that there were more marriages subject to the risk of breakdown. Even if the proportion of marriages that did break down could be shown to have increased, it might merely be that the marriages were subjected to greater risks and not that there was any moral decline.[57] The commission points out that divorce is merely one of several possible consequences of a marriage breakdown. The examples of England of the time before 1857 and of present-day Italy are adduced to show that parties may also merely part, or may enter a formal separation agreement, or may obtain a judicial separation or a maintenance order. In contrast to earlier investigations, the commission succinctly stated what should have been obvious all along:

If a divorce is obtained, it follows and is caused by the breakdown — not vice versa.

And the commission continued:

In so far as it is obtained because the parties wish to establish new unions but want those unions to be marriages rather than "living in sin," the fact that they resort to divorce is not an indication of a waning of the respect for marriage but rather the contrary. From a secular point of view, divorce is socially harmful only when the possibility of obtaining it leads to the break-up of a home which would not have occurred if the parties had known that under no circumstances could the legal tie be severed. No statistics are available to show to what extent, if at all, this is a contributory cause of marital breakdown.[58]

A footnote adds the observation:

If the inability to obtain a divorce is an inducement to marital fidelity, its potency must be weakened by the ease with which names can be changed and an apparently regular establishment set up in another neighborhood.

Obviously, the commission was familiar with the Chicago inquiry and my article published in 1956.[59]

As to the number of marriages, their increase during the past century has been obvious. The risk of breakdown has been increased by the tendency to marry younger and by greater longevity, which in the twentieth century has doubled the average duration of marriage; other factors have been the housing shortage and the emancipation of women and their ability to be financially independent. But,

57. Para. 6.
58. *Ibid.*
59. 9 VAND. L. REV. 633.

despite all this, there is no real evidence that the proportion of marriage breakdown has increased during the century; nor, of course, is there any evidence that it has not. But recent sociological investigation seems to show that marriage as an institution in present-day England is in a fairly healthy state as compared with the past. . . .

Changes in the class structure of society have made divorce (with the resultant possibility of regularizing another union) desired by sections of the population which were formerly content with illicit and fluctuating unions. And the introduction of Legal Aid has made divorce something that they can afford. In spite of all these factors, only about one marriage in ten ends in divorce.[60]

There is thus no cause for alarm, and the commission can proceed soberly to recite the objectives of a "good divorce law," which are said

(i) to buttress, rather than to undermine, the stability of marriage; and
(ii) when, regrettably, a marriage has irretrievably broken down, to enable the empty legal shell to be destroyed with the maximum fairness, and minimum bitterness, distress and humiliation.[61]

In both respects the existing divorce law of England is found to be wanting. The matrimonial offense principle, it is true, has worked. It presents the court with a clear issue and thus enables solicitors with some confidence to advise their clients about their prospects. By laying down the circumstances in which an individual has a right to ask that his marriage be dissolved, the law provides an external buttress to the stability of marriages and deters the setting up of illicit unions because those who contemplate such unions know that there can be no certainty of their being able to carry and have legitimate children.[62]

But the principle is defective because in the majority of divorces fault actually attaches to both parties and the issues tried by the court are superficial. The procedure being, at least in form, litigious and causing embarrassment, it engenders bitterness, impedes conciliation, induces collusive practices, and thus tends to bring into disrepute the law and its administration and induces people to enter upon illicit unions and to procreate bastard children. While the problem of guilt will necessarily continue to play a role in the determination of the financial consequences of the dissolution of a marriage, it is likely to lose its sting when it is removed from the public trial of the issue of the termination itself.

A weighty argument against the principle of marital offense was seen in the fact that its existence in the present law has been one of

60. Paras. 8, 12. Again the commission seems to have drawn on the Chicago inquiry.
61. Para. 15.
62. Para. 24.

the principal causes of the creation of irregular unions and the principal obstacle to their transformation into marriages and to the legitimation of their offspring. No exact statistical data about such unions are available. But the sociological inquiries indicate that some 40 percent of illegitimate children were born into stable unions.

In the fifteen years up to and including 1964 there were 607,000 live illegitimate births in England and Wales. Thirty percent of this is 182,100. As regards the future, the annual number of illegitimate births is now about 64,000 (63,340 in 1964). Thirty percent of this is 19,200. It would seem therefore that, if the law were changed, about 180,000 living illegitimate children (below age 16) would be legitimated and that in each future year some 19,000 children who would otherwise be condemned to permanent illegitimacy might be born in wedlock or subsequently legitimated.[63]

The Archbishop's Group found the case against the marital offense principle "overwhelming," and the Law Commission, too, finds it not adequate to achieve the objective of a good divorce law.[64]

The only alternatives deserving further consideration are thus

1. (a) Breakdown with Inquest,
   (b) Breakdown without Inquest,
2. Divorce by Consent,
3. The Separation Ground.[65]

Breakdown with inquest is the solution proposed by the Archbishop's Group. In the view of the Law Commission, it is practically not feasible, even though it has much to commend it. The Group's proposal that in every case the stories of both parties be heard would founder on the difficulty of enforcing the attendance of an apathetic or absent defendant. The Group itself rejected as utopian the introduction of the defender of the bond. Under the present law, the Queen's Proctor goes into action in no more than about fifty cases a year, i.e., a tiny fraction of the forty thousand or more cases filed annually. Even when the intervention uncovers marital misconduct of the petitioner, the court more often than not exercises its discretion in the petitioner's favor. In 1965, fifty-four interventions by the Queen's Proctor were heard, discretion was exercised in thirty-four of these.[66]

If the inquest were to become a genuine one, time-consuming preliminary inquiries would have to be undertaken by trained personnel; if the whole matrimonial history were to be ascertained, the hearing

63. Para. 36.
64. Paras. 26, 28.
65. Para. 54.
66. Para. 21 n. 32.

itself would take much longer than at present. Public opinion would be unlikely to regard it as an improvement if in every case the whole matrimonial history were to be ventilated in public.

If our divorce laws are to be made more humane, it seems to us that the undefended divorce affords a better model than the dilatory, expensive and distressing defended divorce. . . .

Far more judges, courthouses and court officials would be needed. Persons with the appropriate training as forensic social workers would be unobtainable in sufficient numbers and, if they were obtained, they could be more usefully employed in the probation service, in child care and in marriage guidance.[67]

The commission concedes that the system of breakdown with inquest might provide a remedy in some cases of presently incurable irregular unions,[68] but it finds the system to be affected with the basic

weakness of an elaborate, time-consuming and expensive investigation. . . . The realities of the situation are that unless the marriage had broken down the parties would not be before the court. Conceivably, it may not have broken down irretrievably, but if cohabitation has ended and both parties are convinced that reconciliation is impossible, the chances of saving it are remote. The parties are likely to be better judges of the viability of their own marriage than a court can hope to be, even with the most elaborate and searching inquest.[69]

So the Law Commission proceeded to discuss the system of *Breakdown without Inquest,* i.e., a system in which marriage breakdown is not just one ground for divorce along with acts of marital offense, but the only and exclusive ground, such as it is now in the USSR and the other socialist countries. Under such a system, the commission finds that the judicial decision would have to involve the following four questions:

(a) Has the marriage broken down?
(b) If so, is there any reasonable prospect of reconciliation?
(c) If not, is there any reason of public policy, including in particular justice to the parties and the children, why the marriage should not be dissolved?
(d) If not, what are the appropriate consequential arrangements to be made regarding the parties and the children?[70]

How difficult it is for a court, unaided by an investigatory staff, to find the answer to the first two questions, is shown by Professor Jan

67. Paras. 60, 62.
68. Paras. 66–69.
69. Para. 71.
70. Para. 72.

Górecki's inquiry into the practice of the courts of Poland.[71] How difficult it is even to define the concept of marriage breakdown should be apparent from chapter 11 of the present book. The Law Commission believes that these difficulties can be eliminated if, on proof of a period of separation, the court is prepared to assume a positive answer to question (a) and, in the absence of proof to the contrary, negative answers to (b) and (c).[72]

Normally, neither question (a) nor question (b) requires investigation. Only if something in the pleadings or in the evidence has led the court to think that there is a possibility of reconciliation might the court adjourn the hearing for a limited period. But the court would not attempt an inquest into the marriage. Dispute may arise whether, despite the irreconcilable breakdown, a divorce should be refused in order to do justice to the parties and the children. Normally that would turn on the answer to the final question: the adequacy of the arrangements for the future. The only situation in which an inquest into the marital history might be needed to determine this point would be one in which the wife opposed the divorce on the ground that it would impose hardship on her and the children notwithstanding the fact that the husband has made the most equitable arrangements possible in the circumstances. If such a discretion were conferred, a full inquiry might sometimes be needed. But it would be infrequent. Even in the 7 percent of defended cases there is normally no dispute of the kind — merely one about who should divorce whom.[73]

Under the scheme of breakdown as the one single ground for divorce, petition might be made by either party or jointly by both. Where there are dependent or, as the Law Commission says, infant children, the court would have to satisfy itself that the arrangements proposed for the children were the best possible in the circumstances. Where there are no "infant" children, the court would have to grant the divorce if satisfied that the parties had been living separate and apart for the prescribed period unless, because equitable financial arrangements were not made, the court was bound to refuse the divorce, or unless it ordered an adjournment for attempted reconciliation.[74] As to the length of the period, the commission succinctly declared that

71. DIVORCE IN POLAND 28 (1970); also in 10 ACTA SOCIOLOGICA 68 (1966).
72. Para. 72.
73. Para. 73.
74. Para. 74.

no period of much more than six months prior to the filing of the petition could be regarded as a feasible proposal were breakdown to become the sole ground for divorce. If as short a period as that is regarded as unacceptable, then this proposal ceases to be a practicable one. . . . With a longer period it could be a practicable solution if coupled with other grounds.[75]

If proof is needed for this position, it will be found in the Australian statistics[76] and, we may add, in those of Denmark.[77]

So the commission turned to the next alternative, *Divorce by mutual consent.*

In October 1965, a survey of public attitudes toward divorce was carried out for the *Daily Sketch* by National Opinion Polls, Ltd., which interviewed a sample of 1,010 adults throughout Great Britain. Of these, 80 percent were in favor of divorce by consent, 17 percent against, and 3 percent answered "don't know." Four out of five of those interviewed thus expressed themselves in favor of divorce by consent.[78] But the Law Commission was skeptical. Initially it observed that consent would be no substitute for matrimonial offense as a sole ground for divorce. Standing alone it would do nothing to improve the situation of those who have established stable illicit unions and are at present unable to have their marriages dissolved.[79] But in the majority of cases, the commission conceded, open consent would be substituted for clandestine consent.[80] The danger that the economically weaker party, normally the wife, might be overborne by the stronger, and that accordingly it would not be safe to assume that her signature to an agreement necessarily represented a real and free consent, could, the commission declared, be overcome by some independent verification. As we have seen, such a system seems to work well in the Scandinavian countries.[81] Its absence in Japan seems to result in real hardship for women.[82]

For the allegation that "countries which permit divorce by consent tend to have divorce rates considerably higher than those which do not"[83] no evidence is adduced. Nevertheless, the Law Commission maintained that, unless it were coupled with a minimum period of separation, the availability of divorce by consent might enable mar-

75. Para. 76.
76. Law Commission Report, App. E.
77. *Supra* p. 145.
78. Paras. 51, n. 74; 77 n. 16.
79. Para. 78.
80. Para. 79.
81. *Supra* pp. 141 ff.
82. *Supra* p. 121.
83. Para. 80 (g).

riages to be dissolved which had not broken down irretrievably.[84] The commission does not explain how this allegation might be squared with its statements that "if cohabitation has ended and both parties are convinced that reconciliation is impossible the chances of saving it are remote" and that "the parties are likely to be better judges of the viability of their own marriage than a court can hope to be."[85]

The last alternative regarded as feasible by the Law Commisson is what it calls "the separation ground," which means the adding to the offense grounds for divorce of the present law the new ground of the parties' having lived separate and apart for a stated period of time. The objection of the Archbishop's Group to such a combination of the allegedly incompatible principles of marital offense and breakdown is brushed aside by referring to the existence and satisfactory working of this combination in Austrialia and New England and a brief quotation from Professor Monrad Paulsen's review of *Putting Asunder*.[86] Such a scheme was contained in the bill of Mrs. Eirene White, M.P., that prompted the setting up of the Morton Commission.[87] In recent years, the Law Commission observed, at least one such bill had been introduced in each session of Parliament. The pressure behind these efforts was, the commission stated, prompted by the desire to do something about the serious social problem of the stable illicit unions and their issue.[88]

The commission agreed that the introduction of the new ground of separation would help cure stable illicit unions. In addition, the commission believed that it might take the sting out of situations of marital offense by inducing petitioners to plead the neutral ground of separation rather than create the embarrassment and hostility likely to be implied in the allegation of an offense. To achieve this effect, the minimum period of separation must not be so long, however, as to render the allegation of an offense necessary to obtain a divorce with reasonable speed. But, on the other hand, the minimum period must not be so short as to undermine the stability of marriage.[89] "If both parties are anxious to end their marriage without rancour and without seeking to secure a public finding of guilt or innocence, they may be prepared to wait, it seems to us, as long as two years."[90]

84. Para. 84.
85. Para. 71.
86. NEW SOCIETY, 4 August 1966.
87. *Supra* p. 322.
88. Para. 86.
89. Para. 92
90. Para. 93.

No reasons are stated for this expectation, but it seems that the proposal can be explained by considerations of parliamentary expediency. Apparently, the Law Commission neither expected nor wished Parliament to adopt the system of breakdown without inquest. The proposition that that system is impracticable if the minimum period of separation were to be longer than six months was likely to make parliamentary rejection virtually certain.

Although not expressly saying so, the commission was obviously in favor of adding the separation ground to the traditional offense grounds. In such a context a period of two years is not so shockingly out of line with proposals made or with the laws of Commonwealth countries as to make it appear unacceptable at the very outset.[91] The plan was made even more palatable by the suggestion that the period should be longer — to wit, five years — in the case of contest. But this longer period should apply only where the respondent actually opposes the divorce, but not where he (or she) simply fails to object. Such failures should be treated as equivalent to consent, provided the court is satisfied that the respondent is fully aware of the consequences.

The bill of Mrs. Eirene White, who in 1956 had sought to add the ground of separate living to the traditional matrimonial offense grounds, provided for a period of seven years. In subsequent English bills the length of the period varied between five and seven years. In Sweden, the period is one year when the parties are in agreement and three years otherwise, but in the former case the one year begins to run from the decree of judicial separation, which of necessity must be later than the date of factual separation.[92] Under the American state statutes, the period is between one year and ten years.[93] In Australia it is five years,[94] in New Zealand two years,[95] under the Canadian Divorce Act of 1968, three years.[96]

The period of separation need not necessarily have to be uninterrupted. The commission recommended continuing the scheme of the

91. Para. 97.
92. *Supra* p. 141.
93. *Supra* p. 314.
94. Matrimonial Causes Act 1959, § 28 (m).
95. Matrimonial Proceedings Amendment Act 1968 (Statutes 1968 No. 62).
96. 16 Eliz. 2, c. 24, provides in § 4 (1) (e) that the period of separation is three years, except where the petitioner has deserted the respondent, in which case the period is five years. Upon the expiration of such period permanent breakdown of the marriage shall be deemed to have been established, § 4 (2). The Act took effect on 2 July 1968, Proclamation of the Governor General, of 8 May 1968, at 102, CANADA GAZETTE 184 (1968, Part II, no. 10).

Matrimonial Causes Act, 1965,[97] which provides that resumption of cohabitation with a view to reconciliation does not interrupt a period of desertion or amount to condonation of a marital offense.[98]

Does the scheme thus outlined require additional safeguards?

The commission favored the continuation of the present ban on divorce within the first three years of marriage, subject, as it is at present, to leave by judicial discretion.[99] Also the court should in all cases have the power to adjourn for a limited period if it thinks there is a real likelihood of a reconciliation.[100] It was furthermore made clear that the present absolute and discretionary bars would be inappropriate to petitions brought on the separation ground.

There would be no relevant offence to connive at, conduce to or condone. A mutual agreement to facilitate a divorce on those grounds would be something to encourage rather than the reverse. Nor would the petitioner's adultery, at any rate if subsequent to the separation, appear to be relevant.[101]

Adultery committed before the separation should be merely one factor to be taken into consideration by the court. Delay in bringing suit should be openly recognized to be irrelevant.[102] On the other hand, the commission insisted upon "adequate safeguards to ensure that the petitioner does not wilfully deceive the court." But, while the commission stated the sanction for deceit — judicial discretion to refuse the divorce — it did not spell out what the safeguards against deceit might be, except that the rules of the court should make it clear what a petitioner is called upon to disclose in his petition.

The interests of the children are to continue to be protected as they now are under the Matrimonial Causes Act of 1965. Thereby a decree absolute cannot be granted unless the court is satisfied regarding the arrangements made for the care and upbringing of the children. The commission announced its intention to undertake an investigation into the working of this section in order to see if it could be improved.[103] Future study was also announced for the problems of family property

---

97. Para. 103.
98. §§ 1 (2) and 42 (2). The desire to facilitate reconciliation also inspired the Illinois law of 15 May 1961, Laws 1961, at 487, now Divorce Act, § 21.2, under which the court may allow the parties to a suit for divorce temporarily to resume cohabitation without prejudice to their respective rights.
99. Paras. 19, 106.
100. Para. 107.
101. Para. 108.
102. Para. 109.
103. Para. 110.

and financial relief. In its divorce report the Law Commission had stated its conviction that the economically weaker party, i.e., normally the wife, be free of pressure in the decision of whether or not to veto a divorce after two years of separation, and that she be fully aware of the financial consequences. To this end strict proof of service of the petition would be necessary and the petition should be accompanied by a notice advising the respondent to seek legal advice and explaining how it could be obtained under the Legal Aid Advice Scheme. It might also be possible to devise a procedure whereby, if the court doubted whether the respondent had fully understood the situation, a welfare officer might be instructed to investigate and report.[104]

Such safeguards may protect wives as long as the major part of petitions for divorce are brought by husbands, as, according to the commission, seems to be the case in England. But we may ask whether the English practice might not turn into one like that which has long prevailed here in the United States, where the overwhelming mass of petitions for divorce is brought by women,[105] frequently as the *quid pro quo* for the husband's willingness to purchase his freedom through a generous arrangement for alimony, property, and child custody. An even stricter safeguard was held to be necessary in the case of a separation divorce objected to by the respondent. In accord with the Archbishop's Group the Law Commission recommended a bar for those cases in which the court is not satisfied that the arrangements concerning property, pensions, and maintenance are "equitable."[106]

There still remained the thorny question whether in the case of marriage breakdown as proved by the expiration of the statutory minimum period the divorce might yet be denied upon grounds of public policy. The commission found it helpful to look to the laws of New Zealand and Australia and to the New York law of 1967. In New Zealand three years' separation under a decree, order, or separation agreement was made a discretionary ground for divorce in 1920,[107] but shortly thereafter an absolute bar was established for cases in which the divorce was opposed and the separation found to have been due to the wrongful conduct of the petitioner.[108] In 1953, seven years' simple separation with no prospect of reconciliation was added to the list of grounds of divorce, but also subject to the bar of opposition

---

104. Para. 112.
105. P. H. JACOBSON, AMERICAN MARRIAGE AND DIVORCE 121 (1959); U.S. DEPT. OF HEALTH, EDUCATION, AND WELFARE, DIVORCE STATISTICS ANALYSIS 1963, at 38.
106. Para. 113.
107. Divorce and Matrimonial Causes Amendment Act 1920, §4.
108. Divorce and Matrimonial Causes Amendment Act 1921–22, §2.

because of guilt of the petitioner.[109] Ten years later judicial discretion was substituted for the absolute bar where the separation had lasted seven years and no prospect of reconciliation existed.[110] As the commission observes, these successive changes have not markedly affected the incidence of divorce.[111] Even less, we may add, are they likely to have affected the incidence of marriage breakdown.

In Australia the law of divorce was unified by the Commonwealth Matrimonial Causes Act 1959, which came into force on 1 February 1961. Up to then separation had been a ground in South Australia[112] and Western Australia.[113] Now a divorce can be granted after five years separation if there is no reasonable likelihood of cohabitation being resumed.[114] But a divorce on this ground must be denied if "the court is satisfied that, by reason of the conduct of the petitioner, whether before or after the separation commenced, or for any other reason, it would, in the particular circumstances of the case, be harsh and oppressive to the respondent, or contrary to the public interest, to grant a decree."[115] Further, if the court is of the opinion that it is just and proper for the petitioner to make financial provision for the respondent, it is not to grant a decree until the petitioner has made arrangements to the satisfaction of the court.[116] Australian statistics indicate that adultery and desertion have remained the common grounds for divorce.[117] The Law Commission believes that the shunning of the separation ground is due to its statutory restrictions.[118] The commission wisely refrains from the expression of an opinion whether the statutory provisions have also influenced the total incidence of divorce or of factual marriage breakdown.

Of the New York law of 1966, the commission mentioned § 15, under which a divorce is not to follow a judicial or contractual two years' separation unless the petitioner has duly performed all the terms and conditions of the decree or deed.[119]

The Archbishop's Group wished the court to have the duty to refuse a decree even though breakdown has been proved, if "to grant

109. Divorce and Matrimonial Causes Amendment Act 1953, § 7.
110. Matrimonial Proceedings Act 1963, §§ 29, 30.
111. Para. 87 n. 35.
112. Matrimonial Causes Amendment Act 1938.
113. Supreme Court Amendment Act 1945.
114. Matrimonial Causes Act 1959, § 28 (m).
115. *Id.* § 37 (l).
116. *Id.* § 37 (c).
117. Law Commission Report 62.
118. Para. 88.
119. Para. 89.

it would be contrary to the public interest in justice and in protecting the institution of marriage."[120] The Law Commission agreed with the idea but also recognized that

> any such discretion should be so circumscribed as to give the courts as clear and precise a guidance as possible. This is particularly necessary since divorce jurisdiction is perforce exercised by a great number of different judges — High Court Judges, County Court Judges, and Special Commissioners — and experience with the existing discretions has shown that it is extremely difficult to ensure that they are exercised consistently.[121]

In an effort to devise a more precise formula, the commission analyzed the interests it believed to be at stake:[122] There is first the interest to prevent the respondent, especially the wife respondent, from suffering disproportionate hardship and injustice. Even though the financial arrangements may be fair at the time of the divorce, their enforcement may be jeopardized when the husband remarries and thus contracts new obligations.

> While to refuse a divorce on this ground might be said to discriminate against the poor, it may be argued that on marriage the petitioner has undertaken an obligation to support his wife — at least while she is innocent of any matrimonial offence.

Perhaps the discrimination would work more against the lower middle class than against the poor, among whom maintenance is obtainable with difficulty at best, and not at all in many cases. But should it still be said that, on marrying, a man assumes the duty to support the woman for the entire duration of their joint lives? Is this once powerful idea compatible with the admission of divorce? Is the linking of this duty with divorce justified in a system which seeks to eliminate from the law of divorce the relevancy of the matrimonial offense and recognizes that the determination of guilt in any but a merely formal sense surpasses the ability of the courts? Ought a man be so saddled with the duty to support a woman who under present conditions may be able to support herself? In a country which, as the United Kingdom, has abolished the legal duty of adult children to support their indigent parents, one may even ask whether an ex-husband is nearer than the taxpayers to his ex-wife who is unable to support herself. If it is recognized that society has an interest in regularizing irregular unions, should that interest yield to the interest of an ex-wife to be supported for life by the man who once went through a cere-

---

120. PUTTING ASUNDER, para. 66, at 53.
121. Para. 115.
122. Paras. 114–19.

mony of marriage with her? A provision of the kind could, indeed, smack of discrimination, i.e., of discrimination of men against women.

The Law Commission observed that a divorce might violate a wife respondent's interests of a noneconomic nature: religious opposition to divorce; spiteful desire to deny the husband the freedom of remarriage; hope that some day the husband may yet return; deprivation of status; general anxiety that, with the availability of divorce, husbands of aging wives might be tempted to turn to younger, more attractive women. None of these is regarded by the commission as sufficiently weighty generally to preclude the introduction of the breakdown principle.[123] But this fact does not mean that such interests are necessarily disregarded in the exercise of an ultimate discretion in an individual case.[124] Of the children's interests it is said that they may sometimes suggest the refusal of a divorce, but it is added that in other cases it might be better for them that the marriage be ended.[125] Strong arguments are given for requiring that a petitioner's disregard of his matrimonial obligations be taken into account. "It just would not do to let the petitioner get away with it."[126]

As interests to be weighed against those stated, the Law Commission mentions the public interest in ending empty ties, and the interests of the petitioner, any partner in the petitioner's irregular union, and any children thereof.[127]

On the basis of all these considerations the Law Commission proposes a formula which it says approximates the principles which the Australian and New Zealand courts have worked out. The commission says that the formula should be somewhat as follows:

> The Judge may in his discretion refuse to grant a divorce if satisfied that, having regard to the conduct and interests of the parties and the interests of the children and other persons affected, it would be wrong to dissolve the marriage, notwithstanding the public interest in dissolving marriages which have irretrievably broken down.[128]

This formula tells the judge which interests he has to consider, but it fails to tell him how he ought to balance them against each other. The term "wrong" is used in a moral sense, and in applying a moral standard to complex situations judges, like theologians, philosophers, and other men, may vary. It is the Law Commission's own insight that

---

123. Paras. 42–45.
124. Para. 118 (1).
125. Paras. 118 (2), 47–51.
126. Para. 118 (3).
127. Para. 118 (4).
128. Para. 119.

there appear to be only two practical alternatives. The first is not to have any bar additional to that which, being restricted to cases where equitable financial arrangements are not made, does have the desired precision. The second is to couple it with a wider discretion in which event a measure of imprecision appears unavoidable.[129]

Perhaps the Law Commission might have preferred the alternative of no bar if, in addition to the laws of New Zealand and Australia, it had looked to the laws of Continental countries.

The idea that a wrongdoer ought not to be let to get away with it has prompted the lawmakers of Switzerland, the Federal Republic of Germany, Poland, and other countries to provide specially for such cases an exception from the principle of breakdown. Under article 142, para. 2, of the Swiss Civil Code of 10 December 1907 only the innocent or less culpable spouse can obtain a divorce upon the ground of "deep disruption." Under the Polish Family Code, article 56, § 3, a divorce will not be granted upon the petition of the spouse who is the only guilty one in having caused the breakdown, unless the respondent fails to object or the objection appears under the circumstances to be contrary to the rules of social life. According to § 48, para. 2 of the Marriage Law of the Federal Republic of Germany (Control Council Law No. 16, of 20 February 1946, Control Council Gazette 2.77, as amended by Law of 11 August 1961, BGBl. I 1221), "the objection of the respondent prevents the granting of a divorce upon the ground of disruption evidenced by a separation of at least three years, if the disruption was totally or preponderantly caused by the guilt of the petitioner. The objection is to be disregarded if the respondent does not feel bound by the marriage and is not willing under adequate conditions to continue the marriage."

All these provisions have resulted in uncertainty and dissatisfaction.[130] In West Germany, separation divorce has been almost obliterated by the favor shown to objecting spouses by the Supreme Court.

The Law Commission declared the proposal of the archbishop's group — breakdown with inquest — to be unworkable. Consent divorce was obviously regarded as acceptable to Parliament. Breakdown with-

---

129. Para. 116.
130. H. Hinderling, *Die Bedeutung ds Verschuldens für das Ehescheidungsrecht der Schweiz*, 2 IUS PRIVATUM GENTIUM: FESTSCHRIFT FÜR MAX RHEINSTEIN 993 (1969); Jan Górecki, *supra* note 71, at 108; same *Recrimination in Eastern Europe: an Empirical Study of Polish Divorce Law*, 14 AM.J.COMP.L. 603 (1966); W. MÜLLER-FRIENFELS, EHE UND RECHT 144–45 (1962); E. Wolf, *Zwang zur Ehe*, 22 JURISTEN ZEITUNG 659 (1967), and reply: H. Weinkauff, president emeritus of the Supreme Court, *Zwang zur Ehe?* 23 JURISTEN ZEITUNG 15 (1968).

out inquest was not treated as being impossible outright, but adding the separation ground to certain slightly modified offense grounds apparently seemed to the commission the preferable route of reform, even though it was careful not to say so expressly and to leave the decision to public opinion and Parliament. But the contradictions between two such influential bodies as the Archbishop's Group and the Law Commission were bound to be disturbing. In accordance with wishes expressed during the debate in the House of Lords on 22 November 1966, the members of the Archbishop's Group entered upon discussions with the Law Commission, as the result of which the Commission decided to put forward a number of proposals which agreed with the position of the Group more in form than in substance.[131] Slightly modified they have been embodied in the Divorce Reform Act, 1969.[132] The Law received the Royal Assent on 22 October 1969. It came into operation on 1 January 1971.

While in form adopting the principle of irretrievable breakdown, the Act actually has preserved, although somewhat modified, the traditional offense grounds and added the separation ground to them. In § 1 the Act solemnly declares that the sole ground on which a petition for divorce may be presented to the court by either party shall be that the marriage has broken down irretrievably. But then article 2 continues as follows:

(1) The court . . . shall not hold the marriage to have broken down irretrievably unless the petitioner satisfies the court of one or more of the following facts, that is to say

(a) that the respondent has committed adultery and the petitioner finds it intolerable to live with the respondent;

(b) that the respondent has behaved in such a way that the petitioner cannot reasonably be expected to live with the respondent;

(c) that the respondent has deserted the petitioner for a continuous period of at least two years immediately preceding the presentation of the petition;

(d) that the parties to the marriage have lived apart for a continuous period of at least two years immediately preceding the presentation of the petition and the respondent consents to a decree being granted;

(e) that the parties to the marriage have lived apart for a continuous period of at least five years immediately preceding the presentation of the petition.

---

131. For the text see 117 NEW LAW JOURNAL 827 (1967).

132. Laws 1969, ch. 55. On the new law, see B. PASSINGHAM, THE DIVORCE REFORM ACT 1969 (1970), and G. G. Brown, *Divorce Reform Act 1969*, 120 NEW L.J. 74 (1970). Anon., *Divorce Reform Act 1969*, 120 NEW L.J. 83, 107, 131, 155 (1970); J. L. Barton, *Questions of the Divorce Reform Act 1969*, 86 L.Q.REV. 348 (1970); see also 120 NEW L.J. 192, 209 (1970).

While under this wording a marriage cannot be treated as irretrievably broken down without proof of one of the five situations enumerated, such proof is not irrebuttable evidence of irretrievable breakdown. The court must not grant the divorce if it is satisfied on all the evidence that the marriage has not broken down irretrievably.[133]

Subsection 2 declares it to be the duty of the court "to inquire, so far as it reasonably can, into the facts alleged by the petitioner and into any facts alleged by the respondent." Nothing is said on how the court is to perform this duty or how the limits of the reasonably possible are to be determined.

The situations listed as indicia of irretrievable marriage breakdown are but modifications of the marital offenses and the insanity ground of the old law as it was stated last in § 1 of the Matrimonial Causes Act 1965,[134] the consolidation law in which the provisions of former laws had been coherently restated, and which has remained in effect except those of its provisions which have been expressly repealed or modified by the Act of 1969.[135] Under the new Act, divorce is no longer automatically to follow proof of adultery, but only if the petitioner finds it intolerable to live with the adulterous spouse. But judicial evaluation of the situation is bounded by the rule of § 3 (3):

Where the parties to the marriage have lived with each other for any period or periods after it became known to the petitioner that the respondent had, since the celebration of the marriage,[136] committed adultery, then —

(a) if the length of that period or those periods together was six months or less, their living with each other during that period or those periods shall be disregarded in determining for the purposes of section 2 (1) (a) of this Act whether the petitioner finds it intolerable to live with the respondent; but

(b) if the length of that period or those periods together exceeded six months, the petitioner shall not be entitled to rely on that adultery for the purposes of the said section 2 (1) (a).

The rule of § 2 (1) (b), under which a marriage may be held to have irretrievably broken down "if the respondent has behaved in such a way that the petitioner cannot reasonably be expected to live with the respondent," essentially rephrases the divorce ground of cruelty[137]

133. § 1 (3).
134. Laws 1965, ch. 72.
135. Divorce Reform Act 1969, §§ 11 (2), 9 (1), 9 (2), and schedules 1 and 2.
136. Query: How could adultery be committed before the celebration of the marriage? Are the words "since the celebration of the marriage" meant to indicate the self-evident proposition that A cannot complain of adultery committed by his spouse while that spouse was married to B?
137. Matrimonial Causes Act 1965, § 1 (1) (a) (iii).

so as to express the meaning the House of Lords gave it in holding that the respondent's state of mind and even his mental capacity are irrelevant, and declaring it decisive that the respondent had, even without fault, created a situation that the petitioner could not be called upon to endure.[138] By this practice the principle of offense had already been abandoned. The new statutory provision may be interpreted to have an even broader meaning. In deciding whether or not the petitioner can reasonably be expected to live with the respondent the court is, as in the case of adultery, directed to disregard the fact that the parties have lived with each other in the same household for up to six months after the date of the occurrence of the final incident relied on by the petitioner and held by the court to support his allegation.[139]

Desertion has constituted a ground of divorce ever since Herbert's Act,[140] but the minimum period has now been shortened from three years to two. The idea that parties shall have an opportunity of another try without jeopardizing the right to divorce in the case of failure has found expression in § 3 (5).

The important innovation is the addition to the modified traditional grounds of the new ground, factual separation, for which the minimum periods are those which were suggested by the Law Commission: two years where the parties are in agreement and five years where the respondent does not agree. But contrary to the view expressed by the commission, expiration of the shorter period does not suffice where the respondent simply fails to object. Provision is to be made by rules of court to make sure that, where in pursuance of § 2 (1) (d) the petitioner alleges that the respondent consents to a decree being granted, the respondent has such information as will enable him to understand the consequences of his consent and the steps he must take to indicate that he does consent.[141]

The possibility of a unilateral divorce upon the sole ground of five years' separation was not accepted by Parliament without misgivings about the financial hardships to which it might expose middle-aged women. In the debate in the House of Lords, the Lord Chancellor, Lord Gardiner, conceded that middle-aged women may indeed find

---

138. Gollins v. Gollins, [1963] 3 W.L.R. 170, [1963] 2 All E.R. 966 (H.L.); Williams v. Williams [1963] 3 W.L.R. 215; [1963] 2 All E.R. 994 (H.L.); cf. L. N. Brown, *Cruelty without Culpability or Divorce without Fault*, 26 Mod.L.R. 625 (1963). D. Tolstoy, Divorce and Matrimonial Causes 61 (6th ed. 1967).
139. § 3 (4).
140. Last version: Matrimonial Causes Act 1965, § 1 (1) (a) (ii).
141. § 2 (6).

themselves in a precarious situation. But, so he pointed out, such a woman would hardly be in a better situation without divorce. The husband is likely to fall down on his maintenance payments. Even if he pays, the amount which he is ordered to pay is rarely enough for the wife to live on. So what really matters are the public welfare payments which supplement what she receives from the husband.

The hardship is there whether she is divorced or not. The only additional hardship that can arise upon divorce is the loss of a state widow's pension about which the Lord Chancellor declared that nothing could be done. Probably he was too rash. Why should it not be possible, as it is done in Sweden, to apportion such pensions among successive wives? Besides, under English law, a woman aged sixty or over can, when she is divorced, obtain a social security pension at its full rate of £5 a week even if neither she nor her former husband has retired.[142] In regard to other pensions the Lord Chancellor pointed out that, where a man can say to whom payment should be made after his death, the court will have the power to withhold the divorce unless the husband makes provisions for his wife to the effect that after his death the pension be paid to her as if she were the widow. Besides, Lord Gardiner warned, one ought not to overestimate the frequency with which the problem might arise. In 1967, there were 4,267 women over fifty whose marriages were dissolved, and 2,642 divorced women over fifty who remarried. Eighty-two percent of women divorced in any one year are forty-four or younger, a third of them being twenty-nine or younger. He also pointed out that in New Zealand, of those who take advantage of the five-year separation clause over 40 percent are women.[143] Probably, similar data could have been given from those states of the United States in which a divorce can be obtained unilaterally upon the ground of separation after periods shorter than five years. But such statistics, desirable though they might be, are not available.

Under the new English Act, protection against financial hardship that might follow a divorce obtained upon the separation ground is sought by means of a complex scheme that generally follows the suggestion of the Law Commission.[144]

The new Act no longer speaks of insanity. Under the old law a divorce could be obtained if the respondent was "incurably of unsound

---

142. H. A. Munro, *Retirement Pensions after Divorce*, 121 New L.J. 159 (1971).
143. The Economist, 5 July 1969.
144. It is contained in §§ 4, 5, and 6 of the Act, the full text of which is reproduced in Appendix B, below.

mind and has been continuously under care and treatment for a period of at least five years immediately preceding the presentation of the petition."[145] How will insanity be treated under the separation ground or the intolerable situation ground of the new Act? The answer will depend on the courts, as will the functioning of the new Act in general. To some extent, it is true, the danger of too wide a range of judicial discretion has been avoided by the authoritative definition of marriage breakdown. The vagueness of the term "irretrievable marriage breakdown" has been avoided through the compromise reached between the Archbishop's Group and the Law Commission. But each of the five situations in which alone a marriage may be held to have broken down still contains terms of vagueness requiring judicial interpretation. In what circumstances may a petitioner be held to find it intolerable to live with an adulterous spouse? What kind of behavior is it that will allow a court to hold that a petitioner cannot reasonably be expected to live with the respondent? What is the "cause" or "a just cause" that allows a spouse to walk out on the other without being a deserter? What is "grave financial or other hardship to the respondent," and when would "in all circumstances it be wrong to dissolve a marriage upon the ground of five years' separation"? In what circumstances is a court in cases of a petition based upon the ground of five or two years' separation to refuse the decree because it is not satisfied that the financial provisions made by the petitioner for the respondent are reasonable and fair or the best that can be made in the circumstances?

On the much debated question of conciliation attempts, the Act takes a middle course that avoids the inanity that seems regularly to affect proceedings prescribed as a necessary preliminary to divorce suits, but suggests the desirability of a conciliation attempt for parties willing to try them.[146]

145. Matrimonial Causes Act 1965, § 1 (1) (a) (iv).
146. § 3. (1) Provision shall be made by rules of court for requiring the solicitor for the petitioner for divorce to certify whether he has discussed with the petitioner the possibility of a reconciliation and given him the names and addresses of persons qualified to help effect a reconciliation between parties to a marriage who have become estranged. (2) If at any stage of proceedings for divorce it appears to the court that there is a reasonable possibility of a reconciliation between the parties to the marriage, the court may adjourn the proceedings for such period as it thinks fit to enable attempts to effect such a reconciliation. The power conferred by the foregoing provisions is additional to any other power of the court to adjourn proceedings. The machinery is outlined in a Practice Note issued by the president of the Probate, Divorce and Admiralty Division of the High Court. Where the court considers that there is a reasonable possibility of reconciliation or of amicable settlement of matters of finance or of arrangement for the welfare of the children, the

If the courts wished it they could make divorce more difficult in England than it is today. Legal criteria expressed by higher courts are to be observed by trial courts even in undefended cases. Of course, once these criteria are defined lawyers can be expected to formulate their petitions so as to fit the facts judicially declared to be essential. But English solicitors are reluctant knowingly to induce or allow clients to lie. Some county court judge may feel impelled and may have the time conscientiously to follow the statutory command "so far as [he] reasonably can" to inquire into the fact alleged.[147] The Act provides ample possibilities for the courts to stem the tide of divorce. Whether they are willing and factually able to do so in the cultural climate of present-day England is another question. And if they were to do so, what would be the effect on informal separations and irregular unions?

We have dealt with the English divorce reform so extensively because its long preparation through the Gorell Commission, the Morton Commission, the Archbishop's Group and the Law Commission has resulted in incisive investigation and discussion. The problems that are to be considered in the pluralistic society of high industrialization have probably all been raised at one of these stages or another. The reform act has been drafted with great care and a desire for accuracy. It is a compromise and it had to be one. But it may succeed in eliminating or at least reducing the conflict between the law of the books and the law in action. It signifies an advance of liberalism, but not yet its breakthrough.

NEW YORK

In divorce law reform England was three years later than New York, the American state whose divorce law had long been the most conservative. The New York law had adhered to the principle of offense in its narrowest form: no divorce for any ground other than adultery. In addition, it is true, a marriage could be judicially terminated if one of the spouses had disappeared and for five years no information had

---

court may refer the parties to the court welfare officer. If after discussion with the parties the court welfare officer believes that there is such a reasonable possibility he may either continue to deal with the case himself, or refer the parties to a probation officer, or to a marriage guidance counsellor recommended by the local office of the appropriate organization concerned with marriage guidance and welfare, or to some other appropriate person or body indicated by the special circumstances, for example denominational of the case. Experience is stated to have shown that reconciliation is unlikely to be successful in the absence of readiness to cooperate on the part of the spouses (121 NEW L.J. 221 [1971]).

147. § 1 (2).

been received as to whether he was alive or dead,[148] and for incurable insanity that had existed for five years.[149] A marriage was regarded as automatically terminated upon one spouse's sentence to life imprisonment.[150] Out of delicacy such termination was not called divorce but dissolution of marriage in the Enoch Arden situation, annulment in the case of insanity, and civil death in the last named contingency. The number of these special modes of marriage termination was not insignificant, as shown by the data in table 23. But for "divorce" the sole ground was adultery, actually committed, staged, or faked.

TABLE 23
MARRIAGE TERMINATION IN NEW YORK, 1940–56

	1940	1945	1946	1950	1956
Divorces	7,150 (71)*	10,860 (67)	14,960 (62)	6,604 (57)	4,750 (55)
Dissolutions	590 (6)	850 (5)	950 (4)	418 (3)	300 (3)
Annulments†	2,280 (23)	4,430 (28)	8,350 (34)	4,599 (40)	3,600 (42)

Source: JACOBSON, *supra* note 105, at 113.
* Numbers in parentheses are percent of total.
† Covering all kinds, including annulments because of insanity existing at, and occurring after, the conclusion of the marriage.

Criticism of this uniquely narrow law had been mounting for decades, especially when an occasional scandal publicly demonstrated the routine character of hotel evidence and the professionalization of the "paramour" ladies. But so potent was the legislators' fear of clerical wrath that the legislature without discussion tabled even all the most modest proposals to investigate the problem.[151] Nobody wished to waken the sleeping dogs and through open discussion disturb the longstanding compromise. But, at last the changing cultural climate broke the equilibrium between conservatives and liberals and when, in 1965, the state's highest court openly revealed the inanity of the strict law of the New York books,[152] the way was opened for the reform law of 1966.[153]

In the revised version of § 170 of the Domestic Relations Law the adultery ground was broadened so as to cover not only heterosexual completed coitus but all kinds of sexual activity including homosexual

148. Dom. Rel. Law, § 7a.
149. Dom. Rel. Law, § 7 (5).
150. Penal Law, § 511 (1923); Civil Rights Law § 79a and Dom. Rel. Law § 6 (2).
151. The story is told in detail in N. M. BLAKE, THE ROAD TO RENO (1962).
152. Rosenstiel v. Rosenstiel, 16 N.Y. 2d 64, 209 N.E. 2d 709 (1965).
153. Laws 1966, ch. 254. For an analysis see H. H. FOSTER, JR. & D. J. FREED, DIVORCE REFORM LAW (1970).

and other deviate sexual activity with a person other than the spouse.[154] In addition to the dissolution of marriage automatically resulting from one spouse's being sentenced to life imprisonment a right to divorce has been predicated upon the ground of the partner's imprisonment for three or more consecutive years after marriage.[155] And three new grounds for divorce were added:

1. Cruel and inhuman treatment of the plaintiff by the defendant such that the conduct of the defendant endangers the physical or mental well-being of the plaintiff or renders it unsafe or improper for the plaintiff to cohabit with the defendant.[156]

2. Abandonment for two or more years.[157]

3. Living apart for two or more years pursuant to a decree of separation or to a written agreement executed in the form required for a deed to be recorded and filed in the county clerk's office within thirty days of execution.[158]

The first two of the new grounds constitute cases of marital misconduct of the traditional character, but cruelty is expressly defined as including acts endangering the plaintiff's *mental* well-being. It may be some time before the Court of Appeals is given an opportunity to spell out the meaning of this vague term. Until then a lower court may call mental cruelty anything it chooses in order to indicate that the plaintiff's well-being has been endangered. A court will be within the wording of the statute when it finds that a wife's mental equilibrium is in danger of being hurt by her husband's eating crackers in bed.

The most remarkable feature of the new statute is that it allows divorce upon the modified separation ground which has come to be called the "conversion ground." If pursuant to a judgment of judicial separation or to a separation agreement the parties have actually lived apart for the period specified in the law, either party is entitled to a divorce, provided he has performed the terms and conditions of the judgment or the agreement.[159] A judgment of judicial separation cannot be obtained unless the defendant is proved to have committed a marital offense. But, once the statutory waiting period has expired, the conversion of the separation into a divorce can be applied for not only by the innocent party who has obtained the judicial separation

154. § 170 (4).
155. § 170 (3).
156. § 170 (1).
157. § 170 (5).
158. § 170 (5) (6).
159. *Ibid.*

but also by the party against whom the judgment of separation was pronounced because of his marital offense. That this is the effect of the reform law has been expressly established by the Court of Appeals of New York.[160] When the stage is set for the divorce by a separation agreement, no judicial determination of guilt is made at all. As soon as the waiting period is over, the divorce is to be pronounced as a matter of course upon the application of either party, unless the petitioner has failed to abide by the agreement.

In both cases of conversion divorce the original text of the statute required that the terms of the judgment of separation or of the separation agreement be complied with "duly." But only two years later this requirement was softened so that it now suffices for the petitioner's compliance to have been substantial.[161]

The rigor of the old law was mitigated in further respects. The old bars to divorce — condonation, connivance, and recrimination — at least seem no longer to apply to any grounds for divorce except that of adultery.[162] The former restrictions on the remarriage of a guilty spouse have been abolished.[163]

By amendments enacted shortly after the Reform Act of 1968, divorce was further facilitated. The old scheme of two-step divorce requiring an interlocutory decree and a waiting period of three months was abolished.[164] The waiting period of two years required for a conversion divorce was shortened to one year.[165] The separation agreement need no longer, as originally required, be filed within thirty days after its execution. It may be filed any time prior to the commencement of the action for its conversion into a judgment of divorce.[166]

The new law thus provides three avenues toward divorce:

1. A long-road divorce by mutual consent: the parties make a separation agreement and then wait for one year.

2. A long-road divorce obtained in a contested or in an uncontested unilateral proceeding for judicial separation and followed by a waiting period of one year.

3. A short road divorce obtained (*a*) in a contested or in a unilateral proceeding upon true or faked proof of a marital offense; or (*b*) im-

---

160. Gleason v. Gleason, 308 N.Y. 2d 347, 351; 256 N.E. 2d 513, 516, 519 (1970).
161. Laws 1968, ch. 700.
162. See FOSTER & FREED, *supra* note 153, at 11.
163. Divorce Reform Law § 1 and Laws 1968, ch. 584.
164. Laws 1968, ch. 645.
165. Laws 1970, ch. 335, effective 1 September 1972; the minimum period of abandonment stated in § 170 (2) was also shortened from two years to one year.
166. Laws 1970, ch. 867.

mediately after the execution of a separation agreement falsely dated so as to make it appear to have been made prior to one year before the commencement of the action for its conversion into a judgment of divorce.[167]

The departure from the traditional strictness of the divorce law of New York was not achieved easily and not without concession to conservativism. The Reform Act does not allow divorce without the cooperation or at least the acquiescence of an "innocent" party. In addition it contains an elaborate scheme of compulsory conciliation proceeding and provisions designed to stop migratory divorce.

These safeguards against easy divorce were insisted upon by the conservatives. They may be less effective than they appeared when they were worked into the new law as a compromise. The significant fact is that the new compromise was arrived at openly after full discussions in public and in the legislature, where, *mirabile dictu*, it was adopted by 157 to 7 in the Assembly, and 64 to 1 in the Senate. The vote indicates the representatives' response to massive liberal pressure by influential individuals and, above all, by the press, especially the *New York Times*, and by powerful organizations as diverse as the Association of the Bar of the City of New York, the Protestant Council of the City of New York, the Rabbinical Council of America, the City Club of New York, and the Committee of Catholic Citizens to Support Divorce Reform.

The attack upon the relic of the eighteenth century had been well prepared. After a five year letter-writing campaign the Association of the Bar of New York was moved in July 1964 to appoint a nine-member committee to agitate actively for liberalizing the divorce law. The evasive devices were emphasized prominently: hotel evidence of adul-

---

167. This new form of collusive divorce is made possible through the peculiar wording of § 170 (6): As a preliminary to the commencement of the action for the conversion of the separation agreement into a judgment of divorce, the interested party may file with the clerk of the county of his residence either the full agreement or a short memorandum that includes no more than (*a*) the names and addresses of each party or the parties, (*b*) the date of marriage of the parties, (*c*) the date of the agreement of separation, and (*d*) the date of the subscription and acknowledgment of such agreement of separation. The one-year waiting period does not begin with the date at which the agreement is subscribed and acknowledged, an act that has to be performed before a notary public, but on the date at which it is "executed," i.e., an act for which the presence of a notary is not prescribed. Consequently, parties who do not mind a little lie may "execute" their agreement today in the morning, dating it as having been made one year earlier, "subscribe and acknowledge" it before the notary in the afternoon, and commence the action for divorce the next day. Since there is no oath involved as to the correctness of the date of execution, no perjury is committed.

tery and Reno and Mexican divorces. Of the latter it was stated that their doubtful validity endangered the status of some 200,000 divorcees and of the even larger number of children of their remarriages. The inequality of the situation was pointed out time and again. People of means, like Governor Nelson Rockefeller or Patricia Lawford, could avail themselves of migratory divorce; poor people could not and were forced into immorality. The very fact that Mr. Rockefeller could, in 1962, go through not only a divorce but a migratory one without losing prestige and without thwarting his reelection, was in itself indicative of the changed cultural climate.

In his widely read book, *The Road to Reno*, published in 1962, Professor Nelson M. Blake of the History Department of Syracuse University vividly presented the historical background of American divorce laws and of the make-believe world of the law of New York. In his testimony before the Joint Legislative Committee, Professor Blake showed that the law of 1787 had not been enacted as a device to limit divorce. If it expressed any policy at all, it was that of rendering divorce more easily accessible than it had been under the hit and miss scheme of legislative divorce. Rather than passing a special bill, an assembly committee under the chairmanship of Alexander Hamilton recommended general measures to grant divorce upon proof of adultery.[168] Erwin N. Griswold, then dean of the Harvard Law School, in his testimony before the Joint Legislative Committee elaborated upon the relation between divorce reform and the separation of church and state. The First Amendment, he stated, should limit the extent to which religious objections might be permitted to override efforts of liberalizing the law of divorce.[169] Senator Robert F. Kennedy, a prominent Catholic, came out for the reform.[170] Professor Henry H. Foster, Jr., of New York University School of Law was an indefatigable prime mover of the reform.

While the bill calling for the creation of a joint legislative committee to study New York's substantive law of divorce was pending in the legislature, the Court of Appeals, on 12 July 1965, pronounced its decisions in *Rosenstiel* v. *Rosenstiel* and *Wood* v. *Wood*.[171] Mexican consent divorces were judicially sanctioned. New York's restrictive law was rendered practically worthless. The text of the judicial opinion

168. New York Times, 28 October 1968, at 45 col. 1.
169. New York Times, 2 December 1965, at 46 col. 1.
170. New York Times, 3 February 1966, at 30 col. 2, and 7 February 1966, at 31 col. 4.
171. *Supra* note 152.

amounted to a repeal of New York's law of the books. Mexican mail order divorces and unilateral Mexican divorces, it is true, still remained unrecognized in New York. But all a New Yorker seeking a consent divorce had to do was to travel to El Paso, Texas, step over the bridge to Juárez, stay there for an hour or so, and go through the simple formalities of Chihuahua law. Now the Catholic bishops, organized in the Catholic Welfare Committee and represented by its secretary, Charles J. Tobin, became alarmed. Contrary to their attitude toward earlier efforts of divorce law reform, they had kept silent, but on 1 December 1965, the day after the spokesman of the Committee of the Association of the Bar of the City of New York appeared before the Joint Legislative Committee, the bishops announced their view. They opposed anything tantamount to divorce by consent and proposed incorporation into any reform statute of a scheme of compulsory conciliation and a proctor system similar to that of the defender of the bond, as it exists in the tribunals of the church. Their plan was not to facilitate divorce but to render it more difficult, especially as the new scheme was to be combined with an express outlawing of migratory divorces of any kind, Mexican, Reno, or other. Under such condtions the bishops were ready to accept the new ground of cruelty, but not that of two years' separation. The issue was joined. The outcome was a compromise, but one that was openly worked out in the legislature. Both sides retreated from their initial positions. The conservatives had to give up the proctor scheme and accept the conversion ground, which they had opposed as an avenue to consent divorce obtainable by a guilty party against an unwilling innocent one. As the law now stands, the party found innocent in separation proceedings cannot prevent the conversion of the separation into a divorce by the guilty one. But she can still prevent being divorced if, instead of suing for judicial separation, she just sues for a decree of support.[172]

A conservative victory of doubtful value is the exclusion of a conversion divorce in the case of a purely factual separation. The waiting period can be set in motion only by a judgment of judicial separation or a formalized separation agreement. Since it is not feasible in the United States to obtain a judicial decree or conclude a separation agreement without the assistance of lawyers, the expenses can be considerable for anyone who is not so out and out indigent that he qualifies for legal aid. Since the amendment law of 1970 the requirement that the separation agreement be filed with the county clerk is not

---

172. See FOSTER & FREED, *supra* note 153, at 23.

even a guarantee against collusive shortening of the statutory period of separate living.[173]

The conservatives successfully insisted on additional safeguards against too easy divorce. The delaying device of the interlocutory decree had to be continued from the earlier New York law. Only after the expiration of three months was the decree to become final. But this relic was abolished just two years later [174] on the alleged ground that the reason for requiring a judgment to be interlocutory only was to permit an opportunity for conciliation of the parties before the judgment became final, and that such opportunity was now provided by the new conciliation proceedings.[175] Apparently, it was feared that delay through a further device would encourage flight to Reno.

The two major concessions that had to be included in the Reform Act were the establishment of a system of conciliation as a necessary preliminary to a suit for divorce, and of a scheme to prevent the evasion of that preliminary and of the still restrictive New York law in general by resort to out-of-state migratory divorce.

The movers of the New York divorce law reform knew that they could not succeed without including in the law some system of official conciliation proceedings. So the Wilson-Sutton bill, by which the plan was introduced in the legislature, provided a conciliation system along the lines of the Conciliation Court of Los Angeles, California, the services of which are available when conciliation efforts are desired by one of the parties or both. But in order to satisfy the opposition, New York had to adopt a system patterned upon the model of Wisconsin, under which conciliation proceedings are a necessary preliminary to every suit for divorce.[176] In Wisconsin that system is said to work satisfactorily, or at least to the satisfaction of its ardent advocate, Judge Hansen.[177]

Does the conciliation scheme fulfill the expectations of its sponsors? Observers are skeptical. The conciliation bureaus provide jobs for patronage. But as Foster and Freed observe,[178] the funds that have been appropriated are insufficient to employ staffs large enough to deal with the flood of cases. No formal conciliation *hearing* is said to have been

173. *Supra* pp. 355–56.
174. Laws 1968, ch. 645.
175. Memorandum of the Joint Legislative Committee on Matrimonial and Family Laws, 2 McKinney's Session Laws of New York 2304 (1968).
176. Wis. Stat. Ann. §§ 245.001–248.08 (Supp. 1965).
177. R. W. Hansen, *Wisconsin Family Code — after Five Years*, 18 Okla. L. Rev. 68 (1965).
178. *Supra* note 153, at 6, 27 ff.

held down to the spring of 1970. The informal conciliation *conferences* seem to have been more successful in bringing about settlements of the dollar-and-cents issues, on custody of children, and on visitation rights. The authority to appoint guardians to represent the interests of children has rarely been exercised, however. But, as in Germany, the issuance of certificates stating there is no necessity for further conciliation efforts has become almost a matter of course. Less than 3 percent of divorce cases brought before conciliation bureaus have resulted in reconciliation and in most of New York the figure is said to be closer to one percent. How many of these reconciliations are lasting is unknown.

As the reconciliation scheme is short-circuited in most cases, so the attempted ban on migratory divorces is less important than it may have appeared. It is legally as good as worthless with regard to divorces obtained in Nevada or other places in the United States, and the attraction of Ciudad Juárez has diminished following the 1970 amendment of the divorce laws of Chihuahua.

The conciliation system is elaborate.[179] It is to be administered by a new set of state agencies, called conciliation bureaus, one of which is to be established in each of the nine judicial districts of the Supreme Court. The head of each such bureau is a Supreme Court justice designated by a majority of the justices of the appellate division of the judicial department in which the judicial district is located. He is the chief administrative officer of the bureau, responsible for administering and supervising the affairs of the bureau in accordance with rules and regulations promulgated by the appellate division of the appropriate judicial department. Upon the request of the supervising justice, one or more additional justices may be assigned to assist him in the performance of his duties.

The staff of each conciliation bureau consists of one or more conciliation commissioners and a number of counselors. The conciliation commissioners must be attorneys admitted to practice in New York for at least five years. The counselors are, presumably, to be experts in marriage counseling. The statute says that use may be made of public, religious, and social agencies. It is not clear whether cases are to be referred to such agencies so that conciliation conferences may be conducted through their machinery and on their premises or whether a marriage counselor employed by, or known to, an outside agency

---

179. The basic statute is art. II-B of the Domestic Relations Laws, inserted into it by Laws 1966, ch. 254.

is required to be appointed a member of the staff of the conciliation bureau in order to conduct the conferences in the office of the bureau.

No action for divorce may be sustained unless the plaintiff files a notice of commencement with the conciliation bureau of the district within which he resides. The matter is then assigned to a conciliation commissioner. If there are minor, handicapped, or incompetent children of the marriage, the commissioner may request the supervising justice to appoint an attorney, of at least five years' standing, as special guardian for the children. Within five days after the matter is assigned to him the commissioner shall notify the defendant and all other parties.[180] He is also to fix a date for the conciliation conference, but if the commissioner has been convinced "that there is no necessity for a conference" he simply issues a certificate of no necessity for a conference, the conciliation procedure is ended,[181] and the plaintiff may now proceed with his action for divorce. If the conference is not dispensed with and one of the parties has failed to appear, upon the application of the commissioner or counselor the supervising justice may issue an order of personal appearance, disobedience to which may be punished as contempt of court. If the conciliation commissioner determines that further conferences will be beneficial, he may refer the parties to a counselor. If, on the other hand, the commissioner is of the view that no further purpose will be served by a continuation of conciliation, he is to issue a certificate of no further necessity for conferences and thus terminate the conciliation proceedings. The conciliation conference which is to be held within ten days of reference of the proceedings to a counselor is to be conducted informally. With the consent of the parties, the counselor may make use of the assistance of physicians, psychiatrists, or clergymen of the parties' denomination.

Within, normally, thirty days after the matter has been assigned to him, the counselor must file with the commissioner his final report, in which he may request that the commissioner hold a "conciliation hearing."

The commissioner now, within twenty days, decides either to terminate the conciliation proceedings or to hold a conciliation hearing, which is a more formal and a more formidable affair than a conciliation conference. Attendance at the hearing is mandatory for all parties. Each party is to present evidence, cross-examine witnesses, and be "represented," which probably means "assisted," by an attorney.

---

180. This provision of § 215 I c, para. b (2) apparently means the special guardian that may have been appointed for children.
181. § 215-c, para. b (2).

If the commissioner believes that reconciliation is possible and would best serve the interests of both parties to the marriage, "*and*" any of their children, he shall apply to the supervising justice for an order requiring the parties, for a period not to exceed sixty days, to attempt to effect a reconciliation. If, however, the commissioner finds that no reconciliation is possible, or would not serve the interest of the parties "*or*" their children, he thus reports to the supervising justice and conciliation proceedings are at an end.[182]

The antimigratory divorce weapon of th New York Law of 1966 has been written into § 250 of the Domestic Relations Law.[183] The text follows, with slight modification, the Uniform Divorce Recognition Act, as proposed by the National Conference of Commissioners on Uniform State Laws in 1948.[184] The New York version reads as follows:

Proof that a person obtaining a divorce in another jurisdiction was (a) domiciled in this state within twelve months prior to the commencement of the proceedings therefor, and resumed residence in this state within eighteen months after the date of his departure therefrom, or (b) at all times after his departure from this state and until his return maintained a place of residence within this state, shall be prima facie evidence that the person was domiciled in this state when the divorce proceeding was commenced.

In the Uniform Divorce Recognition Act, the counterpart to this provision constitutes § 2. It is preceded by § 1, which provides that a divorce decree obtained in "another jurisdiction shall be of no force and effect . . . , if both parties to the marriage were domiciled" in the enacting state at the time the proceeding for divorce was commenced. This section clearly claims for the enacting state the exclusive jurisdiction to grant divorce in cases where both parties are domiciliaries. The Uniform Act is silent as to a divorce granted by a jurisdiction in which only the plaintiff is domiciled. Apparently § 2 applies to the proof of domicile in the case mentioned in § 1, and, possibly also to those cases in which only one party was domiciled in the divorcing state. Without some such preceding provision as that contained in § 1 of the Uniform Act, § 2 appears to be suspended in midair. What, after all, is the significance of domicile for the recognition of out-of-state divorces in New York? Shortly before the enactment of the statute, the Court of Appeals had held that Mexican divorces would be recognized

---

182. § 215-c.f.
183. For this much discussed provision, see FOSTER & FREED, *supra* note 153, at 25.
184. About this late, still-born product of the once powerful movement for nationally uniform legislation on divorce, see *supra* chap. 4.

in New York even if both parties were domiciled in New York, provided only that one party had actually placed foot on Mexican soil and the other party had, personally or through an attorney, participated in the proceedings. Is this rule of the *Rosenstiel* case abolished by the statute? The conservatives, upon whose urging § 250 was inserted in the reform act, apparently intended to eliminate that case, along with other opportunities to avoid the safeguards against easy divorce of New Yorkers. But have they succeeded in that intention?

In determining when its own courts are to have jurisdiction in actions for divorce, New York now requires that at least one party have a firm geographical relationship with the state, but the statute uses the term "residence" rather than "domicile." [185] Is residence equivalent to domicile? Furthermore, what is the effect of § 250 on Reno and other American sister-state divorces? In the Williams case [186] the Supreme Court of the United States declared that the divorcing court's finding of domicile is entitled to high respect and that a party who wishes to attack such a finding has the burden of proof. In *Coe* v. *Coe* and *Sherrer* v. *Sherrer*,[187] the Supreme Court of the United States declared a finding of domicile immune against attack by any party who has participated in the divorce proceedings, and in *Johnson* v. *Muelberger*[188] the immunity was declared to extend to third parties. All these decisions are based upon article IV, § 1 of the Constitution of the United States. They thus partake the force of the supreme law of the land against which a state law can have no effect. It can be said with a firm degree of certainty that, with the new § 250 in its law, New York is as unable to prevent New Yorkers from obtaining fully effective consent divorces in Reno or in any other court within the United States as it had been without that provision. The only party that might use § 250 as a weapon against sister-state consent divorces is the public prosecutor. It would be most extraordinary if a New York state's attorney would start a bigamy prosecution. It can be regarded as equally improbable that any New Yorker will be deterred from obtaining a sister-state consent divorce by fear of punishment for bigamy.

What effect § 250 will have on the temptation to seek bilateral divorces in places outside the United States is difficult to predict. New York attorneys may do well to warn clients against the risk of possible nonrecognition. But will parties regard this risk as a sufficiently serious

---

185. § 230.
186. 325 U.S 226, 65 S.Ct 1092, 89 L.Ed. 1577 (1945).
187. 334 U.S. 343, 68 S.Ct 1087, 92 L.Ed. 1429 (1948).
188. 340 U.S. 581, 71 S.Ct 474, 95 L.Ed. 552 (1951).

deterrent? Criminal prosecution for bigamy will hardly enter their consideration. The possibility of collateral attack by a third person may be considered in some situations. Attack by one of the parties is unlikely to be taken into consideration where the divorce is obtained in mutual agreement and the terms have been worked out fairly and carefully. Even in its liberalized form, the New York law with its delays, its conciliation system, and the present uncertainty as to the meaning of the term "cruel and inhuman treatment" may appear unattractive. To some extent, the attractiveness of migratory consent divorce will depend on practice of New York courts and conciliation bureaus. If certificates of no necessity for a conference continue to be obtained with ease at a conveniently accessible place, and if the easily accessible trial courts are generous in finding that the "defendant" by cruel and inhuman treatment has so endangered the mental well-being of the "plaintiff" as to render it "improper for the plaintiff to cohabit with the defendant"[189] the uncontested New York divorce may be no more time-consuming and may, besides, be cheaper than a Reno divorce or other out-of-state divorce. Nevada, in order to protect its business, quickly amended its law. Incompatibility was added to the list of grounds for divorce, and the period for which the parties have to have lived separate and apart was shortened to one year.[190]

The New York attempt to shift the compromise from the courts to the legislature does not hold the promise of full success. The consent divorces can hardly all be channeled into the "long road," with even the shortened separation period of one year. Compulsion to submit to conciliation proceedings before a government officer is even more likely in New York to be an empty formality than it is in Scandinavia, France, Germany, or Switzerland, where the conciliators do not owe their positions to political patronage. To what extent the statutory provision against migratory divorce will be effective, depends upon the courts not only of New York. The last word, at least on intra-United States divorce migration, lies with the Supreme Court of the United States, whose post-*Williams* practice indicates little inclination to close the door to consent divorce.

To some extent the new York law is likely to reduce the number of cases in which parties are separated by judicial decree or merely in fact, without being divorced. Irregular unions may be regularized and

189. § 170 n. 1.
190. Nevada Revised Statutes, § 125.010 as amended Nev.R.S. A 1967.805; see *supra* p. 76.

their offspring legitimated. But insofar as the failure to take out a divorce is due to financial considerations, regularization of the situation may require the availability of free legal aid. While legal aid is likely in the future to be more easily accessible to the "poor," it is too much to expect of the bar that it will agree to have legal aid provided to those who are able to pay but can do so only under hardship and who, instead of paying $500 for a divorce, prefer the cheaper de facto separation, perhaps combined with an inexpensive support decree. Among Negroes, the incentive to divorce may even decrease if the white man's mores should increasingly be repudiated. Expectations that the new New York law will increase the incidence of marriage breakdown among New Yorkers are as unfounded as hopes that its new safeguards will eliminate or reduce the incidence of consent divorce. And consent divorces, it ought to be remembered, constitute some 90 percent of all divorces, in New York as elsewhere.

But the New York divorce reform is remarkable, nevertheless. In the state in which conservative influence had so far prevented any mitigation of the strict divorce law of the books, the compromise that had become inevitable had to be worked out in the courts. In 1966, it was transferred to the legislature, and thus removed into the official ways of democratic process. The liberal forces had gained sufficient strength; the conservatives were no longer strong enough.

The liberal approach to divorce has found conspicuous expression in the insertion in the list of grounds of divorce of the situations of mental cruelty and the conversion ground. Cruelty, it is true, is still defined in restrictive terms. No divorce is to be granted unless the plaintiff has been treated by the defendant so cruelly and inhumanly that the plaintiff's health has been endangered so seriously as to render it unsafe or improper for the plaintiff to cohabit with the defendant. But well-being is expressly stated to include the mental; and when is it "improper" for a spouse to cohabit with the other? The terms here used are vague. They will mean what the courts say they mean, and New York trial judges have been known for their permissive attitude. Of course, this attitude was provoked by the rigor of the old law. But will it be changed under a statute that can be read as officially sanctioning that kind of interpretation that has been placed by the courts of other states upon terms of seemingly equal or even greater stringency? Why should courts of New York be more reluctant than those of California?

Even more remarkable is the abandonment by the New York legislature of the time-honored view that divorce is to be a punishment for misconduct and a reward for innocence. Where a divorce is sought upon the ground of the parties' failure to live together, the question of guilt is no longer asked. The divorce is granted because the marriage has factually broken down, perhaps without anybody's fault. *Divorce sanction* is turned into *divorce faillite*. Where the separation has been initiated by a separation agreement, guilt plays no role either. New York has thus joined the continuously growing number of states abandoning the guilt principle and allowing in the official law divorce on the objective basis of marriage breakdown without inquiry into the question of fault.[191]

191. On the following, see W. E. McCurdy, *Divorce — a Suggested Approach with Particular Reference to Dissolution for Living Separate and Apart*, 9 VAND.L.REV. 685 (1956); W. Wadlington, *Divorce without Fault, without Perjury*, 52 VA.L.REV. 32 (1966).

15
The Liberal Breakthrough, II: California, the Commissioners on Uniform State Laws, and the Federal Republic of Germany

CALIFORNIA

A big, indeed a radical, step in the new direction was taken in the California Law of 1969, which may be read as sanctioning short-road divorces not only in the case of consent but also upon unilateral petition. Radical steps are also proposed in the Draft Uniform Marriage and Divorce Act of the National Conference of Commissioners on Uniform State Laws and in drafts produced in the Federal Republic of Germany, in Sweden, and in the Netherlands.

In California, the new law of divorce or, as it is now called, dissolution of marriage, forms part of a comprehensive revision of a major sector of family law. The Family Law Act also deals with conclusion of marriage, judicial determination of void or voidable marriages, custody and support of children and the relations between husband and wife including marital property rights. By Statutes 1969, chapter 1608, § 8,[1] the act was added to the California Civil Code as part 5 of division 4. Its sections thus have the numbers under which they appear in the Civil Code.

The key provisions on dissolution of marriage are brief. They read as follows:

Sec. 4506. A court may decree a dissolution of the marriage or legal separation on either of the following grounds, which shall be pleaded generally:

---

1. Approved by the governor on 4 September 1969, Calif. Statutes and Amendments to the Codes 1969, vol. 2, p. 3312. A number of provisions of the Family Law Act were amended by chapter 1609 (Statutes, vol. 2, p. 3351), enacted simultaneously with chapter 1608 and approved by the governors on the same day.

(1) Irreconcilable differences, which have caused the irremediable breakdown of the marriage.

(2) Incurable insanity.

Sec. 4507. Irreconcilable differences are those grounds which are determined by the court to be substantial reasons for not continuing the marriage and which make it appear that the marriage should be dissolved.

Sec. 4508. (a) If from the evidence of the hearing and contained in the confidential questionnaire the court finds that there are irreconcilable differences, which have caused the irremediable breakdown of the marriage, it shall order the dissolution of the marriage. . . . If it appears that there is a reasonable possibility of reconciliation, the court shall continue the proceeding for a period not to exceed 30 days. . . . At any time after the termination of such 30-day period, either party may move for the dissolution of the marriage or a legal separation, and the court may enter its judgment decreeing such dissolution or separation.

This text is a compromise that was worked out obviously in a hurry and in the last stage of discussions that had extended over many years and in the course of which the most diverse ideas had been expressed. In the early stages carefully considered plans had been suggested. The version that was ultimately adopted is poorly drafted. Indeed, its literal application is impossible. Any court may give it almost any meaning. If the statute was meant to provide for the termination of the marriage bond in the case of the factual breakdown of the marital community of life, it fails to indicate any standard by which one is to determine the meaning of the vague term of marriage breakdown. But the text makes things worse by requiring that the breakdown be "irremediable" and that it be caused by "irreconcilable differences."

If one were to take literally the words "irremediable" and "irreconcilable," no marriage could ever be judicially dissolved. Human conduct is even less predictable than the weather. Wisely, the weatherman refrains from flatly predicting rain or sunshine and limits himself to the announcement of a higher or lower percentage of probability of measurable precipitation. Even in the case of a profoundly deep split in the marital community, the possibility of reconciliation is never completely excluded, even though the probability may be as low as one-hundredth of 1 percent. So what is meant in the statute is obviously a marriage breakdown with a low probability of being remedied. But how low must the probability be: 20 percent, or 10, or 1, or 49? If one said that the chance of the breakdown's being remedied must be so low that no cure can reasonably be expected, the margin of judicial freedom would not be perceptibly narrowed. The very vagueness of the term "marriage breakdown," with or without such meaningless adjectives as "irremediable,'" has prompted careful legislative draftsmen to supplement statutory pronouncements of the principle of breakdown by modifiers of more clearly ascertainable meaning. Under the new English law marriage breakdown is to be presumed if one party has committed adultery, or if the parties have lived separate from each other for two years, or if one spouse's conduct has created a situation intolerable to the other. In the draft of the minister of justice of the Federal Republic of Germany it is proposed that irremediable breakdown is to be regarded as proved irrefutably if the parties have lived separate for three years, or, if one party objects, for five years. The Scandinavian laws have long contained provisions of this kind. The wide range left to judicial discretion has long been criticized in Switzerland, and how inconvenient it can be has been shown by Górecki's inquiry into the practice of Polish divorce courts.[2] Proposals to make more definite the concept of marriage breakdown by providing for its irrefutable assumption in the case of joint petition or insistent unilateral applications had been proffered in the course of the California discussions. Apparently the proposals seemed too liberal to conservative legislators, whose efforts, in turn, did not appeal to the liberals. The way out thus was a compromise text devoid of any perceptible standard.

To make things worse, the text requires that the "irremediable breakdown" of the marriage be caused by "irreconcilable differences." The meaning of this term is cryptic. The differences meant are apparently those between human beings, specifically those existing between a husband and his wife. But what kind of differences? Probably not differences in height or weight, or in the color of the skin or the hair. But what about differences in health, or in sexual characteristics? What if one spouse is bursting with health and the other debilitated by cancer, or if one desires sexual intercourse twice a day and the other is ready just once a week? Probably the draftsmen, if they had any clear idea at all, thought of differences of character, temperament, or attitude. The fact that the difference in health produced by one party's incurable insanity is added as a separate ground for dissolution of marriage seems to point in this direction. But if this interpretation is correct, dissolution of marriage may be excluded in all cases of purely objective differences between the spouses other than those due to insanity. Even where the marital community has "irremediably" broken down because of the husband's captivity as a prisoner of war or as a

---

2. JAN GÓRECKI, DIVORCE IN POLAND 28 (1970).

political suspect incarcerated by a totalitarian regime, or because of one party's physical disease, the marriage could not be dissolved. Is this an intended result? Furthermore, when are differences "irreconcilable"? What has been said about the impossibility of predicting the irremediability of a marriage breakdown applies with equal strength.

The definition of irreconcilable differences given by the text itself does not help to remove the difficulties. Indeed they are rather increased by the wording: "Irreconcilable differences are those *grounds* which are determined by the court to be substantial reasons for not continuing the marriage and which make it appear that the marriage should be dissolved."

The differences in order to be irreconcilable must thus be "grounds." Of what, we must ask? Standing alone and by itself, the word "grounds" makes no sense. Vaguely thinking of the traditional practice of speaking of grounds for divorce, the draftsmen apparently wished to refer to those *facts* which the following part of the sentence seeks to describe. The interpretation of "grounds" as "facts" is expressly indicated in § 4509, which generally excludes from the proceedings the evidence of specific acts of misconduct, except where at the hearing such evidence is determined by the court to be necessary to establish the existence of irreconcilable differences. As the text reads, facts do not fit the description until they have been determined by the court to do so. If it were taken literally, the sentence would make no sense. How can a court determine whether or not it is to determine that certain facts fit a certain legal description? But since we can assume that the sentence is not meant to be understood literally, the lapsus in logic need not bother us. But what must bother the California courts, the divorce seekers, and the public is the lack of clarity of the standard the courts are meant to apply. What facts are "substantial reasons" for not continuing the marriage? And what is meant by "continuing the marriage": the marital life in common, or the formal marriage bond? What is meant is probably the former, because otherwise it would make no sense to provide that the facts in question must "make it appear that the marriage should be dissolved." Apparently, § 4507 must then be understood as if it read as follows:

"Irreconcilable differences are those facts which are substantial reasons for the parties discontinuing their marital life and which make it appear to the court that the marriage bond should be terminated."

Even when it is read in this way the passage remains ambiguous. The court has to decide whether or not the facts make it appear that the bond should be terminated. Does this determination follow with necessity from the determination that the facts in question are substantial reasons for the parties to discontinue their married life, or is the second determination to be made in addition to the former? In that case the dissolution of the marriage might, or perhaps must, be denied even if there are substantial reasons for the parties' discontinuing their marital life, if the situation fails to appear to the judge sufficiently grave to justify (or to demand?) the termination of the bond. For neither determination, that of the substantiality of the reasons for the parties' discontinuing their marital life, or that of the sufficiency of these reasons for the judicial termination of the bond, does the court find any guidance in the statute. The defect is not even remedied if we assume that the determination, or the determinations, must be made in accordance with reason. In the controversial field of divorce what is reasonable to a liberal may well be unreasonable to a conservative, and vice versa.

If we move on to § 4508, we find ourselves confronted with another riddle:

If from the evidence . . . the court finds that there are irreconcilable differences, which have caused the irremediable breakdown of the marriage, it shall order the dissolution of the marriage.

So far, so good. But then the text continues:

If it appears that there is a reasonable possibility of reconciliation, the court shall continue the proceeding for a period not to exceed 30 days. . . . At any time after the termination of such 30-day period, either party may move for the dissolution of the marriage . . . and the court may enter its judgment decreeing such dissolution.

How can it appear to a court that there is a reasonable possibility of reconciliation when it has already found that there are irreconcilable differences which have caused the irremediable breakdown of the marriage? Either the breakdown is irremediable or there is a reasonable possibility of reconciliation. The two situations mutually exclude each other. So it seems that we must read the two sentences as referring to two different situations. If the court finds that there are *truly* irreconcilable differences which have caused the *truly* irremediable breakdown of the parties' marital life, the court shall order the dissolution of the marriage. But if it appears to the court that the differences are not irreconcilable, it shall continue the proceeding for a period not to exceed thirty days. Then, when that period has expired, either party may move for the dissolution of the marriage and the court may enter its judgment decreeing such dissolution.

Does this mean that the marriage is to be dissolved even though the court has found that the parties' marital life has not irremediably broken down? Is the parties' failure to reach a reconciliation within the period irrefutable evidence of the irremediability of the breakdown? Note that no evidence is required that any effort at reconciliation has actually been made, and that this period of continuance, while it may not exceed thirty days, may be shorter, conceivably as short as one day or one hour. Or has the period always to be thirty days? In its last part the sentence speaks of "such 30-day period," and the "such" cannot but refer back to the preceding words which clearly state that the period is *not to exceed 30* days.

Is it really meant that a California court is to dissolve a marriage upon the unilateral motion of one party when it has found that the marriage has *not* irremediably broken down and a period has elapsed the maximum length of which is thirty days? That would be a breakthrough more radical than liberal.

Perhaps some weight should be attached to the variation of the verbs meant to guide the court. If it is found that there are irreconcilable differences and that they have caused the irremediable breakdown of the marriage, the court "shall" order the dissolution of the marriage. But where it appears that there is a reasonable possibility of reconciliation, the proceeding has been continued, the period set by the court has expired, and one party moves for the dissolution of the marriage, the court "may" enter such a judgment. Is that to mean that in the second case the court has a measure of discretion which it does not have in the former? How would such an interpretation square with the wording of § 4506, the basic provision, where it is also stated that a court *may* decree a dissolution of the marriage on the grounds of either the irremediable breakdown of the marriage caused by irreconcilable differences, or of incurable insanity? It can hardly be assumed that the court is meant to have the power to refuse the decree of dissolution where one or the other of the two grounds is proved. Such an interpretation would be flatly contradicted by the first sentence of § 4508 (a), where it is said that the court *shall* order dissolution if irremediable breakdown is proved. But then we encounter again the verb "may" in § 4510 dealing with the case of proved incurable insanity. So we are forced to conclude that the verbs "may" and "shall" are used interchangeably and without an intention to express a difference of meaning.

Obviously, the statutory text is a compromise hammered together in haste. As it fails to convey a clear meaning, the compromise may appear to be a specially poor one. But considering the subject matter, the compromise may be not so poor as it seems to be. All references to marital misconduct are gone. Apart from the special situation of incurable insanity, there is only one single ground for divorce: irremediable breakdown. True enough, this term is susceptible of a great variety of interpretations, especially when, as the statute says, the breakdown must be caused by irreconcilable differences. A conservative judge may use this formula to deny the dissolution of a marriage in situations in which under the former law a divorce might have been had for the asking, upon true or faked evidence. But are California trial judges likely to be conservative? Few have been so in the past. They have handled the old statute so that a divorce was hardly ever denied and thus the California divorce rate has been one of the highest in the nation. Nothing but the requirement of a minimum residence of one year in the state, and the delay produced by the interposition of an interlocutory decree, prevented California from being a competitor with Nevada. The words "irreconcilable" and "irremediable" have obviously been inserted in the text as a sop to the conservatives. The effect is likely to be as negative as it was in France when, during the Vichy regime, the possibility of obtaining a divorce upon the ground of cruelty, physical or mental, was meant to be limited by inserting into the text of article 231 of the French Civil Code the qualification that the "acts constitute a grave or a repeated violation of the duties and obligations of marriage and render intolerable the continuance of the marital bond" (Law of 2 April 1941, as modified by ordinance of 12 April 1945).

In 1963, the movement to modify the divorce law of California started as an effort not to turn the tide of conservative resistance to divorce but to stem the rising tide of divorce, to lessen the very high divorce rate of the state as a whole and of some counties in particular.

In the United States the ratio of divorces to marriages in 1940 was 16.5 percent and in 1960, 25.6 percent. In California the ratio in 1940 was 51 percent, in 1960, 47 percent. In Sacramento County in 1940 it was 62.7 percent and in 1960, 69.1 percent. In Napa County, the rate per 1,000 population in 1940 was 5.9 divorces and annulments but only 4.6 marriages. The ratio of divorces to marriages was thus 127.3 percent. In 1960, it had dropped to 73.3 percent.[3]

These figures looked alarming, and so did the data on high school

3. Assembly Interim Committee Reports 1964–65, Final Report of the Assembly Interim Committee on Judiciary, Relating to Family Relations (vol. 23, no. 63), 50–51.

student marriages and pregnancies assembled by Professor Judson T. Landis.[4] His inquiry was initiated by the Assembly Judiciary Committee, before which, on 8 January 1964, Governor Edward G. Brown stated his intention to ask the committee to expand its hearings on California domestic relations law. In his message of 4 March 1964 he urged the committee to "make a serious inquiry into [the] *festering* problem."

> Statistics [he said] seem to show clearly how divorce erodes the very foundation of our society — the family. The statistics indicate that some 75 per cent of our juvenile delinquents and more than 50 per cent of the inmates of our penal institutions come from broken homes. These are shocking statistics. They tell of an erosion of our precepts and institutions which are so dependent on the endurance, stability, and sanctity of the home.
> Great civilizations have faltered and ultimately perished and vanished from the earth through moral decadence. These were civilizations without our capacity to communicate. We must utilize our talents and facilities to probe and expose the core of this growing social problem.[5]

As so often before, divorce and breakup of a home were thus regarded as identical. But the Judiciary Committee was impressed by the statistics that had already been presented to it, as well as by the governor's appeal. It continued and expanded its inquiry. By a resolution adopted on 9 March 1964,[6] a special legislature advisory committee on family life and law was established. Its extensive report was transmitted to the speaker and the members of the Assembly on 11 January 1965. This document of 182 printed pages does not deal with the divorce problem as a whole, but with a number of separate aspects as well as related matters.[7]

In connection with plans to safeguard family stability through more adequate laws on marriage and divorce, the committee recommended that the Californian legislature memorialize the United States Congress to enact a constitutional amendment which would authorize Congress to establish minimal residence requirements in the various states of the country. The aim was not the enactment by Congress of a federal law on marriage and divorce but a scheme that would eliminate the possibility through migratory divorce to evade those safeguards which each state would regard as appropriate.

4. *Id.* 54–58.
5. Report, 176.
6. Assembly Journal, p. 1258.
7. Such as a collection of statistical material on registration of divorces, annulments, and decrees of separate maintenance; youthful marriage and parenthood as affecting family stability; matters of property settlement, alimony, and custody; problems of procedure, etc.

Finally, the committee found that

1. Marriage, family life and divorce problems continue to be a major area of concern in California. The number of people affected and the potential disruption of the stability of future generations constitute a serious threat to our society.

2. The incidence of family instability and inadequacy, as reflected in the voluminous number of judicial proceedings which are instituted as a result of family failure, warrants a thorough study of our existing judicial structures and procedures, as well as our statutory enactments, to ascertain methods and laws which will ameliorate present deficiencies.

Hence, the committee recommended "continuance of the present study of marriage and divorce laws, with adequate staff and resources to permit a complete and comprehensive examination."

In response the governor, on 11 May 1966, established the Governor's Commission on the Family. Among its twenty-two members were two state senators and one assemblyman, five judges, six attorneys, one social worker, four physicians with expertise in psychiatry and gynecology, one churchman, and two law professors (Herma Hill Kay and Aidan R. Gough, who was the executive director of the commission).

The governor charged the commission with four responsibilities:

1. to study and suggest revisions, where necessary, of the substantive laws of California relating to the family;
2. to determine the feasibility of developing significant and meaningful courses in family life education to be offered in the public schools;
3. to consider the possibility and desirability of developing uniform national standards of marriage and divorce jurisdiction; and
4. to examine into the establishment of Family Courts on a statewide basis and to recommend the procedures whereby they may function most effectively.

Because of time pressure the commission found it necessary to focus its efforts upon the first and fourth points and to reserve the rest for future study. The report thus concentrated on the substantive and procedural laws of divorce.[8] Just like the Archbishop's Group in England, the California commission recommended the abandonment of the principle of matrimonial offense. The reasons were the same: commission of a matrimonial offense constitutes guilt in a formalistic sense only; guilt in the true sense almost always lies with both parties; the commission of a matrimonial offense does not by itself indicate that the marriage is no longer viable; the necessity of alleging a matrimonial offense creates an atmosphere of hostility in which it is diffi-

---

8. For a summary of the report, see R. C. Dinkelspiel & A. R. Gough, *A Family Court Act for Contemporary California*, 42 ST. B. CAL. J. 363 (1967).

cult to settle the issues of child custody and support, of property settlement and alimony; the commission of an offense can be feigned so that insincerity and perjury may be induced to the detriment of the respect for the law and the courts. The commission added another ground, the incompatibility of the principle of offense with the function of a family court as envisaged by the commission. While it would thus no longer be necessary or sufficient to prove adultery, desertion, cruelty, or any other of the matrimonial offenses enumerated in the existing law of California, it should be possible to obtain a divorce upon the initiative of either party. The proceedings could be assumed normally to last about eight months. The proposed new law was more liberal than those of Sweden or Japan or even the Prussian Code of 1791. The commission also proposed to abolish the interlocutory decree that under the then existing California law had to precede the decree absolute by at least one year, and also to shorten from twelve months the time one or the other of the parties must have resided in the state in order to confer divorce jurisdiction upon its courts. The requirements would thus be eased not only of the official law but also of the law in action.

The commission's extreme liberality in stating the grounds for divorce was counterbalanced by the proposal of an elaborate system of family courts. It is hard to say whether this proposal was meant as a serious check or as window dressing. But so conspicuous was this part of the report that it was apt all but to obscure the section under which a decree of "dissolution" of marriage" should be obtainable upon the unilateral motion of one party who need not specify any particular ground, as soon as some eight months more or less had expired since the filing of the initial petition.

This petition, to be styled "In re the marriage of A and B," was to be called "petition of inquiry." In it the court would be requested to inquire into the continuance of the marriage (§ 017). A family court was to be a division of the superior court of each county. Following the admonition of Paul Alexander and other advocates of the family court plan, the new court was to have comprehensive jurisdiction in all matters of family law, including juvenile delinquency, but, unlike the Japanese system, exclusive of matters of probate and administration of decedents' estates. The judges, it was hoped, would be interested and experienced in family matters. They were to be aided by a staff of professionals trained in counseling. This staff was to go to work when a petition of inquiry had been filed. But it was not to hold an inquest as proposed in *Putting Asunder*. It was rather to proceed like the counselors of a Japanese family court, to explore whether and in what ways a reconciliation might be possible, to help the parties, through efforts of its own or through recommendation of an outside counselor or agency, and, if it appeared that the parties would not decide to be reconciled, consult with them "for the purpose of working out a settlement of the circumstances attendant upon the dissolution of the marriage including the problems of child custody and visitation" (§ 019). The counselor would then submit a report to the judge. If he found that "the legitimate objects of matrimony have been destroyed and that there is no reasonable likelihood that the marriage can be saved," he would immediately make an order dissolving the marriage (§ 028). If the court failed immediately to dissolve the marriage, the proceeding would be continued for a period not to exceed ninety days "during which time the parties *may, if they so desire*, pursue further the possibility of continuing the marriage" (§ 029). "If, at the end of the ninety-day period . . . the decision *of one* or both parties is that the marriage should be terminated, the court shall enter its order, effective when made, dissolving the marriage" (§ 029).[9]

The court proceeding for the dissolution of a marriage by mutual consent or upon unilateral petition was thus to go through a series of stages, beginning with an interview by a counselor and through one or several judicial hearings leading up to the final decree. For each stage definite time limits were set. The total amounted to a minimum of about eight months, but in a busy court with a crowded calendar the period would have been likely to be longer, perhaps even considerably.

The plan of the California governor's commission was a compromise. In one and the same piece of legislation the commission sought to bring together the essentially conservative family court plan and a divorce law of the books that in effect was to be more liberal than even the existing California law in action. While the former tendency was emphasized, the latter required some scrutiny to be discovered.

Although the commission was meticulously anxious to make sure that lawyers would have to, or at least could, participate in all steps of the proceedings, the report did not meet with a friendly reception by the bar. A highly critical article was published in the state bar journal,[10] and the board of governors of the State Bar Association, at its February 1968 meeting, disapproved the proposed Family Court Act in the form in which it was submitted by Assembly bill 230 and Senate

---

9. My italics, in both passages.
10. J. L. Goddard, *The Proposal for Divorce upon Petition and without Fault*, 43 ST. B. CAL. J. 90 (1967).

bill 88 which later was withdrawn from the current legislative session. In its resolution the board of governors referred the report to the State Bar Association Committee on Family Law requesting it to engage in further studies of the report and of several specific problems.

The bar may have been primarily responsible for the elimination from California divorce reform of the family court plan. Helped by taxpayers' desire for economy and the difficulty of finding sufficient numbers of trained personnel, tendencies to broaden the existing scheme of conciliation courts were also stopped.[11]

Conservative forces in California succeeded in preserving the institution of the interlocutory decree. But the time period that must elapse before its transformation into a final decree of dissolution of marriage has been shortened to six months and, this is of importance, that period begins no longer at the date of the interlocutory decree but with that "of service of a copy of summons and petition or of the appearance of the respondent" (§ 4514). In a court with a crowded docket the period may well be over before any decree is rendered so that a decree absolute can be made forthwith.

11. Conciliation courts are established only in those counties the superior court of which determines that the social conditions in the county and the number of domestic relations cases in the courts render conciliation procedures necessary to protect the rights of children and to promote the public welfare by preserving and promoting family life and the institution of marriage and to provide means for the reconciliation of spouses and the amicable settlement of domestic and family controversies (California Code of Civil Procedure, §§ 1733, 1730). In major counties, the conciliation court is to have a staff of expert counselors (§§ 1744–45). In 1970, fourteen of the fifty-eight counties of the state had a conciliation court, among them San Francisco and Los Angeles. Even though no case is pending in court, the services of the conciliation court may be invoked by a parent if the welfare of a minor child may be adversely affected by the dissolution of the marriage of the parent or the disruption of the household (§§ 1760, 1761). If such a petition has been filed, neither party may commence a suit for dissolution of marriage, annulment, or separation until the expiration of thirty days after the hearing (§ 1770). If a suit is already pending, the court may transfer the case to the conciliation court if the welfare of minor children is involved and if there appears some reasonable possibility that a conciliation can be effected (§ 1771). Cases not involving the welfare of children need be accepted only if the work of the court in cases involving children will not be seriously impeded (§ 1772). The California system of conciliation has the special feature that a reconciliation agreement made between the parties may, with the consent of the parties, be reduced to a court order so that it is enforceable as such, if necessary by punishment for contempt of court (§ 1769). The conciliation courts vary in the practice of inducing the parties to enter upon such enforceable conciliation agreements. The Family Law Act of 1969 provides that in those counties which have established a conciliation court, the petitioner shall complete and file a questionnaire and that a responsive pleading which the respondent chooses to file, must be accompanied by a similar document. Both questionnaires shall be confidential. They are solely meant to inform the court of those facts which it needs to know in deciding whether or not to refer the case to the conciliation court (§ 4506).

Elimination from the proceedings of allegation of misconduct and wrangling about guilt is one of the principal aims of the new California law. This desire has found expression not only in the substitution of the objective ground of breakdown for the former misconduct grounds, but also in what constitutes the most far-reaching innovation of the new scheme, the elimination of guilt as a determinant in the decision about property settlement, alimony, and child custody.

The parties are prohibited from presenting evidence of specific acts of misconduct. Only two exceptions are permitted. The court may admit the evidence of specific acts of misconduct which it considers necessary to establish the existence of irreconcilable differences. It may furthermore admit such evidence where child custody is an issue and the evidence is relevant to that issue (§ 4509). In neither of these cases is the issue constituted by misconduct as such. In neither could the court make a decision if it were barred from information about circumstances which might constitute essential indicia.

In its determination of child custody, the court is guided by the following provisions:

§ 4600.
In any proceeding where there is at issue the custody of a minor child, the court may, during the pendency of the proceeding, or at any time thereafter, make such order for the custody of such child during his minority as may seem necessary or proper. If a child is of sufficient age and capacity to reason so as to form an intelligent preference as to custody, the court shall consider and give due weight to his wishes in making an award of custody or modification thereof. Custody should be awarded in the following order of preference:
(a) To either parent according to the best interests of the child, but, other things being equal, custody shall be given to the mother if the child is of tender years.
(b) To the person or persons in whose home the child has been living in a wholesome and stable environment.
(c) To any other person or persons deemed by the court to be suitable and able to provide adequate and proper care and guidance for the child.
Before the court makes any order awarding custody to a person or persons other than a parent, without the consent of the parents, it must make a finding that an award of custody to a parent would be detrimental to the child, and the award to a nonparent is required to serve the best interests of the child. Allegations that parental custody would be detrimental to the child, other than a statement of that ultimate fact, shall not appear in the pleadings. The court may, in its discretion, exclude the public from the hearing on this issue.

California is one of the nine jurisdictions in the United States in which property acquired during marriage through the exertion by either party does not belong to him alone but to both parties as their community property.[12] Property that was owned by a spouse before the conclusion of the marriage, or that is acquired during marriage by inheritance, gift, or testamentary provision, is that spouse's separate property.[13]

When a marriage is judicially dissolved, the distribution of the property and the question of alimony or, as it is called in the California law, support, which may be payable by one spouse to the other, are primarily determined by the parties' own agreement.[14] As anywhere, such agreements are made in the great majority of cases in which there is enough property to make regulation worthwhile. Formerly, where no agreement could be worked out, determination had to be made by the court, in whose decision the question of guilt was of essential importance. Indeed, contesting an action for divorce regularly served no purpose other than that of forestalling an adverse adjudication of guilt and its dollar-and-cent consequences. Through the elimination of guilt from the proceedings settlement negotiations are now greatly facilitated. The parties know that in the absence of agreement each spouse keeps his separate property and the community fund is simply split fifty-fifty (§ 4800). But grounds for negotiation could not be completely eliminated. The equal division of the community property may have to be modified in order to make adjustment as compensation for prior expenditures or mismanagement, or for the awarding to one spouse a particular asset in specie. But guilt is not to be considered when it falls to the court to decide such issues. Nor is guilt to play any role when the court is asked to make a decision on post-marital support. The factors to be considered in that respect are stated in § 4801 as follows:

(a) In any judgment decreeing the dissolution of a marriage or a legal separation of the parties, the court may order a party to pay for the support of the other party any amount, and for such period of time, as the court may deem just and reasonable having regard for the circumstances of the respective parties, including the duration of the marriage, and the ability of the supported spouse to engage in gainful employment without interfering with the interests of the children of the parties in the custody of such spouse. The court may order the party required to make such payment of support to give reasonable security therefor. Any order for support of the other party may

---

12. The other eight community property jurisdictions are Arizona, Idaho, Louisiana, Montana, New Mexico, Puerto Rico, Texas, and Washington.
13. See California Civil Code §§ 5107 ff.
14. See §§ 4802, 4801 (b), 4811.

be modified or revoked as the court may deem necessary, except as to any amount that may have accrued prior to the date of the filing of the notice of motion or order to show cause to modify or revoke. The order of modification or revocation may be made retroactive to the date of filing of the notice of motion or order to show cause to modify or revoke.

(b) Except as otherwise agreed by the parties in writing, the obligation of any party under any order or judgment for the support and maintenance of the other party shall terminate upon the death of the obligor or upon the remarriage of the other party.

(c) Except as otherwise agreed by the parties in writing, the court may, upon petition of either party, modify or revoke any decree or judgment granting any allowance to the other party upon proof that the wife is living with another man and holding herself out as his wife, although not married to such man, or that the husband is living with another woman and holding himself out as her husband, although not married to such woman, except as to any amount that may have accrued prior to the filing of the petition.

(d) When a court orders a person to make specified payments for support of the other party for a contingent period of time, the liability of such person terminates upon the happening of such contingency. If the party to whom payments are to be made fails to notify the person ordered to make such payments, or the attorney of record of such person, of the happening of such contingency and continues to accept support payments, such party shall refund any and all moneys received which accrued after the happening of such contingency, except that such overpayments shall first be applied to any and all support payments which are then in default. The court may, in the original order for support, order the party to whom payments are to be made to notify the person ordered to make such payments, or his attorney of record, of the happening of such contingency.

(e) An order for payment of an allowance for the support of one of the parties shall terminate at the end of the period specified in the order and shall not be extended unless the court in its original order retains jurisdiction.

The full switch made by the 1969 law from misconduct to breakdown pure and simple is radical as far as the law of the book is concerned. For the law in action, it has been less spectacular. In those 90 percent or more of the cases in which the parties were in consent, the interlocutory decree could be had for the asking. Now the period of waiting for the final decree and thus for the freedom of remarriage has been shortened,[15] as has also the period of residence required for the filing of divorce proceedings. Formerly, the plaintiff had to be a resident of the state for one year and of the county for three months.[16] Now the former requirement has been shortened to six months.[17]

The temptation to go the shorter road of a Nevada or other out-of-

---

15. *Supra* p. 378.
16. California Civil Code § 128.
17. § 4530 (a).

state divorce has thus been alleviated. Nevertheless, California has kept on its statute book the Uniform Divorce Recognition Act, which it adopted in 1949. It is now continued in §§ 5000–5004 of the Civil Code. Contrary to New York, where only the second section of the Uniform Law has been adopted and worked into the Divorce Reform Law of 1966, California has adopted the full text, which bluntly states that "a divorce in another jurisdiction shall be of no force and effect in this state if both parties to the marriage were domiciled in this state at the time the proceeding for the divorce was commenced" (§ 5001).

The presumptions of domicile stated in the second section (i.e., § 5002) of the California text are thus not suspended in midair as they are in the New York Domestic Relations Law.[18] But efforts to evade the new California law are likely to be much less frequent than those intended to eliminate the long time span required in New York for a divorce applied for under the separation ground, and to avoid the compulsory arbitration feature of New York. For good measure, the California law also states as § 5004 what is obvious anyway, namely, that "the application of [the Divorce Recognition Act] is limited by the requirements of the Constitution of the United States that full faith and credit shall be given in each state to the public acts, records and judicial proceedings of every other state."

THE NATIONAL CONFERENCE OF COMMISSIONERS ON
UNIFORM STATE LAWS

To stem the rising tide of divorce through unification was one of the motives, or we should rather say, the principal motive, for the establishment of the National Conference of Commissioners on Uniform State Laws.[19] But, in spite of many efforts, nothing of note was achieved and for a long period of time divorce practically disappeared from the agenda of the conference. Nevertheless, the Special Committee on Uniform Divorce and Marriage Laws was kept in existence. In 1965, this committee made a new beginning. Apparently stirred by the events in neighboring New York, Governor Hughes of New Jersey initiated efforts to modernize the divorce law of his state, one of the strictest in the country. The two co-chairmen of the conference committee, both from New Jersey, felt impelled to give nationwide scope to this effort. The report by which they moved the conference to action reflects a spirit different from that which had prompted earlier

18. See *supra* p. 362.
19. *Supra* p. 47.

The Liberal Breakthrough, II

work of the conference.[20] The aim was no longer to be repression. In accord with the English plans, the report suggested the abandonment of the traditional "forms of action" approach under which a divorce was to be granted if, and only if, adultery, desertion, or extreme cruelty has been proved to the court. The authors of the report felt troubled by the prevalence of contrivance and by migratory divorce. Hinting at the case of Governor Rockefeller, they said:

When the wife of a wealthy governor of our greatest state goes 2,500 miles to a foreign jurisdiction for the purpose of consummating a divorce upon which the parties have previously agreed, it is obviously time for something to be done. The artificial limitations on divorce in our most enlightened jurisdiction foster fictions of jurisdiction, perjury and direspect for the law and are equally reprehensible. As debilitating as the existing hodgepodge of laws on divorce and marriage may be for the lives of the participants, the destructive effect upon children is incalculable. If the time for improvement and uniformity in this field were not at hand for the sake of the marriage partners, it is surely at hand for the sake of the children.

In what ways children might suffer from the present state and diversity of the divorce laws, is not spelled out. But when the authors ask whether the proof of adultery shall always be a sensible reason for the dissolution of a marriage, without regard to the destructive effect of that dissolution upon the lives of the children involved, it is apparent that the authors have fallen into the old confusion between breakdown of the home and dissolution of the bond of a marriage which has ceased to function.

For the reasons stated "and others too long to be detailed," the chairman of the committee urged that a new departure be made.

It requires an elimination of the Forms of Action approach to the administration of the divorce laws. It requires an analysis of the entire subject of the custody of children as an integral part of drafting any legislation on the subject of Marriage and Divorce.

To this end are recommended the recruitment of an able paid staff with time to devote to the necessary research and careful drafting. This staff and the Committee should consult with an Advisory Committee consisting of representation from the fields of psychiatry, religion, social work, and every other phase of our society which has a bearing on the issues involved.

A progress report was submitted by the committee one year later. It expressly referred to the completion of the divorce law reform in New York and the repudiation of the principle of marital offense by the Group convoked by the Archbishop of Canterbury. It also recited

---

20. HANDBOOK OF THE NATIONAL CONFERENCE OF COMMISSIONERS ON UNIFORM STATE LAWS, 1965, at 181.

various efforts made by the members of the committee to incite the interest of the public in the cause of divorce law reform and uniformity, and the elaboration of a prospectus and its submission to a number of foundations.[21]

In 1967 a generous grant was made by the Ford Foundation for research, deliberation, and drafting necessary for promulgation of a uniform law that would cover the entire law of the family rather than only the limited field of divorce. Upon the request of the special committee Professor Robert J. Levy of the University of Minnesota prepared a monographic study on conclusion of marriage and on divorce, which constituted a working basis for the committee's endeavors. In his report Levy emphatically rejected the matrimonial offense approach as obsolete and mischievous. A proposal generally to allow consent divorce apparently met with the fear that it might antagonize members of American legislatures. But Levy suggested that consent divorce might be considered for childless couples, to be granted after a reasonable cooling-off period. So Levy concluded that the American uniform law should be predicated clearly and exclusively upon the ground of irremediable marriage breakdown. But recognizing the vagueness of the term, the risk that it might be interpreted in many different ways and that it might be used to deny divorces contrary to present-day views, he proposed that the new law be predicated upon "breakdown with specifics." But what should be the specifics? No clear answer emerged from Levy's discussion of various possibilities, especially those that at one time or another had figured in the discussion in England.

The "specific" of presuming breakdown upon proof of a marital offense was repudiated. Charges of offense should be barred from divorce proceedings once and for all. Presumption of breakdown after a period of separation was not recommended either. Apparently American legislatures were not to be trusted to fix the period realistically short. Levy also declared it inadvisable to complicate the law with safeguards against the granting of divorces that would appear to be contrary to what might be called the public interest. He also declared it to be unwise to withhold an otherwise justified divorce in the alleged interest of the children or because the financial security of a party was not sufficiently assured.

The draft statutes which were presented by Levy and by Professor Herma Hill Kay of the University of California in Berkeley were thus little different from the approach of breakdown pure and simple that was to become the law of California.

21. HANDBOOK, 1966, at 184–87.

The proposed Uniform Marriage and Divorce Act was approved by the National Conference of Commissioners on Uniform State Laws in 1970. It will hardly be considered by any state legislature before it has been examined by the House of Delegates of the American Bar Association, which is expected to act upon it in 1971.

In its part dealing with "dissolution of marriage," the text more or less, but not completely, follows the example of the California law. Irretrievable breakdown pure and simple and without specifics is the only ground upon which a marriage is to be dissolved.[22] Even incurable insanity is no longer mentioned. There is no reference to irreconcilable differences as the cause of the breakdown. No guidance is given for the determination of this vague term. Irretrievable breakdown of marriage means whatever a court chooses it to mean. So it may mean one thing in a liberal court and another in a conservative.

The length of the road to freedom of remarriage also depends on judicial discretion. If both parties have stated under oath or affirmation that the marriage is irretrievably broken, or one of them has so stated and the other has not denied it, the court, after hearing, shall make a finding whether the marriage is irretrievably broken. But if one of the parties has denied under oath or affirmation that the marriage is irretrievably broken, the court shall consider all relevant factors, including the circumstances that gave rise to the filing of the petition and the prospect of reconciliation, and shall either make a finding whether the marriage is irretrievably broken or continue the matter for further hearing not less than thirty or more than sixty days later, or as soon thereafter as the matter may be reached on the court's calendar, and he may suggest to the parties that they seek counseling. At the adjourned hearing, the court shall make a finding whether the marriage is irretrievably broken.[23] The marriage will be dissolved if the court finds that the marriage is irretrievably broken and if, to the extent that it has jurisdiction to do so, the court has considered, approved, or made provision for child custody, child support, the maintenance of either spouse, and the disposition of property.[24]

Obviously, a party is not meant to be guilty of perjury if he has stated under oath that his marriage is irretrievably broken and the

22. § 302 (a) (2).
23. § 305.
24. § 303 (a). Under norms worked out by the Supreme Court of the United States, the court of a state has jurisdiction to dissolve a marriage if the plaintiff is a resident of the state. But it does not have jurisdiction to deal with the other issues unless the defendant is also a resident of the state or there are certain other contacts with the state.

court finds that it is not. The inept wording does not mean that a party has to take an oath to the legal conclusion that his marriage is, or is not, irretrievably broken. One cannot swear but to a state of fact, and the fact to be sworn to here can be but the internal fact of the party's believing that his marriage is or is not irretrievably broken.

But if both parties have sworn to this fact, or if one has sworn to, and the other has not denied it, then what? Their desire for a consent divorce is not binding on the court. Secton 305 (a) does not order the court to find *that* the marriage is irretrievably broken, but *whether* it is. Even though the text does not speak of a finding "whether or not," the possibility of a negative answer is implied in the word "whether." The text says that the finding shall be made by the court. Does that term refer to the judge or may it be understood as possibly referring to a jury? Nowhere does the text exclude the use of juries, which is widely possible, although rarely resorted to, in present American divorce law.

If the petition is contested, the court has the choice either right away to make its finding whether or not the marriage is irretrievably broken, or it may adjourn the case for no less than thirty and no more than sixty days (plus) and thus give the parties an opportunity to seek counseling. At the adjourned hearing it (or a jury?) has then to make its finding whether or not the marriage is irretrievably broken. Note that the judge cannot order the parties to seek counseling. But what is to prevent him from making the petitioner feel that his petition will be denied unless he submits to counseling?

Nothing in the Act expressly precludes the court from ordering adjournment in the case of an uncontested, and additional adjournment in the case of a contested, petition. But its text seems to be so formulated as requiring prompt decision that the road to marriage dissolution can be remarkably short, no longer certainly than it is under the California law of 1969. Perhaps it is expected that irretrievable breakdown will be interpreted as liberally as California judges can be trusted to interpret the term of their statute. But attitudes toward divorce all over the United States are not the same as those of California. Several differences are thus likely to develop just as they exist between Swiss cantons in the application of the breakdown ground of article 142 of the Swiss Civil Code.[25] Perhaps this possibility of diverse interpretation is a special merit of a "uniform" law meant to be applied in a country of great diversity. Local differences of inter-

---

25. See H. HINDERLING, DAS SCHWEIZERISCHE EHESCHEIDUNGSRECHT 10 (2d ed. 1960).

pretation may also be neutralized by the opportunity for migratory divorce opened up by any court's obtaining jurisdiction to dissolve a petitioner's marriage ninety days after he has made himself a resident of the state.[26] But Nevada's requirement of forty-two days of residence is still shorter by forty-eight days.

As far as marriage dissolution is concerned, for the majority of states and especially for their metropolitan courts, adoption of the uniform law would mean hardly more than concordance of the law of the books with the law in action. As in the case of California, the major impact would be felt in the matters of child custody and of dollars-and-cents, and in the negotiations about these issues.

The amicable regulation of these issues by the parties' own agreement is expressly encouraged. The terms of the agreement, except those providing for the custody, support, and visitation of children, are declared to be binding upon the court, unless it finds them unconscionable.[27] The evidence relevant for such a finding must be produced by the parties, on their own motion or on request of the court. If the court finds the agreement unconscionable, it is expressly allowed to request the parties to submit a revised version.[28] The terms on child custody and visitation must be found by the court to correspond to the best interest of each child.[29] In order to be aided in deciding on child custody, visitation, and support, the court is expressly authorized to appoint an attorney to represent the interests of a minor or dependent child and to order either or both parents or, in the case of indigence, a welfare agency, to pay the costs and the attorney's fee and disbursements.[30] The Act thus removes the difficulties which, in proceedings between parents, courts have sometimes felt in trying to prevent the children from being mere objects. Fortunately, it avoids calling the children's representative inappropriately "guardian ad litem," a name that has crept into the practice of the courts.

The Act also seeks to eliminate any later troublesome controversies on the effect of a parties' agreement. If the court has found that the agreement is not unconscionable as to property and maintenance, the terms of the agreement shall be set forth in the decree of dissolution of marriage, unless the agreement provides to the contrary. Even if

---

26. § 302 (a) (1).
27. The meaning of this vague term is not explained. Presumably, it is the same as that which is stated in § 2-302 of the Uniform Commercial Code and explained in the Comment thereto.
28. § 306 (a), (b), and (c).
29. § 402.
30. § 310.

the agreement provides that its terms shall not be set forth in the decree, the Act provides for the avoidance of future trouble in that the decree shall state that the court has found its terms not to be unconscionable.[31] In this connection the Act also speaks of "support." Under the Act's terminology this term seems to mean child support, in contrast to the payments which one spouse may have to make for the support of the other and which in the Act are consistently called "maintenance." While the parties' autonomy to regulate maintenance has no limit other than that of unconscionableness, it seems to be intended to be less broad for their regulation of child support. Under § 309 the court may order either or both parents to pay an amount reasonable or necessary[32] for the support of a child. In making its decision the court is to consider all relevant factors including the financial resources of the child; the standard of living the child would have enjoyed had the marriage not been dissolved;[33] the financial resources of the custodial parent; the financial resources and needs of the noncustodial parent; and the physical and emotional condition of the child, and his educational needs. As all the factors stated are relevant for the welfare of the child, it seems that the court ought to make sure that they are taken care of in the parties' agreement.

All terms of the parties' agreement which are set forth in the decree can be enforced by all remedies available for the enforcement of a judgment, including punishment for contempt of court, but are no longer enforceable as contract terms.[34] The latter provision may create trouble when enforcement is sought in a foreign country whose courts refuse or render difficult the enforcement of American judgments. Except for terms concerning child custody, visitation rights, and child support, the decree may expressly preclude or limit modification of the terms set forth, if the agreement so provides.[35] Parties are thus no longer forced, as they are in some states, to choose between a regulation that is final but requires new action in court in every instance of noncompliance, and the opportunity of simple enforcement but without guarantee of finality of regulation.

31. § 306 (d) (1) and (2).
32. Query: when is the support to be "reasonable" and under what circumstances does it have to be no more than what is "necessary"?
33. Apparently what is meant is the standard upon which the child would have lived if the parents had not separated. Or, when the marriage is dissolved, is the child entitled to only that possibly much lower standard on which he lived with one parent after the parties had separated but before the marriage bond was dissolved?
34. § 306 (c).
35. § 306 (f).

For those cases in which the parties fail to regulate matters by their own agreement, the court has to step in. For the disposition of property the Act seeks to substitute for the present variety of systems an approach which is inspired by the California law of 1969 but which is more flexible and which has to take into account that the system of community property does not exist in most American states, where each spouse simply owns his own property. Were this system strictly applied in cases of divorce, either party would simply keep what he had and the only question that might have to be judicially determined is, Who owns what? Where, as still frequently happens, the husband is the sole or principal breadwinner, acquisitions and savings are in his name, and the wife owns little or nothing. In order to compensate her for perhaps long years in the household and with the children, various devices are presently used, mostly without clear statutory bases and with uncertain outcome. The system of community property has its very basis in the desire to let the wife participate in marital acquests. What the husband earns belongs to both him and her, and in the case of a divorce she departs with her share. Under the pre-1970 California law that share had not necessarily to be 50 percent. Considering guilt, the court could give her more or less. Under the law of 1969, the division has to be half-and-half, but adjustments can be made in special circumstances.[36]

The Uniform Act uses a new terminology which elegantly allows it to be applied in both community property states and other states. Those assets which under the community system normally constitute the community fund are called marital property.[37] In both kinds of states the court has first to set apart for each spouse the assets which are his and then to divide the marital property between them. But, in contrast to the California Law of 1969, the division need not be equal. It is rather to be made "in such proportions as the court deems just after considering all factors such as the contribution of each spouse to the acquisition of the marital property, including the contribution of a spouse as homemaker; the value of the property set apart to each spouse; and the economic circumstances of each spouse at the time the division of property is to become effective, including the desirability of awarding the family home or the right to live therein for reasonable periods to the spouse having custody of any children."

36. See *supra* p. 380.
37. The definition is given in § 307 (b). In a community property state the marital property so defined may not in all cases exactly correspond to the community fund.

The discretion thus given to the court may make adaptation to individual circumstances far easier, but it will not facilitate the parties' own arrangements so easily as does the more clearly foreseeable California scheme.

Where the party favored by an unequal division of the marital property is the wife, the advantage may be evened out by denying or curtailing her claim for maintenance. The Uniform Act does not go quite so far as the 1970 draft of a new divorce law for the Federal Republic of Germany. There it is flatly stated that "after the divorce either spouse has to take care of his maintenance by himself,"[38] a principle which is softened by the statement that "a spouse who is unable to provide his own maintenance is, as long as he is in need, entitled to maintenance by the other spouse, considering, however, such other spouse's ability to do so."[39] The limits of this claim are then spelled out in some detail.

The Uniform Act also treats the right of maintenance not as a matter of course. The court is to grant it *only* if the claimant, who may be the husband or the wife,

lacks sufficient property, *including marital property apportioned to him*, to provide for his reasonable needs, and is unable to support himself through appropriate employment or is the custodian of a child where condition or circumstances make it appropriate that the custodian not be required to seek employment outside the home. . . .

The maintenance order shall be in such amounts and for such periods of time as the court deems just, . . . and after considering all relevant factors including the financial resources of the [claimant], *including marital property apportioned to him*, and his ability to meet his needs independently, including the extent to which a provision for support of a child living with the party includes a sum for that party as custodian; the time necessary to acquire sufficient education or training to enable the [claimant] to find appropriate employment;[40] the standard of living established during the marriage; the duration of the marriage; the age and the physical and emotional condition of [the claimant]; and the ability of the [other spouse] to meet his needs while meeting those of the [claimant].[41]

If these provisions are enacted and followed, "divorce American style" should cease to be a gold-digging tool.

For all three issues — property division, maintenance, and child support — the Uniform Act expressly excludes from the court's considera-

---

38. §8 (1).
39. § 8 (2). Details are spelled out in §§ 9 ff.; see *infra* p. 396.
40. The line of activity which under present fashion is called "self-employment" seems to be included.
41. § 308; my italics.

tion the issue of misconduct.[42] In the determination of custody the court is directed not to "consider conduct of a proposed custodian that does not affect his relationship to the child."[43] Custody is to be awarded — to either parent or to a third person — in accordance with the best interests of the child. The court shall consider all relevant factors including the wishes of the parents and of the child, the interaction and interrelationship of the child with his parents, his siblings, and any other person who may significantly affect the child's interests (the text says "the child's best interests"); the child's adjustment to his home, school and community; and the mental and physical health of all individuals involved.[44] A parent not granted custody is entitled to reasonable visitation rights unless visitation would endanger the child's physical health or significantly impair his emotional development.[45]

As in the California Law, consideration of guilt is thus eliminated, not only from the issue of marriage dissolution, but also from those issues which, while often called ancillary, tend to be the only ones which actually prompt contest and litigation. The heat which allegations of guilt are said to engender is likely to be reduced. The percentage of divorces obtained by mutual consent of the parties is likely to be increased beyond the present average of 93 percent. But marriage instability will not be increased by the shift.

FEDERAL REPUBLIC OF GERMANY

In the heated discussions of divorce that have agitated the past, attention has been centered upon the availability of liberation from the impediment to remarriage, and thus upon the grounds upon which a divorce might be obtained or ought to be barred. With the liberal breakthrough these problems seem to be settled. The unmistakable trend is to open the door to remarriage whenever the existing marriage has turned out to be a failure and has ceased to function. Attention is now beginning to focus on those problems which arise when a home has been broken up. They are still widely treated as consequences of divorce, but more and more they are recognized to be problems consequential to marriage breakdown irrespective of whether or not it is followed by a divorce. Of course, problems of maintenance and child custody have long been handled as such, but the guiding principles have not always been consistent with their treatment in cases of divorce.

In dealing with the "ancillary" issue of maintenance, the divorce laws

42. §§ 307 (a), 308 (b), 309.
43. § 402 (5).
44. § 402.
45. § 407 (a).

have had little to say. American statutes in particular have rarely said more than that the decision ought to be made "justly" or "reasonably." In regard to child custody the courts are rarely told more than that they ought to decide in accordance with the best interests of the child.

There has also been wide room for judicial discretion on the issue of property settlement, except where a state statute simply orders that either spouse is to have what he already owns, thus making it difficult or impossible to let the wife share in the property the husband accumulated while she was tending the household. Almost universally, the courts consider guilt as a major, or even the decisive, factor, guilt mostly in the formalistic sense of marital misconduct constituting the ground for the divorce. It is here that the most significant break is made with the past. The enactments and drafts of the latest, the second, phase of the liberal breakthrough, are paying major attention to the ancillary issues, trying to guide judicial discretion and to enter new, unprecedented paths.

Efforts to deal in an untraditional way with the problem of maintenance have provoked incisive discussions in the Federal Republic of Germany. A carefully worked out scheme is contained in the legislative draft that was submitted to public scrutiny by the Federal Minister of Justice in August 1970.[46] The draft law and the report by which it is accompanied also contain remarkable ideas about divorce itself.

The traditional principle of marital offense is repudiated in the German draft just as it is in the laws of the socialist countries, of England, and of California, and in the drafts of Sweden, the Netherlands, and the Commissioners on Uniform State Laws. Marriage failure is to be the only ground for divorce. Already in the existing law, marriage breakdown is recognized as a ground for divorce, but along with a number of misconduct grounds and hedged in by strict limitations. Under § 48 of the Marriage Law[47] either spouse may apply for a di-

---

46. BUNDESMINISTERIUM DER JUSTIZ, DISKUSSIONSENTWURF EINES GESETZES ÜBER DIE NEUREGELUNG DES RECHTS DER EHESCHEIDUNG UND DER SCHEIDUNGSFOLGEN (1970) (hereinafter cited as Minister's Report). The discussion draft of the Minister of Justice is based upon the proposals made and the report submitted by the commission of experts that was appointed in 1968 (EHERECHTSKOMMISSION BEIM BUNDESMINISTERIUM DER JUSTIZ, VORSCHLÄGE ZUR REFORM DES EHESCHEIDUNGSRECHTS UND DES UNTERHALTSRECHTS NACH DER EHESCHEIDUNG, 1970).

47. Control Council Law No. 16 of 20 February 1946. Section 48, I of this law is practically identical with § 55 of the Marriage Law for Greater Germany of 6 July 1938 (RGBl. I 807). Recognition of separation of at least three years' duration as a ground for divorce was proposed in 1928 by the Judiciary Committee of the German Reichstag (minutes of the meeting of 14 March 1928). Reform of the law of

vorce "if the domestic community of the spouses has been discontinued for three years and if, because of a deep and irremediable disruption of the marital relationship, it cannot be expected that there be reestablished a community of life that would correspond to the nature of marriage."

Guilt or misconduct is not mentioned in this involved formula. But consideration of guilt will be brought in through paragraph 2, which gives the respondent a veto power if the disruption of the marriage has been totally or preponderantly caused by guilty conduct of the petitioner. The court's task is not facilitated by the proviso under which the veto is to be disregarded "if the respondent lacks the feeling of being bound to the marriage and is not willing to continue the marriage although he ought so to be willing under the circumstances."

Making things if possible more difficult, paragraph 3 orders that even in the case of disruption and three years' separation the divorce is to be denied "if the preservation of the marriage is required by the well-understood interests of one or more minor children of the marriage."

The courts have struggled to give meaning to the cryptic terms, and the Supreme Court has interpreted them so as to give broad scope to the veto power of female respondents. Little use is therefore made of the long-road breakup ground, especially since, through an amendment act of 1961, § 55 was given its present wording. In 1950 the breakup ground was the basis of 12.2 percent of all divorces pronounced in the country. In 1968 the percentage had sunk to 4.4. In that year 93 percent of all divorces were pronounced under the general misconduct clause of § 43, which permits a spouse to obtain a divorce "if the other, by serious marital misconduct or through his dishonorable or immoral behavior has disrupted the marriage so deeply that one can no longer expect the restoration of a community of life which would correspond to the nature of marriage." The specific misconduct ground of adultery (§ 42) plays but a small role. It constituted the sole ground in only 1.4 percent of the divorces granted in 1968, and in 3.4 percent it figured as the ground for divorce along with the general misconduct ground of § 43.[48]

Under the proposed law all specific grounds of divorce, including those of mental disease and infectious and loathsome disease would be

---

divorce has been widely discussed ever since and particularly since the end of World War II. The literature on it is immense. Scholarly discussions are E. WOLF, G. LÜKE & H. HAX, SCHEIDUNG UND SCHEIDUNGSRECHT: GRUNDFRAGEN DER EHESCHEIDUNG IN DEUTSCHLAND (1959); and W. MÜLLER-FREIENFELS, EHE UND RECHT (1962).

48. Minister's Report 27–29.

replaced by one single ground, which is called "foundering" (*Scheitern*) of the marriage rather than breakdown (*Zerrüttung*). "A marriage has foundered when the spouses' community of life [*Lebensgemeinschaft*] has ceased to exist and the spouses cannot be expected to restore it" (§ 2). That formula, vague though it is, expresses the underlying idea a bit more clearly than those of the California Law of 1969 or the draft law of the Commissioners on Uniform State Laws. The German plan does not prescribe any period of separation. In fact, it even leaves room for the determination that a marriage has foundered although the parties have continued to live in the same home. But a marriage must be treated as having foundered if the spouses have lived separate for one year or for three years, depending on whether or not the divorce is opposed by one party. If neither party is opposed, the longest period that must elapse between the day of their separation and that of the hearing before the court is one year, but if they are able to convince the court that their marriage has indeed foundered, the divorce may be obtained by the short-road method without any delay. The busy courts of the large cities can be expected to be accommodating. For the three-year period of separation, upon the expiration of which the marriage *must* be treated as having foundered even in the case of one party's opposition, it suffices that the separation has existed uninterruptedly for one year preceding the hearing; the remaining two years can be composed of separate periods of separation that have occurred within the past five years and which together amount to two years (§ 4).

To make the proposal more palatable, its simple system is qualified by a hardship clause. "A marriage should [*soll*] not be dissolved if, because of extraordinary circumstances, the divorce constitutes to the opposing party such a grave hardship that it appears requisite to maintain [the marriage] even though it has foundered" (§ 5). But if the denial of the divorce would constitute an equal hardship to the petitioner, the divorce is to be granted in spite of the hardship to the respondent. Hardship, one would assume primarily to consist in the loss of a pension, of rights of inheritance, or of similar economic detriments. But these are exactly the elements which the court is expressly prohibited from considering. "Marriage must not be degraded into an institution that is merely to guarantee economic security."[49] It is hard to see what noneconomic circumstances could require the preservation of the bond of a marriage that is proved to have foundered.

---

49. *Id.* 5.

Suggestions to continue the present compulsory system of attempting reconciliation, to provide for some new system of official conciliation proceedings, or to make provision for marriage counseling were rejected as useless and impracticable.[50] So also was the idea of excluding divorce during the first years of marriage. Why indeed should one preserve the bond of a marriage of which it becomes clear at the very beginning that it can never be anything but a source of misery for the parties?[51]

Radical though they are, the provisions on grounds for divorce seem not to meet with serious opposition. In the main, although not in all details, they agree with the ideas of what may be called the bar association of the Federal Republic of Germany,[52] the Family Law Commission of the Protestant church in Germany,[53] and even the workshop on marriage law established at the *Kommissariat* of the German bishops of the Roman Catholic church.[54]

But doubts and opposition are being expressed as to the proposed reform of the law of support. In obedience to the constitutional command of equal treatment of the sexes,[55] the draft law, it is true, does not treat alimony as a right of divorced women. It simply speaks of the right of one spouse to obtain alimony from the other, but the problem is of primary importance for women. Criticism has thus been raised concerning the effects which the draft scheme would have on women. In what respects would their position be different from that obtaining under the present law? Would the changes be desirable? Would they be justified?

In the United States, two issues are not always kept distinct from each other — the issue of division of property and the issue of alimony. When dealing with the division of property, one often has to unscramble a tangled mass of property owned by the married couple: which of them owns what? How should assets owned jointly be partitioned between the partners? Alimony, on the other hand, means the payment which one ex-spouse, mostly the husband, has to make to the

---

50. *Id.* 50.
51. *Ibid.*
52. Deutscher Juristentag. 48th Annual Meeting, 22–25 September 1970. Beschlüsse. Zivilrechtliche Abteilung; Verhandlungen des 48. Deutschen Juristentages, vol. II, Part M: Empfiehlt es sich Gründe und Folgen der Ehescheidung neu zu regeln? Reports by W. Müller-Freienfels and P. Nolte.
53. DENKSCHRIFT DER FAMILIENRECHTSKOMMISSION DER EVANGELISCHEN KIRCHE DEUTSCHLANDS, 1969.
54. KOMMISSARIAT DER DEUTSCHEN BISCHÖFE, ERWÄGUNGEN ZUR REFORM DES ZIVILEN SCHEIDUNGSRECHTS DER BUNDESREPUPLIK DEUTSCHLAND, 1970.
55. Basic Law of 1949, art. 3.

other. The two issues could be neatly kept separate if the division of property had just the one function of determining title, and the awarding of alimony were exclusively aimed at providing support. But additional functions enter the consideration, especially of American courts. If upon the parting of their ways either party were to move away with exactly those assets which are his, it might easily happen that the husband took all and the wife was left with nothing. He was the breadwinner for the family. He brought home the earnings. He invested the savings in his name. But the wife was not idle. She ran the household; she brought up the children. It was through her toil that the husband was able to go out into the world and make money. Should she not receive a portion that would correspond to her contribution to the joint enterprise? Systems of community property have been designed for exactly that end. Under such systems the increment of property that is due to the exertions of both spouses outside or inside of the home is treated as belonging to both and will thus be divided between them upon the termination of their life in common. In the United States a community property system exists in only nine jurisdictions.[56] In all the others, the husband owns his property and the wife hers, provided she has any. But courts are reluctant in the case of a divorce to leave a wife without compensation for her toil as housewife and mother. Especially where the marriage has lasted for many years, a court might easily incline to order a husband to turn over some of his property to the wife. Where that method is not feasible, either because it is not considered permissible under the law of the jurisdiction or because the husband does not have much tangible property, the desired effect can be achieved by increasing the alimony award beyond the amount needed strictly for the wife's support. Or, where there are assets, the husband may be ordered instead of making periodical payments of alimony, to pay to her a lump sum as alimony, payable all at once or in installments possibly extending over a long period of time.

Another element that can play a role in both awarding alimony and dividing the property is that of guilt. Traditionally an American ex-wife has been entitled to alimony only where the divorce was obtained by her, which meant, if the husband was guilty of a marital offense, that she is blameless. This tradition is still strong in the United States, but it is not always applied strictly and rigidly. In an increasing number of states awards of alimony have been made officially permissible

---

56. See *supra* p. 380.

by statute or by clear expression in case law. But equivalent effects can be achieved by free judicial handling of the division of property both in states with the majority system of matrimonial property system and in community property states. Conversely, where the divorce is obtained by the wife, courts may feel inclined to punish the husband for his misconduct or to give the wife compensation for the loss of the home, the pain suffered, and other harm caused to her by the husband's wrongdoing. American courts are likely, influenced by such moral considerations, to deny alimony to an adulteress and to be generous to a wife who has, or has been able to give the court the impression of having, been faithful and loyal to a reprobate husband. Such moral judgment may be expressed in a high award of alimony as well as in the mode of property division.

Denial of all alimony to a guilty wife may not only result in hardship to her but may possibly make her a burden upon the taxpayers. Should she not receive from the husband at least the subsistence minimum that corresponds to public welfare checks? But why, on the other hand, should the burden be placed upon the ex-husband and his new family? Why should he be closer to her than the taxpayers? Furthermore, because of what kind of guilt ought a woman be repudiated? Is a wife's adultery still considered just as abhorrent as it was in the past, when not only were moral standards different but no technical means were available to prevent the corruption of the husband's blood line? And what about such modern grounds of divorce as mental cruelty? Is a woman to be left without support merely because she angered her husband by eating crackers in bed? Finally, and most important of all, is formalized, judicially ascertained guilt identical with true, moral guilt? Can such guilt be judicially determined at all? Is there ever any case in which guilt lies solely with one partner? For these reasons guilt is losing weight as the determining element or even as one of the factors determining awards of alimony and division of marital property. Yet even where the divorce is pronounced on one of the non-guilt grounds — separation for a certain period of time, incompatibility — considerations of guilt are likely to creep into the disposition of the issues of alimony and property settlement. But guilt determination, when it is to be more than purely formalistic, is not only beset with difficulties. The knowledge that it will significantly determine the economic future of the parties as well as the decision on child custody poisons divorce procedure and the negotiations between the parties. Charges of guilt must be made and proved, and the party so charged must seek either to disprove them or to buy them off.

Attempts to part amicably are therefore discouraged. Is it necessary that already strained relations be embittered even more? Reflections of this kind have caused the authors of the California Law of 1969 and of the Uniform Law of 1970 to exclude the consideration of guilt completely from the issues of property and alimony and substantially from those of custody and visitation rights. For the same reasons, they seek to eliminate guilt from consideration in the Federal Republic of Germany.

There, it is true, guilt does not play any present role in the division of property. Participation of the wife in the gains made during marriage by the husband is openly achieved under the Equal Rights Law of 18 June 1957 (RGBl. I 609). A comparison is made for each partner of the amount of property he owns at the time of the divorce and of the property he owned at the time of the beginning of the marriage. The difference between the latter and the former is called his increment (*Zugewinn*). The husband's increment is compared with that of the wife, the smaller amount is subtracted from the larger, and the difference is divided by two; by "equalization payment" of one party to the other, each party is to end up with one-half of the difference between the increments.[57] In the process, guilt may be considered in the special case in which the party who has obtained the smaller increment and who therefore claims from the other "equalization payment" has for some considerable period of time, by guilty conduct, failed to comply with those economic duties which are incident to the marital relation (§ 1381).

As to alimony, guilt can be decisive, however. The basic provision of the present law reads as follows:

If the husband has been declared to be the exclusively or predominantly guilty party, he has to pay to his former wife that amount of alimony which is proper under the parties' circumstances of life, insofar as the income from the wife's property and the proceeds from gainful activity are insufficient.

If the wife has been declared to be the exclusively or preponderantly guilty party, she has to pay proper alimony to her former husband insofar as he is not in a position to support himself.[58]

57. Civil Code as amended by the Law of 1957, §§ 1363, 1372–78. The system differs from American systems of community property; while under these systems the assets of each spouse are jointly owned by both as their community fund, under the German system the assets of each spouse remain his separate property. With a few exceptions designed to prevent grave impairment of the expectations of both partners, each is free to manage and alienate his own assets (§§ 1364–70). The system of increment splitting can be contracted out by the parties, who may also choose to have all their assets combined in a fund of community property (§§ 1408 ff.).

58. Marriage Law of 1945, § 58.

If both parties have been found to be equally guilty, a party who is unable to support himself may be awarded a contribution to his support, if and insofar as such an award appears to be equitable (§ 60). The same rule applies where the divorce has been granted on the ground of mental or physical disease or of breakdown combined with separate living and where the court has not declared one or the other party to be guilty (§ 61).

The great majority of divorces are pronounced upon an offense ground.[59] If the wife is declared to be the exclusively or preponderantly guilty party, she is not entitled to any alimony. Even if she is found to be innocent, she may be awarded little or no alimony. The upper limit of possible alimony is the difference between her requirements for living on the standard appropriate to the spouses' circumstances of life and the amount of income she derives from her own property and from earnings she actually receives or could receive from gainful activity in which she could reasonably be expected to engage. The lower limit is constituted by an amount which, if by paying the full amount as just defined, the husband would impair his own proper support, appears to be equitable in accordance with the comparative state of the property, the income of the parties, and their obligations toward third parties, especially the children (§ 59).

Thus if a woman wants to lay any basis for a claim for alimony, she must allege and prove facts under which the husband appears to be exclusively or at least the preponderantly guilty party. If the husband wants to be safe from any duty of alimony, he must allege and prove facts indicating the exclusive or preponderant guilt of the wife. The incentive to obtain a favorable guilt determination in the decree of divorce is strengthened by the fact that under German law the awarding of alimony, including the determination of the amount, belongs to the jurisdiction of a court different from that which pronounces the divorce. But the district court (*Amtsgericht*), which deals with the alimony award, is bound by the finding of guilt expressed in the decree of the circuit court (*Landgericht*), by which the divorce was pronounced. Under German law it is thus more difficult for divorcing parties by their own agreement to settle the alimony issue in advance of a judicial pronouncement on guilt. If, as it seems to be, the percentage of consent divorce is somewhat lower in Germany than in most other countries — 80 percent rather than 90–95 percent — and if more divorce cases are driven up to the Supreme Court in Germany,

---

59. See *supra* p. 393.

the reason seems to lie in this overriding significance of determination of guilt and the peculiar dichotomy of the proceedings.[60]

Under the new German scheme guilt is eliminated from the issue of alimony as it is under the California Law of 1969 and the American Uniform Law of 1970. The discrimination against a guilty wife will therefore disappear. But the innocent wife may fare less well than she does under the present law.

The basic idea is expressed drastically in § 8 I: "After divorce either spouse has to take care of his support by himself." But this radical maxim is modified by the very next paragraph: "If a spouse cannot take care of his support, he has a claim for support against the other spouse. This claim exists for the duration of the need. The other party's ability to pay is to be taken into consideration."

The incidents of the claim are then stated in detail in §§ 9–26, and by these provisions the right of an ex-spouse to claim support from his former partner is limited to those situations of need which are "marriage-conditioned," i.e., those situations in which the need arises just because the claimant was married and the arrangements under which the spouses carried on their married life have impaired the ability of the claimant now, after termination of the marriage, to be self-supporting. A woman's inability to be self-supporting is marriage-conditioned if, upon entering or during marriage, she interrupted her schooling or vocational training, or if she now has to spend her time with the upbringing or education of children of the marriage, or if she is now too old or too infirm through illness to be self-supporting (§§ 10, 11).

60. Determination of child custody also does not belong to the jurisdiction of the divorce court. The court that is to deal with this issue may be different from that which has to deal with alimony as well as from that which has to adjudicate problems of division of property. Divorced parents are supposed to submit to the guardianship court their own proposal as to the custody of their children. From such proposal the court is not to deviate unless a different course is necessary in the interest of the child concerned. If the parents fail to submit a proposal within two months after the decree of divorce has become *res judicata*, or if the court disapproves of the parents' proposal, the court must make the regulation which best corresponds to the interest of the child. *If one parent has been declared to be the exclusively guilty one, the court shall not award him custody, unless there are grave reasons for doing so* (my italics; Civil Code § 1671). Before rendering its decision the court is to hear the report of the Youth Welfare Office (*Jugendamt*), i.e., the government agency which in its district is through its expert staff to deal with matters of juvenile welfare (Juvenile Welfare Law of 11 August 1961, BGBl. I 1206) § 48. As the law stands, guilt is thus a factor playing an important role in the adjudication of custody. The draft law of 1970 still does not deal with the matter. In the coming installment that is to deal with it, consideration of guilt will be reduced to a minimum or perhaps eliminated entirely.

The commission of experts by whom the draft was prepared had proposed that in the first-named situation, where schooling had been interrupted, the claim for support be granted only where the decision not to engage in gainful work or in schooling or vocational training had been motivated by the marriage. In the minister's draft this limitation is removed. The claim is to exist whenever the needy party has not been gainfully active or engaged in schooling or training at any time during marriage. Proving the motive is regarded as too difficult.[61]

The claim for support exists so long and only so long as the ex-wife is in the state of marriage-conditioned inability to support herself. She has no claim if her income from work or capital yields her enough to live on. And if income is not enough, she must use her capital, unless such use would be economic waste or would constitute an inequitable hardship (§ 13 I). Age or sickness can constitute the basis for claiming support if it applies at the time of the divorce or at the termination of the care and education of a child of the parties (§ 11 II). Sickness beginning after that date or later loss of capital or income are risks which the ex-wife has to bear. The Civil Code of 1896 still operated on the idea that, upon marrying, a man assumed the responsibility permanently to provide for the care of his wife, after a divorce as well as during marriage, provided she had been faithful and had not herself committed a marital offense. This idea the minister's report declares to be incompatible with the idea of divorce based on the principle of breakdown, "which is aimed at the parties' freeing themselves of each other as quickly and as completely as possible so that each of them, burdened by the former marriage as little as possible, can enter upon a new course of life." [62]

Another frequently occurring case of marriage-conditioned need is considered in § 12. A divorced spouse, especially a divorced woman, may find her security for old age or disability impaired because while she was married she did not, or not fully, engage in gainful activity and has thus not paid, or not fully paid, the contributions to social security or to a pension or annuity fund. For an analogous reason she may have lost or diminished a pension right to which she is or would have been entitled as a public servant. Such a detriment is marriage-conditioned as is also the case where no or reduced contributions were paid after the divorce because the now needy party could not find an appropriate gainful activity or would not, or not fully, engage in

61. Minister's Report 81.
62. *Id.* 79.

a gainful activity because she had to take care of, or educate, a child of the parties. Insofar as the detriment results in need the other spouse will have to make up the loss. Mostly, the party entitled to this "pension equalization" (*Rentenausgleich*) will, of course, be the wife.

A divorced spouse's duty to support his ex-spouse has an upper limit, which is determined in a two-step process. As long as he is "capable of performance" (*leistungsfähig*), the award of support is limited by the need of the claimant. A divorced person is declared not to be capable of performance "if in view of his earning capacity and his property and upon consideration of his other obligations, he is not capable of paying the support adequate to the claimant's needs without endangering his own support." He must dig into his capital unless such use would be economic waste or would constitute an inequitable hardship to him (§ 17). If the obligor is found to be incapable of performance, his duty does not go beyond that amount which appears equitable in comparison with his own needs and the circumstances of his own financial capacity. In this respect it is remarkable that the needs of the divorced spouse have no absolute priority over those of a family created by remarriage. After all, restoration to the freedom of remarriage is the very purpose of divorce.

Generally, the duty of support is limited to that amount which corresponds to equity, if the marriage was of especially short duration, or if the claimant has been guilty of a serious crime against the ex-spouse or a member of the ex-spouse's near family; or if the claimant has brought about his state of need by his own recklessness (*mutwillig*) (§ 15).

Need on the one side, capacity of performance, tempered if necessary by equity, on the other, determine all awards of support including those based upon impaired security for old age or disability. Differently treated is the claim for "pension equalization" (*Versorgungsausgleich*, §§ 27–32). In the "housewife marriage" of the traditional type, the husband is not only the partner who earns the bread for the family and can thus accumulate acquests in his own name, but he is also the one who acquires those claims for pensions on which he and his wife are supposed to live in old age or when he is disabled. The wife is entitled to derivative widow's benefits only if she is married to the man at the time of his death; and widow's benefits are usually modest. When the husband actually becomes a pensioner, his income is likely to be so reduced that support claims against him are hard to enforce or are actually worthless.

The problem could be solved by treating the running of households as an activity which would entitle housewives to social security benefits of their own and would, of course, also require corresponding contributions to be paid. As much as the present government may be inclined to bring about major social reforms, such a remodeling of the social security system is not in the plans for the immediate future.[63] Besides, social security for housewives would not take care of security rights of different kinds, such as pensions for public service or private annuity insurance. In order to stimulate discussion, the minister's report proposes a scheme similar to that equalizing property increments.[64] For each party a computation is to be made of the value of the security rights he has acquired at the time of the marriage (opening value) and of this value at the time of the divorce (terminal value). For each party the opening value is to be subtracted from the terminal value. To achieve equalization one must assume that each party is entitled to one-half of the sum of the two differences.[65] "The party who has the lower increment is entitled to receive from the other the difference between the pension he actually obtains and that which he would obtain if that share to which he was entitled at the time of the divorce had actually been credited to him."[66] As a general rule the ex-wife cannot claim equalization before she reaches the age at which she is or would be entitled to a pension or before she has been disabled. In addition it is necessary that the other party has actually begun to receive his pension. But if she wishes to obtain immediate cash, she may have the capital value paid to her at the time of the divorce, in a lump sum or in installments, provided the ex-husband is not inequitably burdened thereby.[67]

Whatever is received by a party as pension equalization is, of course, deducted from that item of support which is due as compensation for the omission, during the marriage or the subsequent period of child care, of making the payments necessary to secure full pension rights.[68]

The support scheme of the German discussion draft is more complex than the basic features here reported would suggest. Its major characteristics have been presented because they indicate what far-

63. See Social Report 1970 of the Federal Government (Sozialbericht 1970 der Bundesregierung) Bundestags-Drucksachen VI/643, p. 25, No. 62.
64. *Supra* p. 398.
65. § 27.
66. "Als Ausgleich ist dem benachteiligten Ehegatten der Unterschied zwischen der tatsächlich erlangten Versorgung und einer Versorgung zu zahlen, die er erhalten würde, wenn ihm der ihm gebührende Zusatzanteil im Zeitpunkt der Scheidung gutgebracht worden wäre" (text of § 27).
67. § 32.
68. § 30.

reaching consequences are implied in a shift from traditional fault-divorce to breakdown-divorce. If divorce is no longer to be regarded as repudiation of a spouse guilty of misconduct, but as the opening of the opportunity for seeking happiness in a new marital venture, the pain and suffering that are always connected with marital breakdown must not be aggravated by mutual charges of guilt, nor must the establishment of a new legitimate family be hampered by crushing financial burdens. But, on the other hand, marriage is a joint venture; when it comes to an end, gains and losses ought to be shared equally. It is not easy to achieve these ends, and it is particularly difficult to achieve them where the marriage has been conducted according to the traditional pattern of role assignments, with the husband the breadwinner and his spouse the housewife and mother. The report of the German Minister of Justice contains extensive statistical material which indicates that the stereotype of "housewife marriage" is on its way out in the Federal Republic of Germany.[69] In 1968, of the 26.8 million persons gainfully active in the Federal Republic, 9.6 million, i.e., 36 percent, were women. Of the persons between fifteen and twenty years of age, the percentage of the women gainfully active — 61.2 percent — was practically the same as the 62.2 percent of the men. In the age group of twenty to twenty-five, the percentage among the men of those gainfully active was 87.6 percent; the corresponding percentage among the women was 68.8 percent, and that among the married women was 51.8 percent. For the age group of thirty-five to forty the percentages of persons gainfully active were 98.8 percent of the men, 43.9 percent of all the women, and 38.1 percent of the married women. Even the number and percentages of women with children who are gainfully active, are considerable. In 1962, of the 6.7 million women with children below the age of fourteen, 2.338 million were gainfully active, among them 1.6 million in work other than agriculture or forestry. Among the married women having such children, 33.3 percent were gainfully active. Projections made by the Institute of Labor Market and Vocation Research of the Federal Institution of Labor Relations indicate that in 1980 about 59 percent of the married women can be expected to be gainfully active.

But the pattern of the housewife marriage has not disappeared and it cannot be expected to disappear completely. And housewives are afraid that their husbands may discard them once they have lost the charm of youth. The data presented by the Lord Chancellor in the

---

69. Minister's Report, 73–77.

debate about the English Divorce Reform Act should indicate that such fears are exaggerated.[70] But they exist, and with them exists the fear that under the new law faithful wives may be worse off than under the traditional rules. Although rarely expressed, this fear seems to be the result largely of a feeling that women may have less bargaining power than now when a husband wants to have his freedom. Under the new scheme, support will be frequently limited to the period of retraining for gainful activity. For the woman who is not eliminated from the labor market because of age, support will be a kind of severance pay, similar to *zaisen-bunyo* of Japan or the support that is granted in socialist countries. The Japanese system is a relic from the time of complete male domination. The socialist scheme is a technique to push women into the labor force. In the nonsocialist countries the same process is going on simply as an incident of industrialization. Whether it will result in women's liberation remains to be seen. The transition, at any rate, is painful. So the German draft has come under extensive criticism.[71] Unquestionably it will be modified in numerous respects. But the draft has begun serving the purpose of stirring up discussion and providing a target to shoot at. The draft is indicative of the trend of the present and in its careful elaboration of the consequences which are implied in this trend it deserves attention wherever the trend is apparent.

70. *Supra* p. 350.
71. See DER SPIEGEL (24th Year, no. 49), 30 November 1970, at 70.

16
What to Do About Marriage Breakdown

Experienced observers have long known what we have laboriously tried in this book to prove, namely, that a strict statute law of divorce is not an effective means to prevent or even to reduce the incidence of marriage breakdown. In spite of the facts the old belief is still held widely among the public as well as among lawyers. But it is losing ground. The recent enactments and drafts in the United States and Europe are not attempts to protect the stability of marriage through strictness on divorce. They are expressions of the realization that marriage breakdown has causes other than easy availability of restoration to the freedom of legitimate marriage. Their aim is to eliminate the measure of pain unnecessarily added by traditional law to the suffering which is inevitable in every case of marriage breakup. Does the new attitude mean abandonment of hope and of efforts to protect and promote the stability of marriage? By no means. It rather opens the way for the consideration of more promising avenues. In this concluding chapter I shall try, without stating final solutions, to suggest what these avenues might be and what future means might hold greater promise than the ineffectual tool of strictness in the statute law on divorce.

Evasive practices seem to be universal wherever divorce is not available or available only with difficulty or at high cost. Not only in the United States are abandonment and separation known as "the poor man's divorce."[1] In Chile, the institution of divorce does not exist, but factual marriage breakup occurs nevertheless, and for those who

---

1. See H. H. Foster, Jr., *Common Law Divorce*, 46 MINN. L. REV. 43 (1961); H. H. Foster, Jr., & D. J. Freed, *Unequal Protection: Poverty and Family Law*, 42 IND L.J. 192 (1967); W. O. Weyrauch, *Informal and Formal Marriage*, 28 U. CHI. L. REV. 88 (1960). J. tenBroek, *California's Dual System of Family Law*, 16–17 STAN. L. REV. 614 (1965) (also U. Cal., Berkeley, Dept. Pol. Sci., Reprint Ser. no. 23).

care about respectability and have the necessary means, judicial practice provides a way out. Under Chilean law a marriage ceremony must be performed before the registrar of the municipality or the ward in which one or the other of the parties has resided for the three months just prior thereto.[2] The Supreme Court of Chile has interpreted these provisions as rendering void any marriage concluded at any other place.[3] If parties are in agreement that their marriage has been a failure they can readily find witnesses who, for a standard fee, will testify that neither party resided in the place at which the marriage was celebrated. A decree of nullity will then be obtained as a matter of course.[4]

In Argentina and in Brazil, the institution of divorce also does not exist. But irregular unions are frequent, and those who can afford it resort to the so-called Uruguay marriage. A consent divorce is obtained abroad, where remarriage with the new partner is celebrated as well. Neither in Argentina nor in Brazil is the new relationship a marriage in the legal sense, but the fact that the formalities have been gone through renders it socially respectable.[5]

Before divorce became available to Polish Catholics after World War II, Riga, the capital of Latvia, was the place where one could easily obtain a divorce that had some chance of being recognized as valid in Poland. The various evasive devices that have been resorted to in Italy have been described above in chapter 7. In France and Germany the specialists in divorce geography know how to keep divorce cases out of courts known for strictness and to make them accumulate in those which are known to be easy. Even in ancient Babylonia we are

2. Ley de Matrimonio Civil, 10 January 1884, arts. 9 and 16; Ley No. 4, 808 Sobre Registro Civil, 10 February 1930, art. 35.
3. Decision of 30 July 1925, REVISTA DE DERECHO Y JURISPRUDENCIA, vol. 23, part 1, at 659, and decision of 28 March 1932 (Sabioncello con. Hausmann), REV. DER. JURISPR., vol. 29, part 1, at 351.
4. In 1963 the average number of decrees of nullity obtained this way was estimated to be about 2,000 per year. M. SOMMARIVA UNDURRAGA, DERECHO DE FAMILIA 68, 80, 83 (1963). In this divorceless country the rate of annulments per 1,000 population is thus 0.22 and the 1959 dissolution rate is higher than that of Peru (0.15), and close to those of Canada (0.39), Venezuela (0.23), Greece (0.28), and Scotland (0.33). See UNITED NATIONS DEMOGRAPHIC YEARBOOK, 1968, table 34.
5. On Argentina: information received from Professor J. Arellano Alarcón, Concepción, Chile; as to Brazil, see D. Pierson, *The Family in Brazil*, 16 MARRIAGE AND FAMILY LIVING 308, 311 (1954). According to Professor Arellano, Ciudad Juárez, Chihuahua, Mexico, is the place favored by Argentinians. There is no risk of criminal prosecution for bigamy. Under certain circumstances the parties to the new relationship may be treated as members of a factual partnership. On the strictly legal aspects, see R. GALLARDO, DIVORCIO, SEPARECIÓN DE CUERPOS Y NULIDAD DE MATRIMONIO EN LAS NACIONES LATINO-AMERICANAS 48, 124 (1957).

told of the custom of simply walking out on a distasteful marriage so as to avoid the high fee of a formal divorce, a custom which Urukagina, ruler of Lagash, tried to abolish in 2470 B.C.[6]

Infidelity, abandonment, and separation have never been fully eliminated nor is there a chance that they ever will be. But the frequency of these forms of marriage breakup as well as the frequency of irregular unions depends upon the cultural climate.[7] If such acts are strongly disapproved of morally, they tend to be infrequent, especially in those circles which are concerned about respectability. The contemporary cultural climate of the United States has not developed in that direction. Even among middle classes of suburbia, marriage breakup is no longer taboo. The factual breakup, it is true, is expected to be regularized by a divorce, and a union meant to be more than fleeting still seems to require a marriage certificate in order to be respectable. In England even the Beatles found it advisable to go through the ceremonies of marriage, perhaps for love, perhaps for the sake of social acceptance, perhaps for tax reasons. In the United States and other countries the very respect for marriage demands that the breakup of a marriage be followed by an official act that bestows legitimacy upon the next following union. The Italian situation makes it clear that the impossibility of obtaining such legitimation is not enough to prevent new unions and even less to prevent marriage breakup. The only chance to prevent these factual events is the development of a cultural climate in which they are strongly disapproved of. Could such a climate be created in the United States?

We cannot exclude the possibility of some cataclysmic event by which the current trend toward liberal individualism might be reversed. The country may be devastated by nuclear attack, conquered by an enemy, or shaken by revolution. A prophet may kindle religious fervor among the masses; a dictator may use the tools of propaganda to establish a new creed. All that is possible, and in the sequel the cultural climate of the country may be profoundly affected. But as long as we have an even moderately peaceful life or more or less traditional American democracy, nobody has it in his power to reverse the direction in which the cultural climate has been developing.

If there is little prospect of a reversal of the trend of the American cultural climate as a whole, what prospects are there in those subcultures whose attitudes toward marriage and family are significant?

---

6. G. MANN & A. HEUSS, 1 PROPYLAENWELTGESCHICHTE 546 (1961).
7. *Cf.* B. Bodenheimer, *New Approaches of Psychiatry: Implication for Divorce Reform*, [1970] Utah L. Rev. 191, 207.

The main protagonist for marriage stability has been the Roman Catholic church. Its stout adherence to the dogma of indissolubility has not been merely opposition to remarriage during the lifetime of the partner of a prior marriage, but prevention of factual marriage breakup. The aim has not been fully achieved. But where the faith has been strong, marriage has tended to be stable. The priest, the parents, and other relatives are likely to be listened to before the engagement, the often long duration of which helps the future spouses to know each other's characters, although not their sex patterns. His wife, his children, and the world outside recognize the husband-father as the head of the family. Temptation to adultery is repressed by the sense of sin and the fear of eternal punishment. The virtue of patience is cultivated, disappointments and adversities are accepted as divinely ordained and to be borne. The children are brought up with that sense of responsibility before God by which the home life is inspired. Hierarchic and governmental authority is respected. The highest form of life is that of the priest and the religious who are pledged to obedience and chastity.

Even if that ideal way of social life is not fully attained, the very fact that it is striven for deeply influences the life and structure of society. Families tend to be knit closely, the breakup of a home is sinful and detestable. Temptation to adulterous intercourse is kept at a minimum. Of course, to repeat, the ideal has never actually been attained. The sexual double standards, prostitution, and the mistress system have often enough flourished in Catholic society. Catholic husbands have deserted their wives and abandoned their children. Every now and then a Catholic wife has run away with a lover. Separations have occurred with or without the placet of the church. But in spite of all this, open marriage breakup has tended to be rare in a society in which the faith is strong.

During the past few decades membership in the Catholic church has grown in the United States.[8] Catholic influence has been conspicuous in American public life. Catholic circles have consistently opposed attempts to liberalize the laws on sex, obscenity, abortion, or divorce. But the force of such opposition is weakening. Even in New York the Catholic hierarchy could not prevent the easing of the divorce law. The growing demand for "modernization" forced the convocation of the Second Vatican Council, and modernization means adaptation of the church to industrialization and urbanization and thus to egali-

---

8. In 1950 it was 27,766,141, in 1960 it was 40,871,302, and in 1966 it was 47,873,248, according to the *National Catholic Almanac* for 1951, 1961, and 1970, respectively.

tarianism and democracy. It has been a long way from the Syllabus of Errors, the Anti-Modernist Oath, and the Pronouncement of Papal Infallibility to Vatican II, the formation of labor unions of priests, the demands for relinquishing priestly celibacy, the violent criticism of Paul VI's encyclical on birth control, and the reformulation of long-established dogma in the Dutch Catechism. Catholicism is undergoing profound internal changes. The church may hope to prevent them from getting out of hand. It tries through change, to reestablish its hold and influence. At present, however, it finds itself unable financially to support all the parochial schools it has so steadfastly declared to be indispensable for the preservation of the faith; and the hitherto entirely priestly government of the Catholic universities is being handed over to laymen. The increase in church membership has not been in proportion to the growth of the entire population. Immigrants from Ireland, Poland, Italy, and other Catholic countries no longer form those compact blocs by which the political complexion of the metropolitan centers was once dominated. The grandchildren of the immigrants do not feel repelled by the thought of intermarrying with non-Catholic Americans of different ethnic extraction.

If one looks upon the picture as a whole, one must conclude that Catholic influence on the cultural climate of the United States is not only unlikely to increase but has been decreasing and is likely to continue to decrease. The same observation applies to Protestantism. Fundamentalism is still a power in some parts, especially the South. But it has long been overbalanced by the liberals, whose ranks are swelled by more and more radical protagonists of a new order in which individual conscience replaces authority and tradition. Inhibition of sexual freedom and reluctance to try a new union when hopes of marital felicity have failed in the first one, are no longer insisted upon. Protestant clergymen are found in the front ranks of those who oppose the existing social order as unjust and ripe for destruction. Like their Catholic counterparts they hope to win for the faith those groups whom they regard as oppressed and ready for revolution. But so far they have had little success in stopping the rising tide of indifferentism that is emptying the churches and finding expression in the huge number of Americans who declare themselves to be unaffiliated with any religious denomination.

The orthodox and conservative sections of Judaism neither have sufficient numerical strength nor are they outgoing enough to influence the cultural climate significantly.

Of secular movements none is in sight that could have significant influence either. In the United States neither communism nor socialism has produced such conservative tendencies as those they have developed in the Soviet Union, Italy, and France. Besides, both are too small and too weak to have considerable influence in matters of morals, even in the direction of hostility toward the bourgeois family which has characterized the socialist movement outside the regions in which it has come to power or close to it. Such organizations as temperance groups, anti-vice crusaders, or the Boy Scouts have long ceased to be of major influence upon the cultural climate of the country.

Conservatism has been exhibited by those Negroes who have achieved middle-class status. But among the great masses of Negroes, in the South as well as in the cities of the North, the cultural climate has been different from that of the white middle class. In the days of slavery, a marriage between slaves did not prevent the master from separating the wife from the husband or the children from the parents. A sale might be of an entire family, but just as possibly of single individuals. In such circumstances a feeling for the sanctity or indissolubility of marriage could not develop. It remained comparatively weak after the abolition of slavery, just as it has been weak among white proletarians the world over. To people living at or near starvation level the expense of a marriage license or a marriage ceremony appears unnecessary, not to speak of the cost of divorce that is generally so high as to place it beyond reach. A couple's living together without benefit of clergy does not expose proletarians to contempt in their own circles. Simple walking out, informal separation, or switching of partners is inhibited neither by considerations of respectability nor by the fear of losing rights of property or support, which are uninteresting to the propertyless, nor by attention to criminal sex laws which are not enforced, least of all against members of the lowest class of society. Efforts made through the administration of welfare laws to achieve higher regard for the sex and marriage code of white society have produced some results, but they are weakened by the resistance of the protagonists of Black Power and the allegedly different cultural needs of what is called the black community. The growing strength of these tendencies among young Negroes is likely not only to counteract but to overbalance the eagerness of middle-class Negroes to adopt the standards of the white majority. The liberalizing influence which Negroes have had upon the cultural climate of the nation through their sex-stimulating music will probably be strengthened if the effort at integration should turn out to be successful. It may decrease, however, if the black sector of the American people comes to live in the scheme of apartheid which now seems to be the aim of some of its leaders.

Conservatism is still a force to be reckoned with in the United States. Perhaps it is strong enough to prevent further liberalizing of the divorce laws of the books and thus to render it politically advisable not to disturb the compromise that has been working during the period of equilibrium between conservatism and liberalism. But with that problem we are not concerned in the present context. The question with which we are dealing here is different: Is conservatism likely in the foreseeable future to bring about a change in the cultural climate of the United States that will place effective factual or ideological obstacles in the way of factual marriage breakdown? To this question the answer is negative.

Even though the cultural climate of the United States is unlikely to change, it may still be possible to some, perhaps to a considerable, degree to eliminate or reduce the temptation toward marriage breakup which exists in certain specific situations. What are these situations? How might the injurious elements be removed from them?

The proposition that lack of harmony between the spouses is the basic cause of marriage breakdown may be a tautology. It will appear so if we include situations not only of permanent but also of temporary or assumed disharmony, situations in which a tiff is regarded by an immature spouse as a sign of lasting incompatibility or situations arising from extravagantly romantic expectations about marriage. But exactly because of this tautological nature, the proposition is apt to direct attention to those situations in which incompatibility with its inherent risk of marriage breakdown can typically be found. These situations may be of two kinds: those in which a high risk of incompatibility exists at the very outset; and those in which it develops in the course of a marriage between parties who initially appeared to be well matched. The two types overlap, especially in that situation which is widely regarded as especially risky, that of youthful, of teen-age marriage.

In China, Japan, India, and Islamic countries, child marriage was an established and much practiced institution, not only in ancient times. In Europe of the Middle Ages it was not uncommon either. We read of engagements concluded by princes or noblemen for their infant children and the performance of the marriage ceremonies when the children were around the age of ten. We are not concerned with such cases of cultures totally different from ours.[9]

Between 1890 and 1940 the median age at first marriage for all women who ever married declined slightly — from 22 years to about 21½. But after World War II it dropped to about 20 years. The corresponding figures for men were 26 in 1890, about 24 in 1940, and about 23 in the late 1950s.[10]

Data collected from the Marriage Registration Area (1962–63: 36 states accounting for 62.5 percent of the national total of marriages) indicate that teen-age couples constitute only a minority of all of the marriages which include one teen-age partner. Most of the teen-agers who marry are brides marrying older grooms. In 1963, the rate at which young women (14–19 years of age) married was over three times the rate at which young men in the same age group married.[11] Comparison of the data for 1963 with those for 1960 is said to indicate that young women in their teens not only married at a lower rate in 1963 than in 1960 but also tended to choose older men less frequently.[12]

From 1900 to 1950 the United States population married at age 14–19 increased in the case of males from 39,000 to 175,000 and in the case of females from 421,000 to 895,000.[13]

Because of the lack of nationwide data, correlations between age at marriage and incidence of factual marriage breakdown have so far not been made at all and correlations between age of marriage and incidence of divorce have been made for geographically limited populations only. Since young people are likely to be anxious, after the breakdown of a marriage, to return to the freedom of remarriage, it can be assumed that in their case the number of divorces more nearly

---

9. The claim that child marriage arranged by the parents constitutes the best possible system was made by an Indian physician, Dr. S. Roy, in a letter to the editor, Saturday Review, 19 January 1963, at 23. The relevant passage is reproduced in FOOTE, LEVY & SANDER, CASES AND MATERIALS ON FAMILY LAW 231 (1966). India's low divorce rate is said to constitute the proof. The author overlooks the fact that both child marriage and divorce must be seen in the total complex of the cultural climate of the society in question. Arranged child marriage, Hindu style, would be as impossible in the cultural climate of the United States as divorce was in that of traditional Hinduism.

10. P. H. JACOBSON, AMERICAN MARRIAGE AND DIVORCE 75 (1959); see also [California] Assembly Interim Committee Reports 1963–1965, vol. 23, no. 6, Final Report of the Assembly Interim Committee on Judiciary Relating to Domestic Relations 51 (1965).

11. NAT'L CENTER FOR HEALTH STATISTICS, Ser. 21, no. 16, MARRIAGE STATISTICS ANALYSIS, U.S. 1963, at 7 (1968).

12. *Id.* at 10.

13. JACOBSON, *supra* note 10, at 162.

approximates that of factual marriage breakdown than it does in the case of older people. The published data indicate that marriages concluded at a youthful age have higher divorce rates than marriages concluded at a higher age. Of the twenty-three states participating in the Divorce Registration Area in 1963, only six (Hawaii, Iowa, Missouri, Rhode Island, Tennessee, and Wisconsin) supplied the necessary data. In 1963, in these states the husband had been under the age of 20 at the time of marriage in 19.4 percent of all divorces or annulments, and the percentage for men who at the time of marriage had been from 20 to 24 years old was 39.6 percent. The corresponding percentages for the wives were 48.3 percent below the age of 20 at the time of marriage, and 24.7 percent between 20 and 24. For the total group of divorcing persons, the percentage of those who at the time of marriage had been below 25 years of age was 59 percent of the males and 73 percent of the females.[14]

The Report of the California Interim Committee[15] presents data tending to indicate that the marriages concluded when both parties were below the age of twenty are more likely to end in divorce than any other marriages.

A peculiarly high correlation between youthful age at marriage and high proneness for breakup appears in the statistical comparison of 500 marriages and 500 desertion and nonsupport cases in Philadelphia, undertaken by Hart and Shields,[16] and in Monahan's extensive study of the 52,722 marriages and the 8,040 divorces that occurred in Iowa 1945–47, in cases of white couples, both parties married once only, residence in Iowa at the time of marriage, and both marriage and divorce taking place in the state.[17] It is thus understandable that, as stated by Monahan,[18] the assumption that youthful marriages are particularly susceptible to divorce has general support from "public attitude" and "most sociological authors." But Monahan himself is not fully convinced that the youthful age of the party or parties is necessarily the decisive factor. He points to the probability of higher incidence of forced or shotgun marriages and of such disruptive factors as economic difficulties or parental interference.[19] Similarly, David R.

14. NAT'L CENTER FOR HEALTH STATISTICS, Ser. 21, no. 13, DIVORCE STATISTICS ANALYSIS, U.S. 1963, at 14 (1967).
15. Assembly Interim Committee Reports 1963–1965, vol. 23, no. 6, p. 51 (1965).
16. *Happiness in Relation to Age at Marriage*, 12 J.SOC. HYGIENE 403 (1926).
17. *Does Age at Marriage Matter in Divorce?* 32 SOCIAL FORCES 81 (1953); condensation in FOOTE, LEVY & SANDERS, *supra* note 9, at 227–30.
18. At 82.
19. At 84–86.

Mace observes that "teen-age marriages do not occur among a typical cross section of the teen-age population, but rather among those who are so immature, disturbed, irresponsible or confused that they are likely to encounter marriage difficulties irrespective of the age at which they marry."[20] Such observations are unquestionably true, but they hardly affect the truth of the proposition that in youthful marriages the risk of breakdown is higher than in marriages concluded at a more mature age. As shown in Monahan's study[21] the risk is higher when both parties are below the age of 20 and lowest when at the time of marriage the groom is from 24 to 26 and the bride from 22 to 24. Marriages concluded at this "ideal" age constitute the great majority. Marriages in which both parties are in their teens are rare. Marriages between a younger groom and an older bride are even more infrequent, but marriages between a youthful female and a man of considerably higher age occur with some frequency.[22] These marriages appear to be more threatened the greater the difference in age.

Should one expect that the incidence of family breakdown could be measurably lowered by reducing the incidence of youthful marriages? The answer must be negative if reducing the number of such marriages means to prohibit or inhibit them by legal devices. In every state of the United States as in all modern countries, the law establishes a minimum age below which a person cannot marry. In most places this minimum limit is low.[23] At common law it was the age of 7. A second limit was 14 years for males and 12 for females: a marriage in which one party was below that limit but above the age of 7 was said to be "inchoate and incomplete." The marriage was valid, but it could be retroactively eradicated through disaffirmance by the party under age, provided he did so before or immediately upon reaching the age of consent. But he confirmed the marriage if he continued cohabitation.[24] The nonage party thus had a power of election. Unless he disaffirmed the marriage before or upon reaching the age of consent, the marriage remained in effect, indissoluble, of course, as long as divorce was not available in the jurisdiction.

20. Article published in Minneapolis Star, 1 October 1963, as reported in FOOTE, LEVY & SANDER 230.
21. Table 3.
22. NAT'L CENTER FOR HEALTH STATISTICS, Ser. 21, no. 16, MARRIAGE STATISTICS ANALYSIS, U.S., 1963, at 8 ff. (1968).
23. On the following, see H. H. CLARK, JR., THE LAW OF DOMESTIC RELATIONS IN THE UNITED STATES 77 ff. (1968).
24. Occasionally a power of disaffirmance also belonged to the marriage partner of the party of nonage.

In all American states the common-law age of consent has been increased, in a majority of the states to 18 years for males and 16 for females. But in some states the limit is lower. In a few it is as high as 21 for males and 18 for females. Generally, it is held that a marriage to which one party was below the statutory age of consent can be disaffirmed by that party. But diverse, and frequently confused, views obtain with respect to other questions: can the marriage be annulled upon the petition of the parents of the nonage party? May the marriage be treated as null and void if it has not been affirmed in time by the under-age party? May the ineffectiveness of a nonage marriage which has not been clearly disaffirmed be raised by third persons?

Almost all states have by statute introduced another limitation. No marriage license may be issued for an intended marriage without the written consent of the parent or guardian of a party who is below a certain age limit. This limit is higher than the limit determining the age of consent. When the latter is 18 for males and 16 for females, the limit determining the need of parental consent tends to be 21 for males and 18 for females. Occasionally it is provided that for the consent of the parent or guardian that of a judge may be substituted when a parent's denial of consent appears abusive or harmful to the best interests of the party or parties to the intended marriage. In some other states, the parental consent does not suffice to allow the issuance of the marriage license until it has been approved by a judge. The statutory requirement of parental consent to the issuance of a marriage license is, of course, no safeguard in those fourteen states in which it is still possible to enter upon a common-law marriage, i.e., a marriage that can be concluded without any ceremony and consequently without a license. Even in those states where a ceremony is necessary for the conclusion of a marriage and where no official or minister is allowed to perform a marriage ceremony unless the parties have first obtained a license, if the parties, perhaps by lying about the point of age, have wrongly obtained a license, or if they succeed in having a ceremony performed with a forged license or without any license at all, their marriage is nevertheless valid. It can be disaffirmed neither by the party who should not have obtained the license without the proper consent, nor by a person whose consent should have been obtained. Documentary proof of age is not universally required in the United States. In some states, only one of the parties to the intended marriage has to appear in person before the license issuer. Lying about age is thus not too difficult and young people in love easily yield to the temptation, even under oath, to make false statements. Besides, the diversity of state laws on age limits and on formalities necessary to obtain a marriage license constitutes an invitation to the evasion of the law of the home state. If an out-of-state marriage is attacked later on, the courts are inclined to uphold it if it is valid under the law of the place of contracting even if the parties returned to the home state right after the marriage ceremony.

Present laws establishing age limits are thus far from being fully effective. Could they be changed so as to increase their effectiveness? The answer has to be negative. In many cases of youthful marriage, especially those where both parties are teen-agers, the decision to marry is made when the girl has become pregnant. In the American system of coeducation, dating, and going steady, the temptation to engage in sexual intercourse is high. Techniques of birth control are frequently unknown to or impracticable for youngsters. Where religious or moral inhibitions are weak, the threat of disciplinary measures by the school authorities or even that of delinquency proceedings in a criminal court rarely suffices as a deterrent.[25] Where intercourse results in pregnancy, psychological and social pressures easily induce the parties to conclude a marriage the instability of which can be foreseen, or is actually foreseen by the parties. The parties may even be in agreement that they are not to live together and that a divorce or an annulment is to be obtained immediately after the marriage or after the birth of the child. The stigma of illegitimacy is to be prevented, perhaps also, for the girl, that of being an unwed mother. The pressure is increased by the law when it exempts from punishment for statutory rape the man who goes through a ceremony of marriage with the girl whom he has made pregnant. A marriage concluded under such circumstances can hardly be expected to be harmonious. But should one therefore abolish those laws by which punishment is foregone in the case of marriage? Should the male partner be sent to jail or a penitentiary in all circumstances, even if he is himself a youngster? Such indiscriminate application of the usually serious punishment with which statutory rape is threatened would be widely regarded as shocking. But should punishment for statutory rape be abolished altogether? That would be even more shocking, especially when the man is considerably older than the girl. Should criminal punishment perhaps be abolished just for those cases in which the male partner is an adolescent? This could mean leaving the matter to the unpredictable discretion of juvenile courts or the police. Perhaps, the least unsatisfac-

---

25. On such measures see FOOTE, LEVY & SANDER, *supra* note 9, at 234.

tory solution is the present one, in spite of the great vulnerability of the marriages it brings about. After all, the social problem of the situation has been created by premature intercourse and pregnancy rather than the divorce. The marriage can be deemed to have broken down even before it was concluded. The subsequent divorce is no more than the formalization of that breakdown which not only assures, if that is factually possible, the support of the child and saves it from the stigma of bastardy, but also makes it possible for the parties to enter upon new, more meaningful ventures, sobered by the experience.

So we must conclude that in the cultural climate of present-day America marriages of adolescents cannot be eliminated or even perceptibly reduced by legal means. But some effect, even a considerable one, may be achieved by influencing the subculture of adolescents. A potentially effective means toward this end is education for family living. Such education is basically the task of the parents, who have generally proved not to be up to it. Churches and the public agencies of education, the schools, have to step in. Family life education promises to be particularly effective if it makes candidates for marriage aware of the advisability of seeking premarital counseling, and if such counseling is then, indeed, available.[26]

Marriages of adolescents are not the only ones in which an especially high risk of breakdown is inherent. Common sense and systematic studies indicate that the risk is abnormally high where the social background of the partners is so different that it decisively influences their personality traits. Since the pioneer study of Burgess and Cottrell[27] the literature on marital compatibility has grown to vast proportions. Predictably unharmonious marriages cannot be forbidden. In a free society they should not. But education for family living and premarital counseling can warn the parties of the risk. These devices also are the most effective ones to counteract the risk inherent in hasty marriages. In a more traditionalist cultural climate marriages between parties of heterogeneous background are infrequent, young people are wont to seek the advice of their parents, and a long period of en-

---

26. On the role of family life education, see Assembly Interim Committee Reports 1964–65, Final Report of the Assembly Interim Committee on Judiciary, Relating to Family Relations (vol. 23, no. 6), 29, 54 (A Study of High School Student Marriages, Pregnancies and School Policy, by Judson T. Landis), and 59 (Statement submitted by Lester A. Kirkendall). A list of books used in California high schools is given at 52.

27. Ernest W. BURGESS & LEONARD S. COTTRELL, PREDICTING SUCCESS OR FAILURE IN MARRIAGE 94–106 (Publications of the American Sociological Society, vol. 27, 1935).

gagement gives the parties the opportunity to know and to test the traits of each other's characters. All this has changed in the course of continuously increasing industrialization. The seclusion of marriageable females has long been a quaint historical reminiscence. Social contacts between people of different classes, educational levels, nationality, race, and religion have multiplied; engagements, even short ones, have gone out of fashion. In Continental countries a marriage ceremony cannot be performed before the expiration of the two weeks or so during which the banns must be published. Additional time is frequently needed for the procurement of the documents to be submitted. In most parts of the United States a marriage license can be obtained practically instantaneously and the marriage may be celebrated immediately thereupon.[28] Attempts through statutory establishment of short waiting periods to compel the parties to consider the fateful step at least for a few days have been of little avail. The impatient simply drive to a more accommodating state. Marriages concluded after just a few hours or days of acquaintance are, of course, infrequent. They would not be news if it were otherwise. But still the impression prevails that in modern life marriages are concluded with less consideration than they once were. Unquestionably, the knowledge that in the case of failure a divorce can be obtained with ease has contributed to the development of this inclination to take the step of marrying less seriously. To that extent it is justified to say that divorce breeds divorce. But in the cultural climate that has developed in the course of ever increasing industrialization it was inevitable that the door should be opened wide to the possibility of remarriage after the breakdown of a previous marriage, even if that marriage was an ill-considered one. So once again it seems that the law is impotent to prevent the conclusion of hasty or otherwise ill-considered marriages by restrictions, and that the only remedies promising a measure of success are again family life education and counseling.

Marriage breakdown may, of course, occur even when the mates were not badly matched initially. Breakdown may be caused by tension, friction, temptation, or external circumstances developing during the course of marriage. The fact that a high percentage of all divorces occurs during the early years of marriage may indicate that because of insufficient deliberation the majority of disrupted marriages are doomed from the outset.[29] But there are enough of those in

---

28. See M. RICHMOND & F. S. HALL, MARRIAGE AND THE STATE (1929).
29. In the Divorce Registration Area the percentage of divorces and annulments in 1965 occurring before the end of the second year after the conclusion of the mar-

which the divorce and, one may surmise, the break occur so late that developments taking place in the course of the marriage are likely to have been the cause.[30]

Marriage crises and, possibly, subsequent marriage breakdown may result from divergent developments of the spouses, caused in turn by changing external circumstances to which one spouse fails to adjust. The legislative softening of the German divorce law of 1938 is said to have had as one of its causes the fact that the wives of certain functionaries of the National Socialist movement could not adapt themselves to the sudden rise of their husbands from social insignificance to high positions, great power, and exalted social standing. The marriages broke down under the strain, and the husbands were anxious to be free to remarry companions more suitable to their new positions. In the Russian Revolution breaks occurred between spouses of whom one would fervently embrace the ideals of the new order while the other could not readily abandon the traditional values. In such a mobile society as that of the United States, one spouse may fail to keep pace with the other's rise to high position in the government, the economy, or academic life. Or the spouses' careers stand in the way of a normal family life. The husband may be an attorney bound to the place where he is admitted to practice, while the wife is an actress working at constantly changing locations. Or, one spouse is unable to overcome the shock of experiencing the other's resorting to crime, being convicted, and imprisoned and thus dishonoring the family. Or, one spouse becomes converted to a religion or political faith in which the other does not believe. Or, one spouse continues to grow intellectually and the other fails to keep pace. The causes and forms of divergent personality development are manifold. The law is impotent to prevent such situations. It can, and for a long time actually has, barred escape from the bond of such a marriage. In some cases the impossibility of entering upon a new marriage may actually have induced the partners to suffer in silence or even to make successful efforts to overcome the crisis. But how many cases have there been in which the situation

---

riage was 14.6. Of the two years, the higher percentage, 9.3, occurred during the second year. The percentage of divorces occurring during the third year was 8.6. It decreased for each year following. NAT'L CENTER FOR HEALTH STATISTICS, DIVORCE STATISTICS ANALYSIS, U.S., 1964 and 1965, at 42–43. The percentages for earlier years were similar (*id.* 10).

30. In 1965 the percentage of divorces and annulments occurring in the Divorce Registration Area after the sixteenth year of marriage was 24.4, of those occurring after the twenty-first year of the marriage was 16.3 (*id.* 42–43).

has produced adultery, or the husband's taking a mistress, or separation followed by the establishment of a new but irregular union, or disappearance followed by bigamy? We have no figures. But all signs indicate that the incidence of breakdown, immorality, or irregularity has been high even when the causes of divergent personality development were less frequent and less acute than they are today. By instituting rules on divorce that are repressive or of a penal nature, the law has not been of help in such situations. If anything can help, it is again family life education and counseling. And the same conclusion applies to cases of marital maladjustment due to immaturity or sexual incompatibility. Neuroses, are probably frequent at the present age of mobility, decline of religion and authority, permissive education, professional strain, and the belief that insecurity is greater than ever, although, in fact, it is considerably lower than it ever was in the "good old days."

Something more than providing a good education for family living and a system of competent and easily accessible counseling can be done in some of those economic situations which experience has shown to be conducive to marriage breakdown. Temporary setbacks do not seem to increase the incidence of family breakdown. Such calamities as natural catastrophes, war, mass expulsion, or economic depression seem rather to cement family coherence. Perhaps the even trend of the American divorce rate during the years of the Great Depression was simply due to inability or unwillingness to pay the high cost of divorce. About the incidence in those years of factual marriage breakdown, we have no data. It must have been considerable in those numerous cases in which a husband left the family home in search of a job elsewhere. But a family that weathers a storm together is likely to be highly cohesive. At the end of World War II, when twelve million Germans were expelled from their homes in eastern Europe, families tended to stay together in their flight to the West, as did those who later escaped from East Germany into the Federal Republic. Among these Germans family coherence was found to be very strong, stronger, indeed, that it had been in happier times.[31]

But by never-ending poverty, slum housing, poor education, and lack of recreation, family stability is apt to be affected adversely, just as it is by alcoholism and drug addiction. The chain of causality can be complex. The tensions created by the adverse condtions easily result in crime, delinquency, despair, indifference, promiscuity, quarrel-

---

31. H. SCHELSKY, WANDLUNGEN DER DEUTSCHEN FAMILE IN DER GEGENWART 63 (1954).

ing, family crises, and family breakup.[32] Family instability has been characteristic of the lowest status groups of society: American Negroes, London East-Enders, Paris *clochards*, the "Lumpenproletariat" of Berlin-Wedding. The divorce rate may be high, as among the low-status groups of white Americans, or low where divorce is not needed for respectability or is not within financial reach. The bond of marriage is taken the least seriously by those groups which are so low on the social ladder that their behavior patterns are irrelevant to the guardians of respectability. The bottom groups are those among whom the irregular union is a regular phenomenon. De facto divorce, as it has been called, is typical among American Negroes[33] or the Indians of Bolivia. The "Stockholm marriages," so much discussed in Sweden,[34] owed their name to the fact that they were frequent among working-class people at the time when they had to live on a low proletarian level. In Italy irregular unions rarely occurred among the middle or upper classes before industrialization had changed the cultural climate of the country, or more correctly, of its northern parts. Their number is highest, and they have begun to be respectable, in Turin, Milan, and Florence. In the south they are still limited to the slum dwellers of Naples and Palermo, where those at the bottom still resort to abandonment, prostitution, adultery, "divorce Italian style," or escape northward.

We do not know to what extent, if any, the breakup process among subproletarians is reduced by improvement of social conditions. The most or, perhaps, the only effective way to achieve lasting improvement has been industrialization. But universally increasing industrialization has been accompanied by rising divorce rates and, probably, by rising rates of factual marriage breakdown. The process of industrialization involves so much migration, uprooting of traditional modes of living, obliterating of traditional mores, etc. that we must assume almost with certainty that it not only induces people to regularize situations of actual breakdown which would have occurred in any case, but that it also is a cause, nay, *the* cause, of increased incidence of factual marriage breakdown. The reduction of that incidence which is caused by the rise of the bottom groups of society may thus be upset, or more than upset, by the disupting effects of industrialization. But this factor may lose relevance once the society has reached a high level of mature industrialization. True, in a fully industrialized society, mobility, geo-

---

32. *Cf.* Danon Boileau, *Influence de l'habitat sur l'équilibre psychologique du foyer*, POUR LA VIE 1956, at 307.

33. Foster, *supra* note 1, at 43; Weyrauch, *supra* note 1, at 88.

34. *Supra*, chap. 6.

graphic and social, is higher than in the traditional society of pre-industrialization. Those who are involved in individual mobility remain threatened with anomie. But the social structure as such becomes less unstable and, above all, people learn how to live in the new society and to develop new role patterns. The process is slow and the number of those who fail to adapt to the brave new world is high. Those who feel uncomfortable in the new civilization easily become revolutionaries or escapists. But such individuals are more numerous among the comparatively small group of intellectuals than among those who have come to enjoy the amenities of middle-class living. Student revolutionaries have failed to find support among the workers or their unions in the United States as well as in France, Germany, Great Britain, and Italy. In the period between the end of the transition from a traditionalist to a fully industrialized society and the onset, in the 1960s, of the new phase of industrialization, divorce rates and, we may surmise, the rates of factual breakdown were comparatively stable.[35]

Among the more affluent and better educated groups divorce rates seem to be lower than among groups of lower education or lower income.[36] As among the educated the need of respectability is greatest, we can assume that among them the number of divorces approximates that of cases of factual breakdown, while among the lower groups the number of such cases is certainly higher than the number of divorces. We may have here additional evidence that the trend of increasing frequency of breakdown which appears to accompany industrialization is broken or at least retarded in those groups which have found their place in the new society, while it continues among those who are still caught in the process of transition or have failed to enjoy the full fruits of the new order.

Measures to improve the conditions of the lower classes or of society in general may thus have some stabilizing effect on marriage. This effect, if it occurs at all, is independent of the motives for which such measures are taken. It may be a by-product of a "war on poverty" waged for political reasons or as a general step toward social reform, or of a policy aimed at stopping a decline in the birthrate and the threatened shrinkage of the population. Such a policy has been adopted in France and Sweden. Couples are encouraged to be fertile. Stability

---

35. See *supra* p. 312.
36. A. B. Hollingshead, *Class Differences in Marriage Stability*, 272 ANN. AM. ACAD. POL. SOC. SCI. 39 (1950); W. J. Goode, *Economic Factors and Marital Stability*, 16 AM. SOCIOL. REV. 474 (1951); R. F. WINCH, THE MODERN FAMILY 704 (1963).

of the home and family life are regarded as essential for this end. The implementation of such a "family policy" may remove factors which are apt to cause marriage instability. In other countries, especially the socialist countries and Great Britain, Canada, West Germany, and the United States, measures of this kind constitute parts of an overall policy of revolutionary or evolutionary social reform as demanded by egalitarian democracy.

In the United States, social legislation has been extensive ever since the era of the New Deal when the Supreme Court receded from an initial hostility toward it.[37] Free public education continually expanding to reach higher age groups has been in existence for more than a century. Workmen's compensation laws were enacted around the turn of the century. The New Deal brought social security, insurance against unemployment, minimum wage and maximum hour laws. The National Labor Relations Act fortified the bargaining power of labor. Through public welfare the subsistence minimum was secured for everybody. Through the legislation on aid for dependent children, or as it is now called, aid for families with dependent children (AFDC), a minimum financial basis has been established for the needy among the growing generation, which is also supported by free school lunches, medical examinations, and free immunization. Public housing measures are intended to improve the living conditions of the most needy. The tax burden of married people is alleviated through the privilege of the joint return as well as through income tax exemptions and the marital deduction which lessens the estate tax burden of a surviving spouse and so, by indirection, the necessity of cutting down on living expenses of the ongoing family in order to accumulate savings for the survivor. The public measures are supplemented by the activities of voluntary family service organizations, denominational and secular.

Few, if any, of these extensive social welfare measures have been taken for the express purpose of strengthening family cohesion and thus reducing the incidence of family breakdown. But they all may have these effects by indirection. With some the effect is obvious, as, for instance, housing or unemployment insurance. Others have, in the course of their administration, turned out to weaken rather than strengthen family stability. Such, for instance, was the case of AFDC under the man-in-the-house rule, by which a financial premium was placed upon separation and abandonment. Or what effect does the Soviet Union's extensively provided day care for children have upon

---

37. On this initial hostility, see esp. E. LAMBERT, LE GOUVERNEMENT DES JUGES (1921).

families? By freeing the mother for gainful outside work it decreases the financial dependency of wives upon their husbands and may thus remove an inhibition against the breaking up of a marriage which might otherwise be endured. Whether such endurance would be socially desirable is, of course, a different question. The impact of social welfare measures upon family stability is potentially enormous. Through well-considered use they could constitute an effective device of rational family policy and prove much more effective than manipulation of the laws on divorce. But much research is needed to render these tools more effective and to avoid adverse consequences.

So far little is known either about the effects upon family stability of those legislative and other measures which have been taken in numerous foreign countries but for which the United States does not, or not yet, have exact counterparts. The most conspicuous of these devices is the system of family allowances, which in 1959 existed in no less than thirty-eight countries,[38] among them Canada. Mostly such legislation has been motivated by a desire to reverse a declining trend in the birthrate or simply to encourage fertility. In the Federal Republic of Germany general considerations of social welfare have been emphasized. Financial allowances are paid periodically to the heads of households in which children are brought up. In Sweden an allowance is paid for every child up to sixteen years of age, in France for every child from the second on, but in Brazil no allowances are paid for the first seven children. In detail, the regulations are complex.[39] In systems as elaborate as those of France or Sweden, the laws on family allowances are supplemented by other benefits for families having children or having numerous children, such as free vacations for children, mothers, or both, reduction of railroad fares, free medical care, home helper service in the case of illness of the mother or other emergency, etc. The implementation and constant elaboration of the governmental measures are promoted by private organizations. A powerful network of private and semiprivate *associations familiales* has been established in France,[40] where they are officially represented in the

---

38. H. T. ELDRIDGE, POPULATION POLITICS: A SURVEY OF RECENT DEVELOPMENTS (1954); K. M. Bolte, *Bevölkerung (Politik)*, 2 HANDWÖRTERBUCH DER SOZIALWISSENSCHAFTEN 159 (1959); UNITED NATIONS, DEPARTMENT OF SOCIAL AFFAIRS, ECONOMIC MEASURES IN FAVOR OF THE FAMILY (1952).

39. See, for instance, G. Marty, *La politique juridique française en faveur de la famille*, 9 ANN. DE LA FACULTÉ DE DROIT D'ISTANBUL (8ᵉ année, no. 13), at 199 (1960); G. Karlsson, *Social Policies and Marriage Stability in Sweden*, id. 240.

40. The French family associations are of several types: general family associations, associations of families with numerous children, family associations of specific vocational groups such as civil service personnel, railroad employees, farmers, de-

governmental bodies all the way up to the Ministry of Public Health and Population, and where they exercise considerable influence upon the committees of public health and population of the chambers of the National Assembly. In the Federal Republic of Germany a special cabinet Ministry of Family has been established. On the supranational level, national family associations have formed the *Union internationale des associations familiales*.

TABLE 24
COMPARISON OF DIVORCE RATES, SHOWING POSSIBLE INFLUENCE OF FAMILY POLICIES, 1962–66
(Per 1,000 Population)

	1962	1963	1964	1965	1966
U.S.	2.22	2.27	2.35	2.47	2.54
France	0.65	0.63	0.69	0.72	0.74
West Germany	0.82	0.84	0.91	0.93	0.92
Sweden	1.17	1.12	1.20	1.24	1.32

Source: U.N. DEMOGRAPHIC YEARBOOK, 1968, table 34.

The divorce rates of countries having family allowances and other measures of family policy have all been lower than that of the United States, even countries of so high a degree of industrialization as the Federal Republic of Germany, Sweden, and France (see table 24). To what extent these data reflect an influence of the measures of family policy upon the incidence of marriage breakup is a problem on which no research whatever seems to have been undertaken so far.

Research and experiment should be undertaken to find out whether the alleviation of economic conditions apt to produce tension between spouses promises to be an effective device in reducing the incidence of marriage breakdown. Another avenue ought to be explored too: in what ways can we reduce the psychological tensions which may be a source of marriage breakdown even more significant than economic adversity? Such tensions may be created by sexual maladjustment. Education promises to have prophylactic effects. Therapy may be provided by physicians, especially psychiatrists, the treatment possibly induced through marriage counseling, including premarital counseling.

---

nominational associations (Catholic and Protestant), associations of parents of high school pupils, etc. In each *département* the various family associations are brought together in a *Union départementale des associations familiales*, which sends representatives into a number of national organizations, among them the National Economic Council and the High Commission on Collective Labor Agreements, and the consultative boards on social security, public welfare, social service, etc.

A major cause of marriage breakdown seems to be the uncertainty about the role assigned to women in present-day American society. The mere fact that the great majority of suits for divorce are filed by women does not, of course, suffice to support this view. Irrespective of the wife's role in the decision to break up an existing home, it is simply customary in those negotiations which usually precede the filing of the suit to assign the petitioner's role to the wife. Even if the wife's role as formal petitioner coincides with the role of initiator of the actual break, it does not necessarily follow that the cause of the break has also been the work of the wife. She may have been driven to it by the husband's conduct. But it seems to be true that woman's uncertainty about her place and role in society creates nervous tensions in her which easily result in neurotic behavior and thus in conflict between the spouses. Women have been emancipated from their former legal disabilities. They have been given political rights equal to those of men. The Civil Rights Act of 1964 has also declared women to be entitled to employment opportunities equal to those of men. Careers in the professions and in business are open to women. Above all, women's education is now the same as that of men. Women are told to expect independence, to be the equals of men not only in form but in reality. But they are not. The expectation of full equality and independence is not fulfilled in American life. In fact, it is less real in the United States than in, let us say, the Soviet Union, Germany, or Sweden, where it is not complete either. The American middle-class woman's education directs her toward a professional career, only to find that it is hard for her to penetrate the phalanx of males who resent her intrusion into the sacred precincts of the professions, to say nothing of the ranks of business executives. Certain vocations — teaching, nursing, librarianship, social work — are female domains, but their members suffer from inferiority complexes and the top ranks are reserved for men. Some women also find out that it is hard to combine the two ways of life to which they aspire: professional life and marriage. Once children have arrived, the career has mostly to be given up and the wife finds herself relegated to the home. Thanks to modern household appliances housework does not fill the day, but what housework there is must largely be done without servants, and the college educated woman feels it to be degrading drudgery. On how to educate the children the mother is beset with uncertainty. Children yearn for guidance, for authority, but they cannot find it from parents who have been brought up to disdain authority and hesitate to inculcate moral values whose validity has not been proved, which is, of course, impossible. Soon the children enter kindergarten and school and are taken off the mother's hands for much of the day. The husband is away at work, the wife is left to herself, with free time. She tries to fill it with pursuits she does not really think worth while. So she grows frustrated, plagued by anxiety, irritable, dissatisfied. The virtues of self-denial, humility, patience, resignation, are out of fashion. Rarely is consolation sought, and even more rarely found, in religion. Psychoanalysis is accessible only to the affluent, and an uncertain remedy to those who can afford it. The husband may not be able to satisfy his wife's overly high expectations. So there will be frustration on both sides, tension, and a high risk of breakup.

Dissatisfied people are the most dangerous to peace, political and domestic. Both revolution and marital disharmony thrive on dissatisfaction. More human needs are fulfilled in our time than ever before. Yet dissatisfaction seems also to be more general and more intense. The very fulfillment of once pressing needs has made expectations run ahead of reality. A utopian society free from war and authority, is sincerely believed to be achievable by sinful men. Absurd as it is, many among the young generation are so ignorant of history that they commiserate with themselves as the generation exposed to greater uncertainty and more gruesome risks than any earlier one. So the victims of progressive education take to flight into the escapist realms of drugs, sex, flower power, pacifism, extraparliamentary opposition, romanticism—realms in which lasting satisfaction is not to be found. The hard ways of discipline, self-restraint, acceptance of fate immutable by man, these solely effective ways to find satisfaction here on earth, are disdained. If marital breakdown has indeed come to be more frequent than in the past, here seems to lie the principal cause. To some extent we may be able by measures of social policy, if not to remove, at least to mitigate some of the economic sources of dissatisfaction. Indeed, the development of the cultural climate seems to move in that direction. But is it not that same direction by which the deeper, noneconomic sources of dissatisfaction have been aggravated, by which the discomfort of civilization is intensified? If that is the case, the danger could be banned only by a total reversal brought about by a cataclysmic catastrophe, but not by measures of deliberate policy. But is this truly the situation? Are there really no prospects that within the present stream of cultural development all efforts to reduce dissatisfaction are doomed to failure? We do not know. Little attention has been paid to this basic problem. If we really wish to do something about family breakdown, it is here that our attention should be focused. If research and experiment should indicate that it is possible within the framework of the prevailing cultural climate to reduce human dissatisfaction, more will be done for the preservation of the family and the home, of society and of civilization, than by any tinkering with the laws on divorce.

Measures of social policy may conceivably help to reduce the economic sources of those tensions that are shown by experience to be conducive toward the breakdown of marriages. Tensions may be prevented or alleviated also by help directly extended to individuals through family life education, marriage counseling, and conciliation services.[41]

Family life education means planned and sustained preparation for marriage and parenthood. In marriage counseling people receive advice on how to handle difficulties that have arisen in their married life. Conciliation is that special kind of counseling in which an attempt is made to heal a marital breach that has already occurred. Family life education and marriage counseling are not neatly separated from each other. They are combined in premarital counseling. and in that activity of social agencies which has come to be called family service. In our context, the terms will be used in the following senses:

By *family life education* we shall understand those activities which are aimed at preparing people as yet unmarried for the responsibilities of married life and parenthood. By *marriage counseling* we shall mean those activities which are aimed at helping parties to troubled marriages to understand their difficulties and the sources of them, and thus to deal with them in a rational way. Where marital difficulties have their source in neurotic traits, the marriage counselor may have to resort to *therapy*, ordinarily by advising the client to seek the service of a psychotherapist. By *conciliation* we shall mean those activities which are principally aimed at inducing parties to a marriage which has factually broken down to resume their marital life. The term *family service* is used to refer to those manifold services by which social agencies attempt to help people to avoid or to straighten out family problems of any kind. In addition to education for family life and marriage counseling it includes such activities as educational coun-

---

41. Problems of family life education and marriage counseling are currently discussed in the JOURNAL OF MARRIAGE AND THE FAMILY, 1939–, now published by the National Council on Family Relations. A large number of publications is listed in R. G. LORINCZI, MARRIAGE COUNSELING AND CONCILIATION, KNOWN COURT CONNECTED SERVICES, WITH SUMMARIES OF STATUTES AND A BIBLIOGRAPHY, published by the American Bar Foundation, 1970.

seling, probation services, economic or legal assistance, care of the aged, and medical services.

Marriage counseling and family life education are modern terms, but what they refer to is anything but new. Both activities have been carried on through all the ages in which marriage and the family have existed, i.e., from the very beginning of the human race. But the agents by which these functions once were exercised no longer function so effectively as is needed. New agencies must be called upon to supplement, or where necessary to take the place of, the old.

In some circles in the United States the term family life education has assumed an odious, sinister meaning. The inclusion in school curricula of courses in family life education has been denounced as part of a communist plot to corrupt American youth. But what is meant by these often passionate critics is not family life education as we mean it but a special and not necessarily essential branch of it: sex education. Some parents object to the classroom presentation and discussion of sex in public schools, especially in coeducational classes. Sex education, they maintain, is the task of father or mother rather than teacher. That position may overlook the third alternative — sex education by age mates — but it deserves attention and discussion. At any rate the subject of the controversy — sex education in the schools — must be clearly labeled as such. Indiscriminate attacks on family life education are directed against aims which are dear to the very people by whom the attacks are launched.

Family life education in the comprehensive sense of the term means the development of personality traits and attitudes and the imparting of knowledge which an individual must have if his marriage is to be a stable cell of society, a source of personal satisfaction, and a cradle of the young, all of which it is expected to be in our civilization.

The first goal at which family life education should be aimed is that of injecting reason into the decision of whether or not to marry at all. Some persons simply should not marry. They are unfit for marriage just as there are persons who are unfit for the priest's or the religious' life of chastity. He who considers marriage ought to know himself, ought to consider whether he is sufficiently mature, whether he is able to bear the financial responsibilities. He must know that where one party is sexually impotent or homosexual the marriage is likely to be unsatisfactory. But he must also know that sexual attraction is not enough and that ardent love may not last.

Education toward knowledge of one's own personality must be combined with education toward rationality in the choice of the mate.

Among orthodox Moslems future spouses are not supposed to see each other before they are married. Traditionally, parental arrangement of marriages has been the established system of India, China, and Japan. It functioned because men could find satisfaction with prostitutes and geishas, and women were brought up to be submissive and long-suffering. In Western bourgeois society parentally arranged marriage played a considerable role although it never followed the exclusive pattern presented by Engels, Bebel, and other socialist writers. Property arrangements certainly played a conspicuous part, but parents could not fully neglect their sons' and daughters' own desires and aversions. Since the age of the troubadors and before, the ideal of romantic love has played too important a role in Western lore to be neglected even in the arrangement of marriages,[42] not to speak of the church's emphasis upon the marrying parties' own free will, tempered though it might be by filial piety.[43] Yet, with all freedom, the choice of marriage partners was ordinarily limited to the circle of personal acquaintance or persons known indirectly through family or friends. That circle was not large and was regularly limited to those of the same social class, religion, ethnicity, and education.

In the society of the contemporary industrialized, urbanized world, of coeducation, female emancipation, travel, and youth culture, no limits are set to the circle of possible acquaintances both male and female. Inhibitions toward sexual contact have weakened and temptations and occasions for it have multiplied. With the waning of parental authority and the growing financial independence of the young, the need of parental consent to marriage or even of parental advice in the choice of the marriage partner is disappearing. The young man, the young woman, is anxious to make his own choice. He is induced to believe that it cannot be made for him by anyone else, because in marriage he seeks the fulfillment of values and desires so strictly personal that he, and only he, can feel where they might be found. These values are subtle, more complex, and more delicate than they were in earlier times. In the big city man easily feels lost, life is impersonal, full of risks, dangers, and uncertainties. Society easily appears as a wilderness in which the individual is as helpless as he once was in the jungle. So one yearns for involvement, participation, intimacy. In marriage this desire is expected to find fulfillment, the marital home is to be the haven of refuge from the storms of life, the marriage part-

---

42. D. DE ROUGEMONT, LOVE IN THE WESTERN WORLD (1940).
43. CODEX JURIS CANONICI, canon 1081.

ner is to be that human soul that fully understands, with whom all joys and sorrows, all troubles and worries can be shared, on whose strength one can lean in adversity, whose love will forgive all faults, with whom one can share the delights of taste, the interests of the mind, and the yearnings of the spirit. It is not easy to find a partner who but halfway lives up to such expectations. It is a gamble for young people who are but vaguely aware of their expectations and desires, whose discernment is not yet developed and is apt to be blurred by love and desire. This state of unpreparedness can be corrected. Young people can be prepared for the fateful decision. Certainly, there will always be some who will jump without looking. But some, probably many, can be induced rationally to weigh the pros and cons and, above all, to seek counseling before they make the choice final.

An even more effective alternative could be trial marriage. Serious proposals have been made to institutionalize what has already begun to be carried into practice: marriage with the understanding that no children are to be procreated during the first years and that a divorce be obtained if the relationship should turn out to be unsatisfactory. In many such cases the parties are hardly aware that they are experimenting with an institution which is incompatible with the traditional notion of marriage in the Christian world. Suggestions of open recognition of trial marriage as a legally recognized institution have met with outraged repudiation. English legislation has gone so far as to exclude the possibility of divorce for couples who have been married less than three years, at least in all those cases in which a judge does not find that the denial of the divorce would subject the petitioner to exceptional hardship or that the respondent is exceptionally depraved.[44] American legislatures may still be reluctant openly to admit that consent divorce is freely available in the courts and that use of it is made every year in more than 400,000 cases. They are even more unlikely to admit that trial marriage is practiced in the United States and that its frank recognition might prevent the procreation of children in those 120,000 cases a year in which a marriage is terminated within the first three years of its existence.[45]

44. Matrimonial Causes Act 1965, § 2.
45. The total number of divorces and annulments granted in 1967 was 534,000. The percentage of marriage terminations granted within the first three years of marriage has been consistently somewhat above one-fifth. In 1965, 38.1 percent of all divorces and annulments granted by the courts of the twenty-two states of the Divorce Registration Area were granted before the end of the fourth year of the parties' marriage. The period between the conclusion of the marriage and its factual breakup must, of course, have been considerably shorter. The highest percentages, 8.6 and

Attempts by prescribing waiting periods or other devices of legal compulsion to induce people to think before they jump into marriage have been shown to be ineffective. Even if they worked, the effect upon irresponsible individuals would be insignificant. There are indeed only two devices holding serious promise of success: family life education and premarital counseling, and family life education is the most effective instrument to induce candidates for marriage to make use of premarital counseling.

Preparation for the decision to marry and for the choice of the marriage partner is the first task of family life education. The second is preparation for married life and parenthood. In the innumerable discussions of divorce in recent writing, one will inevitably encounter the complaint about youth's over-romanticism in which love and marriage are glorified as states of perpetual bliss. The slightest tiff, the first quarrel, then brings on a conviction that the marriage is a failure and that it must be dissolved as speedily as possible so that the way may be free for a new try. Hollywood is blamed for having shaped these minds. Hollywood has mended its ways, and its alleged product has hardly ever existed in pure form. But, exaggerated as the image may be, it holds a core of truth. A good many people, and not all of them young, are insufficiently prepared for the shoals of married life. They are surprised by tensions and crises, and they do not know how to meet them. Some people do not realize that tensions and crises are necessary parts of married life, that they are inevitable in even the most harmonious marriage. They do not know that it is of the essence of a good marriage that crises arise and that they are overcome through the common effort of both parties to understand, to be patient, to endure, to stick together, and thus to grow to ever fuller understanding, to become one not only in the flesh but in mind and spirit. Every man and every woman that has ever been married has some day to discover that the partner is not exactly what he was believed to be, that he has faults that had not been expected, and that his attitudes toward life, his actions and reactions, his tastes, predilections, or biases are not exactly the expected ones. That discovery should not come as a shock. People ought to be prepared for it. Preparation should be provided by

---

9.3 percent respectively, occur in the second and third years of marriage; 8.5 percent occur in the fourth, 6.9 percent in the fifth, and 5.2 percent before the first year is over. No children had been born in 84.8 percent of the marriages which were terminated in their first year, 57.5 percent in the second and third years, and 38.5 percent in the fourth and fifth years. NAT'L CENTER FOR HEALTH STATISTICS, DIVORCE STATISTICS ANALYSIS, U.S. 1965, at 42–43, 26. For earlier years the data consistently show the same pattern; see JACOBSON, *supra* note 10, at 144, 147, 129–30.

observation and experience. But since such observation and experience is not necessarily provided by life, it must be provided by education in the sense of both character building and instruction.

Awareness of the inevitability of tensions and crises eases their solution, but it does not necessarily suffice. Acquaintance with or even mastery of techniques of crisis handling does not necessarily suffice either. There must be the will to overcome and the strength to remain calm, to resist panic, to apply reason rather than to be swayed by pride, anger, jealousy, or fear. The development of the personality of a good citizen ought to be the principal aim of all education, which is family life education insofar as it concentrates on family problems. In what circumstances are such problems likely to arise? What forms do they take? What techniques have been shown by experience to be helpful toward sensible solution; and, last but not least, what kind of conflict between spouses indicates such an unbridgeable gap that a clean break is the most wholesome remedy? Not every kind of individual conflict can be anticipated. Each situation requires its own specific way of handling which cannot be indicated without the knowledge of what actually happened. Counseling may be necessary for the intelligent handling of a particular situation. Family life education ought to create awareness of this need and to provide information on where and how to find the appropriate service.

Family life education is, we have seen, nothing new. In all societies, illiterate or literate, the young are continuously educated for family life simply by living in a family or, if they are deprived of a family home of their own, by observing the family pattern of their society. But in the society of the industrialized part of the world transformations have occurred which have rendered the traditional ways insufficient. The need has increased and the facilities have shrunk. Education for family living will continue to be carried on by those who have done so before: parents and grandparents, uncles and aunts, youth leaders, ministers, and teachers. But, under present conditions a larger share has to be carried by the teachers, the schools. In this era of cultural change too many parents have lost direction, are unable or unwilling to give guidance, are far from living an exemplary life. Only a fraction of the young have contact with ministers and mostly these contacts are fragile or the ministers are unprepared. Sunday schools also reach but a part and tend to be cursory. So the schools have to step in and to systematize what they have done before. Their task, like that of the others engaged in the educational process, is twofold: build up character and impart knowledge. The first task is the essential. In the present cultural climate the teachers are as uncertain about basic values as are the people at large. Few are those among them who have the gift of inspiration or the training to do more than instruct in skills and knowledge. But the schools do have influence, fair play is being developed by athletic coaches, civic responsibility by teachers of social studies, rationality in courses on mathematics, and a good portion of information necessary for successful marriage is presented in special courses of education for family living. Such courses are offered in a constantly growing number of schools in the United States, and they have begun to be developed in Scandinavia, West Germany, Switzerland, and the Netherlands. They are fine as far as they go, but few go as far as they should. Besides, special courses, valuable as they can be, do not suffice. Single lectures or short series of special lectures, as they are offered in colleges or high schools, can also be helpful, but suffice even less. What is needed is a school curriculum in which education for family living constitutes an integral part of all teaching, from nursery school all the way up to college. In play, songs, stories children of every age can be shown what makes and what destroys a harmonious home. Biology can be the course for the discussion of sex. In mathematics, problems can deal with household budgeting and such topics as investment and financing purchases of a home and of household items. Home economics obviously deals with nutrition, furnishing the home, or baby care. Shop can develop the skills necessary for repairs on the home, the car, or the radio. In social studies the function of the institutions of marriage and the family appears to be a necessary part of the course. Much can be achieved in courses of English and of foreign languages when the reading material systematically includes such writings as Galsworthy's *Forsyte Saga*, Tolstoy's *The Living Dead*, Strindberg's *The Father*, Ibsen's *Doll's House* or *Ghosts*, or other plays and stories in which marriage and marriage failure constitute the plot. Why did Soames and Irene Forsyte's marriage fail? Was the breakup the best way to solve the tensions? Could another way have been found? What was wrong in the personalities of the heroes? Such discussion, skillfully guided, can go far in waking awareness of the problems of married life and parenthood.

On the level of high school and college the educational effect can be completed by special courses or lecture series directly geared to the problems of adolescents agitated by sex, love, approaching marriage, social conventions (or their lack), dating and going steady, mothers' worries over their daughters' social success. There might also be a more systematic discussion of household management, the problem of how to combine married life with a professional career, or the role of the sexes in the division of labor, of infant care and child guidance, of marital property rights and succession to property on death, of separation, abandonment, divorce, and their financial aspects, and, above all, of the importance of seeking competent counseling in situations of crisis and of how and where to obtain it.

Like family life education, marriage *counseling* is nothing new.[46] Here too, new agencies have had to supplement or take over the task which can no longer be adequately performed by the old ones. Marriage counseling as a specialized profession is a specifically American invention. It is just beginning to appear in Europe, and counseling services are being organized in one form or another especially in England, Scandinavia, and West Germany. In the modest and but slightly effective form of conciliation agencies they have long been in existence in many countries.

Marriage counseling services are carried on by private practitioners and by organized agencies, private and public. They can be tied in with the structure of the courts or of social welfare agencies, or they can be independent. Counseling activities can be carried on in the usually perfunctory way of attempts to reconcile marriage partners already engaged in, or ready to start, proceedings for divorce; or they may be attempts to help clients find a reasonable way to deal with marital difficulties irrespective of whether or not a divorce or separation is in the offing. Counseling may lead to long-term treatment of emotional disturbance, addiction, or mental or physical illness, or into financial rehabilitation. Marriage counseling may be limited to problems strictly marital or it may form part of a comprehensive scheme of family service. All these forms can be found in the United States. Counseling services which are connected with courts have been comprehensively described by Professor Henry H. Foster, Jr.,[47] and by Professor Brigitte Bodenheimer.[48]

In continental Europe submission to conciliation proceedings has

46. The literature about marriage counseling is enormous. A survey of problems and approaches can be conveniently obtained through HANDBOOK OF MARRIAGE COUNSELING, edited by B. N. ARD, JR., and C. C. ARD (1969). This book also contains an annotated bibliography and lists of professional organizations and agencies for referral.

47. *Conciliation and Counseling in the Courts in Family Cases*, 41 N.Y.U. L. REV. 353 (1966). A thoughtful description and evaluation of American institutions is O. v. BUSEKIST, DAS FAMILIENGERICHT IN DEN VEREINIGTEN STAATEN VON AMERIKA (1970).

48. *Supra* note 7.

long been required as a preliminary to proceedings for divorce.[49] Differences exist, of course, in matters of detail. Repeated efforts at conciliation were provided for in the original version of the French Civil Code.[50] With some modification they are still prescribed in Belgium,[51] Luxembourg,[52] and the Netherlands.[53] In France, the Civil Code, as amended by the Law of 18 April 1886 provides for divorce cases an exception from the general rule that in a civil action the complaint be filed by an *avoué*:

> A married person who wishes to begin a suit for divorce must personally present his complaint to the presiding judge of the tribunal or to the judge who acts in that function. Where it has been found that the petitioner is unable to do so, the judge accompanied by the clerk, must himself go to the residence of the petitioner.
>
> When the judge has listened to the petitioner and has addressed to him those observations which he regards as proper, he orders, at the end of the act of petition, that the parties appear before him at a certain date and hour, and he commissions a bailiff [*huissier*] to present the citation to the respondent.[54]

At the time indicated

> both parties must appear personally and the judge hears them in the absence of their attorneys. He addresses to them those observations which he regards appropriate to bring about reconciliation. If it is impossible for a party to come to the judge, the place where the reconciliation is to be attempted is determined by the judge or he issues a commission to hear the party who is so prevented.[55]

If no conciliation is achieved or if the respondent has failed to appear, the judge authorizes the petitioner to file his complaint with the court.[56] But if he regards it proper to do so, the judge may adjourn the case for a period not to exceed six months. He may even order a second adjournment, but the total period of adjournment may not exceed one year.[57]

Once the case is before the court, it may again be adjourned to give the parties another chance to be reconciled, and no time limit is prescribed for this measure. An exception exists only in the rare case in

---

49. For description and analysis, see H. PROETEL, DER SÜHNEVERSUCH IM EHESCHEIDUNGSVERFAHREN (1969).
50. See *supra* chap. 8.
51. Civil Code, arts. 239, 282.
52. Civil Code, arts. 238, 282.
53. Code of Civil Procedure, arts. 816, 819.
54. Civil Code, arts. 234, 235.
55. *Id.*, art. 238.
56. *Id.*, art. 238, paras. 2, 3, 4.
57. *Id.*, art. 238, para. 9.

which divorce is found to be justified because of the respondent's having been sentenced to the "dishonouring punishment of imprisonment."[58] This adjournment is of a special kind. It is authorized to be ordered when after the trial of the case the court has found the petition to be legally justified. Upon the expiration of the period either party is thus entitled immediately to call the other into court so as to have the decree of divorce pronounced. Nothing apparently prevents a court from adjourning, perhaps repeatedly, a divorce case before the completion of the trial. French law thus provides not only for a compulsory conciliation attempt by the presiding judge of the tribunal but also gives ample opportunity to him and the court to induce the parties to seek counseling or even undergo therapy. But in practice little use seems to be made of these opportunities, at least in the metropolitan centers. French authors are inclined to call the conciliation proceedings an empty rite, but in some 15 percent of the cases the conciliation proceedings seem not to be followed by the filing of a complaint.[59] It is not clear, however, in how many of these cases the parties are reconciled or lastingly reconciled, and in how many the failure further to pursue the case is due to inertia, unwillingness to pay the cost, death, or the fact that the complaint is filed by the other party so that it is no longer necessary for the petitioner to go ahead with his.

The Federal Republic of Germany also follows the long tradition of requiring the petitioner for a divorce to submit to a conciliation effort as a premilinary to the suit. But it does not make it necessary for the petitioner in person to hand the petition to the judge and thus to be possibly dissuaded from starting the proceedings at all. In fact it facilitates the initiation of the proceedings by allowing the petitioner, if he wishes to do so, orally to declare his complaint to the clerk of the court,[60] thus excepting him from the general requirement of acting through an attorney, whose service must be used, however, in the subsequent proceedings.[61] German law also expressly empowers the presiding judge of the court to omit conciliation proceedings "if the respondent is outside of the country or if his place of abode is unknown, or if conciliation proceedings are impeded by some other obstacle that cannot be removed without difficulty," or "if it can be fore-

58. *Id.*, art. 246 in the version of the Law of 18 April 1886, and the Ordinance of 12 April 1945.
59. J. CARBONNIER, 1 DROIT CIVIL 431 (1962), citing Gontet, La conciliation en matière civile, dissertation, Paris, 1936, at 129 ff.
60. Code of Civil Procedure, § 608.
61. *Id.* § 78.

seen with certainty that conciliation efforts will not succeed."[62] Both parties are summoned at the appointed date to appear before the presiding judge or the member of the three-man judicial panel designated by him. If the respondent fails to appear, the judge may either issue a new summons or immediately declare the conciliation proceedings to have failed. The judge must so declare if the respondent fails to appear upon the second summons. If a conciliation conference is held, each party may bring along his attorney or any other person by whom he wishes to be assisted, but all such persons, including the attorneys, can be excluded from the hearing by the judge.[63] On the way in which the conference is conducted, the statute is silent. The judge is thus free to the best of his ability and within the time limit allowed by the calendar to engage in meaningful discussion or to let the hearing be an empty formality.

In Sweden, Finland, and Norway submission to conciliation proceedings is required only when both parties apply for judicial separation, the preliminary to long-road divorce,[64] but in Denmark it is also required when the decree is applied for by one party on the ground of the other's alleged misconduct.[65]

In Austria, the situation is similar to that of the Federal Republic of Germany.[66] In Switzerland, several cantons require not only one but two succssive attempts at reconciliation.[67] In Italy, an attempt at conciliation is required in suits for judicial separation.[68]

In the Soviet Union, under the Law of 1944, divorce cases had to proceed in two stages, the first in the people's court and the second in the district court. Corresponding laws were in effect in the other republics of the Soviet Union. The people's court was supposed to investigate the facts and to attempt the conciliation of the parties.[69]

In England, the desirability of conciliation proceedings was considered repeatedly in the lengthy discussions which ultimately resulted

62. *Id.* § 609, para. 1.
63. *Id.* § 610.
64. See *supra* chap. 6. Sweden, Marriage Law, ch. 14, §§ 1 ff.; Finland, Marriage Law, part 3, ch. 3, para. 84a; Norway, Marriage Law, ch. 5, §§ 44, 48.
65. Marriage Law, ch. 7, § 76.
66. First Decree to Implement the Marriage Law of 27 July 1938 (German Reichsgesetzblatt 1938. I 923), § 75.
67. Bern, Code of Civil Procedure, art. 148, para. 2; Fribourg, Introductory Law to the Swiss Civil Code, art. 45; Geneva, Code of Civil Procedure, arts. 434, para. 3, 438, para. 1; Zurich, Code of Civil Procedure, § 254, para. 1; Schaffhausen, Code of Civil Procedure, art. 270, para. 1.
68. Code of Civil Procedure, art. 708.
69. See *supra* chap. 9.

in the Divorce Reform Act 1969. The importance of conciliation services was emphasized in the memorandum that was submitted to the Morton Commission by the Archbishop of Canterbury and again in the Report of the Archbishop's Group. The Law Commission expressed doubts about the effectiveness of conciliation proceedings as a compulsory preliminary to a petition for divorce but declared it desirable that divorce seekers be encouraged voluntarily to seek conciliation services. Following up this idea, the Wilson bill provided that in each petition for divorce the petitioner's socilitor ought to declare that he had informed his client about the desirability of conciliation and had indicated to him where and how such services would be available. In the course of the parliamentary debates this proposal was softened so that under the Act the solicitor does not have to state *that* he has made the appropriate statement to his client but merely *whether* he has made it. A solicitor is thus not bound to recommend or even mention reconciliation in a case in which he regards conciliation attempts as hopeless. In contrast to the English Reform Act, the New York Law of 1966 not only declares conciliation attempts to be indispensable in all cases of divorce but also established an elaborate machinery within the framework of the court system. California, on the other hand, has not followed similar suggestions. The reform act of 1969 merely continues the existing system of conciliation courts, the establishment of which is optional with the local authorities and which are as a rule not to go into action in cases in which no dependent children are involved.

Judgments about the effectiveness of conciliation proceedings in general and about compulsory conciliation in particular are divided. While in France and Germany they are widely held to be of little use, Professor Lüke has interperted the statistics of continuance of petitions as indicating a fairly high degree of effectiveness. But the conclusiveness of these statistics is open to doubt.[70]

American conciliation systems have been praised highly, especially by their initiators. But the favorable judgments have also met with skepticism. Apparently impressive figures of "conciliations achieved," conciliation agreements concluded, or petitions dismissed or not followed up, cannot be regarded as conclusive. As long as there are no studies which follow through a number of years the couples who are or appear to have been reconciled, no valid conclusions can be drawn. No such studies are in existence. Even if they were, they would not

---

70. See *supra*, chap. 13.

indicate to what extent success or failure has been due to such imponderables as the personality, background, or training of the conciliator, or the amenities of the surroundings. Even *a priori* doubts must exist about a service which does not begin before the parties have already separated and one of them has moved to follow up the factual break with the formal seal of a judicial decree of divorce. The trend thus is to have the curative effort begin at an earlier stage, which means that a comprehensive scheme of marriage or family counseling be substituted for the narrowly limited scheme of conciliation. The trend to transform conciliation into counseling is conspicuous in Scandinavia, West Germany, and England, and in the United States the growth of counseling facilities has been conspicuous.

The most useful service a conciliator can render is that of making clients realize that their marital difficulties have their roots in deep-seated personality defects, which can rarely be corrected in ways other than psychotherapy or counseling extending over some period of time. The conciliation service is therefore successful which makes the clients see that they, and perhaps their parents as well, have to change psychologically. This understanding ought to be conveyed not only to those couples who are persuaded to be "reconciled," but also to those who will, or are advised to, go ahead with the divorce and will thus be set free for new marital ventures.[71]

Recognition of the limited effectiveness of efforts to cure a breach that has already occurred has been one of the motives of the family court plan of Judge Paul W. Alexander[72] as well as of the family court scheme of Japan. Marital tensions and the likelihood of an impending marriage breakdown can be indicated by the delinquency of children of the family, by their parents' neglect, their abuse, or similar indicia. If the juvenile court is combined with the court that deals with marital troubles of all kinds as well as with divorce, the danger signals may be recognized in time and counseling services can be applied before the breach has occurred. The idea is sound, but its implementation is not necessarily assured in a court with more than one judge. In Japan it

---

71. See I. A. Burch in R. L. Hunter and I. A. Burch, Annual Report 1969, Divorce Division of the Circuit Court of Cook County [Illinois] 8 (1970). On the use of psychotherapy in marital trouble situations and techniques available, especially techniques other than long-term depth psychoanalysis, see Bodenheimer, *supra* note 7.

72. Among his numerous writings, see *The Follies of Divorce: A Therapeutic Approach to the Problem*, 36 A.B.A.J. 105 (1950); *Legal Science and the Social Sciences: The Family Court*, 21 Mo. L. Rev. 105 (1956); *The Family Court — An Obstacle Race?* 19 U. Pitt. L. Rev. 602 (1958). On Judge Alexander's Court in Toledo, Ohio, see Busekist, *supra* note 47.

seems that in major family courts the judges handling matters of divorce are not necessarily informed about the business of the court's juvenile division. If the aim of providing therapy at the right moment is to be achieved, the various divisions of the court must so cooperate that information about cases is mutually available.

In order to be effective, counseling must be done by competent people. They need not necessarily be specialized marriage or family counselors. A physician, a clergyman, a teacher, or even a lawyer may be competent if, but only if, he has the right personality and the necessary training. No real agreement exists as to what kind of training is best for a counselor. Clearly, the counselor must be well grounded in psychology. Ideally, he ought to be aware of how the many facets of modern life produce marital tension: health, sex, economic life, addiction to drugs and alcohol, housing, and what not. He must also be familiar with those techniques which psychiatry, psychology, social work, medicine and pedagogy are elaborating to guide sound and mature personality development and to correct personality defects. In addition, he ought to know the laws of marriage, of divorce, and of the problems arising from marriage breakdown. The fields and skills are so many that they can rarely if ever be found united in a single individual. Teamwork may be called for, or a well-organized system of referral to competent specialists by an overall counselor who is competent to recognize the need for the specialist's skills. Above all, the marriage counselor himself must be a mature person, patient, sympathetic, open-minded, vigorous, as well as modest, experienced, and wise. A layman may be such a rare person in whom those qualities are combined and have the necessary contacts for referral. Occasionally, a lawyer may be such a person, but if that happens it is not because he is a lawyer. His legal education has not prepared him for counseling and no attempts ought to be made to insert training for counseling into the already overburdened curriculum of the law schools.[73] One of the principal defects of the conciliation schemes of the French, German, and Polish types is the fact that the task is given to a judge, a person well trained in the law but unprepared for the problems of counseling. The well-meaning but not sufficiently competent counselor can do more harm than good. The conscientious attorney will not rush into the filing of a petition for divorce or even for support. He will consider the chances of counseling or conciliation and will urge, perhaps strongly, that his client explore these approaches. Wisely, the English Divorce Reform Act of 1969 re-

---

73. For a thoughtful analysis of the lawyer's role in matters of divorce, see Bodenheimer, *supra* note 7, at 211.

quires the petitioner's solicitor to tell the court whether he has suggested counseling or conciliation efforts to the client. But even more wisely, the Act does not make such efforts a necessary preliminary to a petition for divorce nor does it entrust the judge with the counselor's job. If the judge has reason to believe that the marital break can be healed and, this ought to be understood too, if he has reason to believe that the marriage is worth resuscitation, then he can adjourn the case and thus give the parties the opportunity to try counseling or conciliation through competent channels.

In order to make sure that counseling services are competently staffed, organizational measures must be considered. As counseling develops into a profession, organizations have been founded, standards of professional competency and ethics are being elaborated, and schemes of certification or licensing are emerging. These promising developments deserve attention and support. Above all, funds are necessary to provide competent staffs for the agencies offering counseling and, even more desirable, overall family services. Funds are needed to train the personnel which is not yet available in sufficient numbers. Funds and publicity efforts are needed to make the existence of the facilities known to those they are meant to serve. The media can do much in this respect and so can the churches, civic organizations, and youth groups. But the most effective task of popularization can and has to be done in the course of that comprehensive family life education which must be carried on primarily by the schools. For that task the schools are not yet ready. Teachers have not yet been systematically prepared for it. Not much can be expected of the schools until education for family living has found a firm place in teacher training. It should not be too difficult to establish such a place. In contrast to some tasks with which American schools are presently charged, such as overcoming race segregation, family life education is much like those didactic jobs which the schools have ably performed so far. Family life education can easily be worked into the curricula of schools, be they progressive or old-fashioned or revolutionary. Only, we must not give in to the American vice of impatience. The construction of effective systems of family counseling will take time. Perhaps it will require more time than we have at our disposal. But the extent and the complexity of the tasks should be no excuse for not trying.

For the strengthening of marriage stability, then, effective tools are available. Laws tending to make divorce difficult should not be considered one of them. Social policy and, above all, family counseling and family life education are effective means at our disposal.

Appendix A
Marriage Disruption and Divorce Laws in the United States

In his investigation of the relationship between state laws of divorce and the incidence of marriage breakdown, Dr. Plateris had to face the problems of (1) how to obtain the data on marriage breakdown; (2) how to quantify the differences in the permissiveness of the state divorce laws; and (3) what statistical data to correlate with local differences in the laws, or in the incidence of marriage breakdown, or both, in order to discover possible causes of such differences.[1]

1. Factual separations and abandonments have never been enumerated in the United States. But in the 1950 census married persons whose spouses were present at the date of the enumeration were counted separately from those married persons whose spouses were not present, and among the latter a division was made between those "separated" and "others." A person enumerated as "married – spouse absent – separated" may be presumed to be one who lives apart from his spouse because of marital discord. The sum of persons divorced and persons separated thus provided the percentages in the population used by Plateris as indices of marriage breakdown (p. 151). In order to make the study independent of variations by sex, color, and age, the universe for which percentages were computed was made up of white females, married at least once, and 20 to 54 years of age. For the age groups of 14 through 19, and of above 54 years of age, marital disruption patterns vary considerably from those of the majority group of the population, i.e., of 20 through 54 (p. 34). Census figures show that

---

1. This Appendix is essentially a summary of the findings of Alexander Broel-Plateris set forth in his unpublished doctoral dissertation, "Marriage Disruption of Divorce Law" (Division of Social Sciences, University of Chicago, 1961). Unless otherwise indicated, page references are to this work. See also *supra* p. 306.

in the United States among persons of disrupted marital status the number of females is higher than that of males. According to the 1950 census, there was a surplus of about 300,000 divorced and over 200,000 separated females (p. 39). The number of persons undergoing divorce or separation must, however, be the same for both sexes. To some extent the difference in the census figures may be caused simply by different answers given to the enumerator. But generally the numerical difference is caused by circumstances occurring after the divorce or separation, i.e., death, remarriage, or migration. As these circumstances would be misleading in an inquiry in which the number of persons living in a disrupted marital status is used to define the incidence of marriage disruption, Plateris limited his study to women.

That family patterns among whites and nonwhites differ is well known.[2] Plateris observed from the 1950 census that throughout the United States the percentage of "separated" spouses is much higher among the nonwhites than among the whites: nonwhite males, 6.0 percent, white males, 1.1 percent; nonwhite females, 8.6 percent, white 1.3 percent. As for divorced persons, the percentage figure for the nation is also higher for the nonwhite females, 2.7 percent as against 2.4 percent for whites, but the difference is small, and in the case of the males, the relation is reversed, although by a slim margin — nonwhite, 1.9 percent, white, 2.0 percent. There is a slight margin of white over nonwhite divorced males and females in the southern states, while in New York and Pennsylvania the relation is reversed, probably because in these states the nonwhites are concentrated in the big cities. Because of the differences between color groups, comparison of the incidence of marriage disruption between areas would be misleading unless distribution by color were taken into account. Plateris eliminated this complication by concentrating on the white population. Women who have never been married can obviously neither be separated nor divorced; they were thus also eliminated from the population study.

The number of persons of disrupted marital status residing in a given area does not directly correspond to the number of events of marriage disruption. The place in which a person finds himself on the date of the census may differ from that at which he was when his marriage was disrupted. Migration, death, or new change of marital status may have occurred in the time between.

The high frequency of migration within the United States casts doubt upon the correspondence of percentages of persons of disrupted

2. See E. F. FRAZIER, THE NEGRO FAMILY IN THE UNITED STATES (1940, rev. ed. 1966).

APPENDIX A 446

marital status found within an area and the incidence of disruption in it. But, as Plateris observes,

> Migration can influence the percentages of divorced and separated persons in an area only if there is a difference between the number of in-migrants and out-migrants. It is not migration, both total and the net migration of people of disrupted marital status, that is of importance. Besides, the percentage of persons of disrupted marital status among the net migrants must be different from that of the population into which, or from which, the net migration occurs. If this percentage among the net migrants were identical with that of the population at large, the number of persons of disrupted marital status, and that of the total population would change due to migration, but percentages would remain stable.

Furthermore, in order to produce a relevant difference in percentages, the net migration must be numerous (pp. 161–62).

Data from the 1950 census are interpreted as indicating that differences among the four main regions of the United States (Northeast, North Central, South, and West) in the percentage of the group of persons whose marriages are "broken" because of death, divorce, or separation are primarily due to factors other than migration (p. 165).

As Plateris compares not only percentages of persons of disrupted marital status in the total population of states, but also percentages of such persons found in different residence categories within each state, namely, cities of more than 100,000 population, cities of lower population, farms, and rural places other than farms, he had to consider not only migration from one state into another, or from a foreign country into a state and vice versa, but also intrastate migration from one of the residence categories into another. An assumption that streams in opposite directions cancel each other would not be justified, because it is known that streams of migration follow definite patterns: from country to town, from city to suburb, and from certain states into certain others. In order to determine the influence of migration, Plateris computed coefficients of correlation (p. 162)[3] between percentages of

---

3. Coefficient of correlation: Readers to whom this term is as cryptic as it was to me when I studied Plateris's investigation may be helped by an explanation expressed in lay language: What is the relation of the direction of two or more sets of variables? If one set increases, does the other increase, or does it decrease, or is there no observable regularity? If there is a relationship between increase or decrease, is the change in set B strongly or weakly proportional to that of set A? Francis Galton, Karl Pearson, and others elaborated a mathematical formula by which it is possible to express the strength of the correlation between the direction of two sets of variables as decimal fractions. The value of zero indicates the absence of regularity in the direction of the sets. The value of $+1$ indicates the strongest equality of direction, the value of -1 the strongest regressive direction. In social science investigations values below $+0.05$ and above -0.05 are generally regarded as insignificant. For detailed explanation,

persons divorced, separated, and "disrupted" (i.e., the total of both divorced and separated), on the one side and the following demographic variables on the other: (1) percentage, in a population area, of persons who at the census indicated that they had in-migrated from a different country or from abroad; (2) the "net total migration," i.e., the surplus of persons who in the decade between 1940 and 1950 had migrated into a state over the number of those who had migrated out of it or vice versa; (3) the percentage of persons born in the state in which they resided at the time of the census; and (4) the population increase of each area that occurred between 1940 and 1950 resulting from both natural increase and migration.

The correlation coefficients thus computed are interpreted by Plateris as indicating that areas attracting migrants coincide with areas containing a comparatively high percentage of persons of disrupted marital status. There is no reason, he concludes, to assume that the percentage of such persons among the total number of persons migrating into such areas is significantly higher or lower than their percentage among those who already reside there, or that the number of in-migrating persons of disrupted status is large enough to influence the marital status composition of the area.

Are variations in the percentages of persons divorced and separated due not so much to variability in the rates of divorce and of separation as to the variability in the rates of events which take people out of the ranks of the divorced or separated? These events are, for the divorced, death or remarriage, and, for the separated, death, divorce, or reconciliation. If the latter is true, the variations in the percentage of persons divorced or separated would be more indicative of variations in the rates of these events than of variations in the rates of divorces and separations.

In order to test this hypothesis, Plateris again resorted to the computation of coefficients of correlation. He first correlated the percentage of divorced females with the rate of remarriage of divorcees per 1,000 divorced females in the population of a state. The necessary data were available for twenty-two states (p. 168). He also correlated, upon the basis of data from all states, the percentage of separated females and the divorce rate per 1,000 separated females (pp. 168, 171). In both correlations the coefficients turned out to be statistically insignificant.

---

see J. C. Stanley, *Linear Hypotheses: Analysis of Variance*, 9 INT'L ENC. SOC. SCI. 324 (1969); R. H. Somers, *Statistics, Descriptive: Association*, 15 INT'L ENC. SOC. SCI. 240; H. Kellerer, *Korrelationsanalyse*, 6 HANDWÖRTERBUCH DER SOZIALWISSENSCHAFTEN 198 (1959).

Appendix A

Plateris concluded that variations between states in the percentages of divorced and of separated are not significantly associated with variations in the rates of remarriage of divorced persons or of divorces of persons separated.[4] Thus one ought to reject the hypothesis that the variation between the states in percentage of divorced and the percentage of separated is mainly due to the variability of events removing individuals from these marital status groups (p. 171).

2. As the incidence of divorce and factual marriage breakdown indicated by percentages of persons of disrupted marital status was to be determined for states of strict and for states of permissive divorce law, it became necessary for Plateris to quantify the degrees of strictness or permissiveness of the divorce laws of the several states. Many, if not most states of the United States have two different laws of divorce, the law of the books and the law in action. While it might have been of interest to relate variations in the incidence of marriage breakdown separately with each of these, that task was regarded as not feasible. So I advised Dr. Plateris to limit the correlation to the law in action or, as it turned out, with views held about it by local experts, which were determined preponderantly by their observations of judicial practice, but which were not uninfluenced by the statutory texts. This decision has had an unfortunate result: the investigation does not fully reveal the effectiveness of attempts by means of a strict divorce statute to protect and promote marriage stability. It rather indicates correlations between marriage stability and judicial practice, i.e., an activity which is more highly susceptible than legislation to those social factors which also, and indirectly at that, influence marriage stability. The coefficients computed by Plateris are high for the correlations between permissiveness of divorce law and such variables as those indicating category of residence, ethnicity, social status, and religion. A state's law of the books is the same for all courts in the state. But the law in action varies among metropolitan, urban, and rural districts, according to the skill of the attorneys the parties are able to retain, and even according to predilections of individual judges which are likely to be determined by the cultural climate not so much of the state as a whole but of the particular district or social class. The coefficients of correlations between strictness of the divorce law of the books on the one side and, on the other, family stability and the social variables directly influencing it would probably have been considerably lower than those which were computed for the law in action. If

---

4. No statistical data are available on rates of death of persons divorced or separated, or on rates of reconciliation of persons separated.

Plateris's work is to serve as a basis for conclusions on the effectiveness to be expected of legislative changes of the divorce law, this circumstance ought to be kept in mind.

As Plateris was interested in establishing correlations with the divorce law in action, he was faced with the delicate task of ascertaining its actual shape, which not only is not uniform for all courts of a state or all cases coming before a court but also cannot be determined by simply consulting books. In this predicament, Plateris decided to canvass a number of law experts who could be expected to have informed views about the laws of their particular states. Questionnaires were sent to professors of family law and to the chairmen of the family law sections of state and local bar associations. The questionnaire was as follows:

1. If a resident of your state desires to obtain a decree of divorce which under the circumstances he cannot obtain, or does not wish to seek to obtain, in the state, what are in your opinion the states or territories in which he could obtain a divorce with the least difficulty if he

    a) would move to such other state or territory with the intention to stay there to establish himself as a permanent resident;

    b) would go to such state or territory with the intention to stay there no longer than necessary to obtain a decree of divorce and then to return to your state?

    Please list for each of these situations five jurisdictions in the sequence which corresponds to your impression of the comparative ease with which a decree of divorce can be obtained there.

2. Would you also, please, list those five jurisdictions in which you believe that it is most difficult for a resident of such jurisdiction to obtain a decree of divorce. Please list these states in the sequence which corresponds to your impression of the comparative difficulty with which a decree of divorce can be obtained there.

3. Where do you consider that the comparative ease or difficulty with which a resident can obtain a decree of divorce constitutes the national average in the United States (list five states)?

4. How do you evaluate the comparative ease or difficulty of obtaining a decree of divorce in your own jurisdiction as compared with other jurisdictions in the United States (check one)?
... Very easy   ... Easy   ... Medium   ... Difficult   ... Very difficult

5. How do you evaluate the comparative ease or difficulty of obtaining a decree of divorce in the jurisdictions adjoining your state or territory

    a) as compared with other jurisdictions of the Nation;
    (Very easy, Easy, Medium, Difficult, Very difficult)

    b) as compared with your own jurisdiction?
    (Easier, About the same, More difficult)

APPENDIX A

The questionnaire was accompanied by a letter:

DEAR SIR:

Mr. Alexander Broel-Plateris, a graduate student at the University of Chicago, is presently engaged in a study of the problem of what the relationship is between the comparative difficulty or ease with which a decree of divorce can be obtained in a given state, and the degree of marriage stability actually existing in that state. The figures necessary for the comparison of marriage stability existing in the several jurisdictions of the United States will be obtained from census reports, publications of the Bureau of Vital Statistics, and other sources of statistical data. The comparative difficulty or ease with which a decree of divorce can be obtained in the several states and territories of the United States constitutes the resultant of a number of factors such as the statutory lists of grounds for, and bars to, divorce, the configuration of divorce proceedings, the judicial inclination to receive evidence at face value or to check upon the actual truth of evidence tendered in an uncontested divorce suit, the length of required residence in the state and county, the requirement vel non of personal appearance of the plaintiff, the cost of the proceedings, etc. It is difficult to compare the results of such complex configurations of circumstances. However, lawyers have formed certain impressions as to the comparative ease with which decrees of divorce can be obtained in those jurisdictions about which they have information. It is these impressions of yours and other experienced fellow members of the profession which Mr. Plateris would like to know. Such information would greatly help him to make those comparisons which must be made in order to find out which laws are most likely to be of help in efforts to protect and promote the stability of marriages and families. The discovery of means likely to be useful toward this end constitutes the subject matter of a major research project which is presently carried on by the University of Chicago Comparative Law Research Center in cooperation with the International Association of Legal Science.

In view of your interest in the law of the family I am turning to you for assistance in this project. Your help will be greatly appreciated.

Yours sincerely,

Max Rheinstein
Professor of Law
Director, University of Chicago
Comparative Law Research Center

As one can see, the questions were aimed at obtaining information about two different situations, namely, (1) How difficult, or how easy, is it for a resident of the state to obtain a divorce in that state? (2) How difficult, or how easy, is it for a nonresident of the state to obtain a divorce in that state?

The wisdom of including questions soliciting information about the second situation appears doubtful if one regards as the aim of the investigation the ascertainment of associations between legislative efforts to promote marriage stability and actual marriage stability. Legislatures are not aiming at promoting marriage stability in states other than their own. Also permissiveness for the state's own residents does not necessarily coincide with permissiveness for nonresidents. However, the combination in the questionnaire of two characteristics which do not necessarily coincide, does not appear seriously to have harmed the result of the canvass. The pattern that merges from the sixty-four usable replies corresponds with the impression which the present author, after thirty years of work in family law, has formed in his mind. That test is, of course, a subjective one, but it is no more so than that which the recipients of the questionnaire were asked to apply, and that test was, as Plateris observes, the only one that was practicably available.

The replies are tabulated in Plateris's table 11 (p. 146), from which

TABLE A1
STATES LISTED ACCORDING TO THE EASINESS OF THEIR DIVORCE LAW, 1959

Category and State	Easiness Score	Category and State	Easiness Score
Very permissive		*Medium* — Continued	
Nevada	95	Nebraska	49
Florida	90	Ohio	48
Arkansas	85	North Dakota	46
Idaho	81	Delaware	45
New Mexico	77	Vermont	44
Alabama	76	*Strict*	
California	74	Maryland	42
Wyoming	72	Minnesota	41
Permissive		West Virginia	40
Kentucky	69	Maine	39
Georgia	67	Illinois	37
Arizona	66	Louisiana	36
Oklahoma	64	Virginia	34
Utah	63	Wisconsin	33
Washington	62	New Hampshire	32
Mississippi	60	Michigan	29
South Dakota	59	Dist. of Columbia	28
Oregon	59	*Very Strict*	
Kansas	58	North Carolina	25
Indiana	57	Pennsylvania	22
Medium		Rhode Island	19
Montana	55	Connecticut	16
Tennessee	54	New Jersey	13
Colorado	53	Massachusetts	9
Missouri	52	New York	4
Texas	50	South Carolina	1
Iowa	49		

Source: Plateris, table 12, p. 149, based on table 11, p. 146.

APPENDIX A

he established the order of relative easiness scores stated in his table 12 (p. 149) (see table A1). The scores of this table do not have the precision of results of counting, measuring, or weighing. The unit of measurement is derived from subjective experiences which do not allow full articulation. But, as we have observed, they appear to us to reflect the reality of the law as it is applied in general and as it applies to resident divorce seekers in particular.

3. The comparative permissiveness of the divorce laws having been reduced to a numerical scale, it became possible to investigate the association of this variable with percentages of marriage disruption.

As a first step this association was tested by means of analysis of variance so as to determine the probability that differences are due to chance or whether it is permissible to assume that the characteristics of division in subgroups are significantly associated with the universe. It was found that on the 5 percent level the hypothesis that law is significantly associated with the percentage of females of disrupted marital status can be accepted in nine relationships out of twelve, viz., for "total disrupted," i.e., divorced plus separated in cities over 100,000 and in cities under 100,000, for divorced in cities of both groups and of rural nonfarm population; and for separated in all four residence categories. The three exceptions are total disrupted, rural nonfarm; total disrupted, rural farm; and divorced, rural farm (pp. 189-90).

Total disrupted shows a much lower variance ratio than either divorced or separated, except for rural farm. This fact, together with the observation of percentages in the five classifications of permissiveness of state laws, is regarded as indicating that the more permissive the law, the higher the percentage of divorced and of total disrupted, and the lower that of separated.

As the second step, correlation coefficients were computed between the three types of marriage disruption and the permissiveness scores of the state divorce laws.

The correlation coefficients between law and marriage disruption . . . [table A2] show a pattern similar to that of the variance ratios, but the direction of the association between variables, which could be only inferred from the variance ratios, is clearly shown here. All coefficients are positive for the divorced, negative for the percentages separated and statistically significant for big cities; coefficients for the total disrupted and for the divorced, but not for the separated, are significant for other urban population; for rural non-farm only the coefficient for the divorced is significant, and all coefficients for the rural farm areas are not significant.

Some of those coefficients are very high: in large cities, 36 per cent of the variation of the total disrupted can be explained by variations in divorce laws; this is true for as much as 62 per cent of the variation in the percentage divorced, but only for 19 per cent in the case of the separated. The same percentages of the other urban population are: 22 for total disrupted, 48 for divorced, and only 7 per cent for separated. The percentages of variation in marriage disruption for the rural population that can be explained by variations in law are much lower, and five out of six are statistically not significant. There is, however, one rural coefficient which seems rather surprising: the correlation coefficient between the percentage divorced in the rural farm population and divorce law is practically nil ($r=0.06$), while the correlation between percentage separated and the same law is -0.27; this figure, though statistically not significant, is nevertheless highly indicative and similar to the pattern of variance ratios, where the F score for rural farm percentages of the separated is 3.01, while it is only 0.88 for rural farm percentage of the divorced. The theory that the divorce law is associated with the percentage divorced and, indirectly, with percentage separated does not hold here.

TABLE A2

COEFFICIENTS OF CORRELATION BETWEEN MARRIAGE DISRUPTION AND PERMISSIVENESS SCORES OF STATE DIVORCE LAWS

Residency Category	Total Disrupted	Divorced	Separated
Cities over 100,000	.60	.79	−.44
Urban, cities under 100,000	.47	.69	−.26[a]
Rural nonfarm	.21[a]	.47	−.27[a]
Rural farm	−.11[a]	.06[a]	−.27[a]

Source: Plateris, table 23, computed from data of the 1950 census.
[a] Not significant on 5 percent level.

We have the seemingly absurd situation where permissiveness of divorce law is not correlated with divorces, which are legal acts, but with non-legal facts, namely, separations. This contradiction can be explained by the spatial distribution of the separated population. The Eastern high separation area comprises all states with a very strict and many with strict divorce laws; in this area the percentage of separated among the rural farm population is as a rule higher than in the Western high separation area which has mostly permissive or very permissive divorce laws. As separations are not controlled by law, the comparatively high correlation coefficient between those two variables cannot be interpreted as an index of direct influence of law on separation. This coefficient is rather due to cultural processes which in some parts of the country have brought about simultaneously high separation percentages and difficult divorce law. The correlation coefficients between law and separation for the other three residence categories should be interpreted in the same light.

On the other hand, in the rural farm areas of all states percentages of divorces are comparatively low. It can be thought that the easiness of the divorce law is of little importance, because rural farm people are disinclined

TABLE A3
PERCENTAGES OF DIVORCED AND SEPARATED WHITE MALES, 14 YEARS OF AGE AND OVER, TOTAL AND RURAL FARM POPULATIONS, SELECTED STATES, 1950

	Total Males			Rural Farm Males		
State	Total Disrupted	Divorced	Separated	Total Disrupted	Divorced	Separated
Strict Divorce Law						
Massachusetts[a]	2.7	1.6	1.1	2.3	1.3	1.0
Michigan[a]	3.3	2.3	1.0	1.9	1.3	0.6
New Jersey[a]	2.6	1.2	1.4	2.5	1.0	1.5
New York[a]	2.4	1.0	1.4	2.2	0.8	1.4
South Carolina	2.1	0.8	1.3	1.5	0.4	1.1
Virginia	2.7	1.6	1.1	1.8	0.9	0.9
Mean percentage	2.6	1.4	1.2	2.0	1.0	1.1
Permissive Divorce Law						
Arkansas	2.6	1.8	0.8	2.0	1.2	0.8
Florida	4.3	2.8	1.5	2.9	1.6	1.3
Idaho[b]	3.6	2.7	0.9	2.2	1.6	0.6
Illinois[a]	3.1	2.1	1.0	1.4	0.9	0.5
Nevada[b]	7.7	5.5	2.2	7.3	5.6	1.7
New Hampshire[b]	3.4	2.3	1.1	3.3	2.3	1.0
New Mexico[a]	3.1	2.0	1.1	1.9	1.1	0.8
Mean percentage	4.0	2.7	1.2	3.0	2.0	1.0
Mean percentage excluding Nevada	3.4	2.3	1.1	2.3	1.4	0.8

Source: Plateris, table 2, from U.S. BUREAU OF THE CENSUS, CENSUS OF POPULATION: 1950, vol. 2. CHARACTERISTICS OF POPULATION, parts 4, 10, 12, 13, 21, 22, 28, 29, 30, 31, 32, 33 and 46, table 57.

[a] As the nonwhite male rural farm population age 14 and over was less than 50,000, rural farm data are available for all races only.

[b] As the total nonwhite male population, age 14 and over, was less than 50,000 in the state, data are available for all races only.

to take advantage of opportunities offered by the law for dissolving marriages. Table 23 [here table A2] indicates that the willingness to take advantage of this opportunity increases sharply with the influence of urban way of life [pp. 192–94].

The associations between marriage disruption and law permissiveness scores, and the distribution of the divorced and disrupted population, by state, as found for 1950, was found also to have obtained for 1940.

Plateris's work does not contain a table showing overall percentages by states. Apparently he did not regard such figures as meaningful unless the percentages for each state were broken down into the four residence categories. Statewide data are given only for thirteen selected states, of which six are classified as having a strict divorce law and seven as having a permissive one. His table 2 relates only to white males of 14 years of age and over, and, in addition to the state totals, also lists the percentages for the rural farm population, i.e., the residence area having the lowest percentage of persons of disrupted marriage status. Table A3 shows that the statewide percentages of persons divorced tend to be higher in the permissive than in the strict states. The percentage of persons separated is the same for both groups of states, viz., 1.2 percent. But if one excludes not only Nevada, as Plateris has done, but also the other divorce mill states, Florida and Idaho, the mean for the permissive states is 1.0 percent and thus lower than that of the strict states. The abnormally high percentages of separated persons in Nevada, Idaho, and Florida seem to be caused by the influx into these states of separated persons who are residents of other, presumably strict, states and who have temporarily come to obtain a divorce. Leaving these three states apart, the total disrupted is 3.05 percent rather than 4.0 percent or, if Nevada alone is eliminated, 3.4 percent. The difference between this figure and the 2.6 percent of the strict states is thus considerably less than what appears from Plateris's table. From Plateris's tables 17 and 18, I have compiled the percentage of divorced and separated from the cities above 100,000 population situated in the states listed in table 13 and, for those states which have no such cities, the percentages for the urban areas, i.e., the residence categories with the highest percentages disrupted (table A4). These figures tend to indicate that great permissiveness of the law, while it may be associated with a higher percentage of divorced and slightly higher percentage of total disrupted, is also associated with a lower percentage of separated.

In the permissive states the percentage of divorced is consistently appreciably higher than the percentage of separated. Obviously, a sizable majority of persons whose marriages are disrupted avail themselves of the possibility of obtaining the freedom of remarriage. Among those who in the census appear as separated are clearly a good many for whom this status constitutes a transitory stage prior to divorce. How many remain in the stage of separation, more or less permanently, cannot be ascertained from the census data. Their number is unlikely to be large, except perhaps in the case of Roman Catholics.

In the strict states the pattern is not quite so clear. In most places the percentages of separated are as one would expect them to be, i.e.,

TABLE A4
WHITE FEMALES OF DISRUPTED MARITAL STATUS, LARGE CITIES, 1950
(Percent)

States and Cities	Divorced	Separated
Permissive States		
Arkansas		
Little Rock	6.26	1.54
Idaho	4.36	1.20
New Mexico	4.25	2.20
Alabama		
Birmingham	5.37	1.56
Mobile	4.96	2.31
Montgomery	4.95	1.64
California		
Berkeley	7.97	1.58
Long Beach	7.25	2.18
Los Angeles	8.66	2.69
Oakland	7.38	2.35
Pasadena	8.41	2.68
Sacramento	7.46	2.68
San Diego	6.69	2.18
San Francisco	9.21	2.57
Wyoming	3.75	1.20
Strict States		
South Carolina	2.82	2.97
New York		
Albany	3.48	4.26
Buffalo	2.02	3.10
New York	2.59	2.89
*Rochester	3.25	3.11
Syracuse	2.98	3.44
Utica	2.26	2.99
Yonkers	1.51	2.46
Massachusetts		
*Boston	3.96	3.02
*Cambridge	4.08	2.80
*Fall River	2.96	2.57
*New Bedford	3.97	2.53
*Somerville	3.06	2.55
*Springfield	3.73	2.17
*Worcester	3.96	2.07
New Jersey		
Camden	3.23	4.23
*Elizabeth	2.52	2.39
Jersey City	1.69	2.99
Newark	3.07	3.31
*Paterson	3.14	2.81

TABLE A4 — Continued

States and Cities	Divorced	Separated
Trenton	3.33	4.67
Connecticut		
Bridgeport	2.95	3.15
Hartford	5.00	4.02
*New Haven	2.72	2.50
*Waterbury	2.36	2.07
Rhode Island		
*Providence	4.12	2.47
Pennsylvania		
*Allentown	4.12	3.26
*Erie	3.12	2.84
Philadelphia	2.92	3.34
*Pittsburgh	3.66	2.80
*Reading	5.91	3.44
*Scranton	2.66	2.54
North Carolina		
*Charlotte	4.33	3.31

Source: Plateris, table 17, p. 174: Percentages of ever married white females of disrupted marital status, 14 years old and over, by state and residence category, United States, 1950. Computed from unpublished 1950 census data. Plateris, table 18, p. 176: Percentages of ever married white females of disrupted marital status, 14 years old and over, in cities of 100,000 or more, 1950. Computed from unpublished 1950 census data.

* Cities with higher percentage of divorced than separated.

higher than the percentages of divorced. However, there are some places (marked by an asterisk in table A4) in which the relation is reversed. This situation obtains for all large cities of Massachusetts and for all but one in Pennsylvania. It also holds true for the urban areas other than cities of 100,000 and more in Massachusetts (divorced, 3.06 percent; separated, 1.95 percent) but not of Pennsylvania (divorced 2.17 percent; separated 3.38 percent). The majority of the population of the United States resides in metropolitan and urban areas. These are the areas in which cases of marriage disruption accumulate and also those which show the greatest inclination to transform a separation into a divorce. The pattern indicated in table A4 may thus be accepted as the representative pattern of the United States. Plateris's table 21 (p. 186) shows coefficients of correlation between divorced and separated, between total disrupted and separated, and between total disrupted and divorced for each of the four residence categories in the nation as a whole. It appears that the coefficient of correlation between total dis-

APPENDIX A 458

rupted and separated is lowest (0.21) for the large cities and steadily increases so that it is 0.49 for the other cities, 0.51 for the rural nonfarm, and 0.80 for rural farms. "Thus," Plateris observes, "the importance of the share of separations in total disruptions increases as the urban way of life declines" (p. 187).

4. Plateris's inquiry indicates that a positive association exists between permissiveness of divorce law and the incidence of marriage breakdown. But he cautiously refrains from alleging a cause-and-effect relationship.

The positive association may be the result of such a relationship, but it may just as well be pure coincidence or the effect of other circumstances which are in the same direction causal for both sets of variables. Plateris has taken pains to test these possibilities. The probability of mere coincidence is negated by his test of analysis variance. But the existence of a common set of causes is made to appear probable by his computation of correlation coefficients between law permissiveness scores and incidence of disruption on the one side, and a series of other variables on the other (pp. 210 ff.).

The variables which Plateris considers conceivably significant are:

Percentage among the white women of age 20 to 54:
   (1) of persons never married;
   (2) of widows;
   (3) of married women spouse absent other than separated.

Percentage of other groups in the total population (i.e., both sexes, all age groups, all races) and other miscellaneous factors:
   (4) percentage of married women who have borne no children;
   (5) percentage in the labor force of married women, spouse present;
   (6) percentage of population of 14 years and over with income under $1,500 per person annually;
   (7) percentage of population of 14 years and over with income over $6,000 per person annually;
   (8) percentage in the labor force of white-collar workers, i.e., professional, technical and kindred workers; managers, officials, and proprietors except farm, clerical, and kindred workers, and sales personnel;
   (9) percentage in the labor force employed in manufacturing industries;
   (10) median school years completed by the population 25 years of age and older;
   (11) percentage of foreign-born among the population of 21 years of age and over;
   (12) percentage in the total population of Roman Catholics;
   (13) size of large cities expressed in thousands of population;
   (14) density of population outside of the large cities;
   (15) length of time since admission of the state as a state of the United States;
   (16) percentage of immigrants from different county or abroad;

TABLE A5
CORRELATION COEFFICIENTS BETWEEN MARRIAGE DISRUPTION AND NONLEGAL VARIABLES: LARGE CITIES, OTHER URBAN, RURAL NONFARM, AND RURAL FARM POPULATION, 1950

Nonlegal Variables	Total Disrupted				Divorced				Separated			
	Large Cities	Other Urban	Rural Non-farm	Rural farm	Large Cities	Other Urban	Rural Non-farm	Rural Farm	Large Cities	Other Urban	Rural Non-Farm	Rural Farm
Never married	−.23	−.36	−.28[a]	.31	−.44	−.46	−.35	.16[a]	.45	.07[a]	.02[a]	.38
Widowed	.36	.29	.05[a]	.59	.16[a]	.09[a]	−.28[a]	.31	.41	.43	.42	.72
Spouse absent	.38	.57	.35	.56	.24	.31	.10[a]	.38	.30	.62	.39	.59
Childless wives	.55	.49	.37	.28[a]	.51	.37	.06[a]	.21[a]	.08[a]	.36	.47	.27[a]
Employed wives	.34	.37	.20[a]	.39	.30	.16[a]	−.07[a]	.31	.07[a]	.47	.38	.34
Income under $1,500	.38	.21[a]	.02[a]	.36	.42	.24[a]	...[b]	.18[a]	−.10[a]	.01[a]	.02[a]	.45
Income over $6,000	.36	.02[a]	−.02[a]	−.23[a]	.47	.04[a]	.08[a]	−.05[a]	−.23	−.02[a]	−.12[a]	−.37
Median education	.40	.04[a]	.19[a]	−.05[a]	.56	.26[a]	.48	.29	−.36	−.38	−.32	−.44
In manufacturing	−.54	−.26[a]	.09[a]	.56	−.54	−.40	−.18[a]	.48	.02[a]	.20[a]	.36	.44
White-collar	.41	−.16[a]	−.30	.60	.50	.03[a]	.04[a]	.60	−.19	−.39	−.49	.37
Foreign-born	−.34	−.17[a]	...[b]	.25[a]	−.48	−.20[a]	.16[a]	.36	.31	.01[a]	−.19[a]	.02[a]
Catholics	−.43	−.25[a]	.02[a]	.06[a]	−.58	−.30	.05[a]	.17[a]	.33	.03[a]	−.03[a]	−.10[a]
Size of city	−.06[a]	...	...	...	−.10[a]	...	...	...	.08[a]	...	...	...
Population density	...	.33	−.03[a]	.19[a]	...	−.48	−.23[a]	.10[a]	...	.20[a]	.24[a]	.22[a]
Years in the Union	−.35	−.09[a]	.09[a]	.39	−.58	−.35	−.31	.15[a]	.51	.46	.52	.54

Source: Plateris, table 26, p. 199, computed from the collected data.
[a] Not significant on the 5 percent level.
[b] Less than .005.

(17) percentage among the residents of the state of persons born in that state;
(18) net total migration;
(19) percentage of population increase 1940–50.

Dr. Plateris compiled the coefficients of correlation between marriage disruption and fifteen nonlegal variables (see table A5). Variations in the percentage of persons never married can be regarded as being influential on variations of marriage disruption for two reasons. For one, no person can live in a disrupted marital state unless he has first been married. Second, persons never married tend to be more numerous in young age groups than in older ones. Divorce and, probably, separation too, occur more frequently among younger married people. It may thus be inferred that the incidence of marriage disruption is higher in a population with a low percentage of persons never married.

The percentage of never married is correlated negatively with the percentages of total disrupted and divorced for all residence categories except farms. Plateris interprets this negative correlation as corroboration of the experience that marriages among the younger age groups, where most never married are concentrated, result in comparatively high incidence of disruption. The deviant behavior of the farm population is explained as probably due to the out-migration of single females from farm areas. The association between percentages of the never married and the separated is positive for the large cities and farms, and practically nil for the other urban and other rural areas. As to the farms, the correlation is the same for the separated, the divorced, and the total disrupted.

The correlation between percentages of widowed and disrupted is shown to be positive, although at varying degrees for all categories of residence and of disruption except divorced rural nonfarm. This finding is puzzling. Marriages can be dissolved only by death or divorce. Not only in the United States but also in other industrialized countries, the percentage of marriage dissolutions by divorce has continuously increased. In 1860, 4.1 percent of the marriage dissolutions occurring in the United States were by divorce. In 1946, the percentage reached a peak of 48.4; in 1956 it was still high at 34.6 percent. Obviously, the percentage of marriages dissolved by death correspondingly declined between 1860 and 1946 and then rose again.[5] Of course, since there has been a steady increase in absolute figures of population as well as of marriages concluded and marriages dissolved, the correlation between numbers of dissolution by death and by divorce is likely to be positive. But why a positive correlation should exist between per-

---

5. P. H. JACOBSON, AMERICAN MARRIAGE AND DIVORCE 142, 144 (1959).

centages in the female population of widows and of divorcees is not obvious. Such a correlation is indicated in Plateris's table, but he does not explain it. Perhaps the reason lies in the fact that in recent decades the life expectancy of women has increased beyond that of men [6] so that that cultural climate which favors a higher incidence of marriage breakup simultaneously results in larger percentages of widows among the female population.

The association between percentages in the female population of grass widows and other women of disrupted marital status is strongly positive for all residence categories except, strangely enough, the association between divorced and rural nonfarm. The positive association is easily explained, since the category "spouse absent but not separated" covers such endangered marriages as those of traveling salesmen or of men detained in prison. Plateris states: "The stronger, the more accepted in a subculture is marriage disruption, the easier people drift into the marginal marital status of 'other,' and, further, into marriage disruption" (p. 202).

The association between the percentage of childless married women and those of disrupted marital status is positive throughout. It is, as Plateris observes (p. 202), a case in which the association clearly indicates a causal relationship: childless marriages are more divorce prone than marriages with children. This observation is corroborated by other statistical data.

As an index of the ways in which functions are performed and distributed in the family, Plateris uses the census data about participation of married women in the labor force. A married woman who works outside of the home does not perform housewifely functions in the same way as a married woman who does not work on an outside job. The association between percentage of married women (spouse present) who are participating in the labor force and married women of disrupted marital status is, as one would expect, significantly positive for most residence categories. As Plateris emphasizes, this variable is also indicative of the percentage of women who are not economically dependent on their husbands. Such women are less urgently impelled to endure a distasteful home life. Plateris also points out that a family in which the wife works outside tends to be less integrated (p. 203).

As indices of socioeconomic structure, Plateris uses the census data about size of family income, level of education, percentage of workers in manufacturing industries, and percentage of white-collar workers.

The association between the percentage of low-income families with

---

6. *Id.* 140.

that of total disrupted is significantly positive in large cities and on the farms, that with divorced is significantly positive for the big cities only, and that with the separated for the farms only. The association of high percentage of high-income groups with total disrupted is significantly positive for the big cities only; the same holds true for the association with the percentage divorced; as to the percentage separated, it is significantly negative for the big cities and the farms. As Plateris points out, these findings cannot be interpreted without further studies (p. 203). He warns against the temptation to regard the findings as necessarily indicating that low-income and high-income families are more disruption prone than the middle classes. The figures, after all, do not relate directly to families of one or the other kind, but to variations in the percentage of families of one or another kind in total societies. All that could be concluded from the figures is that in big cities and on farms disruption percentages are higher if the percentage of low- and of high-income families is higher. As the number of high-income families is too small to influence the disruptive role of the group as a whole, one must conclude that a society which contains a higher percentage of high-income families appears to have characteristics which tend to increase the percentage of people living in a status of marriage disruption.

The association of a population's median level of education with percentage divorced and percentage total disrupted is generally positive, but with percentage separated, negative. To us this pattern seems to indicate that in a society with a higher level of education that form of disruption which allows remarriage tends to be preferred over that which tends to be associated with the formation of irregular unions. Plateris takes pains to point out (p. 192) that his finding does not necessarily contradict those studies which indicate that, not just because of their education, better-educated people are less divorce prone.[7]

The fact that groups with higher median education tend to have a higher percentage divorced does not necessarily mean that better educated people divorce more. Moreover, median education does not tell us anything about the distribution of education in a population. The range may be wide or narrow, the form of the distribution may vary. The fact that median education is not significantly associated with total disruption, except for large cities, shows that the positive association of education with divorce is counter-

---

7. Ogburn, *Education, Income and Family Unity*, 53 AM. J. SOCIOL. 474 (1948); W. M. Kephart, *Occupational Level and Marital Disruption*, 20 AM. SOCIOL. REV. 456. See also now J. R. Udry, *Marital Instability by Race, Sex, and Education, Occupation and Income*, in R. F. WINCH & L. W. GOODMAN, eds., SELECTED STUDIES IN MARRIAGE AND THE FAMILY 572 (1968).

balanced by its negative association with separation, thus leaving the percentage total disrupted uncorrelated with education [p. 205].

The correlation of the percentage of the labor force employed in manufacturing shows negative association with the percentages of total disrupted and divorced, except in the farm area, where it is positive, and positive association with the percentages of separated, especially in the two rural residence categories.

Plateris regards it as possible that the percentage of workers in manufacturing industries in rural areas is associated with the influence of the urban way of life, which includes higher divorce rates. The culture of farm areas where part of the population is employed in manufacturing, rather than in agriculture, is more similar to the urban culture than to that of purely agricultural areas (p. 206).

The association of the percentage of white-collar workers in the labor force with various types of marriage disruption Plateris calls "erratic." "A possible explanation," he says, "can be found in the difference of the meaning of the properties of white-collar workers for the social organization and for the stratification of communities, depending on the residence category to which those communities belong" (p. 206).

As an index of ethnicity Plateris uses the census data on foreign-born individuals. The percentage of foreign-born is negatively associated with the percentage of divorced in urban, and positively in rural, areas; with the percentage of separated it is associated positively in large cities and negatively, or not at all, in the country. As a consequence, the association with the percentage of total disrupted is negative in cities, positive on farms, and not apparent in the rural nonfarm area. Plateris offers the following explanation:

> In most cases the percentages foreign-born are much larger in cities than among rural population. Moreover, the immigrants are, as a rule, not fully acculturated into American society and follow marriage and marriage disruption patterns of their own. The settling of immigrants in farm areas may result in a decline of social cohesiveness among the farm population, and in an increased divorce rate, also the percentage foreign-born is highly associated with the percentage of Roman Catholics [p. 207].

In this connection it may be of interest that in the Federal Republic of Germany the disruption rate has been comparatively low among the 10 million expellees who found refuge in the country after the last war. The experience of being uprooted and the necessity of rebuilding an existence in new, unaccustomed surroundings seems to have promoted a high degree of family cohesion.[8]

8. H. SCHELSKY, WANDLUNGEN DER DEUTSCHEN FAMILIE IN DER GEGENWART 63 (1954).

Census data about religion are not available, but data about statewide percentages of Roman Catholics were obtained by Plateris from the *National Catholic Almanac*, 1950. In accordance with expectation, the associations are either significantly negative or, for noncity areas, statistically insignificant. It ought to be observed, however, that the negative association with the percentage of separated is very different from that with the percentage of divorced. In the large cities the coefficient of correlation of Catholics with divorced is −0.58, but with separated it is +0.33.

As indices of general characteristics of the residence categories Plateris used census data about migration, about the size of the cities of residence, and about population density. Finally he used a set of historical data, namely, the number of years since achievement of statehood by the state of residence. Migration has already been considered in connection with the problem of whether the relation between divorce law scores and persons of disrupted, divorced, or separated status present at the census taking was so distorted by migration as to render it useless in an inquiry concerned with the incidence of the events of separation and divorce. Plateris found that the relation had not been so distorted as to render the census data unusable.[9] His inquiry also showed that by and large the percentage of divorced is more strongly associated with migration variables than the percentage of separated, and the association of total disrupted is similar to that of the divorced group (p 153). Plateris then concluded that "where there are comparatively many newcomers little integrated in the community, divorces become frequent, and the separated population tends to divorce, thus giving rise to an increase of the percentage divorced with a simultaneous decline of the separated population" (p. 155).

The coefficients of correlation obtained between the percentages of disrupted and the size of city of residence are all statistically insignificant. Plateris concludes that "it can be assumed that no relationship exists among the variables in question and that the prevalence of divorces, separations and of total marriage disruption in large cities is independent of the number of persons living in such cities" (p. 208).

"Variation in the density [of population] identifies," as Plateris observes, "various types of culture and of social organization. Areas that are not fully settled or that, because of the nature of their soil, cannot be fully settled, can be expected to have social patterns, including patterns of marriage disruption, different from those obtained in densely

---

9. *Supra* p. 447.

settled areas" (p. 208–9). Density of population per square mile is associated negatively with percentages of divorced and total disrupted, but positively with percentages of separated. Possibly this pattern is connected with the fact, mentioned by Plateris, that the thinly populated areas of the United States are in the West, where divorce is by and large easier to obtain and of higher incidence than in the East.

This observation induced Plateris to investigate the correlation between percentages of disrupted and the length of the period since the achievement of statehood by the state of residence. Apparently this inquiry was also stimulated by the observation which Willcox had made about statistical patterns of divorce in the United States.[10] Willcox's findings are summarized by Plateris as follows:

> The first [belt is that] between the Atlantic and the Alleghenies, the second between the Alleghenies and the Mississippi, and the third, West of the Mississippi. Divorce rates increased in each belt from east to west. Only nine states had divorce rates that were not characteristic for the belt of states in which they were located. The six New England states and Florida had rates higher than should be expected from their geographical location, while Louisiana and New Mexico had lower rates [p. 51].

Plateris finds that the regional factor is still important and applies not only to the divorced, but also to the separated. The percentages of separated in the two urban residence categories show a clear-cut pattern.

If the line between high and low prevalence is drawn at 2 percent for large cities and at 1.4 percent for other urban areas, geographical patterns appear, but they are more complex than those described by Willcox, and they are different for the incidence of separation, and of divorce, the former being more strongly associated with location. While divorces are subject to social control, religious, legal, and other, separations are said more directly to reflect the culture of the population. While divorce, on the whole, still follows the pattern observed by Willcox, the separation areas are found roughly to correspond to the cultural regions.

> We find high separation indices in the states that were first settled and have old commercial and industrial traditions dating back to the eighteenth century, in the states where plantation economy and the appropriate type of social stratification have prevailed, in the states where large part of the land is desert, and in the "glamorous" states, such as Florida and California. Low separation percentages are found in the newer states, settled during the nineteenth century, which were historically agricultural, even if they are highly industrialized today.[11]

10. W. F. WILLCOX, THE DIVORCE PROBLEM 37 (1897).
11. *Id.* 185.

When arranged by residence categories the figures are interpreted as indicating that divorce and separation have no uniform pattern of interdependence. So Plateris feels justified in stating that the

> facts imply that the total disruption can best be viewed as the sum of two variables, which are fairly independent one of the other. Various factors contribute to the level of divorces and to the level of separation, while the level of total disruption is a sum of the two. Thus the available figures support the cumulative rather than the complementary hypothesis on the relationship between divorce and separation: the magnitude of marriage disruption is not approximately uniform, but varies between states and residence categories depending on the proportion of the divorced and of the separated in the population [pp. 187–88].

The association between high permissiveness of the divorce law and a high incidence of marriage disruption is found to be strong, especially in the urban areas in which, at the time of the 1950 census, 64.0 percent of the population resided. The findings for the rural nonfarm population (20.7 percent of the population of the United States) are not much different. Only the rural farm population (15.3 percent of the popula-

TABLE A6
CORRELATION COEFFICIENTS BETWEEN PERMISSIVENESS SCORES OF DIVORCE LAW AND NONLEGAL VARIABLES

Nonlegal Variables	Large Cities	Other Urban	Rural Nonfarm	Rural Farm
Never married	−.66	−.71	−.68	−.72
Widowed	.09[a]	.03[a]	.04[a]	−.16[a]
Spouse absent, other than separated	.14[a]	.07[a]	−.17[a]	−.25[a]
Childless married women	.48	.20[a]	−.10[a]	.12[a]
Wives in the labor force	.18[a]	.02[a]	−.28[a]	−.22[a]
Income under $1,500	.47	.40	.40	.27[a]
Income over $6,000	.38	.06[a]	−.14[a]	.14[a]
Median education	.42	.31	.03[a]	.04[a]
In manufacturing	−.54	−.70	−.62	−.61
White-collar workers	.37	.20[a]	−.07[a]	−.40
Foreign-born	−.57	−.46	−.34	−.31
Catholics	−.77	−.45	−.45	−.45
Size of the city	−.14[a]	...	...	...
Population per square mile	...	−.61	−.61	−.61
Years in the Union	−.64	−.58	−.58	−.58
Migrants from different county	.62	.69	.68	.62
Born in state of residence	−.24	−.39	−.39	−.39
Increase 1940–50	.32	.66	−.04[a]	−.14[a]
Net total migration	.30	.18[a]	.18[a]	.18[a]

Source: Plateris, table 27, p. 216, computed from the collected data.
[a] Not significant on the 5 percent level.

TABLE A7
CORRELATION COEFFICIENTS OF MARRIAGE DISRUPTION, DIVORCE LAW, AND SELECTED NONLEGAL VARIABLES: LARGE CITIES, 1950

Residence Categories and Selected Variables	Divorced	Separated	Law	Catholics	Never Married	Median Education	Years in the Union	Foreign-born	Manufacturing	Migrants	Childless Wives	Income under $1,500
Total disrupted	.89	.21	.60	−.43	−.23	.40	−.35	−.34	−.54	.47	.55	.38
Divorced		−.25	.79	−.58	−.44	.56	−.58	−.48	−.54	.60	.51	.42
Separated			−.44	.33	.45	−.36	.51	.31	.02	−.30	.08	−.10
Law easiness scores				−.77	−.66	.42	−.64	−.57	−.54	.62	.48	.47
Catholics					.63	−.25	.41	.73	.48	−.55	−.58	−.38
Never married						−.22	.51	.59	.28	−.54	−.34	−.28
Median education							−.65	−.21	−.54	.62	.15	.16
Years in the Union								.25	.52	−.64	.08	−.22
Foreign-born									.44	−.52	−.50	−.44
In manufacturing										−.76	−.46	−.58
Migrants from different county											.43	.57
Childless married women												.30
Income under $1,500												

Source: Plateris, table 28, p. 213, computed from the collected data.

TABLE A8
CORRELATION COEFFICIENTS OF MARRIAGE DISRUPTION, DIVORCE LAW, AND SELECTED NONLEGAL VARIABLES: OTHER URBAN AREAS, 1950

Residence Categories and Selected Variables	Divorced	Separated	Law	Catholics	Never Married	Median Education	Years in the Union	Foreign-born	Manufac-turing	Migrants	Childless Wives	Income under $1,500	Density
Total disrupted	.88	.49	.47	−.25	−.36	.04	.09	−.17	−.26	.31	.49	.21	−.33
Divorced		.01	.69	−.30	−.46	.26	−.35	−.20	−.40	.44	.37	.24	−.48
Separated			−.26	.03	.07	−.38	.46	.01	.20	−.15	.36	.01	.20
Law easiness scores				−.45	−.71	.31	−.58	−.46	−.70	.69	.20	.40	−.61
Catholics					.55	.04	.13	.77	.35	−.33	−.37	−.51	.60
Never married						−.25	.46	.58	.54	−.68	−.32	−.25	.49
Median Education							−.53	.22	−.40	.44	−.27	−.37	−.19
Years in the Union								.14	.75	−.69	.25	−.17	.54
Foreign-born									.46	−.44	−.48	−.57	.62
In manufacturing										−.88	−.11	−.42	.65
Migrants from different county											.22	.36	−.55
Childless married women												.21	−.13
Income under $1,500													−.54
Population per square mile													

Source: Plateris, table 29, p. 214, computed from the collected data.

tion of the United States) shows a different pattern, which appears to be socioculturally conditioned (pp. 239–40).

Plateris is, of course, careful not to regard the findings of association as proof of causation. The following three forms of causal relationship he says, however, are theoretically possible:

1. A permissive divorce law is a cause of a high incidence of marriage disruption;
2. A high incidence of marriage disruption causes the pressure for a permissive divorce law;
3. A permissive divorce law and a high incidence of marriage disruption mutually strengthen each other (p. 243).

Since there is no way to test these theories on the basis of the collected data, Plateris resorts to an analysis which allows him to transcend the need to select any one of the three causal theories. He computed coefficients of correlation between permissiveness scores of divorce laws and nonlegal variables and, for the big cities and for the other urban areas, those between both marriage disruption and divorce law and certain nonlegal variables (tables 28 and 29 at pp. 213 and 214) (see tables A6, A7, and A8).

The variables produce a web of strong mutual relationships. "Thus it seems," Plateris concludes, "that marriage disruption is associated not so much with individual variables as with a system of interrelated variables which may be considered as indices of the greater whole which can be called social stability of social cohesiveness (p. 215).

In the final step of the investigation the partial and the multiple correlation coefficients were computed for each of the nonlegal variables and the improvements shown over the respective zero-order coefficients between disruption and law permissiveness scores were analyzed (pp. 216–35).

So in his final chapter Plateris can say: "The main characteristic of communities, underlying variations in permissiveness of divorce laws and in the distribution of marriage disruption, seems to be social stability or, conversely, social anomie" (pp. 245–46).

Appendix B
The English Divorce Reform Act of 1969

Sec. 4 (1) The respondent to a petition for divorce in which the petitioner alleges any such fact as is mentioned in paragraph (e) of section 2(1) of this Act may oppose the grant of a decree nisi on the ground that the dissolution of the marriage will result in grave financial or other hardship to him and that it would in all circumstances be wrong to dissolve the marriage.

(2) Where the grant of a decree nisi is opposed by virtue of this section, then, —
 (a) if the court is satisfied that the only fact mentioned in the said section 2(1) on which the petitioner is entitled to rely in support of his petition is that mentioned in the said paragraph (e), and
 (b) if apart from this section it would grant a decree nisi, the court shall consider all the circumstances, including the conduct of the parties to the marriage and the interests of those parties and of any children or other persons concerned, and if the court is of opinion that the dissolution of the marriage will result in grave financial or other hardship to the respondent and that it would in all the circumstances be wrong to dissolve the marriage it shall dismiss the petition.

(3) For the purposes of this section hardship shall include the loss of the chance of acquiring any benefit which the respondent might acquire if the marriage were not dissolved.

Sec. 5. Where the court on granting a decree of divorce held that the only fact mentioned in section 2(1) of this Act on which the petitioner was entitled to rely in support of his petition was that mentioned in paragraph (d), it may, on an application made by the respondent at any time before the decree is made absolute, rescind the decree if it is satisfied that the petitioner misled the respondent (whether intentionally or unintentionally) about any matter which the respondent took into account in deciding to consent to the grant of a decree.

Sec. 6. (1) The following provisions of this section shall have effect where —
 (a) the respondent to a petition for divorce in which the petitioner alleged any such fact as is mentioned in paragraph (d) or (e) of section 2(1)

Laws 1969, ch. 55; see *supra* p. 350.

of this Act has applied to the court under this section for it to consider for the purposes of subsection (2) hereof the financial position of the respondent after the divorce; and

(b) a decree nisi of divorce has been granted on the petition and the court has held that the only fact mentioned in the said section 2(1) on which the petitioner was entitled to rely in support of his petition was that mentioned in the said paragraph (d) or (e).

(2) The court hearing an application by the respondent under this section shall consider all the circumstances, including the age, health, conduct, earning capacity, financial position of the respondent as, having regard to the divorce, it is likely to be after the death of the petitioner should the petitioner die first; and notwithstanding anything in the foregoing provisions of this Act but subject to subsection (3) of this section, the court shall not make absolute the decree of divorce unless it is satisfied —

(a) that the petitioner should not be required to make any financial provision for the respondent, or

(b) that the financial provision made by the petitioner for the respondent is reasonable and fair or the best that can be made in the circumstances.

(3) The court may if it thinks fit proceed without observing the requirements of subsection (2) of this section if —

(a) it appears that there are circumstances making it desirable that the decree should be made absolute without delay, and

(b) the court has obtained a satisfactory undertaking from the petitioner that he will make such financial provision for the respondent as the court may approve.

Index

Administrative divorce, in Denmark, 131, 144
Adultery: and criminal law, 278; in France, 214; in Italy, 180
Agreement, divorce by, in Japan, 109; see also Consent divorce
Alexander, Paul W., 261, 441
Alimony: in California, 380; German draft of 1970, 392, 401; Sweden, 146; Uniform Law, 387, 390
Alteration of status, crime of, in Italy, 186
American Bar Association, 385
Andrews, Stephen Pearl, 43
Annulment of marriage, 21, 91; for insanity, 314; in New York, 96, 353
Anti-Modernist Oath, 285, 410
Archbishop's Group, 324
Argentina, 194, 406
Associations familiales, 425
Australia, 340, 342, 345
Austria, 160, 251

Babylonia, 408
Bebel, August, 222
Beckman, Nils, 148
Beckman, Sven, 126
Belgium, consent divorce in, 213
Bertillon, Jacques, 289
Bigamy, 35, 279
Bishop, Joel Prentice, 39
Blake, Nelson M., 357
Bodio, L., 288
Bonaparte, Napoleon, 209
Bonnald, Marquis de, 213
Box-Tiao method, 303
Brazil, 407

Breakdown: and California Law of 1969, 269; definition of, 264; in England, 333; statistics on, 264; in USSR, 255, 259, 261
Breakdown, ground of, 316; in Germany, 369; in Sweden, 140; in Switzerland, 386
Breakdown, principle of, 328; in England, 336
Breakdown, with inquest, principle of, 330, 334
Broel-Plateris, Alexander, 263, 306, 444
Brown, Edward G., 374

Cahen, Alfred, 292
California, 316; divorce rates in, 373; Family Law Act of 1969, 367; Governor's Commission on the Family, 5, 375; uncontested divorces in, 250
Calvin, Jean, 22, 197
Canada, 131, 340; uncontested divorces in, 251
Canon law, 12, 17, 56, 92, 174
Catholic church in United States, 409
Catholic countries, 194
Catholic doctrine of indissolubility of marriage, 193
Chicago studies, 292
Chihuahua divorces, 87, 358
Child marriage, 412
Chile, 407
Church of England, 324
Ciudad Juárez divorces, 87, 358
Civil marriage: in France, 198; in Italy, 161; in Sweden, 137; in USSR, 223

Index

Civil status, registrations: in France, 204; in Italy, 164, 186
Code Napoléon, 208
Coercion, as ground of nullity, 93
Collusion, 55, 62, 241; in France, 219
Colonial period, 34
Community property, 379, 389, 396, 398
Como-Ticino research, 180, 305
Compromise, in democracy, 252
Comrades' courts, USSR, 239
Conciliation, 429; in California, 371, 378; in England, 351, 440; in France, 437; in Germany, 301, 438; in Italy, 190; in Japan, 110; in New York, 359; in Sweden, 140, 147; in Switzerland, 439; in United States, 440
Concordat, Italian, of 1929, 163
Concubinage, 278; and criminal law, in Italy, 180
Conditional consent to marriage, 174
Consensus maritalis, canon law, 174
Consent divorce, 241, 313; in Belgium, 213; in France, 201, 211, 215, 219; in Germany, 399; in Japan, 109, 111, 248; in Sweden, 139
Consent divorce, principle of: in England, 325, 338; in USSR, 238
Constitution of United States, divorce law amendment, 46
Contested divorces, 248
Conversion ground: in Italy, 190; in New York, 354
Cook County, Ill., uncontested divorces in, 250
Copenhagen divorce, 136
Counseling, 425, 435
Crime of honor, Italy, 186
Croce, Benedetto, 160
Cruelty, 101, 328; in France, 217, 373; and New York Divorce Reform Law of 1966, 365
Cultural climate, 284, 311, 408
Custody: in California, 379; in Germany, 400; and Uniform Law, 387

Damages upon divorce, in Sweden, 147

D'Annunzio, Gabriele, 172
Decree nisi, 61
Decree of nullity, and ecclesiastical tribunals, in Italy, 174
Defender of the bond (*defensor vinculi*), 59; in France, 219
Democracy, compromise in, 252
Denmark, 8, 128, 144; administrative divorce in, 131, 144; adultery as ground of divorce in, 145; divorce rates in, 317; Law of 30 June 1922, 144
Diderot, Denis, 200
Dike, Samuel W., 44
Disappearance, as substitute for divorce, 37
Dissatisfaction, 428
Dissolution of marriage: in California, 367; in Italy, 192; statistics on, 4, 30
Divisible divorce, 80, 385
Divorce faillite, 214
Divorce, grounds for: in Sweden, 142; in United States, 52
Divorce, laws of: Islamic, 9; Italian Law of 1970, 189; "Italian style," 186; Jewish, 11; and military personnel, 82; Roman, 10, 13, 15; United States, 51; variety of, 8
Divorce, rates of: in California, 373; in England, 319, 321; in Germany, 119; in Japan, 119; in New York, 262; in Oklahoma, 262; in USSR, 241; in United States, 119; *see also* Rates of divorce
Divorce Reform Act 1969, England, 347
Divorce sanction, 211
Doane, William C., 46
Dreyfus affair, 215
Dualism, law of books and law in action, 241
Dumas, Alexandre, *fils*, 215
Dwight, Timothy, 28, 42

Ecclesiastical law, Protestant, 23
Ecclesiastical tribunals in Italy, 165, 175

Index

Economic factors of marriage stability, 421
Education and divorce, 423
Emancipation of women, 272
Encyclicals: on Christian marriage, 11; *Quanta Cura*, 163
Engels, Friedrich, 200, 222, 254
England, 317; divorce rates in, 312; Divorce Reform Act 1969, 347; history of, 18, 31; research on marriage stability in, 269; uncontested divorces in, 251
Enlightenment, 199
Equal rights law of 1957, Germany, 398
Error, ground of nullity, 93
Estoppel, 89
Ethics, professional, 104
Exequatur, Italy, 177

Family allowances, 425
Family arbitration tribunals, France, 204
Family associations, 425
Family Code of 1926, RSFSR, 226
Family court, 60; in Japan, 110, 112
Family Court Plan, 261, 441
Family legislation, Sweden, 138
Family life education, 425, 435
Family service, 429
Family system, Japan, 117
Finland, divorce rates in, 312
Fisher, Geoffrey F., 323
Fiume divorces, 172
Foreign decree of nullity, Italy, 177
Foreign divorce of Italians, 173; recognition of, 64, 176
Fortuna-Spagnoli bill, 159, 189
Foster, Henry H., Jr., 357
France, 194; *ancien régime*, 26, 197; cruelty in, 373; Divorce Law of 1792, 201; divorce rates in, 312; Nationality Code of 1945, 170; uncontested divorce in, 251
Fraud, ground of nullity, 94
Frederick II, of Prussia, 25
Free unions, France, 183
French divorces: of Americans, 85; of Italians, 170

French Revolution, 27, 200
Friend of the Court, 60
Full faith and credit clause, 65
Fuorilegge del matrimonio, 159, 181

Gallicanism, 26, 198
German Civil Code of 1896, 218, 294
German expellees, 421
German Marriage Act of 1938–45, 218, 300, 392
Germanic peoples, 14
Germany, 346; breakdown and separation in, 369; cultural climate of, 287; custody in, 400; divorce rates in, 312; draft of 1970, 391; equal rights law of 1957, 398; study in, 293; uncontested divorces in, 251
Goichbarg, 228
Gorecki, Jan, 337
Gorrell Commission, 319
Gospel, 13
Gough, Aidan R., 375
Governor's Commission on the Family, California, 375
Greeley, Horace, 39
Griswold, Erwin N., 357
Guardian ad litem, 387
Gustavus IV of Sweden, 132

Hague Convention on Divorce, 64
Hansen, R. W., 359
Herbert, Alan P., 319
Hotel evidence, 63
Housewife marriage, 404
Housing, 422

Ibsen, Henrik, 136
Illegitimacy, 280; in Italy, 184; in USSR, 229
Illegitimate births, in England, 335
Illinois, 341
Impotence, ground of nullity in Italy, 177
Incompatibility, 316; in French law, 201, 206, 211
Incomplete marriage, Sweden, 137
Informal divorce, Italy, 158
Indissolubility of marriage, Catholic doctrine, 193

Injures graves, 201, 217, 373
Insanity, ground of annulment, 314; ground of divorce, 314, 327, 350
Interlocutory decree, 59, 61
Iowa, 316
Irreconcilable differences, California Law of 1969, 368
Irregular unions, 267; in England, 333; in Italy, 158, 182, 259; in USSR, 242
Italy: attempts to introduce divorce, 188; Civil Code of 1865, 161; Constitution of 1947, 168; cultural climate of, 187, 285; Divorce Law of 1970, 189; indissolubility of marriage and evasive devices, 169

Japan, 8, 109; divorce rates in, 312
Judicial separation, Italy, 179

Karl Johann Bernadotte, king of Sweden, 132
Kay, Herma Hill, 375, 384
Kent, James, 41
King's Proctor, 60, 321

Lagberedningen, 139
Landis, Judson T., 374
Lang, Cosmo Gordon, 318
Lateran Treaties of 1929, 163, 168
Law Commission: England, 331; Sweden, 139
Lawyer as marriage counselor, 442
Legal Aid and Advice Act, 1949, 320
Legislative divorce, 33
Length of marriage before divorce, 432
Lenin, 231
Levy, Robert J., 384
License, marriage, 419
Lichtenberger, James P., 292
Limping marriage, 171
Little divorce, Italy, 188, 191
Loi Bonnald (1816), 213
Loi Naquet (1884), 215
Long road–short road to divorce: in Sweden, 134; in New York, 355
Loren, Sofia, 170, 172
Luther, Martin, 22

Mace, David R., 5
Maintenance, in Uniform Law, 387, 390
Mann Act, 257
Marconi, Guglielmo, 175
Marital property, in Uniform Law, 389
Marriage: celebration of, in Sweden, 129, 137; changing image of, 272; conclusion of, in USSR, 239; counseling, 425, 435; counseling in Sweden, 150; disruption, 306, 444; law reform in Scandinavia, 138; nullity, in canon law, 92, 174; nullity, in Italy, 166, 173
Maryland, uncontested divorces in, 249
Matrimonial actions, Italy, 181
Matrimonial Causes Act: 1857, 318; 1937, 319; 1965, 341; 1967, 331
Matrimonium ratum sed non consumatum, 56, 160
Meiji Code, 117
Mental cruelty, 104
Mental reservation, 174
Mexican divorces, 86, 357; of Italians, 170
Migratory divorce, 45, 63, 241, 407; California Law of 1969, 382; New York Divorce Law of 1966, 362
Misconduct, marital, as ground of divorce, 22, 34
Montesquieu, 199
Montevideo divorces, 407
Morton Commission, 320, 322
Mueller, Gerhard O. W., 269, 318
Mussolini, Benito, 162

Nakodo, 116
Name of illegitimate child, Italy, 183, 185
Napoleonic Code, 208
Naquet, Alfred, 215
National Conference of Commissioners on Uniform State Laws, 47, 382
National Divorce Reform League, 44
National League for the Protection of the Family, 44
Nationality laws, 171

Nayen marriage, 120
Netherlands, 316; divorce rates in, 312
Nevada divorces, 76
New Economic Policy, USSR, 225
New Deal, 50
New England Divorce Reform League, 44
New Morality, 50
New York: debates about divorce, 38; Divorce Reform Law 1966, 343, 352; uncontested divorces in, 250
New Zealand, 340, 342, 345
Norway, divorce rates in, 312
Nullity of marriage, 21, 92; canon law, 92, 174; decree of, ecclesiastical tribunal, Italy, 176; proceedings in ecclesiastical courts, 57

O'Neill, William L., 48
Owen, Robert Dale, 39

Papal infallibility, 410
Parliamentary divorce, 31; in Quebec, 131
Pashukanis, Evgenij Bronislavovich, 228
Pauline privilege, 57
Pension rights of divorced spouse, Sweden, 145
Perturbatio sanguinis, 203
Piccolo divorzio, 188, 191
Pius IX, Pope, 163
Poland, 337, 346, 369
Ponti, Carlo, 170, 172
Poor man's divorce, 406
Population policy, 423
Predicting success of marriage, 418
Pregnancy, motive for marriage, 417
Presumption of validity of last marriage, 36, 270
Privilegium Paulinum, 57, 160
Progressive Era, 49
Prohibition of remarriage, 91
Property settlement, California, 379; German draft of 1970, 395; Uniform Law, 387, 389
Protestant Reformers, 22
Prussia, 25
Putting Asunder, 324

Quarrelsome couples, 129
Quebec, parliamentary divorce in, 131
Queen's Proctor, 60, 321

Radziwill, Caroline Lee, 175
Ramsey, Arthur M., 323
Rape, statutory, 417
Rascel, Renato, 175
Rates of divorce: Denmark, 128; Finland, 128; Iceland, 128; Norway, 128; Sweden, 128, 135; United States, 128
Recognition of ecclesiastical and foreign judgments in Italy, 176
Reconciliation; *see* Conciliation
Records of divorces, 263
Recrimination, 54, 206, 256
Reformers, Protestant, 22
Remarriage, restriction after divorce, 266, 282
Reno divorces, 76
Reservatio mentalis, 174
Richardson-McFarland affair, 43
Riga divorces, 407
Roosevelt, Theodore, 45
Rousseau, Jean-Jacques, 200
Royal dispensation, divorce by, 129, 131
Russia, tsarist, 7; Family Code of 1926, 226

San Marino nullity decrees, Italy, 178
Sansone-Nenni bill, 158
San-san-kudo, 116, 120
Scandinavia, 126; cooperation in legal reform, 136, 138
Secular marriage: in France, 198; in Italy, 161; in Sweden, 137; in USSR, 223
Separation, factual, in Italy, 159
Separation, as ground for divorce, 313, 340; in Australia, 343; in Canada, 343; in England, 322, 339, 351; French law of 4 Floréal an II (1794), 205; in Germany, 369; in New Zealand, 343
Separation, judicial, in Italy, 179
Shotgun marriage, 417
Signatura, Supreme Court of, 166

Index

Social legislation, 421
Soviet Union; *see* USSR
Spain, 194
Stalin law on divorce, 229
Stanton, Elizabeth Cady, 39
Statute law, in United States, 306, 444
Statutory rape, 417
Stockholm marriages, 139, 422
Stoljar, Samuel, 269
Strindberg, August, 136
Sub rosa institution, 257
Support, in California, 380, 392; German draft of 1970, 401
Sveriges Rikes Lag, 1734, 130
Sweden, 8, 126, 316; Church Law 1686, 129; cultural climate of, 287; divorce reform plan, 156; divorce rates in, 312; ecclesiastical ordinance, 1572, 129; Law of 11 November 1915, 140; Royal Edict, 1810, 133
Swiss nullity decrees, in Italy, 177
Switzerland, 305, 346; breakdown ground in, 386; divorce rates in, 312
Syllabus of errors, 163, 285, 410

Teenage marriage, 413
Texas, 316
Theology, Catholic, views on indissolubility of marriage, 193
Third Republic (France), 215
Ticino-Comasco research, 180, 305
Toledo, Ohio, family court in, 261
Tolstoy, Leo, 7
Trial marriage, 432
Turkey, unregistered marriage in, 121

Uncontested divorces, 248

Uniform Act Regulating Annulment of Marriage and Divorce, 47
Uniform Divorce Jurisdiction Act, 47
Uniform divorce law, 45, 382
Uniform Divorce Recognition Act, 362, 382
USSR, 222; decree of 10 Dec. 1965, 233, 237; directive of Supreme Court, of 16 Sept. 1949, 232; divorce law of 8 July 1944, 229; divorce rates in, 312; Law of Marriage and Family 27 June 1968, 233, 237
United States: Chicago study, 306, 444; divorce history, 32; divorce rates in, 312
Unregistered marriage, Japan and Turkey, 120
Urukagina, 408
Uxoricide, in Italy, 186

Virgin Island divorce, 77, 82
Voltaire, 199, 211

Waiting period after divorce, in France, 203, 205
Walker, Lord, 323, 328
Willcox, Walter F., 48, 290
Wives as plaintiffs in divorce cases, 255
Wolf, Ernst, 293
Women, role of, in United States, 427
Woolsey, Theodore, 44
Wright, Carroll D., 45
Wright Report, 290

Zaisen-bunyo, 110, 122, 405
Zwingli, Huldreich, 22

Table of Cases

AMERICAN AND ENGLISH CASES

Aldrich v. Aldrich, 378 U.S. 540, 84 S.Ct. 1687, 12 L.Ed. 2d 1020 (1964)	74
Alton v. Alton, 207 F. 2d 667 (1953)	78, 82
Andrews v. Andrews, 188 U.S. 14, 23 S.Ct. 237, 47 L.Ed. 366 (1903)	65
Atherton v. Atherton, 181 U.S. 155, 21 S.Ct. 544, 45 L.Ed. 794 (1901)	66
Baillet-Latour v. Baillet-Latour, 301 N.Y. 428, 94 N.E. 2d 715 (1950)	100
Bell v. Bell, 181 U.S. 175, 21 S.Ct. 551, 45 L.Ed. 804 (1901)	65
Bergeron v. Bergeron, 287 Mass. 524, 192 N.E. 86 (1934)	89
In re Biersack, 156 N.Y.S. 519, 96 Misc. 161 (1916)	36
Bolala v. Bolala, 68 Ohio App. 63, 33 N.E. 2d 845 (1940)	89
Burch v. Burch, 195 F.2d 799 (1952)	77
Bury's Case, 2 Dyer 179a, 73 Eng.Rep. 394 (1560)	58
Coe v. Coe, 334 U.S. 378, 68 S.Ct. 1094, 92 L.Ed. 1451 (1948)	71, 363
Cook v. Cook, 342 U.S. 126, 72 S.Ct. 157, 96 L.Ed. 164 (1951)	74
Curley v. Curley, 144 Fla. 728, 198 So. 584 (1940)	75
Davis v. Davis, 305 U.S. 32, 59 S.Ct. 3, 83 L.Ed. 26, 118 A.L.R. 1518 (1938)	72
Di Lorenzo v. Di Lorenzo, 174 N.Y. 467, 67 N.E. 63, 63 L.R.A. 92, 95 Am.St.Rep. 609 (1903)	97
Ditson v. Ditson, 4 R.I. 87 (1856)	66
Du Quesnay v. Henderson, 24 Calif. App. 2d 11, 74 P. 2d 294 (1937)	89

Esenwein v. Esenwein, 325 U.S. 279, 65 S.Ct. 1118, 89 L.Ed. 1609, 157 A.L.R. 1396 (1944) — 80

Estin v. Estin, 334 U.S. 541, 68 S.Ct. 1213, 92 L.Ed. 1561 (1948) — 81

Evans v. Evans, 1 Hagg. Cons. Rep. 35, 161 Eng. Rep. 460 (1790) — 102

Fisher v. Fisher, 250 N.Y. 313, 166 N.E. 460, 61 A.L.R. 1523 (1929) — 92

Fulwood's Case, Cro. Cas. 482 (1638) — 93

Gault, in re, 387 U.S. 1, 78 S.Ct. 1428, 18 L.Ed. 2d 527 (1967) — 113

Gleason v. Gleason, 308 N.Y. 2d 347, 256 N.E. 2d 513 (1970) — 355

Golden v. Golden, 41 N.M. 356, 68 P. 2d 928 (1937) — 89

Gollins v. Gollins, [1963] 3 W.L.R. 170, [1963] 2 All E.R. 966 (H.L.) — 349

Granville-Smith v. Granville-Smith, 349 U.S. 1, 75 S.Ct. 553, 99 L.Ed. 773 (1955) — 78

Griswold v. Connecticut, 381 U.S. 479, 85 S.Ct. 1678, 14 L.Ed. 2d 516 (1965) — 257

Haddock v. Haddock, 201 U.S. 562, 26 S.Ct. 525, 50 L.Ed. 867, 5 Am.Cas. 1 (1906) — 66

Hafner v. Hafner, 66 N.Y.S. 2d 442 (1946) — 101

Harford v. Morris, 2 Hagg.Cons.Rep. 423, 161 Eng. Rep. 792 (1776) — 93

Harter v. Harter, 5 Ohio 319 (1832) — 51

In re Johnson's Estate, 301 N.Y. 13, 92 N.E. 2d 44 (1950) — 75

Johnson v. Muelberger, 340 U.S. 581, 71 S.Ct. 474, 95 L.Ed. 552 (1951) — 74, 363

Krause v. Krause, 282 N.Y. 355, 26 N.E. 2d 290 (1940) — 90

Latterner v. Latterner, 51 Nev. 285, 274 P. 194 (1929) — 77

Moss v. Moss, [1897] P. 263 — 94

Mountbatten v. Mountbatten, [1959] 1 All E.R. 99 — 89

Pennoyer v. Neff, 95 U.S. 714, 24 L.Ed. 565 (1877) — 79

People v. Baker, 76 N.Y. 78 (1879) — 67

People v. Dawell, 25 Mich. 247 (1872) — 67

People v. Harlow, 9 Cal. App. 2d 643, 50 P.2d 1052 (1935) — 67

Table of Cases

Reik v. Reik, 109 N.J.Eq. 615, 158 A. 519; 112 N.J.Eq. 234, 163 A. 907   89

Reynolds v. Reynolds, 3 Allen (85 Mass.) 665 (1862)   95

Rosenstiel v. Rosenstiel, 16 N.Y. 2d 64, 209 N.E. 2d 709, 13 A.L.R. 3d 1401 (1965)   87, 91, 100, 257, 357, 363

Ryan v. Wurmbrand-Stuppach, 150 Misc. 251, 281 N.Y.S. 709 (1955)   101

Scott v. Sebright, 12 P.D. 21 (1886)   93

Sherrer v. Sherrer, 334 U.S. 343, 68 S.Ct. 1087, 92 L.Ed. 1429 (1948)   71, 84, 363

Shonfeld v. Shonfeld, 260 N.Y. 477, 184 N.E. 66 (1933)   97

Smith v. Smith, 44 N.Y.S. 2d 826 (1943)   101

Spears v. Spears, 178 Ark. 720, 12 S.W. 2d 876 (1928)   36

State v. Armington, 25 Minn. 29 (1878)   67

State v. Herron, 175 N.C. 754, 94 S.E. 698 (1917)   67

State v. Najjar, 1 N.J. Super. 208, 63 Atl. 2d 807 (1949); 2 N.J. 208, 66 A. 2d 37 (1949)   73, 89

State of New Jersey v. John de Meo, 20 N.J. 1, 118 Atl. 2d 1, 56 A.L.R. 2d 905 (1955)   73, 89

State v. Shulfelt, 107 Vt. 358, 179 Atl. 3 (1935)   67

State v. Westmoreland, 76 S.C. 145 (1906)   67

State v. Williams, I, 220 N.C. 445, 17 S.E. 2d 769 (1940)   68

State v. Williams, II, 224 N.C. 182, 29 S.E. 2d 744 (1944)   69

State v. Woods, 107 Vt. 354, 179 Atl. 1 (1935)   67

Stoll v. Gottlieb, 305 U.S. 165, 59 S. Ct. 134 (1938)   73

Thompson v. Whitman, 85 U.S. (18 Wall.) 457 (1873)   65

Vanderbilt v. Vanderbilt, 354 U.S. 416, 77 S.Ct. 1360, 1 L.Ed. 2d 1450 (1957)   81

Wakefield v. Turner, 17 Hans.Parl.Deb. N.S. 1133 (1827)   93

Walker v. Walker, 45 Nev. 105, 198 P. 433 (1921)   77

Warrender v. Warrender, 42 N.J. 287, 205 A. 2d 123 (1964)   89

Williams v. North Carolina, 317 U.S. 287, 63 S.Ct. 207, 87 L.Ed. 279, 143 A.L.R. 1273 (1942)   67, 79, 84, 257

Williams v. State of North Carolina, 325 U.S. 226, 65 S.Ct. 1092, 89 L.Ed. 1577, 157 A.L.R. 1366 (1945)   69, 79

Table of Cases

Williams v. Williams [1963] 3 W. L.R. 215, [1963] 2 All E.R. 994 (H.L.)	328, 349
Wood v. Wood, 16 N.Y. 2d 64, 209 N.Y. 2d 709, 13 A.L.R. 3d 1401 (1965)	87, 91, 357
Woronzoff-Daschkoff v. Woronzoff-Daschkoff, 303 N.Y. 506, 104 N.E. 2d 877 (1952)	98

FRENCH AND BELGIAN CASES

Bruxelles, 14 August 1834, Pas. belge 1834. 2. 258	216
Ferrari, affair, Rec. Dalloz 1922. I. 137, Rec. Sirey 1923.I.5; Dalloz Heb. 1928. 253, Rec. Sirey 1929. I. 92 (1922/1928)	171
Lewandowski, affair, Rec. Dalloz 1955. 540, J.C.P. 1955. II. 8771, Rev. crit. dr. int. pr. 1955. 320 (1955)	171
Cass. 16 November 1825, Sirey, Rec. gén. 1re série t.8.213	216
Angers, 29 January 1859, D. 1860.2.97, S. 1859. 2. 77	216
Dijon, 30 July 1868, D. 1868. 2. 247	216
Lyon, 4 April 1818, Sirey, Rec. gén. I. 5. 370	216
Metz, 25 May 1869, D. 1869. 2. 202	216
Riom, 5 July 1965, [1966] Rec. Dalloz 549	185

ITALIAN CASES

Cass. 11 June 1934, [1934] Giur. it. I. 1. 745	178
Cass. Sez. unite, 25 July 1949 [1949] Foro it. I. 801	178
Cass. Sez. unite, 6 August 1949, [1949] Foro Ital. I. 1. 1019	173
Cass. Sez. unite, 6 August 1949, [1949] Foro it. I. 908	173
Cass. 16 March 1950, [1950] Foro ital. I. 388	171
Cass. Sez. unite, 27 October 1953, Rep. Giur. civ., Delibazione nos. 47, 49	177
Cass. 16 April 1959, [1959] Foro it. I. 1301, 42 Riv. dir. internaz. 626.	178
Cass. Sez. unite, 19 April 1963, [1963] Giur. it. I. 1. 1965	186
Cass. civ. Sez. unite, 12 March 1970, [1970] Giur. it. I. 1. 1019	173
App. Torino. 28 June 1948, [1948] Foro Ital. I. 909	171